DATE DUE

MAY 2 0 2008		
6/22/09	11:53499884	
JUN 1 9 2013		

Handbook of
Database Security
Applications and Trends

Handbook of
Database Security
Applications and Trends

edited by

Michael Gertz
University of California at Davis
USA

Sushil Jajodia
George Mason University
USA

 Springer

Michael Gertz
University of California at Davis
Dept. of Computer Science
One Shields Avenue
Davis, CA 95616-8562
gertz@cs.ucdavis.edu

Sushil Jajodia
George Mason University
Center for Secure Information Systems
Research I, Suite 417
Fairfax VA 22030-4444
jajodia@gmu.edu

Library of Congress Control Number: 2007934795

ISBN-13: 978-0-387-48532-4
e-ISBN-13: 978-0-387-48533-1

Printed on acid-free paper.

9 8 7 6 5 4 3 2 1

springer.com

Preface

Motivation for the book

Database security has been gaining a great deal of importance as industry, military, and government organizations have increasingly adopted Internet-based technologies on a large-scale, because of convenience, ease of use, and the ability to take advantage of rapid advances in the commercial market. Along with the traditional security aspects of data integrity and availability, there is an increasing interest in research and development in data privacy. This is because today's often mission-critical databases no longer contain only data used for day-to-day processing by organization; as new applications are being added, it is possible for organizations to collect and store vast amounts of data quickly and efficiently and to make the data readily accessible to the public, typically through Web-based applications. Unfortunately, if security threats related to the integrity, availability, and privacy of the data are not properly resolved, databases remain vulnerable to malicious attacks and accidental misuse. Such incidents, in turn, may translate into financial losses or losses whose values are obviously high but difficult to quantify, e.g., the loss of the public's trust in the data management infrastructure and services offered by an organization.

In assembling this handbook, we have had a twofold objective: first, to provide a comprehensive summary of the results of research and development activities in various aspects of database security up to this point, and second, to point toward directions for future work in this important and fruitful field of research.

This handbook offers twenty three essays contributed by a selected group of prominent researchers. Given the dynamic nature of the field of database security, we have attempted to obtain a balance among various viewpoints by inviting multiple contributions on the same topic. We believe that this diversity provides a richness generally not available in one book. In some cases, authors have tried to reconcile their differences by contributing a single essay on a topic.

About the book

Essays in this handbook can be roughly divided into following eight areas:

Foundations of Access Control

- Recent Advances in Access Control by Sabrina De Capitani di Vimercati, Sara Foresti, and Pierangela Samarati
- Access Control Models for XML by Sabrina De Capitani di Vimercati, Sara Foresti, Stefano Paraboschi, and Pierangela Samarati
- Access Control Policy Languages in XML by Naizhen Qi and Michiharu Kudo

Trust Management and Trust Negotiation

- Database Issues in Trust Management and Trust Negotiation by Dongyi Li, William Winsborough, Marianne Winslett, and Ragib Hasan

Secure Data Outsourcing

- Authenticated Index Structures for Outsourced Databases by Feifei Li, Marios Hadjileftheriou, George Kollios, and Leonid Reyzin
- Towards Secure Data Outsourcing by Radu Sion
- Managing and Querying Encrypted Data by Bijit Hore, Sharad Mehrotra, and Hakan Hacıgümüş

Security in Advanced Database Systems and Applications

- Security in Data Warehouses and OLAP Systems by Lingyu Wang and Sushil Jajodia
- Security for Workflow Systems by Vijayalakshmi Atluri and Janice Warner
- Secure Semantic Web Services by Bhavani Thuraisingham
- Geospatial Database Security by Soon Ae Chun and Vijayalakshmi Atluri
- Security Re-engineering for Databases: Concepts and Techniques by Michael Gertz and Madhavi Gandhi

Database Watermarking

- Database Watermarking for Copyright Protection by Radu Sion
- Database Watermarking: A Systematic View by Yingjiu Li

Trustworthy Record Retention and Recovery

- Trustworthy Records Retention by Ragib Hasan, Marianne Winslett, Soumyadeb Mitra, Windsor Hsu, and Radu Sion
- Damage Quarantine and Recovery in Data Processing Systems by Peng Liu, Sushil Jajodia, and Meng Yu

Privacy

- Hippocratic Databases: Current Capabilities and Future Trends by Tyrone Grandison, Christopher Johnson, and Jerry Kiernan
- Privacy-Preserving Data Mining: A Survey by Charu C. Aggarwal and Philip S. Yu
- Privacy in Database Publishing: A Bayesian Perspective by Alin Deutsch
- Privacy Preserving Publication: Anonymization Frameworks and Principles by Yufei Tao

Privacy in Location-based Services

- Privacy Protection through Anonymity in Location-based Services by Claudio Bettini, Sergio Mascetti, and X. Sean Wang
- Privacy-enhanced Location-based Access Control by Claudio A. Ardagna, Marco Cremonini, Sabrina De Capitani di Vimercati, and Pierangela Samarati
- Efficiently Enforcing the Security and Privacy Policies in a Mobile Environment by Vijayalakshmi Atluri and Heechang Shin

Intended audience

This handbook is suitable as a reference for practitioners and researchers in industry and academia who are interested in the state-of-the-art in database security and privacy. Instructors may use this handbook as a text in a course for upper-level undergraduate or graduate students. Any graduate student who is interested in database security and privacy must definitely read this book.

Acknowledgements

We are extremely grateful to all those who contributed to this handbook. It is a pleasure to acknowledge the authors for their contributions. Special thanks go to Susan Lagerstrom-Fife, Senior Publishing Editor for Springer, and Sharon Palleschi, Editorial Assistant at Springer, whose enthusiasm and support for this project were most helpful.

Davis, California, and Fairfax, Virginia *Michael Gertz*
September 2007 *Sushil Jajodia*

Contents

List of Contributors

Charu C. Aggarwal
IBM T. J. Watson Research Center, Hawthorne, NY, e-mail: charu@us.ibm.com

Claudio A. Ardagna
Dipartimento di Tecnologie dell'Informazione, Università degli Studi di Milano,
Crema, Italy, e-mail: ardagna@dti.unimi.it

Vijayalakshmi Atluri
Rutgers University, Newark, NJ, e-mail: atluri@cimic.rutgers.edu

Claudio Bettini
DICo, University of Milan, Italy, e-mail: bettini@dico.unimi.it

Sabrina De Capitani di Vimercati
Dipartimento di Tecnologie dell'Informazione, Università degli Studi di Milano,
Crema, Italy, e-mail: decapita@dti.unimi.it

Soon Ae Chun
City University of New York, College of Staten Island, Staten Island, NY, e-mail:
chun@mail.csi.cuny.edu

Marco Cremonini
Dipartimento di Tecnologie dell'Informazione, Università degli Studi di Milano,
Crema, Italy, e-mail: cremonini@dti.unimi.it

Alin Deutsch
Department of Computer Science and Engineering, University of California San
Diego, La Jolla, CA, e-mail: deutsch@cs.ucsd.edu

Sara Foresti
Dipartimento di Tecnologie dell'Informazione, Università degli Studi di Milano,
Crema, Italy, e-mail: foresti@dti.unimi.it

Madhavi Gandhi
Department of Mathematics and Computer Science, California State University, East Bay, CA, e-mail: madhavi.gandhi@eastbay.edu

Michael Gertz
Department of Computer Science, University of California at Davis, Davis, CA, e-mail: gertz@cs.ucdavis.edu

Tyrone Grandison
IBM Almaden Research Center, San Jose, CA, e-mail: tyroneg@us.ibm.com

Hakan Hacıgümüş
IBM Almaden Research Center, San Jose, CA, e-mail: hakanh@acm.org

Marios Hadjileftheriou
AT&T Labs Inc., e-mail: marioh@research.att.com

Ragib Hasan
Department of Computer Science, University of Illinois at Urbana-Champaign, IL, e-mail: rhasan@cs.uiuc.edu

Bijit Hore
Donald Bren School of Computer Science, University of California, Irvine, CA, e-mail: bhore@ics.uci.edu

Windsor Hsu
Data Domain, Inc., e-mail: windsor.hsu@datadomain.com

Sushil Jajodia
Center for Secure Information Systems, George Mason University, Fairfax, VA, e-mail: jajodia@gmu.edu

Christopher Johnson
e-mail: chrisjohnson@alum.berkeley.edu

Jerry Kiernan
IBM Almaden Research Center, San Jose, CA, e-mail: jkiernan@us.ibm.com

George Kollios
Computer Science Department, Boston University, Boston, MA, e-mail: gkollios@cs.bu.edu

Michiharu Kudo
Tokyo Research Laboratory, IBM, Japan, e-mail: kudo@jp.ibm.com

Dongyi Li
Department of Computer Science, University of Texas at San Antonio, TX, e-mail: dli@cs.utsa.edu

Feifei Li
Department of Computer Science, Florida State University, FL, e-mail: lifeifei@cs.fsu.edu

Yingjiu Li
School of Information Systems, Singapore Management University, 80 Stamford
Road, Singapore, e-mail: yjli@smu.edu.sg

Peng Liu
Pennsylvania State University, PA, e-mail: pliu@ist.psu.edu

Sergio Mascetti
DICo, University of Milan, Italy, e-mail: mascetti@dico.unimi.it

Sharad Mehrotra
Donald Bren School of Computer Science, University of California, Irvine, CA,
e-mail: sharad@ics.uci.edu

Soumyadeb Mitra
Department of Computer Science, University of Illinois at Urbana-Champaign, IL,
e-mail: mitra1@cs.uiuc.edu

Stefano Paraboschi
University of Bergamo, Dalmine, Italy, e-mail: parabosc@unibg.it

Naizhen Qi
Tokyo Research Laboratory, IBM, Japan, e-mail: naishin@jp.ibm.com

Leonid Reyzin
Computer Science Department, Boston University, Boston, MA, e-mail:
reyzin@cs.bu.edu

Pierangela Samarati
Dipartimento di Tecnologie dell'Informazione, Università degli Studi di Milano,
Crema, Italy, e-mail: samarati@dti.unimi.it

Heechang Shin
Rutgers University, Newark, NJ, e-mail: hshin@cimic.rutgers.edu

Radu Sion
Network Security and Applied Cryptography Lab, Stony Brook University, NY,
e-mail: sion@cs.stonybrook.edu

Yufei Tao
Department of Computer Science and Engineering, Chinese University of Hong
Kong, Sha Tin, New Territories, Hong Kong, e-mail: taoyf@cse.cuhk.edu.hk

Bhavani Thuraisingham
University of Texas at Dallas, TX, e-mail: bhavani.thuraisingham@utdallas.edu

Lingyu Wang
Concordia Institute for Information Systems Engineering, Concordia University,
Montreal, QC H3G 1M8, Canada, e-mail: wang@ciise.concordia.ca

X. Sean Wang
Department of Computer Science, University of Vermont, VT, e-mail: xy-
wang@emba.uvm.edu

Janice Warner
Rutgers University, Newark, NJ, e-mail: janice@cimic.rutgers.edu

William Winsborough
Department of Computer Science, University of Texas at San Antonio, TX, e-mail: wwinsborough@acm.org

Marianne Winslett
Department of Computer Science, University of Illinois at Urbana-Champaign, IL, e-mail: winslett@cs.uiuc.edu

Meng Yu
Western Illinois University, Macomb, IL, e-mail: m-yu2@wiu.edu

Philip S. Yu
IBM T. J. Watson Research Center, Hawthorne, NY, e-mail: psyu@us.ibm.com

1

Recent Advances in Access Control

S. De Capitani di Vimercati, S. Foresti, and P. Samarati

Dipartimento di Tecnologie dell'Informazione
Università degli Studi di Milano
26013 Crema, Italy
{decapita,foresti,samarati}@dti.unimi.it

Summary. Access control is the process of mediating every request to resources and data maintained by a system and determining whether the request should be granted or denied. Traditional access control models and languages result limiting for emerging scenarios, whose open and dynamic nature requires the development of new ways of enforcing access control. Access control is then evolving with the complex open environments that it supports, where the decision to grant an access may depend on the properties (attributes) of the requestor rather than her identity and where the access control restrictions to be enforced may come from different authorities. These issues pose several new challenges to the design and implementation of access control systems. In this chapter, we present the emerging trends in the access control field to address the new needs and desiderata of today's systems.

1 Introduction

Information plays an important role in any organization and its protection against unauthorized disclosure (*secrecy*) and unauthorized or improper modifications (*integrity*), while ensuring its availability to legitimate users (*no denials-of-service*) is becoming of paramount importance. An important service in guaranteeing information protection is the *access control* service. Access control is the process of mediating every request to resources and data maintained by a system and determining whether the request should be granted or denied. An access control system can be considered at three different abstractions of control: *access control policy*, *access control model*, and *access control mechanism*. A policy defines the high level rules used to verify whether an access request is to be granted or denied. A policy is then formalized through a *security model* and is enforced by an access control *mechanism*. The separation between policies and mechanisms has a number of advantages. First, it is possible to discuss protection requirements independently of their implementation. Second, it is possible to compare different access control policies as well as different mechanisms that enforce the same policy. Third, it is possible to design access control mechanisms able to enforce multiple policies.

In this way, a change in the access control policy does not require any changes in the mechanism. Also, the separation between model and mechanism makes it possible to formally prove security properties on the model; any mechanism that correctly enforces the model will then enjoy the same security properties proved for the model.

The variety and complexity of the protection requirements that may need to be imposed in today's systems makes the definition of access control policies a far from trivial process. An access control system should be simple and expressive. It should be simple to make easy the management task of specifying and maintaining the security specifications. It should be expressive to make it possible to specify in a flexible way different protection requirements that may need to be imposed on different resources and data. Moreover, an access control system should include support for the following features.

- *Policy combination.* Since information may not be under the control of a single authority, access control policies information may take into consideration the protection requirements of the owner, but also the requirements of the collector and of other parties. These multiple authorities scenario should be supported from the administration point of view providing solutions for modular, large-scale, scalable policy composition and interaction.
- *Anonymity.* Many services do not need to know the real identity of a user. It is then necessary to make access control decisions dependent on the requester's *attributes*, which are usually proved by *digital certificates*.
- *Data outsourcing.* A recent trend in the information technology area is represented by data outsourcing, according to which companies shifted from fully local management to outsourcing the administration of their data by using externally service providers [1, 2, 3]. Here, an interesting research challenge consists in developing an efficient mechanism for implementing selective access to the remote data.

These features pose several new challenges to the design and implementation of access control systems. In this chapter, we present the emerging trends in the access control field to address the new needs and desiderata of today's systems. The remainder of the chapter is organized as follows. Section 2 briefly discusses some basic concepts about access control, showing the main characteristics of the discretionary, mandatory, and role-based access control policies along with their advantages and disadvantages. Section 3 introduces the problem of enforcing access control in open environments. After a brief overview of the issues that need to be addressed, we describe some proposals for trust negotiation and for regulating service access. Section 4 addresses the problem of combining access control policies that may be independently stated. We first describe the main features that a policy composition framework should have and then illustrate some current solutions. Section 5 presents the main approaches for enforcing selective access in an outsourced scenario. Finally, Sect. 6 concludes the chapter.

	Document1	Document2	Program1	Program2
Ann	read, write	read	execute	
Bob	read	read	read, execute	
Carol		read, write		read, execute
David			read, write, execute	read, write, execute

Fig. 1. An example of access matrix

2 Classical Access Control Models

Classical access control models can be grouped into three main classes: *discretionary access control* (DAC), which bases access decisions on users' identity; *mandatory access control* (MAC), which bases access decisions on mandated regulations defined by a central authority; and *role-based access control* (RBAC), which bases access decisions on the roles played by users in the models. We now briefly present the main characteristics of these classical access control models.

2.1 Discretionary Access Control

Discretionary access control is based on the identity of the user requesting access and on a set of rules, called *authorizations*, explicitly stating which user can perform which action on which resource. In the most basic form, an authorization is a triple (s, o, a), stating that user s can execute action a on object o. The first discretionary access control model proposed in the literature is the *access matrix model* [4, 5, 6]. Let S, O, and A be a set of subjects, objects, and actions, respectively. The access matrix model represents the set of authorizations through a $|S| \times |O|$ matrix $\mathcal{A}$. Each entry $\mathcal{A}[s, o]$ contains the list of actions that subject s can execute over object o. Figure 1 illustrates an example of access matrix where, for example, user **Ann** can **read** and **write** **Document1**.

The access matrix model can be implemented through different mechanisms. The straightforward solution exploiting a two-dimensional array is not viable, since $\mathcal{A}$ is usually sparse. The mechanisms typically adopted are:

- *Authorization table.* The non empty entries of $\mathcal{A}$ are stored in a table with three attributes: **user**, **action**, and **object**.
- *Access control list (ACL).* The access matrix is stored by column, that is, each object is associated with a list of subjects together with a set of actions they can perform on the object.
- *Capability.* The access matrix is stored by row, that is, each subject is associated with a list indicating, for each object, the set of actions the subject can perform on it.

Figure 2 depicts the authorization table, access control lists, and capability lists corresponding to the access matrix of Fig. 1.

User	Action	Object
Ann	read	Document1
Ann	write	Document1
Ann	read	Document2
Ann	execute	Program1
Bob	read	Document1
Bob	read	Document2
Bob	read	Program1
Bob	execute	Program1
Carol	read	Document2
Carol	write	Document2
Carol	execute	Program2
David	read	Program1
David	write	Program1
David	execute	Program1
David	read	Program2
David	write	Program2
David	execute	Program2

(a)

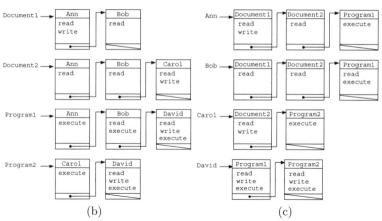

(b)   (c)

Fig. 2. Access matrix implementation mechanisms

From the access matrix model, discretionary access control systems have evolved and they include support for the following features.

- *Conditions.* To make authorization validity depend on the satisfaction of some specific constraints, today's access control systems typically support conditions associated with authorizations. [5]. For instance, conditions impose restrictions on the basis of: object content (content-dependent conditions), system predicates (system-dependent conditions), or accesses previously executed (history-dependent conditions).

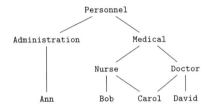

Fig. 3. An example of user-group hierarchy

- *Abstractions.* To simplify the authorization definition process, discretionary access control supports also *user groups* and *classes of objects*, which may also be hierarchically organized. Typically, authorizations specified on an abstraction propagate to all its members according to different *propagation policies* [7]. Figure 3 illustrates an example of user-group hierarchy. Here, for example, an authorization specified for the Nurse group applies also to Bob and Carol.
- *Exceptions.* The definition of abstractions naturally leads to the need of supporting exceptions in authorization definition. Suppose, for example, that all users belonging to a group but u can access resource r. If exceptions were not supported, it would be necessary to associate an authorization with each user in the group but u, therefore not exploiting the possibility of specifying the authorization of the group. This situation can be easily solved by supporting both *positive* and *negative* authorizations: the system would have a positive authorization for the group and a negative authorization for u.

  The introduction of both positive and negative authorizations brings to two problems: *inconsistency*, when conflicting authorizations are associated with the same element in a hierarchy; and *incompleteness*, when some accesses are neither authorized nor denied.

  Incompleteness is usually easily solved by assuming a *default policy*, open or closed (this latter being more common), where no authorization applies. In this case, an open policy approach allows the access, while the closed policy approach denies it.

  To solve the inconsistency problem, different *conflict resolution policies* have been proposed [7, 8], such as:

  - *No conflict.* The presence of a conflict is considered an error.
  - *Denials take precedence.* Negative authorizations take precedence.
  - *Permissions take precedence.* Positive authorizations take precedence.
  - *Nothing takes precedence.* Conflicts remain unsolved.
  - *Most specific takes precedence.* An authorization associated with an element n overrides a contradicting authorization (i.e., an authorization with the same subject, object, and action but with a different sign) associated with an ancestor of n for all the descendants of n. For instance, consider the user-group hierarchy in Fig. 3 and the autho-

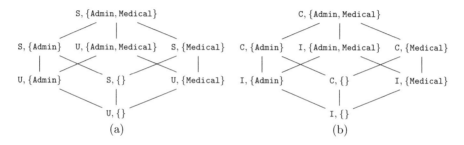

Fig. 4. An example of security (a) and integrity (b) lattices

rizations (Medical,Document1,$+r$) and (Nurse,Document1,$-r$). Carol cannot read Document1, since the Nurse group is more specific than the Medical group.

– *Most specific along a path takes precedence.* An authorization associated with an element n overrides a contradicting authorization associated with an ancestor n' for all the descendants of n, only for the paths passing from n. The overriding has no effect on other paths. For instance, with respect to the previous example, Carol gains a positive authorization from the path ⟨Medical,Doctor,Carol⟩, and a negative one from path ⟨Nurse,Carol⟩.

While convenient for their expressiveness and flexibility, in high security settings discretionary access control results limited for its vulnerability to *Trojan horses*. The reason for this vulnerability is that discretionary access control does not distinguish between *users* (i.e., human entity whose identity is exploited to select the privileges for making the access control decision) and *subjects* (i.e., process generated by a user and that makes requests to the system). A discretionary access control system evaluates the requests made by a subject against the authorizations of the user who generated the corresponding process. It is then vulnerable from processes executing malicious programs that exploit the authorizations of the user invoking them. Protection against these processes requires controlling the flows of information within processes execution and possibly restricting them. Mandatory policies provide a way to enforce information flow control through the use of labels.

2.2 Mandatory Access Control

Mandatory security policies enforce access control on the basis of regulations mandated by a central authority. The most common form of mandatory policy is the *multilevel security policy*, based on the classifications of subjects and objects in the system. Each subject and object in the system is associated with an *access class*, usually composed of a *security level* and a set of *categories*. Security levels in the system are characterized by a total order relation, while categories form an unordered set. As a consequence, the set of access classes is characterized by a partial order relation, denoted $\geq$ and called *dominance*. Given two access classes c_1 and c_2, c_1 *dominates* c_2, denoted $c_1 \geq c_2$, iff the security level of c_1 is greater than or equal to the security level of c_2 and the set of categories of c_1 includes the set of categories of c_2. Access classes together with their partial order dominance relationship form a *lattice* [9].

Mandatory policies can be classified as secrecy-based and integrity-based, operating in a dual manner.

Secrecy-Based Mandatory Policy [10, 11, 12, 13]. The main goal of secrecy-based mandatory policies is to protect data confidentiality. As a consequence, the security level of the access class associated with an object reflects the sensitivity of its content, while the security level of the access class associated with a subject, called *clearance*, reflects the degree of trust placed in the subject not to reveal sensitive information. The set of categories associated with both subjects and objects defines the area of competence of users and data. A user can connect to the system using her clearance or any access class dominated by her clearance. A process generated by a user connected with a specific access class has the same access class as the user.

The access requests submitted by a subject are evaluated by applying the following two principles.

No-Read-Up. A subject s can read an object o if and only if the access class of the subject dominates the access class of the object.

No-Write-Down. A subject s can write an object o if and only if the access class of the object dominates the access class of the subject.

Consider, as an example, the security lattice in Fig. 4(a), where there are two security levels, Secret (S) and Unclassified (U), with S>U, and the set of categories {Admin, Medical}. Suppose that user Ann has clearance $\langle$S,{Admin}$\rangle$ and she connects to the system as the $\langle$S,{}$\rangle$ subject. She is allowed to read objects $\langle$S,{}$\rangle$ and $\langle$U,{}$\rangle$. She can write objects with access class $\langle$S,{}$\rangle$, $\langle$S,{Admin}$\rangle$, $\langle$S,{Medical}$\rangle$, and $\langle$S,{Admin,Medical}$\rangle$.

Note that a user is allowed to connect to the system at different access classes to the aim of accessing information at different levels (provided that she is cleared for it). Otherwise, these accesses would be blocked by the no-write-down principle.

The principles of the secrecy-based mandatory policy prevent information flows from high level subjects/objects to subjects/objects at lower (or incomparable) levels, thus preserving information confidentiality. However, these two principles may turn out to be too restrictive. For instance, in a real scenario data may need to be downgraded (e.g., this may happen at the end of the embargo). To consider also these situations, the secrecy-based mandatory models can allow exceptions for processes that are *trusted* and ensure that the information produced is *sanitized*.

Integrity-Based Mandatory Policy [14]. The main goal of integrity-based mandatory policies is to prevent subjects from *indirectly* modifying information they cannot write. The integrity level associated with a user reflects then the degree of trust placed in the subject to insert and modify sensitive information. The integrity level associated with an object indicates the degree of trust placed on the information stored in the object and the potential damage that could result from unauthorized modifications of the information. Again, the set of categories associated with both subjects and objects defines the area of competence of users and data.

The access requests submitted by a subject are evaluated by applying the following two principles.

No-Read-Down. A subject s can read an object o if and only if the integrity class of the object dominates the integrity class of the subject.

No-Write-Up. A subject s can write an object o if and only if the integrity class of the subject dominates the integrity class of the object.

Consider, as an example, the integrity lattice in Fig. 4(b), where there are two integrity levels Crucial (C) and Important (I), with C>I, and the set of categories {Admin, Medical}. Suppose that user Ann connects to the system as the $\langle C, \{Admin\} \rangle$ subject. She can read objects having integrity class $\langle C, \{Admin\} \rangle$ and $\langle C, \{Admin, Medical\} \rangle$ and she can write objects with integrity class $\langle C, \{Admin\} \rangle$, $\langle C, \{\} \rangle$, $\langle I, \{Admin\} \rangle$, and $\langle I, \{\} \rangle$.

These two principles are the dual with respect to the principles adopted by secrecy-base policies. As a consequence, the integrity model prevents flows of information from low level objects to higher objects. A major limitation of this model is that it only captures integrity breaches due to improper information flows. However, integrity is a much broader concept and additional aspects should be taken into account [15].

Note that secrecy-based and integrity-based models are not mutually exclusive, since it may be useful to protect both the confidentiality and the integrity properties. Obviously, in this case, objects and subjects will be associated with both a security and an integrity class.

A major drawback of mandatory policies is that they control only flows of information happening through *overt channels*, that is, channels operating in a legitimate way. As a consequence, the mandatory policies are vulnerable to *covert* channels [16], which are channels not intended for normal communication but that still can be exploited to infer information. For instance, if a low level subject requests the use of a resource currently used by a high level subject, it will receive a negative response, thus inferring that another (higher level) subject is using the same resource.

2.3 Role-Based Access Control

A third approach for access control is represented by *Role-Based Access Control* (RBAC) models [17, 18]. A *role* is defined as a set of privileges that any user playing that role is associated with. When accessing the system, each user has to specify the role she wishes to play and, if she is granted to play that role, she can exploit the corresponding privileges. The access control policy is then defined through two different steps: first the administrator defines roles and the privileges related to each of them; second, each user is assigned with the set of roles she can play. Roles can be hierarchically organized to exploit the propagation of access control privileges along the hierarchy.

A user may be allowed to simultaneously play more than one role and more users may simultaneously play the same role, even if restrictions on their number may be imposed by the security administrator.

It is important to note that roles and groups of users are two different concepts. A group is a named collection of users and possibly other groups, and a role is a named collection of privileges, and possibly other roles. Furthermore, while roles can be activated and deactivated directly by users at their discretion, the membership in a group cannot be deactivated.

The main advantage of RBAC, with respect to DAC and MAC, is that it better suits to commercial environments. In fact, in a company, it is not important the identity of a person for her access to the system, but her responsibilities. Also, the role-based policy tries to organize privileges mapping the organization's structure on the roles hierarchy used for access control.

3 Credential-Based Access Control

In an open and dynamic scenario, parties may be unknown to each other and the traditional separation between *authentication* and *access control* cannot be applied anymore. Such parties can also play the role of both client, when requesting access to a resource, and server for the resources it makes available for other users in the system. Advanced access control solutions should then allow to decide, on one hand, which requester (client) is to be granted access to the resource, and, on the other hand, which server is qualified for providing the same resource. *Trust management* has been developed as a solution for supporting access control in open environments [19]. The first approaches proposing a trust management solution for access control are PolicyMaker [20] and KeyNote [21]. The key idea of these proposals is to bind public keys to authorizations and to use credentials to describe specific delegations of trust among keys. The great disadvantage of these early solutions is that they assign authorizations directly to users' keys. The authorization specification is then difficult to manage and, moreover, the public key of a user may act as a pseudonym of herself, thus reducing the advantages of trust management, where the identity of the users should not be considered.

The problem of assigning authorizations directly to keys has been solved by the introduction of *digital certificates*. A digital certificate is the on-line counterpart of paper credentials (e.g., a driver licence). A digital certificate is a statement, certified by a trusted entity (the certificate authority), declaring a set of properties of the certificate's holder (e.g., identity, accreditation, or authorizations). Access control models, by exploiting digital certificates for granting or denying access to resources, make access decisions on the basis of a set of properties that the requester should have. The final user can prove to have such properties by providing one or more digital certificates [22, 23, 24, 25, 26].

The development and effective use of credential-based access control models require however tackling several problems related to credential management and disclosure strategies, delegation and revocation of credentials, and establishment of credential chains [27, 28, 29, 30]. In particular, when developing an access control system based on credentials, the following issues need to be carefully considered [22].

- *Ontologies.* Since there is a variety of security attributes and requirements that may need to be considered, it is important to guarantee that different parties will be able to understand each other, by defining a set of common languages, dictionaries, and ontologies.
- *Client-side and server-side restrictions.* Since parties may act as either a client or a server, access control rules need to be defined both client-side and server-side.
- *Credential-based access control rules.* New access control languages supporting credentials need to be developed. These languages should be both expressive (to define different kinds of policies) and simple (to facilitate policy definition).
- *Access control evaluation outcome.* The resource requester may not be aware of the attributes she needs to gain access to the requested resource. As a consequence, access control mechanisms should not simply return a permit or deny answer, but should be able to ask the final user for the needed credentials to access the resource.
- *Trust negotiation strategies.* Due to the large number of possible alternative credentials that would enable an access request, a server cannot formulate a request for all these credentials, since the client may not be willing to release the whole set of her credentials. On the other hand, the server should not disclose too much of the underlying security policy, since it may contain sensitive information.

In the following, we briefly describe some proposals that have been developed for trust negotiation and for regulating service access in open environments.

3.1 Overview of Trust Negotiation Strategies

As previously noted, since the interacting parties may be unknown to each other, the resource requester may not be aware of the credentials necessary for gaining access privileges. Consequently, during the access control process, the two parties exchange information about the credentials needed for access. The access control decision comes then after a complex process, where parties exchange information not only related to the access itself, but also to additional restrictions imposed by the counterpart. This process, called *trust negotiation*, has the main goal of establishing trust between the interacting parties in an automated manner. A number of trust negotiation strategies have been proposed in the literature, which are characterized by the following steps.

- The client first requests to access a resource.
- The server then checks if the client provided the necessary credentials. In case of a positive answer, the server grants access to the resource; otherwise it communicates the client the policies that she has to fulfill.
- The client selects the requested credentials, if possible, and sends them to the server.
- If the credentials satisfy the request, the client is granted access to the resource.

This straightforward trust negotiation process suffers of privacy problems, since both the server discloses its access control policy entirely and the client exposes all her certificates to gain access to a resource. To solve such an inconvenience, a *gradual trust establishment* process can be enforced [31]. In this case, upon receiving an access request, the server selects the policy that governs the access to the service and discloses only the information that it is willing to show to an unknown party. The client, according to its practices, decides if it is willing to disclose the requested credentials. Note that this incremental exchange of requests and credentials can be iteratively repeated as many times as necessary.

PRUdent NEgotiation Strategy (PRUNES) is another negotiation strategy whose main goal is to minimize the number of certificates that the client communicates to the server [30]. It also ensures that the client communicates her credentials to the server only if the access will be granted. Each party defines a set of *credential policies* on which the negotiation process is based. The established credential policies can be graphically represented through a tree, called *negotiation search tree*, composed of two kinds of nodes: *credential nodes*, representing the need for a specific credential, and *disjunctive nodes*, representing the logic operators connecting the conditions for credential release. The root of the tree represents the resource the client wants to access. The negotiation process can be seen as a backtracking operation on the tree. To the aim of avoiding the cost of a brute-force backtracking, the authors propose the *PRUNES* method to prune the search tree without compromising completeness or correctness of the negotiation process. The basic idea is that if a credential has just been evaluated and the state of the system has not changed too much, then it is useless to evaluate again the same credential.

A large set of negotiation strategies, called *disclosure tree strategy* (DTS) family [32], has been also defined and proved to be closed. This means that, if two parties use different strategies from the DST family, they will be able to negotiate trust. A *Unified Schema for Resource Protection* (UniPro) [33] has been proposed to protect the information specified within policies. UniPro gives (opaque) names to policies and allows any named policy P_1 to have its own policy P_2, meaning that the content of P_1 can only be disclosed to parties who satisfy P_2. Another solution is the *Adaptive Trust Negotiation and Access Control* (ATNAC) approach [34]. This method grants (or denies) access on the basis of a *suspicion level* associated with subjects. The suspicion level is not fixed but may vary on the basis of the probability that the user has malicious intents.

It is important to note that in recent, more complicated, scenarios disclosure policies can be defined both on resources and on credentials [22]. In this case, the client, upon receiving a request for a certificate, can answer with a counter-request to the server for another certificate.

3.2 Overview of a Credential-Based Access Control Framework

One of the first solutions providing a uniform framework for credential-based access control specification and enforcement was presented by Bonatti and Samarati [22]. The proposed access control system includes an access control model, a language, and a policy filtering mechanism.

The paper envisions a system composed of two entities: a *client* and a *server*, interacting through a predefined negotiation process. The server is characterized by a set of resources. Both the client and the server have a *portfolio*, which is a collection of credentials (i.e., statements issued by authorities trusted for making them [35]) and declarations (statements issued by the party itself). Credentials correspond to digital certificates and are guaranteed to be unforgeable and verifiable through the public key of the issuing authority.

To the aim of performing gradual trust establishment between the two interacting parties, the server defines a set of *service accessibility rules*, and both the client and the server define their own set of *portfolio disclosure rules*. The service accessibility rules specify the necessary and sufficient conditions for accessing a resource, while portfolio disclosure rules define the conditions that govern the release of credentials and declarations. Both the two classes of rules are expressed by using a logic language. A special class of predicates is represented by *abbreviations*. Since there may exist a number of alternative combinations of certificates allowing access to a resource, *abbreviation predicates* may be used for reducing the communication cost of such certificates. The predicates of the language adopted exploit the current *state* (i.e., parties' characteristics, certificates already exchanged in the negotiation, and requests made by the parties) to take a decision about a release. The information about the state is classified as *persistent state*, when the information is stored at the site and spans different negotiations, and *negotiation state*, when it is acquired during the negotiation and is deleted when the same terminates.

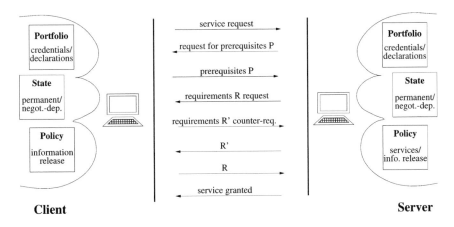

Fig. 5. Client-server negotiation

The main advantage of this proposal is that it maximizes both server and client's privacy, by minimizing the set of certificates exchanged. In particular, the server discloses the minimal set of policies for granting access, while the client releases the minimal set of certificates to access the resource. To this purpose, service accessibility rules are distinguished in *prerequisites* and *requisites*. Prerequisites are conditions that must be satisfied for a service request to be taken into consideration (they do not guarantee that it will be granted); requisites are conditions that allow the service request to be successfully granted. Therefore, the server will not disclose a requisite rule until the client satisfies a prerequisite rule. Figure 5 illustrates the resulting client/server interaction. It is important to highlight here that, before releasing rules to the client, the server needs to evaluate state predicates that involve private information. For instance, the client is not expected to be asked many times the same information during the same session and if the server has to evaluate if the client is considered not trusted, it cannot communicate this request to the client itself.

4 Policy Composition

In many real word scenarios, access control enforcement needs to take into consideration different policies independently stated by different administrative subjects, which must be enforced as if they were a single policy. As an example of policy composition, consider an hospital, where the global policy may be obtained by combining together the policies of its different wards and the externally imposed constraints (e.g., privacy regulations). Policy composition is becoming of paramount importance in all those contexts in which administrative tasks are managed by different, non collaborating, entities.

Policy composition is an orthogonal aspect with respect to policy models, mechanisms, and languages. As a matter of fact, the entities expressing the policies to be composed may even not be aware of the access control system adopted by the other entities specifying access control rules. The main desiderata for a policy composition framework can be summarized as follows [36].

- *Heterogeneous policy support.* The framework should support policies expressed in different languages and enforced by different mechanisms.
- *Support of unknown policies.* The framework should support policies that are not fully defined or are not fully known when the composition strategy is defined. Consequently, policies are to be treated as black-boxes and are supposed to return a correct and complete response when queried at access control time.
- *Controlled interference.* The framework cannot simply merge the sets of rules defined by the different administrative entities, since this behavior may cause side effects. For instance, the accesses granted/denied might not correctly reflect the specifications anymore.
- *Expressiveness.* The framework should support a number of different ways for combining the input policies, without changing the input set of rules or introducing ad-hoc extensions to authorizations.
- *Support of different abstraction levels.* The composition should highlight the different components and their interplay at different levels of abstraction.
- *Formal semantics.* The language for policy composition adopted by the framework should be declarative, implementation independent, and based on a formal semantic to avoid ambiguity.

We now briefly describe some solutions proposed for combining different policies.

4.1 Overview of Policy Composition Solutions

Various models have been proposed to reason about security policies [37, 38, 39, 40]. In [37, 39] the authors focus on the secure behavior of program modules. McLean [40] introduces *the algebra of security*, which is a Boolean algebra that enables to reason about the problem of policy conflict, arising when different policies are combined. However, even though this approach permits to detect conflicts between policies, it does not propose a method to resolve the conflicts and to construct a security policy from inconsistent sub-policies. Hosmer [38] introduces the notion of meta-policies, which are defined as policies about policies. Metapolicies are used to coordinate the interaction about policies and to explicitly define assumptions about them. Subsequently, Bell [41] formalizes the combination of two policies with a function, called *policy combiner*, and introduces the notion of *policy attenuation* to allow the composition of conflicting security policies. Other approaches are targeted to the development of a uniform framework to express possibly heterogeneous policies [42, 43, 44, 45, 46].

A different approach has been illustrated in [36], where the authors propose an algebra for combining security policies together with its formal semantics. Here, a policy, denoted P_i, is defined as a set of triples of the form (s,o,a), where s is a constant in (or a variable over) the set of subjects S, o is a constant in (or a variable over) the set of objects O, and a is a constant in (or a variable over) the set of actions A. Policies of this form are composed through a set of *algebra operators* whose syntax is represented by the following BNF:

$$E ::= \mathbf{id}|E + E|E\&E|E - E|E^\wedge C|o(E,E,E)|E * R|T(E)|(E)$$
$$T ::= \tau\mathbf{id}.E$$

where **id** is a unique policy identifier, E is a policy expression, T is a construct, called *template*, C is a construct describing constraints, and R is a construct describing rules. The order of evaluation of algebra operators is determined by the precedence, which is (from higher to lower) τ, ., + and & and -, * and $\wedge$.

The semantic of algebra operators is defined by a function that maps policy expressions in a set of ground authorizations (i.e., a set of authorization triples). The function that maps policy identifiers into sets of triples is called *environment*, and is formally defined as follows.

Definition 1. *An* environment e *is a partial mapping from policy identifiers to sets of authorization triples. By* $e[X/S]$ *we denote a modification of environment* e *such that*

$$e[X/S](Y) = \begin{cases} S & \text{if } Y = X \\ e(Y) & \text{otherwise} \end{cases}$$

The semantic of an identifier X in the environment e is denoted by $[\![X]\!]_e = e(X)$.

The operators defined by the algebra for policy composition basically reflect the features supported by classical policy definition systems. As an example, it is possible to manage exceptions (such as negative authorizations), propagation of authorizations, an so on. The set of operators together with their semantic is briefly described in the following.

- *Addition* (+). It merges two policies by returning their union.

$$[\![P_1 + P_2]\!]_e = [\![P_1]\!]_e \cup [\![P_2]\!]_e$$

Intuitively, additions can be applied in any situation where accesses can be authorized if allowed by any of the component policies (maximum privilege principle).
- *Conjunction* (&). It merges two policies by returning their intersection.

$$[\![P_1\&P_2]\!]_e = [\![P_1]\!]_e \cap [\![P_2]\!]_e$$

This operator enforces the minimum privilege principle.

- *Subtraction* $(-)$. It deletes from a first policy, all the authorizations specified in a second policy.

$$[\![P_1 - P_2]\!]_e = [\![P_1]\!]_e \setminus [\![P_2]\!]_e$$

Intuitively, subtraction operator is used to handle exceptions, and has the same functionalities of negative authorizations in existing approaches. It does not generate conflicts since P_1 prevails on P_2 by default.
- *Closure* $(*)$. It closes a policy under a set of derivation rules.

$$[\![P * R]\!]_e = \mathbf{closure}(R, [\![P]\!]_e)$$

The closure of policy P under derivation rules R produces a new policy that contains all the authorizations in P and those that can be derived evaluating R on P, according to a given semantics. The derivation rules in R can enforce, for example, an authorization propagation along a pre-defined subject or object hierarchy.
- *Scoping Restriction* $(^\wedge)$. It restricts the applicability of a policy to a given subset of subjects, objects, and actions of the system.

$$[\![P_1^{\wedge}c]\!]_e = \{t \in [\![P]\!]_e \mid t \text{ satisfy } c\}$$

where c is a condition. It is useful when administration entities need to express their policy on a confined subset of subjects and/or objects (e.g., each ward can express policies about the doctors working in the ward).
- *Overriding* (o). It overrides a portion of policy P_1 with the specifications in policy P_2; the fragment that is to be substituted is specified by a third policy P_3.

$$[\![o(P_1, P_2, P_3)]\!]_e = [\![(P_1 - P_3) + (P_2 \& P_3)]\!]_e$$

- *Template* (τ). It defines a partially specified (i.e., parametric) policy that can be completed by supplying the parameters.

$$[\![\tau X.P]\!]_e(S) = [\![P]\!]_{e[S/X]}$$

where S is the set of all policies, and X is a parameter. Templates are useful for representing policies as black-boxes. They are needed any time when some components are to be specified at a later stage. For instance, the components might be the result of a further policy refinement, or might be specified by a different authority.

Due to the formal definition of the semantic of algebra operators, it is possible to exploit algebra expressions to formally prove the security properties of the obtained (composed) policy.

Once the policies have been composed through the algebraic operators described above, for their enforcement it is necessary to provide executable specifications compatible with different evaluation strategies. To this aim, the authors propose the following three main strategies to translate policy expressions into logic programs.

- *Materialization.* The expressions composing policies are explicitly evaluated, by obtaining a set of ground authorizations that represents the policy that needs to be enforced. This strategy can be applied when all the composed policies are known and reasonably static.
- *Partial materialization.* Whenever materialization is not possible since some of the policies to be composed are not available, it is possible to materialize only a subset of the final policy. This strategy is useful also when some of the policies are subject to sudden and frequent changes, and the cost of materialization may be too high with respect to the advantages it may provide.
- *Run-time evaluation.* In this case no materialization is performed and run-time evaluation is needed for each request (access triple), which is checked against the policy expressions to determine whether the triple belongs to the result.

The authors then propose a method (*pe2lp*) for transforming algebraic policy composition expressions into a logic program. The method proposed can be easily adapted to one of the three materialization strategies introduced above. Basically, the translation process creates a distinct predicate symbol for each policy identifier and for each algebraic operator in the expression. The logic programming formulation of algebra expressions can be used to enforce access control. As already pointed out while introducing algebra operators, this policy composition algebra can also be used to express simple access control policies, such as open and closed policy, propagation policies, and exceptions management. For instance, let us consider a hospital composed of three wards, namely *Cardiology*, *Surgery*, and *Orthopaedics*. Each ward is responsible for granting access to data under its responsibility. Let $P_{Cardiology}$, $P_{Surgery}$ and $P_{Orthopaedics}$ be the policies of the three wards. Suppose now that an access is authorized if any of the wards policies state so and that authorizations in policy $P_{Surgery}$ are propagated to individual users and documents by classical hierarchy-based derivation rules, denoted R_H. In terms of the algebra, the hospital policy can be represented as follows.

$$P_{Cardiology} \& P_{Surgery} * R_H \& P_{Orthopaedics}$$

Following this work, Jajodia et al. [47] presented a propositional algebra for policies with a syntax consisting of abstract symbols for atomic policy expressions and composition operators.

5 Access Control Through Encryption

Since the amount of data that organizations need to manage is increasing very quickly, data outsourcing is becoming more and more attractive. Data outsourcing provides data storage at a low rate, allowing the data owner to concentrate its activity on its core business where data are managed by an external service provider. The main drawback of this practice is that the service provider may not be fully trusted. The data owner and final users are usually supposed to trust the provider for managing data stored on its server, and to correctly execute queries on it, but the provider is not fully trusted for accessing data content. To solve this problem, different solutions have been proposed in the literature, mainly based on the use of cryptography as a mechanism for protecting data privacy [1, 2, 3]. Most of the proposals in this area focus on issues related to querying encrypted data, to the aim of avoiding server-side decryption, while minimizing client-side burden in query evaluation. Another drawback of existing proposals is that they assume that any client has complete access to the query results, and therefore the data owner has to be involved for filtering out the data not accessible by the client. This would cause an excessive burden on the owner, thus nullifying the advantages of outsourcing data management. On the other hand, the remote server cannot enforce access control policies, since it may not be allowed to know the access control policy defined by the owner. Since neither the data owner nor the remote server can enforce the access control policy, for either security or efficiency reasons, the data themselves need to implement selective access. This can be realized through *selective encryption*, which consists in encrypting data using different keys and distributing the keys so that users can decrypt only the data they are authorized to access.

The problem of enforcing access control policies through selective encryption has been analyzed both for databases and for XML documents. In the following, we briefly introduce the most important proposals for these two scenarios [48, 49, 50].

5.1 Overview of Database Outsourcing Solutions

Let us consider a system composed of a set $\mathcal{U}$ of users and a set $\mathcal{R}$ of resources. A resource may be a table, an attribute, a tuple, or even a cell, depending on the granularity at which the data owner wishes to define her policy. Since this distinction does not affect access control policy enforcement, we will always refer generically to resources. The access control policy defined by the data owner can be easily represented through a traditional access matrix $\mathcal{A}$, where each cell $\mathcal{A}[u,r]$ may assume either the value 1, if u can access r, or the value 0, otherwise (currently only read privileges have been considered). Figure 6 represents an example of access matrix, where there are four users, namely A, B, C, and D, and four resources r_1, r_2, r_3, and r_4.

A first solution that could be adopted for selectively encrypting data for access control purposes consists in using a different key for each resource, and in communicating each user the set of keys used to protect the resources belonging to her capability list (i.e., the set of resources that the user can access). This solution requires each user to keep a possibly great number of

	r_1	r_2	r_3	r_4
A	1	1	0	1
B	1	1	0	0
C	1	0	1	0
D	0	1	1	0

Fig. 6. An example of binary access matrix

(secret) keys, depending on the number of her privileges. To the aim of reducing the number of keys that each user has to manage, *key derivation methods* can be adopted [51]. A key derivation method allows the computation of an encryption key, by proving the knowledge of another secret key in the system. By adequately organizing encryption keys and adopting a derivation method, it is possible to communicate a small number of keys to users, granting then the possibility of deriving from these keys, those needed for accessing data. Typically, these methods assume the existence of a partial order relationship defined on the set of keys. Given the set of encryption keys $\mathcal{K}$ in the system, and a partial order relationship $\preceq$ defined on it, the pair $(\mathcal{K}, \preceq)$ represents the *key derivation hierarchy* of the system, where $\forall k_i, k_j \in \mathcal{K}$, if $k_j \preceq k_i$ then k_j is derivable from k_i. Consequently, by knowing a key k_i, it is possible to compute the value of any k_j such that $k_j \preceq k_i$. Graphically, a key derivation hierarchy can be represented as a graph, with a vertex for each key in $\mathcal{K}$, and a path from k_i to k_j if $k_j \preceq k_i$. A key derivation hierarchy can however assume three different graphical structures, which in turn influence the key derivation method that can be adopted, as described in the following.

- *Chain of vertexes.* The relation $\preceq$ is a total order relation for $\mathcal{K}$; the value of k_i depends only on the value of the key of its (unique) direct ancestor k_j [52].
- *Tree.* The relation $\preceq$ is a partial order relation for $\mathcal{K}$ such that if $k_i \preceq k_j$ and $k_i \preceq k_l$, then either $k_j \preceq k_l$ or $k_l \preceq k_j$; the value of k_i depends on the value of the key of its (unique) direct ancestor k_j, and on the public label l_i associated with k_i [52, 53, 54].
- *DAG.* Different classes of solutions have been proposed for DAGs [51]. In particular, Atallah et al. [55] introduce an interesting solution that allows insertion an deletion of keys in the hierarchy without the need of redefining the whole set of keys $\mathcal{K}$. This method associates a piece of public information (called *token*) with each edge in the DAG. Given an edge connecting key k_i with k_j, token $T_{i,j} = k_j \oplus h(k_i, l_j)$, where l_j is a publicly available label associated with k_j, h is a secure hash function, and $\oplus$ is the n-ary xor operator.

Damiani et al. [56] propose an access control solution for outsourcing data that is based on the definition of a key derivation hierarchy reflecting the user-group containment relation. Given a set $\mathcal{U}$ of users, a *user-based hierarchy*, denoted UH, is defined as a pair $(P(\mathcal{U}), \preceq)$, where $P(\mathcal{U})$ represents the powerset

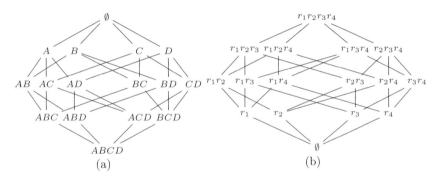

Fig. 7. An example of UH (a) and RH (b)

(i.e., the set of all subsets of $\mathcal{U}$) of $\mathcal{U}$, and contains $2^{|\mathcal{U}|}$ items, and $\preceq$ is defined as the set containment relation, that is, $\forall a, b \in P(\mathcal{U})$, $a \preceq b$ if and only if $b \subseteq a$. Each vertex v_i in UH is associated with a private key k_i. Each user $u_i \in \mathcal{U}$ is then communicated key k_i associated with the vertex representing the singleton set $\{u_i\}$. Each resource r_j is instead encrypted with the key k_j associated with the vertex representing its *acl*. Since partial order relation $\preceq$ is defined on the basis of the set containment relation, any user in the system, by knowing the key of vertex $\{u_i\}$, can derive all and only the keys of vertexes representing sets of users including u_i. Figure 7(a) represents the user hierarchy suitable for the access matrix in Fig. 6. To correctly enforce the given access control policy, r_1 is encrypted with the key of vertex ABC, r_2 with the key of vertex ABD, r_3 with the key of vertex CD, and r_4 with the key of vertex A. Due to this key assignment, any user can access exactly the resources in her capability list. As an example, with respect to the hierarchy in Fig. 7(a), it is easy to see that B can derive the key associated with vertexes AB and BD that in turn can be used for deriving the keys associated with vertexes ABC and ABD, this allowing to access r_1 and r_2, respectively.

In a dual way, it is possible to build a key derivation hierarchy on the basis of the resources in the system. A *resource-based hierarchy*, denoted RH, is defined as a pair $(P(\mathcal{R}), \preceq)$, where $P(\mathcal{R})$ represents the powerset of $\mathcal{R}$, and $\preceq$ is a partial order relation such that $\forall a, b \in P(\mathcal{R})$, $a \preceq b$ if and only if $a \subseteq b$. To correctly enforce the given policy, each user u_i is assigned the key of the vertex representing her capability list, while each resource r_j is encrypted with the key of the vertex representing the singleton set $\{r_j\}$. Considering again the access matrix in Fig. 6, the corresponding resource hierarchy is represented in Fig. 7(b).

Although both the models presented for defining a key derivation hierarchy correctly enforce the access control policy defined by the owner, there is an important difference that should be considered when deciding which structure to adopt. As a matter of fact, UH allows resources to share the same encryption key, while each user has her secret key. By contrast, when adopting RH,

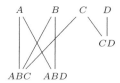

Fig. 8. An example of transformed user hierarchy.

different users can share the same secret key, while resources are all encrypted using a different key. Moreover, since the number of vertexes in the hierarchy depends on the number of users (resources, respectively) in the system, if $\mathcal{U}$ is smaller than $\mathcal{R}$, UH will be probably more convenient than RH. In the following, we focus on the user-based hierarchy, but the discussion is however applicable also to the resource-based hierarchy.

It is easy to note that UH structure defines a great number of keys, some of which may be useful neither for encryption nor for distribution to users. This causes both an expensive key derivation process on the client side, and an excessive storage workload for the server. As a matter of fact, the length of key derivation paths in UH is linear in $|\mathcal{U}|$, and the number of tokens stored on the server grows with $|\mathcal{U}|$.

To the aim of reducing both key derivation costs and, more generally, the size of the key derivation hierarchy, the authors propose to remove from UH all those vertexes that are not necessary for access control enforcement [48]. Therefore, the vertexes that are maintained in the hierarchy are those that represent singleton sets of users and resources' *acls*. These vertexes are then connected in a new hierarchical structure, according to the $\preceq$ partial order relation. The resulting hierarchy should guarantee that any user u_i can compute, from her private key, the keys used to encrypt all and only the resources belonging to her capability list. To this purpose, the authors propose an algorithm that, starting from the set of required vertexes, builds a key derivation hierarchy on which they apply the Atallah et al. key derivation method. To improve the key derivation process for final users, the algorithm tries to minimize the number of tokens in the system. To this aim, other vertexes besides the necessary ones are possibly added to the hierarchical structure. Considering the user hierarchy in Fig. 7, Fig. 8 illustrates the hierarchy corresponding to the access control policy in Fig. 6, and containing only the vertexes needed for a correct enforcement of the policy.

Zych and Petkovic [49] exploit Diffie-Hellman key generation scheme and asymmetric encryption for enforcing selective access on outsourced data. Given a user-based hierarchy, the authors propose to build a *V-graph* starting from it. For each vertex in the V-graph, the number of incoming edges is either 2 or 0, and for any two vertexes, there is at most one common parent vertex. The resulting structure is a *binary tree*, whose leaves represent singleton sets of users, and whose root represents the group containing all the users in the system. Also, any user knows the private key of the vertex representing herself in the hierarchy, and each resource is encrypted with the private key associated with the vertex representing its *acl*. However, differently from other proposals, key derivation goes from leaves to the root of the tree.

5.2 Overview of XML Document Outsourcing Solutions

Besides traditional databases, also XML documents can contain sensitive information, and their outsourcing may cause privacy breaches. As a consequence, it is necessary to develop techniques for enforcing access control on outsourced XML data as well. Although some of the approaches presented for the relational database outsourcing scenario are suited for XML data outsourcing, they do not exploit the main characteristics of XML documents (e.g., their tree structure) and different specific approaches have then been proposed. The solutions presented exploit once again selective encryption as a way for enforcing access control when publishing or outsourcing sensitive data.

Miklau and Suciu [50] propose a way for differentiating the encryption of different portions of an XML document, on the basis of users or groups who can access them. The proposed access control mechanism is enriched by adding metadata XML nodes, adopted to enforce access control rules with conditions on the values contained in the document. Wang et al. [57] present an access control system that both protects data stored in the XML document and the associations among data by introducing association constraints that need to be satisfied by the encryption model adopted.

6 Conclusions

This chapter discussed recent trends in the access control field. We described the basic concepts of access control and investigated different issues concerning the development of an access control system. In particular, we outlined the needs for providing means to: support access control in open environments, where the identities of the involved parties may be unknown; combine authorization specifications that may be independently stated; enforce access control through the use of selective encryption. For these contexts, we described recent proposals and ongoing work.

Acknowledgements

This work was supported in part by the European Union under contract IST-2002-507591, and by the Italian Ministry of Research, within programs FIRB, under project "RBNE05FKZ2", and PRIN 2006, under project "Basi di dati crittografate" (2006099978).

References

1. Hacigümüs, H., Iyer, B., Mehrotra, S., Li, C.: Executing SQL over encrypted data in the database-service-provider model. In: Proc. of the ACM SIGMOD 2002, Madison, Wisconsin, USA (2002)
2. Hacigümüs, H., Iyer, B., Mehrotra, S.: Providing database as a service. In: Proc. of 18th International Conference on Data Engineering, San Jose, California, USA (2002)
3. Damiani, E., De Capitani di Vimercati, S., Jajodia, S., Paraboschi, S., Samarati, P.: Balancing confidentiality and efficiency in untrusted relational DBMSs. In: Proc. of the 10th ACM Conference on Computer and Communications Security (CCS03), Washington, DC, USA (2003)
4. Graham, G., Denning, P.: Protection- principles and practice. In: Proc. of the Spring Jt. Computer Conference. Volume 40., Montvale, NJ, USA (1972) 417–429
5. Harrison, M., Ruzzo, W., Ullman, J.: Protection in operating systems. Communications of the SCM **19**(8) (August 1976) 461–471
6. Lampson, B.W.: Protection. ACM Operating Systems Review **8**(1) (January 1974) 18–24
7. Jajodia, S., Samarati, P., Sapino, M., Subrahmanian, V.: Flexible support for multiple access control policies. ACM Transaction on Database Systems **26**(2) (June 2001) 214–260
8. Lunt, T.: Access control policies: Some unanswered questions. In: Proc. of IEEE Computer Security Foundations Workshop II, Franconia, New Hampshire (1988)
9. Sandhu, R.: Lattice-based access control models. IEEE Computer **26**(11) (1993) 9–19
10. Bell, D., La Padula, L.: Secure computer systems: A mathematical model. Technical Report MTR-2547, Vol 2, MITRE Corp., Bedford, MA (November 1973)
11. Bell, D., La Padula, L.: Secure computer systems: Mathematical foundations. Technical Report MTR-2547, Vol 1, MITRE Corp., Bedford, MA (November 1973)
12. Bell, D., La Padula, L.: Secure computer systems: A refinement of the mathematical model. Technical Report MTR-2547, Vol 3, MITRE Corp., Bedford, MA (April 1974)
13. Bell, D., La Padula, L.: Secure computer systems: Unified exposition and multics interpretation. Technical Report MTR-2997, Vol 4, MITRE Corp., Bedford, MA (July 1975)
14. Biba, K.J.: Integrity considerations for secure computer systems. MTR-3153 rev., MITRE Corp., Vol 1, Bedford, MA (April 1977)
15. Samarati, P., De Capitani di Vimercati, S.: Access control: Policies, models, and mechanisms. In Focardi, R., Gorrieri, R., eds.: Foundations of Security Analysis and Design. LNCS 2171. Springer-Verlag (2001)
16. McLean, J.: Security models. In Marciniak, J., ed.: Encyclopedia of Software Engineering. John Wiley & Sons (1994)
17. Ferraiolo, D., Kuhn, D.: Role-based access control. In: Proc. of the 15th National Computer Security Conference. (1992)
18. Sandhu, R., Coyne, E., Feinstein, H., Youman, C.: Role-based access control models. IEEE Computer **29**(2) (1996) 38–47

19. Security and trust management (2005)
    http://www.ercim.org/publication/Ercim_News/enw63/.
20. Blaze, M., Feigenbaum, J., Lacy, J.: Decentralized trust management. In: Proc.
    of the 17th Symposium on Security and Privacy, Oakland, California, USA (May
    1996)
21. Blaze, M., Feigenbaum, J., Ioannidis, J., Keromytis, A.: The KeyNote Trust
    Management System (Version 2). Internet RFC 2704 edn. (1999)
22. Bonatti, P., Samarati, P.: A unified framework for regulating access and infor-
    mation release on the web. Journal of Computer Security **10**(3) (2002) 241–272
23. Irwin, K., Yu, T.: Preventing attribute information leakage in automated trust
    negotiation. In: Proc. of the 12th ACM Conference on Computer and Commu-
    nications Security, Alexandria, VA, USA (2005)
24. Li, N., Mitchell, J., Winsborough, W.: Beyond proof-of-compliance: Security
    analysis in trust management. Journal of the ACM **52** (2005) 474–514
25. Ni, J., Li, N., Winsborough, W.: Automated trust negotiation using crypto-
    graphic credentials. In: Proc. of the 12th ACM Conference on Computer and
    Communications Security, Alexandria, VA, USA (2005)
26. Yu, T., Winslett, M., Seamons, K.: Supporting structured credentials and sen-
    sitive policies trough interoperable strategies for automated trust. ACM Trans-
    actions on Information and System Security (TISSEC) **6**(1) (February 2003)
    1–42
27. Seamons, K.E., Winsborough, W., Winslett, M.: Internet credential acceptance
    policies. In: Proc. of the Workshop on Logic Programming for Internet Appli-
    cations, Leuven, Belgium (July 1997)
28. Seamons, K.E., Winslett, M., Yu, T., Smith, B., Child, E., Jacobson, J., Mills,
    H., Yu, L.: Requirements for policy languages for trust negotiation. In: Proc.
    of the 3rd International Workshop on Policies for Distributed Systems and Net-
    works (POLICY 2002), Monterey, CA (June 2002)
29. Winslett, M., Ching, N., Jones, V., Slepchin, I.: Assuring security and privacy
    for digital library transactions on the web: Client and server security policies.
    In: Proc. of the ADL '97 — Forum on Research and Tech. Advances in Digital
    Libraries, Washington, DC (May 1997)
30. Yu, T., Ma, X., Winslett, M.: An efficient complete strategy for automated
    trust negotiation over the internet. In: Proc. of the 7th ACM Computer and
    Communication Security, Athens, Greece (November 2000)
31. Seamons, K., Winslett, M., Yu, T.: Limiting the disclosure of access control
    policies during automated trust negotiation. In: Proc. of the Symposium on
    Network and Distributed System Security, San Diego, CA (April 2001)
32. Yu, T., Winslett, M., Seamons, K.: Interoperable strategies in automated trust
    negotiation. In: Proc. of the 8th ACM Conference on Computer and Commu-
    nications Security, Philadelphia, Pennsylvania (November 2001)
33. Yu, T., Winslett, M.: A unified scheme for resource protection in automated
    trust negotiation. In: Proc. of the IEEE Symposium on Security and Privacy,
    Berkeley, California (May 2003)
34. Ryutov, T., Zhou, L., Neuman, C., Leithead, T., Seamons, K.: Adaptive trust
    negotiation and access control. In: Proc. of the 10th ACM Symposium on Access
    Control Models and Technologies, Stockholm, Sweden (June 2005)
35. Gladman, B., Ellison, C., Bohm, N.: Digital signatures, certificates and elec-
    tronic commerce. http://www.clark.net/pub/cme/html/spki.html.

36. Bonatti, P., De Capitani di Vimercati, S., Samarati, P.: An algebra for composing access control policies. ACM Transactions on Information and System Security **5**(1) (February 2002) 1–35

37. Abadi, M., Lamport, L.: Composing specifications. ACM Transactions on Programming Languages **14**(4) (October 1992) 1–60

38. Hosmer, H.: Metapolicies II. In: Proc. of the 15th National Computer Security Conference, Baltimore, MD (October 1992)

39. Jaeger, T.: Access control in configurable systems. Lecture Notes in Computer Science **1603** (2001) 289–316

40. McLean, J.: The algebra of security. In: Proc. of the 1988 IEEE Computer Society Symposium on Security and Privacy, Oakland, CA, USA (April 1988)

41. Bell, D.: Modeling the multipolicy machine. In: Proc. of the New Security Paradigm Workshop, Little Compton, Rhode Island, USA (August 1994)

42. Bertino, E., Jajodia, S., Samarati, P.: A flexible authorization mechanism for relational data management systems. ACM Transactions on Information Systems **17**(2) (April 1999) 101–140

43. Jajodia, S., Samarati, P., Sapino, M., Subrahmanian, V.: Flexible support for multiple access control policies. ACM Transactions on Database Systems **26**(2) (June 2001) 214–260

44. Jajodia, S., Samarati, P., Subrahmanian, V., Bertino, E.: A unified framework for enforcing multiple access control policies. In: Proc. of the 1997 ACM International SIGMOD Conference on Management of Data, Tucson, AZ (May 1997)

45. Li, N., Feigenbaum, J., Grosof, B.: A logic-based knowledge representation for authorization with delegation. In: Proc. of the 12th IEEE Computer Security Foundations Workshop, Washington, DC, USA (July 1999)

46. Woo, T., Lam, S.: Authorizations in distributed systems: A new approach. Journal of Computer Security **2**(2,3) (1993) 107–136

47. Wijesekera, D., Jajodia, S.: A propositional policy algebra for access control. ACM Transactions on Information and System Security **6**(2) (May 2003) 286–325

48. Damiani, E., De Capitani di Vimercati, S., Foresti, S., Jajodia, S., Paraboschi, S., Samarati, P.: An experimental evaluation of multi-key strategies for data outsourcing. In: Proc. of the 22nd IFIP TC-11 International Information Security Conference (SEC 2007), Sandton, South Africa (May 2007)

49. Zych, A., Petkovic, M.: Key management method for cryptographically enforced access control. In: Proc. of the 1st Benelux Workshop on Information and System Security, Antwerpen, Belgium (2006)

50. Miklau, G., Suciu, D.: Controlling access to published data using cryptography. In: Proc. of the 29th VLDB Conference, Berlin, Germany (September 2003)

51. Crampton, J., Martin, K., Wild, P.: On key assignment for hierarchical access control. In: In Proc. of the 19th IEEE Computer Security Foundations Workshop (CSFW'06), Los Alamitos, CA, USA (2006)

52. Sandhu, R.: On some cryptographic solutions for access control in a tree hierarchy. In: Proc. of the 1987 Fall Joint Computer Conference on Exploring Technology: Today and Tomorrow, Dallas, Texas, USA (1987)

53. Gudes, E.: The design of a cryptography based secure file system. IEEE Transactions on Software Engineering **6** (1980) 411–420

54. Sandhu, R.: Cryptographic implementation of a tree hierarchy for access control. Information Processing Letters **27** (1988) 95–98

55. Atallah, M., Frikken, K., Blanton, M.: Dynamic and efficient key management for access hierarchies. In: Proc. of the 12th ACM conference on Computer and Communications Security (CCS05), Alexandria, VA, USA (2005)
56. Damiani, E., De Capitani di Vimercati, S., Foresti, S., Jajodia, S., Paraboschi, S., Samarati, P.: Selective data encryption in outsourced dynamic environments. In: Proc. of the Second International Workshop on Views On Designing Complex Architectures (VODCA 2006). Electronic Notes in Theoretical Computer Science, Bertinoro, Italy, Elsevier (2006)
57. Wang, H., Lakshmanan, L.V.S.: Efficient secure query evaluation over encrypted XML databases. In: Proc. of the 32nd VLDB Conference, Seoul, Korea (September 2006)

2

Access Control Models for XML

S. De Capitani di Vimercati[1], S. Foresti[1], S. Paraboschi[2], and P. Samarati[1]

[1] University of Milan – 26013 Crema, Italy
   {decapita,foresti,samarati}@dti.unimi.it
[2] University of Bergamo – 24044 Dalmine, Italy
   parabosc@unibg.it

Summary. XML has become a crucial tool for data storage and exchange. In this chapter, after a brief introduction on the basic structure of XML, we illustrate the most important characteristics of access control models. We then discuss two models for XML documents, pointing out their main characteristics. We finally present other proposals, describing their main features and their innovation compared to the previous two models.

1 Introduction

The amount of information that is made available and exchanged on the Web sites is continuously increasing. A large portion of this information (e.g., data exchanged during EC transactions) is sensitive and needs to be protected. However, granting security requirements through HTML-based information processing turns out to be rather awkward, due to HTML's inherent limitations. HTML provides no clean separation between the structure and the layout of a document and some of its content is only used to specify the document layout. Moreover, site designers often prepare HTML pages according to the needs of a particular browser. Therefore, HTML markup has generally little to do with data semantics.

To the aim of separating data that need to be represented from how they are displayed, the World Wide Web Consortium (W3C) has standardized a new markup language: the *eXtensible Markup Language* (XML) [1]. XML is a markup meta-language providing semantics-aware markup without losing the formatting and rendering capabilities of HTML. XML's tags' capability of self-description is shifting the focus of Web communication from conventional hypertext to data interchange. Although HTML was defined using only a small and basic part of SGML (Standard Generalized Markup Language: ISO 8879), XML is a sophisticated subset of SGML, designed to describe data using arbitrary tags. As its name implies, extensibility is a key feature of XML; users and applications are free to declare and use their own tags and attributes. Therefore, XML ensures that both the logical structure and content of semantically rich information is retained. XML focuses on the description of information structure and content as opposed to its presentation. Presentation issues are addressed by a separate language, XSL [2] (XML Stylesheet Language), which is also a W3C standard for expressing how XML-based data should be rendered.

Since XML documents can be used instead of traditional relational databases for data storage and organization, it is necessary to think of a security system for XML documents protection. In this chapter, we will focus on access control enforcement. Specifically, in the literature, different access control models have been proposed for protecting data stored in XML documents, exploiting the flexibility offered by the markup language. Even if traditionally access control models can be applied to XML documents, by simply treating them as files, a finer grained access control system is frequently necessary. As a matter of fact, an XML document may contain both sensitive and publicly available information, and it is necessary to distinguish between them when specifying the access control policy.

The remainder of the chapter is organized as follows. Section 2 discusses the basic XML concepts, by introducing DTD, XML Schema, XPath and XQuery syntax and semantics. Section 3 introduces the problem of access control for XML documents, points out the characteristics that an access control model for XML documents should have. Section 4 illustrates in the details two of the first access control models proposed for XML documents, and briefly describes other proposals. Finally, Sect. 5 concludes the chapter.

2 Preliminary Concepts

XML [1] (eXtensible Markup Language) is a markup language developed by the World Wide Web Consortium (W3C) and used for describing semi-structured information. We introduce some of the most important concepts related to XML, which are useful to define an access control system for protecting XML documents.

2.1 Well-Formed and Valid XML Documents

XML document is composed of a sequence of (possibly nested) *elements* and *attributes* associated with them. Basically, elements are delimited by a pair of start and end tags (e.g., <request> and </request>) or, if they have no content, are composed of an empty tag (e.g., <request/>). Attributes represent properties of elements and are included in the start tag of the element with which they are associated (e.g., <request number="10">). An XML document is said to be *well-formed* if its syntax complies with the rules defined by the W3C consortium [1], which can be summarized as follows:

- the document must start with the *prologue* <?xml version="1.0"?>;

- the document must have a *root* element, containing all other elements in the document;
- all open tags must have a corresponding closed tag, provided it is not an empty tag;
- elements must be properly nested;
- tags are case-sensitive;
- attribute values must be quoted.

An *XML language* is a set of XML documents that are characterized by a syntax, which describes the markup tags that the language uses and how they can be combined, together with its semantics. A *schema* is a formal definition of the syntax of an XML language, and is usually expressed through a schema language. The most common schema languages, and on which we focus our attention, are *DTD* and *XML Schema*, both originating from W3C.

Document Type Definition.

A DTD document may be either internal or external to an XML document and it is not itself written in the XML notation.

A DTD schema consists of definition of elements, attributes, and other constructs. An element declaration is of the form `<!ELEMENT` *element_name content*`>`, where *element_name* is an element name and *content* is the description of the content of an element and can assume one of the following alternatives:

- the element contains parsable character data (`#PCDATA`);
- the element has no content (`Empty`);
- the element may have any content (`Any`);
- the element contains a group of one or more subelements, which in turn may be composed of other subelements;
- the element contains parsable character data, interleaved with subelements.

When an element contains other elements (i.e., subelements or mixed content), it is necessary to declare the subelements composing it and their organization. Specifically, sequences of elements are separated by a comma "," and alternative elements are separated by a vertical bar "|". Declarations of sequence and choices of subelements need to describe subelements' cardinality. With a notation inspired by extended BNF grammars, "*" indicates zero or more occurrences, "+" indicates one or more occurrences, "?" indicates zero or one occurrence, and no label indicates exactly one occurrence.

An attribute declaration is of the form `<!ATTLIST` *element_name attribute_def*`>`, where *element_name* is the name of an element, and *attribute_def* is a list of attribute definitions that, for each attribute, specify the attribute name, type, and possibly default value. Attributes can be marked as `#REQUIRED`, meaning that they must have an explicit value for each occurrence of the elements with which they are associated; `#IMPLIED`, meaning that they are optional; #FIXED, meaning that they have a fixed value, indicated in the definition itself.

An XML document is said to be *valid* with respect to a DTD if it is syntactically correct according to the DTD. Note that, since elements and attributes defined in a DTD may appear in an XML document zero (optional elements), one, or multiple times, depending on their cardinality constraints, the structure specified by the DTD is not rigid; two distinct XML documents of the same schema may differ in the number and structure of elements.

XML Schema.

An XML Schema is an XML document that, with respect to DTD, has a number of advantages. First, an XML Schema is itself an XML document, consequently it can be easily extended for future needs. Furthermore, XML Schemas are richer and more powerful than DTDs, since they provide support for data types and namespaces, which are two of the most significant issues with DTD.

An element declaration specifies an element name together with a simple or complex type. A *simple type* is a set of Unicode strings (e.g., decimal, string, float, and so on) and a *complex type* is a collection of requirements for attributes, subelements, and character data that apply to the elements assigned to that type. Such requirements specify, for example, the *order* in which subelements must appear, and the cardinality of each subelement (in terms of maxOccurs and minOccurs, with 1 as default value).

Attribute declarations specify the attributes associated with each element and indicate attribute name and type. Attribute declarations may also specify either a default value or a fixed value. Attributes can be marked as: required, meaning that they must have an explicit value for each occurrence of the elements with which they are associated; optional, meaning that they are not necessary.

Example 1. Suppose that we need to define an XML-based language for describing bank account operations. Figure 1(a) illustrates a DTD stating that each account_operation contains a request element and one or more operation elements. Each account_operation is also characterized by two mandatory attributes: bankAccN, indicating the number of the bank account of the requester; and id, identifying the single update. Each request element is composed of date, means, and notes elements, where only date is required. Element operation is instead composed of: type, amount, recipient, and possibly one between notes and value.

Figure 1(b) illustrates an XML document valid with respect to the DTD in Fig. 1(a).

DTDs and XML documents can be graphically represented as trees.

A DTD is represented as a labeled tree containing a node for each element, attribute, and value associated with fixed attributes. To distinguish elements

```
<!DOCTYPE record[                                   <?xml version="1.0" ?>
  <!ELEMENT account_operation                       <!DOCTYPE record SYSTEM "record.dtd">
    (request, operation+)>                             <account_operation
  <!ATTLIST account_operation                             bankAccN="0012" id="00025">
    bankAccN CDATA #REQUIRED                             <request number="10">
    id CDATA #REQUIRED>                                    <date> 04-20-2007 </date>
  <!ELEMENT request                                       <means> Internet </means>
    (date,means?,notes?)>                                 <notes> urgent </notes>
  <!ATTLIST request number CDATA #REQUIRED>             </request>
  <!ELEMENT operation                                   <operation>
    (type, amount, recipient, (notes|value)?)>            <type> bank transfer </type>
  <!ELEMENT date (#PCDATA)>                               <amount> $ 1,500 </amount>
  <!ELEMENT means (#PCDATA)>                              <recipient> 0023 </recipient>
  <!ELEMENT notes (#PCDATA)>                              <notes> Invoice 315 of 03-31-2007
  <!ELEMENT type (#PCDATA)>                               </notes>
  <!ELEMENT amount (#PCDATA)>                           </operation>
  <!ELEMENT recipient (#PCDATA)>                      </account_operation>
  <!ELEMENT value (#PCDATA)>
]>
```

(a)   (b)

Fig. 1. An example of DTD (a) and a corresponding valid XML document (b)

and attributes in the graphical representation, elements are represented as ovals, while attributes as rectangles. There is an arc in the tree connecting each element with all the elements/attributes belonging to it, and between each #FIXED attribute and its value. Arcs connecting an element with its subelements are labeled with the cardinality of the relationship. Arcs labeled *or* and with multiple branching are used to represent a choice in an element declaration (|). An arc with multiple branching is also used to represent a sequence with a cardinality constraint associated with the whole sequence (?, +, *). To preserve the order between elements in a sequence, for any two elements e_i and e_j, if e_j follows e_i in the element declaration, node e_j appears below node e_i in the tree.

Each XML document is represented by a tree with a node for each element, attribute, and value in the document. There is an arc between each element and each of its subelements/attributes/values and between each attribute and each of its value(s). Each arc in the DTD tree may correspond to zero, one, or multiple arcs in the XML document, depending on the cardinality of the corresponding containment relationship. Note that arcs in XML documents are not labeled, as there is no further information that needs representation. Figure 2 illustrates the graphical representation of both DTD and XML document in Fig. 1.

2.2 Elements and Attributes Identification

The majority of the access control models for XML documents identify the objects under protection (i.e., elements and attributes) through the *XPath* language [3]. XPath is an expression language, where the basic building block is the path expression.

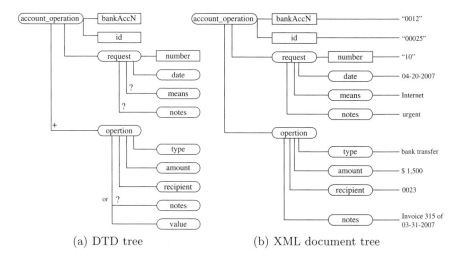

(a) DTD tree   (b) XML document tree

Fig. 2. An example of graphical representation of DTD and XML document

A *path expression* on a document tree is a sequence of element names or predefined functions separated by character / (slash): $l_1/l_2/\ldots/l_n$. Path expressions may terminate with an attribute name as the last term of the sequence. Attribute names are syntactically distinguished by preceding them with special character @. A path expression $l_1/l_2/\ldots/l_n$ on a document tree represents all the attributes or elements named l_n that can be reached by descending the document tree along the sequence of nodes named $l_1/l_2/\ldots/l_{n-1}$. A path expression can be either *absolute*, if it starts from the root of the document (the path expression starts with /); or *relative*, if it starts from a predefined element in the document (the path expression starts with element name). The path expression may also contain operators (e.g., operator . represents the current node, operator .. represents the parent node, operator // represents an arbitrary descending path), functions, and predicates (we refer the reader to [3] for more details).

XPath allows the association of conditions with nodes in a path; in this case the path expression identifies the set of nodes that satisfy all the conditions. Conditional expressions in XPath may operate on the "text" of elements (i.e., character data in elements) or on names and values of attributes. A condition is represented by enclosing it within square brackets, following a label l_i in a path expression $l_1/l_2/\ldots/l_n$. The condition is composed of one or more predicates, which may be combined via **and** and **or** boolean operators. Each predicate compares the result of the evaluation of the relative path expression (evaluated at l_i) with a constant or with another expression. Multiple conditional expressions appearing in the same path expression are considered to be **and**ed (i.e., all the conditions must be satisfied). In addition, conditional expressions may include functions **last()** and **position()** that permit the extraction of the children of a node that are in given positions. Function `last()` evaluates to true on the last child of the current node. Function `position()` evaluates to true on the node in the evaluation context whose position is equal to the context position.

Path expressions are also the building blocks of other languages, such as XQuery [4] that allows to make queries on XML documents through `FLWOR` expressions. A `FLOWR` expression is composed of the following clauses:

- `FOR` declares variables that are iteratively associated with elements in the XML documents, which are identified via path expressions;
- `LET` declares variables associated with the result of a path expression;
- `WHERE` imposes conditions on tuples;
- `ORDER BY` orders the result obtained by `FOR` and `LET` clauses;
- `RETURN` generates the final result returned to the requester.

Example 2. Consider the DTD and the XML document in Example 1. Some examples of path expressions are the following.

- `/account_operation/operation`: returns the content of the `operation` element, child of `account_operation`;
- `/account_operation/@bankAccN`: returns attribute `bankAccN` of element `account_operation`;
- `/account_operation//notes`: returns the content of the `notes` elements, anywhere in the subtree rooted at `account_operation`; in this case, it returns both `/account_operation/request/notes` and `/account_operation/operation/notes`;
- `/account_operation/operation[./type="bank transfer"]`: returns the content of the `operation` element, child of `account_operation`, only if the `type` element, child of `operation`, has value equal to "bank transfer".

The following XQuery extracts form the XML document in Fig. 1(b) all the `account_operation` elements with operation type equal to "bank transfer". For the selected elements, the `amount` and the `recipient` of the operation are returned, along with all `notes` appearing in the selected `account_operation` element.

```
<BankTransf>
{ FOR    $r in document("update_account")/account_operation
  WHERE  $r/operation/type="bank transfer"
  RETURN $r/operation/amount, $r/operation/recipient, $r//notes
}
</BankTransf>
```

3 XML Access Control Requirements

Due to the peculiar characteristics of the XML documents, they cannot be protected by simply adopting traditional access control models, and specific

models need to be defined. By analyzing the existing proposals, it is easy to
see that they are all based on the definition of a set of authorizations that at
least specify the subjects on which they apply, the objects to be protected,
and the action to be executed. The existing XML-based access control models
differentiate on the basis of the subjects, objects, and actions they can support
for access control specification and enforcement.

Subject. Subjects are usually referred to on the basis of their *identities* or
   of the network *location* from which requests originate. Locations can
   be expressed with reference to either the numeric IP address (e.g.,
   150.100.30.8) or the symbolic name (e.g., bank.com) from which the
   request comes.
   It often happens that the same privilege should be granted to sets of
   subjects, which share common characteristics, such as the department
   where they work, or the role played in the company where they work. To
   the aim of simplifying the authorizations definition, some access control
   models allow the specification of authorizations having as subject:
   - a *group of users*, which is a statically defined set of users; groups can
     be nested and overlapping;
   - a *location pattern*, which is an expression identifying a set of physi-
     cal locations, obtained by using the wild character * in physical or
     symbolic addresses;
   - a *role*, which is a set of privileges that can be exploited by any user
     while playing the specific role; users can dynamically decide which role
     to play, among the ones they are authorized to play.
   Also, subjects are often organized in hierarchies, where an authorization
   defined for a general subject propagates to its descendants.

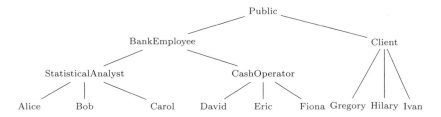

Fig. 3. An example of user-group hierarchy

A hierarchy can be pictured as a *directed acyclic graph* containing a node
for each element in the hierarchy and an arc from element x to element y, if
x directly dominates y. Dominance relationships holding in the hierarchy
correspond to paths in the graph. Figure 3 shows an example of user-group
hierarchy.

Recently proposed models [5] for access control on XML documents introduce the possibility of specifying authorizations on the basis of subject's characteristics, called *credentials*, without even knowing the user's identity and/or location.

Object Granularity. The identification of the object involved in a specific authorization can exploit the possibility given by XML of identifying elements and attributes within a document through path expressions as defined by the XPath language.

Consequently, XML allows the specification of authorizations at a fine grained level. Any portion of a document that can be referred by a path expression can be the object of an authorization. For instance, a single element or a single attribute are objects as well as a whole XML document. It is important to note that not all models support entirely XPath syntax, since it is very expressive and may be difficult to manage. For instance, some models impose restrictions on the number of times that the // operator can appear in a path expression [6], other proposals do not allow predicates to be specified after the // operator [7].

Action. Most of the proposed XML access control models support only *read* operations, since there is not a standard language for XML update. Furthermore, the management of *write* privileges is a difficult task, which needs to take into account both the access control policy and the DTD (or XML Schema) defined for the document. In fact, the DTD may be partially hidden to the user accessing the document, as some elements/attributes may be denied by the access control policy. For instance, when adding an element to the document, the user may even not be aware of the existence of a required attribute associated with it, as she is not entitled to access the attribute itself.

However, some approaches try to also support write privileges that are usually classified as: insert operations, update operations, and delete operations.

In [8], the author proposes to differentiate also read privileges in two categories: the privilege of reading the content of an element, from the privilege of knowing that there is an element in a certain position of the XML document (without knowing the name and content of the element itself). The former authorization class is modeled as read action, while the latter is modeled as position action. In the same paper, the author proposes also to add the possibility, for the security administrator, to propagate privileges *with-grant option*, as in typical database contexts.

We now discuss the basic peculiar features that are supported by the existing XML-based access control models.

Support for Fine and Coarse Authorizations. The different protection requirements that different documents may have call for the support of access restrictions at the level of each specific document. However, requiring the specification of authorizations for each single document would make the authorization specification task too heavy. The system may then support, beside authorizations on single documents (or portions of documents), authorizations on collections of documents [9]. The concept of DTD can be naturally exploited to this end, by allowing protection requirements to refer to DTDs or XML documents, where requirements specified at the level of DTD apply to all those documents instance of the considered DTD. Authorizations specified at DTD level are called *schema level* authorizations, while those specified at XML document level are called *instance level* authorizations.

Furthermore, it is important to be able to specify both organization-wide and domain authorizations, which apply only to a part of the whole organization. To this purpose, some systems [9] allow access and protection requirements to be specified both at the level of the enterprise, stating general regulations, and at the level of specific domains where, according to a local policy, additional constraints may need to be enforced or some constraints may need to be relaxed. Organizations specify authorizations with respect to DTDs; domains can specify authorizations with respect to specific documents as well as to DTDs.

Propagation Policy. The structure of an XML document can be exploited by possibly applying different propagation strategies that allow the derivation of authorizations from a given set of authorizations explicitly defined over elements of DTD and/or XML documents. Some proposals therefore distinguish between two kinds of authorizations: *local*, and *recursive* [9]. Local authorizations defined on an element apply to all its attributes only. A recursive authorization defined on an element applies to its whole content (both attributes and subelements). Recursive authorizations represent an easy way for specifying authorizations holding for the whole structured content of an element (for the whole document if the element is the root node of the document).

The models proposed in [6, 7] assume that negative authorizations are always recursive, while positive authorizations may be either local or recursive.

Besides downward propagation, upward propagation methods have been introduced [10]. Here, the authorizations associated with a node in the XML tree propagate to all its parents.

Some of the most common propagation policies (which include also some resolution policies for possible conflicts) are described in the following [11].

- *No propagation.* Authorizations are not propagated. This is the case of local authorizations.
- *No overriding.* Authorizations of a node are propagated to its descendants, but they are all kept.
- *Most specific overrides.* Authorizations of a node are propagated to its descendants, if not overridden. An authorization associated with a

node n overrides a contradicting authorization[3] associated with any ancestor of n for all the descendants of n.

- *Path overrides.* Authorizations of a node are propagated to its descendants, if not overridden. An authorization associated with a node n overrides a contradicting authorization associated with an ancestor n' for all the descendants of n only for the paths passing from n. The overriding has no effect on other paths.

These policies can be adopted also for the authorization subject hierarchy.

Support of Exceptions. The support of authorizations at different granularity levels allows for easy expressiveness of both fine and coarse grained authorizations. Such an advantage would remain however very limited without the ability of the authorization model to support exceptions, since the presence of a granule (document or element/attribute) with protection requirements different from those of its siblings would require the explicit specification of authorizations at that specific granularity level. For instance, the situation where a user should be granted access to all documents associated with a DTD but one specific instance, would imply the need of stating the authorizations explicitly for all the other documents as well; thereby ruling out the advantage of supporting authorizations at the DTD level. A simple way to support exceptions is by using both *positive* (permissions) and *negative* (denials) authorizations, where permissions and denials can override each other.

The combined use of positive and negative authorizations brings to the problem of how the two specifications should be treated when conflicting authorizations are associated with the same node element for a given subject and action. This requires the support for conflict resolution policies [11].

Most of the models proposed for XML access control adopt, as a conflict resolution policy, the "denials take precedence" policy, meaning that, in case of conflict, access is denied.

Note that, when both permissions and denials can be specified, another problem that naturally arises is the *incompleteness* problem, meaning that for some accesses neither a positive nor a negative authorization exists. The incompleteness problem is typically solved by applying a default *open* or *closed* policy [12].

4 XML Access Control Models

Several access control models have been proposed in the literature for regulating access to XML documents. We start our overview of these models by presenting the first access control model for XML [9], which has then inspired

---

[3] Two authorizations (s, o, a) and (s', o', a') are contradictory if $s = s'$, $o = o'$, and $a = a'$, but one of them grants access, while the other denies it.

many other subsequent proposals. We then illustrate the Kudo et al. [13] model that introduced the idea of using a static analysis system for XML access control. Finally, we briefly describe other approaches that have been studied in the literature to the aim of supporting write privileges and adopting cryptography as a method for access control enforcement.

4.1 Fine Grained XML Access Control System

Damiani et al [9] propose a fine grained XML access control system, which extends the proposals in [14, 15, 16], exploiting XML's own capabilities to define and implement an authorization model for regulating access to XML documents.

We now present the authorizations supported by the access control model and illustrate the authorizations enforcement process.

Authorizations Specification

Access authorization determines the accesses that the system should allow or deny. In this model, access authorizations are defined as follows.

Definition 1 ((Access Authorization)). *An* access authorization $a \in$ Auth *is a five-tuple of the form:* ⟨*subject, object, action, sign, type*⟩, *where:*

- subject $\in$ AS *is the subject for which the authorization is intended;*
- object *is either a URI*∈Obj *or is of the form URI:PE, where URI*∈Obj *and PE is a path expression on the tree of document URI;*
- action=read *is the action being authorized or forbidden;*
- sign $\in \{+,-\}$ *is the sign of the authorization, which can be positive (allow access) or negative (forbid access);*
- type $\in \{$LDH, RDH, L, R, LD, RD, LS, RS$\}$ *is the type of the authorization and regulates whether the authorization propagates to other objects and how it interplays with other authorizations (exception policy).*

We now discuss in more detail each of the five elements composing an access authorization.

Subject. This model allows to identify the subject of an authorization by specifying both her identity and her location. This choice provides more expressiveness as it is possible to restrict the subject authorized to access an object on the basis of her identity and of the location from which the request comes.

Subjects are then characterized by a triple ⟨user-id,IP-address,sym-address⟩, where user-id is the identity with which the user connected to the system, and IP-address (sym-address, respectively) is the numeric (symbolic, respectively) identifier of the machine from which the user connected. The proposed model supports also *user-groups* and *location patterns* and the corresponding hierarchies. Location patterns are however restricted by imposing that multiple wild characters must be continuous, and that they must always appear as rightmost elements in IP patterns and as leftmost elements in symbolic patterns. As a consequence, location pattern hierarchies are always trees. The user-group hierarchy and the location pattern hierarchies need to be merged in a unique structure: the *authorization subject hierarchy* AS, obtained as Cartesian product of the user-group hierarchy, the IP hierarchy, and the symbolic names hierarchy. Any element in the hierarchy is then associated with a user-id (or group), an IP address (or pattern), and a symbolic name (or pattern). When one of these three values corresponds to the top element in the corresponding hierarchy, the characteristics it defines are not relevant for access control purposes, as any value is allowed.

Object. The set of objects that should be protected is denoted as Obj and is basically a set of URIs (Uniform Resources Identifiers) referring to XML documents or DTDs. Reference to the finer element and attribute grains is supported through path expressions, which are specified in the XPath language.

Action. The authors limit the basic model definition to read authorizations only. However, the support of write actions such as insert, update, and delete does not complicate the authorization model. In [9] the authors briefly introduce a method to handle also write operations, using a model similar to the one proposed for read operations.

Sign. Authorizations can be either positive (permissions) or negative (denials), to provide a simple and effective way to specify authorizations applicable to sets of subjects/objects with support for *exceptions*.

Type. The type defines how the authorizations must be treated with respect to propagation at a finer granularity and overriding.

Authorizations specified on an element can be defined as applicable to the element's attributes only (*local* authorizations) or, in a recursive approach, to its subelements and their attributes (*recursive* authorizations). To support exceptions (e.g., the whole content, except a specific element, can be read), recursive propagation from a node applies until stopped by an explicit conflicting (i.e., of different sign) authorization on the descendants, following the "most specific overrides" principle. Authorizations can be specified on single XML documents (instance level authorizations) or on DTDs (schema level authorizations). Authorizations specified on a DTD are applicable (i.e., are propagated) to all XML documents that are instances of the DTD. According to the "most specific overrides" principle, schema level authorizations being propagated to an instance are overridden by possible authorizations specified for the instance. To address situations where this precedence criterion should not be applied, the model allows users to specify instance level authorizations as *soft* (i.e., to be applied unless otherwise stated at the schema level) and schema level

Table 1. Authorization types

Level/Strength	Propagation	
	Local	Recursive
Instance	L	R
Instance (soft statement)	LS	RS
DTD	LD	RD
DTD (hard statement)	LDH	RDH

authorizations as *hard* (i.e., to be applied independently from instance level authorizations). Besides the distinction between instance level and schema level authorizations, this model allows the definition of two types of schema level authorizations: *organization* and *domain* schema level authorizations. Organization schema level authorizations are stated by a central authority and can be used to implement corporate wide access control policies on document classes. Domain schema level authorizations are specified by departmental authorities and describe department policies complementing the corporate ones. For simplicity, these two classes of authorizations are merged by performing a *flat union* (i.e., they are treated in the same way).

The combination of the options above (i.e., local vs recursive, schema vs instance level, and soft vs hard authorizations) introduces the eight authorization types summarized in Table 1. Their semantics dictates a priority order among the authorization types. The priority order from the highest to the lowest is: LDH (local hard authorization), RDH (recursive hard authorization), L (local authorization), R (recursive authorization), LD (local authorization specified at the schema level), RD (recursive authorization specified at the schema level), LS (local soft authorization), and RS (recursive soft authorization).

Access Control Enforcement

Whenever a user makes a request for an object of the system, it is necessary to evaluate which portion of the object (if any) she is allowed to access. To this aim, the system builds a *view* of the document for the requesting subject [9]. The view of a subject on each document depends on the access permissions and denials specified by the authorizations and on their priorities. Such a view can be computed through a *tree labeling* process, followed by a *transformation* process.

Given an access request rq and the requested XML document URI, the tree labeling process considers the tree corresponding to URI and, for each of its nodes, tries to identify if the requesting subject is allowed or denied access. Each node n in the considered tree is associated with a vector $n.veclabel[t]$

that, for each authorization type $t \in \{$LDH, RDH, L, R, LD, RD, LS, RS$\}$, stores the users for which there is a positive ($n.veclabel[t].Allowed$) and negative ($n.veclabel[t].Denied$) authorization of type t that applies to n. The algorithm mainly executes the following steps.

Step 1: *Authorization retrieval.* Determine the set A of authorizations defined for the document URI at the instance and schema levels and applicable to the requester in rq (i.e., the subject of the authorization is the same, or a generalization of the requested subject).

Step 2: *Initial labeling.* For each authorization $a = \langle subject, object, action, sign, type \rangle \in A$, determine the set N of nodes that are identified by $a.object$. Then, for each node n in N, $a.subject$ is added to the list $n.veclabel[a.type].Allowed$ or to the list $n.veclabel[a.type].Denied$ depending if $a.sign$ is $+$ or $-$, respectively.

Since several authorizations, possibly of different sign, may exist for each authorization type, the application of a conflict resolution policy is necessary. The final sign $n.veclabel[t].sign$ applicable to node n for each type t is then obtained by combining the two lists according to the selected conflict resolution policy. The model is applicable and adaptable to different conflict resolution policies. However, for simplicity it is assumed that conflicts are solved by applying the "most specific subject takes precedence" principle together with the "denials take precedence" principle.

Step 3: *Label propagation.* The labels (signs) associated with nodes are then propagated to their subelements and attributes according to the following criteria: (1) authorizations on a node take precedence over those on its ancestors, and (2) authorizations at the instance level, unless declared as soft, take precedence over authorizations at the schema level, unless declared as hard. The nodes whose sign remains undeterminate (ϵ) are associated with a negative sign since the closed policy is applied.

Step 4: *View computation.* Once the subtree associated with the request has been properly labeled with $+$ $-$ signs, it is necessary to compute the document's view to be returned to the requester. Note that, even if the requester is allowed access to all and only the elements and attributes whose label is positive, the portion of the document visible to the requester includes also start and end tags of elements with a negative label, but that have a descendant with a positive label. Otherwise, the structure of the document would change, becoming non compliant with the DTD any more. The view of the document can be obtained by *pruning* from the original document tree all the subtrees containing only nodes with a negative or undefined label. The pruned document may be not valid with respect to the DTD referenced by the original XML document. This may happen, for instance, when attributes marked as #REQUIRED are deleted because the final user cannot access them. To avoid this problem, a *loosening* transformation is applied to the DTD, which simply defines as optional all the elements (and attributes) marked as required in the original

Table 2. An example of access control policies

Subject	Object	Sign	Action	Type
1 Public,*,*	/account_operation/@bankAccN	−	read	LD
2 BankEmployee,*,*	/account_operation	+	read	RD
3 StatisticalAnalyst,*,*	/account_operation	+	read	RD
4 StatisticalAnalyst,*,*	//notes	−	read	LD
5 StatisticalAnalyst,*,*	/account_operation/operation [./type="bank transfer"]	−	read	RD
6 Client,*,*	/account_operation [./@bankAccN=$userAcc]	+	read	R
7 BankEmployee,150.108.33.*,*	/account_operation/@bankAccN	+	read	L
8 StatisticalAnalyst,*,*.bank.com	/account_operation//notes	+	read	L
9 CashOperators,*,*	/account_operation/ request[./means="Internet"]	−	read	R

DTD. DTD loosening prevents users from detecting whether information has been hidden by the security enforcement or was simply missing in the original document [14].

Example 3. Consider the DTD and the XML document in Fig. 1, and the user-group hierarchy in Fig. 3. Table 2 shows a list of access control policies. The first schema-level authorization states that nobody can access attribute @bankAccN of element account_operation (1). Users belonging to BankEmployee and StatisticalAnalyst groups can access the account_operation element (2 and 3), but StatisticalAnalyst group is denied access to //notes (4). Since the fourth authorization is LD, while third authorization is RD, the fourth policy overrides the third one. Furthermore, StatisticalAnalyst group is denied access to /account_operation/operation[./type="bank transfer"], meaning that users belonging to the group cannot access /account_operation/operation if the operation is a bank transfer (5). Consider now the instance-level authorizations. Users belonging to Client group can access the account_operation element, if condition ./@bankAccN=$userAcc holds (variable $userAcc represents the variable containing the bank account number for the requesting user) (6). Also, members of the BankEmployee group and connected from 150.108.33.* can access @bankAccN attribute (7). This authorization overrides the first authorization in the table. Members of the StatisticalAnalyst group and connected from *.bank.com can read /account_operation//notes for the specific instance (8). Finally, CashOperators group is denied access to /account_operation/request[./means="Internet"] (9).

Suppose now that Alice and David submit a request to read the document in Fig. 1(b). Figure 4 illustrates the views returned to Alice and David at the end of the access control process.

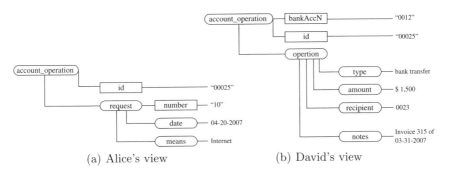

(a) Alice's view   (b) David's view

Fig. 4. Examples of views

4.2 Kudo et al. Static Analysis

Most of the access control systems proposed for XML documents are based on a run-time policy evaluation, that is, any time an access request is submitted to the system, the access control policies are evaluated. However, this run-time policy evaluation may be quite expensive [13]. To avoid this problem, Kudo et al. proposed an access control system based on *static analysis*, which is complemented by a run-time analysis when needed [13].

Authorization Specification

Access authorizations are defined as triples of the form $(s, \pm a, o)$, stating that authorization subject s is (or not, depending on the sign) allowed to perform action a on object o.

An authorization subject may be a user-id, a role, or a group name: the subject name is preceded by a prefix indicating its type. Note that hierarchical structures are not supported by this model. The XPath language is used to define objects in an authorization rule, but functions are not handled by the considered model. Like in [9], the authors limit the basic model definition to read authorizations only, and support both positive and negative authorizations to easily handle exceptions. However, this model does not distinguish between schema and instance level authorizations.

Authorizations specified on an element can be defined as applicable to the element's attributes only (*local* authorizations) or, in a recursive approach, to its subelements and their attributes (*recursive* authorizations). To solve conflicts that may arise on a node, the proposed model can adopt either the "denials take precedence" or the "permissions take precedence" principles, independently from the node on which the conflicting authorizations have been specified. For security reasons, the model presented in the paper limits the analysis to "denials take precedence" principle adoption. The default closed policy is applied when no authorizations are specified.

The framework proposed for static analysis is based on the use of *automata* to compare schemas, authorizations, and queries. The static analysis tries to evaluate anything that does not depend on the specific XML instance and that can be evaluated simply on the basis of the schema and of the access control policy. Formally, an automaton is defined as follows.

Definition 2 ((Non deterministic finite state automaton)). *A non deterministic finite state automaton (NFA) M is a five-tuple of the form* $(\Omega, Q, Q^{init}, Q^{fin}, \delta)$ *where:*

- Ω *is the alphabet;*
- Q *is a finite set of states of* M*;*
- $Q^{init} \subseteq Q$ *is the set of* initial *states of* M*;*
- $Q^{fin} \subseteq Q$ *is the set of* final *states of* M*;*
- $\delta : Q \times \Omega \to Q$ *is the* transition function *of* M*.*

The set of strings accepted by M, denoted $L(M)$, is the language of the automaton.

Given the definition of non deterministic finite state automaton, it is possible to build a NFA corresponding to an arbitrary XPath expression r that does not contain conditions. The NFA accepts a path iff it matches with r. This correspondence is possible since XPath is limited to // operator and conditions are not considered while building the NFA. However, if an XPath expression contains conditions, it is possible to partially capture their semantics by building two NFAs for the given XPath expression r: an *overestimation* $\overline{M[r]}$ and an *underestimation* $\underline{M[r]}$. The former automaton is obtained by assuming all conditions satisfied, while the latter is obtained by assuming all conditions not satisfied.

Static Analysis

The static analysis exploits the definition of automaton and is composed of the following four steps.

Step 1: *Create schema automata.* Given a schema (DTD or XML Schema) that a document should follow, a *schema automaton* M^G is built. This automaton accepts all and only the paths that are allowed by the schema.

Step 2: *Create access control automata.* For each role (group) in the system, a pair of automata is defined: an *underestimate access-control automaton* $\underline{M^\Gamma}$ and an *overestimate access-control automaton* $\overline{M^\Gamma}$. For each role, this pair of automata should accept the set of paths to elements and/or attributes that the role is authorized to access. It is necessary to define both an underestimate and an overestimate automaton since conditions may be added to correctly handle the propagation of positive and negative authorizations along the XML tree. In particular, since the "denials take precedence" principle is adopted, an element is accessible only if it is the descendant of an authorized node, and it is not the descendant of any denied node.

Step 3: *Create query regular expressions.* Given a query expressed in XQuery, the XPath expressions appearing in the query are translated in equivalent *regular expressions* E^r. XPath expressions appearing as argument for the clauses FOR, LET, ORDER, and WHERE are translated in equivalent (possibly overestimated) regular expressions. XPath expressions appearing in the RETURN clause are overestimated and the regular expression generated captures also any descendant of the nodes defined by the XPath expression. Note that recursive queries cannot be handled, since the corresponding regular expression would not be defined.

Step 4: *Compare schema and access control automata with query regular expressions.* Given an XPath expression r, it may be:

- *always granted*, if every path accepted by the query regular expression E^r and by the schema automaton M^G is accepted by the (underestimated) access control automaton $\underline{M^\Gamma}$;
- *always denied*, if no path is accepted by all of the query regular expression E^r, the schema automaton M^G, and the (overestimated) access control automaton $\overline{M^\Gamma}$;
- *statically indeterminated*, otherwise.

Note that, if the schema is not defined, the schema automaton M^G accepts any path.

The proposed static analysis method does not support conditions involving values specified in the XML documents. However, it is possible to extend the model to the aim of partially handling value-based access control. Intuitively, if an access control policy and a query specify the same predicate, it is possible to incorporate the predicate in the underlying alphabet adopted to build NFAs. To this aim, it is necessary a pre-processing phase of the static analysis method that identifies and substitutes predicates with symbols. Even if this solution does not eliminate predicates completely, it improves query efficiency by anticipating some predicate evaluations.

The main advantage of static analysis is that queries can be rewritten on the basis of the XPath expressions they consider. If the query contains a path expression classified as always denied by the fourth step of the static analysis process, it can be removed from the query without evaluation. By contrast, path expressions classified as always granted, simply need to be returned to the requester. Those path expressions that are classified as statically indeterminate have to be run-time evaluated, on the basis of the specific instance they refer to.

The authors provide also a way for easily building a schema (DTD or XML Schema), which can be released without security threats, depending on the authorizations of the requesting user. This method is based on the automata structures previously described. The *view schema* contains only elements visible to the final user, while non accessible elements containing accessible ones are renamed as AccessDenied elements [13].

As a support for the proposal, experimental results are presented demonstrating the efficiency gain due to static analysis with respect to run-time analysis proposed by other approaches.

Example 4. Consider the DTD and the XML document in Fig. 1 and suppose that there are three user-groups: BankEmployee, which are employees of the considered bank institute, StatisticalAnalyst, which are bank employees who make statistics about clients and their operations, and Client, which are people having a bank account at the institute.

Consider a set of authorizations stating that the members of the BankEmployee group can access the whole content of the account_operation element, members of the StatisticalAnalyst group can access the content of the account_operation element but the notes elements, and each client can access the account_operation elements about their bank account. Formally, these authorizations can be expressed as follows.

- group: BankEmployee, /account_operation, + read, recursive
- group: StatisticalAnalyst, /account_operation, + read, recursive
- group: StatisticalAnalyst, //notes, - read, recursive
- group: Client, /account_operation[./@bankAccN=$userAcc], + read, recursive

We first define the schema automaton corresponding to the considered DTD. It is first necessary to define two sets of symbols, representing elements and attributes, respectively.

$\Sigma^E=$ {account_operation, request, operation, date, means, notes, type, amount, recipient, value}
$\Sigma^A=$ {@bankAccN, @Id, @number}

Given Σ^E and Σ^A, it is now possible to define the schema automaton M^G as follows.

- $\Omega=\Sigma^E \cup \Sigma^A$
- $Q=$\{Account_Operation, Request, Operation, Date, Means, Notes, Type, Amount, Recipient, Value\}$\cup\{q^{init}\}\cup\{q^{fin}\}$
- $Q^{init}=\{q^{init}\}$
- $Q^{fin}=$\{Date, Means, Notes, Type, Amount, Recipient, Value\}$\cup\{q^{fin}\}$
- $\delta(q^{init},$account_operation$)=$Account_Operation
  $\delta($Account_Operation,request$)=$Request
  $\delta($Account_Operation,operation$)=$Operation
  $\delta($Request,date$)=$Date
  $\delta($Request,means$)=$Means
  $\delta($Request,notes$)=$Notes
  $\delta($Operation,type$)=$Type
  $\delta($Operation,amount$)=$Amount;

δ(Operation,recipient)=Recipient
δ(Operation,notes)=Notes;
δ(Operation,value)=Value
δ(Account_Operation,@bankAccN)=q^{fin}
δ(Account_Operation,@Id)=q^{fin}
δ(Request,@number)=q^{fin}

The schema automaton defined accepts the same paths allowed by the considered DTD. Specifically, $L(M^G)$ is equal to: /account_operation, /account_operation/@Id, /account_operation/@bankAccN, /account_operation/request, /account_operation/request/@number, /account_operation/request/date, /account_operation/request/means, /account_operation/request/notes, /account_operation/operation, /account_operation/operation/type, /account_operation/operation/amount, /account_operation/operation/recipient, /account_operation/operation/notes, /account_operation/operation/value.

The second step of the static analysis method consists in building the access control automata M^Γ and $\overline{M^\Gamma}$, for each of the three groups of users considered. For the sake of simplicity, we represent only the language of the automaton.

BankEmployee $L(M^\Gamma)$={account_operation}·$(\Sigma^E)^* \cdot (\Sigma^A \cup \{\epsilon\})$
StatisticalAnalyst $L(M^\Gamma)$={account_operation}·$(\Sigma^E)^* \cdot (\Sigma^A \cup \{\epsilon\})\backslash$
  {notes}·$(\Sigma^E)^* \cdot (\Sigma^A \cup \{\epsilon\})$
Client $L(\underline{M^\Gamma})$=$\emptyset \cdot (\Sigma^E)^* \cdot (\Sigma^A \cup \{\epsilon\})$; $L(\overline{M^\Gamma})$={account_operation}·$(\Sigma^E)^* \cdot$
  $(\Sigma^A \cup \{\epsilon\})$

Here, · is the concatenation operator, \ is the set difference operator, ϵ is the nil character, and $(\Sigma^E)^*$ represents any string in Σ^E.

Consider now the XQuery expression introduced in Example 2. The corresponding XPath expressions, classified on the basis of the clause they are represented in, are:

FOR, LET, ORDER BY ,WHERE: /account_operation;
  /account_operation/operation/type
RETURN: account_operation/operation/amount;
  account_operation/operation/recipient;
  account_operation//notes

Here record//notes implies both record/request/notes and record/operation/notes.

On the basis of the static analysis, it is possible to classify the requests submitted by users. As an example, consider the following requests.

- BankEmployee requests /account_operation/operation/type: the request is *always granted*;

- `StatisticalAnalyst` requests `/account_operation//notes`: the request is *always denied*;
- `Client` requests `/account_operation/operation/amount`: the request is *statically indeterminate*.

The last request introduced by the example is statically indeterminate as the path expression `/account_operation[./@bankAccN=$userAcc]` in the access control policy cannot be statically captured by an automaton. To solve this problem, it is possible to rewrite the policy, and all the statical analysis tools, adding two new symbols to the considered alphabet: `account_operation1 = /account_operation[./@bankAccN=$userAcc]` and `account_operation2 = /account_operation[not ./@bankAccN=$userAcc]`.

4.3 Other Approaches

Besides the two access control models described above, a number of other models have been introduced in the literature for controlling access to XML documents.

The first work of Kudo et al. [10] introduce provisional authorizations in XML access control. A *provisional authorization* is an authorization allowing the specification of a security action that the user (and/or the system) has to execute to gain access to the requested resource. A security action may be for example, the encryption of a resource with a given key, or the recording in the log of an access control decision. Due to the problem of run-time policy evaluation, Kudo et al. [6] present a different access control model, based on the definition of an *Access-Condition-Table* (ACT). An ACT structure is statically generated from an access control policy. The ACT contains, for each target path in the XML document, an access condition and a subtree access conditions, which are the conditions that have to be fulfilled to gain access to the node and to its subtree, respectively. By using the ACT, the run-time evaluation of requests is reduced from the whole policy to an access condition. The proposed model has however some disadvantages: it does not scale well, and it imposes limitations on XPath expressions. To overcome these issues the authors propose an alternative structure to ACT, the *Policy Matching Tree* (PMT) [7], which supports real-time updates of both policy and data. In this case, the pre-processing phase consists in building the tree structure on the basis of the access control policy. Whenever a user makes a request, an algorithm visits the path in the tree that matches the request, to compute the correct answer stored in the leaf. To further improve computational efficiency, the authors propose a *function-based* access control model that has a rule function for each authorization in the policy [17]. A rule function is a piece of executable code, which is run any time an access request matches with the rule, and returning the answer for the final user. Function rules can be organized on the basis of the subject or object they refer to: the first solution has been empirically proven to be more efficient.

An alternative solution to the static analysis proposed by Kudo et al. is presented in [18], where the authors propose to store the access control policy in a space and time efficient data structure, called *compressed accessibility map* (CAM). This structure is obtained by exploiting the structural locality of access authorizations, that is, by grouping object having similar access profiles.

Another model proposing a pre-processing phase for access control purposes is introduced in [19], where the pre-processing algorithm, called *QFilter* rewrites these queries by pruning any part that violate access control rules.

The concept of view as the portion of an XML document that can be released to the user (introduced first by Damiani et al. [9]) has been exploited by different models.

The solution proposed by Fan et al. [20] is based on the concept of *security view*. A security view of an XML document provides with each user group both a view of the XML document with all and only the information that the group can access, and a view of the DTD, compliant with the released portion of the XML document. It is important to note that, concretely, each document has one security view, obtained by marking the XML document according with the access control policy. Authorized users are then supposed to make queries over their security view. In the paper, the authors propose both an algorithm for computing security views from an access control policy, and an algorithm for reformulating queries posed on security views to be evaluated on the whole XML document, avoiding materialization.

An alternative method for view generation has also been proposed [21]. This model uses an *authorization sheet* to collect all the authorizations. The authorization sheet is then translated in an XSLT sheet, which grants the generation of the correct view to the user when she asks for (a portion of) the document.

In [22] the authors propose an alternative method to the tree labeling process for view generation, since it may be inefficient if the size of the tree and the number of requests increase. The alternative model stores XML documents in a relational database, which is used to select data on users' request, and to check only selected data against the access control policy, instead of labeling the whole XML tree.

Bertino et al. proposed different works aimed at access control enforcement in XML documents [23, 24, 25, 5]. In particular, they propose a model supporting the use of *credentials* (i.e., sets of attributes concerning a specific user) for subject definition.

Since XML documents represent an alternative to the traditional relational database model, some models adopt solutions proposed for relational databases [8, 26]. In [8] the author proposes to adopt SQL syntax and semantics to XML documents. Each user manages all privileges on her files, and **grants** or **revokes** them to other users, possibly along with the **grant option**.

The model proposed in [26] does not use SQL syntax, but exploits the concept of view as in relational databases to restrict access to data. In this case, views are defined by using the XQuery language, and may be authorization objects. The model supports not only structure-based authorizations, but also rules depending on the context or content of the considered documents by adding conditions in XQuery expressions.

Since relationship among elements/attributes may reveal sensitive information, in [27] the authors propose the definition of access control rules on the relationship among XML elements and attributes (i.e., on arcs in the XML tree). It is then presented a technique to control the view that can be released of the *path* leading to any authorized node in an XML document. The authors introduce also a rule-based formulation of the new class of authorizations.

To the aim of adding semantic meaning to authorizations, RDF (Resource Description Framework) is used as a new way for expressing access control policies [28]. The paper focuses also on the problem of controlling *data associations*, and adds a new object type to the classical model: the association security object. An association security object is an XML subtree whose elements can be accessed only separately. To solve the problem of data associations, the model uses temporal data.

All the models introduced above for access control of XML documents are based on the discretionary access control model [12]. In [29], the authors propose a role-based access control model (RBAC) for XML documents, which exploits the main characteristics of XML data.

In [30] the authors propose the first access control model for XML documents operating client-side. The main difference with respect to the previous proposals is that this method needs to operate on stream data and it is supposed to operate on a system where the server storing data may not be trusted for access control enforcement.

Recently, a new class of methods have been also proposed for access control enforcement for XML documents [5, 31, 32]. These methods consider a data outsourcing scenario, where XML documents are stored on a possibly not trusted server, and are not under the data owner's direct control. In these cases, XML documents themselves should enforce access control, since this task cannot either be executed by the owner or by the storing server. Access control is enforced through selective encryption, that is, by encrypting different portions of the XML tree by using different encryption keys. Consequently, a correct key distribution to users ensures that access control enforcement is correct.

5 Conclusions

The role of XML in the representation and processing of information in current information systems is already significant and is certainly going to see a considerable increase in the next years. The design and implementation of an access control model for XML promises to become an important tool for the construction of modern applications. The research of the last few years presented in this chapter has produced several proposals for the construction of an access control solution for XML data. These results are a robust basis for the work of a standard committee operating within one of the important consortia involved in the definition of Web standards. Thanks to the availability of such a standard, it is reasonable to expect that XML access control models will be used to support the data protection requirements of many applications, making XML access control a common tool supporting the design of generic software systems.

References

1. Bray, T., Paoli, J., Sperberg-McQueen, C.M., Maler, E., Yergeau, F.: Extensible markup language (XML) 1.0 (fourth edition) (August 2006) W3C Recommendation.
2. Berglund, A.: Extensible stylesheet language (XSL) version 1.1 (December 2006) W3C Recommendation.
3. Clark, J., DeRose, S.: XML path language (XPath) version 1.0 (November 1999) W3C Recommendation.
4. Boag, S., Chamberlin, D., Fernndez, M.F., Florescu, D., Robie, J., Simon, J.: XQuery 1.0: An XML query language (January 2007) W3C Recommendation.
5. Bertino, E., Ferrari, E.: Secure and selective dissemination of XML documents. ACM Transaction Information System Security 5(3) (August 2002) 290–331
6. Qi, N., Kudo, M.: Access-condition-table-driven access control for XML databases. In: Proc. of the 9th European Symposium on Research in Computer Security, Sophia Antipolis, France (September 2004)
7. Qi, N., Kudo, M.: XML access control with policy matching tree. In: Proc. of the 10th European Symposium on Research in Computer Security, Milan, Italy (September 2005)
8. Gabillon, A.: An authorization model for XML databases. In: Proc. of the 2004 Workshop on Secure Web Service (SWS04), Fairfax, Virginia (November 2004)
9. Damiani, E., De Capitani di Vimercati, S., Paraboschi, S., Samarati, P.: A fine-grained access control system for XML documents. ACM Transaction Information System Security 5(2) (May 2002) 169–202
10. Kudo, M., Hada, S.: Xml document security based on provisional authorization. In: Proc. of the 7th ACM Conference on Computer and Communications Security (CCS00). (November 2000)
11. Jajodia, S., Samarati, P., Sapino, M., Subrahmanian, V.: Flexible support for multiple access control policies. ACM Transactions on Database Systems 26(2) (June 2001) 214–260
12. Samarati, P., di Vimercati, S.D.C.: Access control: Policies, models, and mechanisms. In Focardi, R., Gorrieri, R., eds.: Foundations of Security Analysis and Design. LNCS 2171. Springer-Verlag (2001)
13. Murata, M., Tozawa, A., Kudo, M., Hada, S.: XML access control using static analysis. ACM Transaction Information System Security 9(3) (August 2006) 292–324

14. Damiani, E., De Capitani di Vimercati, S., Paraboschi, S., Samarati, P.: Design and implementation of an access control processor for XML documents. Computer Networks **33**(1-6) (June 2000) 59–75

15. Damiani, E., De Capitani di Vimercati, S., Paraboschi, S., Samarati, P.: Securing XML documents. In: Proc. of the 7th International Conference on Extending Database Technology (EDBT00), Konstanz, Germany (March 2000)

16. Damiani, E., Samarati, P., De Capitani di Vimercati, S., Paraboschi, S.: Controlling access to XML documents. IEEE Internet Computing **5**(6) (November/December 2001) 18–28

17. Qi, N., Kudo, M., Myllymaki, J., Pirahesh, H.: A function-based access control model for XML databases. In: Proc. of the 2005 ACM CIKM International Conference on Information and Knowledge Management, Bremen, Germany (October - November 2005)

18. Yu, T., Srivastava, D., Lakshmanan, L.V.S., Jagadish, H.V.: Compressed accessibility map: Efficient access control for XML. In: Proc. of the 28th International Conference on Very Large Data Bases (VLDB), Hong Kong, China (August 2002)

19. Luo, B., Lee, D., Lee, W.C., Liu, P.: QFilter: fine-grained run-time XML access control via NFA-based query rewriting. In: Proc. of the 2004 ACM CIKM International Conference on Information and Knowledge Management, Washington, DC, USA (November 2004)

20. Fan, W., Chan, C.Y., Garofalakis, M.: Secure XML querying with security views. In: Proc. of the 2004 ACM SIGMOD International Conference on Management of Data, Paris, France (June 2004)

21. Gabillon, A., Bruno, E.: Regulating access to XML documents. In: Proc. of the Fifteenth Annual Working Conference on Database and Application Security (Das01), Niagara, Ontario, Canada (July 2002)

22. Tan, K.L., Lee, M.L., Wang, Y.: Access control of XML documents in relational database systems. In: Proc. of the 2001 International Conference on Internet Computing, Las Vegas, Nevada, USA (June 2001)

23. Bertino, E., Braun, M., Castano, S., Ferrari, E., Mesiti, M.: Author-X: A Java-based system for XML data protection. In: Proc. of the IFIP TC11/ WG11.3 Fourteenth Annual Working Conference on Database Security, Amsterdam, The Netherlands (August 2000)

24. Bertino, E., Castano, S., Ferrari, E.: Securing XML documents with Author-X. IEEE Internet Computing **5**(3) (May/June 2001) 21–31

25. Bertino, E., Castano, S., Ferrari, E., Mesiti, M.: Specifying and enforcing access control policies for XML document sources. World Wide Web **3**(3) (June 2000) 139–151

26. Goel, S.K., Clifton, C., Rosenthal, A.: Derived access control specification for XML. In: Proc. of the 2003 ACM Workshop on XML Security (XMLSEC-03), New York (October 2003)

27. Finance, B., Medjdoub, S., Pucheral, P.: The case for access control on XML relationships. In: Proc. of the 2005 ACM CIKM International Conference on Information and Knowledge Management, Bremen, Germany (October - November 2005)

28. Gowadia, V., Farkas, C.: RDF metadata for XML access control. In: Proc. of the 2003 ACM Workshop on XML Security (XMLSEC-03), New York (October 2003)

29. Hitchens, M., Varadharajan, V.: RBAC for XML document stores. In: Proc. of the Third International Conference on Information and Communications Security (ICICS01), Xian, China (November 2001)

30. Bouganim, L., Ngoc, F.D., Pucheral, P.: Client-based access control management for XML documents. In: Proc of the 30th VLDB Conference, Tornoto, Canada (September 2004)

31. Miklau, G., Suciu, D.: Controlling access to published data using cryptography. In: Proc. of the 29th VLDB Conference, Berlin, Germany (September 2003)

32. Wang, H., Lakshmanan, L.V.S.: Efficient secure query evaluation over encrypted XML databases. In: Proc. of the 32nd VLDB Conference, Seoul, Korea (September 2006)

3

Access Control Policy Languages in XML

Naizhen Qi and Michiharu Kudo

Tokyo Research Laboratory
IBM, Japan
{naishin,kudo}@jp.ibm.com

Summary. Policy specification for XML data access control has been difficult since the specification languages usually have complicated semantics and syntax. In this chapter, first we introduce the semantics and syntax of two security policy languages and one policy framework. Then we address several tools for policy modeling and generation which help users in capturing security concerns during the design, and developing the security policies and functions during the implementation.

1 Introduction

Since repeated security incidents such as unexpected personal information leakages and identity thefts have been increasing recently, secure data management is becoming a crucial factor for applications and services. A fundamental enforcement of data management is to specify the access control policies to control each request to the data handled by the system and to determine whether the request should be granted or denied. Several expressive and powerful policy specification languages like XACL [9], XACML [10] and WS-Policy [20] have been designed for the specification of XML-based security policies. However, there are also difficulties in policy specification, integration, management, and maintenance owing to the complicated semantics and syntax of these policy languages.

In this chapter, we discuss several access control policy languages designed for fine-grained XML data management, then address several mechanisms and tools for policy modeling and generation. With these tools, the business stakeholders are able to capture and integrate security concerns at a higher business level, and the developers can easily associate the security-related requirements with the security policies and the implementation.

2 Policy Specification Languages

Generally speaking, there are three types of policy representation regarding access authorization: *access control policy specification languages, privacy policy specification languages*, and *formal specification languages*. Access control policy specification languages include XACL, XACML, and Authorization Specification Language (ASL) [11, 12]. Privacy policy specification languages include P3P [15], and EPAL [2]. The XACML also covers some features of privacy policy. Formal specification languages include Alloy [1], Formal Tropos [6], KAOS [5], Larch [7], UML [16][19], and Z [18]. Moreover, as Web services become more and more common in use, the WS-Policy framework[20] for Web services, is also well-known.

In this chapter, we briefly introduce the access control policy specification languages of XACL, XACML, and the Web services governance specification of WS-Policy framework as they can be broadly used in various XML-based systems, and as standardized by specific organizations.

3 Example XML Document and Associated Policy

First, we use a sample XML document and policy to illustrate how to represent fine-grained access control policy for XML documents. The example is a Web-based paper review application that simulates a typical anonymous paper-reviewing process. In addition, all of the access control policies in this chapter are specified for this XML document.

- Authors submit their papers and a chairperson assigns one or more reviewers to each submitted paper.
- The reviewers read and evaluate the papers assigned to them without knowing who the authors are.
- The program committee members read the reviewers' evaluations and decide which papers should be accepted.
- The chairperson makes the final decisions on the accepted papers.
- Each author receives notification of acceptance or rejection.

The review summary XML document stores all of the information and the states for the reviewing process such as the author information and the evaluation results. Figure 1 shows such an XML document that includes one paper submission from Carol, which final decision is to accept reviewed by a reviewer Robert with a rating of 3.5. Any operations regarding the paper review process can be represented as an access to the XML document such as a read access to the paper `id` attribute and an update access to the `result` element.

We need to specify appropriate access control policies that will be enforced on this XML document in order to support the anonymous paper reviewing process. Figure 2 shows an example access control policy specified on the

```
<review_summary>
  <notificationDue>6/30/07 0:0 AM</notificationDue>
  <entry>
    <paper id="0120">XML Policy Model</paper>
    <contents encoding="Base64">4Dxk5lw...</contents>
    <authorName>Carol</authorName>
    <review>
      <reviewerName>Robert</reviewerName>
      <rating>3.5</rating>
    </review>
    <result status="final">Accept</result>
  </entry>
</review_summary>
```

Fig. 1. An example XML document

review XML document. The rule **R1** is the default policy for the chairperson. Rule **R2** gives the write permission on the **result** field to the chairperson. Rule **R3** allows the reviewers to read any node below the **entry** element except for the **authorName** element. Rule **R4** allows the reviewers to update their **rating** element. Rule **R5** allows authors access to their paper submission. Rule **R6** defines the temporal policy with regard to the notification date.

R1: The chairperson can read any elements, attributes and text nodes of the review document.

R2: The chairperson can write the **review** result (accept or reject) in the result field.

R3: Each reviewer can read the **entry** element (and any subordinates nodes) assigned to him except for the **authorName**.

R4: Each reviewer can fill in the **rating** element assigned to him.

R5: Each author can read his own submission **entry** except for the **review** elements.

R6: Each author can read the **result** of his submission after the date of the notification.

Fig. 2. An access control policy example

For example, when the chairperson issues a read access request for the **author Name** element, the access should be permitted according to R1. On the other hand, when a reviewer tries to read the **authorName** element, the access should be denied according to R3. When an author tries to read the **result** element, the access should be permitted only after the notification date has passed according to R6. Therefore, a query like "retrieve complete XML nodes below the document root" must reflect all of the access control policies at the time of the access.

4 XML Access Control Policy Languages

4.1 XACL

The XML Access Control Language (XACL)[9] is a fine-grained access control policy specification language for XML data. It allows application developers to specify policies at the element and attribute levels with various conditional expressions. XACL uses XPath expressions to specify the targets of a policy with either positive or negative permissions. It provides several ways to resolve conflicts between the decisions, either by the *permit-takes-precedence* or the *denial-takes-precedence* resolution policies. The XACL also defines how the access effects propagate on the XML tree structure. By default, a read permission specified on a certain element automatically propagates upward to the root node as well as propagating downward to its descendants.

Policy Syntax and Semantics.

The XACL policies are specified using `xacl` elements and one or more `rule` elements that specify permit or deny authorization conditions. Two or more rules are disjunctively combined according to the pre-defined combining algorithms. The authorization subject is specified using one or more subject descriptors of `group`, `role`, or `userid` under a `subject` element. With regard to the authorization objects, XACL only supports XPath expressions as an `href` attribute of the `object` element. There are four types of authorization actions in XACL, `read`, `write`, `create`, and `delete`. Arbitrary conditional expressions can be specified using the `operation` attributes, the `predicate` elements, or the `parameter` elements below the `condition` elements. Figure 3 expresses Rule R3 of Figure2.

Rule `R3-1` specifies a permissive rule on a `/review_summary/entry` element for the reviewer group with the condition that only the reviewer in charge can access the paper content and the submission information. Since the XACL supports the downward propagation from the target node by default, any subordinate nodes below the `entry` element, e.g. the `authorName` and `reviewerName` elements, are also the target authorization objects of this rule.

In contrast, Rule `R3-2` specifies a denial rule for all reviewers on the */review_summary/entry/authorName* element which enables anonymous paper review policy. Where this rule contradicts the permissive `R3-1` rule, the conflict resolution `denial-takes-precedence` policy, which is supposed to be specified for the `property` element below the `policy` element, denies access to the `authorName`.

Binding Scheme.

How to bind a set of policies written in XACL with target documents is out of the scope of XACL. There are two fundamental approaches. One is the

```
<policy xmlns="http://www.trl.ibm.com/projects/xml/xacl">
  <xacl id="R3-1">
   <object href="/review_summary/entry"/>
   <rule><acl>
     <subject><group>reviewer</group></subject>
     <action name="read" permission="grant"/>
     <condition operation="and">
       <predicate name="compareStr">
         <parameter value="eq"/>
         <parameter><function name="getValue">
           <parameter value="./review/reviewerName/text()"/></function>
           </parameter>
         <parameter><function name="getUid"/></parameter>
       </predicate>
     </condition>
   </acl></rule>
  </xacl>

  <xacl id="R3-2">
   <object href="/review_summary/entry/authorName"/>
   <rule><acl>
     <subject><group>reviewer</group></subject>
     <action name="read" permission="deny"/>
   </rule></acl>
  </xacl>
</policy>
```

Fig. 3. XACL Policy

association at the schema definition (e.g. DTD) level and the other is the association at the level of each specific document. In the DTD-level approach, a set of policies is bound to all documents valid according to the specified DTD. Therefore, one needs to maintain the mapping between a particular DTD and the associated policy. In the document-level approach, a policy is bound to each specific document. In this case, an associated policy, which is encoded as a policy element, may be an element contained within the target document.

Basic Matching Algorithm

The access control system basically takes an authorization request as input and outputs an authorization decision including *provisional actions*. The access control enforcement may consist of the basic matching algorithm and the policy evaluation algorithm.

Input: An authorization request which contains a requested object, a subject for the requester, and the action.
Output: A decision list, which may contain multiple decisions.
   Step 1. Object-Check: Search the associated policy for each xacl element whose object element contains a node specified in the authorization request.

Step 2. Subject-Check: For each xacl element unit, check if the subject and the action are semantically equal to the corresponding specification in the xacl element.

Step 3. Condition-Check: For each of the remaining xacl elements, check if it meets the condition.

Step 4. Decision-Record: Make a decision for each of the remaining xacl elements, where each decision includes the object, the subject, and the action specified in the xacl element, and append all the decisions to the authorization decision list.

Policy Evaluation Algorithm

The policy evaluation algorithm deals with propagation and conflict resolution. We note that this algorithm always outputs exactly one authorization decision.

Input: An authorization request.

Output: A decision of **grant** or **deny**.

Step 1. Propagation Processing: Call the basic matching algorithm for the request and append the propagated access effects to the decision list.

Step 2. Conflict Resolution: If there is a conflict on the request object, resolve with the conflict resolution policy.

Step 2. Default Resolution: If there is no authorization decision in the list, make a decision according to the default policy and append it to the decision list.

Step 3. Select one decision: Select on evaluation result from the list containing at least one decision.

4.2 XACML

XACML [10] is an access control policy specification language standardized by OASIS. XACML defines the format for policy and request/response messages. The scope of this language is to cover access control systems as broadly as possible. Therefore, the XACML core schema is designed to be extensible for yet unknown features.

XACML achieves interoperability of access control policies among heterogeneous computing platforms. The biggest difference from the XACL language is that the XACL focuses on the access control policy only for XML data[1], while the generalized XACML policies support any resources, including XML data.

---

[1] Many portions of XACML policy model is originated from the XACL language

XACML Architecture.

Figure 4 shows an XACML data-flow diagram.
XACML adds one additional component called a `Context Handler` between
PEP and PDP, which supplies sufficient information for any access request using
the `Policy Information Point` (PIP). The interface from PIP to PDP is
defined in XACML as a `Request Context`. PDP retrieves applicable access
control policies from `Policy Administration Point` (PAP) and makes the
decision using the relevant policies and the request context. The decision is
returned back to PEP via `Context Handler`.

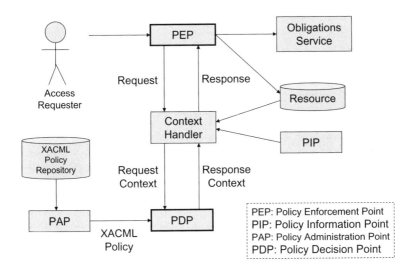

Fig. 4. XACML Architecture

Policy Syntax and Semantics.

Each XACML policy is basically specified using a `Policy` element which consists of a `Target` element that specifies the conditions when the policy is
applicable, and one or more `Rule` elements that contain Boolean expressions
specifying permit or deny authorization conditions. In addition, `Rule` can be
evaluated in isolation to form a basic unit of management and can be reused
in multiple policies when `PolicySet` is used to specify multiple policies simultaneously. XACML also provides a flexible way to extend the semantic
knowledge to support application-specific access control policies with an extensible Rule-combining (or Policy-combining) algorithm.

Figure 5 shows an example[2] for a XACML policy corresponding to the third rule R3 of Figure 2. The `Target` element specifies the applicability of some R by saying that the role of the requesting subject should be *Reviewer-Name* and the requested action should be *read*. The policy R consists of three Rules, R3-1, R3-2, and R3-3.

R3-1 signifies that an access to the `review_summary` element is permitted. Note that this rule does not indicate anything about subordinate nodes, since the `xpath-node-equal` matching function checks the access only for the specified node, which is a `review_summary` element. R3-2 signifies that a read access to an `entry` element and its subordinate nodes is permitted when the name of the requesting subject is identical to the value specified in the `reviewerName` element. The semantics of the propagation to subordinate nodes is handled by the `xpath-node-match` matching function. R3-3 states that a read access to the `authorName` element is denied.

These three rules are combined by the `denial-overrides` algorithm, which basically means that if any rule evaluates to `deny`, then the result of the rule combination should be `deny`. For example, R3-2 permits read access to the `authorName` element while R3-3 explicitly denies the access. Then the `denial -overrides` algorithm concludes that the access to the `entry` element should be denied. In addition, there are several other rule combining algorithms in the XACML specification, such as `first applicable` and `only-one applicable`.

Decision Combining Algorithms

Each rule can specify a rule combining algorithm which defines a procedure for arriving at an authorization decision when the individual results of the evaluations of a set of rules or policies are provided. Various rule combining algorithms, in particular, `Permit-overrides`, `Only-one-applicable`, and `First-applicable`, are supported besides the
`Deny-overrides` algorithm of the previous example.

The `Permit-overrides` algorithm is a procedure such that if there exists any rule that evaluates to `permit`, then the decision is `permit`. However, if all of the rules evaluate to `not applicable`, or some rules evaluate to `deny` but some evaluate to `not applicable`, then the decision is `deny`.

The `Only-one-applicable` algorithm says that if more than one rule applies, then the decision is `indeterminate`. If no rule applies, then the result is `not applicable`. If only-one policy applies, the decision is evaluated by that rule.

The `First-applicable` algorithm is a procedure such that the rules are evaluated in the order of appearance in the policy. The first rule such that the

---

[2] The syntax used in Figure5 is somewhat abbreviated due to space limitations. The exact URI specification of the rule-combining algorithm is "urn:oasis:names:tc:xacml:1.0:rule-combining-algorithm:*deny-overrides*".

```
<Policy xmlns:rs="reviewpaper.xsd" PolicyId="R3"
        RuleCombiningAlgId="deny-overrides">
 <PolicyDefaults><XPathVersion>Rec-xpath-19991116</XPathVersion>
 </PolicyDefaults>
 <Target>
  <Subjects><Subject><SubjectMatch MatchId="string-equal">
    <AttributeValue DataType="string">Reviewer</AttributeValue>
    <SubjectAttributeDesignator AttributeId="role" DataType="string"/>
   </SubjectMatch></Subject></Subjects>
  <Actions><Action><ActionMatch MatchId="string-equal">
    <AttributeValue DataType="string">read</AttributeValue>
    <ActionAttributeDesignator AttributeId="action-id"
DataType="string"/>
  </ActionMatch></Action></Actions>
 </Target>
 <Rule RuleId="R3-1" Effect="Permit">
  <Target><Resources><Resource><ResourceMatch MatchId="xpath-node-equal">
    <AttributeValue DataType="xpath-exp">//rs:review_summary</>
    <ResourceAttributeDesignator AttributeId="resource-id"
DataType="xpath-exp"/>
  </ResourceMatch></Resource></Resources></Target>
 </Rule>
 <Rule RuleId="R3-2" Effect="Permit">
  <Target><Resources><Resource><ResourceMatch MatchId="xpath-node-
match">
    <AttributeValue DataType="xpath-exp">//rs:review_summary/rs:entry</>
    <ResourceAttributeDesignator AttributeId="resource-id"
DataType="xpath-exp"/>
  </ResourceMatch></Resource></Resources></Target>
  <Condition><Apply FunctionId="string-equel">
   <AttributeSelector DataType="xpath-exp"
   RequestContextPath="//rs:review_summary/rs:entry/rs:review/rs:reviewerName
   /rs:text()"/>
   <SubjectAttributeDesignator AttributeId="subject-id"
DataType="xpath-exp"/>
  </Apply></Condition>
 </Rule>
 <Rule RuleId="R3-3" Effect="Deny">
  <Target><Resources><Resource><ResourceMatch MatchId="xpath-node-
match">
    <AttributeValue DataType="xpath-exp">//rs:review_summary/rs:entry
    /rs:authorName</>
    <ResourceAttributeDesignator AttributeId="resource-id"
DataType="xpath-exp"/>
  </ResourceMatch></Resource></Resources></Target>
 </Rule>
</Policy>
```

Fig. 5. XACML access control policy corresponding to R3

access target matches and the optional conditions match, is used to decide the result of the request.

These decision combining algorithms allow administrators to provide various levels of security restrictions on their sensitive data.

Access Request.

XACML defines the format for the request message that provides context for the policy-based decisions. Each request may contain multiple Subject elements and multiple attributes for the Subject, Resource and Action.

Figure 6 shows a sample `XACML Request Context` format where Robert requests a read access for the first `entry` element of the review summary XML document. The request context consisting of three sub-structures, `Subject` information, `Resource` information, and `Action` information, each consisting of one or more attribute type-value pairs. In this example, `subject-id` and `role` are attribute types and `Robert` and `reviewerName` are attribute values, respectively. It is assumed that those attributes are given by a separate authentication mechanism that is out of the scope of the XACML specification.

Regarding to resource information, the `XACML request context` can contain the target XML data as relevant information about the target resource. The `ResourceContent` element contains the `review_summary` XML data with the namespace prefixed by `rs:`. The target XML document is referred to from the access control policy using the `AttributeSelector` function. For example, rule `R3-2` of Figure 5 specifies the path, `//rs:review_summary/rs:entry` `/rs:review/rs:reviewerName/text()`, which refers to `Robert`. This is one of the advantages of the XACML policy model that allows the policy to refer to any of the values of the target XML data as embedded in the `Request Context` and to compare those values against constant values.

Access Response.

The response message defined by XACML provides the format for conveying the Decision (`Deny` or `Permit`) and the Status of an access request evaluation as Figure 7 shows. In our example, the decision is `Deny` since the requested `entry` element contains an `AuthorName` element that should not be accessible to the Reviewer. The `EntireHierarchy` scope parameter specified in the `Resource` of the `XACML Request Context` defines the semantics of the response context such that if any of the descendants nodes of the requested node have one or more access-denial nodes, then the resulting decision should be a denial.

4.3 WS-Policy

WS-Policy Framework [20] is a W3C standard Web services governance specification that enables a service to specify what it expects of callers and how

```
<Request>
  <Subject>
    <Attribute AttributeId="subject-id" DataType="string">
      <AttributeValue>Robert</AttributeValue> </Attribute>
    <Attribute AttributeId="role" DataType="string">
      <AttributeValue>Reviewer</AttributeValue>
    </Attribute>
  </Subject>
  <Resource scope="EntireHierarchy">
    <ResourceContent>
        <rs:review_summary xmlns:rs="urn:review_summary:schema">
          <rs:notificationDue>6/30/07</rs:notificationDue>
          <rs:entry>
            <rs:paper id="0120">XML Policy Model</rs:paper>
            <rs:authorName>Carol</rs:authorName>
            <rs:review><rs:reviewerName>Robert</rs:reviewerName>
            <rs:rating>3.5</rs:rating>
            </rs:review>
            <rs:result status="final">Accept</rs:result>
          </rs:entry>
        </rs:review_summary>
    </ResourceContent>
    <Attribute AttributeId="resource-id" DataType="xpath-expression">
      <AttributeValue>//rs:review_summary/rs:entry[position()=1]
      </AttributeValue>
    </Attribute>
  </Resource>
  <Action>
    <Attribute AttributeId="action-id" DataType="string">
      <AttributeValue>read</AttributeValue>
    </Attribute>
  </Action>
</Request>
```

Fig. 6. XACML Request Context Sample

```
<Response>
  <Result>
    <Decision>Deny</Decision>
  </Result>
</Response>
```

Fig. 7. XACML Response Context Sample

it implements its interface to grant access from callers. WS-Policy is critical to achieve interoperability for the high-level functional operation of the Web services.

Unlike XACL and XACML, WS-Policy defines a wrapper to hold one or more policy assertions. The wrapper itself has limited semantics, leaving the details to the policy assertions from various domains such as `security`, `privacy`, `application priority`, `user account priorities`, and `traffic control`.

Some of these assertions specify traditional requirements and capabilities that will ultimately be manifested on the wire (i.e., security, traffic control).

Some others specify requirements and capabilities that are critical to proper service selection and usage (i.e., privacy, application priority, user account priorities). WS-Policy provides a single policy grammar to allow both kinds of assertions in a consistent manner. However, there are no policy assertions defined for authorization and access control.

Policy Syntax and Semantics.

```
<wsp:Policy xmlns:sp="...">
  <wsp:ExactlyOne>
    <wsp:All>
      <sp:SignedElements>
        <sp:XPath>/S:Envelope/S:Body</sp:XPath>
      </sp:SignedElements>
    </wsp:All>
    <wsp:All>
      <sp:EncryptedElements>
        <sp:XPath>/S:Envelope/S:Body</sp:XPath>
      </sp:EncryptedElements>
    </wsp:All>
  </wsp:ExactlyOne>
</wsp:Policy>
```

Fig. 8. An WS-Policy Example

WS-Policy[3] defines three components: policy expressions, policy assertions, and policy operations (`OnOrMore`, `All`, and `ExactlyOne`). A policy is composed of policy expressions that may each contain only one of the policy operations, policy assertions, or policy reference. The policy expressions can be used as containers for application-specific or service-type-specific policy definitions. In addition, policy operations can be nested and may contain any externally defined content. As an example, Figure 8 gives a simple policy example in the security domain. The policy contains two policy assertions to restrict the elements depicted by the XPath expression `/S:Envelope/S:Body` so they should be either signed or encrypted.

5 Policy Modeling and Generation

XACL, XACML, and WS-Policy are expressive and powerful for policy specification, but also too complicated, especially for the users who are not experts in their use. People also want to be able to address the underlying security concerns in ways that are easy to understand, and so that they can identify the particular technical implementations. Moreover, recently attention has

---

[3] Since in Chapter 13 of *Security and Web Services*, WS-Policy is introduced in details, we do not go deeply into it in this section.

been increasingly given to the techniques and tools required for architecting enterprise-scale software solutions. Many enterprises extend the life of an existing solution by designing new business logic that manipulates existing data resources, presenting existing data and transactions through new channels, integrating previously disconnected systems supporting overlapping business activities, and so on. The design of a high-quality solution therefore also calls for early architectural decisions on privacy and security [4]. Consequently, it is important to

- Model privacy and security concerns as carefully as any other concerns.
- Propagate the security requirements to the security policies and security implementation inexpensively.

5.1 Policy Modeling

Policy modeling is the process to describe and capture a level of abstraction between the security policies and mechanisms, enabling the design of implementation mechanisms to enforce multiple policies in various computing environments without considering the underlying platform of the system and the implementation technologies. During the policy modeling process, system requirements, organizational security and privacy policies, and organizational structures are analyzed to specify access control policies. In particular, organizational complexity introduces the challenge that it is difficult to identify and agree upon a set of roles (or groups) and associated permissions (**grant** or **deny**) within an organization that may have hundreds of roles (or groups).

Several approaches have been proposed in the area of policy modeling with UML. Brose et al. [3] propose integrating access control design into the software development process by extending UML to specify access control policies. This approach does not emphasize the compliance between different levels of the policies, requirements, and system designs. Jurjens proposes in [8] to specify requirements for confidentiality and integrity in analysis models, also on the basis of UML. Their underlying security models are multi-level security and mandatory access control.

In the area of models for RBAC, Lodderstedt et al. [14] proposes a modeling language for integrating the specifications for RBAC into application models. These approaches focus more on system implementation representations that are not easy for the business stakeholders to capture for the enterprise-scale security requirements at a higher business level.

Johnston introduces an approach in [13] that provides a set of primitive modeling elements to allow the users to specify the intention of the security within the requirements process. They generalize the security issues as four domains: **Privacy**, **Authentication**, **Authorization**, and **Audit**. Figure 9 demonstrates the dependencies between these four domains. For example, it is not possible to implement authorization without authentication. On the other hand both authorization and authentication rely on auditing, not for implementation but to ensure that any exceptions are captured for analysis and for non-repudiation. Privacy relies on both authentication and auditing.

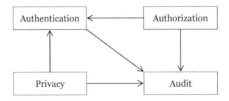

Fig. 9. Dependencies between Security Domains

Primitive intentions that are common in these four domains are addressed and presented as stereotypes that can be applied to the UML elements in capturing the business requirements. Figure 10 shows an example of the specification of an authentication service based on Johnson's approach [13]. In the figure, the messages between the customer and the online bank must be authenticated when the customer performs a wire transfer. The overall security-related concerns can be defined without considering the underlying technologies such as the encryption algorithms and the message formats, etc.

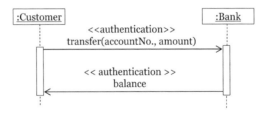

Fig. 10. A Sequence Diagram Example with an <<authentication>> Stereotype

5.2 Policy Generation

With policy modeling, the security intentions are explicitly defined in an abstract manner independent of the underlying platform and the implementation technologies. The software developers can easily capture the security requirements through policy modeling as well. However, the security implementation by hand is difficult and errors often arise if the software developers lack sufficient experience, and therefore the low-level development such as policy definition usually calls for support tools to avoid various problems.

Lodderstedt et al. [14] not only propose a methodology for modeling security policies, they also created an EJB generator which allows software developers to generate EJB applications with fully configured role-based access control including role definitions, method permissions, role assignments, and authorization constraints without specifying the policies by hand. The software developers are therefore able automatically implement the role-based access control enforcement mechanisms without complicated EJB coding.

Differing from Lodderstedt et al. the approach of [14], Satoh et al. [17] propose a framework to create security policies in WS-Policy. The framework enables the users who are not-security experts to configure authentication policies easily in a platform-independent manner on the basis of the application semantics. The key point is that an abstract security qualifier, `Authentication`, is defined to specify an identity that should be authenticated, and then the security qualifier is transformed to a platform-specific security policy using security policy templates. In this approach, the concrete security policies are created using the security policy template for authentication shown in Figure 11, where the parameters are represented using brackets like {DOMAIN_NAME}. *MileageNo*, for example, the real domain name replaces {DOMAIN_NAME} in policy transformation. As a result, the software developers can specify the security policies without detailed knowledge of WS-Policy.

```
<wsp:Policy xmlns:sp="http://...">
  <Authentication>
   <CallerToken>
     <securityDomain domainName="{DOMAIN_NAME}"/>
       {CALLER_TOKEN_ASSERTION}
     <TrustToken method="{TRUSTMETHOD_TYPE}">
       <securityDomain domainName="{DOMAIN_NAME}"/>
         {{TRUST_TOKEN_ASSERTION}}
     </TrustToken>
   </CallerToken>
  </Authentication>
</wsp:Policy>
```

Fig. 11. Security Policy Template

6 Conclusions

In this chapter, we have discussed the main features of two security policy languages and one policy framework. XACL and XACML are expressive and powerful in specifying access control policies for the XML data, while WS-Policy framework focuses more on security-related functional operation of the services. Also, we addressed the policy modeling and generation tools that have been developed to help users in capturing the security requirements during the design, and to develop the security policies and functions during the implementation. However, as more and more enterprises recognize the need for security solutions to protect their data, many problems remain. For example, how to integrate the security functions into the existing systems efficiently and inexpensively, and how to verify the relationships between the security requirements and the implementations.

References

1. D. Jackson. Alloy: A Lightweight Object Modelling Notation. *ACM Transaction on Software Engineering and Methodology*, Vol. 11(2), pp. 256-290, 2002.
2. P. Ashley, S. Hada, G. Karjoth, C. Powers, and M. Schunter: Enterprise Privacy Authorization Language (EPAL 1.1) Specification. IBM Research Report, 2003. Available at *http://www.zurich.ibm.com/security/enterprise-privacy/epal.*
3. G. Brose, M. Koch, and K.-P. Lohr: Integrating Access Control Design into the Software Development Process. In *Proceeding of the 6th International Conference on Integrated Design and Process Technology* (IDPT), 2002.
4. A. Brown, S. Johnston, and K. Kelly: Using service-oriented architecture and component-based development to build Web service applications. Rational Software White Paper. Available at *http://www-128.ibm.com/developerworks/rational/library/content/03July/2000/2169/2169.pdf.*
5. A. Dardenne, A. van Lamsweerde, and S. Fickas: Goal-directed Requirements Acquisition. *Science of Computer Programming*, Vol. 20(1-2), pp. 3-50, 1993.
6. A. Fuxman, R. Kazhamiakin, M. Pistore, and M. Roveri: *Formal Tropos: languages and semantics.* University of Trento and IRST, Trento, Italy, 2003.
7. J.V. Guttag and J.J. Horning, with S.J. Garland, K.D. Jones, A. Modet, and J.M. Wing. Larch: *Languages and Tools for Formal Specification.* Springer-Verlag, 1993.
8. J. Jurjens: Towards Development of Secure Systems using UMLsec. In *Proceedings of Fundamental Approaches to Software Engineering, 4th Internacional Conference*, pp. 187-200, 2001.
9. M. Kudo and S. Hada: XML Document Security based on Provisional Authorization. *7th ACM Conference on Computer and Communications Security*, pp. 87-96, 2000.
10. OASIS eXtensible Access Control Markup Language (XACML). OASIS (2002).
11. S. Jajodia, P. Samarati, M.L. Sapino, and V.S. Subrahmanian: Flexible Support for Multiple Access Control Policies. *ACM Transactions on Database Systems*, Vol. 26(2), pp. 214-260, 2001.
12. S. Jajodia, P. Samarati, and V.S. Subrahmanian: A Logical Language for Expressing Authorizations. In *Proceedings of 1997 IEEE Symposium on Security and Privacy*, pp. 31-42, 1997.
13. S. Johnston: Modeling security concerns in service-oriented architectures. Rational Software White Paper. Available at *http://www-128.ibm.com/developerworks/rational/library/4860.html.* (2004)
14. T. Lodderstedt, D. Basin, and J.Doser: SecureUML: A UML-Based Modeling Language for Model-Driven Security. In *5th International conference on The Unified Modeling Language*, pp. 426-441, 2000.
15. The Platform for Privacy Preferences 1.1 (P3P 1.1). Available at *http://www.w3.org/TR/2006/NOTE-P3P11-20061113/.*

16. J. Rumbaugh, I. Jacobson, and G. Booch: *The Unified Modeling Language Reference Manual*. Addison-Wesley, 1999.
17. F. Satoh, Y. Nakamura, and K. Ono: Adding Authentication to Model Driven Security. *International Conference on Web Services 2006*, pp. 585-594, 2006.
18. J.M. Spivey: *The Z Notation: A Reference Manual. 2nd edition*, Pentice-Hall, Englewood Cliffs, NJ, 1992.
19. The Unified Modeling Language (UML) Version 2.1.1. Available at *http://www.omg.org/technology/documents/formal/uml.htm*
20. Web Services Policy 1.2 - Framework (WS-Policy). Available at *http://www.w3.org/Submission/WS-Policy/*.

4

Database Issues in Trust Management and Trust Negotiation

Dongyi Li[1], William Winsborough[1], Marianne Winslett[2] and Ragib Hasan[2]

[1] Department of Computer Science, University of Texas at San Antonio,
   dli@cs.utsa.edu, wwinsborough@acm.org
[2] Department of Computer Science, University of Illinois at Urbana-Champaign,
   (winslett,rhasan)@cs.uiuc.edu

Summary. Trust management is the process of managing authorization decisions in a decentralized environment where many of the participants do not have pre-established trust relationships, such as logins and passwords, with one another. Trust management is important for enterprise-level and cross-organizational database applications such as supply chain management, enterprise resource planning, and customer relationship management. Trust management research may also interest the database research community because of the former's affinity for a Datalog-based world, in which a query (authorization request) launches a multi-site search for a proof of authorization. To complicate the process, sites have autonomy and may not always cooperate in proof construction; it is not always obvious where to find the facts and rules needed to construct a proof; and attempts to access particular facts and rules may spawn new authorization requests.

1 Introduction to Trust Management

Authorization is one of the most important problems in computer security and privacy. It lies at the heart of meeting the objectives of confidentiality, integrity, and availability. Within a single organization, pre-established trust relationships are used to assign authorizations and prearranged information such as login names and passwords can serve as the basis for making authorization decisions at run time. For instance, an enterprise has pre-established trust relationships with its employees, so it is necessary only to authenticate that a certain resource request is being made by a certain employee for the request to be given appropriate authorization.

On the other hand, when resource provider and resource requester belong to different organizations or have no prior relationship whatsoever, there are no pre-existing trust relationships. This problem can be mitigated slightly by using manual procedures for cross-domain authentication and authorization, such as maintaining local logins and passwords (or lists of X.509 identities) for all employees in a partner company. However, even in the case of cross-organizational resource sharing, this imposes an excessive administrative burden in our world of rapidly changing organizational structures and partnerships. It becomes entirely ad hoc, chaotic, and unmanageable when the requirements for authorization have nothing to do with formal organizational affiliations, such as a senior citizen discount or letting family and friends access an on-line photo album. This is because the approach relies too heavily on pre-established trust relationships.

Over the last 10–15 years, researchers have proposed new techniques that enable on-line parties to establish trust on the fly, as the need arises. Bina *et al.* proposed using characteristics other than identity, attested to by known authorities in digital certificates, as a basis for authorization on the Internet [8]. Blaze *et al.* introduced a complementary approach to authorization based on delegation of privileges and coined the term *trust management* to describe it [11]. Ellison *et al.* introduced a similar scheme called SPKI [22]. Rivest *et al.* introduced a scheme called SDSI [54] that provides an ingenious way to introduce names and bind them to public keys controlled by individuals and groups, which greatly facilitates identifying authorized principals electronically. Following these seminal works, a great deal of work has been done, much of which we will survey in this chapter.

Trust management systems typically use cryptographic credentials to convey information relevant to authorization decisions. The authorization decision determines whether a given set of credentials demonstrate that a given request to access a resource, such as a web or peer-to-peer service, is authorized, which is to say that the access request *complies* with current policy governing that resource. This raises two additional problems that we also survey here. First, the credentials are issued in a decentralized manner, and somehow the relevant credentials need to be collected or otherwise made available to the authorization evaluation process. Second, some credentials carry sensitive, confidential information, and may need to be subject to access control themselves when dealing with an unfamiliar resource provider or requester. The same may also be true of policy: an access control policy may give clues about the nature of the resource it protects. For example, if a patient's prescription can be viewed only by their pharmacist or by their parent, then one can guess that the prescription is for a child. To preserve the privacy of the resources that they protect, policies themselves may need protection just like any other resource. In other words, access to the contents of a policy may need to be governed by another access control policy. These additional authorization decisions can also be based on credentials. Thus, there is a need for a process of credential exchange in which both parties seek to enable a positive authorization decision for the main resource request, while also supporting the additional authorization decisions that may be necessary to achieve this. This process is *trust negotiation* [64, 65], an automated approach to establishing bilateral trust between two parties at run time.

Current and emerging practice implements authorization decisions in middleware or, often, even in the application. Consequently, the goal of this chapter is not to discuss the integration of trust management techniques with database technology. Rather, it is to present problems that arise in designing and implementing trust management systems, many of which are reminiscent of problems from database research. In particular, many trust management systems have foundations based on Datalog, a language used extensively in deductive database systems. Authorization decisions in this class of trust management systems are obtained by evaluating a query involving the client and the requested resource. Evaluation in general requires collecting data and rules from distributed repositories. Our hope is that these and other overlaps will stimulate greater interest in trust management issues on the part of the database community.

The notion of the term "trust management" that we survey in this chapter refers to authorization systems that support principally human agents in defining security policies based on their own judgments of the characteristics of system participants. The focus of research in this area is on providing policy language features and corresponding enforcement mechanisms that meet the needs of policy authors for requirements such as scalability and high assurance in decentralized environments. There is another kind of system sometimes dubbed "trust management" that has a rather different aim, and it is important to be clear that this other type of system is not a subject of this chapter. This sort of system is a bit like a reputation system. It seeks to estimate the trustworthiness of entities within the system by automated or semi-automated means, by compiling and aggregating the evaluations of other parties who have interacted with those entities [34].

The remainder of this chapter is structured as follows. In Section 2 we present the basic notions and aims of trust management. In Section 3 we survey the principal contributions to the field to date. In Section 4 we discuss issues in the evaluation of authorization queries based on considerations such as the distributed definition and storage of credentials and other policy statements. In Section 5 we discuss issues and work in automated trust negotiation. In Section 6 we discuss open issues and trends.

2 What is Trust Management?

Traditional access control models base authorization decisions on the identity of the principal who requests a resource. In an operating system, this identity may be a user name that must appear on an access control list (ACL) associated with a file, if access to the file is authorized. In a large enterprise, an identity may be a distinguished name mentioned in a Public Key Infrastructure (PKI) certificate. In these and similarly closed environments, the identities of all authorized resource requesters are presumed to be known to the resource provider, or at least to some local administrator who aggregates identities into groups or roles to which the resource provider can grant access. However, the number of autonomous services that are administered in a decentralized manner (*i.e.*, within different security domains) has increased enormously on the Internet. As a result, services are often provided to clients whose identities are not previously known to the service provider. Similarly, the participants in a peer-to-peer system need to establish mutual trust in one another. In such a decentralized environment, the traditional access control mechanisms such as ACLs cannot be used to secure the system without excluding vast numbers of valuable and well-intentioned clients and peers.

The trust management (TM) approach, first developed by Blaze *et al.* [11], aims to provide a basis for authorization in highly decentralized environments by enabling resource owners to delegate authority to other entities who will help them identify the appropriate requesters to authorize. In this manner, resource owners and other policy authors can enlist the assistance of appropriate authorities in determining the suitability of individual requesters for authorization.

Trust management relies on *digital credentials*, which are unforgeable statements signed by their issuer. Typically, a digital credential contains an assertion about the properties of one or more principals mentioned in the credential. The best-known standard for digital credentials is X.509v3 [31], though many alternatives exist. Most of these schemes rely on public key cryptography: the credential issuer signs the credential using its private key, and anyone can verify the contents of the credential by obtaining the corresponding public key and checking the signature. In the US, recent legislation such as the Sarbanes-Oxley Act has forced the widespread adoption of the public key infrastructures needed to support digital credentials. Today's digital credentials are typically identity certificates, i.e., they simply say what public key is associated with a particular principal. However, current credential standards already support the inclusion of additional information describing a principal's properties, such as one would need for a digital employee ID, driver's license, or birth certificate.

In TM systems, *security policy* is made by local administrators to specify access control rules on local resources. Blaze *et al.* [10] said that trust management systems combined the notion of specifying security policy with the mechanism for specifying security credentials. The authorization semantics of most TM systems is *monotonic* in the sense that if any given action is approved when given a set of evidence E (*i.e.*, policies and credentials), then it will also be approved when given any superset of E. This means that no negative evidence is allowed in the system. Monotonicity ensures fail-safe behavior in which no potentially dangerous action is allowed by default, simply because of an inability to find negative credentials. This is especially important in decentralized environments due to the many factors that can prevent one from obtaining complete information about all the credentials in the system (network interruption, uncooperative credential repositories, lost information, *etc.*).

Most discussions of TM systems use the terms "certificate" and "credential" more or less interchangeably. However, unlike certificates in public key infrastructure (PKI) systems, such as X.509 or PGP, which bind public keys to identities, certificates and credentials in TM systems do not typically bind public keys to identities, but rather to other information on which authorization decisions are based.

In the early TM systems PolicyMaker [11] and KeyNote [9], the information bound to a key by a credential is essentially an authorization to use a specific resource. In this sense they are quite similar to *capabilities*, which were first introduced by Dennis and Van Horn [20] in the context of operating systems to specify what privileges (*e.g.*, a set of actions on certain objects in the operating systems) the *holder* (*e.g.*, subjects in operating systems) of the capability may use. A delegated capability is copied (or moved) from one holder to another.

Just as the holder of a car key can start the corresponding car, whomever holds a capability can use the privileges it specifies. While an operating system can rely on protected memory to implement assignment and delegation of privileges, in TM systems, credentials are used to bind capabilities to public keys. Credentials may optionally also grant the right to further delegate the capability. Chains of such credentials can be used to document a sequence of delegations of privileges from the resource owner to the requester, and thus can prove that the requester indeed is authorized for the requested resource. Each credential in the chain is signed by using the public key in the previous credential; the first is signed by the resource owner or his designee. The requester proves she is the authorized entity by answering challenges or otherwise demonstrating possession of the public key in the last credential in the chain.

When privileges are specified directly in the credentials, the authorization decision is quite simple. However, additional expressive power can greatly facilitate scalability in environments such as the Internet where service providers may wish to authorize large numbers of principals. Managing the delegation of access rights, for instance, to all students at a given university requires issuing a credential to each student for each resource to which they have access (library, cafeteria, gym, *etc.*). On the other hand, by utilizing credentials that characterize their owners as being students, the same student ID credential can be used to authorize a wide range of actions.

Indeed, later TM systems (*e.g.*, to some extent SPKI/SDSI [18, 54, 22], and certainly RT [46] and Cassandra [5]) use credentials to characterize the holders of the credentials. These credentials need not contain specific authorizations, but provide more general *attributes* of the credential holders (*e.g.*, student, US citizen, licensed driver born in 1960, *etc.*), which can be reused by various resource owners to make their access control decisions. This enables much more scalable policy definition. For instance, anyone who is 21 can purchase alcohol legally. It would be very unsatisfactory to require on-line shoppers to obtain a credential that can be used solely for purchasing alcoholic beverages from a specific vender, as a purely capability-based approach would require. A much more viable solution is to enable all venders of all age-restricted products to utilize any suitable credential that the client already happens to have (*e.g.*, a digital drivers license or passport).

Besides the basic notion of delegation in which one entity gives some of its access rights to another entity, there are two additional delegation idioms that are most often discussed in the designs of trust management systems: *appointment* and *threshold delegation*. In the case of appointment, the appointer has the (appointment) right to confer on another (the appointee) an attribute or right that the appointer may not herself have. (In general, the conferred right can itself be an appointment right.) *Threshold delegation* is also called k-out-of-n ($n \geq 1$ and $n \geq k \geq 1$) delegation, meaning the authority is delegated to n parties, each of which only gets a fragment of it. It is effective only if at least k of these parties issue their requests or exercise their authorities in concert.

Compliance checking (also called *policy evaluation* or *query evaluation*) answers the question: Does a set of credentials prove that a request complies with the security policy associated with a given resource? The process of evaluating a query involves finding a chain of credentials that delegate authority from the resource owner to the requester. This process is also called *credential chain discovery* [47]. As we shall see, it can be helpful to imagine credential chains in graphical terms. To a first approximation, a credential chain can be thought of as a path from the resource provider to the requester in which nodes are principals and edges are credentials. However, the details of such a credential graph depend on the TM system and, in general, a chain may correspond to a richer subgraph structure.

As mentioned earlier, trust negotiation is the process of establishing bilateral trust at run time. Trust negotiation uses verifiable, unforgeable digital credentials that describe principals' properties, together with explicit policies that describe the properties that a principal must possess in order to gain access to a particular resource. When Alice wishes to access a resource owned by Bob, she and Bob follow one of many proposed trust negotiation protocols to determine whether she has the right properties, i.e., whether her credentials satisfy the policy that Bob has specified for access to that resource.

To show how trust negotiation works, let us consider the scenario in Figure 1. Suppose that Alice wants to purchase prescription medication over the web from Bob's pharmacy, which she has never visited before.

Bob's pharmacy sends her its sales policy, which will allow Alice to make the purchase if she presents a prescription issued to her by a doctor licensed to practice medicine in Bob's country.

Since Alice has no prior experience with Bob's pharmacy, she tells Bob that he must prove that he is a licensed pharmacist before she will reveal her prescription. In response, Bob presents a state-issued pharmacist's credential. Alice verifies that the credential is properly signed, and follows a short protocol that allows Bob to prove that he

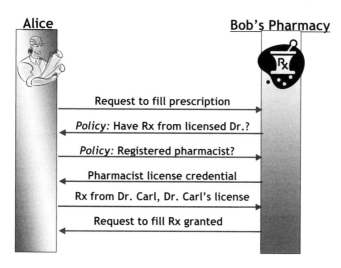

Fig. 1. Example trust negotiation

owns the pharmacist credential.

Alice is now willing to send her prescription to Bob. She sends that along with proof that the prescription was issued by a doctor within the country, in the form of a credential signed by a national agency that attests that her doctor is licensed to practice medicine. Her doctor should have given her this credential the first time she asked for a digital prescription; if he did not, she can query him now (credential discovery) to obtain it.

Bob verifies the signature on the doctor's license certificate, and then verifies that the prescription was signed by the doctor mentioned in the license certificate. He also follows a short protocol that allows Alice to prove that she is the patient mentioned in the credential. Afterwards, Bob's policy has been satisfied, so he allows Alice to purchase the medication.

Under traditional identity-based authorization, Alice and her doctor would have to follow lengthy out-of-band procedures to establish the same level of trust with the pharmacy web site. Both would have to set up accounts beforehand at the pharmacy web site, and Bob would need to see paper credentials to ensure that Alice's doctor really is a doctor. So that Bob can know that the prescription really is for Alice, she will have to give her pharmacy account number to her doctor so that the doctor can mention it in the prescription. Further, the doctor must submit the prescription directly to the site, so that Bob knows that the doctor really did create it. In addition to the hassle of creating accounts and remembering passwords, this traditional approach will severely limit Alice's options for shopping around for the best price. The trust negotiation approach overcomes all of these shortcomings: Alice and Bob meet, disclose their policies, and exchange credentials to establish a trust relationship instantly. Further, all the negotiating steps listed above can be carried out automatically by small software agents acting on their owners' behalf, so that trust establishment is transparent to the human participants.

The pharmacy example shows only one possible way of establishing trust, based on explicit disclosure of credentials and policies. Researchers have investigated many alternative approaches, each with its own advantages and disadvantages, and we will describe them later in this chapter.

3 History

In this section, we survey the principal contributions to date. We will introduce each system by explaining what features it has, what main contributions it makes and the applications its designers had in mind.

3.1 PolicyMaker and KeyNote

PolicyMaker, developed and defined by Blaze *et al.* [11], was the first trust management system. It was designed as a proof of concept for the design principles of trust management with a minimalist prototype implementation. For example, the PolicyMaker system does not take responsibility for cryptographic verification of credentials. Instead, these verifications must be done by the application that call the trust management system.

In PolicyMaker, assertions (security policies and credentials) have the form "<Source> ASSERTS <AuthorityStruct> WHERE <Filter>." ASSERTS and WHERE are keywords in PolicyMaker, while the syntax of the fields <Source>, <AuthorityStruct> and <Filter> are application-dependent. The <Source> field identifies the authority that makes this assertion, the <Author ityStruct> field contains the subjects to whom this assertion applies, and the <Filter> field has an application-specified string "<action string>" that must be satisfied for the assertion to hold. The whole assertion states that the <Source> trusts the subjects to be associated with <action string>.

KeyNote [9, 10] is a direct descendant of PolicyMaker, and follows most of its design principles. However, unlike PolicyMaker whose assertions are fully programmable and application-dependent, KeyNote's [9] assertions are written in a specific, concise and human readable assertion language. The assertion language is defined to be simple and to be supported by a small interpreter. In addition, the expressiveness of the assertions is carefully limited so as to ensure that resource usage is proportional to policy size.

Figure 2 shows a sample KeyNote assertion that states that the authorizer delegates to either of the licensees for read access on file "/etc/passwd." The

KeyNote-Version: 1
Authorizer: rsa-pkcs1-hex: "1234abcd"
Licensee: dsa-hex: "9876dcba" ∥ rsa-pkcs1-hex: "6789defg"
Comment: Authorizer delegates read access to either of the licensees
Condition: ($file == "/etc/passwd" && $access == "read") → {return "OK"}
Signature: rsa-md5-pkcs1-hex: "f00f5673"

Fig. 2. An example KeyNote assertion.

example also illustrates the fact that KeyNote takes responsibility for verifying cryptographic signatures, and thus reduces the workload of the calling applications and better enforces the security policy. Compared to PolicyMaker, KeyNote aims to be a relatively complete software solution for authorization.

KeyNote assertions bind public keys to authorizations for specific security-critical resources. As in capability-based systems, KeyNote's authorization decision procedure is quite straightforward, and does not require resolving the name or identity of the requester. Security-critical actions are given by a set of name, value bindings called an *action environment*, which is specified by the calling application. Assertions contain a *condition* field that expresses constraints on these bindings that must be satisfied for the assertion to participate in a *proof of compliance* with the authorization policy governing the action. For example, in the assertion shown in Figure 2, $access is a name and the constraint on the value assigned to this name is that it must be equal to "read". So if the application binds "action" to "read" whenever the requested operation is a read, then this credential can be used only to grant read access.

3.2 SPKI/SDSI

SPKI/SDSI [18] merged the SDSI [54] and the SPKI [22] efforts together to achieve an expressive and powerful trust management system. SDSI (pronounced "sudsy"), short for "Simple Distributed Security Infrastructure," was proposed as a new public-key infrastructure by Rivest and Lampson. Concurrently, Carl Ellison et al. developed "Simple Public Key Infrastructure," or SPKI (officially pronounced "s-p-k-i" [18], but sometimes informally called "spooky").

SDSI's greatest contribution is its design of local and extended names, which are bound to keys through the use of SDSI name certificates (see below), and which solve the problem of globally unambiguous naming. The owner of each public key can define names local to a name space that is associated with and identified by that key. For example, "K_{Alice} bob" is an example of a local name in which "bob" is an identifier and K_{Alice} is a globally unique key that we assume here belongs to a specific principal, Alice, who has sole authority to define bindings for the local name. Alice can define "K_{Alice} bob" to refer to a particular key "K_{Bob}" by issuing a tuple of the form (K_{Alice}, bob, K_{Bob}, 1). This in effect says that the principal that Alice refers to as bob has the key K_{Bob}. (The "1" just indicates that the certificate is valid.) Given such a binding, a reference to the SDSI name "K_{Alice} bob" can be resolved to the key K_{Bob}, which Bob can prove he controls when he needs to prove that he is the referenced principal.

Whereas a *local name* is a key followed by an identifier, an *extended name* is a key followed by two or more identifiers. The meaning of these are the result of multiple bindings of local names. For instance, if Bob were to issue the certificate (K_{Bob}, friend, K_{Carol}, 1), then the extended name "K_{Alice} bob friend" could be resolved to K_{Carol}. This brings up another important point about SDSI names; they can refer to more than one principal. For instance, Bob could also issue (K_{Bob}, friend, K_{Dave} friend, 1) with the effect that "K_{Alice} bob friend" would refer not only to Carol, but to all of Dave's friends as well. Thus, SDSI names (both local and extended) can denote groups of keys and, equivalently, properties of key owners.

In general, SDSI *name certificates* are 4-tuples of the form (K, A, S, V), in which K is the key used to issue the certificate, "$K\ A$" is the local name being defined, S is either a key, a local name, or an extended name, and V is a certificate validity bit.

A key point about SDSI's use of name spaces is that names that start with different keys are different names, so there is no danger of controllers of different public keys accidentally trying to bind the same name in conflicting ways. In other words, global uniqueness of names can be achieved without necessitating coordination among naming authorities.

While SDSI contributed to SPKI/SDSI name certificates that are used to bind names to public keys, SPKI contributed *authorization certificates*. These are 5-tuples of the form (K, A, D, T, V) in which K is the key issuing the certificate, A is the subject of the certificate, D is a delegation bit which indicates whether the authorization being conveyed to A can be further delegated by A, T is a tag that specifies the authorization being granted, and V is a certificate validity bit. While in the original design of SPKI, A was required to be a key, in SPKI/SDSI, A can also be a SDSI name. For example, a certificate such as (K_{Alice}, K_{Dave} friends, 1, downloadPhotos, 1) might indicate that Alice allows Dave's friends to download photos and to delegate the permission to others. Notice that as principals are added to or removed from the group of Dave's friends, they automatically gain or lose this permission.

3.3 QCM and SD3

QCM [25], short for "Query Certificate Manager," was designed at the University of Pennsylvania as part of the SwitchWare project on active networks. It was designed specifically to support secure maintenance of distributed data sets. For example, QCM can be used to support decentralized administration of distributed repositories housing public key certificates that map names to public keys. In the sense of access control, QCM provides security support for the query and retrieval of ACLs. Although QCM is not designed to be a trust management system, it had significant impact on the TM system SD3 [32, 33] proposed by Trevor Jim. One of the main contributions of QCM that can be adopted by other TM systems is its design of a policy directed certificate retrieval mechanism [25], which enables the TM evaluator to automatically detect and identify missing but needed certificates and to retrieve them from remote certificate repositories. It uses query decomposition and optimization techniques, and discusses its novel solutions in terms of network security, such as private key protection methods.

SD3 [32, 33] is the successor of QCM and inherits design features from QCM, such as the certificate retrieval mechanism in a dynamic decentralized certificate storage system. The SD3 project aimed to make trust management systems easy for applications to use. To this end, SD3 is responsible for verifying cryptographic signatures. In addition, SD3 has a credential retrieval mechanism that enables the evaluation of authorization decisions in the context of distributed credential storage. (We return to this in Section 4.) Finally, in order to guarantee returning a correct answer, SD3 implements certified evaluations, in which a checker checks the evaluator's outcome before passing it to the calling application. Together these features ensure that calling applications need only specify policy, without worrying about how it is enforced.

SD3 enables application developers to write policy statements in an extended Datalog that introduces a notion of name space in which predicates and relations are defined. It extends Datalog with SDSI names. For example, consider the following SD3 rule, which expresses the recursive case in the definition of the transitive closure (T) of the edge relation E: "$T(x, y) \text{:-} K\$E(x, y), T(y, z)$". Here K is a public key, E is a *local relation name*, defined in K's name space, and $K\$E$ is a *global relation name*, the definition of which is independent of the point of evaluation. The presence of this rule in a rule base associated with a given name space says that the pair (x, y) is in the the local relation T if it is in K's E relation. SD3 also allows an IP address A to be paired with its global name, such as $(K@A)\$E$, in which A is the IP address of an evaluation service operated by the principal that has public key K. The address assists in locating the evaluation agent and rule base associated with K, though the authenticity of the rule base is ensured by using K.

We take this opportunity to introduce some Datalog terminology: the atomic formula to the left of the :- ($T(x, y)$ in the example) is called the *head* of the rule or *clause*; the comma-separated list of atomic formulas to the right is called the *body*. These commas represent conjunction.

3.4 *RT*

The *RT* framework [46, 48, 45] is a family of Role-based Trust-management languages that combines the strengths of RBAC (Role-Based Access Control) [1] and the strengths of trust-management systems. Different languages in the family incorporate different features, but all members are designed to permit efficient (polynomial time) evaluation of ordinary authorization queries. Like SD3, RT is based on Datalog. However, rather than writing arbitrary Datalog clauses, the RT policy author uses a distinct RT syntax organized around RT language abstractions whose semantics is given by a formal translation of RT statements (*i.e.*, credentials) into Datalog. This approach enforces an orderly policy-definition discipline while obtaining significant benefits from using what is in effect a subset of Datalog: (1) the semantics are unambiguous and can be constructed in several well understood and equivalent manners (logical entailment, fixpoint, top down, bottom up, *etc.*); (2) authorization queries are easily generalized to ask, for example, which principals are authorized to access a given resource, or which resources a given principal is authorized to access; (3) the complexity of the RT features is easily determined by making use of established complexity results for evaluation of Datalog queries. In addition, the way in which the Datalog clauses generated from RT statements are restricted enables RT credentials to be stored in a manner that is more flexible than is possible with QCM or SD3. As we will see in Section 4, because of these restrictions, RT credentials that are stored with either their subject or their issuer can be located and retrieved as needed during authorization query evaluation. In QCM and SD3, credentials must be stored with their issuers.

The definition and use of roles in RT is based on and extends that of groups in SDSI. Keys are called *principals*. Each principal A controls the definition of a collection of roles of the form $A.R$ in which R is called a *role name* and is either an identifier r or, in members of the RT family of languages that support parameterized roles, an identifier applied to a list of parameters, as in $r(t_1, \ldots, t_k)$. Parameters are quite helpful for the purpose of expressing quantitative attributes, such as age or budget, as well as for enabling roles to express relationships between principals and data objects. For instance, $Alice.read('/usr/alice/research')$ might represent principals allowed to read Alice's research directory.

Certificates in RT are called *statements* or *credentials*. For concreteness, we consider the forms these can take in RT_0. There are four types of credentials that an entity A can issue, each corresponding to a different way of defining the membership of one of A's roles, $A.r$.

- *Simple Member*: $A.r \longleftarrow D$.
  With this credential A asserts that D is a member of $A.r$.
- *Simple Inclusion*: $A.r \longleftarrow B.r_1$.
  With this credential A asserts that $A.r$ includes (all members of) $B.r_1$. This represents a delegation from A to B, as B may cause new entities to become members of the role $A.r$ by issuing credentials defining (and extending) $B.r_1$.
- *Linking Inclusion*: $A.r \longleftarrow A.r_1.r_2$.

$A.r_1.r_2$ is called a *linked role*. With this credential A asserts that $A.r$ includes $B.r_2$, for every B that is a member of $A.r_1$. This represents a delegation from A to all the members of the role $A.r_1$.

- *Intersection Inclusion*: $A.r \longleftarrow B_1.r_1 \cap B_2.r_2$.
  $B_1.r_1 \cap B_2.r_2$ is called an *intersection*. With this credential A asserts that $A.r$ includes every principal who is a member of both $B_1.r_1$ and $B_2.r_2$. This represents partial delegation from A to B_1 and to B_2.

Again to illustrate the technique by which semantics are given to a set of RT_0 credentials, we now present the translation to Datalog. Given a set $\mathcal{C}$ of RT_0 credentials, the corresponding *semantic program*, $SP(\mathcal{C})$, is a Datalog program with one ternary predicate m. Intuitively, $m(A, r, D)$ indicates that D is a member of the role $A.r$. Given an RT statement c, the *semantic program* of c, $SP(c)$, is defined as follows, where identifiers starting with the "?" character are logic variables:

$$SP(A.r \longleftarrow D) = m(A, r, D).$$
$$SP(A.r \longleftarrow B.r_1) = m(A, r, ?X) :- m(B, r_1, ?X).$$
$$SP(A.r \longleftarrow A.r_1.r_2) = m(A, r, ?X) :- m(A, r_1, ?Y), m(?Y, r_2, ?X).$$
$$SP(A.r \longleftarrow B_1.r_1 \cap B_2.r_2) = m(A, r, ?X) :- m(B_1, r_1, ?X), m(B_2, r_2, ?X).$$

SP extends to the set of statements in the obvious way: $SP(\mathcal{C}) = \{SP(c) \mid c \in \mathcal{C}\}$. Now to determine whether a principal D belongs to role $A.r$, one simply evaluates a query (according to any one of a variety of evaluation mechanisms) to determine whether it is the case that $SP(\mathcal{C}) \models m(A, r, D)$.

RT_1 adds parameterized roles to RT_0, and RT_2 adds logical objects to RT_1. Just as roles group together related entities so that their authorizations can be assigned in fewer statements, logical objects logically group together objects so that their permissions can be assigned together. RT^C [44, 45] incorporates constraint systems, carefully selected to preserve query-answering efficiency. Constraints are very helpful for representing ranges of quantitative values and object specifiers such as directory paths. For instance, they can very concisely express policies such as "anyone over 65 is entitled to a senior citizen discount" and "Alice can access the entire directory subtree of /usr/home/Alice". RT^T provides manifold roles and role-product operators, which can express threshold policies and separation-of-duty policies. RT^D provides delegation of role activations, which can express selective use of capacities and delegation of these capacities. RT^D and RT^T can be used, together or separately, with each of RT_0, RT_1, or RT_2. The resulting combinations are written RT_i, RT_i^D, RT_i^T, and RT_i^{DT} for $i = 0, 1, 2$.

SDSI extended names and RT's linked roles both rely on agreement among principals as to the intended meaning of role names ("identifiers" in SDSI). For instance, a linked name such as ABET.accreditedUniversity.student is only meaningful if there is some agreement among ABET-accredited universities as to what it means to be a student. One technique for providing a scalable means of establishing such agreement is based on a structure called an *application domain specification document* (ADSD) [46]. ADSDs contain natural-language descriptions of role names that pertain to a given application domain. They can also be used to specify other technical information useful for ensuring consistent use of these role names, such as how many parameters of what types are required for each role name. ADSDs are made available on the web via a universal resource identifier (a web address) that can serve not only as a locator, but also as an identifier of the vocabulary defined by the ADSD. Credentials that make use of these role names can use this identifier along with the role name to disambiguate the intended meaning.

3.5 OASIS and Cassandra

OASIS [67, 26, 28] and Cassandra [5, 6] are role-based trust management systems that have many design considerations in common. Cassandra was influenced by the OASIS design. However, while OASIS was designed for general purpose use, Cassandra was designed with the goal of supporting the access control policies for a national electronic health record system.

OASIS introduced the notion of appointment. Appointment occurs when a member of some role issues an *appointment credential* that will allow some user to activate another role [67]. Thus appointers belong to roles that resemble administrative roles in RBAC [56].

OASIS uses first-order logic clauses to represent security policy. For example, "$r_1, w_1 \vdash r_4$" is a policy statement that means a user who is active in role r_1 and holds the appointment certificate w_1 can activate the role r_4.

As in RT_1, roles in Cassandra are parameterized. Cassandra represents policy statements as Datalog clauses with constraints. One interesting characteristic of Cassandra is that its expressivity can be tuned by selecting constraint systems having differing complexity (as discussed further in Section 4).

Unlike most trust management systems, OASIS and Cassandra support the notion of a *session*. In this respect, they are unique among the systems we discuss here and thus are perhaps the most justified in calling themselves role-based. Indeed, some researchers have been critical of characterizing languages such as RT as being role-based, because they have no notion of session. On the other hand, the presence of sessions introduces a highly dynamic component of system state into OASIS and Cassandra not present in other trust management systems, which raises serious concerns about scalability in highly distributed systems.

Cassandra makes the interesting choice of implementing some aspects of session state within extensional Datalog relations. There are six predefined predicates in Cassandra: $permits(e, a)$ holds if entity e can perform action a; $canActivate(e, r)$ holds if e can activate role r; $hasActivated(e, r)$ holds if e has activated r; $canDeactivate(e_1, e_2, r)$ holds if e_1 has the power to deactivate e_2's activation of role r; $isDeactivated(e, r)$ holds if role r has been deactivated for entity e; $canReqCred(e_1, e_2.p(\overrightarrow{e}))$ holds if e_1 is permitted to

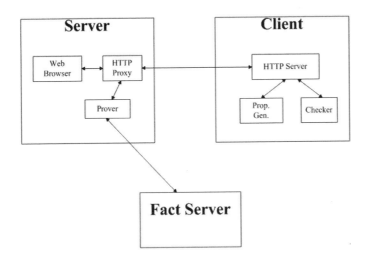

Fig. 3. The PCA system

request credentials issued by e_2 asserting the atomic formula $p(\overrightarrow{e})$. The body of a clause having $canReqCred(e_1, e_2.p(\overrightarrow{e}))$ as its head can specify conditions that must be satisfied before a credential can be disclosed, which is useful in supporting trust negotiation.

3.6 PCA

PCA (Proof Carrying Authorization) [2, 4] was designed primarily for access control in web services. Figure 3 shows the components of the PCA system working in a web browsing environment. HTTP proxies are used to make the whole process of accessing a web page transparent to the web browser. The web browser only knows the final result of either a displayed web page that it attempted to access, or a denial message. The proxy is designed to be portable and easily integrated into the client system without changing anything inside the original web browser. As depicted in Figure 3, the client is responsible for constructing a proof of authorization, which the server need only check for correctness. This substantially reduces the burden imposed on the server by the authorization process.

PCA uses higher-order logic to specify policies and credentials, so that it can be very expressive. Indeed, in general the determination of whether a proof of authorization exists is undecidable, much less tractable. PCA overcomes this issue as follows. First, as mentioned earlier, the server only has to check the proof constructed by the requester, and the checking process is decidable and tractable. Second, on the client side, the proxy is responsible for discovering and retrieving credentials, computing proofs, and communicating

XML:
  < GROUP NAME = "Hospitals" >
    < RULE >
      < INCLUSION ID = "reco" $TYPE$ = "Recommendation"
        FROM = "self" >< \INCLUSION >
    < \RULE >
  < \GROUP >

Prolog:
  $group(X, \text{Hospitals})$: $-$ $cert(Y, X, \text{"Recommendation"}, \text{RecFields})$,
$group(Y, \text{self})$.

Fig. 4. An example TPL rule shown in its concrete XML syntax and its internal Prolog representation.

with the server. To avoid undecidable computations on the client side, the client proxy does not use the full logic; instead, it uses a limited, application-specific logic, in which authorization decisions are tractable.

3.7 TPL

TPL (Trust Policy Language) [27], designed at IBM Haifa Research Lab, was proposed specifically for trust establishment between strangers. TPL is based on RBAC [23, 1] and extends it by being able to map strangers automatically to roles. Unlike other trust management systems [46, 67], TPL's efforts are put only into mapping users to roles, and not into mapping roles to privileges, which simplifies the design. The latter is the responsibility of the application.

The concrete syntax of TPL uses XML to represent security rules. These are then translated by TPL into a standard logic programming language, *viz.*, Prolog. Figure 4 shows an example TPL rule in the portable XML notation and its internal Prolog translation [27].

Using different *transcoders*, TPL is certificate format independent: rules written in XML can be translated and reorganized by the transcoders into any certificate formats, such as X.509 or PGP. In each certificate, the *certificate type* field points to its certificate profile, which selects the proper transcoder to interpret that certificate into its XML rules.

The mandatory components of each certificate are the issuer's public key, the subject's public key, the certificate type, the version of the certificate, the profile URL, the issuer certificate repository, and the subject certificate repository. The last two components were innovative considerations with respect to credential retrieval. First, to enable the TPL system to automatically retrieve relevant certificates from remote repositories, the certificate that is currently being processed should specify the locations of the repositories where the relevant certificates are housed. Second, certificates can be referenced negatively in TPL, which means that TPL is non-monotonic in the sense that adding certificates can diminish authorizations. Thus TPL cannot rely on requesters to present certificates that are referenced negatively. Instead the resource owner specifies a credential "collector" [27], which is a software module configured to know about trusted repositories of negative certificates.

4 Evaluation Problems and Strategies

The trust management engine evaluates authorization queries based on security policies and credentials. Several issues regarding how such evaluation proceeds have been addressed in the evolution of modern TM systems. In this section we consider many of these issues. We defer until Section 5 discussion of issues that bear on the fact that policy and credentials may themselves be sensitive. Other issues, notably certificate revocation, we omit altogether. Topics discussed in this section include the following:

1. **Separating the authorization service from the application provides several advantages.**
   Software components that manage security are subject to very high integrity requirements as their correct functioning is essential to preventing misuse.
2. **Policies should be written in special-purpose languages, not in general-purpose programming languages.**
   This has an obvious impact on the extent to which the trust management engine can efficiently evaluate authorization queries. Finding language constructs that are sufficiently expressive to enable policy objectives to be met, while simultaneously supporting efficient evaluation, has been an important factor in the evolution of TM systems.
3. **Credential discovery and retrieval is an essential part of the authorization problem.**
   One of the important problems for TM systems is that of finding credentials that are not only issued and revoked in a decentralized manner, but whose storage is also distributed. In this environment, there is no central, well-known directory that records and keeps track of locations for each credential in the network, and on which entities can rely to retrieve credentials. If credentials cannot be found when they are needed during evaluation of authorization queries it is not possible to prevent denying some access to resources that should be should be permitted.

It is possible to perform query evaluation with distributed credentials either by bringing the evaluation process to the remote credentials, and thus distributing the evaluation process, or by bringing the remote credentials to a central evaluation point. As we will see in this section, both approaches have been taken by TM systems. Moreover, there are alternatives with respect to where to locate credentials; at a minimum, they can naturally be located with their issuer or with their subject. However, permitting this flexibility raises challenges for ensuring that all credentials can be found by the evaluation process if they are needed, and thus that any access authorized by the current set of valid policy statements can be granted.

4.1 General-Purpose Query Evaluation Engine

As mentioned above, PolicyMaker [10] was the first trust management system *per se*. It aimed to provide a general-purpose, application-independent definition of proof of compliance. The designers identified two main advantages that can be obtained by using a general-purpose compliance checker. First, the design and implementation of an authorization system is not as simple as application programmers might at first imagine, and considerable efficiency can be obtained from reusing a general-purpose authorization engine. Second, it is a generally accepted design principle to minimize the amount of code whose integrity is essential to the secure operation of the system. By clearly separating the role of the application from the role of the compliance checker, PolicyMaker provides a general-purpose application-independent compliance checker that can be explained, formalized and proven correct once and for all. Applications that use PolicyMaker's compliance checker can thus gain high assurance that compliance-checker results depend only on the given query and assertions, and not on any implicit policy decisions or bugs in the design or implementation of the compliance checker. Subsequent TM systems have all followed PolicyMaker's example in these respects.

4.2 Efficiency and Expressivity

In the interest of generality, PolicyMaker [10] put very few restrictions on the specifications of authorizations and delegations. Policies and credentials (collectively called *assertions*) are given by arbitrary executable programs. As long as the underlying programming language is safe in the sense that it is restricted in terms of the I/O operations and resource consumption permitted, there are no restrictions on what programming language is used. The advantage of this is that it is clearly flexible and expressive enough to allow application developers to define authorizations and their delegations however they wish. However, there are also serious shortcomings, including that compliance checking is in general undecidable. No algorithm can, for each set of assertions and each request, decide whether the request is authorized.

PolicyMaker evaluation proceeds by iteratively selecting an assertion and executing it. Each assertion can output a set of "acceptance records" as intermediate results. These are added onto a global append-only *blackboard*. The contents of the blackboard are available to be read by assertions executed subsequently. It is not defined in what order or how many times the assertions should be run by the compliance checker. However, a proof of compliance is given by a (possibly repeating and non-exhaustive) sequence of assertions that, when run by the compliance checker, leaves on the blackboard an acceptance record indicating that the request is approved.

There are several restricted variants of PolicyMaker's proof of compliance problem that are decidable with various complexities. A polynomial variant can be obtained by imposing two complementary restrictions. The first of these is the monotonicity of the assertions themselves. The second involves restricting the resources available to the compliance checker and denying access should any resource limit be exceeded. The authors call it *locally bounded proof of compliance* (LBPOC), which actually subsumes four subordinate restrictions. The first limits the time used to execute each assertion to be a polynomial in the size of the blackboard's content. The second bounds by a constant the number of acceptance records that can be written to the blackboard. The third bounds by a constant the size of acceptance records written on the blackboard. The fourth bounds by a constant the length of the sequence of assertions that make up the proof of compliance. PolicyMaker provides no assistance to the policy author in ensuring that assertions do not violate these restrictions.

There are other drawbacks to basing assertion semantics on program execution semantics rather than on some more declarative approach, such as logic or relational algebra. To understand the meaning of a program-based assertion, a human must mentally simulate its various executions, which can be difficult to do correctly, and the human may find it quite difficult to understand how the effects of different assertions will combine when executed. Furthermore, as we discuss further in later sections, this approach to policy definition provides no assistance in answering questions such as where one can find credentials that may be relevant to evaluating a given query, or in answering more general questions, such as "who are all the principals that are authorized for this resource?"

In addition to becoming more declarative, credentials in later TM systems typically identify a credential subject as well as the credential issuer. The subject is the principal to which the credential is issued and that is characterized by the credential. Explicitly identifying the subject greatly facilitates determining which credentials might be useful at various points in the proof of compliance as it is under construction.

SPKI/SDSI [18] represents authorizations and delegations in structured formats with dedicated fields. Issuers, subjects, delegation bit and authorization tag are specified separately and can easily be recognized by the evaluator. The evaluation is of authorization queries is based on *composition*, a basic operation that takes two valid, compatible certificates as input and outputs another valid certificate. The evaluation algorithm uses composition to compute a closure in a bottom-up manner [18]. The resulting set contains all certificates that can be derived by composition from the given input set. The time complexity of the evaluation algorithm is polynomial in the size of the input set. The closure process must be repeated whenever any certificate is added, expired or revoked, so it is not well suited to be used with a very large and frequently changed certificate pool.

Like SPKI/SDSI [18], KeyNote [9] uses structured assertions. It defines an assertion language that formally captures the decision semantics of a set of credentials and a query (given by an action environment in KeyNote). Monotonicity of KeyNote assertions is inherent in that decision semantics. That said, it has been shown by Li and Mitchell [44] that KeyNote's semantics are sufficiently expressive that it is undecidable to determine the set of all requests that a collection of KeyNote assertions authorizes.

As we have discussed, trust management systems such as SD3 [32] and *RT* [46] use Datalog to represent policies and credentials. Although we do not discuss them here, other trust management languages have also been based on Datalog, including Binder [21] and Delegation Logic [43]. There are many ways in which Datalog can be evaluated. In SD3, evaluation is performed in a top-down manner, much as would be done by a Prolog interpreter, but distributed. In *RT*, evaluation is performed using a special-purpose goal-directed algorithm that combines benefits of top-down and bottom-up evaluation. Datalog can be extended to support constraints on variables ranging over specific domains. If the constraint domains are selected with care, this can be done while preserving the guarantee of polynomial-time query evaluation [44]. The constraints are limited in the sense that they can be used only to define constant bounds on variable values, either in numeric domains or in the domain of finite sequences, such as can be used to represent directory paths or URLs. Constraints over two variables are not permitted. Based on this work, *RT* has been extended to support constraints [45].

Cassandra [5] is another system that uses Datalog with constraints to express semantics of access control. Cassandra approaches the problem of tractability quite differently than does *RT*. Policy authors have the ability to select constraint domains that may not in general support efficient evaluation or even to guarantee termination. In order to ensure that query evaluation does in fact terminate for the clauses actually used as policy statements, the Cassandra system uses a logic programming implementation technique called static groundness analysis. During the course of evaluation, when summarizing the effect of a single clause, the variable environment is projected on to the variables appearing in the head of the clause by existentially quantifying the variables that appear only in the body. The system of constraints that contains existential quantifiers then needs to be simplified so as to eliminate these quantifiers, and it is at this point that the presence of constraints threatens to compromise efficient evaluation. Groundness analysis can be used to ensure that at the time existential quantifier elimination must be performed, certain potentially expensive functions and relational symbols in the constraint will be applied only to constant values, not to unbound variables. This means that these operations can be evaluated before quantifier elimination is performed. It effectively removes these function and relational symbols from the constraint domain on which quantifier elimination must be supported. In this way the designers have made an interesting agreement with the policy writer that says, roughly, you can use all these extra functions and relations when you express your policies, but I will reject the clause if I cannot statically verify that the arguments of those function and relation symbols will be constant by a certain stage in the evaluation of the clause body.

Cassandra's designers, Becker and Sewell [5], discuss a design option similar to the one taken by Clarke et al. with SPKI/SDSI, which precomputes answers to all authorization queries, enabling the results to be cached and reused to make authorization decisions until new credentials are issued or old credentials expire or are revoked. They elect not to take this approach because the policy set is changed every time a role is activated or deactivated. Instead, Cassandra uses Toman's top-down CLP evaluation algorithm [61] based on SLG resolution, which focuses computational effort on one query at a time in the interest of efficiency, as well as using a memoization strategy to avoid inefficiency and non-termination problems suffered by simpler top-down methods.

Higher order logic has also been used to specify policies and credentials. LolliMon [53] is proposed as a typed higher-order linear logic programming language to specify security statements, which is proven to be more expressive and efficient than Datalog or Prolog, especially in dealing with integration of authorization checking and credential retrieval for certificate chain discovery problem. The evaluation process combines bottom-up proof search and top-down proof-search. Every evaluation execution starts and ends in the bottom-up search mode, in which there are switches to and back from top-down mode. Therefore, although the top-down search is still subject to cyclic dependency behaviors, termination can be guaranteed by the property of linear logic. PCA [2] also chooses to use higher-order logic. In order to avoid undecidable computation, the service requester is required to construct and provide the proof and the authorizer only needs to check the proof.

4.3 Credential Retrieval Mechanisms

Early trust management systems [10, 9, 18] assume that all credentials relevant to making a given authorization decision are provided to the system by the calling application. If no proof of compliance can be found, access is denied. There is no consideration of the possibility that the credentials to complete a proof exist, but are simply missing. This may be reasonable for capability-based systems, like KeyNote, in which credentials are issued for authorizing access to a specific resource, so clients can be expected to know what credentials to provide to the application. However, when the credential requirements of a requested resource are less obvious, it may not be obvious what credentials might be needed. For instance, suppose an online ticket sales service has a special offer for students of universities that are members of the NCAA (National Collegiate Athletics Association). In this case, a student might have to present her student ID and a credential issued by the NCAA to her university. Clearly an ideal system would not require the student to figure out what credentials to submit and how to find them.

To be able to assist in ensuring that a proof of compliance can be found when the appropriate credentials do exist, Blaze et al. [10] suggested negative authorization decisions be accompanied by additional information about how a proof might be possible, given additional credentials. Gunter and Jim argued [25] that a better approach is to enlist the assistance of the trust management engine in determining which credentials, should they exist, could prove compliance. Specifically, they observed that doing so can avoid duplication of effort that would be incurred by using a compliance checker that provides hints how a proof might be constructed when sufficient credentials are not presently available. The first kind of duplication is between the calling application and the compliance checker. Whenever the compliance checker returns a negative answer to an authorization query, the application itself undertakes to locate the missing credentials. Then the application again invokes the compliance checker. This process attempts to construct the proof three times, twice by the compliance checker and once by the application when it attempts to collect sufficient credentials to construct a proof. The second form of duplication occurs between different applications that use the TM engine. Each application needs to have its own checking module in order to find and collect missing credentials.

Gunter and Jim observed that these two forms of duplication of effort can be avoided if during the evaluation the trust management engine can take responsibility for discovering which credentials are needed to complete the proof and retrieving them, if they exist.

Thus, trust management systems came to include a credential retrieval mechanism and to interleave credential retrieval operations, be they local or remote, with evaluation steps; corresponding credential repository services are also included. QCM [25] was the first TM system to incorporate credential retrieval; the SD3 [32], RT [49, 53], Minami and Kotz [51], Bauer et al. [3], and PeerAccess [66] systems do so as well. TM engines that support credential retrieval cooperate with each other directly, independently of the calling applications. They discover and retrieve missing credentials as needed to complete the proof.

There are two different approaches to remote credential retrieval taken in the literature. In the first, the request for remote credentials is itself a query in the TM language. It requests the remote TM system to evaluate that query and to return either the answer or credentials required to derive the answer. The remote engine may itself send subqueries to other engines that have credentials required to complete a proof. The first approach is taken by QCM, SD3, Bauer et al., and PeerAccess. In the second approach, the remote TM system is requested only to provide certain credentials that the local engine has determined are needed. The remote system simply returns credentials matching the description given by in the request. It does not participate in collecting further credentials from other sites. The second approach is taken by RT. In the next two subsections, we discuss issues involved in these two approaches.

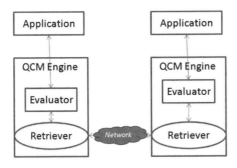

Fig. 5. QCM system

4.4 Distributed Evaluation

As mentioned above, QCM was the first system to incorporate credential retrieval into the evaluation engine. (See Figure 5.) Queries that cannot be solved using locally available credentials are transmitted to other engines belonging to principals whose assertions address the query in question. QCM's credential retriever is designed in such a way that it does not significantly increase the engine's code size because it shares most of its code with the evaluator. In the interest of flexibility, the QCM engine has two modes: verify-only and verify-retrieval. If the calling application chooses verify-only mode, the credential retrieval feature is disabled. This mode is used, for example, to check that the credentials returned from a remote query evaluation do indeed solve the query. In this subsection, we examine several issues that arise in the context of TM systems like QCM and SD3 in which remote engines are invoked to answer subqueries.

When one engine queries another, the latter can reply in one of two ways. Either it can give what QCM calls a *direct reply*, in which the remote engine provides a table of tuples that satisfy the query, or it can provide a proof, a partial proof, or just a set of credentials from which the answer can be deduced. The former are called *extensional answers* and the latter three are called *intensional answers*, by the designers of SD3. In the case of a direct reply, the remote engine typically has to construct a new signed credential containing an assertion (the table) deduced from other credentials. Unlike when providing answers to another TM engine, answers returned by a TM engine to the calling application should be extensional [33].

In addition to supporting extensional answers, SD3 also supports several forms of intentional answers. The server decides which kind of answer to return to the client. For example, in order to avoid bottlenecks and denial of service attacks, the designers of SD3 [33] argue that the server should be able to offer a range of quality of service, corresponding to different forms of answers. In the top level of service, the server evaluates the query fully, communicating with other servers as necessary to do so, and returns a direct reply. A medium service level might return a partial proof along with hints to the client as to other servers that might be able to provide additional relevant credentials. The lowest level just returns relevant credentials held locally.

When one TM system replies to another, integrity and authenticity are normally provided by signing the reply. There are two approaches to signing: on-line signing and off-line signing. Online signing enables the server to sign extensional answers as they are generated. Off-line signing requires the server to return a set of credentials previously signed off line. Off-line signing protects the server's private key, but at the same time requires frequent synchronization and coordination between the trust management server and the off-line signer. Additionally, intentional answers typically require clients to verify more signatures. (QCM uses a technique based on hash trees to decrease the overhead of signing credentials, especially when the set of credentials is very large. This may also reduce the overall effort required to verify credentials in some cases.) QCM allows different servers to choose different signing solutions because neither off-line signing nor on-line signing can be clearly proven superior to the other.

Another issue that must be managed in distributed evaluation arises as a result of cyclic dependencies among the definitions of predicate (*i.e.*, relation) symbols. These can easily lead to repeated subqueries to remote hosts and, if unchecked, can result in nontermination. Two techniques have been proposed to mitigate this problem. QCM [25] uses a timer to detect whether there is a cycle dependency or anything that may have gone wrong if no response is returned within a time-out limit. However, it is not clear what an appropriate time-out period is, so it may possibly lead to denying access to requests that should be authorized. SD3 [32] tags each query with a set of sites that are waiting for it to terminate, so it can always be checked whether the destination site is in this set and may cause a cycle. This method is simple, but may be time consuming and costly in bandwidth.

4.5 Local Evaluation with Distributed Credentials

QCM and its successor SD3 were the first TM systems to address the problem of evaluating authorization policy when credentials (policy statements) are not only issued and revoked in a decentralized manner, but their storage is also distributed. These systems showed that credentials could be stored with their issuers and located as needed during evaluation. In this way it is possible to ensure that every credential in every proof of authorization can be discovered when needed (under basic availability assumptions regarding the network and relevant servers), and thus that it is possible to grant access to all entities that should be authorized according to the set of currently valid policy statements.

However, the assumption that credentials be stored exclusively with their issuers is quite restrictive. In many applications it is more appropriate to store some credentials with their subjects. For example, when a store offers discounts to students at the University of Texas, it may not be reasonable to expect that the university will provide the credentials (student IDs). Firstly, if the student ID includes personally sensitive information, it should be the student who decides whether to give her ID to the store. Secondly, there may be thousands of services that are offered to students, and the university may not be interested in assisting these transactions.

One of the contributions of RT [49] was to devise the first scheme that permits credentials to be stored either at their issuers or at their subjects. RT differs from QCM and SD3 by performing the evaluation process locally and relying on remote servers only to provide credentials relevant to the evaluation process. The evaluation process is based on constructing a graph that represents relationships between different *role expressions*, which is to say, between different principals, roles, linked roles, and intersections. Proofs of role membership are certain subgraphs called *chains*. Nodes in the graph are given by role expressions. Edges represent credentials, as well as some derived relationships. A path connecting two role expressions indicates set containment of the first role expression in the other.

Evaluation of the query asking whether D is a member of $A.r$ begins by introducing nodes representing these two entities and proceeds by adding incident edges. This requires locating the credentials represented by those edges. Speaking very intuitively, credentials are identified as being relevant to extending the graph based on the principals appearing in the nodes. Unfortunately, when trying to extend the graph by including edges incident to a given node, unless the corresponding credentials are stored by principals identified by the node, it is not clear who has the credential. So the evaluation procedure may not be able to find all the credentials that exist and that, if found, would participate in a proof of authorization. (It should be noted that RT's notion of a principal is assumed to provide sufficient information to locate credentials stored "by" the principal.)

We use an example from [49] to better illustrate this problem. Consider the RT_0 credentials shown in Table 1, which are referred to by number in the following. A fictitious web publishing server, EPub, offers a discount to preferred customers of its parent organization EOrg (3). EOrg considers university students to be preferred customers (6). EOrg delegates authority to identify universities to FAB, a Fictitious Accrediting Board (4). The university StateU is accredited by FAB (1). StateU delegates authority to identify students to RegistrarB, which is the registrar of one of StateU's campuses (5). RegistrarB has issued a credential to Alice stating that Alice is a student (2).

These credentials form a chain that shows Alice belongs to EPub.discount. The chain consists of three parts (the expressions are now nodes and the arrows are now edges):

Part (a): EPub.discount ⟵ EOrg.preferred ⟵ EOrg.university.student
Part (b): EOrg.university ⟵ FAB.accredited ⟵ StateU
Part (c): StateU.student ⟵ RegistrarB.student ⟵ Alice

It is natural that credential (4) is a local policy of EOrg and of limited interest to FAB. So it should be stored at its issuer EOrg. Similarly, credentials (3), (5) and (6) should be stored at their issuers. On the other hand, Alice

(1) FAB.university ⟵ StateU
(2) RegistrarB.student ⟵ Alice
(3) EPub.discount ⟵ EOrg.preferred
(4) EOrg.university ⟵ FAB.accredited
(5) StateU.student ⟵ RegistrarB.student
(6) EOrg.preferred ⟵ EOrg.university.student

Table 1.

should hold credential (2) and StateU should be able to provide (1). Otherwise, in order to prove that Alice belongs to EOrg.university.student, one would have to obtain from FAB a complete list of universities, and contact each of these universities to ask whether Alice is one of their students.

This illustrates that storing credentials only with their issuers can be impractical. However, when credentials can be stored with either their issuers or their subjects, serious issues arise with ensuring credentials can be found as needed during evaluation. Suppose credentials (2) and (5) are both stored exclusively with RegistrarB. In this case, the process of elaborating the graph would have no basis on which to identify RegistrarB as being the principal with which these necessary credentials are stored, and the proof of Alice's authorization could not be constructed. Although the credentials exist in the system, they cannot be found in order to make a correct positive authorization decision.

A solution to this problem proposed by [49] balances the advantages of having flexibility in where credentials are stored and the necessity of finding all needed credentials. The solution is based on a type system for credentials that assigns types to role names. The type of a role name indicates, among other things, where to store credentials that define roles with that role name. Well-typing rules are introduced that impose constraints on how role names of various types can be combined within the same credential. These constraints are local to the credentials, yet they have the global effect of ensuring that for every credential chain in the system, each credential in the chain can be discovered and retrieved by a search process that starts from one end of the chain or the other. Since these ends are known based on the authorization query, this means that all queries can be answered correctly. The techniques discussed above were first developed for RT_0, but have subsequently been extended to full RT [50].

The more recent PeerAccess [66] system addresses the same problem through a system of referrals by brokers, issuers, and subjects who are knowledgeable about certain types of credentials. For example, one can imagine a broker rather like a Google for credential search. Parties can have their own favorite brokers that they consult when they do not know where to find a needed credential, or they can take advantage of hints given to them by other parties during proof construction. For example, if someone asks the university for Alice's student credential, the university can suggest that they instead ask Alice or, if the requester *is* Alice, that she contact the university's student ID repository to obtain her ID credential. This facility of PeerAccess, called *proof hints*, can be used to encode the credential retrieval strategies of QCM, SD3, *RT*, and other useful techniques.

5 Automated Trust Negotiation

There are many different algorithms that a set of autonomous parties can follow to establish trust at run time. From just a small sampling, e.g., [14], *idemix* [17], Binder [21], Unipro [68], interactive access control [36], Trust-χ [7], Cassandra [6], Protune [12], OSBE and OAcerts [42, 39], [51], PeerAccess [66], cryptographic-based protocols [41], and [3], we find an amazing diversity of algorithms for the distributed construction of proofs. Some of the simpler algorithms have been described in the previous sections of this chapter; for more sophisticated approaches, space constraints force us to refer the reader to the literature.

However, all recent approaches to trust negotiation do share the following advantages over traditional identity-based approaches to authorization:

- Two previously unacquainted principals can establish *bilateral* trust between themselves at run time.
- The authorization policy for a resource can specify the *properties* that authorized parties must possess, removing the administrative burden of maintaining access control lists of authorized identities.
- Trust establishment does not rely on the existence of any trusted third parties, other than credential issuers.
- In trust negotiation approaches that involve direct disclosure of credentials, trust can be built up gradually through an iterative process, starting with less sensitive properties and moving on to more sensitive ones after a certain level of trust has been established.
- In trust negotiation approaches that do not involve direct disclosure of credentials, trust can be established without either principal learning exactly which properties the other principal possesses.

All approaches to trust negotiation also share a reliance on policy languages with certain properties [58], including the following:

- The policy language must possess a well-defined semantics. This implies that the meaning of the policy in that language must be independent of any particular implementation of the language. Otherwise, two negotiating parties can disagree on whether a particular policy has been satisfied by a set of credentials, leading to chaos.

- As hinted in earlier sections, the language and runtime system should be monotonic in the sense that once a particular level of trust has been reached (e.g., access has been granted), the disclosure of additional credentials should not lower the level of trust. This limits the use of negation in policies in a pragmatic manner. For example, suppose that convicted felons cannot buy guns. This policy can be used as is in trust negotiation, as long as the store owner checks the negated construct (not a convicted felon) by conducting the appropriate credential discovery process himself. In other words, the store owner cannot decide that it is okay to sell Alice a gun, just because she has not supplied a convicted felon credential. The store owner must go out to the national registry of criminals and see whether Alice is listed there. If the runtime system does not support credential discovery and the store owner has not cached the list of criminals before negotiation starts, then the policy cannot be used as written.
- At a minimum, the policy language should also support conjunction, disjunction, transitive closure, constraints on attribute values, and constraints that restrict combinations of multiple credentials (theta-joins, in database terminology).

In the remainder of this section, we discuss ways to support autonomy during negotiation, ways to minimize information leakage during trust negotiation, and implementations of trust negotiation.

5.1 Supporting Autonomy during Trust Negotiation

Most modern trust negotiation (TN) approaches assume that each negotiating party has a significant degree of autonomy in its choice of actions during each step of a negotiation. This assumption mirrors the real world—after all, Alice does not *have* to fill her prescription at Bob's pharmacy—and also helps to make TN algorithms more resilient against attack. When negotiations depend on slavish adherence to the details of a complex algorithm, then a malicious participant can easily attack by deviating from the prescribed behavior, and even a non-malicious participant may have little incentive to cooperate. Any practical TN algorithm must recognize that one cannot just hand a subgoal to an arbitrary party and expect them to produce a proof of it—what is the incentive for them to spend their time in that manner? Similarly, from any discussion of current credential systems, it is clear that their authors intend them to describe properties of entities. However, any database researcher knows that entities, attributes, *and* relationships are all needed to describe the state of the real world. Once credentials are used to describe relationships, simplifying assumptions such as "each credential has one subject" quickly break down. Who is the subject of a marriage certificate? A birth certificate? These certificates describe relationships between several subjects, rather than an attribute of a single subject. While such simplifying assumptions are helpful for getting early TN systems off the ground, at some point they must be abandoned if TN is to scale to arbitrary web services and clients.

In this section, we describe research efforts to abandon the assumption that a negotiating party has exactly one possible message that it can send at each point during a negotiation, dictated by a common distributed proof construction algorithm shared by all participants. Instead, two negotiating parties begin their negotiation by agreeing on a negotiation **protocol**, which is a set of conventions about the types of messages they will send to one another and any restrictions on the ordering of those messages [68]. Within those conventions, each party has freedom to choose the content of its messages. This approach is intended for situations in which parties disclose (send) their credentials and policies to one another.

In addition to a protocol, each negotiating party needs to have a **trust negotiation strategy**, i.e., its own algorithm that determines the content of each message that it sends out, based on its own credentials plus the messages that it has received so far. Every strategy must ensure that all disclosures are **safe**, i.e., if a particular credential is disclosed, then the policy governing access to that credential has already been satisfied by previous disclosures. For example, Alice's prescription should not be disclosed until Bob has proved that he is a pharmacist. Some example strategies:

- Make every possible disclosure of the credentials on hand. In the pharmacy example, this strategy will lead Alice to disclose her doctor's credential immediately—and probably her library card, frequent flyer cards, CPR course certification, and many other irrelevant credentials as well.
- Disclose every credential on hand that is relevant to the negotiation. For example, Alice can disclose every credential of hers that has been mentioned in the policies previously disclosed by the other party.
- Disclose a minimal set of credentials on hand that will advance the state of the negotiation, where "minimal" is defined using set inclusion. The definition of what it means to advance the state of the negotiation can be surprisingly complex [68].
- Disclose a minimal set of credentials on hand that will advance the state of the negotiation, where "minimal" is defined using a system of weights over the credentials. For example, a party can give low weights to the credentials that it does not consider very sensitive, to steer the negotiation toward disclosure of those credentials.
- Use a cryptographic protocol that will allow the two parties to determine whether access is authorized, without letting them learn how the access policy is satisfied (or, in some variants, what the policy was) [16, 17, 30, 15, 24, 39]
- For the less sensitive parts of the negotiation, use one of the direct disclosure strategies mentioned above. For more sensitive aspects, use one of the cryptographic protocols mentioned in the previous item [41].

A negotiating partner may request a credential that a party does not have on hand, but might be able to obtain over the internet at run time through credential discovery. For example, if Alice did not have proof that her doctor was licensed to practice in Bob's country, then she could try to obtain that credential on line. For example, it might be available from a national registry, from the doctor's office, from her insurance company, or from her mother. Alice's negotiation strategy must make the decision about whether to try to look for a missing credential, and guide any subsequent search.

While some approaches to trust negotiation still assume that the two parties agree on the exact strategy that they will use during a negotiation, this is unnecessarily restrictive in general. Agreeing on an exact choice of strategy compromises local autonomy and can leave a principal vulnerable to attack by a negotiating partner who does not follow the agreed-upon strategy. Researchers have shown that for trust negotiation approaches that directly disclose credentials, it is sufficient for the two negotiating parties to agree upon a broad set of strategies that may be used during the negotiation, including strategies described in the first four items in the list above [68]. Each participant has free choice of any strategy from the set, and is still guaranteed that the negotiation will result in trust being established if it is theoretically possible to do so; in other words, all strategies in the set are guaranteed to be **interoperable**. These guarantees apply to the negotiation between the resource requester and provider (i.e., they do not consider ancillary credential discovery searches), and they still apply if policies themselves may contain sensitive information (i.e., the disclosure of a policy is governed by an additional access control policy).

5.2 Avoiding Information Leakage during Trust Negotiation

Researchers recognized early on that negotiation strategies that directly disclose credentials may leak information about credentials and policies that are never disclosed. By observing the behavior of a party, one may also be able to determine what strategy they are using, which can be used as leverage in extracting additional information. We describe some of these leaks in this section.

A credential may contain more information than needed to satisfy a policy. For example, Alice can prove that she is over 21 by presenting a digital driver's license. However, the license also gives her home address, exact date of birth, weight, and other details that are not needed to prove that she is over 21. To address these shortcomings, researchers have proposed versions of digital credentials that allow one to hide information that is irrelevant to the negotiation at hand, such as Alice's home address [29, 60]. More sophisticated (and more expensive) schemes provide even more privacy, by avoiding direct disclosure of credentials. For example, Alice can prove that she is over 21, without disclosing her exact age [16, 17, 30, 15, 39]. These schemes allow Alice to prove to Bob that she has the properties specified in his policy, without Bob learning exactly what properties she has. For example, in the pharmacy example, Bob might learn that Alice is authorized to place an order, without learning who her doctor is. Bob only learns that Alice has some combination of properties that satisfy his policy.

Often, possession or non-possession of a sensitive credential is itself sensitive information. For example, suppose that Alice is a CIA employee, and Bob is looking for people who might be such agents. Bob might query people for their CIA credentials. Even if Alice has a policy to protect the credential, her response for Bob's credentials on receipt of such a request can indicate that she has the credential. In other words, a request for such a credential may cause the recipient to issue counter-requests for credentials needed to satisfy disclosure of the sensitive credential. This, in turn, may indicate that the recipient possesses the sensitive credential. Non-possession may also be sensitive, and termination of a negotiation upon request for a credential can indicate non-possession.

If the value of an attribute in a credential is sensitive, then it is possible for a principal to determine ownership and value of the attribute by the other negotiating principal based on her replies. For example, suppose that Alice has a sensitive *date of birth* field in her driver's license. Now, if Bob's policy has a constraint on age, and upon receipt of Bob's policy, Alice responds by asking for any further credentials from Bob, then Bob can assume that Alice has the attribute that satisfies the constraint. By using a scheme similar to binary search, it is possible for Bob to determine Alice's age, without Alice revealing it to him.

Under many proposed approaches to trust negotiation [14, 62, 68], an attacker can even use a *need-to-know attack* to systematically harvest information about an arbitrary set of credentials that are not even relevant to the client's original request [52]. To do this, the attacker rewrites her policies in such a way that they are logically equivalent to the original policies, but when used during negotiation, they force the victim into a series of disclosures related to the credentials being harvested. Once the harvest is over, the negotiation completes as it would have with the original policies.

The most complete solution to these problems is to adopt a negotiation approach that does not involve direct disclosure of credentials [16, 17, 30, 15, 24, 39]. While these approaches vary in the degree of privacy that they provide, all of them can avoid the leaks cataloged in this section. The price of this improved protection, of course, is significantly longer execution times; thus one may wish to reserve these expensive strategies for policies that are particularly sensitive, and use direct disclosure elsewhere [41]. In general, these TN approaches replace direct disclosure with sophisticated cryptography, usually coupled with special-purpose formats for credentials. These approaches are very interesting in their own right; due to space limitations, we refer the reader to the publications listed above for more information.

In some instances, less expensive forms of protection can be effective against leakage. One approach is that when Bob queries Alice about a sensitive attribute, she does not respond, whether she has that attribute or not [57]. Only after Bob satisfies the conditions to allow disclosure does Alice would disclose the credential or disclose the fact that she does not possess it. This approach is also effective if non-possession is sensitive. However, it relies on the willingness of individuals to behave in the same manner whether or not they possess the sensitive attribute—and for those who do not possess it, there may be little incentive to behave in this manner, as the negotiation will progress faster if they immediately confess that they do not have the attribute.

Another solution with moderate runtime costs involves the use of *acknowledgement policies* [63]. In this scheme, Alice has an acknowledgement policy (ack-policy) for each possible sensitive credential, regardless of whether she has that credential or not. She only discloses whether she has the credential after the ack-policy has been satisfied. This approach also relies on the willingness of people who do not possess a sensitive attribute to act as though they did, even though it will prolong negotiations. The other disadvantage of this approach is that users will have many more policies, and policy specification and maintenance is a huge practical challenge.

Another way to address the problem is to abstract away from requesting specific credentials, and instead request a particular attribute [59]. For example, one can request *age* instead of a *driver's license*. With the help of an ontology of concepts and credential contents, a party can choose which credential to disclose to prove possession of the desired attribute, in such a manner that as little sensitive information as possible is disclosed in the process. For example, Alice might choose to prove her age by disclosing her passport rather than her driver's license, as the latter includes her home address and other sensitive information not present in a passport. The ontology can also be used to help respond to requests for a particular attribute by disclosing either more specific or more general information than was requested. For example, if asked to prove North American residency, a party might instead prove that they live in Mexico.

In all approaches where parties directly disclose credentials to one another, a credential owner has no guarantee that the other party will not show her disclosed credentials and policies to additional parties. In other words, there is no guarantee, or even any suggestion, that others will respect her disclosure policies. PeerAccess [66] addresses this problem by requiring recipients of information to ensure that future recipients of that information also satisfy the original owner's disclosure policies; however, a malicious party could simply ignore this requirement. Another low-cost option is to employ P3P during trust negotiation, as proposed for the privacy-preserving version of the Trust-χ framework for TN [60]. Under this approach, information owners can examine the P3P policies of their negotiation partners, before disclosing any credentials or policies. Of course, a malicious party might not abide by their own P3P policy. In addition, when a credential is forwarded to a third party, the original owner does not have the opportunity to inspect the P3P policy of that party and approve the transfer. If these are significant concerns, then a more expensive TN approach that does not directly disclose credentials or policies is always an option.

5.3 Trust Negotiation Implementations

To date, research on TN has focused mainly on the theoretical issues involved in the negotiation process. While most of the trust management approaches discussed in this chapter have been implemented, and many of them have broken interesting new ground in their implementations, very few of them have been publicly released. Most implementations have been designed as proofs of concept, and were never intended to be used heavily in practice. These theoretical works and proofs of concept have been quite successful, and thus researchers must now begin to address the implementation constraints that act as barriers to the deployment of these systems. Among the systems that support bilateral trust establishment, only Trust-Builder (http://isrl.cs.byu.edu), TrustBuilder2 (http://dais.cs.uiuc.edu/tn), and Trust-χ (http://www.cs.purdue.edu/homes/squiccia/trustx) are currently freely available for download. As TrustBuilder2 was built specifically as a platform for others to reuse and adapt for their own experiments with TN, we describe it briefly here.

TrustBuilder2 is a flexible and reconfigurable Java-based framework for supporting research on the systems aspects of TN approaches to authorization. In TrustBuilder2, the primary components of a TN system—such as strategy modules, compliance checkers, query interfaces, and audit modules—are represented using abstract interfaces, as shown in the architectural diagram in Figure 6. Any or all of these component interfaces can be implemented or extended by users of the TrustBuilder2 system, thereby making the system's functionality extensible. The TrustBuilder2 configuration files can be modified to load these custom components in place of the default system components; this facilitates code reuse and the incorporation of new features without modifications to the underlying runtime system. Further, TrustBuilder2 supports the interposition of user-defined plug-ins at communication points between system components to allow for easy monitoring of system activity or the modification of messages passed between components.

The TrustBuilder2 framework provides an environment for researchers to begin considering the technical issues surrounding the deployment of trust negotiation protocols in production environments and makes several contributions within this space. In addition to the aspects of flexibility described above, the abstract type interfaces used by TrustBuilder2 for representing policies, credentials, and resources ensure that new policy languages, credential formats, and the inclusion of new evidence types can be supported without requiring modifications to existing system components or changes to the TrustBuilder2 framework. This allows users to rapidly implement support for new features, and also provides a framework within which the trade-offs

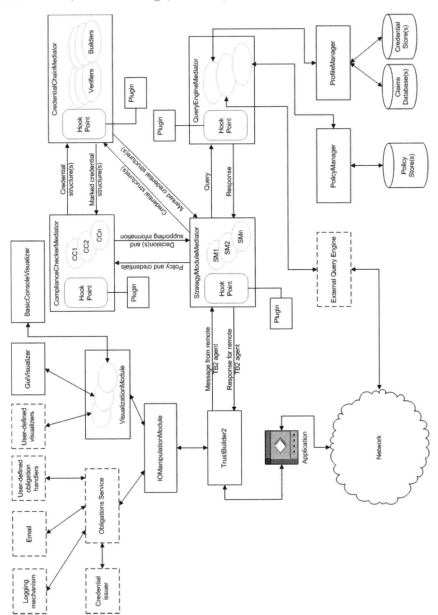

Fig. 6. Internal structure of a TrustBuilder2 trust negotiation agent

between various system configurations can be quantitatively analyzed. Trust-Builder2 allows users to keep the majority of system components constant and change only minor portions of the framework between trust negotiations; for example, a user could execute the same set of negotiations using two different policy compliance checkers. This enables reasonable comparisons to be made between specific system components without requiring modification to the runtime system itself. Further information regarding the specifics of the TrustBuilder2 framework can be found in the programmer documentation and user manuals included with the TrustBuilder2 software distribution.

6 Open Issues and Trends

6.1 Policy Engineering and User Interfaces

The properties of those who can access a resource are specified in the access control policy determined by the resource's owner. Any mistake in the specification or implementation of the policy can potentially be found and automatically exploited by adversaries. Unfortunately, it is very easy to make a mistake when writing a policy. As Cornwell et al. report from their testbed deployment of user-created privacy policies in a pervasive computing environment [19]: "Rules specified at the beginning of the [trials] only captured their policies 59% of the time. [...] Even when using the rules that users ended up with at the end of the experiments and re-running these rules on all 30 (or 45) scenarios, decisions were only correct 70% of the time." The authors suggest that using machine learning techniques to learn users' privacy policies might be more effective.

More generally, software engineering methods to help people write, update, analyze, and understand authorization policies are an open research area. A great amount of research is needed on environments for policy specification, analysis, and debugging; HCI issues in policy engineering, including user-friendly policy languages and interfaces to policy engineering environments [38]; ways to explain authorization decisions to people, and to suggest how they can get a negative decision reversed [35, 13]; and how to compile operational policies from high-level abstract policies.

As a small aid, we expect that many credential issuers will supply suggested default policies to protect the credentials they issue. For example, Alice's doctor's office can supply a suggested policy with each prescription written by the doctor, saying that the prescription should only be disclosed to its owner (Alice) or to a licensed physician. For more complex situations, issuers could offer a Chinese-menu-style set of options. The use of default policies will shield credential bearers from the need to understand policy languages, and will reduce the number of loopholes in their policies.

6.2 Real-world Trust Negotiation Deployments

After several years of research, trust negotiation protocols have yet to make their way into the mainstream; the one exception is the inclusion of *idemix* in the Trusted Platform Module specification, for use in anonymous attestation.

Prior to deploying access control systems based on TN, their systems and architectural properties must be fully explored. Most existing trust negotiation implementations exist largely as proofs of concept designed to illustrate the feasibility of the underlying theory and have performed admirably in this capacity. We need experience with small-scale real-world deployments to really understand what research issues must be addressed before TN can hit the mainstream.

As part of this effort, trust negotiation systems must be hardened against attack and made scalable under heavy load. While initial steps have been made in this direction [55, 40], much more remains to be done.

6.3 Distributed Proof Construction

The process of constructing a proof of authorization is one instance of the general problem of distributed proof construction, which has received a bit of attention in the logic programming community. However, authorization proofs face several construction challenges that have not been fully addressed.

Autonomy in proof methods. Each party is autonomous and may have its own way of constructing proofs, delegating work to others, and choosing what queries to answer and which to ignore. Further, these parameters may change over time; for example, a party may need to ignore low-priority queries during periods of high load, or provide intensional answers instead of its usual extensional answers. In such an environment, how can we orchestrate everyone's individual efforts toward the larger goal of building a single authorization proof?

Sensitive information. As an additional complication, pieces of a proof may be sensitive and not freely disclosable to others. Thus successful proof construction may depend on finding the right party to act as a helper in collecting information. Further, it may be necessary to cloak sensitive information as it passes through the hands of third parties during proof construction [51]. Ideally, we should also have a means of ensuring that others have respected our rules about what they can do with the sensitive information we disclose to them. These are lofty goals, and a great deal of work is needed before they will be met.

Non-monotonicity. As discussed in the previous section, TN systems need to be monotonic in the sense that the arrival of additional evidence will not decrease the level of trust. As explained earlier, this does not mean a policy cannot call for the absence of a particular piece of evidence (e.g., that a credential not be revoked); rather, one has to be very careful about which party checks those negative conditions. The best way to integrate the checking of negative conditions into distributed proof construction is an open problem.

When TN is used in pervasive computing, the current environment may be one factor in authorization decisions. For example, perhaps a student can use a conference room only between 8 AM and 5 PM. The environment can change over time, violating monotonicity. To date, researchers have developed several theoretical approaches to addressing this problem [37]; additional challenges are likely to arise when TN is deployed in such a setting.

References

1. ANSI. American National Standard for Information Technology – Role Based Access Control. ANSI INCITS 359-2004, February 2004.
2. Andrew W. Appel and Edward W. Felten. Proof-carrying authentication. In *CCS '99: Proceedings of the 6th ACM Conference on Computer and Communications Security*, pages 52–62, New York, NY, USA, 1999. ACM Press.
3. Lujo Bauer, Scott Garriss, and Michael K. Reiter. Efficient proving for practical distributed access-control systems. In *12th European Symposium on Research in Computer Security (ESORICS)*, September 2007.
4. Lujo Bauer, Michael A. Schneider, and Edward W. Felten. A general and flexible access-control system for the web. In *Proceedings of the 11th USENIX Security Symposium*, pages 93–108, Berkeley, CA, USA, 2002. USENIX Association.
5. Moritz Y. Becker and Peter Sewell. Cassandra: Distributed access control policies with tunable expressiveness. In *POLICY '04: Proceedings of the Fifth IEEE International Workshop on Policies for Distributed Systems and Networks (POLICY'04)*, page 159, Washington, DC, USA, 2004. IEEE Computer Society.
6. Moritz Y. Becker and Peter Sewell. Cassandra: Flexible trust management, applied to electronic health records. In *CSFW '04: Proceedings of the 17th IEEE Computer Security Foundations Workshop (CSFW'04)*, page 139, Washington, DC, USA, 2004. IEEE Computer Society.
7. Elisa Bertino, Elena Ferrari, and Anna Cinzia Squicciarini. Trust-X: A peer-to-peer framework for trust establishment. *IEEE Transactions on Knowledge and Data Engineering*, 16(7):827–842, 2004.
8. E. Bina, V. Jones, R. McCool, and M. Winslett. Secure Access to Data Over the Internet. In *Conference on Parallel and Distributed Information Systems*, September 1994.
9. Matt Blaze, Joan Feigenbaum, John Ioannidis, and Angelos D. Keromytis. The KeyNote trust-management system, version 2. IETF RFC 2704, September 1999.
10. Matt Blaze, Joan Feigenbaum, John Ioannidis, and Angelos D. Keromytis. The role of trust management in distributed systems. In *Secure Internet Programming*, volume 1603 of *Lecture Notes in Computer Science*, pages 185–210. Springer, 1999.
11. Matt Blaze, Joan Feigenbaum, and Jack Lacy. Decentralized trust management. In *Proceedings of the 1996 IEEE Symposium on Security and Privacy*, pages 164–173. IEEE Computer Society Press, May 1996.
12. Piero Bonatti and Daniel Olmedilla. Driving and monitoring provisional trust negotiation with metapolicies. In *POLICY '05: Proceedings of the Sixth IEEE International Workshop on Policies for Distributed Systems and Networks (POLICY'05)*, pages 14–23, Washington, DC, USA, 2005. IEEE Computer Society.
13. Piero A. Bonatti and Daniel Olmedilla. Policy Language Specification. deliverable I2-D2, ISI- Knowledge-Based Systems, University of Hannover, 2005.

14. Piero A. Bonatti and Pierangela Samarati. A uniform framework for regulating service access and information release on the web. *J. Comput. Secur.*, 10(3):241–271, 2002.
15. R. Bradshaw, J. Holt, and K. E. Seamons. Concealing complex policies with hidden credentials. In *Eleventh ACM Conference on Computer and Communications Security*, October 2004.
16. Stefan Brands. *Rethinking Public Key Infrastructures and Digital Certificates; Building in Privacy*. MIT Press, 2000.
17. Jan Camenisch and Els Van Herreweghen. Design and implementation of the Idemix anonymous credential system. In *ACM Computer and Communication Security*, 2002.
18. Dwaine Clarke, Jean-Emile Elien, Carl Ellison, Matt Fredette, Alexander Morcos, and Ronald L. Rivest. Certificate chain discovery in SPKI/SDSI. *Journal of Computer Security*, 9(4):285–322, 2001.
19. Jason Cornwell, Ian Fette, Gary Hsieh, Madhu Prabaker, Jinghai Rao, Karen Tang, Kami Vaniea, Lujo Bauer, Lorrie Cranor, Jason Hong, Bruce McLaren, Mike Reiter, and Norman Sadeh. User-controllable security and privacy for pervasive computing. In *Eighth IEEE Workshop on Mobile Computing Systems and Applications (HotMobile)*, February 2007.
20. Jack B. Dennis and Earl C. Van Horn. Programming semantics for multiprogrammed computations. *Commun. ACM*, 9(3):143–155, 1966.
21. John DeTreville. Binder, a logic-based security language. In *Proceedings of the 2002 IEEE Symposium on Security and Privacy*, pages 105–113. IEEE Computer Society Press, May 2002.
22. Carl Ellison, Bill Frantz, Butler Lampson, Ron Rivest, Brian Thomas, and Tatu Ylonen. SPKI certificate theory. IETF RFC 2693, September 1999.
23. David F. Ferraiolo, Janet A. Cuigini, and D. Richard Kuhn. Role-based access control (RBAC): Features and motivations. In *Proceedings of the 11th Annual Computer Security Applications Conference (ACSAC'95)*, December 1995.
24. Keith Frikken, Mikhail Atallah, and Jiangtao Li. Attribute-based access control with hidden policies and hidden credentials. *IEEE Transactions on Computers (TC)*, 55(10), 2006.
25. Carl A. Gunter and Trevor Jim. Policy-directed certificate retrieval. *Software: Practice & Experience*, 30(15):1609–1640, September 2000.
26. R. J. Hayton, J. M. Bacon, and K. Moody. Access control in an open distributed environment. In *IEEE Symposium of Security and Privacy*, pages 3–14, '1998.
27. Amir Herzberg, Yosi Mass, Joris Mihaeli, Dalit Naor, and Yiftach Ravid. Access control meets public key infrastructure, or: Assigning roles to strangers. In *Proceedings of the 2000 IEEE Symposium on Security and Privacy*, pages 2–14. IEEE Computer Society Press, May 2000.
28. John A. Hine, Walt Yao, Jean Bacon, and Ken Moody. An architecture for distributed oasis services. In *Middleware '00: IFIP/ACM International Conference on Distributed systems platforms*, pages 104–120, Secaucus, NJ, USA, 2000. Springer-Verlag New York, Inc.
29. J. Holt and K. E. Seamons. Selective disclosure credential sets. *Cryptology ePrint Archive*, 2002.
30. Jason Holt, Robert W. Bradshaw, Kent E. Seamons, and Hilarie Orman. Hidden credentials. In *Workshop on Privacy in the Electronic Society (WPES)*, 2003.

31. Russell Housely, Warwick Ford, Tim Polk, and David Solo. Internet X.509 public key infrastructure certificate and CRL profile. *IETF Request for Comments RFC-2459*, January 1999.

32. Trevor Jim. SD3: A trust management system with certified evaluation. In *Proceedings of the 2001 IEEE Symposium on Security and Privacy*, pages 106–115. IEEE Computer Society Press, May 2001.

33. Trevor Jim and Dan Suciu. Dynamically distributed query evaluation. In *PODS '01: Proceedings of the twentieth ACM SIGMOD-SIGACT-SIGART symposium on Principles of database systems*, pages 28–39, New York, NY, USA, 2001. ACM Press.

34. A. Jsang, R. Ismail, and C. Boyd. A survey of trust and reputation systems for online service provision. *Decision Support Systems*, 43(2):618–644, March 2007.

35. Apu Kapadia, Geetanjali Sampemane, and Roy H. Campbell. KNOW why your access was denied: Regulating feedback for usable security. In *Proceedings of the ACM Conference on Computers and Communication Security (CCS)*, pages 52–61, Washington, DC, Oct 2004.

36. H. Koshutanski and F. Massacci. An interactive trust management and negotiation scheme. In Theo Dimitrakos and Fabio Martinelli, editors, *Formal Aspects of Security and Trust*, pages 139–152. KAP, 2004.

37. Adam J. Lee, Kazuhiro Minami, and Marianne Winslett. Lightweight consistency enforcement schemes for distributed proofs with hidden subtrees. In *12th ACM Symposium on Access Control Models and Technologies (SACMAT 2007)*, June 2007.

38. Adam J. Lee and Marianne Winslett. Open problems for usable and secure open systems. In *Workshop on Usability Research Challenges for Cyberinfrastructure and Tools held in conjunction with ACM CHI*, April 2006.

39. Jiangtao Li and Ninghui Li. OACerts: Oblivious attribute certificates. *IEEE Transactions on Dependable and Secure Computing (TDSC)*, 3(4), 2006.

40. Jiangtao Li, Ninghui Li, XiaoFeng Wang, and Ting Yu. Denial of Service Attacks and Defenses in Decentralized Trust Management. In *2nd IEEE International Conference on Security and Privacy in Communication Networks (SecureComm)*, August 2006.

41. Jiangtao Li, Ninghui Li, and William Winsborough. Automated trust negotiation using cryptographic credentials. *ACM Transactions on Information and System Security (TISSEC)*, 2007.

42. Ninghui Li, Wenliang Du, and Dan Boneh. Oblivious signature-based envelope. In *PODC '03: Proceedings of the twenty-second annual symposium on Principles of distributed computing*, pages 182–189, New York, NY, USA, 2003. ACM Press.

43. Ninghui Li, Benjamin N. Grosof, and Joan Feigenbaum. Delegation Logic: A logic-based approach to distributed authorization. *ACM Transaction on Information and System Security*, 6(1):128–171, February 2003.

44. Ninghui Li and John C. Mitchell. Datalog with constraints: A foundation for trust management languages. In *Proceedings of the Fifth International Symposium on Practical Aspects of Declarative Languages (PADL 2003)*, number 2562 in LNCS, pages 58–73. Springer, January 2003.

45. Ninghui Li and John C. Mitchell. RT: A role-based trust-management framework. In *The Third DARPA Information Survivability Conference and Exposition (DISCEX III)*. IEEE Computer Society Press, April 2003.

46. Ninghui Li, John C. Mitchell, and William H. Winsborough. Design of a role-based trust management framework. In *Proceedings of the 2002 IEEE Symposium on Security and Privacy*, pages 114–130. IEEE Computer Society Press, May 2002.
47. Ninghui Li, William H. Winsborough, and John C. Mitchell. Distributed credential chain discovery in trust management (extended abstract). In *Proceedings of the Eighth ACM Conference on Computer and Communications Security (CCS-8)*, pages 156–165. ACM Press, November 2001.
48. Ninghui Li, William H. Winsborough, and John C. Mitchell. Beyond proof-of-compliance: Safety and availability analysis in trust management. In *Proceedings of IEEE Symposium on Security and Privacy*, pages 123–139. IEEE Computer Society Press, May 2003.
49. Ninghui Li, William H. Winsborough, and John C. Mitchell. Distributed credential chain discovery in trust management. *Journal of Computer Security*, 11(1):35–86, February 2003.
50. Ziqing Mao, Ninghui Li, and William H. Winsborough. Distributed credential chain discovery in trust management with parameterized roles and constraints. In *2006 International Conference on Information and Communications Security (ICICS 2006)*, December 2006.
51. Kazuhiro Minami and David Kotz. Secure context-sensitive authorization. *Journal of Pervasive and Mobile Computing*, 1(1), March 2005.
52. Lars E. Olson, Michael J. Rosulek, and Marianne Winslett. Harvesting Credentials in Trust Negotiation as an Honest-But-Curious Adversary. In *ACM Workshop on Privacy in the Electronic Society (WPES)*, 2007.
53. Jeff Polakow and Christian Skalka. Specifying distributed trust management in Lollimon. In *PLAS '06: Proceedings of the 2006 Workshop on Programming Languages and Analysis for Security*, pages 37–46, New York, NY, USA, 2006. ACM Press.
54. Ronald L. Rivest and Bulter Lampson. SDSI — a simple distributed security infrastructure, October 1996. Available at *http://theory.lcs.mit.edu/~rivest/sdsi11.html*.
55. T. Ryutov, L. Zhou, C. Neuman, T. Leithead, and K. E. Seamons. Adaptive trust negotiation and access control. In *10th ACM Symposium on Access Control Models and Technologies*, June 2005.
56. Ravi S. Sandhu, Venkata Bhamidipati, and Qamar Munawer. The ARBAC97 model for role-based aministration of roles. *ACM Transactions on Information and Systems Security*, 2(1):105–135, February 1999.
57. K. E. Seamons, M. Winslett, T. Yu, L. Yu, and R. Jarvis. Protecting privacy during on-line trust negotiation. In *Proceedings of the 2nd Workshop on Privacy Enhancing Technologies*, April 2002.
58. Kent Seamons, Marianne Winslett, Ting Yu, B. Smith, E. Child, J. Jacobson, H. Mills, and Lina Yu. Requirements for policy languages for trust negotiation. In *Third IEEE International Workshop on Policies for Distributed Systems and Networks (POLICY'02)*, pages 68–79, June 2002.
59. A. C. Squicciarini, E. Bertino, and E. Ferrari. Achieving Privacy with an Ontology-Based Approach in Trust Negotiations. *IEEE Transaction on Dependable and Secure Computing (TDSC)*, 3(1):13–30, 2006.
60. A. C. Squicciarini, E. Bertino, E. Ferrari, F. Paci, and B. Thuraisingham. PP-Trust-X: A System for Privacy Preserving Trust Negotiations. *ACM Transactions on Information and System Security (TISSEC)*, 10(3), July 2007.

61. David Toman. Memoing evaluation for constraint extensions of datalog. *Constraints and databases*, pages 99–121, 1998.
62. William H. Winsborough and Ninghui Li. Towards practical automated trust negotiation. In *Proceedings of the Third International Workshop on Policies for Distributed Systems and Networks (Policy 2002)*, pages 92–103. IEEE Computer Society Press, June 2002.
63. William H. Winsborough and Ninghui Li. Safety in automated trust negotiation. In *Proceedings of the IEEE Symposium on Security and Privacy*, pages 147–160, May 2004.
64. William H. Winsborough, Kent E. Seamons, and Vicki E. Jones. Automated trust negotiation. In *DARPA Information Survivability Conference and Exposition*, volume I, pages 88–102. IEEE Press, January 2000.
65. Marianne Winslett. An introduction to trust negotiation. In *Proceedings of iTrust*, pages 275–283, 2003.
66. Marianne Winslett, Charles C. Zhang, and Piero A. Bonatti. Peeraccess: a logic for distributed authorization. In *CCS '05: Proceedings of the 12th ACM Conference on Computer and Communications Security*, pages 168–179, New York, NY, USA, 2005. ACM Press.
67. Walt Yao, Ken Moody, and Jean Bacon. A model of oasis role-based access control and its support for active security. In *SACMAT '01: Proceedings of the sixth ACM Symposium on Access Control Models and Technologies*, pages 171–181, New York, NY, USA, 2001. ACM Press.
68. Ting Yu, Marianne Winslett, and Kent E. Seamons. Supporting structured credentials and sensitive policies through interoperable strategies for automated trust negotiation. *ACM Transactions on Information System Security*, 6(1):1–42, 2003.

5

Authenticated Index Structures for Outsourced Databases

Feifei Li[1], Marios Hadjieftheriou[2], George Kollios[3], and Leonid Reyzin[3]

[1] Department of Computer Science
Florida State University
lifeifei@cs.fsu.edu
[2] AT&T Labs Inc.
marioh@research.att.com
[3] Computer Science Department
Boston University
gkollios@cs.bu.edu,reyzin@cs.bu.edu

Summary. In an outsourced database (ODB) system the database owner publishes data through a number of remote servers, with the goal of enabling clients at the edge of the network to access and query the data more efficiently. As servers might be untrusted or can be compromised, *query authentication* becomes an essential component of ODB systems. In this chapter we present three techniques to authenticate selection range queries and we analyze their performance over different cost metrics. In addition, we discuss extensions to other query types.

1 Introduction

Today, there is a large number of corporations that use electronic commerce as their primary means of conducting business. As the number of customers using the Internet for acquiring services increases, the demand for providing fast, reliable and secure transactions increases accordingly — most of the times beyond the capacity of individual businesses to provide the level of service required, given the overwhelming data management and information processing costs involved.

Increased demand has fueled a trend towards outsourcing data management and information processing needs to third-party service providers in order to mitigate the in-house cost of furnishing online services [1]. In this model the third-party service provider is responsible for offering the necessary resources and mechanisms for efficiently managing and accessing the outsourced data, by data owners and customers respectively. Clearly, data outsourcing intrinsically raises issues related with trust. Service providers cannot always be trusted (they might have malicious intend), might be compromised (by other parties with malicious intend) or run faulty software (unintentional errors). Hence, this model raises important issues on how to guarantee quality of service in untrusted database management environments, which translates into providing verification proofs to both data owners and clients that the information they process is correct.

Three main entities exist in the ODB model as discussed so far: the data owner, the database service provider (a.k.a. server) and the client. In practice, there is a single or a few data owners, a few servers, and many clients. The data owners create their databases, along with the necessary index and authentication structures, and upload them to the servers. The clients issue queries about the owner's data through the servers, which use the authentication structures to provide provably correct answers. It is assumed that the data owners may update their databases periodically and, hence, authentication techniques should be able to support dynamic updates. In this setting, query authentication has three important dimensions: *correctness*, *completeness* and *freshness*. Correctness means that the client must be able to validate that the returned answers truly exist in the owner's database and have not been tampered with. Completeness means that no answers have been omitted from the result. Finally, freshness means that the results are based on the most current version of the database, that incorporates the latest owner updates. It should be stressed here that result freshness is an important dimension of query authentication that is directly related to incorporating dynamic updates into the ODB model.

There are a number of important costs pertaining to the aforementioned model, relating to the database construction, querying, and updating phases. In particular, in this chapter the following metrics are considered: 1. The computation overhead for the owner, 2. The owner-server communication cost, 3. The storage overhead for the server, 4. The computation overhead for the server, 5. The client-server communication cost, and 6. The computation cost for the client (for verification).

It should be pointed out that there are other important security issues in ODB systems that are orthogonal to the problems considered here. Examples include privacy-preservation issues [2, 3, 4], secure query execution [5], security in conjunction with access control requirements [6, 7, 8, 9] and query execution assurance [10]. Aslo, we concentrate on large databases that need to be stored on external memory. Therefore, we will not discuss main memory structures [11, 12, 13] or data stream authentication [14, 15].

2 Cryptographic Background

In this section we discuss some basic cryptographic tools. These tools are essential components of the authentication data structures that we discuss later.

2.1 Collision-resistant hash functions.

For our purposes, a hash function $\mathcal{H}$ is an efficiently computable function that takes a variable-length input x to a fixed-length output $y = \mathcal{H}(x)$. *Collision resistance* states that it is computationally infeasible to find two inputs $x_1 \neq x_2$ such that $\mathcal{H}(x_1) = \mathcal{H}(x_2)$. Collision-resistant hash functions can be built provably based on various cryptographic assumptions, such as hardness of discrete logarithms [16]. However, we concentrate on using heuristic hash functions that have the advantage of being very fast to evaluate. Specifically we focus on SHA-1 [17], which takes variable-length inputs to 160-bit (20-byte) outputs. SHA-1 is currently considered collision-resistant in practice, despite some recent successful attacks [18, 19]. We also note that any eventual replacement to SHA-1 developed by the cryptographic community can be used instead of SHA-1.

2.2 Public-key digital signature schemes.

A public-key digital signature scheme, formally defined in [20], is a tool for authenticating the integrity and ownership of the signed message. In such a scheme, the signer generates a pair of keys (SK, PK), keeps the secret key SK secret, and publishes the public key PK associated with her identity. Subsequently, for any message m that she sends, a signature s_m is produced by $s_m = \mathcal{S}(SK, m)$. The recipient of s_m and m can verify s_m via $\mathcal{V}(PK, m, s_m)$ that outputs "valid" or "invalid." A valid signature on a message assures the recipient that the owner of the secret key intended to authenticate the message, and that the message has not been changed. The most commonly used public digital signature scheme is RSA [21]. Existing solutions [9, 22, 23, 24] for the query authentication problem chose to use this scheme, hence we adopt the common 1024-bit (128-byte) RSA here. Its signing and verification cost is one hash computation and one modular exponentiation with 1024-bit modulus and exponent.

2.3 A Signature Aggregation Scheme.

In the case when t signatures $s_1, \ldots, s_t$ on t messages $m_1, \ldots, m_t$ signed by the same signer need to be verified all at once, certain signature schemes allow for more efficient communication and verification than t individual signatures. Namely, for RSA it is possible to combine the t signatures into a single aggregated signature $s_{1,t}$ that has the same size as an individual signature and that can be verified (almost) as fast as an individual signature. This technique is called Condensed-RSA [25]. The combining operation can be done by anyone, as it does not require knowledge of SK; moreover, the security of the combined signature is the same as the security of individual signatures. In particular, aggregation of t RSA signatures can be done at the cost of $t - 1$ modular multiplications, and verification can be performed at the cost of $t - 1$

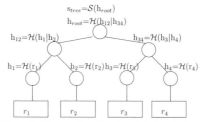

Fig. 1. Example of a Merkle hash tree.

multiplications, t hashing operations, and one modular exponentiation (thus, the computational gain is that $t-1$ modular exponentiations are replaced by modular multiplications). Note that aggregating signatures is possible only for some digital signature schemes.

2.4 The Merkle Hash Tree.

The straightforward solution for verifying a set of n values is to generate n digital signatures, one for each value. An improvement on this straightforward solution is the Merkle hash tree (see Figure 1), first proposed by [26]. It solves the simplest form of the query authentication problem for point queries and datasets that can fit in main memory. The Merkle hash tree is a binary tree, where each leaf contains the hash of a data value, and each internal node contains the hash of the concatenation of its two children. Verification of data values is based on the fact that the hash value of the root of the tree is authentically published (authenticity can be established by a digital signature). To prove the authenticity of any data value, all the prover has to do is to provide the verifier, in addition to the data value itself, with the values stored in the siblings of the path that leads from the root of the tree to that value. The verifier, by iteratively computing all the appropriate hashes up the tree, at the end can simply check if the hash she has computed for the root matches the authentically published value. The security of the Merkle hash tree is based on the collision-resistance of the hash function used: it is computationally infeasible for a malicious prover to fake a data value, since this would require finding a hash collision somewhere in the tree (because the root remains the same and the leaf is different—hence, there must be a collision somewhere in between). Thus, the authenticity of any one of n data values can be proven at the cost of providing and computing $\log_2 n$ hash values, which is generally much cheaper than storing and verifying one digital signature per data value. Furthermore, the relative position (leaf number) of any of the data values within the tree is authenticated along with the value itself. Finally, in [27] this idea is extended to dynamic environments, by dynamizing the binary search tree using 2-3 trees. Thus, insertions and deletions can be handled efficiently by the Merkle hash tree.

Table 1. Notation used.

Symbol	Description
r	A database record
k	A B^+-tree key
p	A B^+-tree pointer
h	A hash value
s	A signature
$|x|$	Size of object x
N_D	Total number of database records
N_R	Total number of query results
P	Page size
f_x	Node fanout of structure x
d_x	Height of structure x
$\mathcal{H}_l(x)$	A hash operation on input x of length l
$\mathcal{S}_l(x)$	A signing operation on input x of length l
$\mathcal{V}_l(x)$	A verifying operation on input x of length l
$\mathcal{C}_x$	Cost of operation x
$\mathcal{VO}$	The verification object

3 Authenticated Index Structures for Selection Queries

Existing solutions for the query authentication problem work as follows. The data owner creates a specialized authenticated data structure that captures the original database and uploads it at the servers together with the database itself. The structure is used by the servers to provide a verification object $\mathcal{VO}$, along with every query answer, which clients can use for authenticating the results. Verification usually occurs by means of using collision-resistant hash functions and digital signature schemes. Note that in any solution, some information that is known to be authentically published by the owner must be made available to the client directly; otherwise, from the client's point of view, the owner cannot be differentiated from any other potentially malicious entity. For example, this information could be the owner's public key of any public signature scheme. For any authentication method to be successful it must be computationally infeasible for a malicious server to produce an incorrect query answer along with a verification object that will be accepted by a client that holds the correct authentication information of the owner.

Next, we illustrate three approaches for query correctness and completeness for selection queries on a single attribute: a signature-based approach similar to the ones described in [9, 24], a Merkle-tree-like approach based on the ideas presented in [28], and an improved embedded tree approach [29]. We present them for the *static scenario* where no data updates occur between the owner and the servers on the outsourced database. We also present *analytical cost models* for all techniques, given a variety of performance metrics.

In particular, we provide models for the *storage, construction, query,* and *authentication* cost of each technique, taking into account the overhead of hashing, signing, verifying data, and performing expensive computations (like modular multiplications of large numbers). The analysis considers range queries on a specific database attribute A indexed by a B^+-tree [30]. The size of the structure is important first for quantifying the storage overhead on the servers, and second for possibly quantifying the owner/server communication cost. The construction cost is useful for quantifying the overhead incurred by the database owner for outsourcing the data. The query cost quantifies the incurred server cost for answering client queries, and hence the potential query throughput. The authentication cost quantifies the server/client communication cost and, in addition, the client side incurred cost for verifying the query results. The notation used is summarized in Table 1. In the rest, for ease of exposition, it is assumed that all structures are bulk-loaded in a bottom-up fashion and that all index nodes are completely full. Extensions for supporting multiple selection attributes are discussed in Section 6.

Aggregated Signatures with B^+-trees

The first authenticated data structure for static environments is a direct extension of aggregated signatures and ideas that appeared in [24, 9]. To guarantee correctness and completeness the following technique can be used: First, the owner individually hashes and signs all consecutive pairs of tuples in the database, assuming some sorted order on a given attribute A. For example, given two consecutive tuples r_i, r_j the owner transmits to the servers the pair (r_i, s_i), where $s_i = \mathcal{S}(r_i|r_j)$ ('|' denotes some canonical pairing of strings that can be uniquely parsed back into its two components; e.g., simple string concatenation if the lengths are fixed). The first and last tuples can be paired with special marker records. Chaining tuples in this way will enable the clients to verify that no in-between tuples have been dropped from the results or modified in any way. An example of this scheme is shown in Figure 2.

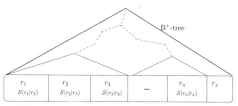

Fig. 2. The signature-based approach.

In order to speed up query execution on the server side a B^+-tree is constructed on top of attribute A. To answer a query the server constructs a $\mathcal{VO}$ that contains one pair $r_q|s_q$ per query result. In addition, one tuple to the left of the lower-bound of the query results and one to the right of the upper-bound is returned, in order for the client to be able to guarantee that no boundary results have been dropped. Notice that since our completeness requirements are less stringent than those of [9] (where they assume that database access permissions restrict which tuples the database can expose to the user), for fairness we have simplified the query algorithm substantially here.

There are two obvious and serious drawbacks associated with this approach. First, the extremely large $\mathcal{VO}$ size that contains a linear number of signatures w.r.t. N_R (the total number of query results), taking into account that signature sizes are very large. Second, the high verification cost for the clients. Authentication requires N_R verification operations which, as mentioned earlier, are very expensive. To solve this problem one can use the aggregated signature scheme discussed in Section 2.3. Instead of sending one signature per query result the server can send one *combined signature* s^π for all results, and the client can use an aggregate verification instead of individual verifications.

By using aggregated RSA signatures, the client can authenticate the results by hashing consecutive pairs of tuples in the result-set, and calculating the product $m^\pi = \prod_{\forall q} h_q \pmod{n}$ (where n is the RSA modulus from the public key of the owner). It is important to notice that both s^π and m^π require a linear number of modular multiplications (w.r.t. N_R). The cost models of the aggregated signature scheme for the metrics considered are as follows:

Node fanout:

The node fanout of the B^+-tree structure is:

$$ f_a = \frac{P - |p|}{|k| + |p|} + 1 \,. \tag{1} $$

where P is the disk page size, $|k|$ and $|p|$ are the sizes of a B^+-tree key and pointer respectively.

Storage cost:

The total size of the authenticated structure (excluding the database itself) is equal to the size of the B^+-tree plus the size of the signatures. For a total of N_D tuples the height of the tree is equal to $d_a = \log_{f_a} N_D$, consisting of $N_I = \frac{f_a^{d_a} - 1}{f_a - 1}$ $(= \sum_{i=0}^{d_a - 1} f_a^i)$ nodes in total. Hence, the total storage cost is equal to:

$$ \mathcal{C}_s^a = P \cdot \frac{f_a^{d_a} - 1}{f_a - 1} + N_D \cdot |s|. \tag{2} $$

The storage cost also reflects the initial communication cost between the owner and servers. Notice that the owner does not have to upload the B$^+$-tree to the servers, since the latter can rebuild it by themselves, which will reduce the owner/server communication cost but increase the computation cost at the servers. Nevertheless, the cost of sending the signatures cannot be avoided.

Construction cost:

The cost incurred by the owner for constructing the structure has three components: the signature computation cost, bulk-loading the B^+-tree, and the I/O cost for storing the structure. Since the signing operation is very expensive, it dominates the overall cost. Bulk-loading the B^+-tree in main memory is much less expensive and its cost can be omitted. Hence:

$$\mathcal{C}_c^a = N_D \cdot (\mathcal{C}_{\mathcal{H}_{|r|}} + \mathcal{C}_{\mathcal{S}_{2|h|}}) + \frac{\mathcal{C}_s^a}{P} \cdot \mathcal{C}_{IO}. \qquad \text{(3)}$$

$\mathcal{VO}$ construction cost:

The cost of constructing the $\mathcal{VO}$ for a range query depends on the total disk I/O for traversing the B^+-tree and retrieving all necessary record/signature pairs, as well as on the computation cost of s^π. Assuming that the total number of leaf pages accessed is $N_Q = \frac{N_R}{f_a}$, the $\mathcal{VO}$ construction cost is:

$$\mathcal{C}_q^a = (N_Q + d_a - 1 + \frac{N_R \cdot |r|}{P} + \frac{N_R \cdot |s|}{P}) \cdot \mathcal{C}_{IO} + \mathcal{C}_{s^\pi}, \qquad \text{(4)}$$

where the last term is the modular multiplication cost for computing the aggregated signature, which is linear to N_R. The I/O overhead for retrieving the signatures is also large.

Authentication cost:

The size of the $\mathcal{VO}$ is equal to the result-set size plus the size of one signature:

$$|\mathcal{VO}|^a = N_R \cdot |r| + |s|. \qquad \text{(5)}$$

The cost of verifying the query results is dominated by the hash function computations and modular multiplications at the client:

$$\mathcal{C}_v^a = N_R \cdot \mathcal{C}_{\mathcal{H}_{|r|}} + \mathcal{C}_{m^\pi} + \mathcal{C}_{\mathcal{V}_{|n|}}, \qquad \text{(6)}$$

where the modular multiplication cost for computing the aggregated hash value is linear to the result-set size N_R, and the size of the final product has length in the order of $|n|$ (the RSA modulus). The final term is the cost of verifying the product using s^π and the owner's public key.

It becomes obvious now that one advantage of the aggregated signature scheme is that it features small $\mathcal{VO}$ sizes and hence small client/server communication cost. On the other hand it has the following serious drawbacks: 1. Large storage overhead on the servers, dominated by the large signature sizes, 2. Large communication overhead between the owners and the servers that cannot be reduced, 3. A very high initial construction cost, dominated by the cost of computing the signatures, 4. Added I/O cost for retrieving signatures, linear to N_R, 5. An added modular multiplication cost, linear to the result-set size, for constructing the $\mathcal{VO}$ and authenticating the results, 6. The requirement for a public key signature scheme that supports aggregated signatures. For the rest of the chapter, this approach is denoted as Aggregated Signatures with B^+-trees (ASB-tree). The ASB-tree has been generalized to work with multi-dimensional selection queries in [24, 31].

The Merkle B-tree

Motivated by the drawbacks of the ASB-tree, we present a different approach for building authenticated structures that is based on the general ideas of [28] (which utilize the Merkle hash tree) applied in our case on a B^+-tree structure. We term this structure the Merkle B-tree (MB-tree).

As already explained in Section 2.4, the Merkle hash tree uses a hierarchical hashing scheme in the form of a binary tree to achieve query authentication. Clearly, one can use a similar hashing scheme with trees of *higher fanout and with different organization algorithms*, like the B^+-tree, to achieve the same goal. An MB-tree works like a B^+-tree and also consists of ordinary B^+-tree nodes that are extended with one hash value associated with every pointer entry. The hash values associated with entries on leaf nodes are computed on the database records themselves. The hash values associated with index node entries are computed on the concatenation of the hash values of their children. For example, an MB-tree is illustrated in Figure 3. A leaf node entry is associated with a hash value $h = \mathcal{H}(r_i)$, while an index node entry with $h = \mathcal{H}(h_1|\cdots|h_{f_m})$, where $h_1, \ldots, h_{f_m}$ are the hash values of the node's children, assuming fanout f_m per node. After computing all hash values, the owner has to sign the hash of the root using its secret key SK.

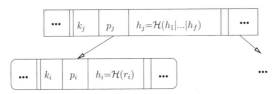

Fig. 3. An MB-tree node.

To answer a range query the server builds a $\mathcal{VO}$ by initiating two top-down B^+-tree like traversals, one to find the left-most and one the right-most query result. At the leaf level, the data contained in the nodes between the two discovered boundary leaves are returned, as in the normal B^+-tree. The server also needs to include in the $\mathcal{VO}$ the hash values of the entries contained in each index node that is visited by the lower and upper boundary traversals of the tree, except the hashes to the right (left) of the pointers that are traversed during the lower (upper) boundary traversals. At the leaf level, the server inserts only the answers to the query, along with the hash values of the residual entries to the left and to the right parts of the boundary leaves. The result is also increased with one tuple to the left and one to the right of the lower-bound and upper-bound of the query result respectively, for completeness verification. Finally, the signed root of the tree is inserted as well. An example query traversal is shown in Figure 4.

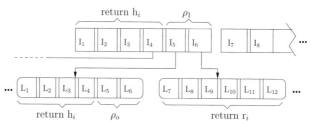

Fig. 4. A query traversal on an MB-tree. At every level the hashes of the residual entries on the left and right boundary nodes need to be returned.

The client can iteratively compute all the hashes of the sub-tree corresponding to the query result, all the way up to the root using the $\mathcal{VO}$. The hashes of the query results are computed first and grouped into their corresponding leaf nodes[4], and the process continues iteratively, until all the hashes of the query sub-tree have been computed. After the hash value of the root has been computed, the client can verify the correctness of the computation using the owner's public key PK and the signed hash of the root. It is easy to see that since the client is forced to recompute the whole query sub-tree, both correctness and completeness is guaranteed. It is interesting to note here that one could avoid building the whole query sub-tree during verification by individually signing all database tuples as well as each node of the B^+-tree. This approach, called VB-tree, was proposed in [22] but it is subsumed by the ASB-tree. Another approach that does not need to build the whole tree appeared in [32]. The analytical cost models of the MB-tree are as follows:

Node fanout:

The node fanout in this case is:

$$f_m = \frac{P - |p| - |h|}{|k| + |p| + |h|} + 1. \tag{7}$$

Notice that the maximum node fanout of the MB-tree is considerably smaller than that of the ASB-tree, since the nodes here are extended with one hash value per entry. This adversely affects the total height of the MB-tree.

---

[4] Extra node boundary information can be inserted in the $\mathcal{VO}$ for this purpose with a very small overhead.

Storage cost:

The total size is equal to:

$$C_s^m = P \cdot \frac{f_m^{d_m} - 1}{f_m - 1} + |s|. \tag{8}$$

An important advantage of the MB-tree is that the storage cost does not necessarily reflect the owner/server communication cost. The owner, after computing the final signature of the root, does not have to transmit all hash values to the server, but only the database tuples. The server can recompute the hash values incrementally by recreating the MB-tree. Since hash computations are cheap, for a small increase in the server's computation cost this technique will reduce the owner/sever communication cost drastically.

Construction cost:

The construction cost for building an MB-tree depends on the hash function computations and the total I/Os. Since the tree is bulk-loaded, building the leaf level requires N_D hash computations of input length $|r|$. In addition, for every tree node one hash of input length $f_m \cdot |h|$ is computed. Since there are a total of $N_I = \frac{f_m^{d_m} - 1}{f_m - 1}$ nodes on average (given height $d_m = \log_{f_m} N_D$), the total number of hash function computations, and hence the total cost for constructing the tree is given by:

$$C_c^m = N_D \cdot C_{\mathcal{H}_{|r|}} + N_I \cdot C_{\mathcal{H}_{f_m|h|}} + C_{\mathcal{S}_{|h|}} + \frac{C_s^m}{P} \cdot C_{IO}. \tag{9}$$

$\mathcal{VO}$ construction cost:

The $\mathcal{VO}$ construction cost is dominated by the total disk I/O. Let the total number of leaf pages accessed be equal to $N_Q = \frac{N_R}{f_m}$, $d_m = \log_{f_m} N_D$ and $d_q = \log_{f_m} N_R$ be the height of the MB-tree and the query sub-tree respectively. In the general case the index traversal cost is:

$$C_q^m = [(d_m - d_q + 1) + 2(d_q - 2) + N_Q + \frac{N_R \cdot |r|}{P}] \cdot C_{IO}, \tag{10}$$

taking into account the fact that the query traversal at some point splits into two paths. It is assumed here that the query range spans at least two leaf nodes. The first term corresponds to the hashes inserted for the common path of the two traversals from the root of the tree to the root of the query sub-tree. The second term corresponds to the cost of the two boundary traversals after the split. The last two terms correspond to the cost of the leaf level traversal of the tree and accessing the database records.

Authentication cost:

Assuming that ρ_0 is the total number of query results contained in the left boundary leaf node of the query sub-tree, σ_0 on the right boundary leaf node, and ρ_i, σ_i the total number of entries of the left and right boundary nodes on level $i, 1 \leq i \leq d_q$, that point towards leaves that contain query results (see Figure 4), the size of the $\mathcal{VO}$ is:

$$
\begin{aligned}
|\mathcal{VO}|^m = \\
(2f_m - \rho_0 - \sigma_0)|h| + N_R \cdot |r| + |s| + \\
(d_m - d_q) \cdot (f_m - 1)|h| + \\
\sum_{i=1}^{d_q-2} (2f_m - \rho_i - \sigma_i)|h| + \\
(f_m - \rho_{d_q-1} - \sigma_{d_q-1})|h|.
\end{aligned}
\tag{11}
$$

This cost does not include the extra boundary information needed by the client in order to group hashes correctly, but this overhead is very small (one byte per node in the $\mathcal{VO}$) especially when compared with the hash value size. Consequently, the verification cost on the client is:

$$
\begin{aligned}
\mathcal{C}_v^m = N_R \cdot \mathcal{C}_{\mathcal{H}_{|r|}} + \sum_{i=0}^{d_q-1} f_m^i \cdot \mathcal{C}_{\mathcal{H}_{f_m|h|}} + \\
(d_m - d_q) \cdot \mathcal{C}_{\mathcal{H}_{f_m|h|}} + \mathcal{C}_{\mathcal{V}_{|h|}}.
\end{aligned}
\tag{12}
$$

Given that the computation cost of hashing versus signing is orders of magnitude smaller, the initial construction cost of the MB-tree is expected to be orders of magnitude less expensive than that of the ASB-tree. Given that the size of hash values is much smaller than that of signatures and that the fanout of the MB-tree will be smaller than that of the ASB-tree, it is not easy to quantify the exact difference in the storage cost of these techniques, but it is expected that the structures will have comparable storage cost, with the MB-tree being smaller. The $\mathcal{VO}$ construction cost of the MB-tree will be much smaller than that of the ASB-tree, since the ASB-tree requires many I/Os for retrieving signatures, and also some expensive modular multiplications. The MB-tree will have smaller verification cost as well since: 1. Hashing operations are orders of magnitude cheaper than modular multiplications, 2. The ASB-tree requires N_R modular multiplications for verification. The only drawback of the MB-tree is the large $\mathcal{VO}$ size, which increases the client/server communication cost. Notice that the $\mathcal{VO}$ size of the MB-tree is bounded by $f_m \cdot \log_{f_m} N_D$. Since generally $f_m \gg \log_{f_m} N_D$, the $\mathcal{VO}$ size is essentially determined by f_m, resulting in large sizes.

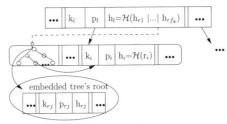

Fig. 5. An EMB-tree node.

The Embedded Merkle B-tree

In this section we present another data structure, the Embedded Merkle B-tree (EMB-tree), that provides a nice, adjustable trade-off between robust initial construction and storage cost versus improved $\mathcal{VO}$ construction and verification cost. The main idea is to have different fanouts for storage and authentication and yet combine them in the same data structure.

Every EMB-tree node consists of regular B^+-tree entries, augmented with an embedded MB-tree. Let f_e be the fanout of the EMB-tree. Then each node stores up to f_e triplets $k_i|p_i|h_i$, and an embedded MB-tree with fanout $f_k < f_e$. The leaf level of this embedded tree consists of the f_e entries of the node. The hash value at the root level of this embedded tree is stored as an h_i value in the parent of the node, thus authenticating this node to its parent. Essentially, we are collapsing an MB-tree with height $d_e \cdot d_k = \log_{f_k} N_D$ into a tree with height d_e that stores smaller MB-trees of height d_k within each node. Here, $d_e = \log_{f_e} N_D$ is the height of the EMB-tree and $d_k = \log_{f_k} f_e$ is the height of each small embedded MB-tree. An example EMB-tree node is shown in Figure 5.

For ease of exposition, in the rest of this discussion it will be assumed that f_e is a power of f_k such that the embedded trees when bulk-loaded are always full. The technical details if this is not the case can be worked out easily. The exact relation between f_e and f_k will be discussed shortly. After choosing f_k and f_e, bulk-loading the EMB-tree is straightforward: Simply group the N_D tuples in groups of size f_e to form the leaves and build their embedded trees on the fly. Continue iteratively in a bottom up fashion.

When querying the structure the server follows a path from the root to the leaves of the external tree as in the normal B^+-tree. For every node visited, the algorithm scans all $f_e - 1$ triplets $k_i|p_i|h_i$ on the data level of the embedded tree to find the key that needs to be followed to the next level. When the right key is found the server also initiates a point query on the embedded tree of the node using this key. The point query will return all the needed hash values for computing the concatenated hash of the node, exactly like for the MB-tree. Essentially, these hash values would be the equivalent of the $f_e - 1$ sibling hashes that would be returned per node if the embedded tree was not used. However, since now the hashes are arranged hierarchically in an f_k-way tree, the total number of values inserted in the $\mathcal{VO}$ per node is reduced to $(f_k - 1)d_k$.

To authenticate the query results the client uses the normal MB-tree authentication algorithm to construct the hash value of the root node of each embedded tree (assuming that proper boundary information has been included in the $\mathcal{VO}$ for separating groups of hash values into different nodes) and then follows the same algorithm once more for computing the final hash value of the root of the EMB-tree.

The EMB-tree structure uses extra space for storing the index levels of the embedded trees. Hence, by construction it has increased height compared to the MB-tree due to smaller fanout f_e. A first, simple optimization for improving the fanout of the EMB-tree is to avoid storing the embedded trees altogether. Instead, each embedded tree can be instantiated by computing fewer than $f_e/(f_k - 1)$ hashes on the fly, only when a node is accessed during the querying phase. We call this the EMB^--tree. The EMB^--tree is logically the same as the EMB-tree, however its physical structure is equivalent to an MB-tree with the hash values computed differently. The querying algorithm of the EMB^--tree is slightly different than that of the EMB-tree in order to take into account the conceptually embedded trees. With this optimization the storage overhead is minimized and the height of the EMB^--tree becomes equal to the height of the equivalent MB-tree. The trade-off is an increased computation cost for constructing the $\mathcal{VO}$. However, this cost is minimal as the number of embedded trees that need to be reconstructed is bounded by the height of the EMB^--tree.

As a second optimization, one can create a slightly more complicated embedded tree to reduce the total size of the index levels and increase fanout f_e. We call this the EMB^*-tree. Essentially, instead of using a B^+-tree as the base structure for the embedded trees, one can use a multi-way search tree with fanout f_k while keeping the structure of the external EMB-tree intact. The embedded tree based on B^+-trees has a total of $N_i = \frac{f_k^{d_k} - 1}{f_k - 1}$ nodes while, for example, a B-tree based embedded tree (recall that a B-tree is equivalent to a balanced multi-way search tree) would contain $N_i = \frac{f_e - 1}{f_k - 1}$ nodes instead. A side effect of using multi-way search trees is that the cost for querying the embedded tree on average will decrease, since the search for a particular key might stop before reaching the leaf level. This will reduce the expected cost of $\mathcal{VO}$ construction substantially. Below we give the analytical cost models of the EMB-tree. The further technical details and the analytical cost models associated with the EMB^*-tree and EMB^--tree are similar to the EMB-tree case and can be worked out similarly.

Node fanout:

For the EMB-tree, the relationship between f_e and f_k is given by:

$$P \geq$$
$$\frac{f_k^{\log_{f_k} f_e - 1} - 1}{f_k - 1}[f_k(|k| + |p| + |h|) - |k|] +$$
$$[f_e(|k| + |p| + |h|) - |k|]. \tag{13}$$

First, a suitable f_k is chosen such that the requirements for authentication cost and storage overhead are met. Then, the maximum value for f_e satisfying (13) can be determined.

Storage cost:

The storage cost is equal to:

$$\mathcal{C}_s^e = P \cdot \frac{f_e^{d_e} - 1}{f_e - 1} + |s|. \tag{14}$$

Construction cost:

The total construction cost is the cost of constructing all the embedded trees plus the I/Os to write the tree back to disk. Given a total of $N_I = \frac{f_e^{d_e} - 1}{f_e - 1}$ nodes in the tree and $N_i = \frac{f_k^{d_k} - 1}{f_k - 1}$ nodes per embedded tree, the cost is:

$$\mathcal{C}_c^e = N_D \cdot \mathcal{C}_{\mathcal{H}_{|r|}} + N_I \cdot N_i \cdot \mathcal{C}_{\mathcal{H}_{f_k|h|}} + \mathcal{C}_{\mathcal{S}_{|h|}} + \frac{\mathcal{C}_s^e}{P} \cdot \mathcal{C}_{IO}. \tag{15}$$

It should be mentioned here that the cost for constructing the EMB^--tree is exactly the same, since in order to find the hash values for the index entries of the trees one needs to instantiate all embedded trees. The cost of the EMB^*-tree is somewhat smaller than (15), due to the smaller number of nodes in the embedded trees.

$\mathcal{VO}$ construction cost:

The $\mathcal{VO}$ construction cost is dominated by the total I/O for locating and reading all the nodes containing the query results. Similarly to the MB-tree case:

$$\mathcal{C}_q^e = [(d_e - d_q + 1) + 2(d_q - 2) + N_Q + \frac{N_R \cdot |r|}{P}] \cdot \mathcal{C}_{IO}, \tag{16}$$

where d_q is the height of the query sub-tree and $N_Q = \frac{N_R}{f_e}$ is the number of leaf pages to be accessed. Since the embedded trees are loaded with each node, the querying computation cost associated with finding the needed hash values is expected to be dominated by the cost of loading the node in memory, and hence it is omitted. It should be restated here that for the EMB^*-tree the expected $\mathcal{VO}$ construction cost will be smaller, since not all embedded tree searches will reach the leaf level of the structure.

Authentication cost:

The embedded trees work exactly like MB-trees for point queries. Hence, each embedded tree returns $(f_k - 1)d_k$ hashes. Similarly to the MB-tree the total size of the $\mathcal{VO}$ is:

$$|\mathcal{VO}|^e = N_R \cdot |r| + |s| +$$
$$\sum_{0}^{d_q-2} 2|\mathcal{VO}|^m + |\mathcal{VO}|^m + \sum_{d_q}^{d_m-1} (f_k - 1)d_k|h|, \qquad (17)$$

where $|\mathcal{VO}|^m$ is the cost of a range query on the embedded trees of the boundary nodes contained in the query sub-tree given by equation (11), with a query range that covers all pointers to children that cover the query result-set. The verification cost is:

$$\mathcal{C}_v^e = N_R \cdot \mathcal{C}_{\mathcal{H}_{|r|}} + \sum_{i=0}^{d_q-1} f_e^i \cdot \mathcal{C}_k + (d_e - d_q) \cdot \mathcal{C}_k + \mathcal{C}_{\mathcal{V}_{|h|}}, \qquad (18)$$

where $\mathcal{C}_k = N_i \cdot \mathcal{C}_{\mathcal{H}_{f_k|h|}}$ is the cost for constructing the concatenated hash of each node using the embedded tree.

For $f_k = 2$ the authentication cost becomes equal to a Merkle hash tree, which has the minimal $\mathcal{VO}$ size but higher verification time. For $f_k \geq f_e$ the embedded tree consists of only one node which can actually be discarded, hence the authentication cost becomes equal to that of an MB-tree, which has larger $\mathcal{VO}$ size but smaller verification cost. Notice that, as f_k becomes smaller, f_e becomes smaller as well. This has an impact on $\mathcal{VO}$ construction cost and size, since with smaller fanout the height of the EMB-tree increases. Nevertheless, since there is only a logarithmic dependence on f_e versus a linear dependence on f_k, it is expected that with smaller f_k the authentication related operations will become faster.

4 Authentication Index Structures in Dynamic Settings

In this section we analyze the performance of all approaches given dynamic updates between the owner and the servers. In particular we assume that either insertions or deletions can occur to the database, for simplicity. The performance of updates in the worst case can be considered as the cost of a deletion followed by an insertion. There are two contributing factors for the update cost: computation cost such as creating new signatures and computing hashes, and I/O cost.

Aggregated Signatures with B$^+$-trees

Suppose that a single database record r_i is inserted in or deleted from the database. Assuming that in the sorted order of attribute A the left neighbor of r_i is r_{i-1} and the right neighbor is r_{i+1}, for an insertion the owner has to compute signatures $\mathcal{S}(r_{i-1}|r_i)$ and $\mathcal{S}(r_i|r_{i+1})$, and for a deletion $\mathcal{S}(r_{i-1}|r_{i+1})$. For k consecutive updates in the best case a total of $k+2$ signature computations are required for insertions and 1 for deletions if the deleted tuples are consecutive. In the worst case a total of $2k$ signature computations are needed for insertions and k for deletions, if no two tuples are consecutive. Given k updates, suppose the expected number of signatures to be computed is represented by $E\{k\}$ ($k \leq E\{k\} \leq 2k$). Then the additional I/O incurred is equal to $\frac{E\{k\} \cdot |s|}{P}$, excluding the I/Os incurred for updating the B^+-tree structure. Since the cost of signature computations is larger than even the I/O cost of random disk accesses, a large number of updates is expected to have a very expensive updating cost. The total update cost for the ASB-tree is:

$$\mathcal{C}_u^a = E\{k\} \cdot \mathcal{C}_s + \frac{E\{k\} \cdot |s|}{P} \cdot \mathcal{C}_{IO}. \tag{19}$$

The Merkle B-tree

The MB-tree can support efficient updates since only hash values are stored for the records in the tree and, first, hashing is orders of magnitude faster then signing, second, for each tuple only the path from the affected leaf to the root need to be updated. Hence, the cost of updating a single record is dominated by the cost of I/Os. Assuming that no reorganization to the tree occurs the cost of an insertion is $\mathcal{C}_u^m = \mathcal{H}_{|r|} + d_m(\mathcal{H}_{f_m|h|} + \mathcal{C}_{IO}) + \mathcal{S}_{|h|}$.

In realistic scenarios though one expects that a large number of updates will occur at the same time. In other cases the owner may decide to do a delayed batch processing of updates as soon as enough changes to the database have occurred. The naive approach for handling batch updates would be to do all updates to the MB-tree one by one and update the path from the leaves to the root once per update. Nevertheless, in case that a large number of updates affect a similar set of nodes (e.g., the same leaf) a per tuple updating policy performs an unnecessary number of hash function computations on the predecessor path. In such cases, the computation cost can be reduced significantly by recomputing the hashes of all affected nodes only once, after all the updates have been performed on the tree. A similar analysis holds for the incurred I/O as well.

Clearly, the total update cost for the per tuple update approach for k insertions is $k \cdot \mathcal{C}_u^m$ which is linear to the number of affected nodes $k \cdot d_m$. The expected cost of k updates using batch processing can be computed as follows. Given k updates to the MB-tree, assuming that all tuples are updated uniformly at random and using a standard balls and bins argument, the probability that leaf node X has been affected at least once is $P(X) = 1 - (1 - \frac{1}{f_m^{d_m-1}})^k$ and the expected number of leaf nodes that have been affected is $f_m^{d_m-1} \cdot P(X)$. Using the same argument, the expected number of nodes at level i (where $i = 1$ is the leaf level and $1 \leq i \leq d_m$) is

$f_m^{d_m - i} \cdot P_i(X)$, where $P_i(X) = [1 - (1 - \frac{1}{f_m^{d_m - i}})^k]$. Hence, for a batch of k updates the total expected number of nodes that will be affected is:

$$E\{X\} = \sum_{i=0}^{d_m - 1} f_m^i [1 - (1 - \frac{1}{f_m^i})^k]. \tag{20}$$

Hence, the expected MB-tree update cost for batch updates is

$$\mathcal{C}_u^m = k \cdot \mathcal{H}_{|r|} + E\{X\} \cdot (\mathcal{H}_{f_m|h|} + \mathcal{C}_{IO}) + \mathcal{S}_{|h|}. \tag{21}$$

In order to understand better the relationship between the per-update approach and the batch-update, we can find the closed form for $E\{X\}$ as follows:

$$\sum_{i=0}^{d_m - 1} f_m^i (1 - (\frac{f_m^i - 1}{f_m^i})^k)$$
$$= \sum_{i=0}^{d_m - 1} f_m^i (1 - (1 - \frac{1}{f_m^i})^k)$$
$$= \sum_{i=0}^{d_m - 1} f_m^i [1 - \sum_{x=0}^{k} \binom{k}{x} (-\frac{1}{f_m^i})^x]$$
$$= \sum_{i=0}^{d_m - 1} f_m^i - \sum_{i=0}^{d_m - 1} \sum_{x=0}^{k} \binom{k}{x} (-1)^x (\frac{1}{f_m^i})^{x-1}$$
$$= k d_m - \sum_{x=2}^{k} \binom{k}{x} (-1)^x \sum_{i=0}^{d_m - 1} (\frac{1}{f_m^i})^{x-1}$$
$$= k d_m - \sum_{x=2}^{k} \binom{k}{x} (-1)^x \frac{1 - (\frac{1}{f_m^{d_m}})^{x-1}}{1 - (\frac{1}{f_m})^{x-1}}$$

The second term quantifies the cost decrease afforded by the batch update operation, when compared to the per update cost.

For non-uniform updates to the database, the batch updating technique is expected to work well in practice given that in real settings updates exhibit a certain degree of locality. In such cases one can still derive a similar cost analysis by modelling the distribution of updates.

The Embedded MB-tree

The analysis for the EMB-tree is similar to the one for MB-trees. The update cost for per tuple updates is equal to $k \cdot \mathcal{C}_u^e$, where $\mathcal{C}_u^e = \mathcal{H}_{|r|} + d_e \log_{f_k} f_e \cdot (\mathcal{H}_{f_k|h|} + \mathcal{C}_{IO}) + \mathcal{S}_{|h|}$, once again assuming that no reorganizations to the tree occur. Similarly to the MB-tree case the expected cost for batch updates is equal to:

$$\mathcal{C}_u^e = k \cdot \mathcal{H}_{|r|} + E\{X\} \cdot \log_{f_k} f_e \cdot (\mathcal{H}_{f_k|h|} + \mathcal{C}_{IO}) + \mathcal{S}_{|h|}. \tag{22}$$

Discussion

For the ASB-tree, the communication cost for updates between owner and servers is bounded by $E\{K\}|s|$, and there is no possible way to reduce this cost as only the owner can compute signatures. However, for the hash based index structures, there are a number of options that can be used for transmitting the updates to the server. The first option is for the owner to transmit only a delta table with the updated nodes of the MB-tree (or EMB-tree) plus the signed root. The second option is to transmit only the signed root and the updates themselves and let the servers redo the necessary computations on the tree. The first approach minimizes the computation cost on the servers but increases the communication cost, while the second approach has the opposite effect.

5 Query Freshness

The dynamic scenarios considered before reveal a third dimension of the query authentication problem, that of *query result freshness*. When the owner updates the database, a malicious or compromised server may still retain an older version of the data. Since the old version was authenticated by the owner already, the client will still accept any query results originating from an old version as authentic, unless the latter is informed by the owner that this is no longer the case. In fact, a malicious server may choose to answer queries using any previous version, and in some scenarios even a combination of older versions of the data. If the client wishes to be assured that queries are answered using the latest data updates, additional work is necessary.

This issue is similar to the problem of ensuring the freshness of signed documents, which has been studied extensively in the context of certificate validation and revocation. There are many approaches which we do not review here. The simplest is to publish a list of revoked signatures, one for every expired version of the database. More sophisticated ones are: 1. Including the time interval of validity as part of the signed root of the authenticated structures and reissuing the signature after the interval expires, 2. Using hash chains to confirm validity of signatures at frequent intervals [33].

Clearly, all signature freshness techniques impose a cost which is linear to the number of signatures used by any authentication structure. The advantage of the Merkle tree based methods is that they use one signature only — that of the root of the tree — which is sufficient for authenticating the whole database. Straightforwardly, database updates will also require re-issuing only the signature of the root.

6 Extensions

This section extends our discussion to other interesting topics that are related to the query authentication problem.

Multi-dimensional Selection and Aggregation Range Queries. The same ideas that we discussed before can be used for authenticating multi-dimensional range queries. In particular, any tree based multi-dimensional index structure, like the R-tree, can be used to create verification objects for multi-dimensional data. The tree is extended with hash values that are computed using both the hash values of its children nodes in the tree and the multi-dimensional information that is used to navigate the tree. For the R-tree, this means that the hash value for a node N will contain all the hash values and the MBR's of the children nodes of N. Signature based approaches can be also used [34, 31]. Furthermore, aggregation queries can be authenticated using aggregation trees [35, 36]. The only difference is that the aggregate value of each subtree should be included in the computation of the hash values. That is, for each node N of an aggregation tree we add the aggregate value of the subtree that starts at N and we include this in the hash value of the node [37].

General Query Types. The authenticated structures presented before can support other query types as well. We briefly discuss here a possible extension of these techniques for join queries. Other query types that can be supported are projections and relational set operations.

Assume that we would like to provide authenticated results for join queries such as $R \bowtie_{A_i = A_j} S$, where $A_i \in R$ and $A_j \in S$ (R and S could be relations or result-sets from other queries), and authenticated structures for both A_i in R and A_j in S exist. The server can provide the proof for the join as follows: 1. Select the relation with the smaller size, say R, 2. Construct the VO for R (if R is an entire relation then the $\mathcal{VO}$ contains only the signature of the root node from the index of R), 3. Construct the $\mathcal{VO}$s for each of the following selection queries: for each record r_k in R, $q_k = $"SELECT * FROM S WHERE $r.A_j = r_k.A_i$". The client can easily verify the join results. First, it authenticates that the relation R is complete and correct. Then, using the $\mathcal{VO}$ for each query q_k, it makes sure that it is complete for every k (even when the result of q_k is empty). After this verification, the client can construct the results for the join query and be sure that they are complete and correct.

7 Conclusion

In this chapter we presented three approaches to authenticate range queries in ODBs. The first approach is based on signature chaining and aggregation, the second on combining a Merkle hash tree with a B+-tree and the third is an improved version of the hash tree approach. We discussed advantages and disadvantages of each approach and we gave an analytical cost model for each approach and different cost metrics. Finally, we discussed the performance of each method under a dynamic environment and we gave extensions of these techniques to other query types. A interesting future direction is to enhance the proposed methods to work efficiently for complex relational queries. Another direction is to investigate authentication techniques for other types of databases beyond relational databases.

References

1. Hacigumus, H., Iyer, B.R., Mehrotra, S.: Providing database as a service. In: Proc. of International Conference on Data Engineering (ICDE). (2002) 29–40
2. Hore, B., Mehrotra, S., Tsudik, G.: A privacy-preserving index for range queries. In: Proc. of Very Large Data Bases (VLDB). (2004) 720–731
3. Agrawal, R., Srikant, R.: Privacy-preserving data mining. In: Proc. of ACM Management of Data (SIGMOD). (2000) 439–450
4. Evfimievski, A., Gehrke, J., Srikant, R.: Limiting privacy breaches in privacy preserving data mining. In: Proc. of ACM Symposium on Principles of Database Systems (PODS). (2003) 211–222
5. Hacigumus, H., Iyer, B.R., Li, C., Mehrotra, S.: Executing SQL over encrypted data in the database service provider model. In: Proc. of ACM Management of Data (SIGMOD). (2002) 216–227
6. Miklau, G., Suciu, D.: Controlling access to published data using cryptography. In: Proc. of Very Large Data Bases (VLDB). (2003) 898–909
7. Rizvi, S., Mendelzon, A., Sudarshan, S., Roy, P.: Extending query rewriting techniques for fine-grained access control. In: Proc. of ACM Management of Data (SIGMOD). (2004) 551–562
8. Bouganim, L., Ngoc, F.D., Pucheral, P., Wu, L.: Chip-secured data access: Reconciling access rights with data encryption. In: Proc. of Very Large Data Bases (VLDB). (2003) 1133–1136
9. Pang, H., Jain, A., Ramamritham, K., Tan, K.L.: Verifying completeness of relational query results in data publishing. In: Proc. of ACM Management of Data (SIGMOD). (2005) 407–418
10. Sion, R.: Query execution assurance for outsourced databases. In: Proc. of Very Large Data Bases (VLDB). (2005) 601–612
11. Anagnostopoulos, A., Goodrich, M., Tamassia, R.: Persistent authenticated dictionaries and their applications. In: ISC. (2001) 379–393
12. Goodrich, M., Tamassia, R., Triandopoulos, N., Cohen, R.: Authenticated data structures for graph and geometric searching. In: CT-RSA. (2003) 295–313
13. Tamassia, R., Triandopoulos, N.: Computational bounds on hierarchical data processing with applications to information security. In: ICALP. (2005) 153–165
14. Li, F., Yi, K., Hadjieleftheriou, M., Kollios, G.: Proof-infused streams: Enabling authentication of sliding window queries on streams. In: Proc. of Very Large Data Bases (VLDB). (2007)
15. Papadopoulos, S., Yang, Y., Papadias, D.: CADS: Continuous authentication on data streams. In: Proc. of Very Large Data Bases (VLDB). (2007)
16. McCurley, K.: The discrete logarithm problem. In: Proc. of the Symposium in Applied Mathematics, American Mathematical Society (1990) 49–74
17. National Institute of Standards and Technology: FIPS PUB 180-1: Secure Hash Standard. National Institute of Standards and Technology (1995)
18. Wang, X., Yin, Y., Yu, H.: Finding collisions in the full sha-1. In: CRYPTO. (2005)
19. Wang, X., Yao, A., Yao, F.: New collision search for SHA-1 (2005) Presented at the rump session of Crypto 2005.
20. Goldwasser, S., Micali, S., Rivest, R.L.: A digital signature scheme secure against adaptive chosen-message attacks. SIAM Journal on Computing **17**(2) (1988) 96–99

21. Rivest, R.L., Shamir, A., Adleman, L.: A method for obtaining digital signatures and public-key cryptosystems. Communications of the ACM (CACM) **21**(2) (1978) 120–126
22. Pang, H., Tan, K.L.: Authenticating query results in edge computing. In: Proc. of International Conference on Data Engineering (ICDE). (2004) 560–571
23. Mykletun, E., Narasimha, M., Tsudik, G.: Authentication and integrity in outsourced databases. In: Symposium on Network and Distributed Systems Security (NDSS). (2004)
24. Narasimha, M., Tsudik, G.: Dsac: Integrity of outsourced databases with signature aggregation and chaining. In: Proc. of Conference on Information and Knowledge Management (CIKM). (2005) 235–236
25. Mykletun, E., Narasimha, M., Tsudik, G.: Signature bouquets: Immutability for aggregated/condensed signatures. In: European Symposium on Research in Computer Security (ESORICS). (2004) 160–176
26. Merkle, R.C.: A certified digital signature. In: Proc. of Advances in Cryptology (CRYPTO). (1989) 218–238
27. Naor, M., Nissim, K.: Certificate revocation and certificate update. In: Proceedings 7th USENIX Security Symposium (San Antonio, Texas). (1998)
28. Martel, C., Nuckolls, G., Devanbu, P., Gertz, M., Kwong, A., Stubblebine, S.: A general model for authenticated data structures. Algorithmica **39**(1) (2004) 21–41
29. Li, F., Hadjieleftheriou, M., Kollios, G., Reyzin, L.: Dynamic authenticated index structures for outsourced databases. In: Proc. of ACM Management of Data (SIGMOD). (2006)
30. Comer, D.: The ubiquitous B-tree. ACM Computing Surveys **11**(2) (1979) 121–137
31. Cheng, W., Pang, H., Tan, K.: Authenticating multi-dimensional query results in data publishing. In: DBSec. (2006)
32. Nuckolls, G.: Verified query results from hybrid authentication trees. In: DBSec. (2005) 84–98
33. Micali, S.: Efficient certificate revocation. Technical Report MIT/LCS/TM-542b, Massachusetts Institute of Technology, Cambridge, MA (1996)
34. Narasimha, M., Tsudik, G.: Authentication of outsourced databases using signature aggregation and chaining. In: DASFAA. (2006) 420–436
35. Lazaridis, I., Mehrotra, S.: Progressive approximate aggregate queries with a multi-resolution tree structure. In: Proc. of ACM Management of Data (SIGMOD). (2001) 401–412
36. Tao, Y., Papadias, D.: Range aggregate processing in spatial databases. IEEE Transactions on Knowledge and Data Engineering (TKDE) **16**(12) (2004) 1555–1570
37. Li, F., Hadjieleftheriou, M., Kollios, G., Reyzin, L.: Authenticated index sturctures for aggregation queries in outsourced databases. Technical report, CS Dept., Boston University (2006)

6

Towards Secure Data Outsourcing

Radu Sion

Network Security and Applied Cryptography Lab
Computer Science, Stony Brook University
sion@cs.stonybrook.edu

Summary. The networked and increasingly ubiquitous nature of today's data management services mandates assurances to detect and deter malicious or faulty behavior. This is particularly relevant for outsourced data frameworks in which clients place data management with specialized service providers. Clients are reluctant to place sensitive data under the control of a foreign party without assurances of confidentiality. Additionally, once outsourced, privacy and data access correctness (data integrity and query completeness) become paramount. Today's solutions are fundamentally insecure and vulnerable to illicit behavior, because they do not handle these dimensions.

In this chapter we will explore the state of the art in data outsourcing mechanisms providing strong security assurances of (1) *correctness*, (2) *confidentiality*, and (3) data access *privacy*.

There exists a strong relationship between such assurances; for example, the lack of access pattern privacy usually allows for statistical attacks compromising data confidentiality. Confidentiality can be achieved by data encryption. However, to be practical, outsourced data services should allow expressive client queries (e.g., relational joins with arbitrary predicates) without compromising confidentiality. This is a hard problem because decryption keys cannot be directly provided to potentially untrusted servers. Moreover, if the remote server cannot be fully trusted, protocol correctness become essential.

Here we will discuss query mechanisms targeting outsourced relational data that (i) ensure queries have been executed with integrity and completeness over their respective target data sets, (ii) allow queries to be executed with confidentiality over encrypted data, (iii) guarantee the privacy of client queries and data access patterns. We will then propose protocols that adapt to the existence of *trusted hardware* — so critical functionality can be delegated securely from clients to servers. We have successfully started exploring the feasibility of such solutions for providing assurances for query execution and the handling of binary predicate JOINs with full privacy in outsourced scenarios.

The total cost of ownership of data management infrastructure is 5–10 times greater than the hardware costs, and more data is produced and lives digitally every day. In the coming years, secure, robust, and efficient outsourced data management will be demanded by users. It is thus important to finally achieve outsourced data management a trustworthy solution, viable in both personal-level and large corporate settings.

1 Introduction

Today, sensitive data is being managed on remote servers maintained by third party outsourcing vendors. This is because the total cost of data management is 5–10 times higher than the initial acquisition costs [61]. In such an outsourced "database as a service" [72] model, *clients* outsource data management to a "database service provider" that provides online access mechanisms for querying and managing the hosted data sets.

This is advantageous and significantly more affordable for parties with limited abilities to manage large in-house data centers of potentially large resource footprints. By comparison, database service providers [1–6, 6–9, 11–15] – ranging from corporate-level services such as the IBM Data Center Outsourcing Services to personal level database hosting – have the advantage of expertize consolidation. More-over, they are likely to be able to offer the service much cheaper, with increased service availability (e.g. uptime) guarantees.

Notwithstanding these clear advantages, a data outsourcing paradigm faces significant challenges to widespread adoption, especially in an online, untrusted environment. Current privacy guarantees of such services are at best declarative and often subject customers to unreasonable fine-print clauses— e.g., allowing the server operator (and thus malicious attackers gaining access to its systems) to use customer behavior and content for commercial, profiling, or governmental surveillance purposes [52]. Clients are naturally reluctant to place sensitive data under the control of a foreign party without strong security assurances of *correctness*, *confidentiality*, and data access *privacy*. These assurances are essential for data outsourcing to become a sound and truly viable alternative to in-house data management. However, developing assurance mechanisms in such frameworks is challenging because the data is placed under the authority of an external party whose honest behavior is not guaranteed but rather needs to be ensured by this very solution.

In this chapter, we will explore the challenges of designing and implementing robust, efficient, and scalable relational data outsourcing mechanisms, with strong security assurances of *correctness*, *confidentiality*, and data access *privacy*. This is important because today's outsourced data services are fundamentally insecure and vulnerable to illicit behavior, as they do not handle all three dimensions consistently and there exists a strong relationship between such assurances: e.g., the lack of access pattern privacy usually allows for statistical attacks compromising data confidentiality. Even if privacy and confidentiality are in place, to be practical, outsourced data services should allow sufficiently expressive client queries (e.g., relational operators such as JOINs with arbitrary predicates) without compromising confidentiality. This

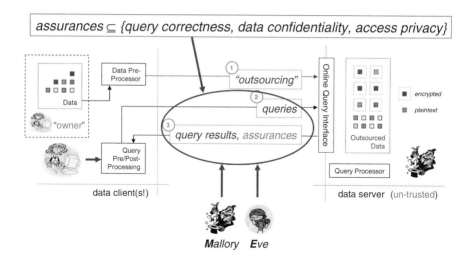

Fig. 1. Secure Data Outsourcing. Clients require assurances of correctness, confidentiality and access privacy.

is a hard problem because in most cases decryption keys cannot be directly provided to potentially untrusted database servers. Moreover, result completeness and data integrity (i.e., correctness) become essential. Therefore, solutions that do not address these dimensions are incomplete and insecure.

We will explore designs for outsourced relational data query mechanisms that (i) ensure queries have been executed with *integrity and completeness* over their respective target data sets, (ii) allow queries to be executed with *confidentiality* over encrypted data, and (iii) guarantee the *privacy* of client queries and data access patterns:

Correctness. Clients should be able to verify the integrity and completeness of any results the server returns. For example, when executing a JOIN query, they should be able to verify that the server returned *all* matching tuples.

Confidentiality. The data being stored on the server should not be decipherable either during transit between the client and the server, or at the server side, even in the case when the server is malicious.

Access Privacy. An intruder or a malicious server should not be able to perform statistical attacks by exploiting query patterns. For example, it should not be able to compromise data confidentiality by correlating known public information with frequently queried data items.

We will discuss how to design protocols that adapt to the existence of *trusted hardware* — so critical functionality can be delegated securely from clients to servers and increased assurance levels can be achieved more efficiently. Moreover, it is important to design for scalability to large data sets and high query throughputs. We note that client *authentication* and *authorization*, two important but orthogonal security dimensions, are extensively addressed in existing research, discussed in both this book and elsewhere [22, 27, 31, 33, 39, 68, 75, 79, 80, 88, 90, 102, 103, 105, 123]; therefore they and are not the main focus here. The assurances discussed here naturally complement these dimensions in providing increased end-to-end security.

2 Designing Secure Data Outsourcing Mechanisms.

2.1 Model

In our discourse, we will consider the following concise yet representative interaction model. Sensitive data is placed by a client on a database server managed by a *database service provider*. Later, the client or a third party will access the outsourced data through an online query interface exposed by the server. Network layer confidentiality is assured by mechanisms such as SSL/IPSec.

We will represent both the server and the client as interactive polynomial-time Turing Machines; we write CLI for the client and SERV for the server machine. A client can interact with the server and issue a sequence of update or processing queries $(Q_1, \ldots, Q_i)$. We call such a sequence of queries a *trace* $\mathcal{T}$. After executing a query Q, the client Turing Machine either outputs $\top$ or $\bot$, indicating whether the client accepts or rejects the server's response (denoted as $D_{\mathcal{T},Q}$); in the first case, the client believes that the server replied honestly. We write $\text{CLI}(\mathcal{T}, Q, D_{\mathcal{T},Q}) \in \{\top, \bot\}$ to denote the output of the client as a result of the server's execution of trace $\mathcal{T}$ and query Q yielding the result $D_{\mathcal{T},Q}$.

A server's response D is said to be *consistent* with both $\mathcal{T}$ and Q, if an honest server, after starting with an empty database and executing trace $\mathcal{T}$ honestly, would reply with D to the query Q. Two traces $\mathcal{T}$ and $\mathcal{T}'$ are called *similar* with respect to Q, written as $\mathcal{T} \approx_Q \mathcal{T}'$, if the query Q yields the same answer when queried after a trace $\mathcal{T}$ or $\mathcal{T}'$, i.e., $D_{\mathcal{T},Q} = D_{\mathcal{T}',Q}$.

The data server is considered to be un-trusted, potentially malicious, compromised or simply faulty. Given the possibility to get away undetected, it will attempt to compromise data confidentiality, infer data access patterns and return incorrect query results. In certain cases we will assume reasonable computational limits such as the inability to factor large numbers or find cryptographic hash collisions. We will not make any limiting assumptions on the DBMS. In particular we will accommodate both multi-processor and distributed query processing DBMS. We will collaborate with other researches to investigate how to accommodate non-relational data integration [17] but mention that this does not constitute the subject of this work.

The main performance constraint we are interested in is *maintaining the benefits of outsourcing*. In particular, for a majority of considered operations, if they are more efficient (than client processing) in the unsecured data outsourcing model – then they should still be more efficient in its secured version. We believe this constraint is essential, as it is important to identify solutions that validate in real life.

We note the existence of a large number of apparently more elegant cryptographic primitives that could be deployed that would fail this constraint. In particular, experimental results indicate that often, individual data-item operations on the server should *not* involve any expensive modular arithmetic such as exponentiation or multiplication. We believe it is imperative to resist the (largely impractical) trend to use homomorphisms in server side operations unless absolutely necessary – as this often simplifies protocols in theory but fails in practice due to extremely poor performance, beyond usability.

Throughout this chapter we reference active secure hardware such as the IBM 4758 PCI [18] and the newer IBM 4764 PCI-X [19] cryptographic coprocessors [21]. The benefits of deploying such hardware in un-trusted remote data processing contexts can be substantial, because the server can now run important parts of the secure client logic. Additionally, the secure hardware's proximity to the data will reduce communication overheads. Practical limitations of such devices however, make this a non-trivial task. To explain this, we briefly survey the processors.

The 4764 is a PowerPC - based board and runs embedded Linux. The 4758 is based on a Intel 486 architecture and is preloaded with a compact runtime environment that allows the loading of arbitrary external certified code. The CPUs can be custom programmed. Moreover, they (4758 models 2 and 23 and 4764 model 1) are compatible with the IBM Common Cryptographic Architecture (CCA) API [20]. The CCA implements common cryptographic services such as random number generation, key management, digital signatures, and encryption (DES/3DES,RSA). Both processors feature tamper resistant and responsive designs [56]. In the eventuality of illicit physical handling, the devices will simply destroy their internal state (in a process powered by internal long-term batteries) and then shutdown. Tamper resistant designs however, face major challenges in heat dissipation. This is one of the main reasons why secure coprocessors are significantly constrained in both computation ability and memory (main heat producer) capacity, often being orders of magnitude slower that the main CPUs in their host systems. For example, at the higher end, the 4758s feature 100Mhz CPUs and 8MB+ of RAM.

These constraints require careful consideration in achieving efficient protocols. Simplistic implementations of query processors *inside* the SCP J are bound to fail in practice simply due to lack of performance. The host CPUs will remain starkly underutilized and the entire cost-proposition of having fast (unsecured) main CPUs and an expensive and slow secured CPU will be defeated. Efficient designs are likely to access the secure hardware just sparsely, in critical portions, not synchronized with the main data flow. Therefore we will pursue designs that use such hardware only as a trusted-aide, while considering its limited I/O and computation throughput. For example, we believe efficient solutions can be achieved by balancing a storage-computation trade-off when main un-secured storage capacity is significantly cheaper than the purchase of additional secure computation elements. In such a model, additional secure metadata structures are constructed over the outsourced data, by both clients and SCPUs. These enable the unsecured main CPU to perform computation-intensive portions of secure queries without requiring trusted hardware support. The cost of constructing these additional *helper* data structures will be amortized over multiple query instances.

We use the term *encryption* to denote any semantically secure (IND-CPA) encryption mechanism [65], unless specified otherwise. We note that the mechanisms introduced here do not depend on any specific encryption mechanism. A *one-way cryptographic hash* $H()$ is a function with two important properties of interest: (i) it is computationally infeasible, for a given value V' to find a V such that $H(V) = V'$ (one-wayness), and (ii) changing even one bit of the hash input causes random changes to the output bits (i.e., roughly half of them change even if one bit of the input is flipped). Examples of potential candidates are the MD5 (fast) or the SHA class of hashes (more secure). *Bloom filters* [35] offer a compact statistical representation of a set of data items and fast set inclusion tests. They are *one-way*, in that, the "contained" set items cannot be enumerated easily. For more details see [65, 113].

2.2 Query Correctness

Informally, we will call a query mechanism *correct* if the server is bound to the sequence of update requests performed by the client. Either the server responds correctly to a query or its malicious behavior is immediately detected by the client:

Definition 1. *A query protocol is correct, if (except with* negligible *probability [65]) for all traces* $\mathcal{T}$ *and* $\mathcal{T}'$ *with* $\mathcal{T}' \not\approx_Q \mathcal{T}$, *any query* Q *and server response* $D_{\mathcal{T}',Q}$, *we have* $\text{CLI}(\mathcal{T}, Q, D_{\mathcal{T}',Q}) = \bot$.

In applied settings, *correctness* in database outsourcing can be often decomposed into two protocol properties, namely *data integrity* and *query completeness*. Data integrity guarantees that outsourced data sets are not tampered with by the server. Completeness ensures that queries are executed against their entire target data sets and that query results are not 'truncated" by servers.

Existing work focuses mostly on solutions for simple one-dimensional range queries, and variants thereof. In a publisher-subscriber model, Devanbu et al. deployed Merkle trees to authenticate data published at a third party's site [54], and then explored a general model for authenticating data structures [97,98]. Hard-to-forge verification objects are provided by publishers to prove the authenticity and provenance of query results.

In [104], mechanisms for efficient integrity and origin authentication for simple selection predicate query results are introduced. Different signature schemes (DSA, RSA, Merkle trees [100] and BGLS [37]) are explored as potential alternatives for data authentication primitives. Mykletun et al. [57] introduce *signature immutability* for aggregate signature schemes – the difficulty of computing new valid aggregated signatures from an existing set. Such a property is defeating a frequent querier that could eventually gather enough signatures data to answer other (un-posed) queries. The authors explore the applicability of signature-aggregation schemes for efficient data authentication and integrity of outsourced data. The considered query types are simple selection queries.

Similarly, in [94], digital signature and aggregation and chaining mechanisms are deployed to authenticate simple selection and projection operators. While these are important to consider, nevertheless, their expressiveness is limited. A more comprehensive, query-independent approach is desirable. Moreover, the use of strong cryptography renders this approach less useful. Often simply transferring the data to the client side will be faster.

In [108] *verification objects* VO are deployed to authenticate simple data retrieval in "edge computing" scenarios, where application logic and data is pushed to the edge of the network, with the aim of improving availability and scalability. Lack of trust in edge servers mandates validation for their results – achieved through verification objects.

In [77] Merkle tree and cryptographic hashing constructs are deployed to authenticate the result of simple range queries in a publishing scenario in which data owners delegate the role of satisfying user queries to a third-party un-trusted publisher. Additionally, in [95] virtually identical mechanisms are deployed in database outsourcing scenarios. [53] proposes an approach for signing XML documents allowing untrusted servers to answer certain types of path and selection queries.

Drawbacks of these efforts include the fact that they operate in an unrealistic "semi - honest" adversarial model. As a result, for example, data updates are not handled properly and the mechanisms are vulnerable to "universe split" attacks discussed in section 2.2.

Moreover, deploying expensive cryptographic operations (e.g., aggregate signatures, homomorphisms) has the potential to defeat the very purpose of outsourcing. Unless the actual query predicates are comparably compute intensive, often simply transferring the *entire* database and executing the query on the client will be faster. This is the case simply because securely server - processing a bit will be more expensive that the bit transfer over a network. A detailed argument can be found in [118] and in section 2.4. Maybe most importantly, existing solutions operate under un-realistic "cooperating" server assumptions. For example, they are unable to address data updates. More specifically, at the time of a client update, the server is assumed to *cooperate* in also updating corresponding server-side security checksums and signature chains. A truly malicious server however, can choose to ignore such requests and compromise future correctness assurances by omitting the updated data from the results (causing an "universe split"). This drastically limits the applicability of these mechanisms.

We started to explore query correctness by first considering the query expressiveness problem. Thus, in [114] we proposed a novel method for proofs of *actual* query execution in an outsourced database framework for *arbitrary* queries. The solution prevents a "lazy" or malicious server from incompletely (or not at all) executing queries submitted by clients. It is based on a mechanism of runtime query "proofs" in a challenge - response protocol. For each batch of client queries, the server is "challenged" to provide a *proof of query execution* that offers assurance that the queries were actually executed with completeness, over their entire target data set. This proof is then checked at the client site as a prerequisite to accepting the actual query results as accurate.

The execution proofs are built around an extension to the *ringer* concept first introduced in [67]. Its core strength derives from the non-"invertibility" of cryptographic hash functions. In other words, a successful fake execution proof requires the "inversion"[1] of a cryptographic hash or a lucky guess. The probability of the lucky guess is known, controllable and can be made arbitrary small. If, as part of the response to a query execution batch, the server includes a correct, verifiable query execution proof, the client is provided with a (tunable) high level of assurance that the queries in the batch were executed correctly. This constitutes a strong counter-incentive to "lazy", (e.g., cost-cutting) behavior.

We implemented a proof of concept and experimentally validated it in a real-world data mining application, proving its deployment feasibility. We analyzed the solution and show that its overheads are reasonable and far outweighed by the added security benefits. For example an assurance level of over 95% can be achieved with less than 25% execution time overhead.

Future Work: Powerful Adversary. Arbitrary Queries. Data Updates.

As the above query execution proofs only validate server-side *processing* but not also actual returned results, handling truly malicious adversaries will require different mechanisms. Moreover, while compute-intensive query scenarios are extremely relevant in data-mining applications, a more general solution should consider general types of queries with less computation load per data tuple (e.g., aggregates such as SUM, COUNT). Handling these is especially challenging due to the large size of the query space, the hardness of building general purpose authenticators and the hardness of predicting future query loads.

We believe future work should focus on two research directions: (1) the design of secure query (de)composition techniques coupled with specialized

---

[1] We informally define "inversion" of hash functions as finding at least one input that hashes to a target output.

query - specific metadata that enables correctness assurance protocols for a set of primitive queries, and (2) mechanisms for trusted hardware.

In (1), additional server-side storage will be traded for efficient correctness assurances. At outsourcing time, in a pre-processing phase, clients generate query and predicate - specific metadata that will be stored on the server, authenticated by minimal state information maintained by clients. For each considered primitive predicate and type of query (e.g., simple range query), its corresponding "correctness metadata" will allow the client (or a trusted proxy such as a secure CPU) to assess the correctness of individual results. We call such primitive queries for which correctness can be assessed, "correctness-assured".

It is important to build on existing work [57, 77, 94, 95, 104], to reduce the computational footprint on the server, and allow consistent handling of updates in the presence of a truly malicious server. For example, we believe incremental hashing paradigms can be deployed to persist client-side authentication information. This will allow a client to efficiently authenticate returned signature values, thus detecting any malicious behavior even after updates.

Another future work item will be to design techniques that decompose or rewrite complex queries into a subset of the primitive queries considered above. Consider the following simple, yet illustrative query listing all account holders with account rates less than the Federal Reserve's base rate on January 1st, 2006:

```
SELECT accounts.name FROM accounts WHERE accounts.rate <
(SELECT federalreserve.baserate FROM federalreserve
WHERE convert(char(10),federalreserve.date,101)='01/01/2006')
```

Its correctness can be efficiently assessed by requiring the server to prove correctness for the inner query first, followed by the outer query. Similar decompositions can be applied to any correctness-assured nested queries. Nevertheless, often such query decomposition or rewriting cannot be achieved with efficiency for arbitrary queries in fully unsecured environments. For example, it is not trivial to extend correctness - assured simple range predicates to even marginally more complex multi-dimensional range queries such as

```
SELECT X.a FROM X WHERE X.b > 10 AND X.c > 20
```

It is important to investigate composition mechanisms that allow the utilization of metadata ensuring correctness of either simple range predicate (e.g., X.b > 10 or X.c > 20), to guarantee correctness for the composite predicate.

To achieve correctness assurances for a larger class of queries we propose to consider mechanisms that leverage the presence of active secure hardware such as secure co-processors (SCPUs). Achieving efficiency however, is an extremely challenging task. Trivially deploying query processor functionality inside power - constrained SCPUs is simply not scalable in practice due to limited communication and computation throughputs. We believe protocols that combine the query decomposition approach in (1) with SCPU processing for required, yet unavailable correctness-assured primitive queries constitute a promising avenue of future research. As a result, SCPU processing will be minimal and amortized over multiple query instances.

As an example, in the above multi-dimensional range query, a trusted SCPU hosted by the server will instruct the main server CPU to execute and prove correctness for the first predicate (X.b > 10) and then evaluate the second predicate (X.c > 20) securely on the result. Heuristics could be deployed to evaluate which of the individual predicates would result in a smaller result set so as to minimize the SCPU computation. Optionally, the process will also generate associated metadata for the joint predicate and cache it on the server for future use, effectively amortizing the cost of this query over multiple instances.

Operating in an *unified client model* [54, 104] assumes the existence of a single client accessing the data store at any one time. In multi-threaded data-intensive application scenarios however, such a model is often of limited applicability. It is important to allow multiple client instances or even different parties to simultaneously access outsourced data sets.

This is challenging because allowing different parties to access the same data store may require the sharing of secrets among them. This is often not a scalable proposition, in particular considering different administrative domains. Moreover, data updates require special consideration in such a scenario due to what we call the *"universe split"* phenomenon. We explain this in the following.

In single - client settings, to efficiently handle incoming data updates, update-able metadata structures can be designed, e.g., leveraging such mechanisms as the incremental hashing paradigm of Bellare and Micciancio [26]. Recently we have demonstrated the feasibility of such methods in the framework of network data storage. In [117] outsourced documents were incrementally authenticated with efficient checksums allowing updates, document additions and removals in constant time.

However, when two clients simultaneously access the same data sets, a malicious server can chose to present to each client a customized version of the data universe, by keeping the other client's updates hidden from the current view. We believe other authors have encountered this issue in different settings, e.g., by Li et al. [91] in an un-trusted networked file system setting[2]. Naturally, if mutually aware of their accesses, the clients can use an external authenticated channel to exchange transactional state on each other's updates. This can occur either during their access, if simultaneous, or asynchronously otherwise. Periodically executing such exchanges will significantly decrease the probability of undetected illicit "universe split" server behavior. Over multiple transactions, undetected malicious behavior will become unsustainable.

In practice, such awareness and online interaction assumptions are not always acceptable, and often the only potential point of contact between clients

---

[2] In their work universe splitting would be the inverse of "fetch-consistency"

is the database server itself. One solution to this problem is to design alternative protocols that leverage the existence of active secure hardware such as secure co-processors (SCPU). The SCPU will authenticate clients securely and also persist transactional state, including a minimal amount of checksum information used to authenticate transaction chains of committed client updates. The unique vendor-provided SCPU public key and its associated trust chain provide an authenticated communication channel between the SCPU and database clients. The clients will use this channel to retrieve up to date transactional state at the initiation of each server interaction. This will defeat "universe split" attacks. Servers are unable to impersonate SCPUs without access to the secrets in its tamper-proof storage.

2.3 Data Confidentiality

Confidentiality constitutes another essential security dimension required in data outsourcing scenarios, especially when considering sensitive information. Potentially un-trusted servers should be able to process queries on encrypted data on behalf of clients without compromising confidentiality. To become practical, any such processing mechanism requires a certain level of query expressiveness. For example, allowing only simple data retrieval queries will often not be sufficient to justify the outsourcing of the data – the database would then be used as a passive data repository. We believe it is important to efficiently support complex queries such as joins and aggregates with confidentiality and correctness.

Hacigumus et al. [71] propose a method to execute SQL queries over partly obfuscated outsourced data. The data is divided into secret partitions and queries over the original data can be rewritten in terms of the resulting partition identifiers; the server can then partly perform queries directly. The information leaked to the server is claimed to be 1-out-of-s where s is the partition size. This balances a trade-off between client-side and server-side processing, as a function of the data segment size. At one extreme, privacy is completely compromised (small segment sizes) but client processing is minimal. At the other extreme, a high level of privacy can be attained at the expense of the client processing the queries in their entirety. Moreover, in [76] the authors explore optimal bucket sizes for certain range queries. Similarly, data partitioning is deployed in building "almost"-private indexes on attributes considered sensitive. An untrusted server is then able to execute "obfuscated range queries with minimal information leakage". An associated privacy-utility trade-off for the index is discussed. As detailed further in section 2.3 the main drawbacks of these solutions lies in their computational impracticality and inability to provide strong confidentiality.

One of the main drawbacks of such mechanisms is the fact that they leak information to the server, at a level corresponding to the granularity of the partitioning function. For example, if such partitioning is used in a range query, to execute rewritten queries at the partition level, the server will be required to precisely know the range of values that each partition contains. Naturally, increasing partition sizes tends to render this knowledge more fuzzy. This, however, requires additional client side work in pruning the (now) larger results (due to the larger partitions). Even if a single data tuple matches the query, its entire corresponding partition will be transferred to the client. On the other hand, reducing partition size will immediately reveal more information to the server, as the smaller number of items per partition and the knowledge of the covered range will allow it to determine more accurately what the likely values are for each tuple. Additionally, for more complex queries, particularly joins, due to the large segments, such methods can feature an communication overhead larger than the entire database, hardly a practical proposition.

Nevertheless, these efforts illustrate a trade-off between confidentiality and overheads: large partitions reveal less but require more computation on the client, small partitions reveal more but increase efficiency. Ultimately, however, unless partitions are very large (in which case the purpose of outsourcing is likely defeated by the additional overheads) true confidentiality cannot be achieved by such partitioning schemes. Statistical security needs to be replaced by efficient, yet stronger mechanisms. In the following we show how this can be achieved not only for range queries but also for more complex joins.

In ongoing work [42] we explore a low-overhead method for executing binary predicate joins with confidentiality on outsourced data. It handles *general* binary join predicates that satisfy certain properties: for any value in the considered data domain, the *number* of corresponding "matching" pair values (for which the predicate holds) is (i) finite, and (ii) the average of its expected value is upper bound. We call these predicates *expected finite match* (EFM) predicates.

Such predicates are extremely common and useful, including discrete data scenarios, such as ranges, inventory and company asset data-sets, forensics, genome and DNA data (e.g., fuzzy and exact Hamming distances), and health-care databases (e.g., bacteria to antibiotics matches). For illustration purposes let us consider the following discrete time – range join query that joins arrivals with departures within the same hour (e.g., in a train station):

```
SELECT * FROM arrivals,departures
WHERE departures.time - arrivals.time < 60
```

For any finite time granularity (e.g. minutes) the join predicate above is an EFM predicate (e.g., with an AEMS of 60). Performing such joins at the server side on encrypted data, is the main functionality desired here.

To analyze the *confidentiality assurances* of this solution we will consider here a server that is *curious*: given the possibility to get away undetected, it will attempt to compromise data confidentiality (e.g., in the process of query execution). Naturally, it should **not** be able to evaluate predicates (i) without the permission of the client, (ii) on two values of the same attribute, and (iii) on data not specified/allowed by the client – specifically, no inter-attribute transitivity should be possible. Additionally it should not be able to (iv) evaluate other predicates on "unlocked" data. This also means that no additional information should be leaked in the process of predicate evaluation. For example, allowing the evaluation of $p(x, y) := (|x - y| < 100)$, should not reveal $|x - y|$.

One solution relies on the use of predicate-specific metadata that clients place on the server together with the main data sets. This metadata does not reveal anything about the main data fields and stays in a "locked" state until its corresponding data is involved in a join. The client then provides "unlocking" information for the metadata and the server is able to perform *exactly* the considered query, without finding out any additional information. In the following we briefly outline this. For more details see [42].

Let N be a public security parameter, and K a symmetric (semantically secure) encryption key. For each column A, let $R_1^A \neq R_2^A$ be two random uniform values in $\{0,1\}^N$. In a client *pre-processing* phase, for each confidential data attribute A with elements a_i, $i = 1..n$, the client computes an obfuscation of a_i, $O(a_i) := H(a_i) \oplus R_1^A$. For all values $y \in P(a_i) := \{y|p(a_i, y) = true\}$, the client computes $H(y) \oplus R_2^A$. and stores it into a Bloom filter specific to a_i, $BF(a_i)$. It then outsources $\{E_K(a_i), O(a_i), BF(a_i)\}$ to the server. To allow a join of two columns A and B on the predicate p, the client sends the server the value $q_{AB} = R_2^A \oplus R_1^B$. For each element a_i in column A and b_j in column B, the server computes $T_{b \to a} := O(b_j) \oplus q_{AB} = H(b_j) \oplus R_2^A$. It then outputs all tuples $< E_K(a_i), E_K(b_j), \ldots >$ for which $BF(a_i)$ contains $T_{b \to a}$. The following can be shown:

Theorem 1. *The server cannot perform join operations on initially stored data.*

Theorem 2. *The server cannot perform transitive joins.*

Theorem 3. *Given a binary EFM predicate p, for any matching pair of values returned as a result of a join, $< x' = E_K(a_i), y' = E_K(b_j) >$, no additional information about a_i and b_j or their relationship can be inferred by the server, other than the fact that $p(a_i, b_j) = true$.*

The solution handles *data updates* naturally. For any new incoming data item, the client pre-processing can be executed per-item and its results simply forwarded to the server. Additionally, in the case of a multi-threaded server, multiple clients (sharing secrets and keys) can access the same data store simultaneously.

We note also that *multiple predicate evaluations* are also accommodated naturally. Confidentiality can be provided for the attributes involved in binary EFM predicates. In the following database schema, the association between patients and diseases is confidential but any other information is public and can be used in joins. To return a list of New York City patient names and their associated antibiotics (but not their disease) the server will access both confidential (disease) and non-confidential (name,zip-code) values. In the following, only the predicate $md()$ – associating antibiotics with diseases – will operate on confidential data:

```
SELECT patients.name,antibiotics.name FROM patients,antibiotics
WHERE md(patients.disease,antibiotics.name)
   AND patients.zipcode = 10128
```

This will be achieved (as discussed above) by encrypting the `patients.disease` attribute and generating metadata for the `antibiotics` relation (which contains a list of diseases that each antibiotic is recommended for).

Additional predicate instances and applications of this solution are explored in [42], including mechanisms for Hamming distance evaluations and DNA fuzzy match predicates. Moreover, we show that the computation overheads of the solution are small. In initial evaluations, throughputs of well beyond 0.5 million predicate evaluations per second can be accommodated.

Future Work: Arbitrary Predicates. Policies. Query Composability.
In future work, we believe it is important to pursue arbitrary query types and multi-assurance compositions. For example we would like to understand how to endow the above method with correctness assurances and data access privacy as discussed in sections 2.2, 2.4 respectively.

Moreover, it is important to analyze the applicability of the protocols for general types of predicates. We believe a recursive decomposition approach can be applied to handle multiple argument EFM predicates. Transformations from arbitrary predicates to a canonical EFM form should be explored. In a first stage this is easy to achieve by simply discretizing queries over continuous data domains. As this will introduce small errors in results (of a magnitude inverse proportional to the quantization), this process needs to be designed such that the errors will result only in the *addition* of a small, controllable, number of non-matching tuples. These will then be pruned by the client.

To fully leverage the potential offered by confidentiality assurances, it is important to investigate an integration with security policy frameworks [60, 111]. This will allow for more complex specifications over the space of data sets, access rights, confidentiality policies and principals. For example, such specifications could include relaxation of expensive DBMS - maintained access control for data sets that are already encrypted.

Exploring novel notions of confidential query "composability" in the presence of multiple confidential data sources and associated secrets (e.g., cryptographic keys) is another avenue of future research. We believe this can be achieved by deploying intra-server secure multi-party computation (SMC) protocols [55, 58, 59, 63, 78] mediated by secure hardware. The presence of secure hardware will result in more efficient, practical SMC. This will ultimately allow for multi-source confidential data integration.

2.4 Data Access Privacy

In existing protocols, even though data sets are stored in encrypted form on the server, the *client query access patterns* leak essential information about the data. A simple attack can correlate known public information with *hot* data items (i.e., with high access rates), effectively compromising their confidential nature. In competing business scenarios, such leaks can be extremely damaging, particularly due to their unpredictable nature.

This is why, to protect confidentiality, it is important to also provide assurances of access pattern privacy. No existing work has tackled this problem yet for relational frameworks. It is thus essential to explore query protocols that leak minimal information about the currently executing query. Access patterns to data tuples become less meaningful when access semantics are unknown to the server. For example the binary predicate join method proposed above does not require the server to know the actual join predicates. Achieving such goals for *arbitrary* relational queries will be a challenging proposition in today's query processors, potentially requiring fundamental changes in base query processing.

To achieve these goals we first turn to existing research. *Private Information Retrieval* (PIR) protocols were first proposed as a theoretical primitive for accessing individual items of outsourced data, while preventing servers to learn anything about the client's access patterns [47]. Chor et al. [48] proved that in information theoretic settings in which queries do not reveal any information about the accessed data items, a solution requires $\Omega(n)$ bits of communication. To avoid this overhead, they show that for multiple *non-colluding* databases holding replicated copies of the data, PIR schemes exist that require only sub-linear communication overheads. This multi-server assumption however, is rarely viable in practice.

In single-server settings, it is known that PIR requires a full transfer of the database [47, 49] for computationally unbounded servers. For bounded adversaries however, *computational* PIR (cPIR) mechanisms have been proposed [40, 41, 45, 86, 87, 93, 96, 122]. In such settings however, it is trivial to establish an $O(n)$ lower bound on server processing, mandating expensive trapdoor operations per bit, to achieve access privacy. This creates a significant privacy - efficiency trade-off between the required server computation cycles and the time to actually transfer the data and perform the query at the client site.

We explore this trade-off in [118] where we discuss single-server computational PIR *for the purpose of preserving client access patterns leakage.* We show that deployment of non-trivial single server private information retrieval protocols on real (Turing) hardware is orders of magnitude more time-consuming than trivially transferring the entire database to the client. The deployment of computational PIR in fact *increases* both overall execution time, and the probability of *forward* leakage, when the deployed present trapdoors become eventually vulnerable – e.g., today's access patterns will be revealed once factoring of today's values will become possible in the future.

We note that these results are beyond existing knowledge of mere "impracticality" under unfavorable assumptions. On real hardware, *no* existing non-trivial single server PIR protocol could have possibly had outperformed the trivial client-to-server transfer of records in the past, and is likely not to do so in the future either. Informally, this is due to the fact that it is more expensive to PIR-process one bit of information than to transfer it over a network.

PIR's aim is to simply transfer one single remote bit with privacy. We showed above that theoretical lower bounds prevent current cryptography to offer efficient solutions in practical settings. Arguably, for more complex query processing this will also be the case. Thus it is important to design practical solutions that have the potential to break the PIR computation-privacy trade-off. We believe a very promising avenue for further research relies on deploying secure hardware hosted by the server, allowing the delegation of client-logic in closer data proximity.

And because (as discussed above) trivial "run client "proxy" inside secure CPU" approaches are likely to be impractical – as typically such hardware is orders of magnitude slower than main CPUs – any solution needs to deploy SCPUs efficiently, to defeat statistical correlation attacks on data access patterns.

3 Related Work.

Extensive research has focused on various aspects of DBMS security, including access control techniques as well as general information security issues [29,31, 51,73,75,80,81,90,106,107,110,112], many of which are discussed elsewhere in this book. Additionally, increasing awareness of requirements for data storage security mechanisms and support can be found with DBMS vendors such as IBM [10] and Oracle [16].

3.1 Database as a Service

The paradigm of providing a database as a service recently emerged [72] as a viable alternative, likely due in no small part to the dramatically increasing availability of fast, cheap networks. Given the global, networked, possibly hostile nature of the operation environments, security assurances are paramount. **Data Sharing.** Statistical and *Hippocratic* databases aim to address the problem of allowing aggregate queries on confidential data (stored on *trusted* servers) without additional information leaks [24,25,50,51,89] to the queries. In [125] Zhang et al. discuss privacy in information sharing scenarios in a distributed multi-party context, where each party operates a private database. An leakage measure is defined for information sharing and several privacy multi-party protocols deploying commutative encryption are defined.

3.2 XML Sharing

In [30] Bertino et al. discuss a solution for access control to XML data. They deploy multi-key encryption such that only the appropriate parts of outsourced XML documents can be accessed by principals. In [32] (also in [28]), they propose a mechanism deploying watermarking [23,69,92,115,116,120] to protect ownership for outsourced medical data. Similarly, Carminati et al. ensure the confidentiality of XML in a distributed peer network by using access rights and encryption keys associated with XML nodes [43]. They enforce the authenticity and integrity of query answers using Merkle signatures [100]. This complicates outsourcing of new documents as new Merkle trees will need to be generated. To ensure query correctness, the server also stores encrypted query templates containing the structure of the original documents. This solution is insecure because it leaks decryption keys and content access patterns.

3.3 Secure Storage

Encrypted Storage. Blaze's CFS [34], TCFS [44], EFS [101], StegFS [99], and NCryptfs [124] are file systems that encrypt data before writing to stable storage. NCryptfs is implemented as a layered file system [74] and is capable of being used even over network file systems such as NFS. SFS [70] and BestCrypt [82] are device driver level encryption systems. Encryption file systems and device drivers protect the confidentiality of data, but do not allow for efficient queries, search, correctness, or access privacy assurances.
Integrity-Assured Storage. Tripwire [84,85] is a user level tool that verifies stored file integrity at scheduled intervals of time. File systems such as I^3FS [83], GFS [62], and Checksummed NCryptfs [119] perform online real-time integrity verification. Venti [109] is an archival storage system that performs integrity assurance on read-only data. SUNDR [91] is a network file system designed to store data securely on untrusted servers and allow clients to detect unauthorized accesses as long as they see each other's file modifications.

3.4 Searches on Encrypted Data

Song et al. [121] propose a scheme for performing simple keyword search on encrypted data in a scenario where a mobile, bandwidth-restricted user wishes to store data on an untrusted server. The scheme requires the user to split the data into fixed-size words and perform encryption and other transformations. Drawbacks of this scheme include fixing the size of words, the complexities of encryption and search, the inability of this approach to support access pattern privacy, or retrieval correctness. Eu-Jin Goh [64] proposes to associate indexes with documents stored on a server. A document's index is a Bloom filter [35] containing a codeword for each unique word in the document. Chang and Mitzenmacher [46] propose a similar approach, where the index associated with documents consists of a string of bits of length equal to the total number of words used (dictionary size). Boneh et al. [36] proposed an alternative for senders to encrypt e-mails with recipients' public keys, and store this email on untrusted mail servers. They present two search protocols: (1) a non-interactive search-able encryption scheme based on a variant of the Diffie-Hellman problem that uses bilinear maps on elliptic curves; and (2) a protocol using only trapdoor permutations, requiring a large number of public-private key pairs. Both protocols are computationally expensive. Golle et al. [66] extend the above idea to conjunctive keyword searches on encrypted data. They propose two solutions. (1) The server stores capabilities for conjunctive queries, with sizes linear in the total number of documents. They claim that a majority of the capabilities can be transferred offline to the server, under the assumption that the client knows beforehand its future conjunctive queries. (2) Doubling the size of the data stored by the server, which reduces the communication overheads between clients and servers significantly. The scheme requires users to specify the exact positions where the search matches have to occur, and hence is impractical. Brinkman et al. [38] deploy secret splitting of polynomial expressions to search in encrypted XML.

4 Acknowledgments

The author is supported partly by the NSF through awards CT CNS-0627554, CT CNS-0716608 and CRI CNS 0708025. The author also wishes to thank Motorola Labs, IBM Research, CEWIT, and the Stony Brook Office of the Vice President for Research.

References

1. Activehost.com Internet Services. Online at http://www.activehost.com.
2. Adhost.com MySQL Hosting. Online at http://www.adhost.com.
3. Alentus.com Database Hosting. Online at http://www.alentus.com.
4. Datapipe.com Managed Hosting Services. Online at http://www.datapipe.com.
5. Discountasp.net Microsoft SQL Hosting. Online at http://www.discountasp.net.
6. Gate.com Database Hosting Services. Online at http://www.gate.com.
7. Hostchart.com Web Hosting Resource Center. Online at http://www.hostchart.com.
8. Hostdepartment.com MySQL Database Hosting. Online at http://www.hostdepartment.com/mysqlwebhosting/.
9. IBM Data Center Outsourcing Services. Online at http://www-1.ibm.com/services/.
10. IBM Data Encryption for DB2. Online at http://www.ibm.com/software/data/db2.
11. Inetu.net Managed Database Hosting. Online at http://www.inetu.net.

12. Mercurytechnology.com Managed Services for Oracle Systems. Online at `http://www.mercurytechnology.com`.

13. Neospire.net Managed Hosting for Corporate E-business. Online at `http://www.neospire.net`.

14. Netnation.com Microsoft SQL Hosting. Online at `http://www.netnation.com`.

15. Opendb.com Web Database Hosting. Online at `http://www.opendb.com`.

16. Oracle: Database Encryption in Oracle 10g. Online at `http://www.oracle.com/database`.

17. The IBM WebSphere Information Integrator. Online at `http://www.ibm.com/software/data/integration`.

18. IBM 4758 PCI Cryptographic Coprocessor. Online at `http://www-03.ibm.com/security/cryptocards/pcicc/overview.shtml`, 2006.

19. IBM 4764 PCI-X Cryptographic Coprocessor (PCIXCC). Online at `http://www-03.ibm.com/security/cryptocards/pcixcc/overview.shtml`, 2006.

20. IBM Common Cryptographic Architecture (CCA) API. Online at `http://www-03.ibm.com/security/cryptocards//pcixcc/overcca.shtml`, 2006.

21. IBM Cryptographic Hardware. Online at `http://www-03.ibm.com/security/products/`, 2006.

22. Martin Abadi, Michael Burrows, Butler Lampson, and Gordon Plotkin. A calculus for access control in distributed systems. *ACM Trans. Program. Lang. Syst.*, 15(4):706–734, 1993.

23. Andre Adelsbach and Ahmad Sadeghi. Advanced techniques for dispute resolving and authorship proofs on digital works. In *Proceedings of SPIE Electronic Imaging*, 2003.

24. Rakesh Agrawal, Jerry Kiernan, Ramakrishnan Srikant, and Yirong Xu. Hippocratic databases. In *Proceedings of the International Conference on Very Large Databases VLDB*, pages 143–154, 2002.

25. Rakesh Agrawal and Ramakrishnan Srikant. Privacy-preserving data mining. In *Proceedings of the ACM SIGMOD*, pages 439–450, 2000.

26. M. Bellare and D. Micciancio. A new paradigm for collision-free hashing: Incrementality at reduced cost. In *Proceedings of EuroCrypt*, 1997.

27. Steven M. Bellovin. Spamming, phishing, authentication, and privacy. *Communications of the ACM*, 47(12):144, 2004.

28. E. Bertino. Data hiding and security in an object-oriented database system. In *Proceedings of the 8th IEEE International Conference on Data Engineering*, 1992.

29. Elisa Bertino, M. Braun, Silvana Castano, Elena Ferrari, and Marco Mesiti. Author-X: A Java-Based System for XML Data Protection. In *IFIP Workshop on Database Security*, pages 15–26, 2000.

30. Elisa Bertino, Barbara Carminati, and Elena Ferrari. A temporal key management scheme for secure broadcasting of xml documents. In *Proceedings of the 9th ACM conference on Computer and communications security*, pages 31–40, 2002.

31. Elisa Bertino, Sushil Jajodia, and Pierangela Samarati. A flexible authorization mechanism for relational data management systems. *ACM Transactions on Information Systems*, 17(2), 1999.

32. Elisa Bertino, Beng Chin Ooi, Yanjiang Yang, and Robert H. Deng. Privacy and ownership preserving of outsourced medical data. In *Proceedings of the International Conference on Data Engineering*, 2005.

33. Ray Bird, Inder Gopal, Amir Herzberg, Phil Janson, Shay Kutten, Refik Molva, and Moti Yung. The kryptoknight family of light-weight protocols for authentication and key distribution. *IEEE/ACM Trans. Netw.*, 3(1):31–41, 1995.

34. M. Blaze. A Cryptographic File System for Unix. In *Proceedings of the first ACM Conference on Computer and Communications Security*, pages 9–16, Fairfax, VA, 1993. ACM.

35. B. H. Bloom. Space/time trade-offs in hash coding with allowable errors. *Commun. ACM*, 13(7):422–426, 1970.

36. D. Boneh, G. Di Crescenzo, R. Ostrovsky, and G. Persiano. Public key encryption with keyword search. In *Proceedings of Eurocrypt 2004*, pages 506–522. LNCS 3027, 2004.

37. D. Boneh, C. Gentry, B. Lynn, and H. Shacham. Aggregate and verifiably encrypted signatures from bilinear maps. In *EuroCrypt*, 2003.

38. R. Brinkman, J. Doumen, and W. Jonker. Using secret sharing for searching in encrypted data. In *Secure Data Management*, 2004.

39. M. Burrows, M. Abadi, and R. Needham. A logic of authentication. In *SOSP '89: Proceedings of the twelfth ACM symposium on Operating systems principles*, pages 1–13, New York, NY, USA, 1989. ACM Press.

40. C. Cachin, S. Micali, and M. Stadler. Computationally private information retrieval with polylog communication. In *Proceedings of EUROCRYPT*, 1999.

41. C. Cachin, S. Micali, and M. Stadler. Private Information Retrieval with Polylogarithmic Communication. In *Proceedings of Eurocrypt*, pages 402–414. Springer-Verlag, 1999.

42. Bogdan Carbunar and Radu Sion. Arbitrary-Predicate Joins for Outsourced Data with Privacy Assurances, 2006. Stony Brook Network Security and Applied Cryptography Lab Tech Report 2006-07.

43. B. Carminati, E. Ferrari, and E. Bertino. Assuring security properties in third-party architectures. In *Proceedings of International Conference on Data Engineering (ICDE)*, 2005.

44. G. Cattaneo, L. Catuogno, A. Del Sorbo, and P. Persiano. The Design and Implementation of a Transparent Cryptographic Filesystem for UNIX. In *Proceedings of the Annual USENIX Technical Conference, FREENIX Track*, pages 245–252, Boston, MA, June 2001.

45. Y. Chang. Single-Database Private Information Retrieval with Logarithmic Communication. In *Proceedings of the 9th Australasian Conference on Information Security and Privacy ACISP*. Springer-Verlag, 2004.

46. Y. Chang and M. Mitzenmacher. Privacy preserving keyword searches on remote encrypted data. Cryptology ePrint Archive, Report 2004/051, 2004. http://eprint.iacr.org/.

47. B. Chor, O. Goldreich, E. Kushilevitz, and M. Sudan. Private information retrieval. In *IEEE Symposium on Foundations of Computer Science*, pages 41–50, 1995.

48. B. Chor, O. Goldreich, E. Kushilevitz, and M. Sudan. Private information retrieval. In *Proceedings of FOCS*. IEEE Computer Society, 1995.

49. Benny Chor, Eyal Kushilevitz, Oded Goldreich, and Madhu Sudan. Private information retrieval. *J. ACM*, 45(6):965–981, 1998.

50. Chris Clifton, Murat Kantarcioglu, AnHai Doan, Gunther Schadow, Jaideep Vaidya, Ahmed Elmagarmid, and Dan Suciu. Privacy-preserving data integration and sharing. In *The 9th ACM SIGMOD workshop on Research issues in data mining and knowledge discovery*, pages 19–26. ACM Press, 2004.

51. Chris Clifton and Don Marks. Security and privacy implications of data mining. In *Workshop on Data Mining and Knowledge Discovery*, pages 15–19, Montreal, Canada, 1996. Computer Sciences, University of British Columbia.

52. CNN. Feds seek Google records in porn probe. Online at http://www.cnn.com, January 2006.

53. Premkumar T. Devanbu, Michael Gertz, April Kwong, Chip Martel, G. Nuckolls, and Stuart G. Stubblebine. Flexible authentication of XML documents. In *ACM Conference on Computer and Communications Security*, pages 136–145, 2001.

54. Premkumar T. Devanbu, Michael Gertz, Chip Martel, and Stuart G. Stubblebine. Authentic third-party data publication. In *IFIP Workshop on Database Security*, pages 101–112, 2000.

55. W. Du and M. J. Atallah. Protocols for secure remote database access with approximate matching. In *Proceedings of the 1st ACM Workshop on Security and Privacy in E-Commerce*, 2000.

56. Joan G. Dyer, Mark Lindemann, Ronald Perez, Reiner Sailer, Leendert van Doorn, Sean W. Smith, and Steve Weingart. Building the ibm 4758 secure coprocessor. *Computer*, 34(10):57–66, 2001.

57. Einar Mykletun and Maithili Narasimha and Gene Tsudik. Signature Bouquets: Immutability for Aggregated/Condensed Signatures. In *Proceedings of the European Symposium on Research in Computer Security ESORICS*, pages 160–176, 2004.

58. Joan Feigenbaum, Yuval Ishai, Tal Malkin, Kobbi Nissim, Martin Strauss, and Rebecca N. Wright. Secure multiparty computation of approximations. In *ICALP '01: Proceedings of the 28th International Colloquium on Automata, Languages and Programming,*, pages 927–938, 2001.

59. M. Freedman, K. Nissim, and B. Pinkas. Efficient private matching and set intersection. In *In Advances in Cryptology EUROCRYPT*, pages 1–19, 2004.

60. Irini Fundulaki and Maarten Marx. Specifying access control policies for xml documents with xpath. In *The ACM Symposium on Access Control Models and Technologies*, pages 61–69. ACM Press, 2004.

61. Gartner, Inc. Server Storage and RAID Worldwide. Technical report, Gartner Group/Dataquest, 1999. www.gartner.com.

62. S. Ghemawat, H. Gobioff, and S. T. Leung. The Google File System. In *Proceedings of the 19th ACM Symposium on Operating Systems Principles (SOSP '03)*, pages 29–43, Bolton Landing, NY, October 2003. ACM SIGOPS.

63. Bart Goethals, Sven Laur, Helger Lipmaa, and Taneli Mielikinen. On private scalar product computation for privacy-preserving data mining. In *ICISC*, pages 104–120, 2004.

64. E. Goh. Secure indexes. Cryptology ePrint Archive, Report 2003/216, 2003. http://eprint.iacr.org/2003/216/.

65. O. Goldreich. *Foundations of Cryptography*. Cambridge University Press, 2001.

66. P. Golle, J. Staddon, and B. Waters. Secure conjunctive keyword search over encrypted data. In *Proceedings of ACNS*, pages 31–45. Springer-Verlag; Lecture Notes in Computer Science 3089, 2004.

67. Philippe Golle and Ilya Mironov. Uncheatable distributed computations. In *Proceedings of the 2001 Conference on Topics in Cryptology*, pages 425–440. Springer-Verlag, 2001.

68. Li Gong. Efficient network authentication protocols: lower bounds and optimal implementations. *Distrib. Comput.*, 9(3):131–145, 1995.

69. David Gross-Amblard. Query-preserving watermarking of relational databases and xml documents. In *Proceedings of the Nineteenth ACM SIGMOD-SIGACT-SIGART Symposium on Principles of Database Systems*, pages 191–201, New York, NY, USA, 2003. ACM Press.

70. P. C. Gutmann. Secure filesystem (SFS) for DOS/Windows. `www.cs.auckland.ac.nz/~pgut001/sfs/index.html`, 1994.

71. H. Hacigumus, B. Iyer, C. Li, and S. Mehrotra. Executing SQL over encrypted data in the database-service-provider model. In *Proceedings of the ACM SIGMOD international conference on Management of data*, pages 216–227. ACM Press, 2002.

72. H. Hacigumus, B. R. Iyer, and S. Mehrotra. Providing database as a service. In *IEEE International Conference on Data Engineering (ICDE)*, 2002.

73. J. Hale, J. Threet, and S. Shenoi. A framework for high assurance security of distributed objects, 1997.

74. J. S. Heidemann and G. J. Popek. File system development with stackable layers. *ACM Transactions on Computer Systems*, 12(1):58–89, February 1994.

75. E. Hildebrandt and G. Saake. User Authentication in Multidatabase Systems. In R. R. Wagner, editor, *Proceedings of the Ninth International Workshop on Database and Expert Systems Applications, August 26–28, 1998, Vienna, Austria*, pages 281–286, Los Alamitos, CA, 1998. IEEE Computer Society Press.

76. B. Hore, S. Mehrotra, and G. Tsudik. A privacy-preserving index for range queries. In *Proceedings of ACM SIGMOD*, 2004.

77. HweeHwa Pang and Arpit Jain and Krithi Ramamritham and Kian-Lee Tan. Verifying Completeness of Relational Query Results in Data Publishing. In *Proceedings of ACM SIGMOD*, 2005.

78. Piotr Indyk and David Woodruff. Private polylogarithmic approximations and efficient matching. In *Theory of Cryptography Conference*, 2006.

79. S. Jajodia, P. Samarati, and V. S. Subrahmanian. A Logical Language for Expressing Authorizations. In *IEEE Symposium on Security and Privacy*, pages 31–42, Oakland, CA, May 04-07 1997. IEEE Press.

80. S. Jajodia, P. Samarati, and V. S. Subrahmanian. A logical language for expressing authorizations. In *IEEE Symposium on Security and Privacy. Oakland, CA*, pages 31–42, 1997.

81. S. Jajodia, P. Samarati, V. S. Subrahmanian, and E. Bertino. A unified framework for enforcing multiple access control policies. In *SIGMOD*, 1997.

82. Jetico, Inc. BestCrypt software home page. `www.jetico.com`, 2002.

83. A. Kashyap, S. Patil, G. Sivathanu, and E. Zadok. I3FS: An In-Kernel Integrity Checker and Intrusion Detection File System. In *Proceedings of the 18th USENIX Large Installation System Administration Conference (LISA 2004)*, pages 69–79, Atlanta, GA, November 2004. USENIX Association.

84. G. Kim and E. Spafford. Experiences with Tripwire: Using Integrity Checkers for Intrusion Detection. In *Proceedings of the Usenix System Administration, Networking and Security (SANS III)*, 1994.

85. G. Kim and E. Spafford. The Design and Implementation of Tripwire: A File System Integrity Checker. In *Proceedings of the 2nd ACM Conference on Computer Commuications and Society (CCS)*, November 1994.

86. E. Kushilevitz and R. Ostrovsky. Replication is not needed: single database, computationally-private information retrieval. In *Proceedings of FOCS*. IEEE Computer Society, 1997.

87. E. Kushilevitz and R. Ostrovsky. One-way trapdoor permutations are sufficient for non-trivial single-server private information retrieval. In *Proceedings of EUROCRYPT*, 2000.

88. Butler Lampson, Martín Abadi, Michael Burrows, and Edward Wobber. Authentication in distributed systems: theory and practice. *ACM Trans. Comput. Syst.*, 10(4):265–310, 1992.

89. Kristen LeFevre, Rakesh Agrawal, Vuk Ercegovac, Raghu Ramakrishnan, Yirong Xu, and David J. DeWitt. Limiting disclosure in hippocratic databases. In *Proceedings of the International Conference on Very Large Databases VLDB*, pages 108–119, 2004.

90. Li, Feigenbaum, and Grosof. A logic-based knowledge representation for authorization with delegation. In *PCSFW: Proceedings of the 12th Computer Security Foundations Workshop*, 1999.

91. J. Li, M. Krohn, D. Mazières, and D. Shasha. Secure Untrusted Data Repository (SUNDR). In *Proceedings of the 6th Symposium on Operating Systems Design and Implementation (OSDI 2004)*, pages 121–136, San Francisco, CA, December 2004. ACM SIGOPS.

92. Yingjiu Li, Vipin Swarup, and Sushil Jajodia. A robust watermarking scheme for relational data. In *Proceedings of the Workshop on Information Technology and Systems (WITS)*, pages 195–200, 2003.

93. H. Lipmaa. An oblivious transfer protocol with log-squared communication. Cryptology ePrint Archive, 2004.

94. Maithili Narasimha and Gene Tsudik. DSAC: integrity for outsourced databases with signature aggregation and chaining. Technical report, 2005.

95. Maithili Narasimha and Gene Tsudik. Authentication of Outsourced Databases using Signature Aggregation and Chaining. In *Proceedings of DASFAA*, 2006.

96. E. Mann. Private access to distributed information. Master's thesis, Technion - Israel Institute of Technology, 1998.

97. C. Martel, G. Nuckolls, P. Devanbu, M. Gertz, A. Kwong, and S. Stubblebine. A general model for authenticated data structures. Technical report, 2001.

98. Charles Martel, Glen Nuckolls, Premkumar Devanbu, Michael Gertz, April Kwong, and Stuart G. Stubblebine. A general model for authenticated data structures. *Algorithmica*, 39(1):21–41, 2004.

99. A. D. McDonald and M. G. Kuhn. StegFS: A Steganographic File System for Linux. In *Information Hiding*, pages 462–477, 1999.

100. R. Merkle. Protocols for public key cryptosystems. In *IEEE Symposium on Research in Security and Privacy*, 1980.

101. Microsoft Research. Encrypting File System for Windows 2000. Technical report, Microsoft Corporation, July 1999. www.microsoft.com/windows2000/ techinfo/howitworks/security/encrypt.asp.

102. Fabian Monrose and Aviel D. Rubin. Authentication via keystroke dynamics. In *ACM Conference on Computer and Communications Security*, pages 48–56, 1997.

103. Fabian Monrose and Aviel D. Rubin. Keystroke dynamics as a biometric for authentication. *Future Generation Computer Systems*, 16(4):351–359, 2000.

104. E. Mykletun, M. Narasimha, and G. Tsudik. Authentication and integrity in outsourced databases. In *ISOC Symposium on Network and Distributed Systems Security NDSS*, 2004.

105. Roger M. Needham and Michael D. Schroeder. Using encryption for authentication in large networks of computers. *Commun. ACM*, 21(12):993–999, 1978.

106. M. Nyanchama and S. L. Osborn. Access rights administration in role-based security systems. In *Proceedings of the IFIP Workshop on Database Security*, pages 37–56, 1994.

107. Sylvia L. Osborn. Database security integration using role-based access control. In *Proceedings of the IFIP Workshop on Database Security*, pages 245–258, 2000.

108. HweeHwa Pang and Kian-Lee Tan. Authenticating query results in edge computing. In *ICDE '04: Proceedings of the 20th International Conference on Data Engineering*, page 560, Washington, DC, USA, 2004. IEEE Computer Society.

109. S. Quinlan and S. Dorward. Venti: a new approach to archival storage. In *Proceedings of the First USENIX Conference on File and Storage Technologies (FAST 2002)*, pages 89–101, Monterey, CA, January 2002. USENIX Association.

110. David Rasikan, Sang H. Son, and Ravi Mukkamala. Supporting security requirements in multilevel real-time databases, citeseer.nj.nec.com/david95supporting.html, 1995.

111. Shariq Rizvi, Alberto Mendelzon, S. Sudarshan, and Prasan Roy. Extending query rewriting techniques for fine-grained access control. In *Proceedings of the 2004 ACM SIGMOD international conference on Management of data*, pages 551–562. ACM Press, 2004.

112. Ravi S. Sandhu. On five definitions of data integrity. In *Proceedings of the IFIP Workshop on Database Security*, pages 257–267, 1993.

113. B. Schneier. *Applied Cryptography: Protocols, Algorithms and Source Code in C*. Wiley & Sons, 1996.

114. Radu Sion. Query execution assurance for outsourced databases. In *Proceedings of the Very Large Databases Conference VLDB*, 2005.

115. Radu Sion, Mikhail Atallah, and Sunil Prabhakar. Relational data rights protection through watermarking. *IEEE Transactions on Knowledge and Data Engineering TKDE*, 16(6), June 2004.

116. Radu Sion, Mikhail Atallah, and Sunil Prabhakar. Ownership proofs for categorical data. *IEEE Transactions on Knowledge and Data Engineering TKDE*, 2005.

117. Radu Sion and Bogdan Carbunar. Indexed Keyword Search with Privacy and Query Completeness, 2005. Stony Brook Network Security and Applied Cryptography Lab Tech Report 2005-07.

118. Radu Sion and Bogdan Carbunar. On the Computational Practicality of Private Information Retrieval. In *Proceedings of the Network and Distributed Systems Security Symposium*, 2007. Stony Brook Network Security and Applied Cryptography Lab Tech Report 2006-06.

119. G. Sivathanu, C. P. Wright, and E. Zadok. Enhancing File System Integrity Through Checksums. Technical Report FSL-04-04, Computer Science Department, Stony Brook University, May 2004. www.fsl.cs.sunysb.edu/docs/nc-checksum-tr/nc-checksum.pdf.

120. J. Smith and C. Dodge. Developments in steganography. In A. Pfitzmann, editor, *Proceedings of the third Int. Workshop on Information Hiding*, pages 77–87, Dresden, Germany, September 1999. Springer Verlag.

121. D. Xiaodong Song, D. Wagner, and A. Perrig. Practical techniques for searches on encrypted data. In *SP '00: Proceedings of the 2000 IEEE Symposium on Security and Privacy (S&P 2000)*. IEEE Computer Society, 2000.

122. J. Stern. A new and efficient all-or-nothing disclosure of secrets protocol. In *Proceedings of Asia Crypt*, pages 357–371, 1998.

123. Thomas Y. C. Woo and Simon S. Lam. Authentication for distributed systems. *Computer*, 25(1):39–52, 1992.

124. C. P. Wright, M. Martino, and E. Zadok. NCryptfs: A Secure and Convenient Cryptographic File System. In *Proceedings of the Annual USENIX Technical Conference*, pages 197–210, San Antonio, TX, June 2003. USENIX Association.

125. Nan Zhang and Wei Zhao. Distributed Privacy Preserving Information Sharing. In *Proceedings of the International Conference on Very Large Databases VLDB*, 2005.

7

Managing and Querying Encrypted Data

Bijit Hore[1], Sharad Mehrotra[1], and Hakan Hacıgümüş[2]

[1] Donald Bren School of Computer Science
University of California, Irvine {bhore,sharad}@ics.uci.edu
[2] IBM Almaden Research Center hakanh@acm.org

Summary. Encryption is a popular technique for ensuring confidentiality of sensitive data. While data encryption is able to enhance security greatly, it can impose substantial overhead on the performance of a system in terms of data management. Management of encrypted data needs to address several new issues like choice of the appropriate encryption algorithms, deciding the key management architecture and key distribution protocols, enabling efficient encrypted data storage and retrieval, developing techniques for querying and searching encrypted data, ensuring integrity of data etc. In this chapter, we give an overview of the state-of-the-art in some of these areas using the "Database As a Service" (DAS) as the prototype application. We especially concentrate on techniques for querying encrypted data and summarize the basic techniques proposed for SQL queries over encrypted relational data, keyword search over encrypted text data and XPath queries over encrypted XML data. We also provide brief summaries of works relating to other issues mentioned above and provide further references to the related literature.

1 Introduction

The proliferation of a new breed of data management applications that store and process data at remote service-providers' locations leads to a new concern, that of security. Especially when sensitive information is contained in the data, ensuring its confidentiality is a key concern in such a model. In a typical setting of the problem, the confidential portions of the data are stored at the remote location in an encrypted form at all times. For example, in a DAS setting data encryption becomes important when the client chooses to hide away certain contents from server-side entities. Two new challenges emerge: (i) Efficient encryption algorithms for relational data. (ii) Supporting queries on the encrypted relational data. While supporting a fully functional RDBMS over encrypted data is a challenge that remains far from being met, other specialized application domains fitting this model have emerged over the past few years. An application that has driven a lot of research in the cryptographic community is that of keyword-matching over encrypted text data. For instance, such schemes can be used to build a *secure email server* where the server stores emails of account holders in encrypted format and allows users to search emails based on keywords without having to decrypt the documents on the server. The returned emails could then be decrypted on the client machine. Another new breed of applications that have emerged more recently can be classified as "secure personal storage" applications [33, 35]. These applications let individuals store a variety of data on remote servers and access them over the network securely from any place. For instance pVault stores and manages an individual's passwords for his online accounts. It also provides support for high-entropy password generation and mobile access. DataVault is another application that makes a secure network drive available to individuals. It utilizes standard unsecure storage facilities on the web, for example Gmail for data storage and provides encryption and navigational support on them. It provides mobile, seamless access to one's files and directories from remote locations. While these specialized classes of applications are far less complex than supporting entire RDBMS functionalities as envisaged in the DAS framework, they share many common features with it. Some other pieces of work exists that have addressed similar issues for XML data [45, 34]. In case of XML, not only the data but structure is also important, which brings up new kinds of challenges.

In the remaining part, we will take DAS to be a prototypical application and present an overview of the various issues involved in managing encrypted data in its context. Depending on the nature of the underlying data (relational, text or XML) encryption techniques and query mechanisms vary. We will highlight these differences and provide short discussions as and when these issues are discussed in the subsequent sections.

In section 2, we start by describing the architecture of a typical DAS system and give an overview of the different approaches for querying encrypted data. Then we summarize the techniques proposed in [26] for query processing over encrypted relational data. In section 2.4 we outline one of the techniques proposed for searching encrypted text data and in section 2.5 we present a brief summary of one technique proposed to handle queries over encrypted XML data. In section 2.4 we give a brief overview of privacy analysis for the partitioning/generalization based secure index creation. In section 3 we describe various other issues that need to be addressed in encrypted data management, like choice of encryption function, key management, authenticity and integrity checking etc. Finally, in section 4 we conclude and point out some of the open problems that need to be addressed.

2 DAS - Storing & Querying Encrypted Data

The DAS model offers a variety of data management functionalities in the form of service to clients. It is an emerging alternative to in-house data management that overcomes many of the above listed challenges of traditional architectures.

A key concern in such an application is that of confidentiality of the sensitive information in the database residing on the server. In many cases, some or all of the data might be considered sensitive and needs to be protected from any kind of unauthorized access on the server side. "Unauthorized access" could refer to a break-in by hackers or an access by a legitimate, but malicious insider, for example a database administrator. A solution is to encrypt the sensitive portions or data where only the client has the access to the key. As a result one needs to address a variety of new issues related to encrypted data management, like support for encryption algorithms, key management, query execution on encrypted data etc. By far, non-trivial query processing on the encrypted data is the most challenging new problem that arises in such applications. A variety of techniques for executing queries over relational, textual and XML data have been developed in literature. We will summarize some of these techniques in this section. We start by describing the security model in a typical DAS application.

2.1 DAS setup & security model

In a typical setting of a DAS application, there is a data-owner, one or more clients of the data (can be same as the owner) and a server. The owner stores the data on the server and the clients may query/modify parts of this data remotely according to their access rights. In a typical setting, some portions of the data (e.g., some of the attributes of a relational table) are sensitive and need to be protected from the *adversaries*. An adversary is some individual/organization who has malicious intention and particularly the entity from whom the sensitive information needs to be kept hidden. In DAS applications, the client/owner side environment is assumed to be secure and trusted therefore the main threat is from server-side adversaries. In most models the service provider is assumed to carry out the data processing tasks honestly, and the main concern is regarding a malicious insider who might get access to the data (e.g., a malicious database administrator) and use this to harm the owner or the client. In such a scenario the sensitive portions of the data must remain encrypted at all times on the server and the secret encryption key should remain with the client. Data is only decrypted on the client side. This is called the *passive* or *curious* adversary model and is by far the most widely assumed security model. In another scenario, the server-side might be completely trustworthy, but in order to protect the data from becoming accessible to an outside hacker, the minimum requirement might be to keep the data encrypted on disk (since for the majority of the time, that is where the data resides).

Protecting against active adversaries is obviously more difficult and requires greater effort on the client's part to ensure proper functioning of the system. Authenticity and integrity checking becomes important in this scenario and we will describe some of the work in this area in section 3.

Now, we look at some of the approaches proposed in literature for querying encrypted relational data.

2.2 Querying Encrypted Relational Data

Consider a user Alice who outsources the database consisting of the following two relations:

```
EMP (eid, ename, salary, addr, did)
DEPARTMENT (did, dname, mgr)
```

The fields in the *EMP* table refer to the employee id, name of the employee, salary, address and the id of the department the employee works for. The fields in the *DEPARTMENT* table correspond to the department id, department name, and name of the manager of the department. In the DAS model, the above tables will be stored at the service provider. Since the service provider is untrusted, the relations must be stored in an encrypted form. Unless specified otherwise, we will assume that data is encrypted at the row level; that is, each row of each table is encrypted as a single unit. Thus, an encrypted relational representation consists of a set of encrypted records.

The client[3] may wish to execute SQL queries over the database. For instance, Alice may wish to pose following query to evaluate "total salary for employees who work for Bob". Such a query is expressed in SQL as follows:

```
SELECT  SUM(E.salary) FROM EMP as E, DEPARTMENT as D
WHERE E.did = D.did AND D.mgr = "Bob"
```

An approach Alice could use to evaluate such a query might be to request the server for the encrypted form of the *EMP* and *DEPARTMENT* tables. The client could then decrypt the tables and execute the query. This however, would defeat the purpose of database outsourcing, reducing it to essentially a remote secure storage. Instead, the goal in DAS is to process the queries directly at the server without the need to decrypt the data. Before we discuss techniques proposed in the literature we note that processing such queries requires mechanisms to support the following basic operators over encrypted data:

- **Comparison operators** such as $=, \neq, <, \leq, =, \geq, >$ These operators may compare attribute values of a given record with constants (e.g., *DEPARTMENT.sal* > 45000 as in selection queries) or with other attributes (e.g., *EMP.did* $=$ *DEPARTMENT.did* as in join conditions).
- **Arithmetic operators** such as addition, multiplication, division that perform simple arithmetic operations on attribute values associated with a set of records in one or more relations. Such operators are part of any SQL query that involves aggregation.

---

[3] Alice in this case since we have assumed that the client and the owner is the same entity.

The example query given above illustrates usage of both classes of operators. For instance, to execute the query, the *mgr* field of each record in the *DEPARTMENT* table has to be compared with "Bob". Furthermore, records in the *DEPARTMENT* table whose *mgr* is "Bob" have to be matched with records in *EMP* table based on the *did* attribute. Finally, the *salary* fields of the corresponding record that match the query conditions have to be added to result in the final answer.

The first challenge in supporting SQL queries over encrypted relational representation is to develop mechanisms to support comparison and arithmetic operations on encrypted data. The techniques developed in the literature can be classified into the following two categories.

Approaches based on new encryption techniques: These techniques can support either arithmetic and/or comparison operators directly on encrypted representation. Encryption techniques that support limited computation without decryption have been explored in cryptographic literature in the past. Amongst the first such technique is the *privacy homomorphism* (PH) developed in [39, 16] that supports basic arithmetic operations. While PH can be exploited to compute aggregation queries at the remote server (see [27] for details), it does not allow comparison and, as such, cannot be used as basis for designing techniques for relational query processing over encrypted data. In [4], the authors developed a data transformation technique that preserves the order in the original data. Such a transformation serves as an *order-preserving* encryption and can therefore support comparison operators. Techniques to implement relational operators such as selection, joins, sorting, grouping can be built on top of the order preserving encryption. The encryption mechanism, however, cannot support aggregation at the server. While new cryptographic approaches are interesting, one of the limitation of such approaches has been that they are safe only under limited situations where the adversary's knowledge is limited to the ciphertext representation of data. These techniques have either been shown to break under more general attacks (e.g., PH is not secure under chosen plaintext attack [6, 10]), or the security analysis under diverse types of attacks has not been performed.

Information-hiding based Approaches: Unlike in encryption based approaches, such techniques store additional auxiliary information along with encrypted data to facilitate evaluation of comparison and/or arithmetic operations at the server. Such auxiliary information, stored in the form of indices (which we refer to as *secure indices*) may reveal partial information about the data to the server. Secure indices are designed carefully exploiting information hiding mechanisms (developed in the context of statistical disclosure control) [48, 47, 1] to limit the amount of information disclosure. The basic techniques used for disclosure control are the following [47, 1]:

1. **Perturbation:** For a numeric attribute of a record, add a random value (chosen from some distribution, like normal with mean 0 and standard deviation σ) to the true value.

2. **Generalization:** Replace a numeric or categorical value by a more general value. For numeric values, it could be a range that covers the original value and for categorical data, this may be a more generic class, e.g., an ancestor node in a taxonomy tree.

3. **Swapping:** Take two different records in the data set and swap the values of a specific attribute (say, the salary value is swapped between the records corresponding to two individuals).

Of all the disclosure-control methods, the one that has been primarily utilized to realize DAS functionalities is that of generalization. The nature of disclosure in information hiding based schemes is different from that in cryptographic schemes. In the latter, the disclosure risk is inversely proportional to the difficulty of breaking the encryption scheme and if broken, it means there is complete disclosure of the plaintext values. In contrast, the information disclosure in information hiding approaches could be partial or probabilistic in nature. That is, there could be a non-negligible probability of disclosure of a sensitive value given the transformed data, e.g., the bucket identity might give a clue regarding the actual value of the sensitive attribute.

In this section, we will primarily concentrate on the information hiding based approach and show how it has been utilized to support SQL queries. As will be clear, information hiding approaches can be used to support comparison operators on the server and can hence be the basis for implementing SPJ (select-project-join) queries. They can also support sorting and grouping operators. Such techniques, however, cannot support aggregation at the server. A few papers [27, 24] have combined an information hiding approach with PH to support both server-side aggregation as well as SPJ queries. Of course, with PH being used for aggregation, these techniques become vulnerable to diverse types of attacks. In the remainder of the section, we will concentrate on how information hiding techniques are used to support SPJ queries. We will use the query processing architecture proposed in [22, 26] to explain the approach.

Query Processing Architecture for DAS [26]

Figure 1 illustrates the control flow for queries in DAS where information hiding technique is used to represent data at the server. The figure illustrates the three primary entities of the DAS model: *user*, *client* and *server*. The client stores the data at the server which is hosted by the service provider and this is known as the *server-side*. The data is stored in an encrypted format at the server-side at all times for security purposes. The encrypted database is augmented with additional information (secure indexes) that allows certain amount of query processing to occur at the server without jeopardizing data privacy. The client also maintains *metadata* for translating user queries to the appropriate representation on the server, and performs post-processing on server-query results. Based on the auxiliary information stored, the original

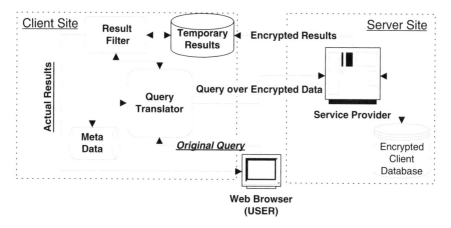

Fig. 1. Query Processing in DAS

query over un-encrypted relations are broken into (1) a server-query over encrypted relations which run on the server, and (2) a client-query which runs on the client and post-processes the results returned after executing the server-query. We achieve this goal by developing an algebraic framework for query rewriting over encrypted representation.

2.3 Relational Encryption and Storage Model

For each relation

$$R(A_1, A_2, \ldots, A_n)$$

one stores on the server an encrypted relation:

$$R^S(etuple, A_1^S, A_2^S, \ldots, A_n^S)$$

where the attribute *etuple* stores an encrypted string that corresponds to a tuple in relation R. Each attribute A_i^S corresponds to the index for the attribute A_i and is used for query processing at the server. For example, consider a relation *emp* below that stores information about employees.

eid	ename	salary	addr	did
23	Tom	70K	Maple	40
860	Mary	60K	Main	80
320	John	50K	River	50
875	Jerry	55K	Hopewell	110

The *emp* table is mapped to a corresponding table at the server:

$$emp^S(etuple, eid^S, ename^S, salary^S, addr^S, did^S)$$

It is only necessary to create an index for attributes involved in search and join predicates. Without loss of generality, one can assume that an index is created over each attribute of the relation.

Partition Functions: To explain what is stored in attribute A_i^S of R^S for each attribute A_i of R the following notations are useful. The domain of values $(\mathcal{D}_i)$ of attribute $R.A_i$ are first mapped into partitions $\{p_1, \ldots, p_k\}$, such that these partitions taken together cover the whole domain. The function *partition* is defined as follows:

$$partition(R.A_i) = \{p_1, p_2, \ldots, p_k\}$$

As an example, consider the attribute *eid* of the *emp* table above. Suppose the values of domain of this attribute lie in the range $[0, 1000]$. Assume that the whole range is divided into 5 partitions, represented as:

$$partition(emp.eid) = \{[0, 200], (200, 400], (400, 600], (600, 800], (800, 1000]\}$$

Different attributes may be partitioned using different partition functions, or they might be partitioned together using a multidimensional model. The partition of attribute A_i corresponds to a splitting of its domain into a set of buckets. The strategy used to split the domain into a set of buckets has profound implications on both the efficiency of the resulting query processing as well as on the disclosure risk of sensitive information to the server. For now, to explain the query processing strategy, we will make a simplifying assumption that the bucketization of the domain is based on the equi-width[4] partitioning (though the strategy developed will work for any partitioning of the domain). We will revisit the efficiency and disclosure risks in the following subsections.

Identification Functions: An identification function called *ident* assigns a random, unique identifier $ident_{R.A_i}(p_j)$ to each partition p_j of attribute A_i. Figure 2 shows the identifiers assigned to the 5 partitions of the attribute *emp.eid*. For instance, $ident_{emp.eid}([0, 200]) = 2$, and $ident_{emp.eid}((800, 1000]) = 4$.

Fig. 2. Partition and identification functions of *emp.eid*

Mapping Functions: Given the above partition and identification functions, a mapping function $Map_{R.A_i}$ maps a value v in the domain of attribute A_i to the identifier of the partition to which v belongs: $Map_{R.A_i}(v) = ident_{R.A_i}(p_j)$, where p_j is the partition that contains v. Later we describe a more general approach where a value might be assigned to multiple buckets [30] (probabilistically). This can be shown to achieve a greater degree of security than the

---

[4] where the domain of each bucket has the same width

more rigid case where partitions are non-overlapping. We describe the work in [30] later in this section. The mapping information is stored on the client to enable query translation (i.e., from plaintext queries to server-side queries). More details about query translation can be found in [21, 26].

Storing Encrypted Data: For each tuple $t = \langle a_1, a_2, \ldots, a_n \rangle$ in R, the relation R^S stores a tuple:

$$\langle encrypt(\{a_1, a_2, \ldots, a_n\}), Map_{R.A_1}(a_1), Map_{R.A_2}(a_2), \ldots, Map_{R.A_n}(a_n)\rangle$$

where *encrypt* is the function used to encrypt a tuple of the relation. For instance, the following is the encrypted relation emp^S stored on the server:

etuple	eid^S	$ename^S$	$salary^S$	$addr^S$	did^S
1100110011110010...	2	19	81	18	2
1000000000011101...	4	31	59	41	4
1111101000010001...	7	7	7	22	2
1010101010111110...	4	71	49	22	4

The first column *etuple* contains the string corresponding to the encrypted tuples in *emp*. For instance, the first tuple is encrypted to "1100110011110..." that is equal to $encrypt(23, Tom, 70K, Maple, 40)$. The second is encrypted to "1000000000011101..." equal to $encrypt(860, Mary, 60K, Main, 80)$. The encryption function is treated as a black box and any block cipher technique such as AES, Blowfish, DES etc., can be used to encrypt the tuples. We discuss some of the issues related to choice of encryption function in the next section. The second column corresponds to the index on the employee ids. For example, value for attribute *eid* in the first tuple is 23, and its corresponding partition is $[0, 200]$. Since this partition is identified to 2, we store the value "2" as the identifier of the *eid* for this tuple.

Decryption Functions: Given the operator E that maps a relation to its encrypted representation, its inverse operator D maps the encrypted representation to its corresponding decrypted representation. That is, $D(R^S) = R$. In the example above, $D(emp^S) = emp$. The D operator may also be applied on query expressions. A query expression consists of multiple tables related by arbitrary relational operators (e.g., joins, selections, etc). Decryption will regenerate the whole record.

Mapping Conditions

To translate specific query conditions in operations (such as selections and joins) to corresponding conditions over the server-side representation, a translation function called Map_{cond} is used. These conditions help translate relational operators for server-side implementation, and how query trees are translated. For each relation, the server-side stores the encrypted tuples, along with the attribute indices determined by their mapping functions. The client stores the meta data about the specific indices, such as the information about the partitioning of attributes, the mapping functions, etc. The client utilizes this information to translate a given query Q to its server-side representation Q^S, which is then executed by the server. More details can be found in [26].

Translating Relational Operators

Now let us give an idea of how relational operators are implemented in [26]. We illustrate the implementation of the selection and join operators in the proposed architecture. The strategy is to partition the computation of the operators across the client and the server such that a superset of answers is generated by the operator using the attribute indices stored at the server. This set is then filtered at the client after decryption to generate the true results. The goal is to minimize the work done at the client (as much as possible). We use R and T to denote two relations, and use the operator notations in [17].

The Selection Operator (σ): Consider a selection operation $\sigma_C(R)$ on a relation R, where C is a condition specified on one or more of the attributes $A_1, A_2, \ldots, A_n$ of R. A straightforward implementation of such an operator is to transmit the relation R^S from the server to the client. Then the client decrypts the result using the D operator, and implements the selection. This strategy, however, pushes the entire work of implementing the selection to the client. In addition, the entire encrypted relation needs to be transmitted from the server to the client. An alternative mechanism is to partially compute the selection operator at the server using the indices associated with the attributes in C, and push the results to the client. The client decrypts the results and filters out tuples that do not satisfy C. Specifically, the operator can be rewritten as follows:

$$\sigma_C(R) = \sigma_C\left(D(\sigma^S_{Map_{cond}(C)}(R^S))\right)$$

Note that the σ operator that executes at the server is adorned with a superscript "S". All non-adorned operators execute at the client. The decryption operator D will only keep the attribute *etuple* of R^S, and drop all the other A_i^S attributes. We explain the above implementation using an example $\sigma_{eid<395 \wedge did=140}(emp)$. Based on the definition of $Map_{cond}(C)$ discussed in the previous section, the above selection operation will be translated into

$$\sigma_C\left(D(\sigma^S_{C'}(emp^S))\right)$$

where the condition C' on the server is:

$$C' = Map_{cond}(C) = \left(eid^S \in [2,7] \wedge did^S = 4\right)$$

The Join Operator ($\bowtie$): Consider a join operation $R \overset{\bowtie}{C} S$. The join condition C could be either an equality condition (in which case the join corresponds to an equijoin), or could be a more general condition (resulting in theta-joins). The above join operation can be implemented as follows:

$$R \stackrel{\bowtie}{C} T = \sigma_C\Big(D\big(R^S \stackrel{\bowtie^S}{Map_{cond}(C)} T^S\big)\Big)$$

As before, the S adornment on the join operator denotes the fact that the join is to be executed at the server. For instance, join operation

$$emp \stackrel{\bowtie}{emp.did=mgr.did} mgr$$

is translated to:

$$\sigma_C\Big(D\big(emp^S \stackrel{\bowtie^S}{C'} mgr^S\big)\Big)$$

where the condition C' on the server is condition C_1 defined in Section 2.3.

Now we show how the above operators are used to rewrite SQL queries for the purpose of splitting the query computation across the client and the server.

Query Execution

Given a query Q, the goal is to split the computation of Q across the server and the client. The server will use the implementation of the relational operators discussed in the previous subsection to compute "as much of the query as possible", relegating the remainder of the computation to the client. Query processing and optimization have been extensively studied in database research [20, 12, 41]. The objective is to come up with the "best" query plan for Q that minimizes the amount of work to be done at the client site. In this setting, the cost of a query consists of many components – the I/O and CPU cost of evaluating the query at the server, the network transmission cost, and the I/O and CPU cost at the client. As an example, consider the following query over the emp table than retrieves employees whose salary is greater that the average salary of employees in the department identified by $did = 1$.

```
SELECT emp.name FROM emp
WHERE  emp.salary > (SELECT AVG(salary)
FROM emp WHERE did = 1);
```

The corresponding query tree and some of the evaluation strategies are illustrated in Figures 3 to 6. The first strategy (Figure 4) is to simply transmit the emp table to the client, which evaluates the query. An alternative strategy (Figure 5) is to compute part of the inner query at the server, which selects (as many as possible) tuples corresponding to $Map_{cond}(did = 1)$. The server sends to the client the encrypted version of the emp table, i.e., emp^S, along with the encrypted representation of the set of tuples that satisfy the inner query. The client decrypts the tuples to evaluate the remainder of the query. Yet another possibility (Figure 6) is to evaluate the inner query at the

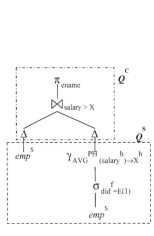

Fig. 3. Original query tree

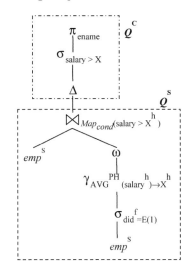

Fig. 4. Replacing encrypted relations

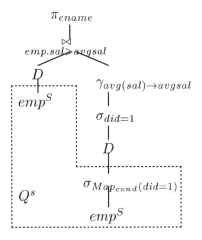

Fig. 5. Doing selection at server

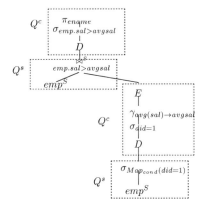

Fig. 6. Multiple interactions between client and server

server. That is, select the tuples corresponding to the employees that work in department $did = 1$. The results are shipped to the client, which decrypts the tuples and computes average salary. The average salary is encrypted by the client and shipped back to the server, which then computes the join at the server. Finally, the results are decrypted at the client.

Supporting Aggregation Operators in Queries: The various query translation techniques discussed above are designed explicitly for relational operators that perform comparisons. While information hiding techniques work for relational operators, they do not work for arithmetic operators such as aggregation. Notice that in the previous query there is an aggregation but that aggregation is done at the client side after decryption. If aggregation is to be performed at the server side, the information hiding approach has to be augmented with an encryption approach that supports arithmetic operations on encrypted representation. [27] illustrates how *privacy homomorphisms* (PH) [39, 16] can be combined with the basic approach described above for this purpose. Additional complexities arise since the information hiding technique does not exactly identify the target group to be aggregated (i.e., the server side results typically contain false positives). The paper develops algebraic manipulation techniques to separate an aggregation group into two subsets a set that *certainly* qualifies the conditions specified in the query, and a set that *may or may not* satisfy the selection predicates of the query (i.e., could contain false positives). The first set can be directly aggregated at the server using PH while the tuples belonging to the second category will need to be transmitted to the client side to determine if they indeed satisfy the query conditions.

Query Optimization in DAS: As in traditional relational query evaluation, in DAS multiple equivalent realizations for a given query are possible. This naturally raises the challenge of query optimization. In [24], query optimization in DAS is formulated as a cost-based optimization problem by introducing new query processing functions and defining new query transformation rules. The intuition is to define transfer of tuples from server to the client and decryption at the client as operators in the query tree. Given different hardware constraints and software capabilities at the client and the server different cost measures are applied to the client-side and server-side computations. A novel query plan enumeration algorithm is developed that identifies the least cost plan.

Now, having given a summary of the various techniques for handling encrypted relational data we move onto encryption of text data.

2.4 Keyword search on encrypted text data

In this section we discuss approaches proposed in the literature to support keyword based retrieval of text documents. The majority of the techniques proposed in literature are cryptographic in nature. Let Alice be the data owner who has a collection of text documents $D = \{D_1, \ldots, D_n\}$. A document D_i is modelled as a set of keywords $D_i = \{W_1^{D_i}, \ldots, W_{n_i}^{D_i}\}$, each word $w \in \mathcal{W}$, and $(\mathcal{W})$ is the set of all possible keywords. Alice stores her document collection at a service provider. Since the service provider is not trusted, documents are stored encrypted. Each document is encrypted at the word level as follows: Each document is divided up into equal length "words". Typically each such word corresponds to an English language word where extra padding (with '0' and '1' bits) are added to make all words equal in length. Periodically Alice may pose a query to the server to retrieve a subset of documents. The query itself is a set of keywords and the answer corresponds to the set of documents that contain all the keywords in the query. More formally, the answer to a query q is given by:

$$Ans(q) = \{D_i \in D | \forall k_j \in q, k_j \in D_i\}$$

The goal is to design techniques to retrieve answers while not revealing any information beyond the presence (or absence) of the keywords (of the query) in each document.

A few different variations of the basic keyword-search problem have been studied over the past years [8, 18, 44, 11, 19, 7, 46]. The authors in [44, 11] study the basic problem where a private-key based encryption scheme is used to design a matching technique on encrypted data that can search for any word in the document. Authors in [8] provide a safe public-key based scheme to carry out "non-interactive" search on data encrypted using user's public-key for a select set of words. [18] proposes a document indexing approach using bloom filters that speeds up the keyword search algorithm but could result in some false-positive retrievals. The work in [19, 7] propose secure schemes for conjunctive keyword search where the search term might contain the conjunction of two or more keywords. The goal here again is to avoid any leakage of information over and above the fact that the retrieved set of documents contain all the words specified in the query.

In this section, we describe a private-key based approach which is motivated by [44] and was amongst the first published solutions to the problem of searching over encrypted text data. The approach described incurs significant overhead, requiring $O(n)$ cryptographic operations per document where n is the number of words in the document.

Private-Key based Search Scheme on Encrypted Text Data

Consider a data owner Alice who wishes to store a collection of documents with Bob (the service provider). Alice encrypts each document D prior to storing it with Bob. In addition, Alice creates a secure index, $I(D)$, which is stored at the service provider that will help her perform keyword search. The secure index is such that it reveals no information about its content to the adversary. However, it allows the adversary to test for presence or absence of keywords using a *trapdoor* associated with the keyword where a trapdoor is generated with a secret key that resides with the owner. A user wishing to search for documents containing word w, generates a trapdoor for w which can then be used by the adversary to retrieve relevant documents.

The secure index is created over the keywords in D as follows. Let document D consist of the sequence of words $w_1, \ldots, w_l$. The index is created by computing the bitwise XOR (denoted by the symbol $\oplus$) of the clear-text with a sequence of pseudo-random bits that Alice generates using a stream cipher. Alice first generates a sequence of pseudo-random values $s_1, \ldots, s_l$ using a stream cipher, where each s_i is $n - m$ bit long. For each pseudo-random string s_i, Alice computes a pseudo-random function $F_{k_c}(s_i)$ seeded on key k_c which generates a random m-bit sequence[5]. Using the result of $F_{k_c}(s_i)$, Alice computes a n-bit sequence $t_i :=< s_i, F_{k_c}(s_i) >$, where $< a, b >$ denotes concatenation of the string a and b). Now to encrypt the n-bit word w_i, Alice computes the XOR of w_i with t_i, i.e., ciphertext $c_i := w_i \oplus t_i$. Since, only Alice generates the pseudo-random stream $t_1, \ldots, t_l$ so no one else can decrypt c_i.

Given the above representation of text document, the search mechanism works as follows. When Alice needs to search for files that contain a word w, she transmits w and the key k_c to the server. The server (Bob) searches for w in the index files associated with documents by checking whether $c_i \oplus w$ is of the form $< s, F_{k_c}(s) >$. The server returns to Alice documents that contain the keyword w which can then be decrypted by Alice.

The scheme described above provides secrecy if the pseudo-random function F, the stream cipher used to generate s_i, and the encryption of the document D are secure(that is, the value t_i are indistinguishable from truly random bits for any computationally bounded adversary). Essentially, the adversary cannot learn content of the documents simply based on ciphertext representation.

While the approach described above is secure, it has a fundamental limitation that the adversary learns the keyword w_i that the client searches for. The search strategy allows the adversary to learn which documents contain which keywords over time using such query logs. Furthermore, the adversary can launch attacks by searching for words on his own without explicit authorization by the user thereby learning document content.

A simple strategy to prevent server from knowing the exact search word is to pre-encrypt each word w of the clear text separately using a deterministic encryption algorithm E_{k_p}, where the key k_p is a private key which is kept hidden from the adversary. After this pre-encryption phase, the user has a sequence of E-encrypted words $x_1, \ldots, x_l$. Now he post-encrypts that sequence using the stream cipher construction as before to obtain $c_i := x_i \oplus t_i$, where $x_i = E_{k_p}(w_i)$ and $t_i =< s_i, F_{k_c}(x_i) >$. During search, the client, instead of revealing the keyword to be searched, Computes $E_{k_p}(w_i)$ with the server.

The proposed scheme is secure and ensures that the adversary does not learn document content from query logs. The scheme is formalized below.

---

[5] **Pseudo-random functions:** A pseudo-random function denoted as $F : K_F \times X \to Y$, where K_F is the set of keys, X denotes the set $\{0, 1\}^n$ and Y denotes the set $\{0, 1\}^m$. Intuitively, a pseudo-random function is computationally indistinguishable from a random function - given pairs $(x_i, f(x_1, k)), \ldots, (x_m, f(x_m, k))$, an adversary cannot predict $f(x_{m+1}, k)$ for any x_{m+1}. In other words, F takes a key $k \in K_F$ the set of keys, a n bit sequence $x \in X$ where X is the set $\{0, 1\}^n$ and returns a m bit sequence $y \in Y$ where Y is the set $\{0, 1\}^m$.

- k_p: Denotes the private-key of the user. $k_p \in \{0, 1\}^s$ which is kept a secret by the user.
- k_c: Denotes a key called the *collection key* of the user. $k_c \in \{0, 1\}^s$ and is publicly known
- **Pseudo-Random Function:** $F : \{0, 1\}^s \times \{0, 1\}^{n-m} \rightarrow \{0, 1\}^m$, is a pseudo-random function that takes a $n - m$ bit string, a s-bit key and maps it to a random m-bit string. F is publicly known.
- **Trapdoor function**: Let T denote a *trapdoor* function which takes as input, a private-key k_p and a word w and outputs the trapdoor for the word w, i.e., $T(k_p, w) = E_{k_p}(w)$ where E is a deterministic encryption function. For a given document, we denote the trapdoor for the ith word by t_i.
- **BuildIndex(D, k_p, k_c)**: This function is used to build the index for document D. It uses a pseudo-random generator G which outputs random string of size s. The pseudo-code of the function is given below.

Algorithm 1 : *BuildIndex*

1: Input: D, k_p, k_c;
2: Output: I_D /* The index for the document*/
3:
4: $I_D = \phi$;
5: **for** all $w_i \in D$ **do**
6:     Generate a pseudo-random string s_i using G;
7:     Compute trapdoor $T(w_i) = E_{k_p}(w_i)$;
8:     Compute ciphertext $c_i = T(w_i) \oplus \langle s_i, F_{k_c}(s_i) \rangle$;
9:     $I_D = I_D \cup c_i$;
10: **end for**
11: Return I_D;

- **SearchIndex(I_D, T(w))**: Given the document index and the trapdoor for the word w being searched, the *SearchIndex* functionality returns the document D if the word w is present in it. The pseudo-code is given below.

Algorithm 2 : *SearchIndex*

1: Input: $I_D, T(w)$;
2: Output: D or ϕ
3:
4: **for** all $c_i \in I_D$ **do**
5:     **if** $c_i \oplus T(w)$ is of the form $\langle s, F_{k_c}(s) \rangle$ **then**
6:         Return D;
7:     **end if**
8: **end for**
9: Return ϕ;

Speeding up encrypted keyword data

The approach described above to search over encrypted text has a limitation. Essentially, it requires $O(n)$ comparisons (cryptographic operations) at the server to test if the document contains a given keyword, where n is the number of keywords in the document. While such an overhead might be tolerable for small documents and small document collections, the approach is inherently not scalable. Authors in [18] overcome this limitation by exploiting *bloom filters* for indexing documents. More details about the bloom filter based approach can be found in [18, 21].

2.5 Search over Encrypted XML Data

While management and querying of XML data have been addressed extensively, there has been relatively little work in the area of encrypted XML data management [45, 34]. The new angle that becomes important in case of XML data is the structural information in the data. In [45] the problem of supporting XPath queries in the DAS model is considered where the underlying data is in XML format and propose a Xpath expressions based method to specify *security constraints* (SCs). They distinguish between two kinds of constraints, one where the goal is to hide the values at the tree nodes and another where one needs to hide the association between different attributes. For example, in a medical database containing patient data, an user might want to protect the information of the following nature: The insurance information of each patient; which SSN matches which patient's name; association between patient and disease etc. Such constraints can be specified in the form of XPath expressions and may be classified as either *node-type constraints* or *association-type constraints*. SCs can be enforced by hiding away the contents of some subset of nodes in the XML tree by encrypting their content. When association between two elements need to be hidden, encrypting any one of the nodes can enforce the SC. The optimization problem then requires one to determine a minimal set of nodes that need to be encrypted in order to satisfy all the SCs. But [45] employs deterministic encryption schemes where a plaintext value is always mapped to the same ciphertext. Deterministic encryption is not secure due to its vulnerability to statistical attacks. To avoid this the authors propose using decoy values to hide the true frequencies.

The query processing follows the typical DAS approach we outlined in the previous sections, wherein some metadata is stored on the server along with the encrypted data to enable server-side query processing. The authors propose using two indexes, one is the *structural index* to enable tree traversal and the second one is a *value index* for enabling attribute value based queries like range queries. The former is called the *discontinuous structural interval (DSI) index*, which associates each node of the tree with intervals from a range of an ordered domain (e.g., from $[0, 1]$). The interval sizes are chosen in a random manner so as not to give away any information about the number of children of a node. The DSI index is stored using two tables on the server-side which enables retrieval of subtrees of the XML document tree without revealing the structure.

For searching on values from an ordered domain (e.g., for range queries), the authors use an "order-preserving encryption" scheme [4] to transform the values from their original domain to a new domain. Since the order is preserved, one can use B-trees on these modified values to implement range-queries. To prevent against frequency-based attacks, the authors insert some s_i (small number) copies of each ciphertext c_i corresponding to a value v_i. But this process imposes an overhead due to the increases dataset size and the corresponding performance degradation has not been sufficiently analyzed. Also, the proposed scheme seems to be requiring a large number of "keys" (depending on the frequency range of values), thereby imposing a significant overhead of key management. Further, this scheme is unsafe under known plaintext attack (due to the usage of order-preserving encryption scheme [4]) thereby making it vulnerable to many attack scenarios where some plaintext-ciphertext pairs may be revealed to an adversary.

The query processing on the server is carried out using the structural and value indices which yields a superset of the true set of nodes satisfying the query predicates. These encrypted nodes are then returned to the client where a post-processing step discards the false-positives. Further details and proofs can be found in [45].

2.6 Privacy Aware Bucketization

In the previous section we discussed how DAS functionality can be realized when data is represented in the form of buckets. Such a bucketized represen-tation can result in disclosure of sensitive attributes. For instance, given a sensitive numeric attribute (e.g., salary) which has been bucketized, assume that the adversary somehow comes to know the maximum and minimum val-ues occurring in the bucket B. Then he can be sure that all data elements in this bucket have a value that falls in the range $[min_B, max_B]$, thereby leading to partial disclosure of sensitive values for data elements in B. If, the adver-sary has knowledge of distribution of values in the bucket, he may also be able to make further inference about the specific records. A natural question is how much information does the generalized representation of data reveal that is, given the bucket label, how well can the adversary predict/guess the value of the sensitive attribute of a given entity? Intuitively, this depends upon the granularity at which data is generalized. For instance, assigning all values in the domain to a single bucket will make the bucket-label completely non-informative. However, such a strategy will require the client to retrieve every record from the server. On the other extreme, if each possible data value has a corresponding bucket, the client will get no confidentiality although the records returned by the server will contain no false positives. There is a natu-ral trade-off between the performance overhead and the degree of disclosure.

Such a tradeoff has been studied in [30] where authors develop a strategy to minimize the disclosure with constraint on the performance degradation[6].

Let us take the case where bucket based generalization is performed over a single dimensional ordered data set, e.g., a numeric attribute and the query class is that of 1-dimensional range queries. The authors in [30] propose *entropy* and *variance* of the value distributions in the bucket as appropriate measure of (the inverse) disclosure risk. Entropy captures the notion of uncertainty associated with a random element chosen with a probability that follows a certain distribution. The higher the value of entropy of a distribution (i.e., larger the number of distinct values and more uniform the frequencies, larger is the value of the entropy), greater is the uncertainty regarding the true value of the element. For example, given a domain having 5 distinct values and the data set having 20 data points, the entropy is maximized if all 5 values appear equal number of time, i.e. each value has a frequency of 4.

In a secure index-based scheme, the adversary only sees the bucket label B of a data element t. Therefore, if the adversary (somehow) learns the distribution (frequencies) of values within B, he can guess the true value (say v^*) of t with a probability equal to the fractional proportion of elements with value v^* within the bucket. The notion of uncertainty regarding the true value can be captured in an aggregate manner by the entropy of the value distribution within B. Entropy of a discrete random variable X taking values $x_i = 1, \ldots, n$ with corresponding probabilities $p_i, i = 1, \ldots, n$ is given by:

$$Entropy(X) = H(X) = - \sum_{i=1}^{n} p_i log_2(p_i)$$

If the domain of the attribute has an order defined on it as in the case of a numeric attribute, the above definition of entropy does not capture the notion of distance between two values. In the worst case model, since the value distribution is assumed to be known to the adversary, greater the spread of each bucket distribution, better is the protection against disclosure. Therefore, the authors propose *variance* of the bucket distribution as the second (inverse) measure of disclosure risk associated with each bucket. That is, higher the variance of the value distribution, lower is the disclosure risk.

$$Variance(X) = \sum_{i=1}^{n} p_i(x_i - E(X))^2, \text{ where } E(X) = \frac{1}{n} \sum_{i=1}^{n} p_i x_i$$

After specifying these measures of disclosure-risk, [30] propose a 2-phase algorithm for creating the secure indices. The goal is to provide the data owner

---

[6] Notice the dual of the problem   maximize performance with a constraint on information disclosure   would also be addressed once we agree on the metric for information disclosure. However, such an articulation of the problem has not been studied in the literature.

a tunable algorithm that allows him to select a desired degree of tradeoff between performance and security. In the first phase, the values appearing in the attribute are divided into an user-specified (say M) number of buckets such that the average number of false-positives is minimized over all possible range queries (i.e., queries with range predicates on the specified attribute). The buckets so created might not meet the required security criteria (i.e., some minimum level of entropy and variance) and therefore in a second pass, the values within these optimal buckets are re-distributed in a "controlled manner" into a new set of M buckets so as to increase the value of entropy and variance of the bucket level distributions while admitting only up to a specified maximum degree of performance degradation. The tunable (user-chosen) parameter specifies this maximum allowed degree of quality degradation.

Similar measures of disclosure-risk have been proposed for privacy preserving data publishing [36]. There too, the key technique for achieving anonymity is data generalization which is akin to the partitioning approach in [30]. For more discussion on the choice of the privacy measures and details of the partitioning and redistribution algorithms the interested reader can refer to [30].

Discussion

In this section only single dimensional data was considered. Most real data sets have multiple attributes with various kinds of dependencies and correlations between the attributes. There may be some kinds of functional dependencies (exact or partial) and correlations as in multidimensional relational data or even structural dependencies as in XML data. Therefore, knowledge about one attribute might disclose the value of another via the knowledge of such associations. The security-cost analysis for such data becomes significantly different. Also, in this section, the analysis that was presented, was carried out for the worst-case scenario where it was assumed that the complete value distribution of the bucket is known to an adversary. In reality it is unrealistic to assume that an adversary has exact knowledge of the complete distribution of a data set. Moreover, to learn the bucket-level joint-distribution of data, the required size of the training set (in order to approximate the distribution to a given level of accuracy) grows exponentially with the number of attributes/dimensions. This makes the assumption of "complete bucket-level" knowledge of distribution even more unrealistic for multidimensional data. [31] proposes a new approach to analyze the disclosure risk for multidimensional data and extends the work in [30] to this case.

3 Trust, Encryption, Key-management, Integrity & Data Confidentiality

Having discussed the querying aspects of encrypted data , let us look at some basic security related issues that need to be addressed in a DAS application.

There are 3 basic models of trust that are widely studied in literature. The first model is that of "complete trust" where the server-side is completely trusted by the client to implement the required functionalities (e.g., query execution) and has complete faith on its security measures. In this scenario encryption might not be required at all and therefore, the data management issues are quite similar to those arising in standard DBMS systems. The second scenario is that of "partial trust", where though the service-provider is trusted to implement functionalities correctly, the sensitive information might be accessible to some adversary in the following two scenarios: (i) Some server-side entities (e.g., administrators) who may have the authority to access the data, but cannot be trusted completely to maintain confidentiality. (ii) The security measures on the server-side (e.g., network security) cannot be guaranteed to be completely safe from unauthorized access by outside hackers. In both these scenarios, the goal is to ensure the confidentiality of sensitive data by preventing its misuse by either legitimate or unauthorized users. The third model of trust is where the server is not trusted to even implement all functionalities correctly (truthfully). We refer to this as the "untrusted model". In this case additional steps need to be taken by the client to ensure authenticity of data and correctness of query results.

We start by discussing some of the issues that need to be considered while selecting the encryption function, especially with respect to relational data. Then, we summarize the techniques proposed in literature for integrity and authentication for the untrusted server model.

3.1 Encrypting relational data

The appropriate encryption algorithm to support in a relational database system is decided based on its performance characteristics. An important factor that dictates the performance is the data granularity at which encryption is supported. In a typical RDBMS, the encryption granularity could be at the field, the row or the page level. Authors in [22] report that embedding encryption within relational databases entails a significant startup cost. Row/page level encryption amortize this cost over larger data and therefore are more preferable than field-level encryption in general. Another criteria to consider while choosing the encryption algorithm is software versus hardware level encryption. Whereas software level encryption allows more flexibility in terms of algorithm selection and granularity control, hardware-based solutions are much faster, but can support only a small set of algorithms, like DES [15] and AES [2]. Therefore depending upon the application and trust model, a choice has to be made whether to use hardware or software level encryption. Authors in [26] experimentally determine that a row-level symmetric key based encryption scheme offers the best tradeoff between performance and object granularity. In general, the 3 important issues to keep in mind are (1) How fast is the encryption function, is it implementable at the hardware level; (2) how to perform key management; (3) at what granularity to encrypt data.

The main challenge is to introduce security functionality without incurring too much of overhead in terms of both performance and storage.

Encryption algorithms: Symmetric key encryption schemes like *AES* [2], *DES* [15] and *Blowfish* [40] are some of the popular algorithms for encrypting relational data. Encrypting the same amount of data using fewer large blocks is more efficient than using several smaller blocks. This is mainly due to the start-up cost associated with the initialization of the encryption algorithm. While Blowfish and DES work with 8-byte data blocks, AES works with 16-bytes blocks. Authors in [32] compare the performance of the above three algorithms and report that Blowfish is the fastest, but has a large startup cost. AES has the best average-case performance out of all the 3. We will discuss the key-management issues later.

Some other schemes in literature propose using public-key encryption algorithms (e.g., RSA) which avoids the problem of secure key distribution that is faced by symmetric key encryption schemes. Nonetheless symmetric key schemes are orders of magnitude faster in practice [32], and therefore are more preferable.

Encryption granularity: In general, finer encryption granularity affords more flexibility in allowing the server to choose what data to encrypt. The obvious encryption granularity choices are: (i) *Field-level*, which is the smallest achievable granularity; each attribute value of a tuple is encrypted separately. (ii) *Record/row level* where each row is encrypted separately. This allows one to retrieve individual rows without decrypting the whole table. (iii) *Attribute/column level* encryption where one chooses to encrypt only certain sensitive attributes in a table. (iv) *Page/block level* encryption could also be used. This is geared towards automating the encryption process. Whenever a page/block of sensitive data is stored on disk, the entire block is encrypted.

Efficient storage for encrypted data: Authors in [32] investigate the performance issues associated with storage of encrypted data on the disk. They propose the "Partitioned Plaintext and Ciphertext" (PPC) model for supporting storage of encrypted data. The basic idea is to cluster the non-sensitive and sensitive data separately in order to minimize the number of encryption operations. The PPC scheme logically breaks each page into two minipages, based on plaintext and ciphertext attributes. PPC takes advantage of the n-ary storage model (NSM) while enabling efficient encryption. Therefore implementing PPC on existing DBMS's that use NSM requires only modifications to the page layout. Within a page, each record is broken down into two parts, the plaintext attributes which do not require encryption and the ciphertext part that requires encryption. Both minipages are organized as NSM pages. Small changes need to be made to the buffer manager and catalog files in order to accommodate this change.

3.2 Authentication & Integrity issues

When a client queries the data on the server, he expects in return a set of records satisfying the query predicates. A query on a single relational table having m rows for instance, may require any one of the possible 2^m possible different subsets to be retrieved. The problem then is that of facilitating secure and efficient authentication of all possible query replies. Authors in [37] look at the problem when the server cannot be trusted with the integrity of the data. In other words, if the malicious server or an adversary inserts fake records into the database or modifies existing records, the client wants to detect this efficiently, without spending too much resources. This work concentrates only on simple query predicates involving relational operators like $=$, $<$, $\leq$, $\geq$, and $>$.

Data integrity and authentication can be provided at different levels of granularity. In principle, integrity checks can be at the level of a table, a column, a row (record), or an individual field (attribute) value in a row. Record-level integrity checking is thought to be the best choice to balance the tradeoff between flexibility of query answering and overhead of integrity checking. The authors look at 3 different scenarios: unified client model (where the client and data owner are one and the same entity), multiple clients-single owner and multiple clients-multiple owners.

The simplest approach for a client scenario is to store for each record a *message authentication code* (MAC) of that record. MAC is a keyed hash of the record's content. The secret key is known only to the client and therefore computable only at the client. The MAC-s tend to be small and of constant length, therefore making them easier to handle. Then with a query response, the server inserts a single integrity check computed as a hash (not a keyed hash) of all record-level MAC-s in the query reply which the client can verify. With a very high probability such hashes will be collision-free, i.e., distinct for different sets of records. The advantage of this approach is that bandwidth overhead is minimal and the computation overhead at the client is low.

The MAC-s are attractive for the unified client model, but in multi owner and multi querier models, one would require the MAC key to be shared between all the entities. This means non-repudiation for the queriers cannot be achieved. Instead of MAC-s, public-key digital signatures can be used for integrity checking (verification), i.e., the record content is encrypted using the owner's private key and verified by the client by decrypting it with the owner's public key.

In using public key algorithms for verification, the efficiency issues become a key concern due to their substantially higher complexity. The proposed solution is to carry out some form of *signature aggregation* which allows the client to aggregate multiple individual signatures into one unified signature. Authors in [37] suggest two aggregation based signature verification schemes, one uses the RSA encryption algorithm and the other uses elliptic-curve and bilinear mappings to aggregate multiple signatures into one. The *condensed-*

RSA scheme uses the multiplicative homomorphic property of RSA to combine multiple signatures generated by a single signer into one "condensed" signature. The result can then be verified quickly by comparing it with the product of the signatures of each record returned to the client in response to his query. In case of multiple owners the client has to verify the different sets of records (i.e., corresponding to the different owners) separately. The second scheme is similar to the first and we point the the interested reader to [37] for the technical details. Further work on authentication and query completeness can be found in [23, 43].

3.3 Key Management in DAS

There have been several proposals for key-management in DAS applications [28, 29, 14]. We briefly summarize the schemes proposed in [28].

The data owner first decides the key-assignment granularity, as to whether it will be at the database level, table level or row-level. The first choice generates a single key for the whole database. In the second case, tables within the database maybe grouped based on some criteria and one key generated for each group. In the third option, grouping is carried out at the record level within tables and each group of records are encrypted with a separate key. Note that the key assignment granularity is different from the encryption granularity. For instance, a single key might be used for the whole database, but encryption may be carried out at the row level. The key generation process itself is classified into two classes: *pre-computation* based and *re-computation* based approaches. In the first case, all keys are generated ahead of time and stored in the *key registry* of the system. In the second case, instead of the key, the key generating information is stored, e.g., *seed* for the random key generating function. In DAS key generation can be carried out at the client-side or at a third-party trusted server. Key registry is the data structure (table) that stores the information about the keys, namely the key-Id, key correspondence information (i.e., the database object to which the key is assigned), key mode (pre-computation or re-computation) and key-material (the actual key or the seed with which to compute the key). Besides key generation, the other issue addressed is that of key updates. The authors investigate the compatibility of key updates along with other data transactions (read/write/update). The efficiency issues related to key-updates is tackled separately in [29].

4 Summary & Related Work

In this chapter, we summarized some of the work done in encrypted data management in the context of database as a service model. Much of the existing work on querying encrypted data have studied the problem in one of the three contexts: keyword search over encrypted text documents, SQL search over encrypted relational data, and XPATH queries over XML data. Since the initial work [44, 26] in these areas, many extensions to the problem have been considered. We briefly mention these advances that we have not covered so far to provide interested readers with references.

Besides extending the data model, some researchers have considered relaxing assumptions made by the basic DAS model itself. The basic DAS model, as discussed in this chapter, assumes "curious but honest" adversary, but such an assumption might not necessarily hold in certain situations. In particular, the service provider may return erroneous data. An error in the result to a query may manifest itself in two ways – the returned answers may be tampered by the service provider, or alternatively, the results returned by the service provider may not be the complete set of matching records. The problem of integrity of the returned results was first studied in [26] for the untrusted server model. Any authentication mechanism adds additional processing cost at the client, and therefore authentication mechanisms using Merkle Hash trees and group signatures that attempt to reduce such an overhead have been studied in [38]. The authors have developed techniques for both the situation where the client (i.e., the user who poses the query) is the same as well as different from the data owner.

Another avenue of DAS research has been to exploit secure coprocessor to maintain confidentiality of outsourced database [5]. Unlike the basic DAS model in which the client is trusted and the service provider is entirely untrusted, in the model enhanced with a secure coprocessor, it is assumed that the service provider has a tamper proof hardware – a secure coprocessor – which is attached to the untrusted server and has (limited) amount of storage and processing capabilities. Data while outside the secure processor must be in the encrypted form, it could be in plaintext within the coprocessor without jeopardizing data confidentiality. Exploiting a secure coprocessor significantly simplifies the DAS model since now intermediate query results do not need to be transmitted to the clients if further computation requires data to be in plaintext. Instead, secure coprocessor can perform such a function, therefore significantly reducing network overheads and optimizing performance. Another additional advantage is that such a model can naturally support situations where the owner of the database is different from the user who poses the query. Another very similar approach using "smart cards" was proposed in [9].

There are several interesting proposals for designing systems that support querying and management of encrypted data [3, 9, 13]. [3] proposes a "two-server" model where data vertical data partitioning and selective attribute encryption is used for enabling confidentiality. [9] proposes an architecture that uses a small trusted hardware (a "smart card") to carry out computation over plaintext data while the bulk storage and processing is carried out by the untrusted server which has only access to the encrypted data. [13] propose a secure B+-tree based indexing approach to query data kept on a single untrusted server and analyze the disclosure risk in terms of inference-based attacks where the adversary has different degrees of background knowledge.

4.1 Open Issues & Future Trends

While much progress in research has been made over the past few years on DAS, we believe that many further challenges remain before the vision outlined in [26] of a secure data management service that simultaneously meets the data confidentiality and efficiency requirements. A few of the many practical challenges that still remain open are the following: (1) techniques to support dynamic updates – some initial approaches to this problem have been studied in [25], (2) mechanisms to support stored procedures and function execution as part of SQL processing, and (3) support for a more complete SQL - e.g., pattern matching queries. Furthermore, given multiple competing models for DAS (e.g., the basic model, the model with secure coprocessor, model with two servers) there is a need for a detailed comparative study that evaluates these approaches from different perspectives: feasibility, applicability under diverse conditions, efficiency, and achievable confidentiality. Furthermore, a detailed security analysis including the nature of attacks as well as privacy guarantees supported by different schemes needs to be carried out. Various other security issues need deeper analysis, like parameter selection for security (e.g., how much entropy, how much variance) and structural information hiding for XML data. Furthermore, wherever cryptographic primitives are used, special most of the works do not address issues related algorithm selection, choice of key-length, key-generation, distribution and revocation. These issues definitely require greater attention than they have received till this point.

A large number of security breaches in databases happen due to insider attacks, a fruitful avenue of research in secure data management would be to enable *secure database administration*. The goal is to determine what information needs to be revealed to administrators that allow them to carry out their tasks while hiding away as much excess information as possible that may potentially disclose some sensitive information.

5 Acknowledgements

This work has been possible due to the following NSF grants: 0331707 and IIS-0220069.

References

1. N.R. Adam, J.C. Worthmann Security-control methods for statistical databases: a comparative study In *ACM Computing Surveys, Vol 21, No. 4*, 1989.
2. Advanced Encryption Standard, NIST. FIPS PUB 197. (2001)
3. G. Aggarwal, M. Bawa, P. Ganesan, H. Garcia-Molina, K. Kenthapadi, U. Srivastava, D. Thomas, Y. Xu. Two Can Keep a Secret: A Distributed Architecture for Secure Database Services In *Proc. of CIDR* 2005.

4. R. Agrawal, J. Kiernan, R. Srikant, Y. Xu Order Preserving Encryption for Numeric Data In *Proc. of SIGMOD* 2004.
5. R. Agrawal, D. Asonov, M. Kantarcioglu, Y. Li Sovereign Joins In *ICDE* 2006.
6. N. Ahituv, Y. Lapid, S. Neumann Processing Encrypted Data In *Communications of the ACM*, 1987 Vol. 30, 9, pp.777-780
7. L. Ballard, S. Kamara, F. Monroe Achieving Efficient conjunctive keyword searches over encrypted data. In *ICICS* 2005.
8. D. Boneh, G. di Crescenzo, R. Ostrovsky, and G. Persiano Public Key Encryption with Keyword Search. In *Advances in Cryptology - Eurocrypt 2004* (2004). volume 3027 of *Lecture Notes in Computer Science*, pp. 506-522. Springer-Verlag, 2004.
9. L. Bouganim, and P. Pucheral. Chip-Secured Data Access: Confidential Data on Untrusted Servers In *Proc. of VLDB* 2002.
10. E. Brickell, Y. Yacobi On Privacy Homomorphisms In *Proc. Adavances in Cryptology-Eurocrypt'87*
11. Y. Chang and M. Mitzenmacher Privacy preserving keyword searches on remote encrypted data. In *Third International Conference on Applied Cryptography and Network Security (ACNS 2005)*, volume 3531 of *Lecture Notes in Computer Science*, pp. 442-455. Springer-Verlag, 2005.
12. S. Chaudhuri. An overview of query optimization in relational systems. In *Proc. of ACM Symposium on Principles of Database Systems (PODS)*, 1998.
13. E. Damiani et al. Balancing Confidentiality and Efficiency in Untrusted Relational DBMSs In *CCS*, 2003.
14. E. Damiani et al. Key Management for Multi-User Encrypted Databases In *StorageSS*, 2005.
15. Data Encryption Standard (DES), NIST. FIPS 46-3. (1993)
16. J. Domingo-Ferrer A New Privacy Homomorphism and Applications In *Information Processing Letters*, 6(5):277-282, 1996.
17. H. Garcia-Molina, J. Ullman, and J. Widom. *Database Systems: The Complete Book.* Prentice Hall, 2002.
18. E-J. Goh Secure Indexes. Technical report 2003/216, In IACR ePrint Cryptography Archive, (2003). See http://eprint.iacr.org/2003/216.
19. P. Golle, J. Staddon, B. Waters Secure conjunctive keyword search over encrypted data. In *Applied Cryptography and Network Security (ACNS 2004)*, volume 3089 of *Lecture Notes in Computer Science*, pp. 31-45. Springer, 2004.
20. G. Graefe. Query eveluation techniques for large databases. *ACM Computing Surveys*, 25(2):73–170, 1993.
21. H. Hacıgümüş, B. Hore, B. Iyer, S. Mehrotra Search on Encrypted Data. In *Secure Data Management in Decentralized Systems*, Springer US, 2007.
22. H. Hacıgümüş, B. Iyer, and S. Mehrotra. Providing Database as a Service. In *Proc. of ICDE*, 2002.
23. H. Hacıgümüş, B. Iyer, and S. Mehrotra. Ensuring the Integrity of Encrypted Databases in Database as a Service Model. In *Proc. of 17th IFIP WG 11.3 Conference on Data and Applications Security*, 2003.
24. H. Hacıgümüş, B. Iyer, S. Mehrotra Query Optimization in Encrypted Database Systems, In *DASFAA*, 2005.
25. H. Hacıgümüş. Privacy in Database-as-a-Service Model. *Ph.D. Thesis, Department of Information and Computer Science, University of California, Irvine*, 2003.
26. H. Hacıgümüş, B. Iyer, C. Li and S. Mehrotra Executing SQL over encrypted data in the database-service-provider model. In Proc. SIGMOD, 2002.

27. H. Hacıgümüş, B. Iyer, and S. Mehrotra Efficient Execution of Aggregation Queries over Encrypted Relational Databases. In *DASFAA*, 2004.
28. H. Hacıgümüş, Sharad Mehrotra Performance concious key management in Encrypted Databases In *DBSec*, 2004.
29. H. Hacıgümüş, Sharad Mehrotra Efficient Key Updates in Encrypted Database Systems In *Secure Data Management*, 2005.
30. B. Hore, S. Mehrotra, and G. Tsudik. A Privacy-Preserving Index for Range Queries. In *Proc. of VLDB* 2004.
31. B. Hore. Storing and Querying Data Securely in Untrusted Environments. *Ph.D. Thesis, Department of Information and Computer Science, University of California, Irvine*, 2007.
32. B. Iyer, S. Mehrotra, E. Mykletun, G. Tsudik, and Y. Wu A Framework for Efficient Storage Security in RDBMS In *Proc. of EDBT* 2004.
33. R. C. Jammalamadaka, S. Mehrotra, and N. Venkatasubramanian PVault: A Client-Server System Providing Mobile Access to Personal Data In *StorageSS*, 2005.
34. R. Jammalamadaka, S. Mehrotra Querying Encrypted XML Documents In *IDEAS*, 2006.
35. R.C. Jammalamadaka, R. Gamboni, S. Mehrotra, K. Seamons, N. Venkatasubramanian gVault:A Gmail Based Cryptographic Network File System. In proceedings of *21st Annual IFIP WG 11.3 Working Conference on Data and Applications Security*, 2007.
36. A. Machanavajjhala, J. E. Gehrke, D. Kifer, M. Venkitasubramaniam l-Diversity: Privacy Beyond k-Anonymity. In *ICDE*, 2006.
37. E. Mykletun, M. Narasimhan, G. Tsudik Authentication and Integrity in Outsourced Databases In *NDSS*, 2004.
38. M. Narasimhan, G. Tsudik DSAC: Integrity of Outsourced Databases with Signature Aggregation and Chaining In *CIKM*, 2005.
39. R. Rivest, R.L. Adleman and M. Dertouzos. On Data Banks and Privacy Homomorphisms. In *Foundations of Secure Computations*, 1978.
40. B. Schneier. Description of a New Variable-Length Key, 64-Bit Block Cipher (Blowfish). Fast software Encryption, Cambridge Security Workshop Proceedings. (1993) 191-204.
41. P. Sellinger, M. Astrahan, D. D. Chamberlin, R. A. Lorie, and T. G. Price. Access Path Selection in Relational Database Management Systems. In *Proc. of ACM SIGMOD*, 1979.
42. E., Shmueli, R. Waisenberg, Y., Elovici, E. Gudes Designing Secure Indexes for Encrypted Databases Secure Data Management, 2004.
43. R. Sion Query Execution Assurance for Outsourced Databases In *VLDB* 2005.
44. D. Song and D. Wagner and A. Perrig. Practical Techniques for Search on Encrypted Data. In *Proc. of IEEE SRSP*, 2000.
45. H. Wang, L. Lakshmanan Efficient Secure Query Evaluation over Encrypted XML Databases In *VLDB*, 2006.
46. B. Waters, D. Balfanz, G. Durfee, and D. Smetters Building and encrypted and searchable audit log. In *NDSS* (2004).
47. L. Willenborg, T. De Waal Elements of Statistical Disclosure Control *Springer*, 2001.
48. L. Willenborg, T. De Waal Statistical Disclosure Control in Practice *Springer-Verlag*, 1996.

8

Security in Data Warehouses and OLAP Systems

Lingyu Wang[1] and Sushil Jajodia[2]

[1] Concordia Institute for Information Systems Engineering
Concordia University
Montreal, QC H3G 1M8, Canada
wang@ciise.concordia.ca

[2] Center for Secure Information Systems
George Mason University
Fairfax, VA 22030-4444, USA
jajodia@gmu.edu

Summary. Unlike in operational databases, aggregation and derivation play a major role in on-line analytical processing (OLAP) systems and data warehouses. Unfortunately, the process of aggregation and derivation can also pose challenging security problems. Aggregated and derived data usually look innocent to traditional security mechanisms, such as access control, and yet such data may carry enough sensitive information to cause security breaches. This chapter first demonstrates the security threat from aggregated and derived data in OLAP systems and warehouses. The chapter then reviews a series of methods for removing such a threat. Two efforts in extending existing inference control methods to the special setting of OLAP systems and warehouses are discussed. Both methods are not fully satisfactory due to limitations inherited from their counter parts in statistical databases. The chapter then reviews another solution based on a novel preventing-then-removing approach, which shows a promising direction towards securing OLAP systems and data warehouses.

1 Introduction

With rapid advancements in computer and network technology, it becomes a common practice for organizations to collect, store, and analyze vast amounts of data quickly and efficiently. On-line analytical processing (OLAP) systems and data warehouses of today are used to store and analyze everything – vital or not – to an organization. The security of data warehouses and OLAP systems is crucial to the interest of both organizations and individuals. Stolen organizational secrets may cause serious and immediate damages to an organization. Indiscriminate collection and retention of data represents an extraordinary intrusion on privacy of individuals. Security breaches in governmental data warehouses may lead to losses of information that translate into financial losses or losses whose values are obviously high but difficult to quantify (for example, national security). Unlike in traditional databases, information stored in data warehouses is typically accessed through decision support systems, such as OLAP systems. OLAP systems help analysts to gain insights to different perspectives of large amounts of data stored in a data warehouse. Due to the sheer volume of data, OLAP systems heavily depend on aggregates of data in order to hide insignificant details and hence to accentuate global patterns and trends. As the underlying data model, a data cube [15] can nicely organize multi-dimensional aggregates formulated by dimension hierarchies. Although security breaches in a data warehouse are possible in many ways, the most challenging threat is from insiders who have legitimate accesses to data through OLAP queries. Unfortunately, most of today's OLAP systems lack effective security measures to safeguard the data accessed through them. Existing security mechanisms can at best alleviate security breaches but cannot completely remove the threat. *Data sanitization* has long been recognized as insufficient for protecting sensitive data by itself due to potential linking attacks [24]. *Access control* techniques, although mature in traditional data management systems, are usually not directly applicable to OLAP systems and data warehouses due to the difference in data models.

Moreover, OLAP systems and underlying data warehouses are especially vulnerable to indirect *inferences* of protected data. The aggregation process used by OLAP systems does not completely destroy sensitive information. The remaining vestiges of sensitive information, together with knowledge obtained through out of bound channels, can cause disclosures of such information. Although studied since 1970s in statistical databases, *inference control* for on-line systems is largely regarded as impractical due to its negative-in-tone complexity results [7]. Most restriction-based inference control methods adopt a *detecting-then-removing* approach. The detection of inferences must take into accounts all combinations of answered queries, which implies complicated on-line computations and constant bookkeeping of queries. Even at such a high cost, each method usually applies to only a few unrealistically simplified cases, such as with only one aggregation type. These facts partially explain why inference control is absent in most commercial OLAP systems. On the other hand, off-line inference control methods have long been used in releasing census tables, which demonstrates that the threat of inferences is real.

This chapter starts by demonstrating the security threat to data warehouses caused by inferences using OLAP queries. Various requirements in designing security measures for such systems are discussed. Armed with this understanding, the chapter then takes steps to meet the stated requirements. Two efforts in extending existing inference control methods to the special setting of OLAP systems are reviewed. The results show that the threat of unauthorized accesses and indirect inferences known in relational databases is still possible even when users are restricted to OLAP queries. Although improved performance is obtained by exploring unique characteristics of OLAP queries, both methods are not fully satisfactory due to limitations inherited from their counter parts in statistical databases. The chapter then reviews another solution, which adopts a *preventing-then-removing* approach. This latter solution can thwart both unauthorized accesses and indirect inferences of sensitive data, and the solution can potentially be applied to a broach range of settings in terms of aggregation types and sensitivity criteria. The solution thus shows a promising direction towards security OLAP systems and data warehouses.

The rest of the chapter is organized as follows. Section 2 reviews background knowledge and related work. Section 3 discusses the threat of inferences and the security requirements. Section 4 outlines a three-tier security architecture for OLAP systems. Section 5 then reviews methods for controlling inferences in such systems. Finally, Section 6 concludes the chapter.

2 Background

In this section, we first review background knowledge such as data warehouses and OLAP systems. We then review other research efforts relevant to our discussions in this chapter.

2.1 Data Warehouses and OLAP Systems

A centralized data warehouse is usually used to store enterprise data. The data are organized based on a *star schema*, which usually has a *fact table* with part of the attributes called *dimensions* and the rest called *measures*. Each dimension is associated with a *dimension table* indicating a dimension hierarchy. The dimension tables may contain redundancy, which can be removed by splitting each dimension table into multiple tables, one per attribute in the dimension table. The result is called a *snowflake schema*. A data warehouse usually stores data collected from multiple data sources, such as transactional databases throughout an organization. The data are cleaned and transformed to a common consistent format before they are stored in the data warehouse. Subsets of the data in a data warehouse can be extracted as data marts to meet the specific requirements of an organizational division. Unlike in transactional databases where data are constantly updated, typically the data stored in a data warehouse are refreshed from data sources only periodically.

Coined by Codd et. al in 1993 [9], OLAP stands for On-Line Analytical Processing. The concept has its root in earlier products such as the IRI Express, the Comshare system, and the Essbase system [29]. Unlike statistical databases which usually store census data and economic data, OLAP is mainly used for analyzing business data collected from daily transactions, such as sales data and health care data [27]. The main purpose of an OLAP system is to enable analysts to construct a mental image about the underlying data by exploring it from different perspectives, at different level of generalizations, and in an interactive manner. Popular architectures of OLAP systems include *ROLAP* (relational OLAP) and *MOLAP* (multidimensional OLAP). ROLAP provides a front-end tool that translates multidimensional queries into corresponding SQL queries to be processed by the relational backend. MOLAP does not rely on the relational model but instead materializes the multidimensional views. Using MOLAP for dense parts of the data and RO-LAP for the others leads to a hybrid architecture, namely, the *HOLAP* or hybrid OLAP.

As a component of decision support systems, OLAP interacts with other components, such as data mining, to assist analysts in making business decisions. While data mining algorithms automatically produce knowledge in a pre-defined form, such as association rule or classification. OLAP does not directly generate such knowledge, but instead relies on human analysts to observe it by interpreting the query results. On the other hand, OLAP is more flexible than data mining in the sense that analysts may obtain all kinds of patterns and trends rather than only knowledge of fixed forms. OLAP and data mining can also be combined to enable analysts in obtaining data mining results from different portion of the data and at different level of generalization [17]. The requirements on OLAP systems have been defined differently, such as the FASMI (Fast Analysis of Shared Multidimensional Information) test [23] and the Codd rules [9]. Some of the requirements are especially relevant to this chapter. First, to make OLAP analysis an interactive process, the OLAP system must be highly efficient in answering queries. OLAP systems usually rely on extensive pre-computations, indexing, and specialized storage to improve the performance. Second, to allow analysts to explore the data from different perspectives and at different level of generalization, OLAP organizes and generalizes data along multiple dimensions and dimension hierarchies. The data cube model we shall address shortly is one of the most popular abstract models for this purpose.

Data cube was proposed as a SQL operator to support common OLAP tasks like histograms and sub-totals [15]. Even though such tasks are usually possible with standard SQL queries, the queries may become very complex. The number of needed unions is exponential in the number of dimensions of the *base* table. Such a complex query may result in many scans of the base table, leading to poor performance. Because sub-totals are very common in OLAP queries, it is desired to define a new operator for the collection of such sub-totals, namely, *data cube*.

Figure 1 depicts a fictitious *data cube*. It has two *dimensions*: *time* and *organization* with three and four *attributes*, respectively. We regard *all* as a special attribute having one attribute value *ALL*, which depends on all other attribute values. The attributes of each dimension are partially ordered by the *dependency relation* $\preceq$ into a *dependency lattice* [18], that is, *quarter* $\preceq$ *year* $\preceq$ *all* and *employee* $\preceq$ *department* $\preceq$ *branch* $\preceq$ *all*. The product of the two lattices gives the dependency lattice of cuboids. Each element of the dependency lattice is a tuple $< T, O >$, where T is an attribute of the *time* dimension and O is an attribute of the *organization*. Attached to each such tuple $< T, O >$ is an empty two-dimensional array, namely, a *cuboid*. Each *cell* of the cuboid $< T, O >$ is also a tuple $< t, o >$, where t and o are *attribute values* of the attribute T and O, respectively. The dependency relation extends to be among cells. For example, a cell $< Y1, Bob >$ depends on the cells $< Q1, Bob >$, $< Q2, Bob >$, $< Q3, Bob >$, and $< Q4, Bob >$. Hence, all cells also form a dependency lattice.

A base table with the schema (*quarter, employee, commission*) is used to populate the data cube with values of a *measure* attribute *commission*. Each record in the base table, a triple (q, e, m), is used to populate a cell $< q, e >$ of the *core cuboid* $< quarter, employee >$, where q, e, and m are values of the attributes *quarter*, *employee*, and *commission*, respectively. Some cells of $< quarter, employee >$ remain empty (or having the *NULL* value), if corresponding records are absent in the base table. If multiple records correspond to the same cell, since the two attributes *quarter* and *employee* are not necessarily a key of the base relation, they are aggregated using the *aggregation function* SUM. All cuboids are then populated using the same aggregation function. For example, in the cuboid $< year, employee >$, a cell $< Y1, Bob >$ takes the value 8500, which is the total amount of the four cells it depends on, $< Q1, Bob >$, $< Q2, Bob >$, $< Q3, Bob >$, and $< Q4, Bob >$. An empty cell is deemed as zero (which depends on the aggregation function) in aggregation.

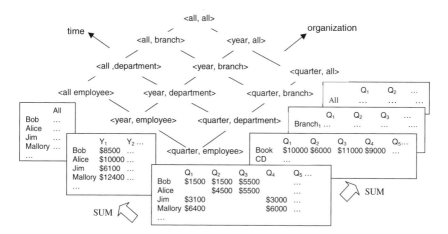

Fig. 1. An Example of Data Cubes

2.2 Related Work

Although the need for security and privacy in data warehouses and OLAP systems has long been identified [5, 27, 28], today's commercial OLAP products usually provide insufficient security measures [27]. In contrast, access control is mature in relational databases. In relational databases, accesses to sensitive data are regulated based on various models. The discretional access control (DAC) uses owner-specified grants and revokes to achieve an owner-centric control of objects [16]. The role-based access control (RBAC) simplifies access control tasks by introducing an intermediate tier of roles that aggregates and bridges users and permissions [25]. The flexible access control framework (FAF) provides a universal solution to handling conflicts in access control policies through authorization derivation and conflict resolution logic rules [20].

Inference control has been studied in statistical databases and census data for more than thirty years [1, 12, 35]. The proposed methods can roughly be classified into *restriction-based* techniques and *perturbation-based* techniques. Restriction-based inference control methods prevent malicious inferences by denying unsafe queries. Those methods determine the safety of queries based on the minimal number of values aggregated by a query [12], the maximal number of common values aggregated by different queries [13], and the maximal rank of a matrix representing answered queries [8]. The perturbation-based techniques prevent inference by inserting random noises to sensitive data [30], to answers of queries [4], or to database structures [26].

Cell suppression and *partitioning* most closely relate to the methods we shall introduce. To protect census data released in statistical tables, cells that contains small COUNT values are suppressed, and possible inferences of the suppressed cells are then detected and removed using linear programming-based techniques. The detection method is effective for two-dimensional cases but becomes intractable for three or more dimensional tables [10, 11]. *Partitioning* defines a partition on sensitive data and restricts queries to aggregate only complete blocks in the partition [7, 37]. Similarly, *microaggregation* replaces clusters of sensitive values with their averages [21, 35]. Partitioning and microaggregation methods usually assume a specific type of aggregations. Moreover, their partitions are not based on dimension hierarchies inherent to data and hence may contain many blocks that are meaningless to a user.

Perturbation-based methods have been proposed for preserving privacy in data mining [2]. Random noises are added to sensitive values to preserve privacy, while the statistical distribution is approximately reconstructed from the perturbed data to facilitate data mining tasks. Protecting sensitive data in OLAP is different from that in data mining. Unlike most data mining results, such as classifications and association rules, the results of OLAP usually cannot be obtained from distribution models alone. The methods proposed in [3] can approximately reconstruct COUNTs from perturbed data with statistically bound errors, so OLAP tasks like classification can be fulfilled. However, potential errors in individual values may prevent an OLAP user from gaining trustful insights into small details of the data, such as outliers. The methods we shall introduce do not perturb data so any answer will always be precise and trustful.

Secure multi-party data mining allows multiple distrusted parties to cooperatively compute aggregations over each other's data [31, 14]. Cryptographic protocols enable each party to obtain the final result with minimal disclosures of their own data. This problem is different from inference control, because the threat of inferences comes from what users know, not from the way they know it. The *k-anonymity* model enables sensitive values to be released without threatening privacy [24, 36]. Each record is indistinguishable from at least $k - 1$ others because they all have exactly the same identifying attribute values. An adversary can link an individual in the physical world to at least (the sensitive values of) k records, which is considered a tolerable privacy threat. Inference control and the k-anonymity model can be considered as dual approaches. The information theoretic approach in [22] formally characterizes insecure queries as those that bring a user with more confidence in guessing possible records [22]. However, such a *perfect-secrecy* metric will not tolerate any partial disclosure, such as those caused by aggregations.

3 Security Requirements

In this section, we first demonstrate the threat of indirect inferences in OLAP systems. We then describe various requirements in designing security measures for such systems.

3.1 The Threat of Inferences

Unlike in traditional databases where unauthorized accesses are the main security concern, an adversary using an OLAP system can more easily infer prohibited data from answers to legitimate queries. Example 1 illustrates an *one dimensional* (or 1-d for short) inference where the sensitive cell is inferred using exactly one of its descendants.

Example 1 (1-d Inference). In Figure 1, suppose an adversary is prohibited from accessing the cuboid $\langle quarter, employee \rangle$ but is allowed to access its descendant $\langle quarter, department \rangle$. Further suppose the empty cells denote the values that the adversary already knows through outbound channels. The adversary can then infer $\langle Q5, Bob \rangle$ as exactly the same value in $\langle Q5, Book \rangle$ (that is, 3500).

A *multi-dimensional* (or m-d) inference is the complementary case of 1-d inferences. That is, a cell is inferred using two or more of its descendants, and neither of those descendants causes 1-d inferences. Example 2 illustrates an m-d inference in a two-dimensional SUM-only data cube. Example 3 and 4 illustrate m-d inferences with MAX-only, and with SUM, MAX, and MIN.

Example 2 (m-d Inferences with SUM). Suppose now an adversary is prohibited from accessing the core cuboid in Figure 1 but is allowed to access its descendants ⟨*quarter, department*⟩ and ⟨*year, employee*⟩. The adversary can no longer employ any 1-d inference to infer data in the first year, because each cell in ⟨*quarter, department*⟩ and ⟨*year, employee*⟩ has at least two ancestors in the core cuboid. However, an m-d inference is possible as follows. the adversary first sums the two cells ⟨*Y*1, *Bob*⟩ and ⟨*Y*1, *Alice*⟩ in the cuboid ⟨*year, employee*⟩ and then subtracts from the result (that is, 18500) the two cells ⟨*Q*2, *Book*⟩ and ⟨*Q*3, *Book*⟩ (that is, 11000). The final result yields a sensitive cell ⟨*Q*1, *Bob*⟩ as 1500.

Example 3 (m-d Inferences with MAX). Suppose now an adversary is prevented from knowing the values in the empty cells. The core cuboid then seems to the adversary full of unknown values. As we shall show later, such a data cube will be free of inferences if the aggregation function is SUM. However, the following m-d inference is possible with MAXs. The MAX values in cells ⟨*Y*1, *Mallory*⟩ and ⟨*Q*4, *Book*⟩ are 6400 and 6000, respectively. From those two values the adversary can infer that one of the three cells ⟨*Q*1, *Mallory*⟩, ⟨*Q*2, *Mallory*⟩, and ⟨*Q*3, *Mallory*⟩ must be 6400, because ⟨*Q*4, *Mallory*⟩ must be no greater than 6000. Similarly, an adversary infers neither ⟨*Q*2, *Mallory*⟩ and ⟨*Q*3, *Mallory*⟩ can be 6400. The sensitive cell ⟨*Q*1, *Mallory*⟩ is then successfully inferred as 6400.

Example 4 (Inferences with SUM, MAX and MIN). Now suppose an adversary can ask queries using SUM, MAX, and MIN on the data cube. Following Example 3, ⟨*Q*1, *Mallory*⟩ is 6400. The MAX, MIN, and SUM values of the cell ⟨*Y*1, *Mallory*⟩ are 6400,6000, and 12400, respectively. From those three values the adversary can infer the following. That is, ⟨*Q*2, *Mallory*⟩,⟨*Q*3, *Mallory*⟩, and ⟨*Q*4, *Mallory*⟩ must be 6000 and two zeroes, although he/she does not know exactly which is 6000 and which are zeroes. The MAX,MIN, and SUM values of ⟨*Q*2, *Book*⟩, ⟨*Q*3, *Book*⟩ and ⟨*Q*4, *Book*⟩ then tell the adversary the following facts. In ⟨*quarter, employee*⟩, two cells in *Q*2 are 1500 and 4500; those in *Q*3 are 5500 and 5500; those in *Q*4 are 3000 and 6000; and the rest are all zeroes. The adversary then concludes that ⟨*Q*4, *Mallory*⟩ must be 6000, because the values in *Q*3 and *Q*2 cannot be. Similarly, the adversary can infer ⟨*Q*4, *Jim*⟩ as 3000, and consequently infer all cells in ⟨*quarter, employee*⟩.

3.2 The Requirements

As illustrated in above examples, a security solution for OLAP systems must combine access control and inference control to remove security threats. At the same time, providing security should not adversely reduce the usefulness of data warehouses and OLAP systems. A practical solution must achieve a balance among following objectives.

- *Security:* Sensitive data stored in underlying data warehouses should be guarded from both unauthorized accesses and malicious inferences. Such a definition of security considers not only the information a user can directly obtain from an OLAP system, but also those that he/she can derive using answers to seemingly irrelevant queries.

- *Applicability:* The security provided by a solution should not rely on any unrealistic assumptions about OLAP systems. In particular, assumptions made in statistical databases are usually not unacceptable in OLAP applications. A desired solution should cover a wide range of scenarios without the need for significant modifications.

- *Efficiency:* The name of OLAP itself indicates the interactive nature of such systems. Most queries should be answered in a matter of seconds or minutes. A significant portion of the OLAP literature has been devoted to meeting such stringent performance requirements. A desired security must be computationally efficient, especially with respect to on-line overhead.

- *Availability:* Data should be readily available to legitimate users who have sufficient privileges. A solution must place security upon justifiable restrictions of accesses in the sense that removing the restrictions will either lead to security breaches or render the method computationally infeasible.

- *Practicality:* A practical security solution should not demand significant modifications to the existing infrastructure of an OLAP system. A solution should take advantage of any query-processing mechanisms and security mechanisms that are already in place.

The main challenge, however, lies in the inherent tradeoff between above objectives. To have provable security and justifiable availability in varying settings of OLAP systems usually implies complicated on-line computations, which are expensive and hard to implement. The methods we shall describe in this chapter represent efforts towards a balance among these objectives.

4 A Three-Tier Security Architecture

Security in statistical databases usually has two tiers, that is, sensitive *data* and aggregation *queries.* Inference control mechanisms check each aggregation query to decide whether answering the query, in addition to previously answered queries, may disclose any protected data through inferences. However, applying such a two-tier architecture to OLAP systems has some inherent drawbacks. First, checking queries for inferences at run time may bring unacceptable delay to query processing. The complexity of such checking is usually high due to the fact that m-d inferences must be checked against *sets* of queries instead of each individual query. Second, inference control methods cannot take advantage of the special characteristics of an OLAP application under the two-tier architecture. For example, OLAP queries are usually answered using materialized views, such as data cubes. As we shall show, the

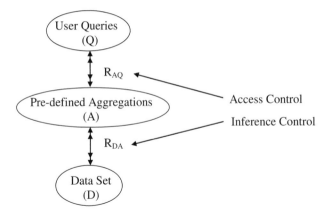

Fig. 2. A Three-Tier Inference Control Architecture

on-line overhead of inference control can be dramatically reduced if this fact can be explored.

The methods we shall review are based on a three-tier security architecture. As illustrated in Figure 2, this architecture introduces an intermediate *aggregation tier* between the data tier and the query tier. More specifically, the architecture has three tiers and three relations, and the aggregation tier must satisfy three properties. First, inference control is enforced between the aggregation tier and the data tier such that the former is secure with respect to the latter. Access control then helps to enforce that only safe aggregations will be used to compute results to queries. Second, the size of the aggregation tier must be comparable to the data tier. Third, the problem of inference control can be partitioned into blocks in the data tier and the aggregation tier such that security only need to be ensured between each corresponding pair of blocks in the two tiers.

The three-tier architecture helps to reduce the performance overhead of inference control in several aspects. The first property of the model implies that the aggregation tier can be pre-computed such that the computation-intensive part of inference control can be shifted to off-line processing. The on-line part is to enforce access control based on whether a query can be rewritten using the aggregation tier (that is, security through views). Second, the last two properties both reduce the size of inputs to inference control algorithms and consequently reduce the complexity. Note that an aggregation tier can be designed to meet the second property, but the size of the query tier is inherently exponential in the size of the data tier. The third property also *localizes* inference control tasks to each block of the data tier so a failure in one block will not affect other blocks.

5 Securing OLAP Data Cubes

The data cube is a natural data model for OLAP systems and underlying data warehouses. This section reviews several methods in safeguarding OLAP data cubes against both unauthorized accesses and indirect inferences.

5.1 SUM-only Data Cubes

This section describes two efforts inspired by previous inference control methods in statistical databases. As an inherited limitation, only SUMs are considered. Moreover, only the core cuboid is considered as sensitive. We show that improved results can be obtained by exploring the unique structures of data cubes.

Cardinality-Based Method

The *cardinality-based* method by Dobkin et. al [13] determines the existence of inferences based on the number of answered queries. In a data cube, aggregations are pre-defined based on the dimension hierarchy, and what may vary is the number of empty cells, that is previously known values. Recall that in Section 3.1, Example 1 illustrated a straightforward connection between 1-d inferences and the number of empty cells in a data cube. That is, an 1-d inference is present when an adversary can access any cell that has exactly one ancestor in the core cuboid. A similar but less straightforward connection also exists between m-d inferences and the number of empty cells, as we shall show in this here.

The model for inferences in this case is similar to that given by Chin et. al [8], but the queries are limited to data cube cells. Here we only consider one-level dimension hierarchy where each dimension can only have two attributes, that is the attribute in core cuboid and the *all*. For each attribute of the core cuboid, we assume an arbitrary but fixed order on its domain. Although an attribute may have infinitely many values, we shall only consider the values that appear in at least one non-empty cell in the given data cube instance. The number of such values is thus fixed. From the point of view of an adversary, the value in any non-empty cell is unknown, and hence the cell is denoted by an unknown variable. The central tabulation in Table 1 rephrases part of the core cuboid in Figure 1.

Table 1 also includes cells in descendants of the core cuboid, namely, the *aggregation cuboids*. These are $\langle all, employee \rangle$, $\langle quarter, all \rangle$, and $\langle all, all \rangle$, as we only consider one-level dimension hierarchy. For SUM-only data cubes, the dependency relation can be modeled as linear equations. At the left side of those equations are the unknown variables in the core cuboid, and at the left side the values in the aggregation cuboids. Table 2 shows a system of nine equations corresponding to the nine cells in the aggregation cuboids.

Next we obtain the reduced row echelon form (RREF) M_{rref} of the coefficients matrix through a sequence of elementary row operations [19], as shown

Table 1. Modeling A Core Cuboid

	Q_1	Q_2	Q_3	Q_4	ALL
Bob	x_1	x_2	x_3		8500
$Alice$		x_4	x_5		10000
Jim	x_6			x_7	6100
$Mallory$	x_8			x_9	12400
ALL	10000	6000	11000	9000	36000

Table 2. Modeling the Aggregation Cuboids

$$
\begin{pmatrix}
1\ 1\ 1\ 0\ 0\ 0\ 0\ 0\ 0 \\
0\ 0\ 0\ 1\ 1\ 0\ 0\ 0\ 0 \\
0\ 0\ 0\ 0\ 0\ 1\ 1\ 0\ 0 \\
0\ 0\ 0\ 0\ 0\ 0\ 0\ 1\ 1 \\
1\ 0\ 0\ 0\ 0\ 1\ 0\ 1\ 0 \\
0\ 1\ 0\ 1\ 0\ 0\ 0\ 0\ 0 \\
0\ 0\ 1\ 0\ 1\ 0\ 0\ 0\ 0 \\
0\ 0\ 0\ 0\ 0\ 0\ 1\ 0\ 1 \\
1\ 1\ 1\ 1\ 1\ 1\ 1\ 1\ 1
\end{pmatrix}
\times
\begin{pmatrix}
x_1 \\ x_2 \\ x_3 \\ x_4 \\ x_5 \\ x_6 \\ x_7 \\ x_8 \\ x_9
\end{pmatrix}
=
\begin{pmatrix}
8500 \\ 10000 \\ 6100 \\ 12400 \\ 10000 \\ 6000 \\ 11000 \\ 9000 \\ 36000
\end{pmatrix}
$$

in Table 3. From M_{rref} it can be observed that the system of linear equations in Table 2 has infinitely many solutions. This means that an adversary cannot infer the *entire* core cuboid from the given aggregation cuboids. However, the first row vector of M_{rref} being a unit vector (that is, it has a single 1) indicates that the value of x_1 must remain the same among all the solutions to the system of equations. Consequently, the adversary can infer Bob's commission in Q_1.

Table 3. The Reduced Row Echelon Form M_{rref}

$$
\begin{pmatrix}
1\ 0\ 0\ 0\ \ 0\ \ 0\ 0\ 0\ \ 0 \\
0\ 1\ 0\ 0\ -1\ 0\ 0\ 0\ \ 0 \\
0\ 0\ 1\ 0\ \ 1\ \ 0\ 0\ 0\ \ 0 \\
0\ 0\ 0\ 1\ \ 1\ \ 0\ 0\ 0\ \ 0 \\
0\ 0\ 0\ 0\ \ 0\ \ 1\ 0\ 0\ -1 \\
0\ 0\ 0\ 0\ \ 0\ \ 0\ 1\ 0\ \ 1 \\
0\ 0\ 0\ 0\ \ 0\ \ 0\ 0\ 1\ \ 1 \\
0\ 0\ 0\ 0\ \ 0\ \ 0\ 0\ 0\ \ 0 \\
0\ 0\ 0\ 0\ \ 0\ \ 0\ 0\ 0\ \ 0
\end{pmatrix}
$$

The existence of at least one unit row vectors in M_{rref} is indeed the necessary and sufficient condition for any unknown variable to have the same value among all the solutions [8]. We shall adopt this notion to model inferences in SUM-only data cubes. Notice that for the special case of 1-d inferences, as shown in Example 1, the coefficients matrix itself would have a unit row vector (which will certainly also appear in M_{rref}). It is well-known that the RREF of a $m \times n$ matrix can be obtained by a Gauss-Jordan elimination with complexity $O(m^2 n)$ [19].

The number of empty cells can only determine the existence of 1-d inferences in two extreme cases. First, if the core cuboid has no empty cell, then trivially it is free of 1-d inferences as long as all the attributes have more than one value. The second straightforward result says that any data cube whose core cuboid has fewer non-empty cells than the given upper bound $2^{k-1} \cdot d_{max}$, where k is the number of dimensions and d_{max} is the greatest domain size among all dimensions, will always have 1-d inferences. If the number of empty cells falls between the two bounds, then the existence of 1-d inferences can no longer be determined simply based on the number of empty cells.

Although less straightforward, there is only a connection between existence of m-d inferences and the number of empty cells (a lengthy proof of Theorem 1 can be found in [34]). Similar to the case of 1-d inferences, any data cube with a core cuboid having no empty cells is free of m-d inferences. To relax this rigid result, Theorem 1 gives a tight upper bound on the number of empty cells for a data cube to remain free of m-d inferences. The bound is tight in the sense that we can no longer tell whether m-d inferences are present from the number of empty cells, once this number goes beyond the bound. Notice that the bound only guarantees the absence of m-d inferences, while 1-d inferences may still be present as long as the core cuboid has empty cells.

Theorem 1 (m-d Inferences). *In any k-dimensional data cube with one-level dimension hierarchy, let C_c be the core cuboid and C_{all} be the collection of all aggregation cuboids. Suppose the ith attribute of C_c has d_i values, and let d_u and d_v be the two smallest among the d_i's, then C_{all} does not cause any m-d inferences to C_c, if the number of empty cells in C_c is less than $2(d_u - 4) + 2(d_v - 4) - 1$ and $d_i \geq 4$ for all $1 \leq i \leq k$; for any integer $w \geq 2(d_u - 4) + 2(d_v - 4) - 1$, there always exists a data cube with w empty cells that causes m-d inferences.*

These connections between inferences and the number of empty cells have following implications. First, a data cube with no empty cells being free of inferences means that the threat of inferences is absent if the adversary does not know any cell from outbound channels. Second, a data cube can still be free of m-d inferences, if it has fewer empty cells than the given upper bound; however, the data cube needs to be checked for 1-d inferences. Hence, if an adversary knows about a few cells in the core cuboid, inferences can still be easily controlled. Third, a data cube having more empty cells than a given bound always has inferences. That is, a data cube cannot be protected from an adversary who already knows most of the cells. Finally, if the number of empty cells falls between the given bounds, we can no longer tell whether inferences are possible by only looking at the number of empty cells.

The above results can be used to compute inference-free aggregations based on the three-tier architecture. The data tier corresponds to the core cuboid; the aggregation tier corresponds to a collection of cells in aggregation cuboids that are free of inferences; the query tier includes any query that can be rewritten using the cells in the aggregation tier. To compute the aggregation tier, we first partition the core cuboid based on dimension hierarchies. We then apply the above sufficient conditions to find blocks that are free of inferences. The union of those blocks then forms the aggregation tier. It is straightforward that the aggregation tier satisfies the three properties of the three-tier architecture. Computing the aggregation tier has a linear time complexity in nature since it only requires counting the number of empty cells in each block. This is an improvement over previously known methods, such as transforming a matrix to its RREF [8].

Parity-Based Method

The second method is based on a simple fact that even number is closed under the operation of addition and subtraction. The nature of an m-d inference is to keep adding or subtracting (strictly speaking, set union and set difference) sets of cells until the result yields a single cell. Suppose now all the sets have even number of cells, then how to add and subtract those sets to obtain *one* cell would be significantly more difficult, although still possible as we shall show shortly. We consider the *multi-dimensional range* (or MDR for short) query, which can be regarded as an axis-parallel box. We use the notation $q^*(u, v)$ to denote an MDR query, where u and v are any two given cells. Table 4 gives examples of MDR queries and their answers. By restricting MDR queries to only include even number of cells, it may seem that inferences are hard to obtain. However, if we add up the answers to the last four queries and subtract from it the answer to the first query, then dividing the result by two gives us Bob's commission in Q_2, that is $x_2 = 500$.

Table 4. Examples of Multi-dimensional Range Queries

The Core Cuboid

	Q_1	Q_2	Q_3	Q_4
Bob	x_1	x_2	x_3	
Alice		x_4	x_5	x_6

MDR Queries

MDR Query	Answer
$q^*(\langle Q_1, Bob\rangle, \langle Q_4, Alice\rangle)$	6500
$q^*(\langle Q_1, Bob\rangle, \langle Q_2, Bob\rangle)$	1500
$q^*(\langle Q_2, Alice\rangle, \langle Q_3, Alice\rangle)$	2000
$q^*(\langle Q_3, Alice\rangle, \langle Q_4, Alice\rangle)$	1500
$q^*(\langle Q_3, Bob\rangle, \langle Q_3, Alice\rangle)$	2500

The model of inferences in SUM-only data cube needs to be enhanced with the new concept of *derivability* and *equivalence* between sets of queries.

Intuitively, if a set of queries is derivable from another set, then the answers to the former can be computed using the answers to the latter. By definition, if a set of queries is derivable from another set of queries, then the former is free of inferences if the latter is so, while the converse is not necessarily true. To determine whether the collection of even MDR queries, denoted as Q^*, causes any inferences, we find another collection of queries that are equivalent to Q^* and whose inferences are easier to detect. Intuitively, the collection of even MDR queries contains redundancy that can be removed by decomposing the queries into the smallest even range queries, that is *pairs* of cells. For example, in Table 4 the query $q^*(\langle Q_2, Bob\rangle, \langle Q_3, Alice\rangle)$ is derivable from $\{q^*(\langle Q_2, Bob\rangle, \langle Q_3, Bob\rangle), q^*(\langle Q_2, Alice\rangle, \langle Q_3, Alice\rangle)\}$, and hence is redundant in terms of causing inferences.

It is not always apparent whether we can find an appropriate collection of pairs equivalent to Q^*. First, the collection of pairs included by Q^*, as shown in Table 5, is *not enough* for this purpose. The query $q^*(\langle Q_1, Bob\rangle, \langle Q_4, Alice\rangle)$ is not derivable from the pairs included by Q^*. Second, the collection of all possible pairs is *too much*. For example, the pair $\{\langle Q_1, Bob\rangle, \langle Q_3, Bob\rangle\}$ is not derivable from Q^*. Fortunately, Theorem 2 shows that there always exists a set of pairs equivalent to the collection of even MDR queries (the proof can be found in [33]). The proof of the theorem includes an algorithm that constructs the desired set of pairs Q^p for any given data cube.

Table 5. The Collection of Even MDR Queries Q^* For The Data Cube in Table 4

Pairs	$q^*(\langle Q_1, Bob\rangle, \langle Q_2, Bob\rangle)$	$q^*(\langle Q_2, Bob\rangle, \langle Q_3, Bob\rangle)$
	$q^*(\langle Q_2, Bob\rangle, \langle Q_2, Alice\rangle)$	$q^*(\langle Q_2, Alice\rangle, \langle Q_3, Alice\rangle)$
	$q^*(\langle Q_3, Alice\rangle, \langle Q_4, Alice\rangle)$	$q^*(\langle Q_3, Bob\rangle, \langle Q_3, Alice\rangle)$
Non-pairs	$q^*(\langle Q_1, Bob\rangle, \langle Q_4, Alice\rangle)$	$q^*(\langle Q_2, Bob\rangle, \langle Q_3, Alice\rangle)$

Theorem 2. *Given any data cube, let the core cuboid be C_c and the collection of even MDR queries be Q^*, then a set of pairs $Q^p = \{\{u, v\} \mid u \in C_c, v \in C_c, u \neq v\}$ can always be found in $O(\mid C_c \mid \cdot \mid Q^* \mid)$ time, such that $Q^* \equiv_d Q^p$ is true.*

For example, in Table 5, the algorithm groups cells included by the query into pairs. For $q^*(\langle Q_1, Bob\rangle, \langle Q_4, Alice\rangle)$, it first group cells along one dimension and have $\{\langle Q_1, Bob\rangle, \langle Q_2, Bob\rangle\}$ and $\{\langle Q_2, Alice\rangle, \langle Q_3, Alice\rangle\}$. It then groups the remaining two cells $\langle Q_3, Bob\rangle$ and $\langle Q_4, Alice\rangle$ into a third pair. Similarly, it processes the other queries in Table 5. The final result Q^p will include all the pairs given in Table 5 plus $\{\langle Q_3, Bob\rangle, \langle Q_4, Alice\rangle\}$, as shown in Table 6. It can be verified that the Q^p in Table 6 is indeed equivalent to the Q^* in Table 5. First, any query in Q^* can be derived by adding up the corresponding pairs in Q^p. Second, each pair in Q^p can be derived by subtracting queries in Q^*.

Table 6. A Collection of Pairs $\mathcal{Q}^p$ Equivalent To The Even MDR Queries in Table 5

In $\mathcal{Q}^*$	$\{\langle Q_1, Bob\rangle, \langle Q_2, Bob\rangle\}$	$\{\langle Q_2, Bob\rangle, \langle Q_3, Bob\rangle\}$
	$\{\langle Q_2, Bob\rangle, \langle Q_2, Alice\rangle\}$	$\{\langle Q_2, Alice\rangle, \langle Q_3, Alice\rangle\}$
	$\{\langle Q_3, Alice\rangle, \langle Q_4, Alice\rangle\}$	$\{\langle Q_3, Bob\rangle, \langle Q_3, Alice\rangle\}$
Not In $\mathcal{Q}^*$	$\{\langle Q_3, Bob\rangle, \langle Q_4, Alice\rangle\}$	

Knowing that $\mathcal{Q}^*$ is equivalent to $\mathcal{Q}^p$, we only need to decide if the latter causes any inference. We first denote $\mathcal{Q}^p$ as an undirected simple graph $G(C_c, \mathcal{Q}^p)$. That is, the core cuboid is the vertex set and the collection of pairs $\mathcal{Q}^p$ is the edge set. We then apply Chin's result that a collection of pairs is free of inferences iff the corresponding graph is a bipartite graph (that is, a graph with no cycle composed of odd number of edges) [37]. The existence of odd cycles can easily be decided with a breadth-first search, taking time $O(|C_c| + |\mathcal{Q}^p|)$. As an example, the graph corresponding to the $\mathcal{Q}^p$ given in Table 6 will have an odd cycle of three edges, corresponding to the inference described earlier.

The parity-based method can be enforced based on the three-tier inference control architecture described earlier. A partition of the core cuboid based on dimension hierarchies composes the data tier. We then apply the parity-based method to each block in the partition to compute the aggregation tier. The query tier includes any query that is derivable from the aggregation tier. The relation R_{AD} and R_{QA} between the three tiers are simply the derivable relation. The first property of the aggregation tier is satisfied because the number of pairs in $\mathcal{Q}^p$ must be $O(n^2)$, where n is the size of the core cuboid. The last two conditions are satisfied in a straightforward way.

5.2 Generic Data Cubes

The two methods we just described can only deal with SUM-only data cubes, which is a limitation inherited from statistical databases. Chin has shown that even to detect inferences caused by queries involving both MAXs and SUMs is intractable [6]. This section describes a method that does not directly detect inferences, but instead first prevents m-d inferences and then removes 1-d inferences. This approach enables the method to deal with data cubes with generic aggregation types, and it also significantly reduces the complexity because 1-d inferences are generally easy to detect by examining each query separately. In contrast, m-d inferences are hard to detect because they are caused by combinations of queries instead of each individual query.

Access Control

Limiting access control to the core cuboid is not always appropriate. Values in aggregation cuboids may also carry sensitive information. For example, in Figure 1 a user may need to be prohibited from accessing any employee's yearly or more detailed commissions. This requirement makes the values in both the core cuboid $\langle quarter, employee \rangle$ and the aggregation cuboid $\langle year, employee \rangle$ sensitive. The data cube is thus partitioned along the dependency lattice into two parts. As another example, the previous requirement may only need to be applied to the first year data, whereas data in other years can be freely accessed. That is, the data cube should also be partitioned along the time dimension.

To meet such security requirements, we describe a framework for specifying authorization objects in data cubes. The function $Below()$ partitions the data cube along the dependency lattice, and the function $Slice()$ partitions the data cube along dimensions. An object is simply the intersection of the two. For example, the above security requirements can now be specified as $Object(L, S)$, where $L = \{\langle year, employee \rangle\}$ and S includes all the cells in the first four quarters of the core cuboids. The cells included by $object(L, S)$ must be included by one of the two cuboids in $Below(L)$, that is $\langle year, employee \rangle$ and $\langle quarter, employee \rangle$; the cell must also be in the first year, that is their first attribute must be one of the following values: Q_1 through Q_4, Y_1, or ALL.

The object specification satisfies the following desired property. First, for any cell in an object, the object will also include all the ancestors of that cell. Intuitively, ancestors of a sensitive cell contain more detailed information and should also be regarded as sensitive. For example, if an object includes the cuboid $\langle year, employee \rangle$, then it also includes the core cuboid , because otherwise an adversary may compute the former from the latter. Second, the definition can be easily extended to objects specified with multiple pairs $O = \{L_i, S_i\}$ due to the fact that $Below()$ is distributive over set union. That is, $Below(L_1 \cup L_2) = Below(L_1) \cup Below(L_2)$. The union of the objects $Object(L_i, S_i)$ thus composes a new object $Object(O)$.

Lattice-Based Inference Control

We do not assume specific models of inferences. Instead, we consider inferences that satisfy given algebraic properties. More specifically, given any two set of cells in a data cube, denoted as S and T, we say a cell c is *redundant* with respect to T if S includes both c and all its ancestors in any single cuboid; a cell c is *non-comparable* to T, if for every $c' \in T$, c is neither ancestor nor descendant of c'. We say a definition of inference is *reducible*, if for any $c \in S$ that is either redundant or non-comparable (or both) then S causes inferences to T iff $S - \{c\}$ does so. That is, reducible inferences can be checked without considering any redundant or non-comparable cells. For example, the inference in SUM-only data cubes, as discussed in the previous section, is indeed reducible. For example, suppose S denotes the union of $\langle all, employee \rangle$ and $\langle year, employee \rangle$, and suppose T includes the cells of $\langle quarter, employee \rangle\rangle\}$ in the first four quarters. Then the cell in $\langle all, employee \rangle$ is *redundant* and the cell $\langle Y_2, Bob \rangle$ is *non-comparable*.

Intuitively, a redundant cell in S can be ignored, because it can be computed from other cells in S. This implies that we only consider *distributive* aggregation functions [15], such as SUM, MAX, MIN, COUNT, or non-distributive functions that can be converted to distributive ones, such as AVERAGE to a pair (SUM,COUNT). By ignoring non-comparable cells, we shall only consider the inference caused by descendants. This assumption may not hold if outbound knowledge can correlate cells that do not depend on each other. To simplify our discussion, we first consider a special case where the set S in any $Object(L, S)$ is a complete cuboid. The object $Object(L, S)$ is thus simply (the union of) the cuboids in $Below(L)$. For example, in Figure 3 the lower curve in solid line depicts such an object $Below(\{\langle a^1, b^1, c^2, d^2 \rangle, \langle a^1, b^2, c^1, d^2 \rangle\})$ in a four-dimensional data cube. Let T be the object and S be its complement to the data cube. To remove inferences from S to T, we first find a subset of S that is free of m-d inferences to T and at the same time is maximal for this purpose. We then remove 1-d inferences from this subset.

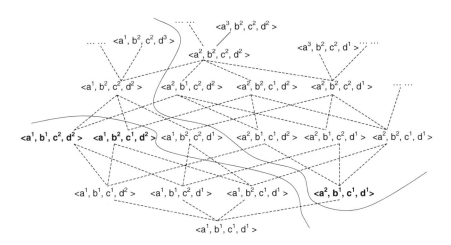

Fig. 3. An Example of Preventing m-d Inferences

The definition of reducible inferences can help to find a maximal subset of S that is free of m-d inferences to T. Roughly speaking, with respect to each cuboid in T, we can remove all the redundant and non-comparable cuboids from S such that only a set of *minimal descendants* need to be considered. For example, in Figure 3, only the two minimal descendants $\langle a^2, b^1, c^1, d^1 \rangle$ and $\langle a^1, b^2, c^2, d^1 \rangle$ need to be examined for inferences. However, checking whether the set of minimal descendants cause m-d inferences may still incur high complexity, and we want to avoid such checking. We take a more aggressive approach by only allowing accesses to one minimal descendant. For example, we can choose to allow $\langle a^2, b^1, c^1, d^1 \rangle$ and remove $\langle a^1, b^2, c^2, d^1 \rangle$ from S. We also need to remove other cuboids that are not redundant, such as $\langle a^1, b^2, c^2, d^2 \rangle$ and $\langle a^1, b^2, c^2, d^3 \rangle$. The result is a subset of S that includes all the descendants of $\langle a^2, b^1, c^1, d^1 \rangle$, namely, a *descendant closure*, as illustrated by the upper curve in Figure 3.

The descendant closure has only one minimal descendant of the core cuboid, and hence is free of m-d inferences to the core cuboid. The property actually holds for any other cuboid in T. That is, for any $c \in T$, only one minimal descendant of c appears in this subset of S, and hence m-d inferences to c are no longer possible. On the other hand, it is easy to observe that the upper curve cannot be modified to include any of the cuboids between the current two curves in Figure 3 without inducing possible m-d inferences. More generally, as long as a cuboid c_r satisfies that all its ancestors are included by T, the descendant closure of c_r will be the maximal result for preventing m-d inferences. Moreover, the descendant closure turns out to be the only choice, if any subset of S is to prevent the need for checking m-d inferences and at the same time being maximal for that purpose. These results are summarized in Theorem 3 (the proof can be found in [32]).

Theorem 3. *In any data cube, let $\mathcal{L}$ be the collection of all cuboids. Given any $L \subseteq \mathcal{L}$, any $C \subseteq \mathcal{L} - Below(L)$ can satisfy both that each cuboid not in C has exactly one descendant in C that is not redundant, and any superset of C must include more than one descendant of some cuboid in $Below(L)$, iff C is the descendant closure of some cuboid c_r satisfying that c_r is not in $Below(L)$ but all of its ancestors are in $Below(L)$.*

The results in Theorem 3 can be extended to the general case where the object is specified by a set of cells instead of a set of cuboids. The key issue in such an extension is that $Slice(S_i)$'s may overlap, and it would be prohibitive if we need to compute a descendant closure for each of their intersections. Fortunately, the set intersection of descendant closures is always another descendant closure. This property guarantees that no m-d inferences are possible to the cells included by multiple slices. However, obtaining the maximal result in Theorem 3 is intractable in the general case, and is no easier than the maximum independent set problem.

After m-d inferences are prevented, we still need to remove 1-d inferences. It may seem to be a viable solution to simply restrict any cell that causes 1-d inferences. However, the restricted cells themselves then become targets of inferences. Hence, we must adopt the following iterative procedure to remove 1-d inferences. First, we check each cell and add those that cause 1-d inferences to the object so they will be prohibited by access control. Second, we control m-d inferences to this new object by applying the results in Theorem 3 again. By repeating the two steps, we gradually remove all 1-d inferences. The procedure terminates in at most m steps, where m is the number cuboids. The final result is a set of cells that are guaranteed to be free of inferences to the object.

The lattice-based inference control method can be implemented based on the three-tier inference control model given in Section 4. The authorization object computed through the above iterative process comprises the data tier. The complement of the object is the aggregation tier since it does not cause any inferences to the data tier. The first property of the three-tier model is satisfied because the number of cuboids is constant compared to the number of cells, and hence the size of the aggregation tier must be polynomial in the size of the data tier. Because the aggregation tier is a collection of descendant closures of single cuboids, the aggregation tier naturally forms a partition on the data tier, satisfying the second property. The aggregation tier apparently satisfies the last property.

6 Conclusion

This chapter has discussed the security requirements of OLAP systems and data warehouses. We have argued that the most challenging security threat lies in that sensitive data stored in a data warehouse may be disclosed through seemingly innocent OLAP queries. We then described three methods specifically proposed for securing OLAP data cubes. The first two methods have been inspired by existing inference control methods in statistical databases. We have shown that better results can be obtained by exploring the unique structures of data cube queries, although both methods also inherit limitations from their counterparts in statistical databases. Finally, the lattice-based method aimed to remove many limitations of previous methods. The method adopted a preventing-then-removing approach to avoid the infeasible task of detecting m-d inferences. The method also based itself upon algebraic properties instead of on specific models of inferences, which helped to broaden the scope of inference control. All the proposed methods could be implemented on the basis of a three-tier inference control architecture that is especially suitable for OLAP systems.

Acknowledgements

This material is based upon work supported by National Science Foundation under grants CT-0627493, IIS-0242237, and IIS-0430402; and by Natural Sciences and Engineering Research Council of Canada under Discovery Grant N01035. Any opinions, findings, and conclusions or recommendations expressed in this material are those of the authors and do not necessarily reflect the views of the sponsoring organizations.

References

1. N.R. Adam and J.C. Wortmann.   Security-control methods for statistical databases: a comparative study. *ACM Computing Surveys*, 21(4):515–556, 1989.

2. R. Agrawal and R. Srikant. Privacy-preserving data mining. In *Proceedings of the Nineteenth ACM SIGMOD Conference on Management of Data (SIG-MOD'00)*, pages 439–450, 2000.

3. R. Agrawal, R. Srikant, and D. Thomas. Privacy-preserving olap. In *Proceedings of the Twenty-fourth ACM SIGMOD Conference on Management of Data (SIGMOD'05)*, pages 251–262, 2005.

4. L.L. Beck. A security mechanism for statistical databases. *ACM Trans. on Database Systems*, 5(3):316–338, 1980.

5. B. Bhargava. Security in data warehousing (invited talk). In *Proceedings of the 3rd Data Warehousing and Knowledge Discovery (DaWak'00)*, 2000.

6. F.Y. Chin. Security problems on inference control for sum, max, and min queries. *Journal of the Association for Computing Machinery*, 33(3):451–464, 1986.

7. F.Y. Chin and G. Özsoyoglu. Statistical database design. *ACM Trans. on Database Systems*, 6(1):113–139, 1981.

8. F.Y. Chin and G. Özsoyoglu. Auditing and inference control in statistical databases. *IEEE Trans. on Software Engineering*, 8(6):574–582, 1982.

9. E.F. Codd, S.B. Codd, and C.T. Salley. Providing olap to user-analysts: An IT mandate. White Paper, 1993. E.F. Codd Associates.

10. L.H. Cox. On properties of multi-dimensional statistical tables. *Journal of Statistical Planning and Inference*, 117(2):251–273, 2003.

11. D.E. Denning. *Cryptography and data security*. Addison-Wesley, Reading, Massachusetts, 1982.

12. D.E. Denning and J. Schlörer. Inference controls for statistical databases. *IEEE Computer*, 16(7):69–82, 1983.

13. D. Dobkin, A.K. Jones, and R.J. Lipton. Secure databases: protection against user influence. *ACM Trans. on Database Systems*, 4(1):97–106, 1979.

14. W. Du and Z. Zhan. Building decision tree classifier on private data. In *Proceedings of the 2002 IEEE International Conference on Data Mining (ICDM'02)*, 2002.

15. J. Gray, A. Bosworth, A. Bosworth, A. Layman, D. Reichart, M. Venkatrao, F. Pellow, and H. Pirahesh. Data cube: A relational aggregation operator generalizing group-by, cross-tab, and sub-totals. *Data Mining and Knowledge Discovery*, 1(1):29–53, 1997.

16. P. Griffiths and B.W. Wade. An authorization mechanism for a relational database system. *ACM Transactions on Database Systems*, 1(3):242–255, September 1976.

17. J. Han. OLAP mining: Integration of OLAP with data mining. In *IFIP Conf. on Data Semantics*, pages 1–11, 1997.

18. V. Harinarayan, A. Rajaraman, and J.D. Ullman. Implementing data cubes efficiently. In *Proceedings of the Fifteenth ACM SIGMOD international conference on Management of data (SIGMOD'96)*, pages 205–227, 1996.

19. K. Hoffman. *Linear Algebra*. Prentice-Hall, Englewood Cliffs, New Jersey, 1961.

20. S. Jajodia, P. Samarati, M.L. Sapino, and V.S. Subrahmanian. Flexible support for multiple access control policies. *ACM Transactions on Database Systems*, 26(4):1–57, dec 2001.

21. J.M. Mateo-Sanz and J. Domingo-Ferrer. A method for data-oriented multivariate microaggregation. In *Proceedings of the Conference on Statistical Data Protection'98*, pages 89–99, 1998.

22. G. Miklau and D. Suciu. A formal analysis of information disclosure in data exchange. In *Proceedings of the 23th ACM SIGMOD Conference on Management of Data (SIGMOD'04)*, 2004.

23. N. Pendse. The olap report - what is olap. OLAP Report Technical Report, 2001. http:// www.olapreport.com / fasmi.htm.

24. P. Samarati. Protecting respondents' identities in microdata release. *IEEE Transactions on Knowledge and Data Engineering*, 13(6):1 010–1027, 2001.

25. R.S. Sandhu, E.J. Coyne, H.L. Feinstein, and C.E. Youman. Role-based access control models. *IEEE Computer*, 29(2):38–47, 1996.

26. J. Schlörer. Security of statistical databases: multidimensional transformation. *ACM Trans. on Database Systems*, 6(1):95–112, 1981.

27. A. Shoshani. OLAP and statistical databases: Similarities and differences. In *Proceedings of the Sixteenth ACM SIGACT-SIGMOD-SIGART Symposium on Principles of Database Systems (PODS'97)*, pages 185–196, 1997.

28. G. Pernul T. Priebe. Towards olap security design - survey and research issues. In *Proceedings of 3rd ACM International Workshop on Data Warehousing and OLAP (DOLAP'00)*, pages 114–121, 2000.

29. Pedersen T.B. and Jense C.S. Multidimensional database technology. *IEEE Computer*, 34(12):40–46, 2001.

30. J.F. Traub, Y. Yemini, and H. Woźniakowski. The statistical security of a statistical database. *ACM Trans. on Database Systems*, 9(4):672–679, 1984.

31. J. Vaidya and C. Clifton. Privacy preserving association rule mining in vertically partitioned data. In *Proceedings of the eighth ACM SIGKDD international conference on Knowledge discovery and data mining (KDD'02)*, pages 639–644, 2002.

32. L. Wang, S. Jajodia, and D. Wijesekera. Securing OLAP data cubes against privacy breaches. In *Proceedings of the 2004 IEEE Symposium on Security and Privacy (S&P'04)*, pages 161–175, 2004.

33. L. Wang, Y.J. Li, D. Wijesekera, and S. Jajodia. Precisely answering multidimensional range queries without privacy breaches. In *Proceedings of the Eighth European Symposium on Research in Computer Security (ESORICS'03)*, pages 100–115, 2003.

34. L. Wang, D. Wijesekera, and S. Jajodia. Cardinality-based inference control in data cubes. *Journal of Computer Security*, 12(5):655–692, 2004.

35. L. Willenborg and T. de Walal. *Statistical disclosure control in practice*. Springer Verlag, New York, 1996.

36. C. Yao, X. Wang, and S. Jajodia. Checking for k-anonymity violation by views. In *Proceedings of the Thirty-first Conference on Very Large Data Base (VLDB'05)*, 2005.

37. C.T. Yu and F.Y. Chin. A study on the protection of statistical data bases. In *Proceedings of the ACM SIGMOD International Conference on Management of Data (SIGMOD'77)*, pages 169–181, 1977.

9

Security for Workflow Systems

Vijayalakshmi Atluri[1] and Janice Warner[2]

[1] Rutgers University, Newark, NJ atluri@cimic.rutgers.edu
[2] Rutgers University, Newark, NJ janice@cimic.rutgers.edu

Summary. Workflow technology is often employed by organizations to automate their day-to-day business processes. The primary advantage of adopting workflow technology is to separate the business policy from the business applications so that flexibility and maintainability of business process reengineering can be enhanced. Today's workflows are not necessarily bound to a single organization, but may span multiple organizations where the tasks within a workflow are executed by different organizations.

In order to execute a workflow in a secure and correct manner, one must ensure that only authorized users should be able to gain access to the tasks of the workflow and resources managed by them. This can be accomplished by synchronizing the access control with the specified control flow dependencies among tasks. Without such synchronization, a user may still hold privileges to execute a task even after its completion, which may have adverse effects on security. In addition, the assignment of authorized users to tasks should respect the separation of duty constraints specified to limit the fraud. Another challenging issue in dealing with workflows spanning multiple organizations is to ensure their secure execution while considering conflict-of-interest among these organizations. Another issue that is of theoretical interest is the safety analysis of the proposed authorization models and their extension in this area. In this book chapter, we review all the above security requirements pertaining to workflow systems, and discuss the proposed solutions to meet these requirements.

1 Introduction

Organizations constantly reengineer and optimize their business processes to reduce costs, deliver timely services, and enhance their competitive advantage in the market. Reengineering involves assessment, analysis, and redesign of business processes, including introducing new processes into existing systems, eliminating redundant processes, reallocating sharable resources, and optimizing the process. Business processes are supported via information systems that include databases that create, access, process and manage business information.

As advances in information systems take place to facilitate business transactions, organizations are seeking ways to effectively integrate and automate their business processes. The advent of database technology has made the change of data more adaptive by successfully separating the access of data from the applications. However, any change and enhancement to the business policies would entail modifying application codes, as the business policy is still often hard-coded in applications rather than accessible to all systems. Workflow systems are a step in the direction of providing both automation and reengineering functionalities. The fundamental idea of workflow technology is to separate the business policy from the business applications to enhance flexibility and maintainability of business process reengineering. This separation facilitates reengineering at the organizational level without delving into the application details. Other advantages include supporting resource allocation and dynamically adapting to workload changes. As a testament to the recognition of these benefits, workflow systems are today used in numerous business application domains including office automation, finance and banking, software development, healthcare, telecommunications, manufacturing and production, and scientific research.

Workflow management aims at modeling and controlling the execution of business processes involving a combination of manual and automated activities in an organization. A workflow is defined as a set of coordinated activities that achieves a common business objective [1]. Thus, a workflow separates the various activities of a given organizational process into a set of well-defined activities, called *tasks*. A task is a described piece of work that contributes toward the accomplishment of a process [23, 15]. Tasks may be carried out by humans, application programs, or processing entities according to the organizational rules relevant to the process represented by the workflow. Tasks that build up the workflow are usually related and dependent upon one another, which in turn are specified by a set of execution constraints called task dependencies. These task dependencies play a key role in supporting various workflow specifications such as concurrency, serialization, exclusion, alternation, compensation and so on. To ensure the correctness of workflow execution, tasks need to be executed in a coordinated manner based on these dependency requirements. A workflow management system (WFMS) is a system that supports process specification, enactment, monitoring, coordination, and administration of workflow process through the execution of software, whose order of execution is based on the workflow logic [1]. In the following, we provide an example workflow to facilitate understanding of tasks and dependencies.

Example 1. Consider a travel reimbursement processing workflow [2] as shown in Figure 1. This workflow consists of four tasks: preparing a claim (T_1), approving the claim (T_2), issuing a check (T_3) and notifying the employee in case the claim is denied (T_4).

Coordinating constraints between the tasks are represented by dependencies shown above the arrows connecting the tasks. The task dependency "bs"

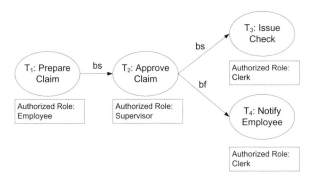

Fig. 1. Example Workflow

means that the next task begins if the previous task successfully completes. The task dependency "bf" means that the next task begins if the previous task completes in failure. A check will be issued (T_3) if the claim is approved (T_2 is completed in success). Otherwise, the employee will be sent a notification (T_4).

Each task is also associated with processing entities who are authorized to perform the task. Specifically, task T_1 can be executed by any employee, task T_2 must be executed by a supervisor, and tasks T_3 and T_4 are to be executed by clerks.

Workflow or business process management systems are widely available as complete systems or software that can be added to other systems in order to integrate them. Major providers of business process management systems include SAP NetWeaver, Bea's WebLogic Integration, Sunguard Carnot, IBM FlowMark, Intalio BPMS, Lombari TeamWorks, Seagull LegaSuite, Oracle BPEL, Savvion Business Manager, and Ultimus BPM. Features include design and lay-out of workflow including creation of rules for task assignment such as those shown in the example with which assignments of tasks can be made based on individual authorization, group authorization or role.

2 Security Requirements in Workflow Systems

In addition to the traditional security requirements such as confidentiality, integrity, availability and authentication, a number of security measures need to be taken into account while building a secure workflow system. In the following, we enumerate these and discuss the issues and solutions proposed by researchers in the following sections.

- *Authorization* - Refers to enforcing access control to ensure only authorized individuals/roles are allowed to execute tasks within a workflow by adhering to the workflow dependencies

- *Separation of Duty* - These are additional constraints associated with the workflow to limit the abilities of agents to reduce the risk of fraud.
- *Delegation* Refers to the delegation of authority to execute a task.
- *Conflict-of-interest* - Refers to preventing the flow of sensitive information flow among competing organizations participating in the workflow.
- *Safety analysis* - Refers to the analysis of studying the propagation of authorizations from the current state. This helps in answering questions such as whether a subject (user) can gain access to execute a task.

3 Workflow Authorization Model

A workflow deals with coordinated execution of tasks that involve processing of each of the tasks in the workflow by executing agents (humans or programs). To execute a task, relevant privileges on required objects have to be granted to appropriate subjects. Agents authorized to execute a task should gain access on the required objects only when the task is to be executed. Considering once again example 1, an employee should not be able to change the prepared claim after it has been approved by his supervisor. Atluri and Huang proposed a Workflow Authorization Model (WAM) [5] that is capable of specifying authorizations in such a way that subjects gain access to required objects only during the execution of the task, thus synchronizing the authorization flow with the workflow. To achieve this synchronization, WAM uses the notion of an Authorization Template (AT) that can be associated with each task. AT is comprised of the static parameters of the authorization that can be defined during the design of the workflow. A task may have more than one AT associated with it in the case where there is more than one type of object to be processed or more than one executing agent needed to perform the task. WAM dynamically assigns authorizations to support workflow activities in a way that the time interval associated with the required authorization to perform a task changes according to the time during which the task actually executes. When the task starts execution, its AT(s) are used to derive the actual authorization. When the task finishes, the authorization is revoked. This is accomplished by placing an object hole in the AT.

A new authorization is granted to an executing agent only when an object hole is filled with an appropriate object. Besides specifying authorizations on tasks to specific individuals, alternatively, one may also specify them in terms of roles. Roles represent organizational agents who perform certain job functions. Users, in turn, are assigned to appropriate roles based on their qualifications. Specifying authorizations on roles is not only convenient but reduces the complexity of access control because the number of roles in an organization is significantly smaller than that of users. Moreover, the use of roles as authorization subjects (instead of users) avoids having to revoke and re-grant authorizations whenever users change their positions and /or duties within the organization. In workflow environments, role-based authorization also facilitates dynamic load balancing when a task can be performed by several individuals. Most commercials WFMSs support role-based authorizations.

The synchronization of the workflow and the authorization flow, as accomplished by WAM, is illustrated with the following example:

Example 2. Consider the workflow in example 1. Suppose the associated executing agents for performing tasks T_1, T_2 and T_3 are John, Mary, and Ken respectively. The authorization templates associated with the tasks would be: $AT(T_1) = (employee, (claim \circ), prepare)$, $AT(T_2) = (supervisor, (claim \circ), approve)$ and $AT(T_3) = (clerk, (claim \circ), issue)$. When John initiates a claim, the hole (i.e., $\circ$) in $AT(T_1)$ will be filled with the object being processed by T_1. As soon as the object hole in the authorization template is filled with the claim form, John receives the authorization to prepare it. Assume he starts this at time 40. At this point, John is granted the authorization to prepare the claim. Suppose he finishes it and sends it to his supervisor at time 47. The authorization template then generates the authorization (John, claim1, prepare, [40,47]), which means the authorization is revoked as soon as he finishes his task. When he finishes T_1, the object was send to T_2, i.e., for approval. Now the hole in $AT(T_2)$ is filled with this object. When the claim (the instance is claim1) arrives to Mary at 47, an authorization to approve is given to Mary. However, John no longer holds the authorization on this instance of the claim any more. When Mary finishes the approval task, say at 82, her authorization is revoked, thus generating (Mary, claim1, approve, (47,82)). Finally, when Mary approves the claim, the hole in $AT(T_2)$ and filled in $AT(T_3)$, and appropriate authorizations are generated. In this fashion, WAM synchronizes the authorization flow with the progression of the workflow.

4 Separation of Duty

By using authorization templates, one can ensure that access to resources to perform relevant tasks is only given along with the progression of the workflow. In addition to this simple authorization specification as to who is allowed to perform a task and when, workflow designers often specify separation of duty constraints primarily to minimize risk due to fraudulent activities. These constraints, also know as Separation of Duty (SOD) constraints, are rules stating that the executing agent for one task is constrained from performing another task. Considering once again example 1, such a constraint could be that the tasks "prepare claim" and "issue check" should not be executed by the same user [24]. Constraints can also be specified to obtain the opposite effect of separation of duty, that is to specify a binding constraint. An example of a binding constraint is that the person assigned to one task should also be assigned to another.

While this example is an *intra-instance* SOD constraint, more complex constraints specified over multiple workflow instances, called *inter-instance* constraints may be necessary. Broadly speaking, SOD constraints can be categorized as follows.

- *Intra-instance* constraints [18, 10, 9] are specified on a workflow schema and therefore apply to a single instance. While some of these constraints can be enforced at the time of workflow schema specification, others can only be enforced at run-time. Based on this criteria, these can be categorized as follows.
  - *Static constraints:* These constraints can be evaluated without executing the workflow. Examples of such constraints include: (i) At least three roles must be involved in executing the workflow. (ii) The same role must execute tasks T_1 and T_2.
  - *Dynamic constraints:* These constraints can be evaluated only during the execution of a workflow, because they express restrictions based on the execution history of an instance of the workflow. If John belongs to role R_1 and has performed task T_1, then he cannot perform T_2. The constraint mentioned above in the context of claim processing is a dynamic constraint.
  - *Hybrid constraints:* These are constraints whose satisfiability can be partially verified without executing the workflow. An example of such a constraint would be, task T_2 must be executed by a role dominating the role, which executes task T_3.
- *Inter-instance* constraints are specified on instances rather than on the workflow schema. These can either be specified on multiple instances of the same workflow that can only be enforced at run-time, or can be specified on the history of *all* the workflow instances and therefore are not necessarily limited to one workflow. Although the motivation to recognize such constraints is to limit fraud, note that they can also be used for the purpose of workload and resource distribution.

Several researchers have proposed constraint specification languages for describing these types of constraints [11, 27, 12, 21, 16, 28]. Given a set of constraints, we now need to ensure that a workflow can be executed. Specifically, one needs to ensure that a workflow specification with constraints is satisfiable, that the conditions and constraints are actually satisfied during execution. Finally, one must ensure that given a set of task assignments, the workflow can complete - that is there are enough users available to complete the workflow tasks given the constraints.

In [10], Bertino et al. present a language to express different types of intra-instance authorization constraints as clauses in a logic program, and propose solutions to verify the consistency of the constraint specification and to assign users and roles to tasks of the workflow in a such a way that no constraints are violated.

Crampton et al. [14, 26] provide a simpler reference model for those cases where tasks can be partially ordered. They define a workflow reference model which determines whether a workflow can complete if a particular user is assigned to a particular task. The reference monitor works by considering only those tasks that directly flow from the task in question.

Wainer et al. [27] describe a permission system that is used in conjunction with a workflow management system. When a task is to be executed, the WFMS queries the permission system as to which users are authorized to perform the task. The permission system has an organizational model including business rules and constraints, organizational assignments (i.e., who is in what group or department or division) and project assignments. It can be an Enterprise Resource Planning (ERP) component. Proposals like this one help to move business policies away, not only from applications, but even from workflow systems, allowing consistent utilization of business policies across all applications. This proposed approach can work with any of the constraint checking models.

Hung and Karlapalam [19] define a multi-level state machine to address workflow security at three levels: workflow, control and data. At the workflow level, the state machine is concerned with task authorization and assignment/revocation of needed permissions. The control level is involved with monitoring events during the execution of a task. Finally, the data level is concerned with actually information object access. Associated with each task in a workflow are the data objects needed and the order in which the objects should be accessed. The data level enforces the rules associated with access to the data objects.

Atluri and Warner [7] identify the need to further coordinate or check runtime workflows with other conditions and constraints that might apply on the people or objects one might want to associate with the workflow instance. In particular, they describe the need to check task dependencies conditions and conditional authorization constraints against role activation constraints as introduced by Bertino et al. in [8]. Role activation constraints are constraints that limit when a role can be activated. Discussed in [8] were temporal constraints such that a role could only be activated during certain periods of time. For example, a consultant role might only be activated during the timeframe of a contract. Alternatively, role activation constraints might be introduced based on environmental or variables of the activity being performed. For example, one might constrain a user from activating a Area Manager role from a remote computer for fear of intellectual property leakage over the Internet.

Atluri and Warner [28] further describe the need to be able to constrain participation in tasks based upon historical participation in tasks. This is particularly important if a set of users can perform both tasks involving submitting a request and approving a request. In a single instance of the workflow, SoD can be accomplished by forbidding the same user form performing both tasks. However, over several instances, a group of individuals can collude where they continue to participate in the two tasks but different people perform the submission task and different people perform the approval task. To address this issue, the authors propose predicates to specify inter-instance workflow constraints and adapt consistency checking such that a historical record of task assignments is kept and consulted when making assignment decisions. In the following, we elaborate the general approach.

4.1 Static User/Role-task Assignment

The approach proposed in [10] uses advance planning of user/role-task assignment so that run-time assignments can be performed more quickly. The planning phase consists of finding all potential assignments given the constraints and ensures that assignments can be consistently made such that a workflow can complete. Example 3 illustrates an example.

Example 3. Figure 2 shows a research paper review process consisting of three tasks.

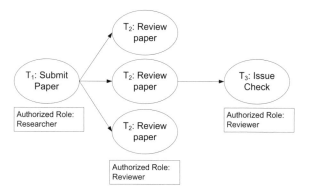

Fig. 2. Example Workflow with Constraints

Task T_1 is the paper submission task. Task T_2 is the paper review task which needs to be performed by three separate members of the reviewer role. Task T_3 is the acceptance decision task. It is performed by a member of the reviewer role but the member can not have performed task T_2. Of course, neither T_2 or T_3 can be performed by the person who performed task T_1. The approach in [11] assesses whether all tasks can successfully be executed given various assignment options. Figure 3 shows how assignment of user U_1 impacts assignment to an instance of task T_2 impacts the workflow.

While in this simple example, it is very easy to see that there must be at least four members of the review role to successfully accomplish the workflow, much more complex scenarios with more tasks, user membership in multiple roles and additional constraints are the norm and the process of planning by

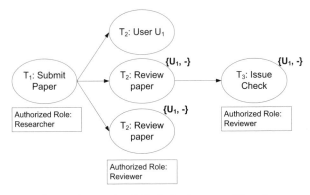

Fig. 3. Example of Task Assignment Planning

assessing potential assignments allows the workflow to proceed in run-time at a quicker pace with a guarantee of the ability to assign all tasks to individuals.

4.2 Constraint Consistency and Enforcement

The workflow authorization model in [11] includes static checking of authorization consistency as a first step. The overall process for checking constraints across workflow instances and for assigning users to tasks is given as a four step process [28]:

- Static Enhancement of the Constraint Base when the workflow is defined - In this phase, constraints that can be derived from other constraints are created and overlapping conditions are rectified.
- Static Inconsistency Identification and Analysis - In this step, constraints and conditions are checked to ensure that different rules do not result in a user or role being authorized and denied from performed a task. This step is performed both when a workflow is defined and when new rules are added.
- Run-time Inconsistency Identification and Analysis - This step is performed whenever a task instance is initiated if there are constraint conditions met by the parameters of the instance.
- Run-time updating of the Constraint Base - Performed whenever assignments are made which constrain assignments for future instances of the workflow.

Step 1 is only performed when a workflow is defined. When a workflow instance is begun, step 3 is initiated. Steps 2 through 4 are repeated whenever new rules are added to the constraint base because of what occurred during a workflow instance. Figure 4 shows a schematic of the process and an example is given below.

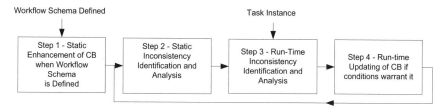

Fig. 4. Overall Constraint Consistency Checking when Inter-instance Workflow Constraints Exist

Example 4. Suppose we have a two task workflow where T_2 is an approval task for task T_1. Both tasks can generally be done by role R_A consisting of members John, Lisa, Paul, Pam and Sam. When the workflow concerns a high-valued customer, Starco, someone from role R_B must perform task T_2. Role R_B's members are Robert and Jane. Now suppose we have the following constraints:

C_1: Sam and Paul are related *(This is not a constraint per se but a fact that is used by other constraints.)*
C_2: Pam and Robert are related.
C_3: A user can only execute two instances of task T_2.
C_4: A user cannot execute task T_2 when someone who has a relationship with them has performed task T_1 in any other instance for the same customer.
C_5: Someone from role R_B must perform task T_2 when the customer is "StarCo".

Once the workflow schema is defined as above, Step 1 is performed and results in the constraint base being enhanced with the following constraint, which can be derived from constraints 1 and 2 above.

C_6: Sam and Pam are related.

In Step 2, we consider if any conditions overlap. None do, so the set of permitted roles/users and denied roles/users for tasks T_1 and T_2. are determined. Permitted roles and users for task T_1 are $\{R_A\}$ and $\{$John, Lisa, Paul, Pam, Sam$\}$, respectively. Permitted roles and users for task T_2 are $\{R_A, R_B\}$ and $\{$John, Lisa, Paul, Pam, Sam, Robert, Jane$\}$, respectively. There are no denied users or roles.

Now suppose a workflow instance for customer StarCo is begun. Step 3 is initiated. Pam is assigned to task T_1 and Robert to task T_2.

Suppose Robert has already performed task T_2 for StarCo in another instance of this workflow. Step 4 is initiated and results in a new constraint specific to Robert:

C_7: Robert is restricted from performing task T_2 when the customer is StarCo.

Now suppose a new instance of the workflow is begun with StarCo as customer again. The process of assignment and consistency checking would be repeated. Eventually, there may be no one in role R_B who can perform task T_2 when the customer is StarCo due to constraint C_5. This is called a depletion anomaly.

5 Delegation of Authority

Delegation is an important concept often applied in workflow systems to ensure that work can be completed even if the users/roles to perform a specific task are not available. It is usually accomplished by a user (delegator) delegating a task to another user (delegatee). For example, managers may delegate tasks to their subordinates either because they find themselves short on time, because they want to give the subordinate more responsibility or want to train the subordinate to perform the task.

In [3], the model proposed in [10] has been enhanced to allow delegation. Specifically, the ability to delegate tasks to users, roles to users and roles to roles were introduced. To handle interactions between delegations and workflow authorization constraints, consistency checking and task assignment were enhanced as follows. First, when a delegation is requested, a static check is performed to make sure there is no delegation cycle such that task assignment would return to the delegator because of other delegations previous accepted. A second static check is made to ensure that the delegation is not inconsistent with authorization constraints when the delegation is to a specific person. That is, no user obliged to perform a task should be allowed to delegate and no user who is restricted from doing a task should be the recipient of a delegation of that task. At run-time, delegations are further evaluated to make actual assignments when the delegation is of a role or to a role.

Because there is usually some reason for delegation, it should be possible to delegate under certain conditions. Specifically, when delegating a task to a user who is otherwise not authorized to perform the task, the following conditions would help ensure that the user is only authorized when absolutely necessary:

- **Temporal Delegation Conditions** - They allow a user to constraint delegation of a task to a defined time interval. This allows the delegator to set up a delegation to apply at some time in the future for some period of time as specified in the condition. For example, a user might delegate a task during the two hours when she is going to a meeting. Alternatively, a user might delegate a task for the week he will be on vacation. The time interval may also be period, such as every Wednesday.
- **Workload Delegation Conditions** - They allow a user to constrain delegation of a task to a workload level. In other words, workload conditions allow the delegator to define a delegation that will only take place

if assigned workload exceeds a certain level. For the potential delegatee, it allows a rejection to be constrained by the workload that the potential delegatee already has. For example, a user might set up a delegation for tasks assigned once he already has five tasks in his queue.

• **Value Delegation Conditions** - They allow a user to constrain delegation of a task depending upon attributes of the task such as the customer associated with the task or the transaction dollar amount associated with the task. Therefore, a requirement of the workflow management system would be that workflow attributes be specified. For example, in processing an insurance claim, a task associated with Mary Smith's claim which ordinarily might be assigned to any member of the insurance agent role, might be delegated to Jack Jones, a client representative, because he is currently addressing issues with other claims from Ms. Smith. As another, example, a manager might delegate a task to a subordinate with the monetary value of the associated contract is less than $100,000.

The conditions limit delegation to certain points in time based either on temporal conditions, workload or value. Similar constraints can be applied to allow a delegator to revoke a delegation. In either case, if a user is given permissions due to a delegation, one must be concerned if in the middle of the workflow, the conditions no longer apply or the delegation is revoked. If the delegatee has not begun the task and is not yet assigned, no harm is done. They are just removed from any planning set of authorized personnel for the delegated task. If the task is already assigned but not completed, the workflow consistency must be rechecked to see if it can still complete given that the delegatee is no longer authorized. For example, if the delegator is constrained from performing a task because of a separation of duty constraint concerning another task that he has already completed, there may be no one else to perform the task that was previously delegated. Occurrence of such cases should be checked, given that the assignment was made based on the availability of the delegatee. If the task is begun, it should be completed.

Another concern with delegation, is that a delegatee should never be allowed to perform a task that the delegator is not authorized to perform because of other constraints that apply - whether separation of duty, role activation or any other business policy rule. For example, let us say that we have a two task workflow where T_1 is a submission and T_2 is an approval and there is a separation of duty constraint between the two tasks. Suppose Harry delegates task T_2 to Sally. If Harry performs task T_1, Sally should not be allowed to perform task T_2 because Harry is constrained from performing task T_2 in this instance and that constraint should be passed to Sally along with the delegation.

Atluri and Warner [7] introduce the above conditional delegation whereby task or role delegation may be constrained to particular time periods or when workflow variables are within a particular range. These conditions must also be checked against task dependencies and role activation constraints to ensure that a workflow instance can complete successfully given availability of human resources. Similar to [3], the modified workflow authorization consistency process, given all the conditions and constraints, consists of a static phase where temporal and value-based conditions are examined for overlaps. Where there are overlaps, consistency is checked such that a user is not both in the set of users who can perform a task and in the set of users restricted from performing a task. A planning graph is created with all conditions included that need to be checked at run-time (temporal and value-based conditions). At run-time users are assigned to tasks who meet the conditions. If they have submitted delegations, the delegations are evaluated and final assignments are made.

6 Conflict-of-Interest

Execution of inter-organization workflows may raise a number of security issues including conflict of interest among competing organizations, especially when they are executed by mobile software agents without using a centralized control flow. In such a decentralized environment, the entire workflow is sent to the first task execution agent which executes its task and then sends the remaining workflow to the next task execution agent. The workflow moves from agent to agent as the workflow progresses. If the task execution agents belong the the same conflict of interest group, knowledge may be passed to them that would give one or more agents an unfair advantage over other agents. The Chinese wall policy for information flow in a commercial sector, proposed by Brewer and Nash [13], states that information flow from one company to another that cause conflict of interest for individuals within these organization should be prevented. The policy enforced is that people are allowed access to information not in conflict with any other information that they already possess. The company information is categorized into mutually disjoint conflict of interest classes. The following example illustrates the problem.

Example 5. Consider a business travel planning process that makes reservations for a flight, hotel and rental car. The workflow that depicts the travel agent process (shown in figure 5 consists of the tasks: T_1: Input travel information, T_2: Reserve a ticket with Continental Airlines, T_3: if T_2 fails or if the ticket costs more than \$400, reserve a ticket with Delta Airlines, T_4: if the ticket at Continental costs less than \$400 or if the reservation at Delta fails, purchase the ticket at Continental, T_5: if Delta has a ticket, purchase it at Delta, T_6: Reserve a room at the Sheraton if there is a flight reservation, and T_7: Rent a car at Hertz. Such a process are not unusual where users can set a maximum price and preferences for airlines possibly because of frequent flyer perks.

Assume that each task is executed by the appropriate agent (e.g., T_2 by Continental, T_3 by Delta, etc.). Now consider the dependencies between T_2 and T_3 or between T_4. If a mobile agent is used to execute the workflow, after

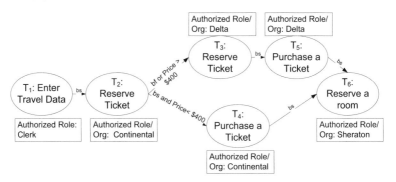

Fig. 5. Example Inter-organizational Workflow

the execution of T_2, Continental must send the remaining workflow to Delta, based on the outcome of T_2. Continental, however, because it has access to the workflow logic, has knowledge that if it has no ticket or if the ticket costs more than $400, Delta Airlines may get the business. Knowing this, Continental has an unfair advantage and may manipulate the price of the ticket, reducing it just under $400.

Atluri et al. in [4] proposed a decentralized workflow Chinese Wall security model to resolve such problems by portioning the workflow in a restrictive manner. The model uses the notion of self-describing workflows and WFMS stubs. Self-describing workflows are partitions of a workflow that carry sufficient information so that they can be managed by a local task execution agent rather than a central WFMS. A WFMS stub is a light-weight component that can be attached to a task execution agent, which is responsible for receiving the self-describing workflow, modifying it and re-sending it to the next task execution.

Web Services are now being touted as the way to coordinate business entities in an inter-organizational business process. A Web Service is a collection of operations that are network-accessible through standardized XML messaging though an interface. In order to created business processes, web services would need to be combined. However, research on the orchestration of web services to form complex business processes is still in its early stages. Research on determining security policies that should apply to the overall process is even further behind and is still at the architectural level [22]. Among other security concerns to address are data privacy, data integrity and audit all of which become more difficult problems when the organization involved in the workflow may be unfamiliar to each other, selected by a third party creator of the overall process. Not only is policy integration needed but languages and mechanisms for exchanging policy information and information about those who will participate in the business process still need to be developed. Kang et al. [20] gave one possible view of how peer-to-peer negotiation of workflow could be done. Their solution allow each organization to have their policies apply to their own tasks. Task access control is thus distributed and autonomous. In the case where constraints need to be set between tasks executed by different organization, a workflow monitor is defined. The monitor records workflow-specific events during runtime and responds to queries from the task-specific access control modules at the various organizations involved in the distributed inter-organizational workflow.

7 Workflow Safety Analysis

Safety analysis refers to ensuring that rights are not propagated unintentionally either directly or indirectly through the granting of permission to some other resource. The safety problem, first identified by Harrison, Ruzzo and Ullman [17], can be stated as the following question: "Is there a reachable state in which a particular subject possesses a particular privilege for a specific object?"

Atluri and Huang [6] showed how colored Petri nets can be used to analyze the safety of the WAM. Petri nets provide a combination of specification and modeling tools to depict the system behavior (thorough its graphical representation), and formal verification tools (through its rich theoretical foundation). Thus, using Petri nets allows a smooth transition from the conceptual level to an implementation of a workflow. In addition, as a graphical tool, Petri nets have the advantage of visually depicting properties, relationships and restrictions among tasks of a given work. Analysis of workflows using Petri nets helps one to understand the implications of the authorization policies. Although each policy may appear innocent in isolation, their cumulative effect may lead to an undesirable authorization state. Their process determines given an initial authorization state and a set of security policies specified by authorization rules, all the reachable authorization states.

Safety analysis becomes especially important when task authorizations may be delegated and revoked as discussed by Schaad et al. [25]. To address the issue, they proposed a model-checking based approach for automated analysis of delegation and revocation functionalities in the context of a workflow requiring static and dynamic separation of duty properties. Using finite state machine to represent the workflow to which they applied a definition of possible delegation and revocation scenarios. The analysis on the state machine will determine whether a set of delegations and/or revocations may be safely accepted.

8 Open Issues

Interoperability and integration are the main research areas of concentration for workflow security. Workflow management systems are maturing but integration with identity management systems, applications, and enterprise resource planning systems is still rather ad-hoc. Workflow management systems separate business process control from applications, making it easier to reuse applications for various business processes. Similarly, it is desirable to separate workflow management from overall business policy management and identity management. However, interactions between security constraints and business rules need to be considered when user-task assignments are performed. Moreover, control of authorizations and permissions can be set across the organization and the workflow management system would only need to be concerned with constraints that apply specifically to the workflow and could consult the policy management system for general authorization questions.

Even less mature is work on inter-organizational workflows. Existing workflow systems do not easily integrate to form allow for formation of a single business process. Instead, inter-organizational workflows are cobbled together from separate, disparate business processes within each organization. Transaction oriented interfaces exist that use the XML-based ebXML business process interface for support of transactions between organizations. This supports inter-organizational interactions by standardizing interfaces. From a security perspective, constraints can currently only be applied at the organizational level. No standard way exists for external organizations to specify constraints on assignment of individuals. Moreover, adhering to the individual organization's business rules and security constraints is essential while composing inter-organizational workflows. A more challenging issue would be to accomplish the composition when individual organizational policies (security as well as business) are sensitive and therefore cannot be revealed.

When processes are created in an ad-hoc manner, participating organizations need also to be concerned with evaluating the risk of working with other participating organizations for the successful completion of the workflow. Trust management issues include being able to assess the credibility of the participants as well as the results of their portion of the process. Contractual obligations must be established, monitored and assessed and audit trails must be available to all participants. Secure, available and reliable information on business process execution has not been deeply addressed in terms of inter-organizational business processes or workflows.

Finally, many of the research ideas presented in this chapter have not been implemented and the problems they solve are still not addressed in existing systems. Specifically, while role based access control and enforcement of the SOD constraints to a limited extent have been implemented in some commercial systems, much of that has been done as application code. As a result, their safety is not tractable.

References

1. Workflow reference model. Technical report, Workflow Management Coalition, 1994.
2. V. Atluri. Security for workflow systems. *Information Security Technical Report*, 6(2):705–716, 2001.
3. V. Atluri, E. Bertino, E. Ferrari, and P. Mazzoleni. Supporting delegation in secure workflow management systems. *IFIP WG 11.3 Conference on Data and Application Security*, August 2003.
4. Vijayalakshmi Atluri, Soon Ae Chun, and Pietro Mazzoleni. A chinese wall security model for decentralized workflow systems. In *CCS '01: Proceedings of the 8th ACM conference on Computer and Communications Security*, 2001.
5. Vijayalakshmi Atluri and Wei-Kuang Huang. An Authorization Model for Workflows. In *Proceedings of the Fifth European Symposium on Research in Computer Security, in Lecture Notes in Computer Science, No.1146, Springer-Verlag*, September 1996.
6. Vijayalakshmi Atluri and Wei-Kuang Huang. A Petri Net Based Safety Analysis of Workflow Authorization Models. *Journal of Computer Security*, 8(2/3):209–240, 2000.
7. Vijayalakshmi Atluri and Janice Warner. Supporting conditional delegation in secure workflow management systems. In *SACMAT*, 2005.
8. Elisa Bertino, Piero Andrea Bonatti, and Elena Ferrari. Trbac: A temporal role-based access control model. *ACM Transactions on Information and System Security (TISSEC)*, 4(3):191–203, 2001.
9. Elisa Bertino, Elena Ferrari, and Vijayalakshmi Atluri. A Flexible Model Supporting the Specification and Enforcement of Role-based Authorizations in Workflow Management Systems. In *Proc. of the 2nd ACM Workshop on Role-based Access Control*, November 1997.
10. Elisa Bertino, Elena Ferrari, and Vijayalakshmi Atluri. An Approach for the Specification and Enforcement of Authorization Constraints in Workflow Management Systems. *ACM Transactions on Information Systems Security*, 2(1), February 1999.
11. Elisa Bertino, Elena Ferrari, and Vijayalakshmi Atluri. An Approach for the Specification and Enforcement of Authorization Constraints in Workflow Management Systems. *ACM Transactions on Information Systems Security*, 2(1), February 1999.
12. R. Botha and J. Eloff. Separation of duties for access control enforcement in workflow environments. *IBM Systems Journal*, 40(3), 2001.
13. D.F.C. Brewer and M.J. Nash. The chinese wall security policy. In *IEEE Symposium on Security and Privacy*, 1989.
14. J. Crampton. A reference monitor for workflow systems with constrained task execution. In *SACMAT 05*, 2005.
15. Dimitrios Georgakopoulos, Mark F. Hornick, and Amit P. Sheth. An overview of workflow management: From process modeling to workflow automation infrastructure. *Distributed and Parallel Databases*, 3(2):119–153, 1995.
16. V. Gligor, S. Gavrila, and D. Ferraiolo. On the formal definition of separation-of-duty policies and their composition. *IEEE Symposium on Research in Security and Privacy*, 1998.

17. Michael A. Harrison, Walter L. Ruzzo, and Jeffrey D. Ullman. Protection in operating systems. *Commun. ACM*, 19(8), 1976.
18. Wei-Kuang Huang and Vijayalakshmi Atluri. Analyzing the Safety of Workflow Authorization Models. In *Proc. of the 12th IFIP WG 11.3 Workshop on Database Security*, July 1998.
19. Patrick C. K. Hung and Kamalakar Karlapalem2. A secure workflow model. In *AISW2003*, 2003.
20. Myong H. Kang, Joon S. Park, and Judith N. Froscher. Access control mechanisms for inter-organizational workflows. In *SACMAT*, 2001.
21. K. Knorr and H. Stormer. Modeling and anlying separation of duties in workflow environments. In *IFIP TC11 Sixtgeenth Annual Working Conference on Information Security*, 2001.
22. Hristo Koshutanski and Fabio Massacci. Interactive access control for web services. *SEC*, pages 151–166, 2004.
23. Marek Rusinkiewicz and Amit P. Sheth. Transactional workflow management in distributed systems (invited paper). In *Proceedings of the First International Workshop on Advances in Databases and Information Systems, Moscow, Russia, May 23 - 26, 1994*, pages 18–33, 1994.
24. Ravi S. Sandhu. Transaction Control Expressions for Separation of Duties. In *Fourth Computer Security Applications Conference*, pages 282–286, 1988.
25. Andreas Schaad, Volkmar Lotz, and Karsten Sohr. A model-checking approach to analysing organisational controls in a loan origination process. In *SACMAT '06: Proceedings of the eleventh ACM symposium on Access control models and technologies*, 2006.
26. K. Tan, J. Crampton, and C. Gunter. The consistency of task-based authorization constraints in workflow systems. In *Proceedings of the 17th IEEE Computer Security Foundations Workshop (CSFW04*, 2004.
27. J. Wainer, P. Barthelmess, and A. Kumar. W-rbac: A workflow security model incorporating controlled overriding of constraints. In *International Journal of Cooperative Information Systems*, volume 12, 2003.
28. Janice Warner and Vijayalakshmi Atluri. Inter-instance authorization constraints for secure workflow management. In *SACMAT*, 2006.

10

Secure Semantic Web Services

Bhavani Thuraisingham

University of Texas at Dallas
bhavani.thuraisingham@utdallas.edu

Summary. Web Services refer to the technologies that allow for making connections. Semantic web consists of technologies that enable machine understandable web pages. Web services make use of semantic web technologies to understand the web pages, conduct reasoning and take actions. Such web services are semantic web services. For many applications the semantic web services have to be secure. In this chapter we discuss secure web services, secure semantic web technologies and finally discuss the integration of secure web services with secure semantic web technologies to develop secure semantic web services.

1 Introduction

As stated in [1], Web Services refer to the technologies that allow for making connections. Services are what you connect together using Web Services. Examples of web services are query service and directory service. A service is the endpoint of a connection. Also, a service has some type of underlying computer system that supports the connection offered. The combination of services - internal and external to an organization - make up a service-oriented architecture.

While many developments have been made on web services, there are now some efforts on securing web services. Access control and security assertion languages are being developed that are based on XML (eXtensible Markup Language). However current web services are not capable of understanding the web pages and taking actions. Therefore, Tim Berners Lee developed the notion of a semantic web that facilitates machine understandable web pages [2]. There are now efforts on integrating web services with the semantic web technologies to produce semantic web services. However these semantic web services have to be secure.

In this chapter we provide an overview of secure web services, secure semantic web and the application of secure semantic web technologies for secure web services to develop secure semantic web services. The organization of this chapter is as follows. Secure web services are discussed in section 2. Secure semantic web technologies are discussed in section 3. Integrating secure web services and secure semantic web technologies are discussed in section 4. The chapter is summarized in section 5. For more details on securing the semantic web we refer to [3].

2 Web Services Security

2.1 Overview

In this section we will provide an overview of web services security. As stated in section 1, web services refer to the technologies that allow for making connections. Web services are being adopted now for numerous applications on the web. It is through these web services that we can now conduct business on the web as well as execute transactions. For many of these applications, it is important that the services be secure.

The organization of this section is as follows. In section 2.2 we provide an overview of web services. The developments in secure web services is discussed in section 2.3. Some security assertion languages are discussed in section 2.4. Shibboleth, which is a distributed web resource access control system that allows federations to cooperate together to share web based resources is discussed in section 2.5 [4].

2.2 Web Services

A service-oriented architecture (SOA) is essentially a collection of services [5]. These services communicate with each other. The communication can involve either simple data passing or it could involve two or more services coordinating some activity such as planning travel. Some means of connecting services to each other is needed. Service-oriented architectures are not new. The first service-oriented architecture can be considered to be DCOM (distributed component object model) and Object Request Brokers (ORBs) based on the CORBA (common object request broker architecture) specification [6]. If a service-oriented architecture is to be effective, we need a clear understanding of the term service. A service is a function that is well-defined, self-contained, and does not depend on the context or state of other services.

The technology of web services is the most likely connection technology of service-oriented architectures. Web services essentially use XML technology to create a robust connection. A service consumer sends a service request message to a service provider. The service provider returns a response message to the service consumer. The request and subsequent response connections are defined in some way that is understandable to both the service consumer and service provider. A service provider can also be a service consumer. The Web Services Description Language (WSDL) forms the basis for Web Services. WSDL uses XML to define messages. The steps involved in providing and consuming a service are the following.

- A service provider describes its service using WSDL. This definition is published on a directory of services. The directory could use Universal Description, Discovery, and Integration (UDDI). Other forms of directories can also be used.
- A service consumer issues one or more queries to the directory to locate a service and determines how to communicate with that service.
- Part of the WSDL provided by the service provider is passed to the service consumer. This tells the service consumer what the requests and responses are for the service provider.
- The service consumer uses the WSDL to send a request to the service provider.
- The service provider provides the expected response to the service consumer.

The UDDI registry is intended to eventually serve as a means of "discovering" Web Services described using WSDL . The idea is that the UDDI registry can be searched in various ways to obtain contact information and the web services available for various organizations. UDDI registry is a way to keep up-to-date on the web services your organization currently uses. An alternative to UDDI is ebXML Directory. All the messages are sent using SOAP. (SOAP at one time stood for Simple Object Access Protocol; Now, the letters in the acronym have no particular meaning.) SOAP essentially provides the envelope for sending the web services messages. SOAP generally uses HTTP, but other means of connection may be used. Security and authorization is an important topic with web services.

2.3 Secure Web Services

Security and authorization specifications for web services are based on XML and can be found in [7, 8, 9]. Various types of control have been proposed including access control, rights, assertions, and protection [10]. We describe some of them in the next section. The list of specifications includes the following:

- eXtensible Access Control Markup Language (XACML)
- eXtensible Rights Markup Language (XrML)
- Security Assertion Markup Language (SAML)
- Service Protection Markup Language (SPML)
- Web Services Security (WSS)
- XML Common Biometric Format (XCBF)
- XML Key Management Specification (XKMS)

Organization for the Advancement of Structured Information Standards (OASIS) is the standards organization promoting security standards for web services. It is a not-for-profit, global consortium that drives the development, convergence, and adoption of e-business standards. Two standards provided by

OASIS are XACML and SAML. XACML (eXtensible Access Control Markup Language) provides fine grained control of authorized activities. SAML (Security Assertions Markup Language) is an XML framework for exchanging authentication and authorization information. The next section gives details of both XACML and SAML.

2.4 XACML and SAML

SAML provides a single point of authorization. It aims to 'solve the web single sign-on' problem. One identity provider in the group allows access. It has Public/Private Key Foundations. Those who are providing SAML in their products are Microsoft Passport, OpenID (VeriSign) and Global Login System (Open Source). As stated in the SAML specifications, its three main components are the following:

Assertions: SAML has three kinds of assertions. Authentication assertions are those in which the user has proven his identity. Attribute assertions contain specific information about the user, such as his spending limits. Authorization decision assertions identify what the user can do, for example, whether he can buy an item.

Protocol: This defines the way that SAML asks for and gets assertions, for example, using SOAP over HTTP for now, although using other methods in the future.

Binding: This details exactly how SAML message exchanges are mapped into SOAP exchanges.

Outstanding issues for SAML include performance, federations and handling legacy applications. With respect to performance, there is no support for caching and also it has to be implemented over HTTP protocols using SOAP. Furthermore, it does not specify encryption and as a result the policies may be compromised. With respect to federations, SAML does not specify authentication protocols. Furthermore, multiple domains cannot be handled. Therefore, OASIS is examining federated identity management. SAML does not work with legacy applications as it is expensive to retrofit.

XACML combines multiple rules into a single policy. It permits multiple users to have different roles. It provides separation between policy writing and application environment. The goal is to standardize access control languages. Some elements of XACML are the following. Users interact with resources. Every resource is protected by an entity known as a Policy Enforcement Point (PEP). This is where the language is actually used and does not actually determine access. PEP sends its request to a Policy Decision Point (PDP). Policies may or may not be actually stored here, but PDP has the final say on access. A decision is relayed to PEP, which then grants or denies access.

Outstanding issues of XACML include distributed responsibility and policy cross-referencing. With respect to distributed responsibility, what happens when the PEP is responsible for multiple objects? What happens when we can compromise the PDP or spoof its communication? How do we guarantee that we reference the right object? While the system is distributed, a policy is still in only one location. With respect to policy cross-referencing, one policy may access another. Typical issues arise as with inheritance and unions/intersections of related work. The challenge is to deal with conflicts.

Researchers as well as practitioners are working on exchanging both SAML and XACML. In the next section we will discuss Shibboleth, which is a distributed web resource access control system that allows federations to cooperate together to share web based resources. It uses SAML in its implementation.

2.5 Shibboleth

As stated earlier, Shibboleth is a distributed web resource access control system that allows federations to cooperate together to share web based resources [4]. It defines a protocol for carrying authentication information and user attributes from a home to a resource site. The resource site can then use the attributes to make access control decisions about the user. This web based middleware layer uses SAML. Access control is carried out in stages. In stage one the resource site redirects the user to their home site, and obtains a handle for the user that is authenticated by the home site. In stage two, the resource site returns the handle to the attribute authority of the home site and is returned a set of attributes of the user, upon which to make an access control decision.

There are some issues with single sign on with Shibboleth. How does the resource site know the home site of the user? How does it trust the handle returned? Answer is, it is handled by the system trust model. The authentication procedure is as follows: when the resource site asks for the home site from the user, he/she selects it from the list of trusted sites which are already authenticated by certificates. Handles are validated by the SAML signature along with the message. User selects the home site from the list. Home site authenticates the user if he/she is already registered. After the home server authentication, it returns a message with SAML sign to the target resource site. If the sign matches, then the target resource site provides a pseudonym (handle) for the user, and sends an assertion message to the home page to find out if the necessary attributes are available with the user. To ensure privacy, each time the system provides different pseudonyms for the user's identity, it needs the release attribute policy from the user attributes each time to provide control over the authority attributes in the target site. Agreement attribute release policy is between the user and the administrator.

Trust is at the heart of Shibboleth. It completely trusts the target resource site and the origin home site registered in the federation. The disadvantage of the existing trust model is that there is no differentiation between authentication authorities and attribute authorities. There is scope for allowing more sophisticated distribution of trust, such as static or dynamic delegation of authority. Another disadvantage in the existing trust model is that it provides only basic access control capabilities. It lacks the flexibility and sophistication that many applications need to provide access control decisions based on role hierarchies or various constraints such as the time of day or separation of duties.

In the basic Shibboleth, a target site trusts the origin site to authenticate its users and manages their attributes correctly while the original site trusts the target site to provide services to its users. Trust is conveyed using digitally signed SAML messages using target and origin server key pairs. Each site has only one key pair per Shibboleth system. Thus there is only a single point of trust per Shibboleth system. Therefore, there is a need for a finer grained distributed trust model and being able to use multiple origin authorities to issue and sign the authentication and attribute assertions. Multiple authorities should be able to issue attributes to users and the target site should be able to verify issuer/user bindings. The target should be able to state, in its policy, which of the attribute authorities it trusts as well as which attributes to issue to which groups of users. The target site should be able to decide, independently of the issuing site which attributes and authorities to trust when making its access control decisions. Not all attribute issuing authorities need to be part of the origin site. A target site should be able to allow a user to gain access to its resources if it has attributes issued by multiple authorities. The trust infrastructure should support dynamic delegation of authority, so that a holder of a privilege attribute may delegate (a subset of) this to another person without having to reconfigure anything in the system. The target site should be able to decide if it really does trust the origin's attribute repository, and if not, be able to demand a stronger proof of attribute entitlement than that conferred by a SAML signature from the sending web server.

Shibboleth defines various trust models. These models have been implemented using X.509. We can look at trust from two different aspects

- Distribution of trust in attribute issuing authorities.
- Trustworthiness of an origin site's attribute repository.

Further details of the trust models and their implementations as well as authorization and privacy issues are discussed in [11].

3 Security and the Semantic Web

3.1 Overview

We first provide an overview of the semantic web and then discuss the security issues. This will include a discussion of XML security, RDF (Resource Description Framework) security and secure information integration, which are components of the secure semantic web. As more progress is made on investigating these various issues, we hope that appropriate standards would be developed for securing the semantic web. Security cannot be considered in isolation. That is, there is no one layer that should focus on security. Security cuts across all layers and this is a challenge.

The organization of this section is as follows. Semantic web is discussed in section 3.2. Aspects of securing the semantic web are discussed in section 3.3. Security issues for XML, RDF and ontologies are discussed in sections 3.4, 3.5 and 3.6 respectively. Security for rules processing is the subject of section 3.7. Privacy and trust issues are discussed in section 3.8.

3.2 Semantic Web

The World Wide Web consortium (W3C) is specifying standards for the semantic web [12]. These standards include specifications for XML, RDF, and ontologies. Tim Berners Lee proposed a technology stack for the semantic web. Essentially the semantic web consists of layers where each layer takes advantage of the technologies of the previous layer. The lowest layer is the protocol layer and this is usually not included in the discussion of the semantic technologies. The next layer is the XML layer. XML is a document representation language. While XML is sufficient to specify syntax, the semantics such as "the creator of document D is John" is hard to specify in XML. Therefore the W3C developed RDF. RDF uses XML syntax. The semantic web community then went further and came up with specification of ontologies in languages such as OWL. Note that OWL addresses the inadequacies of RDF. In order to reason about various policies, the semantic web community has come up with web rules language such as SWRL (semantic web rules language) and Rules ML (rules markup language). For an overview of the semantic we refer to the book by Antoniou and van Harmelen [13].

Semantic web technologies are being utilized by many applications including web services, information integration, and knowledge management, information sharing and digital libraries. With the use of the semantic web technologies, the applications can understand the web pages, conduct reasoning and make decisions. In this chapter we are interested in one of these applications and that is web services. In particular, our goal is to integrate semantic web technologies with web services and security.

3.3 Securing the Semantic Web

For example, consider the lowest layer. One needs secure TCP/IP, secure sockets, and secure HTTP. There are now security protocols for these various lower layer protocols. One needs end-to-end security. That is, one cannot just have secure TCP/IP built on untrusted communication layers. That is, we need network security. The next layer is XML and XML schemas. One needs secure XML. That is, access must be controlled to various portions of the document for reading, browsing and modifications. There is research on securing XML and XML schemas. The next step is securing RDF. Now with RDF not only do we need secure XML, we also need security for the interpretations and semantics. For example, under certain contexts, portions of the document may be unclassified while under certain other contexts the document may be classified [14, 15].

Once XML and RDF have been secured the next step is to examine security for ontologies and inter-operation. That is, ontologies may have security levels attached to them. Certain parts of the ontologies could be secret while certain other parts may be unclassified. The challenge is how does one use these ontologies for secure information integration? Researchers have done some work on the secure interoperability of databases. We need to revisit this research and then determine what else needs to be done so that the information on the web can be managed, integrated and exchanged securely. Logic, proof and trust are at the highest layers of the semantic web. That is, how can we trust the information that the web gives us?

We also need to examine the inference problem for the semantic web. Inference is the process of posing queries and deducing new information. It becomes a problem when the deduced information is something the user is unauthorized to know. With the semantic web, and especially with data mining tools, one can make all kinds of inferences. Recently there has been some research on controlling unauthorized inferences on the semantic web. We need to continue with such research (see, for example, [16, 17]).

Security should not be an afterthought. We have often heard that one needs to insert security into the system right from the beginning. Similarly security cannot be an afterthought for the semantic web. However, we cannot also make the system inefficient if we must guarantee one hundred percent security at all times. What is needed is a flexible security policy. During some situations we may need one hundred percent security while during some other situations say thirty percent security (whatever that means) may be sufficient.

3.4 XML Security

Various research efforts have been reported on XML security (see for example, [18]). We briefly discuss some of the key points. The main challenge is whether to give access to entire XML documents or parts of the documents. Bertino et al. have developed authorization models for XML. They have focused on access control policies as well as on dissemination policies. They also considered push and pull architectures. They specified the policies in XML. The policy specification contains information about which users can access which portions of the documents. In [18] algorithms for access control as well as computing views of the results are presented. In addition, architectures for securing XML documents are also discussed. In [19] the authors go further and describe how XML documents may be published on the web. The idea is for owners to publish documents, subjects to request access to the documents and untrusted publishers to give the subjects the views of the documents they are authorized to see.

W3C (World Wide Web Consortium) is specifying standards for XML security. The XML security project (see [20]) is focusing on providing the implementation of security standards for XML. The focus is on XML-Signature Syntax and Processing, XML-Encryption Syntax and Processing, and XML Key Management. W3C also has a number of working groups including XML Signature working group (see [21]) and XML encryption working group (see [22]). While the standards are focusing on what can be implemented in the near-term, much research is needed on securing XML documents.

3.5 RDF Security

RDF is the foundations of the semantic web. While XML is limited in providing machine understandable documents, RDF handles this limitation. As a result, RDF provides better support for interoperability as well as searching and cataloging. It also describes contents of documents as well as relationships between various entities in the document. While XML provides syntax and notations, RDF supplements this by providing semantic information in a standardized way.

The basic RDF model has three types: they are resources, properties and statements. Resource is anything described by RDF expressions. It could be a web page or a collection of pages. Property is a specific attribute used to describe a resource. RDF statements are resources together with a named property plus the value of the property. Statement components are subject, predicate and object. So for example, if we have a sentence of the form "John is the creator of xxx", then xxx is the subject or resource, property or predicate is "Creator" and object or literal is "John". There are RDF diagrams very much like say ER diagrams or object diagrams to represent statements. It is important that the intended interpretation be used for RDF sentences. This is accomplished by RDF schemas. A schema is sort of a dictionary and has interpretations of various terms used in sentences.

More advanced concepts in RDF include the container model and statements about statements. The container model has three types of container objects, and they are Bag, Sequence, and Alternative. A bag is an unordered list of resources or literals. It is used to mean that a property has multiple values but the order is not important. A sequence is a list of ordered resources. Here the order is important. Alternative is a list of resources that represent alternatives for the value of a property. Various tutorials in RDF describe the syntax of containers in more detail.

RDF also provides support for making statements about other statements. For example, with this facility one can make statements of the form "The statement A is false" where A is the statement "John is the creator of X". Again one can use object-like diagrams to represent containers and statements about statements. RDF also has a formal model associated with it. This formal model has a formal grammar. For further information on RDF, we refer to the excellent discussion in the book by Antoniou and van Harmelen [13].

Now to make the semantic web secure, we need to ensure that RDF documents are secure. This would involve securing XML from a syntactic point of view. However with RDF we also need to ensure that security is preserved at the semantic level. The issues include the security implications of the concepts resource, properties and statements. That is, how is access control ensured? How can statements, properties and statements be protected? How can one provide access control at a finer grain of granularity? What are the security properties of the container model? How can bags, lists and alternatives be protected? Can we specify security policies in RDF? How can we resolve semantic inconsistencies for the policies? How can we express security constraints in RDF? What are the security implications of statements about statements? How can we protect RDF schemas? These are difficult questions and we need to start research to provide answers. XML security is just the beginning. Securing RDF is much more challenging (see also [23]).

3.6 Security and Ontologies

Ontologies are essentially representations of various concepts in order to avoid ambiguity. Numerous ontologies have been developed. These ontologies have been used by agents to understand the web pages and conduct operations such as the integration of databases. Furthermore ontologies can be represented in languages such as RDF or special languages such as web ontology language (OWL).

Now, ontologies have to be secure. That is, accesses to the ontologies have to be controlled. This means that different users may have access to different parts of the ontology. On the other hand, ontologies may be used to specify security policies just as XML and RDF have been used to specify the policies.

3.7 Secure Query and Rules Processing for the Semantic Web

The layer above the Secure RDF layer is the Secure Query and Rules processing layer. While RDF can be used to specify security policies (see, for example, [23]), the web rules language being developed by W3C is more powerful to specify complex policies. Furthermore, inference engines are being developed to process and reason about the rules (e.g., the Pellet engine developed at the University of Maryland). One could integrate ideas from the database inference controller that we have developed (see [24]) with web rules processing to develop an inference or privacy controller for the semantic web.

The query-processing module is responsible for accessing the heterogeneous data and information sources on the semantic web. Researchers are examining ways to integrate techniques from web query processing with semantic web technologies to locate, query and integrate the heterogeneous data and information sources. We need to examine the security impact of query processing.

3.8 Privacy and Trust for the Semantic Web

Privacy is about protecting information about individuals. Furthermore, an individual can specify say to a web service provider the information that can be released about him or her. Privacy has been discussed a great deal in the past especially when it relates to protecting medical information about patients. Social scientists as well as technologists have been working on privacy issues. However, privacy has received enormous attention during the past year. This is mainly because of the advent of the web, the semantic web, counterterrorism and national security. For example, in order to extract information about various individuals and perhaps prevent and/or detect potential terrorist attacks data mining tools are being examined. We have heard much about national security vs. privacy in the media. This is mainly due to the fact that people are now realizing that to handle terrorism, the government may need to collect data about individuals and mine the data to extract information. Data may be in relational databases or it may be text, video and images. This is causing a major concern with various civil liberties unions (see [25]). Closely related to privacy is anonymity. Some argue that it is important to maintain anonymity.

Recently there has been much work on trust and the semantic web (see the research by Finin et al. [26, 27]). The challenges include how do you trust the information on the web? How do you trust the sources? How do you negotiate between different parties and develop contracts? How do you incorporate constructs for trust management and negotiation into XML and RDF? What are the semantics for trust management?

Researchers are working on protocols for trust management. Languages for specifying trust management constructs are also being developed. Also there is research on the foundations of trust management. For example, if A trusts B and B trusts C, then can A trust C? How do you share the data and information on the semantic web and still maintain autonomy? How do you propagate trust? For example, if A trusts B at say 50% of the time and B trusts C 30% of the time, then what value do you assign for A trusting C? How do you incorporate trust into semantic interoperability? What are the quality of service primitives for trust and negotiation? That is, for certain situations one may need 100% trust while for certain other situations 50% trust may suffice (see also [28]).

Another topic that is being investigated is trust propagation and propagating privileges. For example, if you grant privileges to A, what privileges can A transfer to B? How can you compose privileges? Is there an algebra and calculus for the composition of privileges? Much research still needs to be done here. One of the layers of the semantic web is Logic, Proof and Trust. Essentially this layer deals with trust management and negotiation between different agents and examining the foundations and developing logics for trust management.

4 Integrating Security, Semantic Web and Web Services Technologies

Integration of the web services and the semantic web results in semantic web services. That is, web services to the WWW are semantic web services to the semantic web. Tim Finin and his team have discussed an architecture for semantic web services [29]. They have describes the inadequacies of web services and discussed the need for semantic web services. They state that current technologies allow usage of Web Services. In particular current web services support syntactic descriptions as well as syntactic support for service discovery, composition and execution. They argue that we need semantically marked up content and services, and therefore we need to develop semantic web services. They then define an architecture called the semantic web service architecture, which consists of a set of architectural and protocol abstractions that serve as a foundation for Semantic Web service technologies. These technologies support the following:

- Dynamic Service Discovery, Service Engagement, Service process enactment, Community support services and Quality of service.

Service discovery is the process of identifying candidate services by clients. Matchmakers connect the service requesters to the providers. Ontologies may be needed to specify the services. Service engagement specifies the agreements between the requestor and the provider. Therefore contract negation is carried out during this phase. Once the service is ready to be initiated the service enactment phase begins. As stated in [4] during this phase Requestor determines the information necessary to request performance of service and appropriate reaction to service success or failure. This will also include interpreting the responses and carrying out transitions; Community management services support authentication and security management. Aquatic of service provides support for negotiation as well as tradeoffs say between security and timely delivery of the data.

Security cuts across all these services. Note that the community management service specially calls for authentication and security management. Security services are needed for service discovery, engine segment, and enactment. For example, not all services can be discovered. This will depend on the sensitivity of the service and the security credentials possessed by the requestor. Therefore, security specifications for XML, RDF and OWL have to be examined for semantic web service descriptions.

One needs to integrate the diverse and disparate data sources on the web by invoking secure semantic web services. The data may not be in databases. It could be in files both structured and unstructured. Data could be in the form of tables or in the form of text, images, audio and video. Semantic web technologies such as ontologies are becoming critical for information interoperability.

The challenge for security researchers is how does one integrate the information securely? For example, in [30, 31, 32] the schema integration work of Sheth and Larson was extended for security policies. That is, different sites have security policies and these policies have to be integrated to provide a policy for the federated database system. One needs to examine these issues for the semantic web. Each node on the web may have its own policy. Is it feasible to have a common policy for a community on the web? Do we need a tight integration of the policies or do we focus on dynamic policy integration? How can ontologies play a role in secure information integration? How do we provide access control for ontologies? Should ontologies specify the security policies? How do we minimize the trust placed on information integrators on the web? We have posed several questions. We need a research program to address many of these challenges.

5 Summary and Directions

This paper has provided an overview of web services security and semantic web security including a discussion of the various security standards. We first discussed security issues for web services and then discussed secure semantic web. Finally, we discussed integrating security, web services and semantic web technologies to develop secure semantic web services.

Web services are the services that are invoked to carry out activities on the web. A collection of web services comprise the service oriented architecture. We also discussed aspects of XACML, SAML and Shibboleth, which are related to secure web services. We argued that security must cut across all the layers. Next we provided some more details on securing the semantic web including XML security and RDF security. If the semantic web is to be secure we need all of its components to be secure. Next we discussed privacy and trust for the semantic web.

Web services and service oriented architectures are at the heart of the next generation web. They make use of semantic web technologies to generate machine understandable web pages. This is one of the major developments in the late 1990s and early 2000s. While there are numerous developments on web services, the application of semantic web technologies and securing the web services are major challenges. Furthermore, major initiatives such as the global information gird and the network centric enterprise services are based on web services and service oriented architectures. Therefore securing these technologies as well as making web services more intelligent by using the semantic web will be critical for the next generation web.

References

1. OASIS, http://www.oasis-open.org/home/index.php
2. T. Berners Lee and J. Hendler: The Semantic Web, Scientific American, May 2001.
3. B. Thuraisingham: Building Trustworthy Semantic Web, CRC Press, 2007.
4. Shibboleth, http://middleware.internet2.edu/pki05/proceedings/chadwick-distributed-shibboleth.pdf
5. http://en.wikipedia.org/wiki/Serviceoriented_architecture
6. http://www.omg.org
7. E. Bertino, L. Martino: Security in SOA and Web Services. IEEE SCC 2006.
8. SUN XACML Documentation, http://sunxacml.sourceforge.net/guide.html
9. OpenSAML, http://www.opensaml.org
10. R. Bhatti, E. Bertino, and A. Ghafoor: Trust-based Context aware Access Control Models in Web Services, Proceedings of the Web Services Conference, San Diego, July 2004.
11. http://www.terena.nl/activities/tf-aace/workshop/presentations/Distributed_trust_model1.ppt
12. http://www.w3.org
13. G. Antoniou and F. van Harmelan: A Semantic Web Primer, MIT Press, 2003.
14. B. Thuraisingham: Security Standards for the Semantic Web, Computer Standards and Interface Journal, vol. 27, no. 3, 257–268, Mar. 2005.
15. B. Thuraisingham: Database and Applications Security: Integrating Data Management and Information Security, CRC Press, FL, 2005.
16. C. Farkas, et al.: Inference Problem for the Semantic Web, Proceedings of the IFIP Conference on Data and Applications Security, Colorado, August 2003 (formal proceedings published by Kluwer, 2004)
17. B. Thuraisingham et al.: Administering the Semantic Web, Confidentiality, Privacy and Trust, Journal of Information Security and Privacy, 2006.
18. E. Bertino, et al.: Access Control for XML Documents, Data and Knowledge Engineering, Volume 43, No. 3, 2002.
19. E. Bertino, B. Carminati, E. Ferrari, B. Thuraisingham, A. Gupta: Selective and Authentic Third-Party Distribution of XML Documents. IEEE Trans. on Knowledge and Data Engineering. 16(10): 1263-1278, 2004.
20. http://xml.apache.org/security
21. http://www.w3.org/Signature
22. http://www.w3.org/Encryption/2001
23. B. Carminati, E. Ferrari, B. Thuraisingham: Using RDF for Policy Specification and Enforcement, Proceedings of the DEXA Conference Workshop on Web Semantics, Zaragoza, Spain, 2004.
24. B. Thuraisingham, W. Ford, M. Collins, J. O'Keeffe: Design and Implementation of a Database Inference Controller, Data and Knowledge Engineering Journal, Volume 11, No.3, 1993.
25. B. Thuraisingham: Data Mining, National Security, Privacy and Civil Liberties, ACM SIGKDD 2002.
26. G. Denker, et al.: Security for DAML Web Services: Annotation and Matchmaking. International Semantic Web Conference, 2003.
27. L. Kagal, T. W. Finin, A. Joshi: A Policy Based Approach to Security for the Semantic Web. International Semantic Web Conference 2003, 402–418.

28. T. Yu, M. Winslett: A Unified Scheme for Resource Protection in Automated Trust Negotiation, IEEE Symposium on Security and Privacy, Oakland, CA., May 2003.

29. M. Burstein, Ch. Bussler, M. Zaremba, T. Finin, M.N. Huhns, M. Paolucci, A.P. Sheth, St. Williams: A Semantic Web Services Architecture, IEEE Internet Computing, September-October, 2005

30. A. Sheth, J. Larson: Federated Database Systems, ACM Computing Surveys, Volume 22, No.3, 1990.

31. B. Thuraisingham: Security Issues for Federated Database Systems, Computers and Security, Volume 13, No.6, 1994.

32. B. Thuraisingham: Data Management Systems Evolution and Interoperation, CRC Press, 1997.

11

Geospatial Database Security

Soon Ae Chun[1] and Vijayalakshmi Atluri[2]

[1] College of Staten Island, City University of New York, Staten Island, NY
chun@mail.csi.cuny.edu
[2] Rutgers University, Newark, NJ
atluri@cimic.rutgers.edu

Summary. Geospatial data refers to the resources associated with location information represented by longitude and latitude. Its increasing availability and the tools to integrate and visualize the various types of data facilitate conducting sophisticated analysis and discovering hidden patterns. Therefore, uncontrolled dissemination of geospatial data may have grave consequences for national security and personal privacy. Access control for this data is based on its geospatial location, content and context, the credentials and characteristics of the users requesting access as well as the time at which the data is captured and requested. In this chapter, we review the different access control models proposed by researchers for controlled dissemination of geospatial data. Since geospatial data is increasingly obtained from third party Web services, we also review the security models presented in the area of geospatial Web services.

1 Introduction

Geospatial data, which typically includes maps, aerial and satellite images, is associated with location information represented by longitude and latitude. These maps and remotely sensed satellite imageries may represent diverse data, such as rivers, government boundaries, roads, rainfall, vegetation index, business establishments, monuments, parks, schools, population, etc. The proliferation of the Internet, with the advances in the collection and processing of the geospatial data, has led to its easy creation and dissemination by federal, state and local government agencies as well as by private and non-profit organizations. This geospatial data is often made readily available for public access, and can be shared through a geospatial data clearinghouse or portal in a global as well as local level, e.g. [23, 26, 6].

Geospatial data can be collected, analyzed, manipulated, and integrated and visualized with the help of various Geographic Information Systems (GIS) such as ESRI ArcView, ArcInfo, ENVI and Internet Map Server. They support the end users to comprehend the complex nature of data through analysis, integration and visualization through thematic layers, and can produce more value-added products in diverse formats, e.g. VRML, 3D animations, fly-by animation, and interactive Internet maps. The geospatial data, coupled with the GIS and Global Positioning System (GPS), can benefit both businesses and governments in making decisions such as business facilities and site selection, demographic analyses, route selection, zoning, planning, conservation, natural resource extraction, natural and man-made damage assessment, and national security. Despite these numerous benefits, due to its easy availability and due to the powerful analysis tools for the geospatial data, it may pose serious threats to security and privacy. These geospatial data can be sensitive since objects located in a particular location may be of national importance that are vulnerable to attacks. These may include, for example, cultural landmarks or critical infrastructure facilities such as water distribution, telecommunication, bridges, tunnels, and nuclear plants, which may cause a large scale socio-economic impact in case of failure [5].

In addition to the security threats outlined above, availability of geospatial data sometimes may reveal positional information of a person, which may give rise to privacy threats, as he/she can be easily located and even tracked. Similarly, any sensitive activities conducted on a certain location may need to be kept confidential. In addition to protecting single activities, one may need prevent adversaries to be able to discover patterns and hidden trends of individuals by combining other publicly available geospatial data with the activities conducted at those locations. To ensure the above security and privacy needs, there is a need for specification and enforcement of policies for controlled dissemination of the geospatial data.

Another challenge pertaining to securing geospatial data is due to the increasing use of the geospatial Web service technology to easily share and integrate the geospatial data and applications on demand. Previously, sharing of geospatial data had been much more difficult due to the heterogeneities among their format and metrics. These geospatial Web services allow to easily create geospatial "mash-ups" that are nothing but light-weight applications that help in integrating diverse location based information. Such examples include (i) Google Maps API's that facilitate viewing of various types of information of different locations on Web browsers [15], (ii) Google Earth [14] that provides more or less the entire world's geographic information by empowering its search engine with satellite imagery, maps, terrain and 3D buildings where one can fly-to and zoom-in a certain address, get 3D view of terrain and buildings and search schools, parks, hotels, restaurants and get driving directions, and (iii) Microsoft Virtual Earth [18] that uses Web services in combination with a search engine to provide real time business intelligence information, such as high-resolution bird's eye imagery, the dynamic, drag-and-drop maps or highly-visual path maps.

These geospatial Web Services can be invoked using a set of XML-based standard programs and can be embedded into applications integrating many other kinds of data. Sharing of these Web services should be done in such a way that it preserves the security and privacy specifications of their respective owners. Moreover, these policies for secure sharing should be properly managed so that the right policy can be efficiently located and policy inferences can be easily performed.

In this chapter, we review the access control models presented in the areas of geospatial data maintained by stand alone traditional sources as well as that obtained via geospatial Web services. When making access control decisions, the access control models typically consider the characteristics of the geospatial data (object) and the location of the user (subject). This is because, the security and privacy policies are often based on the object's contents and the subject's location. For instance, access control policies may be specified based on the geospatial object characteristics such as the geographic coverage (area or extent), the thematic content within the area, the zoom-levels to a particular location, the temporal nature of the objects or the requesters, as well as the location of the requester and his/her roles within the area and temporal period. Specifically, we review the access control models for geospatial data objects such as satellite images and vector data, and a geospatial role-based access control model for controlling access to resources depending on the user's geospatial context as in location-based services, and an access control model for the semantic geospatial Web services.

This chapter is organized as follows. In section 2, we present the geospatial object data characteristics and models. In section 3 we discuss different flavors of geospatial access control models. Specifically, in section 3.1, we discuss the geospatial data authorization model presented in [8, 3, 4] where an access request for geospatial objects is controlled by both geotemporal characteristics of requested object and the user's geotemporal context. In section 3.2, we present the Geo-RBAC model [7, 11], that provides access control based on the geospatial roles of the user. Similarly, in section 3.3, we review the location-based conditional access model to control the mobile user's resource access, when the user location service is not always precise and sometimes intermittent. In section 3.4, we discuss the geospatial Web services access control model. Finally, in section 4, we provide conclusions and an insight into future research directions in this area.

2 Geospatial Data Models

Geospatial data can be organized in different ways. The vector and raster models are two principal spatial data organization scheme. The vector model uses the geometry, such as points, lines, polygons, while the raster model uses cells or pixels as spatial units.

2.1 Vector data

The vector model represents geospatial data with two components: spatial attributes and non-spatial attributes. First, the spatial attributes indicate the geometric shape such as points, lines and polygons. Points are represented as pairs of latitude and longitude coordinates, lines as strings of coordinate pairs, and polygons as lines that form closed loops or areas. In addition, the vector model can represent the topological attributes between two geometries, such as adjacency and containment. For instance, a water body or a zoning area can be represented with a polygon. Thus the spatial attributes record data about the location, topology and geometry of geospatial data.

The second component in the vector data is the non-spatial attributes, also called thematic attributes, that refer to non-spatial properties of geospatial data, such as annual rainfall, vegetation type, zoning type, land use, states, census tracts, etc. A thematic layer is a collection of geometries having the same attribute set. Thus we can have a layer of schools as points, and another layer describing roads and bridges as lines and points.

2.2 Raster data

Under the raster data model, the spatial data, such as satellite images, elevation maps, or digitized maps, is represented as a grid of columns and rows, i.e. as a matrix of cells (called pixels). Each layer of grid cells in a raster model records a separate attribute. Each cell carries the non-spatial data, such as rainfall, temperature, vegetation type, etc. Spatial coordinates are not usually explicitly stored for each cell, but implicitly represented with the ordering of the pixels. Typically, each layer contains information about the number of rows and columns and the geographic location of the origin. The spatial resolution of a raster is the size of one the the pixels on the ground. For example, if one pixel corresponds to 3 meter by 3 meter area on the Earth, the data has 3 meter resolution. Different sensors provide images of different resolution levels [24]. For instance, the Advanced Very High Resolution Radiometer (AVHRR) produces images of 1km resolution [20], the Landsat Thematic Mapper (TM) multi-spectral images of 30 meter resolution, the Radar images of 5 to 10 meter resolution, and the IKONOS satellite images of 1 and 4 meter resolution. DigitalGlobe's QuickBird satellite's panchromatic images of 60 cm resolution marks the world's highest resolution commercial satellite imagery.

Satellite images also carry temporal information, designating either the time when the image data was downloaded from a satellite, or the time of data creation. The coverage area of images are different from image to image, depending on the orbits of the polar-orbiting satellites. The satellite images also require georegistration that registers each image with a known coordinate system (e.g. longitude, latitude) and reference units (e.g. degrees), and assigns coordinates to the left, right, top and bottom corners of the image. One satellite may have several sensors capturing information in different frequency bands. The information in these bands can be further processed bands to produce different layers, such as water, vegetation and the like.

3 Geospatial Access Control Models

3.1 GSAM: Geospatial Data Authorization Model

The geospatial image access model needs to support the following types of "spatio-temporal policies," which are specified based on spatio-temporal characteristics of both the subject and object.

- P_1: All users can view 10 meter or lower resolution images.
- P_2: 1 meter resolution images of the parcel located in "120 James Street, Newark, New Jersey" can be accessed only by the current owner of this parcel.
- P_3: Only military personnel positioned in Afghanistan can zoom-in to 1 meter resolution images over Afghanistan captured after September 11, 2001.
- P_4: The police officers positioned in Bergen County are allowed to access 1 meter resolution images of the nuclear power plant located at [-81.37227, 28.54623].

The Geospatial Data Access Model (GSAM) [8, 3] presents the formalism required to specify the authorization policies as above. It employs the notion of geotemporal roles. The prototype system that implements GSAM has been presented in [4].

Geotemporal Role

Geotemporal roles are used to specify a set of subjects possessing spatial and temporal credentials indicating that each role is associated with a certain valid region and temporal interval. In other words, while a user may assume a specific role in a traditional RBAC no matter where the user is, a user may assume different geotemporal roles depending on the user's location and time. Thus, roles are also geo-referenced, and users are assigned to a geotemporal role if they possess the required credentials. For instance, a role "doctor in New York City" is different from a role "doctor in Los Angeles." Similarly, a doctor in the morning shift may be different from a doctor in the evening shift. Mobile users can also assume these geotemporal roles as the users move around and satisfy the specified requirements. In other words, geotemporal roles are assigned to users depending on the context a user is in.

Formally, a geotemporal role in a scene can be represented as a pair $\langle r, sc \rangle$, where r is a traditional role as specified in the RBAC role hierarchy, and sc is a scene that is associated with geospatial and temporal extents. Each sc can be organized as a hierarchy in its own domain. For example, an incident domain may have scenes like fire, flood, earthquake, while a shopping domain may have scenes of mall, retail-shop, wholesale area, market, etc. Each sc can be instantiated with a scene expression such as scene name, or a specific geotemporal extent, such as $\langle label, lt, lg, h, w, [t_b, t_e] \rangle$ where *label* is a descriptive scene name, such as "New York City", "mall" or "fire," and $\langle lt, lg, h, w \rangle$ denotes latitude, longitude, height and width of a bounding box covering a geographic area of the scene and $[t_b, t_e]$ denotes the temporal period of the scene. Figure 1 shows the geotemporal role hierarchy that is associated with a generic scene type or with a scene that is located in a particular location or an area.

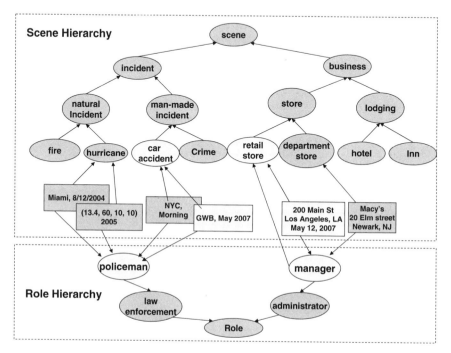

Fig. 1. Geotemporal Role hierarchy

Examples of geotemporal roles include: $\langle manager, retail\ store \rangle$ denotes any manager at a retail store scene regardless of the location of the store, while $\langle manager, 200\ Main\ Street,\ LA,\ May\ 12,\ 2007 \rangle$ denotes any manager whose location is at this particular store located in 200 Main Street in LA on May 12, 2007. Geotemporal roles can be represented as a logical expression, called geotemporal role expression *re*.

Geotemporal Object

Each geotemporal object belongs to an object type, which can be organized into a geotemporal object type hierarchy, as shown in Figure 2. Each geotemporal object type is associated with a set of attributes, which include a unique identifier, the type of geospatial object, the latitude, longitude, height, width, resolution, timestamp (either image download time or last update time), and the thematic link to the data set associated with the object. A geotemporal object is specified with a geotemporal object expression *ge* that is a logical expression of object attributes and their values.

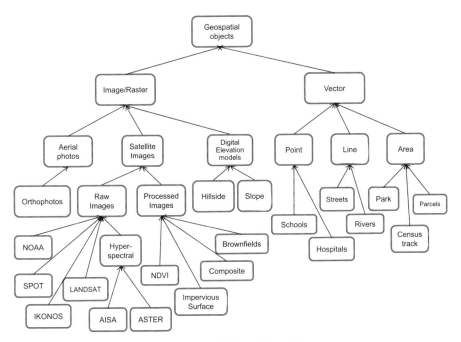

Fig. 2. Geospatial Object Type Hierarchy

Geotemporal Permissions

The permissions on the geotemporal objects include viewing, copying and maintenance modes. The viewing modes include permissions such as view, view-thumbnail and view annotation, zoom-in, overlay, identify, animate and fly-by. View allows a user to see an image object covering a certain geographic area, zoom-in allows a user to view an image covering a certain geographic area at a specific higher resolution level, overlay allows users to generate composite images, where a composite image is constructed from multiple images by first georegistering and then overlaying them one on top of another, identify allows the user to view the tabular data linked to an image, animate allows a user to obtain a time series of images and integrate them to show the changes in the images, and fly-by allows a user to traverse from one location to another a multi-resolution browsing from low resolution images to high resolution images, or vice versa.

The copying modes, download and download-data, allow source files to be downloaded. Unlike the text data where the display privilege implies the copying privilege, the viewing and copying are distinguished as separate privileges with geospatial data since the objects displayed on the Web browser often are image gif files, but not the original source files. The maintenance modes include insert, delete, update and compose. The users with compose privilege can create and insert value-added images, using images in the database.

Geospatial Authorization

An authorization is represented as a 5-tuple $\langle re, ge, privilege, period, sign \rangle$ that specifies whether the set of subjects represented by re has an access privilege to an object or a set of objects represented by ge during the period. The sign is indicates allow or deny the privilege.

Access Control Evaluation

The user's access request can be represented as a tuple $r = \langle gtc, gto, p \rangle$ where gtc is a geotemporal credential expression of the user with the contextual information such as the current location and time the user is situated in, gto is a geotemporal object expression that can include a particular image type, a spatial area with certain temporal footprint, and p is a permission type.

The geotemporal credentials are matched with the geotemporal role expression in the policy statement, and when the spatial and temporal extents are included in the geotemporal role extents, the role is activated. Given the activated roles and its corresponding policies, the requested object gto is matched with the authorized geotemporal expression in the policy. The matching operations between the requested and policy geotemporal extents include predicates to check the spatial and temporal relationships such as containment, total and partial overlap, meet, and no-overlap. When the geotemporal extent gto is contained, or totally or partially overlapping with the object's geotemporal extents ge in the authorization, and the requested permission matches with the one in the authorization, the authorization is allowed. In case of partial overlap, only the overlapping area of the object should be delivered, which requires post-processing of the retrieved objects, such as cropping of images and mosaicking of multiple cropped objects.

3.2 GEO-RBAC: Geospatial Role-based Access Control

In this section, we present different approaches where location-aware applications require access control on spatial data. There are many approaches on context-aware and spatially-aware access control [10, 9, 28, 25, 2]. We present one approach called Geo-RBAC where the map vector data and user's positions are considered to protect resources in location aware applications. Some examples of access policies that can be supported under this model include:

- P1: Only the environmental scientists currently making observations in the river within the New Jersey Meadowlands area can enter the observed fish counts into the database.
- P2: A surveyor working on a street in Newark can change the data on the illegal waste deposits in the region where he is located.

In Geo-RBAC, the protected resources are mostly vector data that are modeled with geometric shapes and associated locations.

Geometric Model and Spatially aware Objects

An object on the Earth is represented by a geometric shape, a point, a line or a polygon. Each geometric object is tied to the Earth coordinates. A point describes a single location, a line represents an ordered sequence of points, and a polygon is an ordered sequence of closed lines. GEO is the set of all geometrics contained in a reference space called Minimum Bounding Box (MBB).

Objects to be protected consists of data about entities of the real world that may occupy a position. These entities are called features. Features represent the spatial and non-spatial attributes. Spatial features have name and location, i.e. geometry, while non-spatial features are not associated with any location. An example of a feature is *Newark* which can be associated with a polygon or point geometry. The features are can have feature types such as *Road, Town, Lake, Car*.

Spatial Role

A spatial role is defined as a pair $\langle r, e \rangle$ where r is a role name and e is the spatial extent determined by the boundaries of the space in which the role can be assumed by the user. Role extent can be a feature. A role *surveyor* can be associated to different extents, resulting in different spatial roles, e.g. $\langle surveyor, city\ of\ Rome \rangle$, and $\langle surveyor, city\ of\ Newark \rangle$, are two spatial roles.

Positional Model

The actual user position that can change in time is modeled with either a *real position*, that is actual geometry such as a point or a polygon, and/or a *logical position*, i.e. spatial feature (such as city). There is a one-to-many *mapping function* that can map the real position to logical positions.

Geo-RBAC Model

The spatially aware role based access control model consists of role schema and role instance, permissions, users, and sessions.

- Role Schema and Role Instance: A role schema defines the role name for a set of spatial roles, the spatial constraints where roles can be enabled, and specifies logical locations and real position for the users who may assume the role. A role instance is a role fulfilling the constraints defined in the role schema. Thus the spatial role is the role name in the schema with a specific spatial feature. The spatial role is represented with $\langle r, ext, loc, m \rangle$ where r is a role name, ext is feature type of the role extent, loc a feature of logical position and m the mapping function relating real positions to logical positions.

  An example of a role schema $\langle Surveyor, RoadNetwork, PointonRoad, m \rangle$, represents a surveyor in a position on a road network. Given a role schema, a role instance is created when the role extent is assigned with a particular feature. For instance, a role instance could be a surveyor on a road in Newark.

- Permissions: These are operations performed on spatial objects, such as *get traffic information* over Urban-Road-Network features, *notify* over accident features, or *find* operation over Monument features. Given a set of operations and a set of objects, permissions are represented as a pair $\langle operation, object \rangle$.

Geo-RBAC Access Control

The access control is specified as a set of assignment relations between permissions to spatial roles, between users and spatial roles:

- User-to-Spatial Role Assignment: This mapping relationship assigns a set of users to spatial role instances. Inverse relationship (i.e. Spatial role-to-User assignment) maps spatial role instances to sets of users.
- Permission to Spatial role assignments: The mappings can be specified between the permission to spatial role schema and between spatial role instances to permissions.

Access Request Evaluation

An access request is represented as a tuple $\langle s, rp, p, o \rangle$ where the user of session s located at a real position rp wants to perform operation p on object o. When permission (p, o) belongs to permission assignment specifications to the enabled role at the user's real position, the access request is granted.

This access control evaluation occurs in the following fashion: When a user starts a new session, a number of roles should be enabled to be included in the session role set. But in order to enable these session roles, the user's logical location should be within the role's spatial extent. In order to find out the logical location of the user using user's real position, the location mapping function in the role schema is used to identify the logical location of the user. To determine enabled roles in a session, containment between user's logical position and role extent has to be evaluated. For each enabled role, the set of permissions assigned to the corresponding role schema is determined. If there are such permission assignment rules for an enabled role, then the access request is granted.

3.3 LBAC: Location-based Access Control

For secure access to data by mobile users, it is important to consider the user's dynamic location to identify the roles allowed and denied. As opposed to focusing on the spatial data objects such as raster or vector data resources, the spatially aware or context-aware based access control focuses on the access to resources based on the physical location of the user. Some of the access policies include:

- P_1: System administrators are authorized to configure the mobile network if they are in the server farm room, they are alone in such an area, and move at walking speed at most.
- P_2: The CEO is authorized to access mobile network statistics if there is nobody close by and she is not in a competitor location.
- P_3: Guests can read mobile network statistics if there is nobody close by and they are in a corporate location.

In [2], Location-based Access Control (LBAC) considers the physical location and the credentials of the requester in determining to allow or deny access. The context data about location and timing are made available by third parties (e.g. mobile phone operators in a mobile network) through service interfaces called *Location Services*. Thus a LBAC system evaluating a policy sends requests to external services. However, the mobile network technology does not provide an exact location measure, which a Location Service performs, and has a degree of uncertainty due to technological limitations and possible environmental effects.

Location-based Predicates

Location-based predicates are used to describe the locational constraints of the user, such as position, movement and interaction predicates described below.

- Position-based conditions on the location of the user are used to evaluate whether a user is in a certain building or city or in the proximity of other entities; For instance, *inarea(user, area) and disjoint(user,area, min, max)* verify the user is within or outside the area of *area*, and *distance(user,*

entity, min, max) checks whether the distance between user and entity lies between min and max).
- Movement-based conditions on the mobility of the users, such as their *velocity, acceleration,* or *direction.*
- Interaction-based conditions relating to multiple users or entities; for instance, the number of users within a given area, i.e. *density* evaluates if the number of people in the area is within certain max and min number, or *relative-density* predicate evaluates if the number of people surrounding users are within the maximum and minimum area.

However, the verification of these predicates depends on the accuracy of the location technology, thus it considers Service Level Agreement (SLA), such as confidence and timeout. Thus, the locational predicates are evaluated to either true or false with the confidence value and timeout, ⟨ *Boolean-value, confidence, timeout*⟩. The confidence value expresses the level of reliability of the Location Service result according to accuracy, and the timeout represents the time validity of the location values that may change rapidly.

For example, *inarea(Alice, Newark) = [True,0.9,2007-11-09 11:10am]* states that the Location Service assesses as true the fact that Alice is located in Newark with a confidence of 90%; and that such an assessment is to be considered valid until 11:10am of November 9, 2007.

Subject

Subjects are represented with subject expression, which is a Boolean conditional predicate to refer to a set of subjects depending on whether they satisfy certain conditions. The conditions are evaluated with the user's profile, location, the user's membership in groups or active roles.

Object

Objects are represented with a Boolean object expression, which refers to a set of objects that satisfy the conditions in the object expression where conditions evaluate membership of the object in categories, and values of properties on metadata.

Action

Action is the action (or class of actions) that is allowed or denied.

LBAC Policy Rules

An access control rule is represented with a triple ⟨*subj expr, obj expr, action*⟩, where *subj-expr* refers to the conditional expression for subjects, *obj-expr* refers to the conditional expression for objects, and *action* refers to a privilege mode.

LBAC Policy Evaluation and Enforcement

A user's access request is represented with $\langle user\ id,\ SIM,\ action,\ object\ id\rangle$, where *user id* is the optional identifier of the user who makes the request, SIM is user's optional SIM card number, *action* is the action that is being requested, and *object id* is the identifier of the object.

In the first phase, the Access Control Engine evaluates the policy P collecting all the rules A in P that are applicable to the request. The set A of applicable rules contains those rules $r \in P$ for which *action(r)* corresponds to the action specified in the access request, and *object id* satisfies the conditions specified in *obj-expr(r)*.

In order to evaluate the location-based predicates that appear in rules, the access control engine needs to submit the query to the Location Service provider for response. The Location Service returns the results in the form of $\langle Boolean\ value,\ confidence,\ timeout\rangle$. Given the response, the access control engine determines whether or not the value returned by the Location Service can be considered valid for the purpose of controlling access. Such an evaluation depends on parameters timeout and confidence returned by the Location Service. For responses with expired timeout, it automatically triggers the re-evaluation of the predicate regardless of the other parameter values. For unexpired responses, the engine evaluates the responses with respect to the confidence value. The evaluation maintains the extended truth table that maintains the acceptable confidence level for each predicate with minimum and maximum thresholds. If the confidence level in response is greater than maximum threshold in the truth table, the returned value is confirmed. If the confidence level is less than the minimum threshold, then the returned value is evaluated to false. If the returned confidence level falls between the maximum and minimum thresholds, the engine submits the re-evaluation query to the Location Service, since it is not clear if the returned results are reliable enough. The truth table for each predicate also maintains the maximum retry for the evaluation. Complex predicate expressions are evaluated with each predicate evaluation results with logical operations.

3.4 Geospatial Web Services Access Control

The geospatial data created by different organizations and individuals being made available rises the challenges related to sharing and interoperating the geospatial resources. Towards this end, the efforts on standardization of metadata [13] have been made, and more recently, the Web services technology facilitates an easy access to distributed geospatial data over the Internet. Web service standards developed by OGC (Open Geospatial Consortium) [22] allow the Geospatial data interoperability and access via discovery, composition and invocation of Geospatial Web Services. It provides standards on Web Feature Service (WFS), Web Map Service (WMS) and Web Coverage Service

(WCS) as well as Web Image Classification service and Web Coordinate Transformation Services. These Web services allow the access of OGC compliant data services around the globe with geographic region, temporal and thematic specifications. In addition, these Web can be dynamically composed together to produce value-added data products.

The OpenGIS Catalog Service for Web (CSW) [21] is a standard supporting the registry and discovery of geospatial data, where data providers register their capabilities using metadata that can be used for service discovery by the users. Some of the catalog services include "getCapabilities", "DescribeRecord", "GetDomain", "GetRecords", "GetRecordbyID", etc. Web Coverage Services include "getCapabilities", "describeCoverage" and "getCoverage". For instance, "describeCoverage" will provide information of an image data such as bounding box, resolution and spatial reference system. Web Feature Services support "getFeatureType", "getFeature", "getGmlObject" and "getCapabilities" to access and interchange the vector data that is a set of attributes, represented with (name, type and value) tuples where one attribute has a geometry as its value. Web Map Services include "getMap", "getFeatureInfo" or "getCapabilities". For instance, "getMap" service supports the map as images in PNG, JPG or GIF format, that can be layered.

The following example shows the "GetGmlObject" request for the name of a town whose identifier is "t1" with traversing to the second level of the nested XLink:

```
<?xml version="1.0" encoding="UTF-8"?>
<wfs:GetGmlObject
  xmlns:wfs="http://www.opengis.net/wfs"
  xmlns:ogc="http://www.opengis.net/ogc"
  xmlns:gml="http://www.opengis.net/gml"
  xmlns:xsi="http://www.w3.org/2001/XMLSchema-instance"
  xsi:schemaLocation="http://www.opengis.net/wfs ../wfs/1.1.0/WFS.xsd"
  service="WFS"
  version="1.1.0"
  outputFormat=" text/xml; subtype=gml/3.1.1"
  traverseXlinkDepth="*"
  traverseXlinkExpiry="2">
  <ogc:GmlObjectId gml:id="t1"/>
</wfs:GetGmlObject>
```

The query response contains one result with the town name "West Orange" that is directed to a point feature "townhall" located in a particular position, as shown in the following.

```
<Town gml:id="t1">
  <gml:name>West Orange</gml:name>
  <gml:directedNode orientation="+"> <!-- xlink:href="#n1" ..
    <gml:Node gml:id=n1>
      <gml:pointProperty xlink:href="http://www.westorgane.nj.us/
          /gps.gml#townHall/">
        <gml:Point gml:id="townHall">
          <gml:pos>147 234</gml:pos>
        </gml:Point>
      </gml:pointProperty>
    </gml:Node>
  </gml:directedNode>
</Town>
```

Geo-XACML: Geospatial Extensible Access Control Markup Language

One aspect of the security concern with the digital geographic content (geo-data) and services that are easily available over the networks is to manage their Intellectual Property, i.e. managing the rights of data producers and users who are licensed to use, distribute, copy and alter, etc. The Geospatial Digital Rights Management Reference Model (GeoDRM RM) defines the framework for web service mechanisms and rights languages to articulate, manage and protect the rights of all participants in the geographic information marketplace, including the owners of intellectual property and the users who wish to use it [27]. It specifies GeoLicense that contains grant-related information *(Principal, Right, Resource, Condition)* as well as license issuer information *langle digital-signature, other-info⟩*. Thus, a GeoLicense is the container expressing the rights to use a specified geospatial resource, for a given geographical space, over a specific period of time, subject to other conditions. For example, a GeoLicense may express the rights to view, print, copy and update all road maps of Chicago area for 2006. The identity for users, resources, licenses, rights and processes is often associated with elements in URL, URI, URN, WSDL, and digital signatures.

For Web services access control management in Service Oriented Architectures, the OASIS defined standard, the eXtensible Access Control Markup Language (XACML) [19], defines a core schema and corresponding namespace for expressing authorization policies in XML for objects that are themselves identified in XML. However, XACML does not have the capabilities to express geo-specific constraints on access rights, relevant for access control for geographic data.

The GeoXACML [17, 16], geospatial extension to the XACML Policy Language, has been proposed to allow specifications of geometry attribute values, condition functions to test topological relationships between geometries, and OpenGIS Web Service and Coordinate Reference System (CRS) specific resource attribute designators. The geometry attribute values supported by geoXACML include *{Point, LineString, LinearRing, Polygon, Multipoint}*. The functions for testing topological relations include *{disjoint, touches, crosses, within, contains, overlaps, intersects, equals}*.

Since GeoXACML uses the same policy language as XACML with additional support for geospatial features and and geospatial condition functions, a policy decision node, supporting GeoXACML policies, is capable of performing authorization decisions on XACML policies as well.

The GeoXACML policy is expressed as a set of rules each of which is expressed in a tuple *(Grant-type, (Subjects, Resources, Actions), Condition)*. It specifies that if conditions are satisfied, then a grant type such as "permit" or "deny" is given to *(Subjects, Resources, Actions)*, denoting *Subjects* can perform *Actions* on geospatial *Resources*. The following GeoXACML illustrates an example of a geospatial policy statement that grants a field engineer to access a feature type "roads" within the area specified in the polygon specified in the condition.

```
<Rule Effect="Permit" RuleId="rule-2.2">
<Description>Field-Engineer can request features of type
'tiger:tiger_roads' </Description>
<Target>

 <Subjects>
  <Subject>
  <SubjectMatch MatchId="urn:oasis:names:tc:xacml:1.0:function:string-equal">
    <AttributeValue DataType="http://www.w3.org/2001/XMLSchema#string">
     Field-Engineer</AttributeValue>
    <SubjectAttributeDesignator AttributeId="urn:oasis:names:tc:xacml:1.0:
      subject:subject-id" DataType="http://www.w3.org/2001/XMLSchema#string"
      SubjectCategory="urn:oasis:names:tc:xacml:1.0:
      subject-category:access-subject" /> </SubjectMatch>
  </Subject>
 </Subjects>
 <Resources> <Resource>
   <ResourceMatch MatchId="urn:oasis:names:tc:xacml:1.0:function:
     integer-less-than">
    <AttributeValue DataType="http://www.w3.org/2001/XMLSchema#integer">
     0</AttributeValue>
    <AttributeSelector DataType="http://www.w3.org/2001/XMLSchema#integer"
     RequestContextPath="count(//wfs:Query[@typeName='tiger:tiger_roads'])"/>
   </ResourceMatch>
 </Resource> </Resources>
 <Actions>
  <Action>
   <ActionMatch MatchId="urn:oasis:names:tc:xacml:1.0:function:string-equal">
   <AttributeValue DataType="http://www.w3.org/2001/XMLSchema#string">GetFeature
   </AttributeValue>
   <ActionAttributeDesignator AttributeId="urn:oasis:names:tc:xacml:1.0:
     action:action-id" DataType="http://www.w3.org/2001/XMLSchema#string"/>
   </ActionMatch>
  </Action>
 </Actions>
</Target>
<Condition FunctionId="urn:oasis:names:tc:xacml:1.0:function:all-of">
  <Function FunctionId="http://www.geoxacml.org/1.0/function#within"/>
 <AttributeValue DataType="http://www.opengis.net/gml#polygon">
  <gml:Polygon xmlns:gml="http://www.opengis.net/gml" gid="P2" srsName="EPSG:4326">
  <gml:exterior> <gml:LinearRing>
  <gml:posList dimension=2>-74.28798767828596,40.72400955310945 -74.12552621736093,
   40.72260599837143 -74.12552621736093,40.614883172228936 -74.28939123302396,
   40.61558494959794 -74.28798767828596,40.72400955310945 -74.28798767828596,
   40.72400955310945 -74.28798767828596,40.72400955310945</gml:posList>
  </gml:LinearRing> </gml:exterior>
  </gml:Polygon>
 </AttributeValue>
 <AttributeSelector DataType="http://www.opengis.net/gml#box"
   MustBePresent="false" RequestContextPath="//ogc:BBOX/gml:Box"/>
</Condition>
</Rule>
```

Geospatial Semantic Web Services Access Control

In [1], secure access to geospatial resources by clients or other Web services in the context of dynamic composition is proposed using the Geospatial Semantic Web Services that facilitates reasoning on security enforcement engines. In contrast to the XML-based standards and first-order logic-based access controls, it defines the axioms in OWL DL (Web Ontology Language-Description

Logics) [12] for policy specification. The policy framework is founded on three atomic concepts defined in OWL DL.

```
<owl:Class rdf:about="#Action"/>
<owl:Class rdf:about="#Condition"/>
<owl:Class rdf:about="#Resource"/>
```

Policy actions are Web Services that make the resources available and perform manipulations on the resources. Policy conditions are contextual events such as road topology or location data, and a resource can refer to the spatial extents of an object such as "building" with a polygon with a set of points. The access policies for a client are defined with OWL geospatial access control ontology, which enables reasoning engine to carry out conflict checks for possible loopholes. The spatial resources are organized with different levels of ontologies. First, it has the domain specific ontology, e.g. county ontology with spatial resources such as school, municipal building, park, etc., as primary concepts, and instances of these concepts as West Orange High School, City Government, etc. In addition, each of these concepts refer to the external upper ontology on the geospatial ontologies, that shows the geospatial related concepts and their relationships such as "features" has spatial extent to concepts such as polygon or line, and each polygon consists of a set of coordinates that form a closed ring. Figure 3 shows the relationships among different types of ontologies.

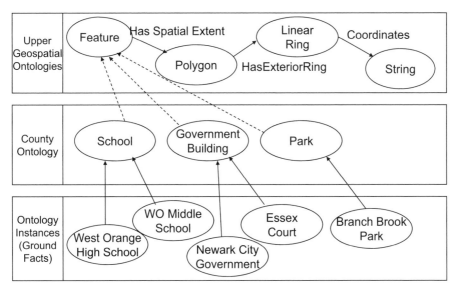

Fig. 3. County Ontology Hierarchy

This approach is intended to provide the ability to enforce the policy with semantic reasoning. This semantics-aware security enforcement should be able to reason and dynamically compose services even though there is no explicit policy specification. For example, a provider network can provide two geospatial services: movie theater finder Web service and a live traffic Web service. For a premium subscriber requesting for movie theaters in a particular zip code area, the provider can choose to overlay traffic information on the displayed map even though it was not explicitly requested or the subscriber is not an explicit client of the traffic service. In addition, the policy on accessing the location information (or map or building plan) of a Newark City government building, and the policy on accessing court buildings can be specified on the concept level of government building, rather than individually listing these policy rules separately. Also, the reasoning engine should be able to detect the conflicts among different policies using the concept hierarchies and relationships.

4 Conclusion and Future Directions

This chapter presents different access control models and approaches for geospatial data resources, such as GSAM (Geospatio-temporal Authorization Model) for multi-resolution satellite images, Geo-RBAC for location aware access to feature and map data, access control for imprecise location-based services for context aware access and GeoXACML access control approaches for geospatial Web Services, and Semantics-aware access control for geospatial Semantic Web Services. In addition, it discusses the issues and the current development in Geospatial Resource Digital Rights Management.

Both GeoXACML and secure Semantic Web Services access control presented above do not consider the specification of the subject role that is also spatially referenced, but focus on the specifications of the geospatial resources and geospatial conditions. An extension of GeoXACML and semantic RDF version can be made to specify the geospatial roles as presented in the GSAM and GEO-RBAC models presented in sections 3.1 and 3.2, and the authorization engine is needed to verify the spatial roles.

The future approaches should focus on privacy issues that arise due to the combination of ubiquitous computing devices and location tracking devices, such as GPS, GPRS, etc. The data generated from these devices, combined with the geospatial data, give rise to much more serious issues on privacy infringement, such as the visualization of the locations from different timelines. The future security research focus should address these location tracking as well as the activities associated with the locations in the track.

Another direction that the research community should pay attention to is to verify the policy composability and consistency in the dynamic ad-hoc geospatial composition that involve multiple coalition organizations. Furthermore, collections of geospatial data from multiple databases within an agency or from multiple agencies taken together may be sensitive, while individually they are not necessarily of sensitive nature.

References

1. Ashraful Alam, Ganesh Subbiah, Bhavani Thuraisingam, and Latifur Khan. Reasoning with semantics-aware access control policies for geospatial web services. In *SWS '06: Proceedings of the 3rd ACM workshop on Secure web services*, pages 69–76, New York, NY, USA, 2006. ACM Press.
2. Claudio A. Ardagna, Marco Cremonini, Ernesto Damiani, Sabrina De Capitani di Vimercati, and Pierangela Samarati. Supporting location-based conditions in access control policies. In *ASIACCS '06: Proceedings of the 2006 ACM Symposium on Information, computer and communications security*, pages 212–222, New York, NY, USA, 2006. ACM Press.
3. Vijayalakshmi Atluri and Soon Ae Chun. An Authorization Model for Geospatial Data. *IEEE Transactions on Dependable and Secure Computing*, 1(4):238–254, 2004.
4. Vijayalakshmi Atluri and Soon Ae Chun. A Geotemporal Role-based Authorization System. *International Journal of Information and Computer Security*, 1(1/2):143–168, 2007.
5. John C. Baker, Beth E. Lachman, David R. Frelinger, Kevin M. O'Connell, Alexander C. Hou, Michael S. Tseng, David Orletsky, and Charles Yost. Mapping the Risks: Assessing the Homeland Security Implications of Publicly Available Geospatial Information. Technical report, RAND National Defense Research Institute, RAND Corporation, 2004.
6. Tom Barclay, Jim Gray, and Don Slutz. Microsoft TerraServer: a spatial data warehouse. In *SIGMOD '00: Proceedings of the 2000 ACM SIGMOD international conference on Management of data*, pages 307–318, New York, NY, USA, 2000. ACM Press.
7. Elisa Bertino, Barbara Catania, Maria Luisa Damiani, and Paolo Perlasca. GEO-RBAC: a spatially aware RBAC. In *Proceeding of the 10th ACM Symposium on Access Control Models and Technologies (SACMAT 2005)*, pages 29–37, 2005.
8. Soon Ae Chun and Vijayalakshmi Atluri. Protecting Privacy from Continuous High-resolution Satellite Surveillance. In *Data and Application Security, Development and Directions, IFIP TC11/ WG11.3 Fourteenth Annual Working Conference on Database Security*, pages 233–244, 2000.
9. Michael J. Covington, Prahlad Fogla, Zhiyuan Zhan, and Mustaque Ahamad. A Context-Aware Security Architecture for Emerging Applications. In *Proceedings of 18th Annual Computer Security Applications Conference (ACSAC'2002)*, pages 249–260, 2002.
10. Michael J. Covington, Wende Long, Srividhya Srinivasan, Anind K. Dey, Mustaque Ahamad, and Gregory D. Abowd. Securing context-aware applications using environment roles. In *Proceedings of the 6th ACM Symposium on Access Control Models and Technologies (SACMAT 2001)*, pages 10–20, 2001.
11. Maria Luisa Damiani, Elisa Bertino, Barbara Catania, and Paolo Perlasca. GEO-RBAC: A spatially aware RBAC. *ACM Transactions of Information Systems Security*, 10(1), 2007.

12. Deborah L. McGuinness and Frank van Harmelen. Owl web ontology language overview: W3c recommendation 10. Technical report, W3C, 2004. http://www.w3.org/TR/owl-features/.
13. Federal Geographic Data Committee. Geospatial Metadata Standards.
14. Google . Google Earth, 2007. http://earth.google.com.
15. Google . Google Maps API, 2007. http://www.google.com/apis/maps/documentation/.
16. Andreas Matheaus. Declaration and enforcement of finegrained access restrictions for a service-based geospatial data infrastructure. In *Proceedings of tenth ACM symposium on Access control models and technologies*, 2005.
17. Andreas Matheus. Geospatial extensible access control markup language (geoxacml). Technical report, Open Geospatial Consortium, Inc., 2007. http://xml.coverpages.org/OGC-07-026-RFC-Submission-GeoXACML-ImplementationSpecification.pdf.
18. Microsoft Corporation. Microsoft Virtual Earth, 2007. http://www.microsoft.com/virtualearth/default.mspx.
19. Tim Moses. eXtensible Acess Control Markup Language (XACML) Version 2.0. Technical report.
20. National Oceanic and Atmospheric Administration (NOAA). NOAA KLM User's Guide, 2000. http://www2.ncdc.noaa.gov/docs/klm/html/c3/sec3-1.htm.
21. Douglas Nebert, Arliss Whiteside, and Panagiotis Vretanos. OpenGIS Catalogue Service Implementation Specification Version 2.0.2. Technical report, Open Geospatial Consortium, Inc., 2007. http://www.opengeospatial.org/standards/cat.
22. Open Geospatial Consortium, Inc. OpenGIS Web Map Service Implementation Specification, 2006. http://www.opengeospatial.org/standards/wms.
23. UNEP: United Nations Environmental Programme. Geo Data Portal, 2006. http://geodata.grid.unep.ch/.
24. Satellite Imaging Corporation. Satellite Imaging Sensors, 2001. http://www.satimagingcorp.com/satellite-sensors.html: Accessed in 2007.
25. Alessandra Toninelli, Rebecca Montanari, Lalana Kagal, and Ora Lassila. A Semantic Context-Aware Access Control Framework for Secure Collaborations in Pervasive Computing Environments. In *The Semantic Web - Proceedings of the 5th International Semantic Web Conference (ISWC 2006)*, pages 473–486, 2006.
26. USDA. USDA Geospatial Data Gateway, 2006. http://gcmd.nasa.gov/records/USDA_Geo_Gateway.html.
27. Graham Vowles. Geospatial Digital Rights Management Reference Model (Geo-DRM RM) Version 1.0.0. Technical report.
28. Guangsen Zhang and Manish Parashar. Dynamic Context-aware Access Control for Grid Applications. In *Proceedings of the 4th International Workshop on Grid Computing (GRID 2003)*, pages 101–108, 2003.

12

Security Re-engineering for Databases: Concepts and Techniques

Michael Gertz[1] and Madhavi Gandhi[2]

[1] Department of Computer Science
University of California at Davis, CA
gertz@cs.ucdavis.edu
[2] Department of Mathematics and Computer Science
California State University, East Bay, CA
madhavi.gandhi@eastbay.edu

Summary. Despite major advancements in access control models and security mechanisms, most of today's databases are still very vulnerable to various security threats, as shown by recent incident reports. A reason for this that existing databases used in e-businesses and government organizations are rarely designed with much security in mind but rely on security policies and mechansims that are added over time in an ad-hoc fashion. What is needed in such cases is a coherent approach for organizations to first evaluate the current secrutiy setup of a database, i.e., its policies and mechanisms, and then to re-design and improve the mechanisms in a focused way, that is, to apply an evolutionary rather than a revolutionary approach to improving database security.

In this book chapter, we present important principles and techniques of such a security re-engineering approach. Our focus is on the detection and prevention of insider misuse, which is still the biggest threat to security. We show how techniques such as focused auditing, and data and user profiling are integrated into a single methodological framework for database security evaluation. This framework is supported by an access path model, which provides information about data and user behavior, access correlations, and potential vulnerabilities. Based on the information obtained in this approach, we illustrate how security can be strengthened using standard database functionality.

1 Introduction

In most of today's information system infrastructures employed by e-businesses and government organizations, database management systems (DBMSs) serve as the back-end for managing and delivering often mission-critical and sensitive data. Although such infrastructures are comprised of many components, such as networks and application servers, we conjecture that the data managed in databases is often the most valuable asset to an organization. The data typically have been curated and maintained over many years, and their loss or corruption would be much more difficult (and costly) to compensate for than the failure of some other infrastructure components.

Over the past twenty years, there have been significant advancements in database security (see, e.g., [12, 50, 51]), ranging from sophisticated, expressive access control models to privacy and trust management. Although some of these concepts have found their way into today's (primarily commercial) DBMSs, database systems are still facing numerous security threats aimed at tampering with the integrity, availability, and confidentiality of the data.

There are several reasons for this situation. First, there is a substantial time lag between the proposal of a better database security technique and its realization in a new release of a DBMS. Even then, the new technologies need to be learned and used appropriately to further secure a database. Second, and more importantly, the shortcomings of appropriately securing databases stem from circumstances that are also found all too often in other computer security settings. These include

- *Lack of clearly defined security policies.* If security policies are not well understood or not clearly stated, they cannot be effectively implemented using database security mechanisms, leaving the database system open to security threats.
- *Poor security design.* As with many other types of computing systems, for databases too security is often an afterthought. Security policies are formulated and implemented in an ad-hoc fashion, leading to an incoherent overall database security design and thus resulting in potential vulnerabilities that can be exploited by malicious users and intruders.
- *Dynamic nature of applications and user tasks/roles.* Over time, database users are added or removed and applications are added, upgraded, or removed, often leaving the implementation of associated security policies at the database back-end untouched. Outdated and obsolete security policies and corresponding enforcing security mechanisms pose a critical threat to database security.

Several other reasons can be given, such as the evolution of database structures and schemas to accommodate new applications and associated security requirements or simply the incorrect usage of the database and its (administrative) tools.

One of the most significant problem contributing to the current situation in better securing databases is that of *insider misuse*. That is, legitimate users of an application or database who (maliciously) tamper with the integrity and confidentiality of the data. As stated in [26, 48], insider misuse is still the biggest threat to security not only in database systems. Clearly, if security policies are not designed and implemented in a coherent and consistent fashion, intrusions and insider misuse pose a great threat to database security.

As becomes evident from the above observations, in order for an organization to strengthen the security of its database (potentially using new security concepts and techniques), first, the status of the security of the existing "legacy" database needs to be evaluated. This should be done with a particular focus on potential vulnerabilities that give rise to insider misuse, which is primarily caused by not adhering to the principle of least privilege [11, 31].

In this book chapter, we present the fundamental concepts and techniques to support different security re-engineering tasks for relational databases. The proposed approach is *data-driven*, meaning that a comprehensive evaluation of the security of a given database necessitates the evaluation of the quality of the data to be protected first. Only if it is known that the mission-critical and sensitive data is of good quality (which is often not the case in practice, see, e.g., [9, 18]), suitable data and user profiling techniques can be deployed. Otherwise, statistical models representing the normal behavior of users and data, which are to be monitored and enforced by respective mechanisms, is skewed due to poor quality data underlying the model generation. The data and user profiling techniques we present employ selective database auditing using standard database functionality and well-known profiling techniques based on data mining approaches.

We further present a methodological framework, called the *access path model*, in which administrators and security personnel can discover, annotate, and evaluate access paths. An access path represents the current (admissible) ways in which application users can operate on the data managed in a database. Correlating data accesses and user accounts (represented in the form of profiles) at the database layer and application layer is crucial in order to strengthen or replace current security policies. A feature of the access path model is that it allows to back-track accesses to and operations on database relations to application users by correlating user profiles and audit trails managed at the database and application layers. The information extracted from such access exploration and analysis tasks is then used in the re-design of existing or the implementation of new security mechanisms. Our primary objective here is to provide a comprehensive overview of existing and novel techniques and in particular their integration into a single coherent framework for the security re-engineering of databases.

The remainder of the chapter is organized as follows. In Section 2, we review some basic concepts underlying the notion of intrusion detection, with a particular focus on insider misuse. In Section 3, we then present basic principles of database auditing techniques and discuss the concepts of data and user profiling in databases. The access path model is discussed in Section 4. Based on the information obtained through employing the access path model, in Section 5, we summarize basic database security reconfiguration approaches. After a review of related work in Section 6, we conclude the chapter with a summary and outlook in Section 7.

2 Insider Misuse and Anomaly Detection

An overarching theme in computer security, which has been studied for more than 20 years and also motivates the need for security re-engineering concepts and techniques for databases, is *intrusion detection* [1, 20, 34, 38, 44]. In general, an intrusion is considered an activity that violates the security policy of a system. *Intrusion detection systems* (IDSs) are based on the assumption that the behavior of an intruder is different from that of an authorized user and that respective unauthorized activities can be detected and reacted upon. One typically distinguishes among host-based IDSs, network-based IDSs and application-based IDSs. All these systems are based on the analysis of audit data, which are collected by some audit procedures and describe events of interest at different levels of granularity, an aspect we will elaborate on in Section 3.1. A host-based IDS uses audit data produced by operating system calls on a local host, such as process executions, resource consumptions, and file accesses. Network-based IDS, on the other hand, are placed in a network and monitor all network traffic. They analyze packages for particular signatures and try to detect and prevent inappropriate network usages. Application-based IDSs can be considered a special class of host-based IDSs. They collect and analyze audit data specific to a particular application, application component or function realized on one or more hosts [23, 54].

One could argue that a database management system (DBMS) is a particular type of such applications. However, as we will discuss in the following sections, traditional application-based IDS techniques are not sufficient to realize an effective intrusion detection system for a DBMS. For this, it is important to understand the methodologies IDSs employ for the detection of security policy violations. These methods are discussed next.

2.1 Misuse Detection

Misuse detection is one of two classes of intrusion detection approaches. Misuse detection is based on *signatures* that describe the characteristics of known system attacks and vulnerabilities. The signatures are typically derived from security policies. Mechanisms implementing a misuse detection approach monitor the system, network, or application for any activities that match the specified signatures, e.g., a specific sequence of system calls or a particular type of packet traffic between two hosts.

Although misuse detection approaches work very well for known attacks and misuse patterns, they fail in dealing with new attacks and security threats. These misuse detection approaches need to continuously update the signatures of security threats and vulnerabilities in order to effectively prevent intrusions.

2.2 Anomaly Detection

Most of the approaches to intrusion detection typically combine misuse detection with anomaly detection. Anomaly detection approaches are the most popular and effective ones, as they are based on the normal behavior of a subject, e.g., a user, system component, or application. In anomaly detection, information about repetitive and usual behavior is collected and suitably represented as statistical models of normal behavior, e.g., in the form of *profiles*. Current user or system activities are then compared to such profiles. If the activities significantly deviate from the profile, the activities are considered intrusive [8, 32, 34, 38, 44]. Deviations from the normal behavior indicate potential violations of a security policy or an intrusion and thus might trigger respective responses.

The advantage of anomaly detection over misuse detection is that previously unseen attacks and activities have a better chance of being detected. Clearly, the effectiveness of an anomaly-based IDS depends on how well normal behavior is modeled and how tight thresholds are set to indicate a deviation from the normal behavior, aiming to reduce false positives (activities that are not normal but do not violate a security policy) and avoiding false negatives (suspicious activities that are considered normal).

It is obviously desirable to adopt techniques suggested for misuse-based and anomaly-based detection techniques, which almost exclusively have been realized in the context of host-based and network-based IDSs, for database management systems and surrounding infrastructure, that is, applications and the network. A major problem the development of a database intrusion detection system is facing, however, is that of insider misuse, an aspect we discuss in more detail next as it drives most of the security re-engineering approach we present in this paper.

2.3 Insider Misuse

The notion of intrusion intuitively refers to subjects that gain access to a system to which they have no legitimate access otherwise. Such intrusions occur by exploiting system vulnerabilities or by simply cracking or stealing accounts of legitimate users. Once the subject has access to a system, the subject then is considered a legitimate user by the system and has all the privileges and rights associated with that user; the intruder is now considered an *insider.* Thus, one objective of a security re-engineering approach to database systems can be framed as "effectively detecting and preventing insider misuse".

As several recent reports clearly indicate, traditional intrusion detection techniques and systems are not sufficient in dealing with insider misuse [5, 6, 26, 43, 48]. In particular, the CSI/FBI reports state that *"The threat from inside the organization is far greater than the threat from outside the organization"* and *"Inside jobs occur about as often as external attacks"* [26, 48]. Clearly, the problem of insider misuse is aggravated in the context of database systems that manage large collections of sensitive and often mission-critical data. There are many sources for potential insider misuse, ranging from the frequently mentioned "disgruntled employee" who maliciously tampers with the integrity of the data, to outside hackers, criminals, and spies that gain unauthorized access to the data [19, 49].

Some key observations that drive our security re-engineering approach can be informally stated as follows. First, traditional host-based and network-based IDSs are ineffective in dealing with insider misuse at the database level. This is because users typically have legitimate access to the database and applications, and misuse patterns are not reflected at the network or system level but at a much finer level of granularity in the database (e.g., deletions and modifications of tuples). However, it seems reasonable to combine such IDSs with a database-based anomaly and misuse detection approach. Second, excessive database and application privileges assigned to legitimate users can be exploited by the users as well as intruders that gain access to user accounts, an aspect often mentioned in the above reports. This aspect obviously relates to the principle of least privilege [11, 31], that is, no subject should be assigned more privileges than those that are necessary and sufficient to carry out their tasks.

In the following, we discuss the first steps of a security re-engineering approach to databases, consisting of the profiling of the data managed in the database and the users operating on the data. In Section 4, we then discuss how these steps are embedded in a methodological security re-engineering framework.

3 Data and User Profiling

The basic technique underlying the detection of intrusions and insider misuse, and subsequently the re-engineering of security mechanisms, is to monitor what types of actions users perform on a database system. In the following, we take a data-centric view on this and detail different profiling approaches. In Section 3.1, we first elaborate on some standard database auditing techniques as important prerequisite for profiling. In Sections 3.2 and 3.3, we then discuss how audit data is used to profile data and users, respectively.

3.1 Auditing

In the context of database systems, auditing is the process of monitoring and recording selected database event and activities [25, 42]. Auditing is primarily used to provide for accountability, the validation of security policies, and to capture and review the observed behavior of applications, users and database objects. Auditing is also often a requirement for organizations that have to comply with federal laws and regulations such as the Health Insurance Portability and Accountability Act (HIPAA) of 1996, Sarbanes-Oxley Act of 2002, and the Graham-Leach-Bliley Act (GLBA) of 1999. In the latter cases, auditing primarily serves the purpose of establishing accountability (who performed what operations on what objects at what points in time) and the reconstruction of events [41]. NIST has established six components of security audit criteria [3], which can directly be adopted to database systems. The activities are the (1) selection of security audit events, (2) security audit data generation, (3) security audit event storage, (4) audit review, (5) security audit analysis, and (6) automatic response. Figure 1 illustrates the sequence of these criteria as an approach to using auditing techniques for evaluation activities, which is preceded by an extra step, the analysis of application specific security requirements.

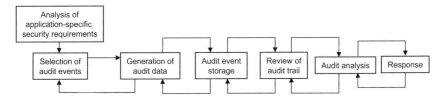

Fig. 1. Activities according to the NIST security audit criteria.

Most of today's commercial and open-source DBMS provide audit mechanisms and architectures that support such activities and which mostly vary in terms of the granularity of access information that can be recorded in audit trails. For example, database triggers provide a convenient means to record information about SQL insert, update, and delete statements against database relations, including the recording of old and new values of updated tuples. Activities related to the creation, modification, and deletion of database objects resulting from SQL data definition language (DDL) statements can be audited as well, often referred to as the auditing of accesses with respect to *system privileges*. Some database systems even offer mechanisms that go beyond simple SQL statement level auditing by monitoring data accesses based on content, such as Fine-Grained Auditing (FGA) introduced with Oracle 9i. This is in particular useful when access information about SQL select statements needs to be recorded (see, e.g., [30]).

In addition to database triggers and the SQL `audit` command supported by many DBMS, another useful technique are stored procedures. Instead of individual SQL insert, update and delete statements issued from an application, stored procedures are called. A stored procedure then executes the data modification statements and also records (in auxiliary relations) some extra context information about the modifications such the current user role, other users currently running database sessions, or the number of records that have been modified through these statements.

In general, audit mechanisms for the monitoring of SQL statements, access privileges used, database schema objects and fine-grained access information can manage audit information in two ways: (1) within the database as a database audit trail (typically a table in the data dictionary) or (2) in an operating system audit trail, where audit information is written to a file outside the database, unaccessible to database users. Typical information recorded in an audit trail includes the database user name, role and object privileges used, name of the database object accessed, session and transaction id, SQL text of the statement that triggered the auditing, and type of operation performed. It should be noted that enabling any type of audit mechanism has an impact on the performance of the database, no matter whether these are triggers or audit mechanisms enabled through the SQL `audit` command. Thus, any audit strategy targeting the security evaluation of a database has to carefully analyze the various security requirements imposed on the database and the specific objectives of the strategy. In the following two sections, we first discuss some basic building blocks for such a strategy: the profiling of data and users. In Section 4, we then present a methodology that embeds these techniques in a more comprehensive and strategy-driven framework.

3.2 Data Profiling

Most approaches to misuse detection are *user-centric*. Their objective is to determine how users typically behave in terms of operations on the database and how their current behavior deviates from previous behavior. We conjecture that for the security re-engineering of databases, the evaluation and strengthening of security has to take a *data-centric* view. That is, first the behavior of the data being managed in the database needs to be evaluated before techniques are employed to detect and evaluate the (potentially anomalous) behavior of users. There are several reasons for such an approach. First, accidental or malicious tampering with the security and integrity of data is often only detected at the data level, that is, when erroneous, missing, extra, or anomalous data are discovered. This aspect leads to the second argument, where one would like to back-trace anomalous data to users who operate on the data, something that is not trivial in particular in the case of shared database user accounts, which is common in many application settings and will be discussed in Section 4. Finally, and most importantly, approaches to establishing some normal user behavior typically assume that the data users operate on are normal, i.e., the data are correct and of good quality, something that is often not the case for production databases where evaluating and maintaining the quality of data is a major concern [9, 18].

Snapshot Profiles

The first step in security re-engineering for databases is to determine and evaluate the properties of data that is to be protected from misuse. Given a database schema consisting of a set of relations $\mathcal{R}$, those relations are investigated that manage mission-critical or sensitive data. Similar to the approaches suggested in [25] and [56], for a given relation $R \in \mathcal{R}$ with attributes

$A_1, \ldots, A_n$, the values for individual attributes A_i are analyzed. This analysis includes determining the distribution and frequency of attribute values, e.g., in the form of histograms, and the minimum and maximum values and lengths for numerical and alpha-numerical attributes, respectively.

Such a simple analysis, which can be done using SQL statements at the relation level, can reveal quite a lot of useful information, for example, outliers that do not conform to certain properties the data are assumed to have. The analysis can also be extended to sets of tuples from one or more relations where now tuples and combinations thereof are analyzed and correlations among attribute values are determined using standard association analysis techniques (see, e.g., [57]). Assume, for example, two relations $R_1(A, C)$ and $R_2(B, D)$ with a foreign key dependency $R_2.B \rightarrow R_1.A$. For any two matching tuples $t_1 \in R_1, t_2 \in R_2$, an association can describe that the value of $t_1.C$ always determines the range of the attribute value $t_2.D$. The association rules discovered are then evaluated and compared to what is expected from the data. In principle, many of the analysis tasks resemble standard actions employed in the evaluation of the quality of the data [9, 18]. It should also be noted that in production databases, most of the above information is typically readily available. This is in particular the case where statistics for relations are periodically maintained to provide cost-based query optimizer with information for choosing efficient query evaluation plans. Statistical information about the relations is then available in the database's data dictionary.

For data profiling, it is assumed that the above analysis tasks are performed on a snapshot of the database, that is, at a particular point in time. This can be done in a batch-mode when the workload of the database is low (e.g., during night), or by using a stand-by or recent backup database. For large-scale databases with hundreds of relations, clearly not all relations are analyzed but only those that are relevant to specific security policies or those that contain sensitive or mission-critical data as indicated in the initial step in Figure 1. The snapshot profiles for these individual relations or parts thereof (e.g., sets of tuples that have some specific properties or contain particularly sensitive information) are managed in separate relations, specifically designed for access to database security mechanisms (see Section 5). In the most simple case, a snapshot profile for a relation $R \in \mathcal{R}$ determined at a particular point in time t, denoted $DataProf(R, t)$, is a collection of measure-value pairs that describe properties of attributes of R. The measure is related to the data, e.g., number or frequencies of different attribute values, and the measure value denotes what has been computed for a measure.

The above discussion makes one point very clear: developing a misuse detection approach on top of a database for which the quality of the data is not known or the data is of poor quality is likely to be not practical. That is, if the normal behavior of users is to be determined, erroneous, missing, or extra data in the underlying relations can significantly skew the statistical models describing the normal behavior of users in terms of accesses to the data. Therefore, it is essential to "clean" the data, i.e., removing (if possible) all the data that is of poor quality and to set up mechanisms that help prevent data of poor quality in the future. For this, mechanisms as simple as integrity constraints that restrict the admissible values of attributes can be very effective. More complex properties of the data, e.g., admissible relationships between attribute values of one or more relations can be realized as well, mostly using database triggers. The discovery of integrity constraints and their enforcement using standard database functionality thus plays an important role in the security re-engineering of databases, because they can effectively detect and prevent potential misuse patterns, no matter whether these patterns stem from accidental or intentional misuse.

Temporal Profiles and Access Properties

Snapshot profiles describe properties of some relations' data at a single point in time, that is, for a given database instance. In order to further evaluate the security of the database and to develop respective enforcing security mechanisms, however, it is important to get a good understanding of how the data behave and evolve over time. For this, we distinguish two objectives:

1. determining the behavior of the data over time, and
2. determining the behavior of accesses to the data over time.

The first objective can be realized by periodically taking snapshot profiles and analyzing sequences of snapshot profiles for certain trends. Key to such an approach is the appropriate choice of time-granularities, that is, instants in time when to perform the snapshot profiling, an aspect that heavily depends on the particular application setting of the database. Assume for a relation $R \in \mathcal{R}$, snapshot profiles $DataProf(R, t_1), \ldots DataProf(R, t_k)$ have been determined at times $t_1, \ldots, t_k$. The goal of the analysis of these profiles then is to discover trends in the behavior of the data. These trends, managed in temporal profiles with a measure/value pair structure similar to snapshot profiles, can include coarse grained properties such the increase or decrease ratio of the number of tuples in R between consecutive timestamps t_i and t_{i+1} as well as more fine-grained properties such as the significant variations in the frequency and/or distribution of attribute values. The outcome of this analysis is again evaluated and verified with respect to the expected behavior of the data. The purpose of this type of trend analysis is less to derive further security mechanisms but to gain confidence in individual snapshot profiles and the properties of relations and data at respective points in time. Again, these profiling tasks can go hand in hand with the process of managing statistics for relations for query optimization purposes (here now, such statistics are maintained over time, again in auxiliary relations).

The task much closer related to misuse and anomaly detection is the management and profiling of accesses to the relations over time. In the most simple case, once some anomalous data or data behavior have been discovered, one might naturally ask "what user is responsible for this behavior of the data?".

Of course, such information cannot be obtained from the relations but requires auditing techniques introduced in Section 3.1.

Assume a relation $R \in \mathcal{R}$ for which access properties is to be determined. First, a suitable time-granularity is chosen for the auditing approach, such as just one hour or a whole week. Next, audit mechanisms are designed and enabled that record access information about SQL insert, update, delete, and select statements against R. If only the frequency of such statements over a period of time is of interest, then normal auditing based on the SQL audit command is sufficient, and no database triggers are employed. However, if more fine grained information about the data modification statements is of interest, triggers have to be employed to record for each such SQL statement what tuples have been inserted, deleted, or modified, the latter also recording the old and new values of updated tuples.

Gathering fine-grained information about SQL select statements is much harder to deal with. To our knowledge, there is no DBMS that provides mechanisms to record how many and what tuples have been retrieved by a select statement, but only the plain, text-based SQL query plus some additional information such as access time and user account. Thus, excessive and possibly anomalous reads against a database are hard to capture as part of a misuse detection strategy. The only viable solution to this problem is to embed some extra code in application programs (e.g., at the client side) and stored procedures (at the database side) that make use of cursors to retrieve and process individual result tuples from an SQL select query.

In the following, we denote the access profile for a relation R for a time interval $[t_i, t_j]$ by $AccessProf(R, t_i, t_j)$. The profile manages information (as measure/value pairs) about the frequencies of all insert, delete, and update statements, including information about individual tuples, and the frequency of select statements against R. Note that for each individual statement, all standard audit information as outlined in Section 3.1 is recorded as well. Figure 2 illustrates the structure and content of a relation used to manage information about accesses to some relation $R(A_1, A_2, A_3)$. Note that in the ideal case, respective profiles and audit trails are not managed in the production database but in another database that allows to analyze and evaluate audit and profile information without interfering with the production database. Oracle's Audit-vault product is a good example of such an approach [2].

timestamp	user	operation	new tuple	old tuple
09-01-07 09:12:14	scott	insert	(3,8,12)	–
09-01-07 09:12:15	scott	insert	(4,9,7)	–
09-01-07 09:13:01	smith	update	(3,8,12)	(3,8,13)
09-01-07 09:13:02	jones	delete	–	(4,9,7)
...	...	...	...	...

Fig. 2. Snapshot of the basic information recorded for a data access profile for a given database relation, including old and new values of modified tuples.

Upon the completion of an audit window for a relation R, the relation's access profile is analyzed to evaluate access patterns of interest. This can easily be done using standard SQL statements that involve `group by` and sorting. For example, for insert statements, one can determine typical values or value ranges of inserted attributes. Similarly, for delete statements, one can compute characteristic properties of the deleted tuples. For update statements, it is furthermore possible to analyze the modifications at a much more fine-grained level. For example, one can determine the average, maximum, and minimum change of an updated attribute. Here again, knowing the security policies and typical behavior of data in the relation is of much help in designing constraint mechanisms that prevent accidental or intentional anomalous updates. As an illustrative example, assume an employee relation with an attribute *Salary*. If it is known that salaries can only be increased by no more than 20% and not decreased by more than 10%, and these properties are also reflected in the access profile for the relation, then suitable triggers enforcing this property can be implemented.

In summary, the data profiling approach provides data administrators with both static (one-time) and temporal properties of relations and accesses to relations. The information obtained during the profiling not only helps in understanding the behavior of mission-critical and sensitive data, but it can also be used to derive semantic integrity constraints, which, if suitably implemented, further help preventing potentially anomalous data modifications.

3.3 User Profiling

Following the data profiling tasks presented in the previous sections, the next step is to associate users with the behavior of the data and eventually determine models describing the normal behavior of users. Profiling of users or, more precisely, their behavior over time, has been the focus of several related work in the context of relational databases, e.g., [13, 15, 29, 56], fraud detection, e.g., [21, 22], and intrusion detection, e.g., [33, 36, 53, 60].

In order to suitably approach the user profiling task, it is important to understand the notion of a user in a database system. Underlying access control models in databases is the notion of *authorization identifier (AuthID)*, which is either the identifier of a database user or a database role name. According to the SQL:1999 standard [39], when an SQL session is initiated (e.g., an application connects to the database using a valid database user account), the authorization identifier is then determined by the DBMS. In the following, whenever we refer to a user, we mean a valid database user account used by either a person or an application. There are typically different types of users:

- *Database Administrators (DBAs)*. These types of users possess various system privileges to manage physical database objects (e.g., the creation of database files), logical objects (e.g., the creation and deletion of relations, views, triggers etc.), user accounts, database roles and privileges, and system parameters and settings.

- *Application Developers.* These users are primarily responsible for the design, implementation, and maintenance of the database schemas (including structures such as indexes and stored procedures) underlying different applications.
- *Application Users.* Unlike the other two classes of users, application users do not have any system privileges, i.e., they are not allowed to manage database objects, but are only allowed to operate on the data of an application schema using insert, update, delete, and select statements or the execution of stored procedures.

Although DBAs have the most comprehensive and powerful set of privileges to perform operations on any database structure and object, profiling their behavior in terms of SQL DML statements against individual relations is not that meaningful, as they will rarely perform such operations. In general, profiling the behavior of DBAs is complicated as they are typically responsible for setting up an audit and profiling framework. Also, there is rarely a fine-grained typical behavior that can be derived from auditing all operations a DBA issues against a database as operations exclusively should comprise the management of logical and physical database objects, and not individual tuples in relations associated with application schemas. We will revisit this aspect again in a later section. A similar argument can be made for application developers. Applications are typically develop not on a production database serving mission-critical applications, but on a development database where the security is likely of less concern. Only in rare circumstances, application developers should perform management related operations on application schemas hosted at the production database, e.g., when structures are transitioned from the development database to the production database.

In the following, we are primarily concerned with profiling techniques for application users with respect to individual relations. Assume a set $\mathcal{U}_{db}$ of database users and a relation R with data access profile $AccessProf(R, t_i, t_j)$ for a time window $[t_i, t_j]$. In order to analyze and evaluate what operations users in $\mathcal{U}_{db}$ performed on R, one can start off with a simple SQL group by statement to see the types and frequencies of operations each user performed on R. Clearly, not all users in $\mathcal{U}_{db}$ will have issued operations against R during the time window, also because they simply do not have any privileges to access R.

Following this kind of aggregating user-centric access information, one now focuses on the behavior of a particular user $u \in \mathcal{U}_{db}$ who operated on R. There are basically two meaningful ways by which entries in $AccessProf(R, t_i, t_j)$ can be organized for u: by session and/or by database role. Typically, every operation occurs as part of a user session, which starts when a user connects to the database and has some kind of id. In a database session, the user can enable different database roles, depending on whether roles are supported by the DBMS and, if supported, have been assigned to the user. Both types of information is recorded in audit trails that keep track of accesses to relations.

Using this information, it is then possible to extract sequences of operations from $Access(R, t_i, t_j)$ that are delimited by role changes, that is, in a session, the user switched roles. For example, the first part of a particular user session may contain 10 operations the user executed with role ro_1 and then 20 operations with role ro_2, all operations against relation R. Extracting all information relevant to a user u can easily be done using SQL query statements against $AccessProf(R, t_i, t_j)$.

Of particular interest in profiling users, of course, is to determine their typical behavior. So one might ask "what is the typical sequence of operations, role enablings, and particular modifications a user is performing in a given session?". For this, existing data mining techniques can be used, for example, temporal sequence learning [33]. User sessions then can be compared and evaluated in terms of similarity, typical patterns, and anomalous access patterns. Note, however, that the above profiling tasks all refer to a single relation R. The construction of more complex profiles and their analysis will be detailed in the next section.

In general, the above techniques show that it is important to determine precise metrics of interest for the user profiling approach. That is, one has to establish clear objectives that can be computed from a data access profile. For example, if the time window underlying a data access profile $AccessProf(R, t_i, t_j)$ covers a whole week from Monday to Sunday, then the profile of a user u with respect to the relation R, denoted, $UserProf(R, u, t_i, t_j)$ may include information about the following measures: (1) number and duration of sessions, (2) names of roles that have been enabled during a session, including timestamps of when roles where enabled, (3) number of operations against R per session and role setting, (4) typical sequence of operations in a session (per role), (5) typical values of attributes inserted or modified, and typical properties of tuples deleted. As done for the other types of profiles introduced in the previous sections, a user profile $UserProf(R, u, t_i, t_j)$ can be managed as measure-value pairs (in auxiliary relations) for easy inspection and use by security mechanisms. It should also be noted that the above tasks can be extended to capture information about the execution of stored procedures by a user.

The above is not a comprehensive list but shows some important measures that can easily be computed from access profiles and presented to personnel conducting the security re-engineering process. The main purpose here is to provide such personnel with insights into who performs what types of operations in what settings on a given relation. In particular, these profiles can serve as a starting point for a more comprehensive user evaluation and profiling approach, as detailed in the next section.

4 Access Path Model

A typical production-type database setup may contain thousands of database objects, hundreds of users and roles and, consequently, many complex access privilege structures. Furthermore, several applications may operate on a single database and its objects using different accounts and privileges. In order to apply a security re-engineering approach to such a complex setting, it is essential to have a good methodology that helps administrators and security personnel to suitably approach the tasks of data and user profiling, analysis and correlation of profiles, and re-design of security policies and mechanisms.

In this section, we present the access path model, which helps accomplishing these tasks in a focused manner. In Section 4.1, we outline the specific problem setting and the objectives the access path model addresses. In Section 4.2, we introduce the components of the access path model. Section 4.3 then discusses how the model is used to accomplish different security re-engineering tasks.

4.1 Problem Setting and Objectives

As discussed in the previous sections, if erroneous or anomalous data have been discovered, one would like to identify the user(s) who operated on these data. There are several aspects that make it very difficult to establish such correlations. First, a complex information system infrastructure can consist of multiple layers, typically several applications on top of a single database, with numerous users at both the application and database layer, including persons, application users, and database users. Most approaches to anomaly and misuse detection assume that the notion of a user is well-defined, typically a user directly operating on the data. However, what precisely constitutes a user in a more complex setting such as outlined above? A person, an application account, or a database account (possibly having several database roles)? What if users and/or applications share accounts? How can accesses to the data be traced back to users? As accesses to the data occur through several layers, starting with a person or application, which, in turn, performs operations on the database, correlating anomalous data and data behavior with a person is not a trivial task. However, in order to adhere to the principle of accountability, being able to determine such correlations is a must.

To address these problems, we propose the *access path model*. The objective of the access path model is to help administrators and security personnel in a focused re-engineering approach to database systems. This is accomplished by a methodology to describe, annotate, explore, and correlate so-called access paths. An *access path*, which will be described more formally below, basically specifies in which way a person operates on the data managed in a DBMS. Different components of an access path are annotated with data and user profiles and allow for an easy comparison of access correlations at the different layers of access. The access path model provides a comprehensive framework and methodology for a security re-engineering approach to databases, with a focus on misuse and anomaly detection driven by data and user profiles.

4.2 Model Components

The access path model consists of several components that help describing correlations between users and accesses at different layers. Figure 3 gives an overview of the basic components, with applications and a single database as back-end being the core components.

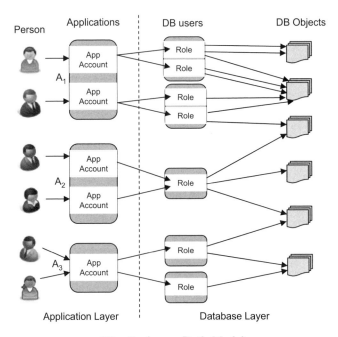

Fig. 3. Access Path Model

In this figure, there are three applications and several persons who have access to the applications based on some application accounts. We assume that a person does not directly connect to the database (e.g., at the database server) but through an application once the she has been authenticated at the application layer. We also make this assumption for DBAs, who operate on the database only using administrative tools (applications). The connection to the database occurs through database user accounts, which then, based on the database privileges assigned to the accounts, are allowed to perform operations on database objects. For the sake of simplicity, we only consider operations on database relations, which are shown on the right. One could also include other types of database objects, such as views or stored procedures, which can be queried and executed, respectively, from a database user account. The figure shows several cases that are typical in real-world settings. We first discuss these cases in more detail, and then elaborate on how an instance of the access path model is obtained before we cover some more formal properties of the model.

Application Layer Figure 3 shows three applications A_1, A_2, and A_3 to which some persons have access. At application A_1, each user has a separate application account, and each application account is associated with a database user account. At application A_2, again each user has a separate application account, but the application uses only one database account. For application A_3, two persons share an application account, and the application uses different database accounts. An important observation from the latter two cases is that *accounts are shared*, which obviously causes problems in correlating data accesses to a particular person.

Database Layer With each database user account, one or more database roles are associated. For application A_1, each application user account corresponds to a database user account, and each database user account has two roles. For application A_2, there is only one (default) role for the database account through which all accesses to the database occur.

More formally, an *instance* of the access path model consists of a set of paths $\mathcal{P} \subset \mathcal{U}_p \times \mathcal{U}_a \times (\mathcal{U}_{db} \times \mathcal{R}_{db}) \times \mathcal{DB}_{obj}$, with the vertices defined as follows.

- $\mathcal{U}_p$ is a set of persons, typically those who possess a (shared) application account.
- $\mathcal{U}_a$ is a set of application accounts.
- $\mathcal{U}_{db}$ is a set of database user accounts, and $\mathcal{R}_{db}$ is a set of database roles; an account/role pair $(u_{db}, r_{db}) \in \mathcal{U}_{db} \times \mathcal{R}_{db}$ specifies that the account u_{db} has been assigned the role r_{db}. Several roles can be associated with one database account u_{db}.
- $\mathcal{DB}_{obj}$ is a set of database objects such as relations, views, and stored procedures managed in the database.

Role hierarchies [24] are not explicitly represented in the access path model, because only individual roles are enabled by users.

How are these sets obtained for creating an instance of the access path model for a particular application and database setting? For this, one has to recognize that the security re-engineering tasks described thus far not only concern the database that is eventually to be better secured but the whole infrastructure on top of the database, in particular all applications. That is, all applications that operate on the database should be known. Consequently, for each application, the application accounts $\mathcal{U}_a$ should be determined. If a good security policy enforcement and maintenance strategy is in place at the organization, then it should also be known what persons $\mathcal{U}_p$ have what application accounts $\mathcal{U}_a$. This is admittedly one of the most complicated tasks in the security re-design, because the set of applications and their user accounts as well as persons possessing accounts can be very dynamic. Determining what application accounts make use of what database account requires an inspection of the application programs, in case respective information is not documented somewhere else. This process establishes application related sub-paths $\mathcal{P}_{app} \subset \mathcal{U}_p \times \mathcal{U}_a$.

Information about database user accounts $\mathcal{U}_{db}$, roles $\mathcal{R}_{db}$, and database objects $\mathcal{DB}_{obj}$ can easily be obtained by querying the database's data dictionary. If a database account $u_{db} \in \mathcal{U}_{db}$ has directly been assigned some privileges on object $o_{db} \in \mathcal{DB}_{obj}$, then sub-paths from u_{db} to o_{db} labeled with these privileges can be determined. Similarly, if u_{db} has been assigned a role $r_{db} \in \mathcal{R}_{db}$, then respective sub-paths are introduced from that role to database objects the role is allowed to operate on. For the sake of simplicity, we again only consider privileges with respect to relations and assume that if an account u_{db} or role r_{db} has insert, update, delete, or select privileges on a relation, then there is only one suitably labeled sub-path from u_{db} and r_{db} to o_{db}, respectively. If the same role r_{db} has been assigned to several database accounts, then the sub-paths from r_{db} to database objects are only given once but there are individual paths from these database accounts to r_{db}.

Figure 4 illustrates a case where a person u_p has an application account u_a, and the application uses the database account u_{db} to connect to the database. Two roles r_{db} and r'_{db} are assigned to the account u_{db}, each with privileges on different database objects $o_1, \ldots, o_5$.

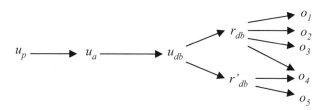

Fig. 4. Instance of some access paths starting from a person u_p using an application account u_a, which, in turn, has two roles r_{db}, r'_{db} with access privileges to some database objects $o_1, \ldots, o_5$.

Gathering information about sub-paths from persons to database user accounts and roles and representing these access structures and access correlations to administrators can be supported by some kind of security re-engineering workbench that, among other tasks such as the selective profiling of data and users, allows to visualize different access paths. This simple representation of access information can lead to some interesting insights, all of which relate to the discovery of potential vulnerabilities in the current security setup of the applications and the database. These include

- *unused application accounts* for which no person exists who makes use of that account,
- *unused database accounts* for which no application account exists that uses the database account, and
- *unused database roles* that have not been assigned to any user or have no privileges associated with them.

Unused user accounts or default accounts, which often come with applications and database servers, always pose a security risk. In particular for default accounts default passwords are used that can easily be guessed by an intruder (see, e.g., [30, 42]). Even though the information gathering determines that there is a correlation between accounts, say an application can use two different database accounts, this does not necessarily mean that these database accounts are actually all used. A similar argument can be made for database roles. An instantiation of the access path model and representing the different access paths from the information available at the application and database layer resembles more like a *static analysis* of admissible access correlations. The instantiation does not reveal any information about the how access paths and sub-paths are actually used. This is where the data and user profiling techniques are employed to further evaluate accesses and to detect potential vulnerabilities, as discussed next.

4.3 Annotating and Exploring Access Paths

Assume a partially instantiated access path model for some applications and database where no access correlations between database accounts/roles and database objects have been made yet. In order to focus on evaluating the security of mission-critical and sensitive database objects and relations in particular, only respective relations are considered first in exploring access correlations. Is is assumed that for a given database schema such relations can be identified based on existing security policies and regulations. In the following, let $\mathcal{DB}_{obj}$ denote only such critical relations.

Now, for each relation $R \in \mathcal{DB}_{obj}$, a snapshot profile $DataProf(R, t_i)$ is determined at time t_i. This process follows exactly the tasks presented in Section 3.2. Respective profiles are inspected, evaluated and subsequently access profiles $AccessProf(R, t_i, t_j)$ are established for a time window $[t_i, t_j]$.

The profiles obtained in this way are now used to *annotate* components of the access path model instance comprised of vertices (representing accounts, roles, and objects) and edges (representing access correlations). Each relation $R \in \mathcal{DB}_{obj}$ is annotated with its snapshot profile $DataProf(R, t_i)$ and access profile $AccessProf(R, t_i, t_j)$. It is assumed that a snapshot profile is captured at the same time t_i the collection of access information for R during the time window $[t_i, t_j]$ is initiated. From an access profile $AccessProf(R, t_i, t_j)$ and its user profiles $UserProf(R, u_{db}, t_i, t_j)$ then access sub-paths from database accounts/roles to the relation R are established. Each such sub-path $((u_{db} \longrightarrow$

r_{db}) $\longrightarrow$ R) is annotated with access information specific to the database user u_{db} and role r_{db}, respectively. The process is repeated for the other relations in $\mathcal{DB}_{obj}$ until all sub-paths from database accounts/roles to the relations $\mathcal{DB}_{obj}$ have been annotated with respective access information.

After completing instantiating access correlations at the database layer, i.e., sub-paths of the form $((u_{db} \longrightarrow r_{db}) \longrightarrow R)$, the next step is to obtain more fine-grained information about access correlations between application users and database accounts, and to annotate respective paths with this information. Although some database systems provide information about the remote database calls in their audit trails, audit trails typically do not provide sufficient information to exactly associate a particular application account or even person with an operation against a relation. While a simple access correlation between an application account and a database account can be determined by inspecting database calls in the application programs, more fine grained information can only be obtained by *audit log correlation* (see, e.g., [4]). A particular case of interest is when accounts are shared, as illustrated in Figure 3 for applications A_2 and A_3. For example, in the case of accesses to the database from application A_2, if it is known that the database account u_{db} has been used to perform some operations on a relation R, one would like to know what application account (and thus possibly what person) was responsible for these operations. If the application keeps a log for maintaining logons, authentication events and calls of, e.g., remote procedures, then such a correlation can be established based on an appropriate comparison of the timestamps in the application logs and the database audit trail. In the ideal case, a respective technique would be able to associate an application account (and application session) with exactly one user session in a user profile. Such fine-grained information then is used to annotate sub-paths connecting application accounts with database accounts.

The above annotation techniques for different components of access paths demonstrate that a focused, data-centric discovery of access correlations in a complex information system infrastructure is feasible using existing techniques for data and user profiling as well as for log correlation. In particular, the techniques show the utility of a reverse engineering approach to extract access information at different components and to present this information to security personnel for further explorations. Such explorations and subsequent security re-engineering tasks can take various forms, the most important one dealing with *unused privileges* violating the principle of least privilege.

Using access profile information associated with database accounts and relations, it is now possible to evaluate how a database account u_{db} operates on a relation R over time. For example, during the instantiation of access path components using information from the data dictionary, an access correlation $u_{db} \longrightarrow R$ is established. Assume this edge represents update and select permission u_{db} has on R. If the access profile for this path component only contains information about select statements again R and the time window has been chosen appropriately, then the account u_{db} likely does not need the update privilege on R. Similar scenarios can be devised for the case of database roles where u_{db} does not use all the privileges associated with a role r_{db}. If such a behavior can be found for all other users of that role, then respective privileges should be revoked from r_{db}. The access path model provides a convenient framework to explore such correlations and establish profiles on demand (though information needs to be collected over a time window) in order to evaluate known security policies or to get better insights into the exact user and access behavior.

5 Security Reconfiguration

We now detail and summarize some basic tasks to reconfigure the security setting and mechanisms of a database system using the information obtained from data and user profiling and access path correlations presented in the previous sections. We assume that appropriate (coordinated) authentication and auditing mechanisms are in place at the application and database layer.

The objective of the reconfiguration of security mechanisms is to constrain the behavior of database users and roles such they have exactly those privileges necessary and sufficient to perform their tasks. In other words, the mechanisms should realize the principle of *least privilege* [11, 31]. The problem with most security mechanisms in database systems in achieving this objective, however, is that they basically rely solely on the SQL **grant** statement, which in general does not allow to specify fine-grained access policies. This means, for example, that if a user is only allowed to insert tuples that have some well-defined properties, this admissible behavior cannot be specified using the **grant** statement. In general, this leaves plenty of room for malicious or accidental misuse of privileges by insiders.

Integrity Constraints. As discussed in Section 3.2, semantic integrity constraints provide an effective mechanism to constrain attribute values and combinations thereof to admissible ones. Most static integrity constraints can be implemented easily, e.g., through database triggers or **check** clauses in relation schemas. These mechanisms can be used to prevent inadmissible attribute values a user tries to (maliciously) insert or modify. Recall that such mechanisms also have the side-effect of helping maintaining the quality of the data, an important prerequisite for evaluating the security of a database.

Unused Accounts and Roles. The access path model provides a framework to detect unused database accounts and roles. In particular unused accounts are vulnerable to misuse and thus should be locked or simply deleted. Similarly, unused roles should be deleted, because they likely implement obsolete policies. The deletion of roles can also have implications on the re-design of role-hierarchies.

Unused Privileges. As indicated at the end of Section 4, unused privileges can be detected once access sub-paths have been annotated with respective access profiles. As the content of an access profile clearly depends on the time window for which information has been collected, care has to be taken to ensure that the suspected unused privilege is not used only on rare occasions. In this case, it is likely that this privilege should then be associated with a separate role and not with a role for which the privilege has been determined as inactive during the time window. The revocation of unused or obsolete privileges and roles from users and roles clearly helps a lot in achieving the goal of least privilege.

Discovery and Re-design of Database Roles. Database roles help in administering privileges associated with complex tasks [24, 45], i.e., activities by different types of application users. Assume that for a set of mission-critical relations data and user access profiles have been determined. Respective access paths in the access path model can now be analyzed to determine whether there are similarities among accesses to the relations by these different database users. If no roles (or only some default role) have been associated with these users in the context of respective accesses, database roles (and role hierarchies) can be introduced to better capture similar privileges used by these accounts and to ease the management of privileges.

There has recently been a great interest in mining roles from permission assignments (see, e.g., [52, 58]). Such approaches can be extended to include more fine-grained access information, such as those represented by access profiles. The design and evaluation of roles and role hierarchies as well as a security analysis focusing just on roles [35] is a topic on its own that can effectively be integrated in our security re-engineering approach.

Derivation of Database Views. One of the most effective mechanisms to achieve the principle of least privilege is to have database views, and to give database users privileges on these views rather than the underlying relations. The derivation of such views is not an easy task and requires a careful analysis of access profiles. Assume a database user u_{db} who has been granted select, insert, and update privileges on a relation R. The access profile for u_{db} might show that the user only selects certain types of tuples and the tuples she modifies have similar characteristics. The description of these tuples, represented in the user profile for u_{db}, then can be used to derive a view V that contains only tuples the user typically operates on. The privileges u_{db} has on R are then revoked, and the user is assigned respective privileges on the view V. More complex views can be derived as well for SQL select statements that refer to more than one relation.

The idea of view derivation from access profiles is relatively unexplored as it is a non-trivial task to precisely describe the data (based on user profiles) that are necessary and sufficient for the user to perform her legitimate tasks. A practical problem might be that an access profile does not cover a large enough time window, and the view derived from the profile then would prevent the user from performing tasks she only does on rare occasions. Note that most of today's DBMSs address the view update problem by providing so-called *instead-of triggers* that can execute some SQL modification statements on base relations whenever a modification statement is issued against a view. Thus, views can even be used in the context of SQL data modification statements.

Stored Procedures. A major limitation of discretionary access control models in relational databases is that SQL **grant** statements for assigning privileges to users and roles are often too coarse-grained. Some of these limitations can be circumvented by view privileges instead of privileges on base relations, as outlined above. However, oftentimes granting access to some relations (and views) depends on *context information* that cannot easily be specified in a view definition. Such context information might include concurrent database user sessions, time information, and the origin of database requests (e.g., application hosts). There has been some substantial work on more expressive access control models that take such context information into account and therefore provide more dynamic access control mechanisms (see, e.g., [10, 16, 17, 27, 28]).

As indicated in Section 3.1, stored procedures provide a powerful means to collect context information (e.g., for auditing purposes) when the procedures are called from application programs instead of plain SQL data modification statements. In the same way, stored procedures can be used to gather context information about its current execution, and one can use this information to make fine-grained access control decisions. For example, when a stored procedure is supposed to perform an update issued by an application, SQL queries in the procedure's body then can query data dictionary relations or call other (remote) procedures, and subsequently make a decision on whether or not the update operation is admissible. Clearly, using stored procedures might require modifications to some application code in that procedures are called instead of plain SQL DML statements. In general, stored procedures seem to be an effective means that help in dealing with misuse prevention, rather than just misuse detection (as done by analyzing audit trails after the fact).

The choice of an appropriate security re-design strategy for a particluar vulnerability discovered in analyzing access paths depends on several factors. First and foremost, there is the issue of database performance. Integrity constraints, triggers, stored procedures and even auditing occur some overhead in verifying conditions or executing additional code. Here again it is important to balance the efficient and reliable performance of the database and it applications with the various security requirements. As the access path model allows to gradually detect and analyze vulnerabilities, driven by specific security foci, re-designed security mechanisms can be gradually implemented and evaluated for performance. In general, the aspect of performance impact security mechanisms have on a database is rarely discussed in related work but leaves an interesting area for further investigation and re-design strategies.

6 Related Work

Compared to the numerous research and development activities in the context of intrusion detection systems for host and network based systems, there is only little work on misuse and anomaly detection for databases and security evaluation approaches in particular. Only Castano et al. [12] give a detailed though idealized description of the steps and approaches in database security design. An extension of Entity-Relationship (ER) modeling concepts to address security and authorization features has been proposed by Oh and Navathe [46].

Chung et al. [13, 14] proposed a technique specifically designed for detecting anomalies and misuse in database systems. In their approach, typical user access patterns are discovered from audit data using association rule mining. It is assumed that users typically access data that is semantically related, an aspect that can easily be captured and utilized based on relationships (e.g., foreign key dependencies) in the underlying database schema. Distances measures are introduced to determine if an observed user data access is within the normal, previously observed boundaries, and if not, an alarm is raised indicating a possible misuse. This approach has been extended in [15] to discover security policies at different levels of granularity and access patterns. In [25], the aspect of monitoring mission critical data for integrity and availability is discussed in detail. In particular, different audit approaches are presented.

Some more recent work on anomaly detection are by Spalka and Lehnhardt [56] and Kamra et al. [29]. Spalka and Lehnhardt introduce the concept of delta relations, which are derived from attributes of relations and basically represent data profiles, to detect anomalies in user operations on the data. In particular, they provide a prototypical implementation of their system using the Microsoft SQL Server 2000. In the approach proposed by Kamra et al., information about user queries to the database system is exploited to build access profiles, which are then compared to new queries based on some distance metrics to determine potential anomalies. That is, profiles are built using the syntactic information from SQL queries rather than from the data SQL statements operate on. It is an interesting and useful approach to detecting anomalous access pattern, and it would be worthwhile to investigate how the access patterns can be used to re-design underlying security mechanisms. Nabar et al. propose a similar approach to query auditing in [40].

Most of the approaches to user and data profiling make extensive use of data mining techniques (see, e.g., [57]) tailored to audit data collected at different components of computing system infrastructure. The edited book by Barbara and Jajodia [8] give an excellent overview of different data mining techniques with a specific focus on intrusion and anomaly detection, although primarily for the network and operating system layer and not for databases. Further data analysis techniques in the context of data and user profiling have already been discussed in Section 3.3.

Other related work that proposes specific techniques to detect and prevent tampering with the integrity and confidentiality of the data managed in a DBMS include the work by Liu and colleagues [37, 59] in which they describe the concepts and a prototype for an intrusion tolerant database. An interesting idea to further protect a database has been proposed by Bai et al. [7], where they describe the concept of a database firewall that helps continuing some database services even if the database is under attack. The work by Snodgrass et al. [47, 55] focuses specifically on the tampering with database audit logs in the context of forensic analysis, an important aspect relevant to our approach, because data and profiling techniques heavily rely on correctly recorded audit data.

Although most of the above work focus on intrusion and anomaly detection approaches in database system, none of them considers a coherent approach in which user profiles and access patterns discovered from audit data and queries are used to re-design security mechanisms in a coherent and methodological fashion. An interesting and important future research direction thus would be the investigation on how some of the techniques proposed in these approaches can be used to further enrich a security re-design technique for databases and to derive security enforcing mechanisms that go beyond those proposed in this chapter.

7 Conclusions and Future Directions

As with any complex software system, poor configuration practices cause vulnerabilities that can be exploited by intruders and insiders. This is equally true for DBMSs where the main focus of standard configuration practices is on the efficient and fault-tolerant operation of the database serving data to applications. Security policies and mechanisms are often only implemented or revised in an ad-hoc fashion when responding to changing application and user requirements, leading to an incoherent and potentially inconsistent database security maintenance and design approach.

Strengthening the security of a database is a non-trivial task, given that many of today's databases used in e-businesses and government organizations are extremely complex in terms of the amount of data served to a variety of applications in a networked information system infrastructure. In this chapter, we presented some fundamental concepts and techniques that help administrators and security personnel to gradually evaluate and improve the security of a database. For the evaluation of security policies, we have shown how data, user, and access profiles obtained from audit trails can effectively be explored and analyzed using the access path model. In this model, diverse access correlations between components at the application and database layer can be investigated and compared to current security requirements and expected practices.

An important feature of the proposed approach is that it allows a gradual and focused re-design of security policies and mechanisms. This is achieved by a data-driven evaluation strategy in which accesses to mission-critical and sensitive data are evaluated first for potential vulnerabilities and insider misuse. We have shown different security re-design strategies, as simple as integrity constraints and as complex and powerful as stored procedures or derived views that precisely contain the data users typically operate on.

The proposed approach motivates several research and development activities that concentrate on securing today's databases in an evolutionary approach. First and foremost, tools are necessary administrators and security personnel can employ for a security re-design approach, including tools that perform most of the data mining tasks on profiles and establish similarity measures between user profiles, leading to the discovery of roles and role-hierarchies. Recent research has developed many of such tool components, which now have to be integrated in a coherent fashion to provide all the functionality for a comprehensive security re-design approach. Second, there is a great potential in well-founded methods that derive database view specifications from a collection of user and access profiles. That is, given a collection of queries (and potentially result tuples) against one or more base relations, what "minimal" views can be queried that contain the same tuples as the queries against the base relations. In general, we think that views, especially those that furthermore include query context information, provide an interesting alternative to implementing expressive access control models using today's database technology.

Acknowledgment. This work is in part supported by the NSF award IIS-0242414.

References

1. Conference series on Recent Advances in Intrusion Detection (RAID), http://www.raid-symposium.org/.
2. Oracle audit vault.
   http://www.oracle.com/technology/products/audit-vault/index.html
3. Common Criteria for Information Technology Security Evaluation (Version 3.1). Technical report, 2006
   http://www.commoncriteriaportal.org/public/expert/index.php?menu=2.
4. Cristina Abad, Jed Taylor, Cigdem Sengul, William Yurcik, Yuanyuan Zhou, and Kenneth E. Rowe. Log correlation for intrusion detection: A proof of concept. In *19th Annual Computer Security Applications Conference (ACSAC 2003)*, pages 255–265, 2003.
5. Ant Allen. Intrusion Detection Systems (IDS): Perspective. Technical report, Gartner Research Report DPRO-95367, Technical Overview, January 2002.
6. Robert H. Anderson. *Research and Development Initiatives Focused on Preventing, Detecting, and Responding to Insider Misuse of Critical Defense In-*

formation Systems. Conference Proceedings CF-151-OSD. RAND Corporation, 1999.

7. Kun Bai, Hai Wang, and Peng Liu. Towards database firewalls. In *9th Annual IFIP WG 11.3 Working Conference on Data and Applications Security (DBSec05)*, pages 178–192, 2005.

8. Daniel Barbara, Julia Couto, Sushil Jajodia, and Ningning Wu. An architecture for anomaly detection. In Daniel Barbara and Sushil Jajodia (eds.), *Applications of Data Mining in Computer Security*, pages 63–76. Kluwer Academic Publishers, 2002.

9. Carlo Batini and Monica Scannapieco (eds.). *Data Quality: Concepts, Methodologies and Techniques (Data-Centric Systems and Applications)*. Springer, 2006.

10. Elisa Bertino, Claudio Bettini, Elena Ferrari, and Pierangela Samarati. An access control model supporting periodicity constraints and temporal reasoning. *ACM Transactions on Database Systems*, 23(3):231–285, 1998.

11. Matt Bishop. *Computer Security: Art and Science*. Addison-Wesley, 2002.

12. Silvana Castano, Maria Grazia Fugini, , Giancarlo Martella, and Pierangela Samarati. *Database Security*. Addison-Wesley Professional, 1994.

13. Christina Yip Chung, Michael Gertz, and Karl N. Levitt. DEMIDS: A misuse detection system for database systems. In *Third Working Conference on Integrity and Internal Control in Information Systems, IFIP TC11 Working Group 11.5*, Kluwer, pages 159–178, 1999.

14. Christina Yip Chung, Michael Gertz, and Karl N. Levitt. Misuse detection in database systems through user profiling. In *Recent Advances in Intrusion Detection (RAID'99)*, 1999.

15. Christina Yip Chung, Michael Gertz, and Karl N. Levitt. Discovery of multilevel security policies. In *FIP TC11/ WG11.3 Fourteenth Annual Working Conference on Database Security (DBSec00)*, Kluwer, pages 173–184, 2000.

16. Michael J. Covington, Wende Long, Srividhya Srinivasan, Anind K. Dey, Mustaque Ahamad, and Gregory D. Abowd. Securing context-aware applications using environment roles. In *6th ACM Symposium on Access Control Models and Technologies (SACMAT 2001)*, pages 10–20, 2001.

17. Vino Fernando Crescini and Yan Zhang. PolicyUpdater: a system for dynamic access control. *International Journal of Information Security*, 5(3):145–165, 2006.

18. Tamraparni Dasu and Theodore Johnson, editors. *Exploratory Data Mining and Data Cleaning*. Wiley-Interscience, 2003.

19. Department of Defense. DoD insider threat mitigation, Insider threat integrated process team, Final report of the insider threat integrated process team. Technical report, Washington, DC, 2000.

20. Carl Endorf, Gene Schultz, and Jim Mellander. *Intrusion Detection and Prevention*. McGraw-Hill Osborne Media, 2003.

21. Tom Fawcett and Foster J. Provost. Combining data mining and machine learning for effective user profiling. In *Proceedings of the Second International Conference on Knowledge Discovery and Data Mining (KDD96)*, pages 8–13, 1996.

22. Tom E. Fawcett and Foster Provost. Fraud Deection. In *Handbook of data mining and knowledge discovery*, pages 726–731. Oxford University Press, Inc., 2002.

23. Amgad Fayad, Sushil Jajodia, and Catherine D. McCollum. Application-level isolation using data inconsistency detection. In *15th Annual Computer Security Applications Conference (ACSAC 1999)*, page 119, 1999.

24. David F. Ferraiolo, Ravi S. Sandhu, Serban I. Gavrila, D. Richard Kuhn, and Ramaswamy Chandramouli. Proposed NIST standard for role-based access control. *ACM Transactions on Information and System Security*, 4(3):224–274, 2001.

25. Michael Gertz and George Csaba. Monitoring mission critical data for integrity and availability. In *IFIP TC11/WG11.5 Fifth Working Conference on Integrity and Internal Control in Information Systems (IICIS02)*, Kluwer, pages 189–201, 2002.

26. Lawrence A. Gordon, Martin P. Loeb, William Lucyshyn, and Robert Richardson. 2005 CSI/FBI computer crime and security survey. Technical report, Computer Security Institute, 2005.

27. R. J. Hulsebosch, Alfons H. Salden, Mortaza S. Bargh, P. W. G. Ebben, and J. Reitsma. Context sensitive access control. In *10th ACM Symposium on Access Control Models and Technologies (SACMAT05)*, pages 111–119, 2005.

28. James Joshi, Elisa Bertino, Usman Latif, and Arif Ghafoor. A generalized temporal role-based access control model. *IEEE Trans. Knowl. Data Eng.*, 17(1):4–23, 2005.

29. Ashish Kamra, Evimaria Terzi, and Elisa Bertino. Detecting anomalous access patterns in relational databases. *To appear in The VLDB Journal*, 2007.

30. David Knox. *Effective Oracle Database 10g Security by Design*. McGraw Hill Professional, 2004.

31. Carl E. Landwehr. Computer security. *International Journal of Information Security*, 1(1):3–13, 2001.

32. Terran Lane and Carla E. Brodley. Temporal sequence learning and data reduction for anomaly detection. In *ACM Conference on Computer and Communications Security*, pages 150–158, 1998.

33. Terran Lane and Carla E. Brodley. Temporal sequence learning and data reduction for anomaly detection. *ACM Transactions on Information and System Security*, 2(3):295–331, 1999.

34. Wenke Lee and Salvatore J. Stolfo. A framework for constructing features and models for intrusion detection systems. *ACM Transactions on Information and System Security*, 3(4):227–261, 2000.

35. Ninghui Li and Mahesh V. Tripunitara. Security analysis in role-based access control. *ACM Transactions on Information and System Security*, 9(4):391–420, 2006.

36. Yingjiu Li, Ningning Wu, Xiaoyang Sean Wang, and Sushil Jajodia. Enhancing profiles for anomaly detection using time granularities. *Journal of Computer Security*, 10(1/2):137–158, 2002.

37. Peng Liu. Architectures for intrusion tolerant database systems. In *18th Annual Computer Security Applications Conference (ACSAC 2002)*, pages 311–320, 2002.

38. John McHugh. Intrusion and intrusion detection. *International Journal of Information Security*, 1(1):14–35, 2001.

39. Jim Melton and Alan R. Simon. *SQL: 1999 - Understanding Relational Language Components (The Morgan Kaufmann Series in Data Management Systems)*. Morgan Kaufmann, 2001.

40. Shubha U. Nabar, Bhaskara Marthi, Krishnaram Kenthapadi, Nina Mishra, and Rajeev Motwani. Towards robustness in query auditing. In *Proceedings of the 32nd International Conference on Very Large Data Bases (VLDB06)*, pages 151–162, 2006.
41. Arup Nanda and Donald K. Burleson. *Oracle Privacy Security Auditing*. Rampant Techpress, 2003.
42. Ron Ben Natan. *Implementing Database Security and Auditing: Includes Examples for Oracle, SQL Server, DB2 UDB, Sybase*. Elsevier Digital Press, 2005.
43. Peter G. Neumann. The challenges of insider misuse, Papers prepared for the workshop on preventing, detecting, and responding to malicious insider misuse, 16-18 August 1999, at RAND, Santa Monica, CA. Technical report, SRI Computer Science Lab, 1999.
44. Peng Ning and Sushil Jajodia. Intrusion detection systems basics. In Hossein Bidgoli (ed.), *Handbook of Information Security*, volume 3, pages 685–700. Wiley, 2006.
45. Sejong Oh, Ravi S. Sandhu, and Xinwen Zhang. An effective role administration model using organization structure. *ACM Transactions on Information and System Security*, 9(2):113–137, 2006.
46. Yong-Chul Oh and Shamkant B. Navathe. Seer: Security enhanced entity-relationship model for modeling and integrating secure database environments. In *14th International Conference on Object-Oriented and Entity-Relationship Modelling (ER95)*, pages 170–180, 1995.
47. Kyriacos Pavlou and Richard T. Snodgrass. Forensic analysis of database tampering. In *Proceedings of the 2006 ACM SIGMOD international conference on management of data*, pages 109–120, 2006.
48. Richard Power. 2002 CSI/FBI computer crime and security survey. *Computer Security Issues & Trends*, 8(1), 2002.
49. Marcus K. Rogers. Internal security threats. In Hossein Bidgoli (ed.), *Handbook of Information Security*, volume 3, pages 3–17. Wiley, 2006.
50. Arnon Rosenthal and Marianne Winslett. Security of shared data in large systems: State of the art and research directions. Tutorial at *ACM SIGMOD International Conference on Management of Data*, pages 962–964, 2004.
51. Pierangela Samarati and Sabrina De Capitani di Vimercati. Access control: Policies, models, and mechanisms. Tutorial Lectures in *Foundations of Security Analysis and Design* Springer, Springer, LNCS 2171, pages 137–196, 2000.
52. Jürgen Schlegelmilch and Ulrike Steffens. Role mining with ORCA. In *10th ACM Symposium on Access Control Models and Technologies (SACMAT05)*, pages 168–176, 2005.
53. Alexandr Seleznyov and Oleksiy Mazhelis. Learning temporal patterns for anomaly intrusion detection. In *Proceedings of the 2002 ACM symposium on Applied computing*, pages 209–213, 2002.
54. Robert Selby Sielken. Application intrusion detection. Master thesis, Department of Computer Science, University of Virginia, May 1999.
55. Richard T. Snodgrass, Shilong (Stanley) Yao, and Christian S. Collberg. Tamper detection in audit logs. In *Proceedings of the 30th International Conference on Very Large Data Bases*, pages 504–515, 2004.
56. Adrian Spalka and Jan Lehnhardt. A comprehensive approach to anomaly detection in relational databases. In *19th Annual IFIP WG 11.3 Working Conference on Data and Applications Security (DBSec05)*, pages 207–221, 2005.

57. Pang-Ning Tan, Michael Steinbach, and Vipin Kumar, editors. *Introduction to Data Mining.* Addison-Wesley, 2006.
58. Jaideep Vaidya, Vijayalakshmi Atluri, and Qi Guo. The role mining problem: finding a minimal descriptive set of roles. In *12th ACM Symposium on Access Control Models and Technologies (SACMAT07)*, pages 175–184, 2007.
59. Hai Wang and Peng Liu. Modeling and evaluating the survivability of an intrusion tolerant database system. In *11th European Symposium on Research in Computer Security (ESORICS06)*, pages 207–224, 2006.
60. Dit-Yan Yeung and Yuxin Ding. User profiling for intrusion detection using dynamic and static behavioral models. In *Advances in Knowledge Discovery and Data Mining, 6th Pacific-Asia Conference (PAKDD 2002)*, pages 494–505, 2002.

13

Database Watermarking for Copyright Protection

Radu Sion

Network Security and Applied Cryptography Lab
Computer Science, Stony Brook University
sion@cs.stonybrook.edu

Summary. As increasing amounts of data are produced, packaged and delivered in digital form, in a fast, networked environment, one of its main features threatens to become its worst enemy: zero-cost verbatim copies. The ability to produce duplicates of digital Works at almost no cost can now be misused for illicit profit. This mandates mechanisms for effective rights assessment and protection.

One such mechanism is based on *Information Hiding*. By concealing a resilient rights holder identity "signature" (*watermark*) within the digital Work(s) to be protected, Information Hiding for Rights Assessment (*Watermarking*) enables ulterior court-time proofs associating particular Works with their respective rights holders.

One main challenge is the fact that altering the Work in the process of hiding information could possibly destroy its value. At the same time one has to be concerned with a malicious adversary, with major incentives to remove or alter the watermark beyond detection – thus disabling the ability for court-time proofs – without destroying the value of the Work – to preserve its potential for illicit profit.

In this chapter we explore how Information Hiding can be deployed as an effective tool for Rights Assessment for discrete digital data. More specifically, we discuss numeric and categorical relational data.

1 Introduction

Mechanisms for privacy assurances (e.g., queries over encrypted data) are essential to a viable and *secure* management solution for outsourced data. On a somewhat orthogonal dimension but equally important, we find the requirement to be able to *assert and protect rights* over such data.

Different avenues are available, each with its advantages and drawbacks. Enforcement by legal means is usually ineffective, unless augmented by a digital counterpart such as Information Hiding. *Digital Watermarking* as a method of Rights Assessment deploys Information Hiding to conceal an indelible "rights witness" ("rights signature", watermark) within the digital Work to be protected (see Figure 1). The soundness of such a method relies on the assumption that altering the Work in the process of hiding the mark does not destroy the value of the Work, while it is difficult for a malicious adversary ("Mallory") to remove or alter the mark beyond detection without doing so. The ability to resist attacks from such an adversary, mostly aimed at removing the watermark, is one of the major concerns in the design of a sound solution.

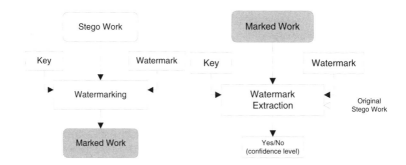

Fig. 1. Introduction: (a) *Digital Watermarking* conceals an indelible "rights witness" ("rights signature", watermark) within the digital Work to be protected. (b) In court, a detection process is deployed to prove the existence of this "witness" beyond reasonable doubt (confidence level) and thus assess ownership.

There exists a multitude of semantic frameworks for discrete information processing and distribution. Each distinct data domain would benefit from the availability of a suitable watermarking solution.

Significant research efforts [2] [3] [8] [11] [14] [15] [22] [24] have been invested in the frameworks of signal processing and multimedia Works (e.g., images, video and audio).

Here we explore Information Hiding as a rights assessment tool for *discrete* data types i.e., in a relational database context. We explore existing watermarking solutions for numeric and categorical data types.

The Chapter is organized as follows. In Section 2 we explore the broader issues and challenges pertaining to steganography for rights protection. Then, in Sections 3 and 4 solutions for numeric respectively categorical data types are introduced. Related work is discussed in Section 5. Section 6 briefly discusses the current state of the art and Section 7 concludes.

2 Model

Before we proceed however, let us first understand how the ability to prove rights in court relates to the final desiderata, namely to *protect* those rights. After all, doesn't simply publishing a summary or digest of the Work to be protected – e.g., in a newspaper, just before releasing the Work – do the job?

It would seem it enables one to prove later in court that (at least a copy of) the Work was in one's possession at the time of release. In the following we address these and other related issues.

2.1 Rights Protection through Assessment

The ability to prove/assess rights convincingly in court constitutes a deterrent to malicious Mallory. It thus becomes a tool for rights protection if counter-incentives and legal consequences are set high enough. But because Information Hiding does not provide a means of actual access control, the question of rights protection still remains. *How* are rights protected here?

It is intuitive that such a method works only if the rightful rights-holder (Alice) actually knows about Mallory's misbehavior **and** is able to prove to the court that: (i) Mallory possesses a certain Work X and (ii) X contains a "convincing" (e.g., very rare with respect to the space of all considered similar Works) and "relevant" watermark (e.g., the string "(c) by Alice").

What watermarking itself does not offer is a direct deterrent. If Alice does not have knowledge of Mallory's illicit possession of the Work and/or if it is impossible to actually prove this possession in court beyond reasonable doubt, then watermarking cannot be deployed directly to prevent Mallory. If, however, Information Hiding is aided by additional access control levels, it can become very effective.

For example, if in order to derive value from the given Work (e.g., watch a video tape), Mallory has to deploy a known mechanism (e.g., use video player), Information Hiding could be deployed to enable such a proof of possession, as follows: modify the video player so as to detect the existence of a watermark and match it with a set of purchased credentials and/or "viewing tickets" associated with the player's owner. If no match is found, the tape is simply not played back.

This scenario shows how watermarking can be deployed in conjunction with other technologies to aid in managing and protecting digital rights. Intuitively, a certain cost model is assumed here: the cost of reverse engineering this process is far higher than the potential derived illicit gain.

This illustrates the game theoretic nature at the heart of the watermarking proposition and of information security in general. Watermarking is a game with two adversaries, Mallory and Alice. At stake lies the value inherent in a certain Work X, over which Alice owns certain rights. When Alice releases X, to the public or to a licensed but potentially un-trusted party, she deploys watermarking for the purpose of ensuring that one of the following holds:

- she can always prove rights in court over any copy or valuable derivate of X (e.g., segment thereof)
- any existing derivate Y of X, for which she cannot prove rights, does not preserve any significant value (derived from the value in X)

- the cost to produce such an un-watermarked derivate Y of X that is still valuable (with respect to X) is higher than its value

Newspaper Digests

To achieve the above however, Alice could publish a summary or digest (e.g., cryptographic hash) of X in a newspaper, thus being able to claim later on at least a time-stamp on the possession of X. This could apparently result in a quite effective, albeit costly, alternative to Watermarking the Work X.

There are many simple reasons why it would not work, including (i) scalability issues associated with the need for a trusted third party (newspaper), (ii) the cost of publishing a digest for each released Work, (iii) scenarios when the fact that the Work is watermarked should be kept secret (stealthiness) etc.

Maybe the most important reason however, is that Mallory can now claim that his ownership of the Work precedes X's publication date, and that Alice simply modified it (i.e., a stolen copy) and published a digest thereof herself. It would then be up to the court to decide if Mallory is to be believed or not, hardly an encouraging scenario for Alice. This could work if there existed a mechanism for the mandatory publication of digests for each and every valuable Work, again quite likely impractical due to both costs and lack of scalability to a virtually infinite set of data producers and Works.

Deploying such aids as rights assessment tools makes sense only in the case of the Work being of value only un-modified. In other words if it does not tolerate any changes, without losing its value, and Mallory is caught in possession of an identical copy, Alice can successfully prove in court that she possessed the original at the time of its publication (but she cannot prove more). Considering that, in the case of watermarking, the assumption is that, no matter how small, there are modifications allowed to the Works to be protected, in some sense the two approaches complement each other. If no modifications are allowed, then a third-party "newspaper" service might work for providing a time-stamp type of ownership proof that can be used in court.

Steganography and Watermarking

There exists a fundamental difference between Watermarking and generic Information Hiding (steganography) from an application perspective and associated challenges. Information Hiding in general (and covert communication in particular), aims usually at enabling Alice and Bob to exchange messages in a manner as resilient and stealthy as possible, through a hostile medium where Malory could lurk. On the other hand, Digital Watermarking is deployed by Alice as a court proof of rights over a Work, usually in the case when Mallory benefits from using/selling that very same Work or maliciously modified versions of it.

In Digital Watermarking, the actual value to be protected lies in the Works themselves whereas pure steganography usually makes use of them as simple value "transporters". In Watermarking, Rights Assessment is achieved by demonstrating (with the aid of a "secret" known only to Alice – "watermarking key") that a particular Work exhibits a rare property ("hidden message" or "watermark"). For purposes of convincing the court, this property needs to be so *rare* that if one considers any other random Work "similar enough" to the one in question, this property is "very improbable" to apply (i.e., bound false-positives rate). It also has to be *relevant*, in that it somehow ties to Alice (e.g., by featuring the bit string "(c) by Alice").

There is a threshold determining the ability to convince the court, related to the "very improbable" assessment. This defines a main difference from steganography: from the court's perspective, specifics of the property (e.g., watermark message) are not important as long as they link to Alice (e.g., by saying "(c) by Alice") and, she can prove "convincingly" it is she who induced it to the (non-watermarked) original.

In watermarking the emphasis is on "detection" rather than "extraction". Extraction of a watermark, or bits of it, is usually a part of the detection process but just complements the process up to the extent of increasing the ability to convince in court. If recovering the watermark data in itself becomes more important than detecting the actual existence of it (i.e., "yes/no" answer) then, from an application point of view, this is a drift toward covert communication and pure Information Hiding (steganography).

2.2 Consumer Driven Watermarking

An important point about watermarking should be noted. By its very nature, a watermark modifies the item being watermarked: it inserts an indelible mark in the Work such that (i) the insertion of the mark does not destroy the value of the Work, i.e., it is still useful for the *intended purpose*; and (ii) it is difficult for an adversary to remove or alter the mark beyond detection without destroying this value. If the Work to be watermarked cannot be modified without losing its value then a watermark cannot be inserted. The critical issue is not to avoid alterations, but to limit them to acceptable levels with respect to the intended use of the Work.

Thus, an important first step in inserting a watermark, i.e., by altering it, is to identify changes that are acceptable. Naturally, the nature and level of such change is dependent upon the application for which the data is to be used. Clearly, the notion of value or utility of the data becomes thus central to the watermarking process. For example, in the case of software, the value may be in ensuring equivalent computation, whereas for natural language text it may be in conveying the same meaning – i.e., synonym substitution is acceptable. Similarly, for a collection of numbers, the utility of the data may lie in the actual values, in the relative values of the numbers, or in the distribution (e.g., normal with a certain mean). At the same time, the concept of value of watermarked Works is necessarily relative and largely influenced by each semantic context it appears in. For example, while a statistical analyst would be satisfied with a set of feature summarizations (e.g., average, higher-level moments) of a numeric data set, a data mining application may need a majority of the data items, for example to validate a classification hypothesis.

It is often hard to define the available "bandwidth" for inserting the watermark directly. Instead, allowable distortion bounds for the input data can be defined in terms of consumer metrics. If the watermarked data satisfies the metrics, then the alterations induced by the insertion of the watermark are considered to be acceptable. One such simple yet relevant example for numeric data, is the case of *maximum allowable mean squared error* (MSE), in which the usability metrics are defined in terms of mean squared error tolerances as $(s_i - v_i)^2 < t_i, \forall i = 1, ..., n$ and $\sum (s_i - v_i)^2 < t_{max}$, where $\mathbb{S} = \{s_1, ..., s_n\} \subset \mathbb{R}$, is the data to be watermarked, $\mathbb{V} = \{v_1, ..., v_n\}$ is the result, $\mathbb{T} = \{t_1, ..., t_n\} \subset \mathbb{R}$ and $t_{max} \in \mathbb{R}$ define the guaranteed error bounds at data distribution time. In other words $\mathbb{T}$ defines the allowable distortions for individual elements in terms of MSE and t_{max} its overall permissible value.

Often however, specifying only allowable change limits on individual values, and possibly an overall limit, fails to capture important semantic features associated with the data – especially if the data is structured. Consider for example, age data. While a small change to the age values may be acceptable, it may be critical that individuals that are younger than 21 remain so even after watermarking if the data will be used to determine behavior patterns for under-age drinking. Similarly, if the same data were to be used for identifying legal voters, the cut-off would be 18 years. Further still, for some other application it may be important that the relative ages, in terms of which one is younger, not change. Other examples of constraints include: (i) *uniqueness* – each value must be unique; (ii) *scale* – the ratio between any two number before and after the change must remain the same; and (iii) *classification* – the objects must remain in the same class (defined by a range of values) before and after the watermarking. As is clear from the above examples, simple bounds on the change of numerical values are often not enough.

Structured collections, present further constraints that must be adhered to by the watermarking algorithm. Consider a data warehouse organized using a standard Star schema with a fact table and several dimension tables. It is important that the key relationships be preserved by the watermarking algorithm. This is similar to the "Cascade on update" option for foreign keys in SQL and ensures that tuples that join before watermarking also join after watermarking. This requires that the new value for any attribute should be unique after the watermarking process. In other words, we want to preserve the relationship between the various tables. More generally, the relationship could be expressed in terms of an arbitrary join condition, not just a natural join. In addition to relationships between tuples, relational data may have constraints within tuples. For example, if a relation contains the start and end times of a web interaction, it is important that each tuple satisfies the condition that the end time be later than the start time.

There exists a trade-off between the desired level of marking resilience and resistance to attacks, and the ability to preserve data quality in the result, with respect to the original. Intuitively, at the one extreme, if the encoded watermark is to be very "strong" one can simply modify the *entire* data set aggressively, but at the same time probably also destroy its actual value. As data quality requirements become increasingly restrictive, any applied watermark is necessarily more vulnerable. Often we can express the available bandwidth as an increasing function of allowed alterations. At the other extreme, a disproportionate concern with data quality will hinder most of the watermarking alterations, resulting in a weak, possibly non-existent encoding.

Naturally, one can always identify some use that is affected by even a minor change to any portion of the data. It is therefore important that (i) the main intended purpose and semantics that should be preserved be identified during watermarking and that (ii) *the watermarking process not interfere with the final data consumer requirements.* We call this paradigm *consumer driven watermarking.*

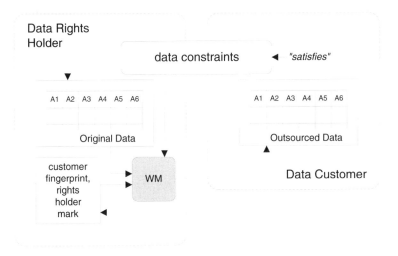

Fig. 2. In *consumer-driven watermarking* a set of data constraints are continuously evaluated in the encoding process to ensure quality of the result.

Some of the solutions discussed here are consumer driven enabled through feedback mechanisms (see Figure 2) that allow the watermarking process to "rollback" modifications that would violate quality constraints in the result on a step by step basis. This ensures the preservation of desired quality metrics with respect to the original un-watermarked input Work.

2.3 Discrete Data vs. Multimedia

An established body of research [2] [3] [8] [11] [14] [15] [22] [24] has resulted from work on Information Hiding and Watermarking in frameworks such as signal processing and multimedia (e.g., images, video and audio). Here we explore Information Hiding as a rights assessment tool for *discrete* data types.

Let us briefly explore the relationship between the challenges and techniques deployed in both frameworks. Because, while the terms might be identical, the associated models, challenges and techniques are different, almost orthogonal. Whereas in the signal processing case there usually exists a large noise bandwidth, due to the fact that the final data consumer is likely human – with associated limitations of the sensory system – in the case of discrete data types this cannot be assumed and data quality assessment needs to be closely tied with the actual watermarking process (see Section 2.2).

Another important differentiating focus is the emphasis on the actual ability to convince in court as a success metric, unlike most approaches in the signal processing realm, centered on bandwidth. While bandwidth is a relevant related metric, it does not consider important additional issues such as malicious transforms and removal attacks. For rights assertion, the concerns lie not as much with packing a large *amount* of information (i.e., watermark bits) in the Works to be protected, as with being able to both *survive* removal attacks and *convince* in court.

Maybe the most important difference between the two domains is that, while in a majority of watermarking solutions in the multimedia framework, the main domain transforms are signal processing primitives (e.g., Works are mainly considered as being compositions of signals rather than strings of bits), in our case data types are mostly discrete and are not naturally handled as continuous signals. Because, while discrete versions of frequency transforms can be deployed as primitives in information encoding for digital images [8], the basis for doing so is the fact that, although digitized, images are at the core defined by a composition of light reflection signals and are consumed as such by the final human consumer. By contrast, arbitrary discrete data is naturally discrete [1] and often to be ingested by a highly sensitive semantic processing component, e.g., a computer rather than a perceptual system tolerant of distortions.

2.4 Relational Data

For completeness let us briefly overview main components of a relational model [7]. In such a model, relations between information items are explicitly specified: data is organized as "a number of differently sized *tables*" [7] composed of "related" rows/columns. A table is a collection of *rows* or records

---

[1] Unless we consider quantum states and uncertainty arising in the spin of the electrons flowing through the silicon.

and each row in a table contains the same *fields*. Certain fields may be designated as data *keys* (not to be confused with "cryptographic keys") when a functional dependency or key constraint, holds for the table. Often, indexing is deployed to speed up searches on values of such primary key fields. Data is structured logically into valued *attributes*. From this perspective, a table is a collection of such attributes (the columns of the table) and models a *relation* among them. The data rows in the tables are also called *tuples*. Data in this model is manipulated using a *relational algebra*. Main operations in this algebra are set operations (e.g., union, intersection, Cartesian product), selection (of some tuples in tables) and projection (of some columns/attributes).

Rights protection for such data is important in scenarios where it is sensitive, valuable and about to be outsourced. A good example is a data mining application, where data is sold in pieces to parties specialized in mining it, e.g., sales patterns database, oil drilling data, financial data. Other scenarios involve for example online B2B interactions, e.g., airline reservation and scheduling portals, in which data is made available for direct, interactive use (see Figure 3). Given the nature of most of the data, it is hard to associate rights of the originator over it. Watermarking can be used to solve this issue.

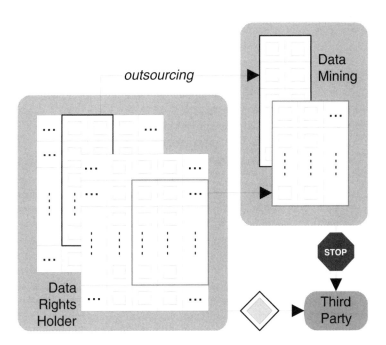

Fig. 3. Rights Assessment is important when valuable data is outsourced to a third party.

2.5 The Adversary

Watermarking is a game between the watermarker and malicious Mallory. In this game, the watermarker and Mallory play against each other within subtle trade-off rules aimed at keeping the quality of the result within acceptable bounds. It is as if there exists an impartial referee (the data itself) moderating each and every "move". As discussed above, it is important to make this "referee" an explicit part of the marking process (consumer-driven paradigm). It is also important to understand Mallory and the adversarial setting.

Once outsourced, i.e., out of the control of the watermarker, data might be subjected to a set of attacks or transformations; these may be malicious – e.g., with the explicit intent of removing the watermark – or simply the result of normal use of the data. An effective watermarking technique must be able to survive such use. In a relational data framework important attacks and transformations are:

A1. Sampling. The attacker (Mallory) can randomly select and use a subset of the watermarked data set that might still provide value for its intended purpose ("subset selection"). More specifically, here we are concerned with both (**A1.a**) horizontal and (**A1.b**) vertical data partitioning – in which a valuable subset of the *attributes* are selected by Mallory.

A2. Data Addition. Mallory adds a set of tuples to the watermarked set. This addition is not to significantly alter the useful properties of interest to Mallory.

A3. Alteration. Altering a subset of the items in the watermarked data set such that there is still value associated with the result. In the case of numeric data types, a special case needs to be outlined here, namely (**A3.a**) a linear transformation performed uniformly to all of the items. This is of particular interest as it can preserve significant valuable data-mining related properties of the data.

A4. Ulterior Claims of Rights. Mallory encodes an additional watermark in the already watermarked data set and claims rights based upon this second watermark.

A5. Invertibility Attack. Mallory attempts to establish a plausible (watermark,key) pair that matches the data set and then claims rights based on this found watermark [8,9].

Given the attacks above, several properties of a successful solution surface. For immunity against **A1**, the watermark has to be likely encoded in overall data properties that survive sampling, e.g., confidence intervals, statistical bias. With respect to (**A1.b**) special care has to be taken such that the mark survives this partitioning. The encoding method has to feature a certain attribute-level property that could be recovered in such a vertical partition of the data. We believe that while vertical data partitioning attacks are possible and also very likely in certain scenarios, often value is to be found in the association between a set of relation attributes. These attributes are highly likely to survive such an attack, as the final goal of the attacker is to produce a still-valuable result. If the assumption is made that the attack alterations do not destroy the value of the data, then **A3** could be handled by encoding the primitive mark in resilient global data properties. As a special case, **A3.a** can be resisted by a preliminary normalization step in which a common divider to all the items is first identified and applied.

While powerful, for arbitrary watermarks, the invertibility attack **A5** can be defeated by requiring the encoded string to be relevant (e.g. "(c) by Mallory") and the encoding to be "convincing" (see Section 2.1). Then the probability of success of invertibility searches becomes upper bound.

In order to defeat **A4**, the watermarking method has to provide the ability to determine encoding precedence, e.g., if it can be proved in court that one watermark encoding was "overwritten" by a later one. Additionally, in the case of such a (court time) dispute, the parties could be requested to present a portion of the original, un-watermarked data. Only the rightful rights holder would be able to produce such a proof, as Mallory could only have access to already watermarked data.

It is worth also noting that, intuitively, if, in the process of watermarking, the data is altered to its usability limits, any further alteration by a watermarker is likely bound to yield an unusable result. Achieving this might be often desirable [2] and has been explored by Sion et. al. in a proof of concept implementation [34] as well as by Li et. al. in [20] (this is discussed in more detail elsewhere in this book). The challenges of achieving such a desiderata however, lies in the impossibility to define absolute data quality metrics that consider all value dimensions of data.

3 Numeric Types

In this section we explore watermarking solutions in the context of relational data in which one or more of the attributes are of a numeric type. Among existing solutions we distinguish between *single-bit* (the watermark is composed of a single bit) and *multi-bit* (the watermark is a string of bits) types. Orthogonally, the encoding methods can be categorized into two; we chose to call them *direct-domain* and *distribution* encodings. In a direct-domain encoding, each individual bit alteration in the process of watermarking is directly correlated to (a part of) the encoded watermark. In distribution encodings, the encoding channel lies often in higher order moments of the data (e.g., running means, hierarchy of value averages). Each individual bit alteration impacts these moments for the purpose of watermark encoding, but in itself is not directly correlated to any one portion of the encoded watermark.

---

[2] This is formulated as the "optimality principle" in [26], as well as previous results such as [28] and [31].

Single Bit Direct Domain Encoding

In [1, 16] Kiernan, Agrawal et.al. propose a direct domain encoding of a single bit watermark in a numeric relational database.

Overview. Its main algorithm proceeds as follows. A subset of tuples are selected based on a secret criteria; for each tuple, a secret attribute and corresponding least significant (ξ) bit position are chosen. This bit position is then altered according to yet another secret criteria that is directly correlated to the watermark bit to be encoded. The main assumption is, that changes can be made to any attribute in a tuple at any least significant ξ bit positions. At watermark detection time, the process will re-discover the watermarked tuples and, for each detected accurate encoding, become more "confident" of a true-positive detection.

There are a set of important assumptions underlying this method. Maybe the most important one is that "the relational table being watermarked is such that if all or a large number of the ξ least significant bits of any attribute are dropped or perturbed, then the value of the data is significantly reduced. However, it is possible to change a small number of the bits and not decrease the value of the data significantly" [16].

The authors make an argument for this being a reasonable assumption as such techniques have been used by publishers of books of mathematical tables for a long time – e.g., by introducing small errors in published logarithm tables and astronomical ephemerides to identify pirated copies [15]. Examples of real-world data sets that satisfy such an assumption are given, including tables of parametric specifications (mechanical, electrical, electronic, chemical, etc.), surveys (geological, climatic, etc.), and life sciences data (e.g., gene expression).

Solution Details. For consistency, the original notation is used: a database relation R with the following schema is $R(P, A_0, \ldots, A_{\nu-1})$, is assumed, with P the primary key attribute. All ν attributes $A_0, \ldots, A_{\nu-1}$ are candidates for marking: the values are assumed such that small changes in the ξ least significant bits are imperceptible. γ denotes a control parameter that determines the average number ω of tuples marked ($\omega = \frac{\eta}{\gamma}$), where η is the number of tuples in the database. $r.X$ is used to denote the value of attribute X in tuple r, α denotes a "significance level" and τ a "threshold" for the test of "detecting a watermark". $\mathcal{K}$ is a key known only to the database owner, and there exists $\mathcal{G}$, a pseudo-random sequence number generator [23] (next($\mathcal{G}$) denotes the next generated sequence number).

Note: There are a set of changes between the initial proposed scheme in [16] and its journal version [1]. Here we discuss the (more robust) journal version.

Watermark insertion is illustrated in Figure 4. The main steps of the algorithm are as follows. Initially (step 2) the random sequence generator is initialized such that its output is distinct for any given distinct tuple value. This mechanism is deployed in order to achieve a certain tuple ordering independence of the encoding. The output of $\mathcal{G}$ is then used to determine: (i) if

---

1) **foreach** tuple $r \in R$ **do**
2)   seed $\mathcal{G}$ with $r.P$ concatenated with $\mathcal{K}$
3)   **if** $(\text{next}(\mathcal{G}) \bmod \gamma = 0)$ **then** // mark this tuple
4)   attribute_index $i = \text{next}(\mathcal{G}) \bmod \nu$ // mark attribute A_i
5)   bit_index $j = \text{next}(\mathcal{G}) \bmod \eta$ // mark j^{th} bit
6) $r.A_i = \text{mark}(\text{next}(\mathcal{G}), r.A_i, j)$
7) mark(random_number i, value v, bit_index j) **return** value
8)   **if** (i is even) **then**
9)   set the jth least significant bit of v to 0
10)   **else**
11)   set the jth least significant bit of v to 1
12)   **return** v

Fig. 4. Watermark insertion for the single-bit encoding of [1, 16].

the current tuple is to be watermarked (step 3), (ii) which attribute value to mark (step 4), (iii) which bit within that attribute's value to alter (step 5), and (iv) what new bit-value to assign to that bit-position in the result (step 6, invocation of mark()). This encoding guarantees that, in order to entirely remove a watermark, Mallory is put in the position of guessing correctly the marked tuples, attributes and altered bit positions.

Once R is published, the data owner, Alice, would like to determine whether the (similar) relation S published by Mallory has been pirated from R. The sets of tuples and of attributes in S are assumed to be strict subsets of those in R. Additionally, Mallory is assumed not to drop the primary key attribute or change the value of primary keys. Then watermark detection is a direct inverse of insertion. It proceeds as follows (see Figure 5).

Alice starts by identifying the bits that should have been marked by the insertion algorithm. To do so, it executes the operations described in lines 1 through 5 of the insertion algorithm (steps 3 through 6). The assumption is that the original database primary key is preserved in S. Each such identified bit is tested for a match with the value that should have been assigned by the insertion algorithm. Each match is counted. If the resulting count is either too small or too large, piracy is suspected. In the case of too small a number, the method assumes that somehow Mallory has identified the marked bits and systematically flipped each one.

In other words, the insertion algorithm is modulated on a set of successive independent coin tosses. A detection algorithm over ω bits will yield a number of matches with a binomial distribution $(\omega, 1/2)$ for the null hypothesis of non-piracy. Naturally, in the absence of piracy, the expected number of matches is $\frac{\omega}{2}$. The paper proposes to suspect piracy if the observed number of matches m is so large or so small that its probability under the null hypothesis is highly unlikely.

1) totalcount = matchcount = 0
2) **foreach** tuple $s \in S$ **do**
3)   seed $\mathcal{G}$ with $s.P$ concatenated with $\mathcal{K}$
4)   **if** (next($\mathcal{G}$) mod $\gamma = 0$) **then** // tuple was marked
5)   attribute_index i = next($\mathcal{G}$) mod ν // A_i was marked
6)   bit_index j = next($\mathcal{G}$) mod η // j^{th} bit was marked
7)   totalcount = totalcount + 1
8)   matchcount = matchcount + match (next($\mathcal{G}$,$s.A_i$,j)
9) τ = threshold(totalcount,α)
10) **if** ((matchcount $< \tau$) **or** (matchcount $>$ totalcount - τ)) **then**
11) *suspect piracy*
12) match(random_number i, value v, bit_index j) **return** integer
13)   **if** (i is even) **then**
14)   **return** 1 **if** the jth least significant bit of v is 0 **else return** 0
15)   **else**
16)   **return** 1 **if** the jth least significant bit of v is 1 **else return** 0

Fig. 5. Watermark detection for the single-bit encoding of $[1, 16]$.

This can be modeled by first fixing an acceptable value for the *significance level* $\alpha \in (0, 1)$ and then computing a threshold $\tau \in (0, \frac{\omega}{2})$ such that the probability of $m < \tau$ or $m > \omega - \tau$ under the null hypothesis is less than or equal to α.

The authors discuss additional extensions and properties of the solution including the following:

- Incremental Updatability: Updates can be handled independently of the existing watermark as the selection and marking criteria are self-sufficient and only depend on the primary key value.
- Blind Watermarking: The method does not require the availability of the un-watermarked data at detection time.
- Varying Parameters: The assumption that any two attributes are marked at the same rate can be removed. Different attributes can be marked at different rates because the attributes may tolerate different error rates and, if the rate parameters are secret, Mallory's task become even more difficult. Additionally, the number of bits available for marking can be varied from one attribute to another.
- Relations Without Primary Keys: The authors also discuss extensions aimed at handling the case of relations without primary keys. This is an important problem as it has the potential to overcome the required assumption of unchanged primary key values in the watermarked data at detection time. In the case of no primary key, the authors propose to designate another attribute, or a number of most significant bit-portions of the currently considered one, as a primary key. This however presents a significant vulnerability due to the very likely existence of duplicates

in these values. Mallory could mount a statistical attack by correlating marked bit values among tuples with the same most significant bits. This issue has been also considered in [18] where a similar solution has been adopted. This, is discussed in more detail elsewhere in this book.

3.1 Multi-Bit Watermarks

While there likely exist applications whose requirements are satisfied by single-bit watermarks, often it is desirable to provide for "relevance", i.e., linking the encoding to the rights holder identity. This is especially important if the watermark aims to defeat against invertibility attacks (**A5**).

In a single-bit encoding this can not be easily achieved. Additionally, while the main proposition of watermarking is not covert communication but rather rights assessment, there could be scenarios where the actual message payload is of importance.

One apparent direct extension from single-bit watermarks to a multi-bit version would be to simply deploy a different encoding, with a separate watermark key, for each bit of the watermark to be embedded. This however, might not be possible, as it will raise significant issues of inter-encoding interference: the encoding of later bits will likely distort previous ones. This will also make it harder to handle ulterior claim of rights attacks (**A4**).

In the following we discuss multi-bit watermark encodings. We briefly discuss a direct-domain encoding [19] that extends the work by Kiernan, Agrawal et. al. [1, 16] and then explore a distribution-encoding method by Sion et. al. [27, 29, 30, 32, 33] and [34].

Multi-Bit Direct Domain Encoding

In [19] Li et. al. extend the work by Kiernan, Agrawal et. al. [1, 16] to provide for multi-bit watermarks in a direct domain encoding. This is discussed in extended detail elsewhere in this book. Here we briefly summarize. The scheme functions as follows. The database is parsed and, at each bit-encoding step, one of the watermark bits is randomly chosen for embedding; the solution in [1, 16] is then deployed to encode the selected bit in the data at the "current" point. The "strength of the robustness" of the scheme is claimed to be increased with respect to [1, 16] due to the fact that the watermark now possesses an additional dimension, namely length. This should guarantee a better upper bound for the probability that a valid watermark is detected from unmarked data, as well as for the probability that a fictitious secret key is discovered from pirated data (i.e., invertibility attacks **A5**). This upper bound is said to be independent of the size of database relations thus yielding robustness against attacks that change the size of database relations.

Multi-Bit Distribution Encoding

Encoding watermarking information in resilient numeric distribution properties of data presents a set of advantages over direct domain encoding, the most important one being its increased resilience to various types of numeric attacks. In [27, 29, 30, 32, 33] and [34], Sion et. al. introduce a multi-bit distribution encoding watermarking scheme for numeric types. The scheme was designed with both an adversary and a data consumer in mind. More specifically the main desiderata were: (i) watermarking should be consumer driven – i.e., desired semantic constraints on the data should be preserved – this is enforced by a feedback-driven rollback mechanism, and (ii) the encoding should survive important numeric attacks, such as linear transformation of the data (**A3.a**), sampling (**A1**) and random alterations (**A3**).

Overview. The solution starts by receiving as user input a reference to the relational data to be protected, a watermark to be encoded as a copyright proof, a secret key used to protect the encoding and a set of data quality constraints to be preserved in the result. It then proceeds to watermark the data while continuously assessing data quality, potentially backtracking and rolling back undesirable alterations that do not preserve data quality.

Watermark *encoding* is composed of two main parts: in the first stage, the input data set is securely partitioned into (secret) subsets of items; the second stage then encodes one bit of the watermark into each subset. If more subsets (than watermark bits) are available, error correction is deployed to result in an increasingly resilient encoding. Each single bit is encoded/represented by introducing a slight skew bias in the tails of the numeric distribution of the corresponding subset. The encoding is proved to be resilient to important classes of attacks, including subset selection, linear data changes and random item(s) alterations.

Solution Details. The algorithm proceeds as follows (see Figure 6): **(a)** User-defined queries and associated guaranteed query usability metrics and bounds are specified with respect to the given database (see below). **(b)** User input determines a set of attributes in the database considered for watermarking, possibly all. **(c)** From the values in each such attribute select a (maximal) number of (e) unique, non-intersecting, secret subsets. **(d)** For each considered subset, **(d.1)** embed a watermark bit into it using the single-bit encoding convention described below and then **(d.2)** check if data constraints are still satisfied. If data constraints are violated, **(d.3)** retry different encoding parameter variations or, if still no success, **(d.4)** try to mark the subset as invalid (see single-bit encoding convention below), or if still no success **(d.5)** ignore the current set[3]. Repeat step (d) until no more subsets are available.

Several methods for subset selection (c) are discussed. In one version, it proceeds as follows. The input data tuples are sorted (lexicographically) on a

---

[3] This leaves an invalid watermark bit encoded in the data that will be corrected by the deployed error correcting mechanisms (e.g. majority voting) at extraction time.

wm(attribute, wm_key, mark_data[],
    plugin_handler, db_primary_key, subset_size, v_{false}, v_{true}, c)
    sort_attribute $\leftarrow$ **sort_on_normalized_hash**(wm_key,db_primary_key,wm_key)
    for (i=0; i $<$ $\frac{length(attribute)}{subset\_size}$;i++)
        subset_bin $\leftarrow$ **next** subset_size elements from sort_attribute
        compute rollback_data
        encode(mark_data[i % mark_data.length], subset_bin, v_{false}, v_{true}, c)
        propagate changes into attribute
        if (not goodness_plugin_handler.isSatisfied(new_data,changes)) **then**
            rollback rollback_data
            continue
        else
            commit
            map[i] = true
            subset_boundaries[i] = subset_bin[0]
    return map, subset_boundaries

Fig. 6. Watermark Embedding (version using subset markers and detection maps shown).

---

secret keyed cryptographic hash H of the primary key attribute (K). Based on this value, compose a criteria (e.g., $H(K, key)$) mod $e = 0$) for selecting a set of "special" tuples such that they are uniformly distributed and average a total number of $e = length(attribute)/$ subset_size. These special tuples are going to be used as subset "markers". Each subset is defined as the elements between two adjacent markers, having on average subset_size elements. The detection phase will then rely on this construction criteria to re-discover the subset markers. This process is illustrated in Figure 6.

Encoding the individual mark bits in different subsets increases the ability to defeat different types of transformations including sampling (**A1**) and/or random data addition (**A2**), by "dispersing" their effect throughout the data, as a result of the secret ordering. Thus, if an attack removes 5% of the items, this will result in each subset S_i being roughly 5% smaller. If S_i is small enough and/or if the primitive watermarking method used to encode parts of the watermark (i.e., 1 bit) in S_i is made resilient to these kind of minor transformations then the probability of survival of most of the embedded watermarks is accordingly higher. Additionally, in order to provide resilience to massive "cut" attacks, the subsets are made to be of sizes equal to a given *percent* of the overall data set, i.e., not of fixed absolute sizes.

Note: If enough additional storage is available, these subsets can be in fact constructed differently: given a secretly keyed cryptographic hash function with discrete output values in the interval $[1, e]$, apply it, for each tuple, to the primary key attribute value and let its output determine which subset the tuple belongs to. This would both alleviate the need to deploy subset markers as well as likely offering more resilience to attacks. This simple and nice improvement was suggested to one of the authors during a discussion with a Purdue graduate student (whose identity he cannot remember but whom he invites forward for credit) attending the 2005 Symposium on Security and Privacy.

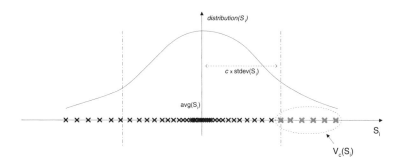

Fig. 7. In the single-bit mark encoding convention, the encoding of the watermark bit relies on altering the size of the "positive violators" set, $v_c(S_i)$.

Once constructed, each separate subset S_i will be marked separately with a single bit, in the order it appears in the actual watermark string. The result will be a e-bit (i.e., $i = 1, \ldots, e$) overall watermark bandwidth in which each bit is "hidden" in each of the marked S_i. If the watermark is of size less than e, error correction can be deployed to make use of the additional bandwidth to increase the encoding resilience.

The single-bit distribution encoding proceeds as follows. Let b be a watermark bit that is to be encoded into S_i and $\mathbb{G}$ represent a set of user specified change tolerance, or usability metrics. The set $\mathbb{G}$ will be used to implement the consumer-driven awareness in the watermark encoding.

Let $v_{false}, v_{true}, c \in (0, 1)$, $v_{false} < v_{true}$ be real numbers (e.g., $c = 90\%$, $v_{true} = 10\%$, $v_{false} = 7\%$). c is called *confidence factor* and the interval (v_{false}, v_{true}) *confidence violators hysteresis*. These are values to be remembered also for watermark detection time. They can be considered as part of the encoding key. Let $avg(S_i)$ and $\delta(S_i)$ be the average and standard deviation, respectively, of S_i. Given S_i and the real number $c \in (0, 1)$ as above, $v_c(S_i)$ is defined as the *number of items of S_i that are greater than* $avg(S_i) + c \times \delta(S_i)$. $v_c(S_i)$ is called the number of positive "violators" of the c confidence over S_i, see Figure 7.

The single-bit **mark encoding convention** is then formulated: given S_i, c, v_{false} and v_{true} as above, $mark(S_i) \in \{true, false, invalid\}$ is defined to be *true* if $v_c(S_i) > (v_{true} \times |S_i|)$, *false* if $v_c(S_i) < v_{false} \times |S_i|$ and *invalid* if $v_c(S_i) \in (v_{false} \times |S_i|, v_{true} \times |S_i|)$.

In other words, the watermark is modeled by the percentage of positive confidence violators present in S_i for a given confidence factor c and confidence violators hysteresis (v_{false}, v_{true}). Encoding the single bit (see Figure 8), b, into S_i is therefore achieved by minor alterations to some of the data values in S_i such that the number of positive violators $(v_c(S_i))$ is either (a) less than $v_{false} \times |S_i|$ if $b = 0$, or (b) more than $v_{true} \times |S_i|$ if $b = 1$. The alterations are then checked against the change tolerances, $\mathbb{G}$, specified by the user.

---

encode(bit, set, v_{false}, v_{true}, c)
    compute $avg(set)$, $\delta(set)$
    compute $v_c(set)$
    if $v_c(set)$ **satisfies** desired bit value **return** *true*
    if (bit)
        compute $v_* \leftarrow v_{true} - v_c(set)$
        alter v_* items close to the stddev boundary so that they become $> v_{true}$
    else
        (!bit) case is similar
    compute $v_c(set)$
    if $v_c(set)$ **satisfies** desired bit value **return** *true*
    else rollback alterations (distribution shifted too much?)
    return *false*

Fig. 8. Single Bit Encoding Algorithm (illustrative overview).

At detection time the secret subsets are reconstructed and the individual bits are recovered according to the single-bit mark encoding convention. This yields the original e-bit string. If e is larger than the size of the watermark, error correction was deployed to increase the encoding resilience. The watermark string can be then recovered by applying error correction decoding to this string, e.g., majority voting for each watermark bit. This process is illustrated in Figure 9.

In [27, 33] and [34] the authors discuss a proof of concept implementation. It is worth mentioning here due to its consumer-driven design (see Figure 10). In addition to a watermark to be embedded, a secret key to be used for embedding, and a set of relations/attributes to watermark, the software receives as input also a set of external *usability plugin modules*. The role of these plugins is to allow user defined query metrics to be deployed and queried at run-time without recompilation and/or software restart. The software uses those metrics to re-evaluate data usability after each atomic watermarking step.

Constraint metrics can be specified either as SQL queries, stored procedures or simple Java code inside the plug-in modules. Constraints that arise from the schema (e.g., key constraints), can easily be specified in a form sim-

det(attr, wm_key, db_primary_key, subset_sz, v_{false}, v_{true}, c, map[], subset_bnds[])
   srt_attr ← **sort_on_normalized_crypto_hash**(wm_key,db_primary_key,wm_key)
   read_pipe ← null
   do { tuple ← **next_tuple**(srt_attr) }
   until (**exists** idx **such that** (subset_bnds[idx] == tuple))
   curr_subset ← idx
   while (**not**(srt_attr.**empty**())) **do**
      do {
         tuple ← **next_tuple**(srt_attr)
         read_pipe = read_pipe.**append**(tuple)
      } **until** (**exists** idx **such that** (subset_bnds[idx] == tuple))
      subset_bin ← (at most subset_sz elements of read_pipe, excluding last read)
      read_pipe.**remove_all_remaining_elements_but_last_read**()
      if (map[curr_subset]) **then**
         mark_data[curr_subset] ← **decode** (subset_bin, v_{false}, v_{true}, confidence)
         if (mark_data[curr_subset] != DECODING_ERROR)
            then map[curr_subset] ← true
      curr_subset ← idx
   return mark_data, map

Fig. 9. Watermark Detection (version using subset markers shown).

ilar to (or derived from) SQL *create table* statements. In addition, integrity constraints (e.g., such as *end_time* being greater than *begin_time*) can be expressed. A tolerance is specified for each constraint. The tolerance is the amount of change or violation of the constraint that is acceptable. This is an important parameter since it can be used to tailor the quality of the water-mark at the expense of greater change in the data. As mentioned earlier, if the tolerances are too low, it may not be possible to insert a watermark in the data. Various forms of expression are accommodated, e.g., in terms of arbitrary SQL queries over the relations, with associated requirements (usability metric functions). For example, the requirement that the result of the join (natural or otherwise) of two relations does not change by more than 3% can be specified.

Once usability metrics are defined and all other parameters are in place, the watermarking module (see Figure 10) initiates the process of watermarking. An undo/rollback log is kept for each atomic step performed (i.e., 1-bit encoding) until data usability is assessed and confirmed by querying the currently active usability plugins. This allows for rollbacks in the case when data quality is not preserved by the current atomic operation.

To validate this consumer driven design the authors perform a set of experiments showing how, for example, watermarking with classification preservation can be enforced through the usability metric plugin mechanisms. Moreover, the solution is proved experimentally on real data to be extremely re-

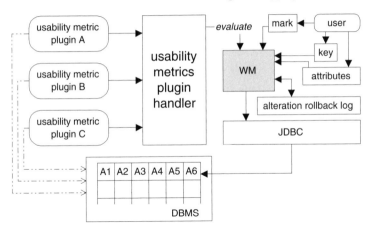

Fig. 10. Overview of the **wmdb.*** package.

silient to random alterations and uninformed alteration attacks. This is due to its distribution-based encoding which can naturally survive such alterations. For example, altering the *entire* watermarked data set within 1% of its original values only yields a distortion of less than 5% in the detected watermark.

The authors also propose a set of improvements and discuss several properties of the solutions.

- Embedding Optimizations: As the encoding resilience is dependent on a set of parameters (e.g., c, $subset\_size$, v_{false}, v_{true}), an automatic fine-tuning mechanism for searching a near-optimum in this parameter space is proposed. Additionally, the watermarking process could be trained to be resilient to a set of transformations expected from any potential attacker.
- Blind Watermarking: The method does not require the availability of the un-watermarked data at detection time.
- On-the-Fly Updatability: The authors also discuss mechanisms for handling dynamic data updates. Several scenarios of interest are: (i) updates that add fresh tuples to the already watermarked data set, (ii) updates that remove tuples from the already watermarked data and (iii) updates that alter existing tuples.

4 Categorical Types

So far we have explored the issue of watermarking *numeric* relational content. Another important relational data type to be considered is categorical data. Categorical data is data drawn from a discrete distribution, often with a finite domain. By definition, it is either non-ordered (nominal) such as gender or city, or ordered (ordinal) such as high, medium, or low temperatures. There are a multitude of applications that would benefit from a method of rights protection for such data. In this section we propose and analyze watermarking relational data with *categorical* types.

Additional challenges in this domain derive from the fact that one cannot rely on arbitrary small (e.g., numeric) alterations to the data in the embedding process. Any alteration has the potential to be significant, e.g., changing DE-PARTURE_CITY from "Chicago" to "Bucharest" is likely to affect the data quality of the result more than a simple change in a numeric domain. There are no "epsilon" changes in this domain. This completely discrete characteristic of the data requires discovery of fundamentally new bandwidth channels and associated encoding algorithms.

4.1 The Adversary Revisited

We outlined above a set of generic attacks in a relational data framework. Here we discuss additional challenges associated with categorical data types.

A3. Alteration. In the categorical data framework, subset alteration is intuitively quite expensive from a data-value preservation perspective. One has also to take into account semantic consistency issues that become immediately visible because of the discrete nature of the data.

A6. Attribute Remapping. If data semantics allow it, re-mapping of relation attributes can amount to a powerful attack that should be carefully considered. In other words, if Mallory can find an even partial value-preserving mapping (the resulting mapped data set is still valuable for illicit purposes) from the original attribute data domain to a new domain, a watermark should hopefully survive such a transformation. The difficulty of this challenge is increased by the fact that there likely are many transformations available for a specific data domain. This is thus a hard task for the generic case. One special case is primary key re-mapping.

4.2 A Solution

In [25], [36] Sion et. al. introduce a novel method of watermarking relational data with categorical types, based on a set of new encoding channels and algorithms. More specifically, two domain-specific watermark embedding channels are used, namely (i) *inter-attribute associations* and (ii) *value occurrence frequency-transforms* of values.

Overview. The solution starts with an initial user-level assessment step in which a set of attributes to be watermarked are selected. In its basic version, watermark encoding in the *inter-attribute association* channel is deployed for each attribute pair (K, A) in the considered attribute set. A subset of "fit" tuples is selected, as determined by the association between A and K. These tuples are then considered for mark encoding. Mark encoding alters the tuple's value according to secret criteria that induces a statistical bias in the distribution for that tuple's altered value. The detection process then relies on discovering this induced statistical bias.

The authors validate the solution both theoretically and experimentally on real data (Wal-Mart sales). They demonstrate resilience to both alteration and data loss attacks, for example being able to recover over 75% of the watermark from under 20% of the data.

Solution Details. For illustration purposes, let there be a set of discrete attributes $\{A, B\}$ and a primary data key K, not necessarily discrete. Any attribute $X \in \{A, B\}$ can yield a value out of n_X possibilities (e.g., city names, airline names). Let the number of tuples in the database be N. Let $b(x)$ be the number of bits required for the accurate representation of value x and $msb(x, b)$ its most significant b bits. If $b(x) < b$, x is left-padded with $(b - b(x))$ zeroes to form a b-bit result. Similarly, $lsb(x, b)$ is used to denote the least significant b bits of x. If by wm denotes a watermark to be embedded, of length $|wm|$, $wm[i]$ will then be the i-th bit of wm. Let $set\_bit(d, a, b)$ be a function that returns value d with the bit position a set to the truth-value of b. In any following mathematical expression let the symbol "&" signify a *bit-AND* operation. Let $T_j(X)$ be the value of attribute X in tuple j. Let $\{a_1, ..., a_{n_A}\}$ be the discrete potential values of attribute A. These are distinct and can be sorted (e.g., by ASCII value). Let $f_A(a_j)$ be the normalized (to 1.0) occurrence frequency of value a_j in attribute A. $f_A(a_j)$ models the de-facto occurrence probability of value a_j in attribute A.

The encoding algorithm (see Figure 11) starts by discovering a set of "fit" tuples determined directly by the association between A and the primary relation key K. These tuples are then considered for mark encoding.

$\mathbf{wm\_embed\_alt}(K, A, wm, k_1, e, \text{ECC})$
$\quad wm\_data \leftarrow ECC.encode(wm, wm.len)$
$\quad idx \leftarrow 0$
$\quad \mathbf{for}\ (j \leftarrow 1;\ j < N;\ j \leftarrow j + 1)$
$\quad\quad \mathbf{if}\ (H(T_j(K), k_1)\ \text{mod}\ e = 0)\ \mathbf{then}$
$\quad\quad\quad t \leftarrow set\_bit(H(T_j(K), k_1), 0, wm\_data[idx])$
$\quad\quad\quad T_j(A) \leftarrow a_t$
$\quad\quad\quad embedding\_map[T_j(K)] \leftarrow idx$
$\quad\quad\quad idx \leftarrow idx + 1$
$\quad \mathbf{return}\ embedding\_map$

Fig. 11. Encoding Algorithm (alternative using embedding map shown)

Step One. A tuple T_i is said to be "fit" for encoding iff $H(T_i(K), k_1)$ mod $e = 0$, where e is an adjustable encoding parameter determining the percentage of considered tuples and k_1 is a secret $max(b(N), b(A))$-bit key. In other words, a tuple is considered "fit" if its primary key value satisfies a certain secret criteria (similar criteria are found in various frameworks, e.g., [16]). The fit tuples set will then contain roughly $\frac{N}{e}$ elements.

The "fitness" selection step provides several advantages. On the one hand this ensures secrecy and resilience and, on the other hand, it effectively "modulates" the watermark encoding process to the actual attribute-primary key association. Additionally, this is the place where the cryptographic safety of the hash one-wayness is leveraged to defeat invertibility attacks (**A5**). If

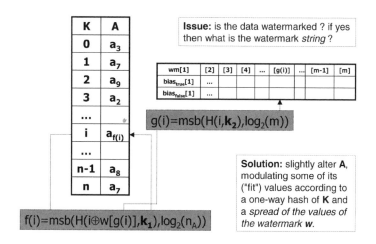

Fig. 12. Overview of multi-bit watermark encoding.

the available embedding bandwidth $\frac{N}{e}$ is greater than the watermark bit-size $|wm|$, error correcting codes (ECC) are deployed that take as input a desired watermark wm and produce as output a string of bits wm_data of length $\frac{N}{e}$ containing a redundant encoding of the watermark, tolerating a certain amount of bit-loss, $wm\_data = ECC.encode(wm, \frac{N}{e})$.

Step Two. For each "fit" tuple T_i, we encode one bit by altering $T_i(A)$ to become $T_i(A) = a_t$ where

$$t = set\_bit(msb(H(T_i(K), k_1), b(n_A)), 0, wm\_data[msb(H(T_i(K), k_2), b(\frac{N}{e}))])$$

and k_2 is a secret key $k_2 \neq k_1$. In other words, a secret value of $b(n_A)$ bits is generated – depending on the primary key and k_1 – and then its least significant bit is forced to a value according to a corresponding position in wm_data (random, depending on the primary key and k_2). The new attribute value is thus selected by the secret key k_1, the associated relational primary key value and a corresponding bit from the watermark data wm_data.

In the decoding phase (see Figure 13), the first aim is to discover the embedded wm_data bit string. The same criteria for discovering "fit" tuples is used. For each "fit" tuple T_i, with $T_i(A) = a_t$, its corresponding entry in the result bit string is set to $(t\&1)$

$$wm\_data[msb(H(T_j(K), k_2), b(\frac{N}{e}))] \leftarrow (t\&1)$$

Once wm_data (possibly altered) is available, the error correcting mechanism is invoked to generate the "closest", most likely, corresponding watermark $wm = ECC.decode(wm\_data, |wm|)$.

---

wm_dec_alt(K,A,k_1,e,ECC,$embed\_map$)
  for $(j \leftarrow 1; j < N; j \leftarrow j + 1)$
    if $(H(T_j(K), msb(k, b(K)))) \bmod e = 0)$ **then**
    determine t such that $T_j(A) = a_t$
    $wm\_data[embed\_map[T_j(K)]] = t\&1$
    $wm \leftarrow ECC.decode(wm\_data, wm.length)$
  return wm

Fig. 13. Decoding Algorithm (alternative using embedding map shown)

The authors propose a natural extension to the above solution aimed at defeating vertical partitioning attacks (**A1.b**). Instead of relying on the association between the primary key and A, the extended algorithm considers *all* pairs of attributes and embeds a watermark separately in *each* of these associations. Additionally, if data constraints allow, the authors propose watermarking each and every attribute pair by first building a closure for the set of attribute pairs over the entire schema that minimizes the number of encoding interferences while maximizing the number of pairs watermarked. To solve the issue of interference, maintaining a mark "interference graph" is proposed.

The proposed extension features a particular issue of concern in certain cases of multi-attribute embeddings where two non-key attributes are used in the encoding, i.e., mark(A,B). Because of the correlation between the watermarking alteration (the newly selected value $T_i(B) = b_t$) and its actual location (determined by the fitness selection, $H(T_i(A), k_1)$ and e), sometimes Mallory can mount a special attack with the undesirable result of revealing some of the mark bit embedding locations. This occurs if the fitness criteria decides that a particular value of A yields a tuple fit and that value of A

appears then in multiple (statistically significant number of) different tuples. This is possible only if A is not a primary key but rather another categorical attribute, with repeating duplicate values.

The authors propose a set of solutions to this issue, including composing the actual watermark encoding out of a combination of several different sub-encodings, each in turn using a different k_1 value. Each such sub-encoding will ignore all tuples with previously seen values of the attribute A (in the fitness criteria). While each of these "low impact" encodings would be weaker than the original solution, their combined "sum" can be made arbitrarily strong, by increasing their number. At the same time correlation attacks would be defeated, as each of the encodings would use a different key thus making such attacks impossible "across" the encodings.

The authors further discuss additional extensions and properties of the solution, including the following.

- Consumer-Driven Design: The solution features a consumer-driven design. Each property of the database that needs to be preserved is written as a constraint on the allowable change to the dataset. The watermarking algorithm is then applied with these constraints as input and re-evaluates them continuously for each alteration. A backtrack log is kept to allow undo operations in case certain constraints are violated by the current watermarking step.
- Incremental Updatability: The solution supports incremental updates naturally. As updates occur to the data, the resulting tuples can be evaluated on the fly for "fitness" and watermarked accordingly.
- Blind Watermarking: The method does not require the availability of the un-watermarked data at detection time.
- Minimizing Alteration Distance: An interesting problem to consider is the case when, for a given "fit" tuple, certain alterations would be preferred to others (e.g., changing "Chicago, O'Hare" into "Chicago" is preferred to "Las Vegas"). The authors propose to handle this scenario by a modified encoding procedure that naturally accommodates and minimizes such an "alteration distance" metric.
- Extreme Vertical Partitioning: To counter extreme vertical partitioning attacks in which only a single attribute A is preserved in the result, the authors propose to encode a watermark in one of the only remaining characteristic properties, namely the value occurrence frequency distribution for each possible value of A. To do so a scheme of watermarking for numeric sets [30] can be applied in this "frequency" domain.
- Multi-Layer Self-Reinforcing Watermarks: To counter the scenario where Mallory gains knowledge, e.g., during a court hearing, of a multiply-used encoding key, the authors propose to embed multiple (i) weak watermarks with different secret keys and reveal in court only a certain subset of these, or (ii) *self-re-enforcing* pairs of watermarks $(w_1, w_2)_i$ with different keys

$(k_1^1, k_2^1, k_1^2, k_2^2)_i$ such that, for example, altering w_2 will result in enforcing w_1.

- Multiple Data Sources: The paper also points out that the solution handles recovering watermarks from data derived from multiple data sources. This scenario is of particular interest for example in the case of an equiJOIN performed between two data sets. Because watermarks rely on a bias in the association between attributes, they can be naturally retrieved from such JOIN result under certain reasonable assumptions.

- Categorical and Numerical Data Types: Watermarking at the intersection of categorical and numerical types is also explored. It is of interest to provide a rights assessment mechanism that could not only prove rights but also that the associated data sets were actually produced "together"; this is relevant for example if the intrinsic value of the data lies in the actual *combination* of the two data types. The authors introduce initial ideas.

- Bijective Attribute Re-mapping: To handle a scenario in which categorical attributes are re-mapped through a bijective function to a new data domain, the authors propose to discover the inverse mapping. This is possible if the initial data domain features distinguishing properties (e.g., value occurrence frequency histogram) that are likely to be preserved in the mapped result.

5 Related Work

So far we have discussed a set of relational data types and associated watermarking methods enabling future rights assessment proofs. We now survey a number of related research efforts that explore Information Hiding and Watermarking for relational data in other security contexts such as privacy enforcement and license violators tracing.

5.1 Privacy and Rights Protection

In [4] Bertino et. al. explore issues at the intersection of two important dimensions in data-centric assurance, namely rights assessment and privacy, in the broader context of medical data. A unified framework is introduced that combines binning and watermarking techniques for the purpose of achieving both data privacy and the ability to assert rights.

The system design borrows components from existing work. More specifically, the binning method (for k-anonymity) is built upon an earlier approach of generalization and suppression by allowing a broader concept of generalization. Similar to the *consumer-driven* paradigm discussed earlier in this chapter, to ensure data usefulness, binning is constrained by usage metrics that define maximal allowable information loss. An initial binning stage is followed then by watermarking. The framework then deploys a version of the encoding for categorical types [36] by Sion et. al. in a hierarchical fashion, for the purpose of defeating a data generalization attack of concern in this framework. The paper then explores whether watermarking can adversely interfere with binning and conclude that the interaction is safe. Experiments were conducted aimed at validating the robustness of the proposed framework.

5.2 Fingerprinting

Another example application of Resilient Information Hiding as a tool aiding rights management, is its deployment to "track" license violators by hiding a specific mark inside the Work, uniquely identifying the party it was sold/outsourced to. This application is commonly referred to as *fingerprinting*. If the Work would then be found in the public domain, that mark could be used to assess the source of the leak.

One significant matter of concern in fingerprinting are collusion attacks. In a collusion attack, multiple attackers "collude" by obtaining multiple copies of the same Work (e.g., by purchasing it separately under different identities) watermarked with different marks, in the hope of "combining" the different copies into a single un-watermarked version. Defending against this attack is not possible in the general case when the number of colluding partners cannot be upper bounded. If this upper bound can be determined however, several results provide appropriate coding techniques that allow tracing even in the case of collusion under minimal assumptions [5] [6] [13].

For relational data, the issue of fingerprinting has been discussed by Li et. al. in [21] where they propose to deploy their multi-bit watermarking method [19] for this very purpose. To handle collusion attacks the authors defer to research in [5] [6] [13]. This work is discussed in more detail elsewhere in this book.

5.3 Tamper Detection through Fragile Watermarking

In [17] Li et. al. explore the issue of detecting malicious alterations to data by embedding a "fragile" watermark in the data. While in this chapter we presented watermarking as a technique deploying Information Hiding for the purpose of rights assessment, in this context, "watermark" is attached to a different semantics. Whereas in rights assessment, a watermark features resilience to value-preserving data alterations, for the purposes of tamper detection, the "watermark" will be "fragile" so as to become a detector for exactly such alterations. The authors also propose to allow this watermark to point at the locations where alterations have occurred in the data.

At an overview level, the method proceeds as follows. The data is partitioned into secret subsets; a keyed cryptographic hash of each such subset (in effect the traditional message authentication code MAC) is then embedded in the group by re-ordering its items with respect to a canonical ordering, based on a cryptographic hash of their primary key attribute. The encoding is claimed fragile enough to be impacted by even minor alterations to the data with reasonable probabilities. Additionally, the encoding can pinpoint at the exact location of the alteration with the granularity of a subset.

Compared with traditional authentication techniques (e.g., appending signatures of MACs) such a technique can become of relevance, e.g., when the overhead of storing and managing the signatures or MACs for a large number of entities is not negligible. This is why it is important to further explore and understand fragile watermarking scenarios. This work is discussed in more detail elsewhere in this book.

5.4 Query Learnability and Consumer-Driven Watermarking

In [12] Gross-Amblard introduce interesting theoretical results investigating alterations to relational data (or associated XML) in a consumer-driven framework in which a set of parametric queries are to be preserved up to an acceptable level of distortion.

The author first shows that the main difficulty preserving such queries "is linked to the informational complexity of sets defined by queries, rather than their computational complexity" [12]. Roughly speaking, if the family of sets defined by the queries is not *learnable* [37], no query-preserving data alteration scheme can be designed.

In a second result, the author shows that under certain assumptions (i.e., query sets defined by first-order logic and monadic second order logic on restricted classes of structures – with a bounded degree for the Gaifman graph or the tree-width of the structure) a query-preserving data alteration scheme exists.

This research is important as it has the potential to enable a better understanding of consumer-driven watermarking designs. For example, as database instances are often having a bounded degree Gaifman graph (or a bounded tree-width), these can now be measured and the information capacity of a query-preserving alteration channel can be computed. This is of interest in the case of extremely restrictive constraints, e.g., when it is not clear if watermarking can yield enough resilience.

6 State of The Art and the Future

Watermarking in relational frameworks is a relatively young technology that has begun its maturity cycle towards full deployment in industry-level applications. Many of the solutions discussed above have been prototyped and validated on real data. Patents have been filed for several of them, including Agrawal et.al. [1, 16] and Sion et.al. [29, 30, 32, 33] [34] [25, 27, 36]. In the next few years we expect these solutions to become available commercially, tightly integrated within existing DBMS (e.g., DB2 [10]) or as stand-alone packages that can be deployed simultaneously on top of multiple data types and sources.

Ultimately, we believe the process of resilient information hiding will become available as a secure mechanism for not only rights protection but also data tracing and authentication in a multitude of discrete data frameworks.

7 Conclusions

In this chapter we explored how Information Hiding can be successfully deployed as a tool for Rights Assessment for discrete digital Works. We analyzed solutions for resilient Information Hiding for relational data, including numeric and categorical types.

A multitude of associated future research avenues present themselves in a relational framework, including: the design of alternative primary or pseudo-primary key independent encoding methods, a deeper theoretical understanding of limits of watermarking for a broader class of algorithms, the ability to better defeat additive watermark attacks, an exploration of zero-knowledge watermarking etc.

Moreover, while the concept of on-the-fly quality assessment for a consumer-driven design has the potential to function well, another interesting avenue for further research would be to augment the encoding method with direct awareness of semantic consistency (e.g., classification and association rules). This would likely result in an increase in available encoding bandwidth, thus in a higher encoding resilience. One idea would be to define a generic language (possibly subset of SQL) able to naturally express such constraints and their propagation at embedding time.

Additionally, of particular interest for future research exploration, we envision cross-domain applications of Information Hiding in distributed environments such as sensor networks, with applications ranging from resilient content annotation to runtime authentication and data integrity proofs.

8 Acknowledgments

The author is supported partly by the NSF through awards CT CNS-0627554, CT CNS-0716608 and CRI CNS 0708025. The author also wishes to thank Motorola Labs, IBM Research, CEWIT, and the Stony Brook Office of the Vice President for Research.

References

1. Rakesh Agrawal, Peter J. Haas, and Jerry Kiernan. Watermarking relational data: framework, algorithms and analysis. *The VLDB Journal*, 12(2):157–169, 2003.

2. Michael Arnold, Stephen D. Wolthusen, and Martin Schmucker. *Techniques and Applications of Digital Watermarking and Content Protection*. Artech House Publishers, 2003.
3. Mauro Barni and Franco Bartolini. *Watermarking Systems Engineering: Enabling Digital Assets Security and Other Applications*. Marcel Dekker, 2004.
4. Elisa Bertino, Beng Chin Ooi, Yanjiang Yang, and Robert H. Deng. Privacy and ownership preserving of outsourced medical data. In *Proceedings of the International Conference on Data Engineering*, pages 521–532, 2005.
5. D. Boneh and J. Shaw. Collusion-secure fingerprinting for digital data. *Lecture Notes in Computer Science*, 963:452–464, 1995.
6. D. Boneh and J. Shaw. Collusion-secure fingerprinting for digital data. *IEEE Transactions on Information Theory*, 44(5):1897–1905, 1998.
7. E.F. Codd. A Relational Model of Data for Large Shared Data Banks. *Communications of the ACM*, 13(6):377–387, 1970.
8. I. Cox, J. Bloom, and M. Miller. Digital watermarking. In *Digital Watermarking*. Morgan Kaufmann, 2001.
9. Scott Craver, Nasir Memon, Boon-Lock Yeo, and Minerva M. Yeung. Resolving rightful ownerships with invisible watermarking techniques: Limitations, attacks, and implications. *IEEE Journal of Selected Areas in Communications*, 16(4):573–586, 1998.
10. The IBM DB2 Universal Database. Online at http://www.ibm.com/software/data/db2.
11. Joachim Eggers and Bernd Girod. *Informed Watermarking*. Kluwer Academic Publishers, 2002.
12. David Gross-Amblard. Query-preserving watermarking of relational databases and xml documents. In *Proceedings of the Nineteenth ACM SIGMOD-SIGACT-SIGART Symposium on Principles of Database Systems*, pages 191–201, New York, NY, USA, 2003. ACM Press.
13. H. Guth and B. Pfitzman. Error and collusion secure fingerprinting for digital data. In *Proceedings of the Information Hiding Workshop*, 1999.
14. Neil F. Johnson, Zoran Duric, and Sushil Jajodia. *Information Hiding: Steganography and Watermarking - Attacks and Countermeasures*. Kluwer Academic Publishers, 2001.
15. S. Katzenbeisser and F. Petitcolas (editors). *Information Hiding Techniques for Steganography and Digital Watermarking*. Artech House, 2001.
16. J. Kiernan and R. Agrawal. Watermarking relational databases. In *Proceedings of the 28th International Conference on Very Large Databases VLDB*, 2002.
17. Yingjiu Li, Huiping Guo, and Sushil Jajodia. Tamper detection and localization for categorical data using fragile watermarks. In *DRM '04: Proceedings of the 4th ACM workshop on Digital rights management*, pages 73–82, New York, NY, USA, 2004. ACM Press.
18. Yingjiu Li, Vipin Swarup, and Sushil Jajodia. Constructing a virtual primary key for fingerprinting relational data. In *DRM '03: Proceedings of the 2003 ACM workshop on Digital rights management*, pages 133–141, New York, NY, USA, 2003. ACM Press.
19. Yingjiu Li, Vipin Swarup, and Sushil Jajodia. A robust watermarking scheme for relational data. In *Proceedings of the Workshop on Information Technology and Systems (WITS)*, pages 195–200, 2003.

20. Yingjiu Li, Vipin Swarup, and Sushil Jajodia. Defending against additive attacks with maximal errors in watermarking relational databases. In *Proceedings of the IFIP WG 11.3 Working Conference on Data and Application Security*, pages 81–94, 2004.
21. Yingjiu Li, Vipin Swarup, and Sushil Jajodia. Fingerprinting relational databases: Schemes and specialties. *IEEE Transactions on Dependable and Secure Computing*, 2(1):34–45, 2005.
22. Chun-Shien Lu. *Multimedia Security: Steganography and Digital Watermarking Techniques for Protection of Intellectual Property*. Idea Group Publishing, 2004.
23. Bruce Schneier. *Applied Cryptography: Protocols, Algorithms and Source Code in C*. Wiley & Sons, 1996.
24. Husrev T. Sencar, Mahalingam Ramkumar, and Ali N. Akansu. *Data Hiding Fundamentals And Applications: Content Security in Digital Multimedia*. ELSEVIER science and technology books, 2004.
25. Radu Sion. Proving ownership over categorical data. In *Proceedings of the IEEE International Conference on Data Engineering ICDE*, 2004.
26. Radu Sion. *Rights Assessment for Discrete Digital Data, Ph.D. dissertation*. Computer Sciences, Purdue University, 2004.
27. Radu Sion. wmdb.*: A suite for database watermarking (demo). In *Proceedings of the IEEE International Conference on Data Engineering ICDE*, 2004.
28. Radu Sion and Mikhail Atallah. Attacking digital watermarks. In *Proceedings of the Symposium on Electronic Imaging SPIE*, 2004.
29. Radu Sion, Mikhail Atallah, and Sunil Prabhakar. On watermarking numeric sets. Online at `https://www.cerias.purdue.edu/tools_and_resources/bibtex_archive/`, 2001.
30. Radu Sion, Mikhail Atallah, and Sunil Prabhakar. On watermarking numeric sets. In *Proceedings of IWDW 2002, Lecture Notes in Computer Science*. Springer-Verlag, 2002.
31. Radu Sion, Mikhail Atallah, and Sunil Prabhakar. Power: Metrics for evaluating watermarking algorithms. In *Proceedings of IEEE ITCC 2002*. IEEE Computer Society Press, 2002.
32. Radu Sion, Mikhail Atallah, and Sunil Prabhakar. Watermarking databases. Online at `https://www.cerias.purdue.edu/tools_and_resources/bibtex_archive/`, 2002.
33. Radu Sion, Mikhail Atallah, and Sunil Prabhakar. Rights protection for relational data. In *Proceedings of the ACM Special Interest Group on Management of Data Conference SIGMOD*, 2003.
34. Radu Sion, Mikhail Atallah, and Sunil Prabhakar. Relational data rights protection through watermarking. *IEEE Transactions on Knowledge and Data Engineering TKDE*, 16(6), June 2004.
35. Radu Sion, Mikhail Atallah, and Sunil Prabhakar. Resilient rights protection for sensor streams. In *Proceedings of the Very Large Databases Conference VLDB*, 2004.
36. Radu Sion, Mikhail Atallah, and Sunil Prabhakar. Ownership proofs for categorical data. *IEEE Transactions on Knowledge and Data Engineering TKDE*, 2005.
37. L. G. Valiant. A Theory of the Learnable. In *Proceedings of the Symposium on the Theory of Computing*, pages 436–445, 1984.

14

Database Watermarking: A Systematic View

Yingjiu Li

School of Information Systems, Singapore Management University
80 Stamford Road, Singapore 178902
yjli@smu.edu.sg

Summary. In this chapter, a systematic review of database watermarking is provided. The existing database watermarking approaches are classified along six dimensions: data type, distortion to underlying data, sensitivity to database attacks, watermark information, verifiability, and data structure. At the end of this chapter, some open issues are discussed.

1 Introduction

The motivation for database watermarking is to protect databases, especially those published online (e.g., parametric specifications, surveys, and life sciences data), from tampering and pirated copies. A watermark can be considered to be some kind of information that is embedded into underlying data for tamper detection, localization, ownership proof, and/or traitor tracing purposes. Database watermarking techniques complement the Database Protection Act [24] and are becoming increasingly important as people realize that "the law does not now provide sufficient protection to the comprehensive and commercially and publicly useful databases that are at the heart of the information economy" [5].

Basic watermarking processes

Database watermarking consists of two basic processes: watermark insertion and watermark detection, as illustrated in Figure 1. For watermark insertion, a key is used to embed watermark information into an original database so as to produce the watermarked database for publication or distribution. Given appropriate key and watermark information, a watermark detection process can be applied to any suspicious database so as to determine whether or not a legitimate watermark can be detected. A suspicious database can be any watermarked database or innocent database, or a mixture of them under various database attacks.

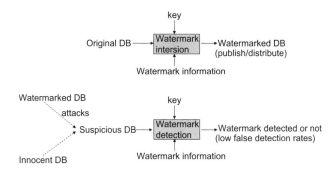

Fig. 1. Basic watermarking processes

Difference from multimedia watermarking

While the basic processes in database watermarking are quite similar to those in watermarking multimedia data (which has long been rigorously studied [10, 11, 4]), the approaches developed for multimedia watermarking cannot be directly applied to databases because of the difference in data properties. In general, database relations differ from multimedia data in significant ways and hence require a different class of information-hiding mechanisms. Unlike multimedia data whose components are highly correlated, database relations consist of independent objects or tuples. The tuples can be added, deleted, or modified frequently in either benign updates or malicious attacks. No existing watermarking techniques for multimedia data are designed to accommodate such tuple operations.

Classification model

The existing database watermarking schemes can be classified along various dimensions, including:

- *Data type*: Different schemes are designed for watermarking different types of data, including numerical data and categorical data.
- *Distortion to underlying data*: While some watermarking schemes inevitably introduce distortions/errors to the underlying data, others are distortion-free.
- *Sensitivity to database attacks*: A watermarking scheme can be either *robust* or *fragile* to database attacks. A scheme is robust (fragile, respectively) if it is difficult to make an embedded watermark undetectable (unchanged, respectively) in database attacks, provided that the attacks do not degrade the usefulness of the data significantly.
- *Watermark information*: The watermark information that is embedded into a database can be a single-bit watermark, a multiple-bit watermark, a fingerprint, or multiple watermarks in different watermarking schemes.

- *Verifiability*: A watermark solution is said to be *private* if the detection of a watermark can only be performed by someone who owns a secret key and can only be proven once to the public (e.g., to the court). After this one-time proof, the secret key is known to the public and the embedded watermark can be easily destroyed by malicious users. A watermark solution is said to be *public* if the detection of a watermark can be publicly proven by anyone, as many times as necessary.

- *Data structure*: Different watermarking schemes are designed to accommodate different structural information of the underlying data, including relational databases (with or without primary keys), data cubes, streaming data, and XML data.

Based on the above classification model, a systematic review of database watermarking is presented in the rest of this chapter. The review covers typical watermarking schemes as well as some new results, not intended to be complete, but rather to present a coherent picture from the author's point of view. The reader is referred to another chapter in this book for a complementary review on database watermarking schemes. For consistency reasons, the same notation is used as much as possible in this interpretation of different schemes (thus the interpretation may not be exactly the same as those given in the literature). In particular, this interpretation uses a cryptographically secure pseudo-random sequence generator $\mathcal{S}$ seeded with a secret key $\mathcal{K}$ in concatenation with some other input X. Given a sequence of numbers $\mathcal{S}_1, \mathcal{S}_2, \ldots$ generated by $\mathcal{S}$, it is computationally infeasible to derive the secret key nor to predict the next number in the sequence. Alternatively, one can use a keyed hash message authentication code $HMAC$ to generate the sequence with different secret keys (i.e., $\mathcal{S}_i = HMAC(\mathcal{K}_i, X)$).

2 Data Type

2.1 Watermarking Numerical Data

The first well-known database watermarking scheme was proposed by Agrawal and Kiernan [1] for watermarking numerical values in relational databases. The fundamental assumption is that the watermarked database can tolerate a small amount of errors: it is acceptable to change a small number of ξ least significant bits in some numeric values; however, the value of data is significantly reduced if a large number of the bits are changed. The basic idea is to ensure that those bit positions contain specific values determined by a secret key $\mathcal{K}$. The bit pattern constitutes a watermark.

For watermark insertion, the scheme scans each tuple r in a relation R and seeds a cryptographically secure pseudo-random sequence generator $\mathcal{S}$ with the secret key $\mathcal{K}$ in concatenation with the tuple's primary key $r.P$. Let $\mathcal{S}_i$ be the i-th number generated by $\mathcal{S}$. If $\mathcal{S}_1$ satisfies $(\mathcal{S}_1 \mod \gamma = 0)$, then the current tuple r is selected, otherwise the tuple is ignored, where γ

is a watermarking parameter used to control the percentage of tuples being selected. Because $\mathcal{S}_1$ is pseudo-random, roughly η/γ tuples are selected, where η is the total number of tuples in relation R. Then, for each selected tuple, the scheme selects one attribute with index ($\mathcal{S}_2 \mod \nu$) out of ν watermarkable numerical attributes indexed from 0 to $\nu - 1$. For the selected attribute of a selected tuple, the scheme selects one bit with index ($\mathcal{S}_3 \mod \xi$) out of ξ least significant bits indexed from 0 to $\xi - 1$, where ξ is a watermarking parameter used to control the error that each numerical value can tolerate. The scheme then assigns the selected bit of the selected attribute in the selected tuple with a mark value ($\mathcal{S}_4 \mod 2$). With a probability of $1/2$, the underlying bit value is changed in this process. Due to the use of a cryptographically secure pseudo-random sequence generator, it is computationally infeasible for an attacker, without knowing the secret key, to derive where the watermark bits are embedded, what the mark bits are, and the correlations among the embedded locations and the embedded values.

For watermark detection, the scheme scans all the tuples in a suspicious database relation R', locates the marked bit positions, and computes the mark values at those bit positions exactly as in watermark insertion. To detect a watermark, the scheme compares the computed mark values to the corresponding bit values stored in R'. A watermark is detected if the percentage of matches in such comparison is greater than τ, where $\tau \geq 0.5$ is a parameter that is related to the assurance of the detection process.

This scheme is suitable for watermarking some numerical data since the errors introduced in the watermarking process are under control. Parameter ξ is used to control the errors introduced to individual values; parameter γ is used to control the fraction of the numerical values that are modified in watermark insertion. These two parameters can be adjusted to constrain watermarking errors within measurement tolerance in many numerical data sets such as meteorological data, gene expression data, parameter data on semiconductor parts, and forest cover data [1].

2.2 Watermarking Categorical Data

Since any bit change to a categorical value may render the value meaningless, Agrawal and Kiernan's scheme [1] cannot be directly applied to watermarking categorical data. To solve this problem, Sion [21] proposed to watermark a categorical attribute by changing some of its values to other values of the attribute (e.g., "red" is changed to "green") if such change is tolerable in certain applications.

Sion's scheme is equivalent to Agrawal and Kiernan's scheme in selecting a number of tuples for watermarking a categorical attribute A. The scheme scans each tuple r and seeds a pseudo-random sequence generator $\mathcal{S}$ with a secret key $\mathcal{K}$ in concatenation with the tuple's primary key $r.P$. If $\mathcal{S}_1$, the first number generated by $\mathcal{S}$, satisfies ($\mathcal{S}_1 \mod \gamma = 0$), then the current tuple r is selected, otherwise the tuple is ignored, where γ controls the percentage of tuples selected. Given η tuples in relation R, roughly η/γ values of attribute A are selected for watermark insertion.

For each selected tuple r, exactly one bit is chosen from watermark information wm_data and is embedded to $r.A$, where the watermark information wm_data consists of roughly η/γ bits generated from a shorter watermark wm using error correcting code (ECC). The bit position that is chosen is determined by mapping S_2 uniformly to the range of wm_data indexes (this can be done by using a pseudo-random number generator or using an embedding map as stated in [21]). To embed the chosen bit b, the current categorical value $r.A$ is changed to another valid value of A, which is chosen from a list L_A of all valid values of A. In this process, any value a can be chosen from L_A (to replace $r.A$) as long as a's index in L_A has the least significant bit b. This flexibility in value selection can be exploited to maintain certain distribution properties of A in watermark insertion.

For watermark detection, a number of tuples are selected the same way as in watermark insertion, based on S_1. Then, for each selected tuple r, a bit position in wm_data is located the same way as in watermark insertion, based on S_2. The corresponding bit value in wm_data is extracted from the least significant bit of the index of $r.A$ in the list L_A. After all of the tuples are processed, the ECC takes as input wm_data and produces the corresponding wm. The ECC can tolerate certain errors in detecting wm_data and still produce the same wm in watermark detection.

This watermarking scheme has been applied to binned medical data in a hierachical manner so as to protect copyright in the presence of generalization attack that is specific to the binned data [2].

3 Distortion

While the watermarking errors introduced to numerical values can be made small, thus tolerable to certain data applications as illustrated in [1], the errors introduced to categorical data can be significant, at least to individual values. In [13], Li, Guo, and Jajodia introduced a distortion-free scheme for watermarking categorical data (it can also be directly applied to watermarking numerical data with no errors). In this solution, all η tuples in a database relation R are first securely divided into g groups according to a secret key $\mathcal{K}$. A different watermark is embedded and verified in each group independently. As a result, any modifications to the watermarked data can be detected and localized to the group level with high probabilities.

3.1 Distortion-Free Watermarking

Algorithms 1 and 2 describe the watermark insertion process. First, a (keyed) tuple hash and a (keyed) primary key hash are computed for each tuple r_i using a HMAC function. The tuple hash values are computed based on a fixed order of attributes. Based on the primary key hash values, all tuples are securely divided into g groups. The grouping is only a virtual operation, which means that it does not change the physical position of the tuples. After grouping, all tuples in each group are sorted according to their primary key hash. Like grouping, the sorting operation does not change the physical position of tuples either. Each group is then watermarked independently.

Algorithm 2 shows the embedding process in each group. A (keyed) group hash value is computed based on the tuple hash values in a sorted order. A watermark, the length of which is equal to the number of tuple-pairs in the current group, is extracted from the group hash value. To embed the watermark, for each tuple pair, the order of the two tuples are changed or unchanged (physically in the original database) to represent a corresponding watermark bit 1 or 0, where 0 is encoded by the ascendant order and 1 by the descendant order. Since only the order of the tuples is changed, the watermark insertion does not introduce any error to the underlying data.

Algorithm 1 Watermark embedding

1: For all $k = 1, \ldots g$, $q_k = 0$
2: **for** $i = 1$ to η **do**
3:    $h_i = HMAC(\mathcal{K}, r_i)$ // tuple hash
4:    $h_i^p = HMAC(\mathcal{K}, r_i.P)$ // primary key hash
5:    $k = h_i^p \bmod g$
6:    $r_i \rightarrow \mathcal{G}_k$ // Virtual operation: assign tuple r_i to group k
7:    $q_k + +$
8: **end for**
9: **for** $k = 1$ to g **do**
10:    watermark embedding in $\mathcal{G}_k$ // See algorithm 2
11: **end for**

Algorithms 3 and 4 describe the watermark detection process. As in watermark insertion, the primary key hash is computed for each tuple and all tuples are divided into groups. Each group is processed independently. In a group, the tuples are first sorted according to their primary key hash values. Like watermark insertion, the sorting is a virtual operation and does not involve order change of any tuples. Based on the tuple hash of the sorted tuples, a group hash value is computed. Then, a watermark W is extracted from the group hash. The watermark W is the one that is supposed to have been embedded if the underlying data were watermarked. On the other hand, a binary string W' is extracted from the tuples in this group. For every tuple pair, if their tuple hash values are in ascendant order, the corresponding bit in W' is extracted to be zero; otherwise, it is one. If W' matches W, the data in the group are authentic; otherwise, the data in this group have been modified or tampered with.

Algorithm 2 Watermark embedding in $\mathcal{G}_k$

1: sort tuples in $\mathcal{G}_k$ in ascendant order according to their primary key hash values// Virtual operation
2: $\mathcal{H} = HMAC(\mathcal{K}, h_1')$; $\mathcal{H} = HMAC(\mathcal{K}, \mathcal{H}|h_2')$; ... $\mathcal{H} = HMAC(\mathcal{K}, \mathcal{H}|h_{q_k}')$ // group hash, where $h_i'(i = 1, \cdots q_k)$ is the tuple hash of the ith tuple after ordering
3: $W = extractBits(\mathcal{H}, q_k/2)$ // See lines 10-17
4: **for** $i = 1, i < q_k, i = i + 2$ **do**
5:    **if** $W[i/2] == 1$ **then**
6:       switch the position of r_i and r_{i+1} physically in DB
7:    **end if**
8: **end for**
9:
10: function $extractBits(\mathcal{H}, \ell)\{$
11: **if** length($\mathcal{H}$) $\geq \ell$ **then**
12:    W = concatenation of first ℓ selected bits from $\mathcal{H}$ // in most cases, $\mathcal{H}$ is longer than ℓ
13: **else**
14:    $m = \ell$ - length($\mathcal{H}$)
15:    W = concatenation of $\mathcal{H}$ and extractBits($\mathcal{H}$, m)
16: **end if**
17: return $W\}$

Algorithm 3 Watermark detection

1: For all $k = 1, \ldots g$, $q_k = 0$
2: **for** $i = 1$ to η **do**
3:    $h_i = HMAC(\mathcal{K}, r_i)$
4:    $h_i^p = HMAC(\mathcal{K}, r_i.P)$
5:    $k = h_i^p \bmod g$
6:    $r_i \to \mathcal{G}_k$
7:    $q_k + +$
8: **end for**
9: **for** $k = 1$ to g **do**
10:    watermark verification in $\mathcal{G}_k$ // See algorithm 4
11: **end for**

In this solution, the number g of groups is used to make a tradeoff between security and localization. On the one hand, the smaller the value of g, the larger the probability of detecting modifications in watermark detection, and the more secure the proposed scheme. On the other hand, this leads to a larger group size; thus, one can localize modifications less precisely as there are more tuples in each group.

3.2 Embedding Capacity

Li, Guo, and Jajodia's scheme embeds one bit for each pair of selected tuples; thus, $q_k/2$ bits are embedded into each group of q_k selected tuples.

Algorithm 4 Watermark verification in $\mathcal{G}_k$

1: sort tuples in $\mathcal{G}_k$ in ascendant order according to their primary key hash //
   Virtual operation
2: $\mathcal{H} = HMAC(\mathcal{K}, h'_1)$; $\mathcal{H} = HMAC(\mathcal{K}, \mathcal{H}|h'_2); \ldots \mathcal{H} = HMAC(\mathcal{K}, \mathcal{H}|h'_{q_k})$ //
   group hash, where $h'_i (i = 1, \cdots q_k)$ is the tuple hash of the ith tuple after ordering
3: $W = extractBits(\mathcal{H}, q_k/2)$ // See lines 10-17 in Algorithm 2
4: **for** $i = 1, i < q_k, i = i + 2$ **do**
5:     **if** $h_i \leq h_{i+1}$ **then**
6:         $W'[i/2] = 0$
7:     **else**
8:         $W'[i/2] = 1$
9:     **end if**
10: **end for**
11: **if** $W' == W$ **then**
12:     $\mathcal{V} = TRUE$
13: **else**
14:     $\mathcal{V} = FALSE$
15: **end if**

The embedding capacity can be further increased such that at most $\ln q_k!$ bits can be embedded into each group of q_k selected tuples. The increase in embedding capacity is illustrated in Table 1.

Table 1. Embedding capacity

q_k	10	20	30	40	50	60	70	80	90	100
$q_k/2$	5	10	15	20	25	30	35	40	45	50
$\ln q_k!$	15	42	74	110	148	188	230	273	318	363

Given a group of q_k selected tuples, a group hash $\mathcal{H}$ is calculated the same way as in Algorithm 2. Then, a watermark $W = extractBits(\mathcal{H}, \ln q_k!)$ of length $\ln q_k!$ is derived from $\mathcal{H}$. The watermark W is embedded into this group by permuting the order of the tuples. The new order π can be easily calculated using Myrvold and Ruskey's linear permutation unranking algorithm [19] based on W:

1. $\pi = (0, \ldots, q_k - 1)$
2. $unrank(q_k, W, \pi)$ // see lines 4-5 below
3. return π

4. function $unrank(q_k, W, \pi)$ // W is in integer form
5. if $q_k > 0$ then swap $\pi[q_k - 1]$ and $\pi[W \mod q_k]$; $unrank(q_k - 1, \lfloor W/q_k \rfloor, \pi)$

The tuples in this group are re-arranged such that π indicates the order of their tuple hash values.

In watermark detection, a group of q_k tuples are selected and the order π of their tuple hash values is identified, where π is a permutation of $(0, \ldots, q_k-1)$. A watermark W' can be derived from π using Myrvold and Ruskey's linear permutation ranking algorithm [19]:

1. let π^{-1} be a binary vector such that $\pi^{-1}[\pi[i]] = i$ for $i = 0, \ldots q_k - 1$
2. $W' = \text{rank}(q_k, \pi, \pi^{-1})$ // see lines 4-7 below
3. return W' in binary form

4. function $\text{rank}(q_k, \pi, \pi^{-1})$
5. if $q_k = 1$ then return 0
6. $s = \pi[q_k-1]$; swap $\pi[q_k-1]$ and $\pi[\pi^{-1}[q_k-1]]$; swap $\pi^{-1}[s]$ and $\pi^{-1}[q_k-1]$
7. return $s + q_k * \text{rank}(q_k-1, \pi, \pi^{-1})$

Based on the tuple hash of the sorted tuples, a group hash value is computed. Then, a watermark W is extracted from the group hash. If W matches W', the tuples in this group are authentic; otherwise, the data in this group have been modified or tampered with.

4 Sensitivity

Watermarking schemes can be classified to be either *robust* or *fragile* according to their sensitivity to typical database attacks. A scheme is robust (fragile, respectively) if it is difficult to make an embedded watermark undetectable (unchanged, respectively) in the presence of database attacks, provided that the attacks do not degrade the usefulness of the data significantly (otherwise, there is no need to protect the data nor to detect the watermark). Robust watermarks are usually used for copyright protection, ownership proof, or traitor tracing, while fragile watermarks can be used for tamper detection and localization.

Typical database attacks

To confuse watermark detection, various database attacks may be launched to watermarked databases. Typical database attacks include *tuple/ attribute insertion/ deletion/ reorganization*, *value modification/ suppression* (including random/ selective bit-flipping/ value-rounding), *invertibility attack* (attacker successfully discovers a fictitious watermark which is in fact a random occurrence from a watermarked database), *additive attack* (attacker embeds some additional watermarks into a watermarked database), and the *brute-force attack* against the secret key. The brute-force attack can be thwarted by assuming that the key is long enough (e.g., 160 bits) in watermarking.

False detection rates

The sensitivity of a watermarking scheme can be measured by the following false detection rates in watermark detection.

- For robust watermarking, we have
  - *False hit*: the probability of the original watermark being detected from unmarked data or a fictitious watermark being detected from watermarked data (i.e., invertibility attack).
  - *False miss*: the probability of not detecting the original watermark from watermarked data.
- For fragile watermarking, we have
  - *False hit*: the probability of the original watermark being detected from unmarked data.
  - *False miss*: the probability of not detecting any change to the embedded watermark from watermarked data.

The false detection rates in watermark detection must be low enough (e.g., 10^{-9}) in order for the detection result to be used as proof in court. The false miss rate should be investigated in the presence of various database attacks. Since the fragile watermark is not used for copyright protection, the invertibility attack is not meaningful.

4.1 Robust Watermarking

The robustness of watermarking can be achieved by using majority vote in watermark detection, as in Agrawal and Kiernan's scheme, or using ECC code, as in Sion's scheme. For simplicity reasons, we focus on Agrawal and Kiernan's scheme.

Consider Bernoulli trials with probability p of success and q of failure. Let $b(k; m, p) = \binom{m}{k} p^k q^{m-k}$ be the probability that m Bernoulli trials result in k successes and $m - k$ failures, where $\binom{m}{k} = \frac{m!}{k!(m-k)!}, 0 \leq k \leq m$. Let $B(k; m, p) = \sum_{i=k+1}^{m} b(i; m, p)$ be the probability of having *more than k* successes in m Bernoulli trials. In Agrawal and Kiernan's scheme, a watermark is detected if more than τ in percentage of the embedded bits are detected correctly. If the watermark detection is applied to unmarked data (or watermarked data with a different secret key), the detection can be considered as Bernoulli trials with a probability of $1/2$ that a correct value will be found in a specific bit position. Assuming ω bits are checked in watermark detection, then the false hit rate is $B(\lfloor \tau\omega \rfloor; \omega, 0.5)$. The false hit rate is extremely low if τ and ω are reasonably large. For example, the false hit rate can be as low as 10^{-10} for $\tau \geq 0.6$ and $\omega \geq 1000$.

The false miss rate can be analyzed under various attack scenarios. A typical modification attack is that an attacker randomly flips every least significant bit with a probability $p < 0.5$ (if $p \geq 0.5$, one can flip every bit back before watermark detection). For the detection algorithm to fail to recover the correct watermark, at least $\omega - \lfloor \tau\omega \rfloor$ embedded bits must be toggled. Thus, the false miss rate is $B(\omega - \lfloor \tau\omega \rfloor - 1; \omega, p)$. An attacker has to flip a significant portion of tuples in order to get a high probability of success in this attack.

Agrawal and Kiernan's scheme relies on the following assumptions to maintain its robustness. First, the watermarked relation has a primary key attribute that either does not change or else can be recovered. The rationale behind this is that a primary key attribute contains essential information and that modification or deletion of this information will substantially reduce the value of the data. With this assumption, the watermark detection is robust against tuple insertion/deletion and it is not affected by tuple reorganization. Second, the names of some, if not all, of the watermarked attributes either do not change or else can be recovered in watermark detection. Under the above two assumptions, the scheme is robust against attribute operations including insertion, deletion, and reorganization.

4.2 Fragile Watermarking

The purpose of fragile watermarking is not to protect copyright, but to detect and localize possible attacks that modify a distributed or published database. Li, Guo, and Jajodia's scheme [13] is an example of fragile watermarking scheme. This scheme embeds a watermark by manipulating the order of the tuples in each group, where the watermark is computed by hashing all tuple values in a group. Any change to the underlying data can be detected with a high probability in watermark detection. Assuming that q is the number of tuples in a group, the false hit/miss rate is $\frac{1}{2^{\frac{q}{2}}}$ in Li, Guo, and Jajodia's scheme, and $\frac{1}{2^{\ln q!}}$ in its extended version with the maximal embedding capacity.

Li, Guo, and Jajodia's fragile watermarking scheme can be further extended to encode watermark information not only to the order of tuples, but also to the order of attributes. The fundamental assumption is that re-shuffling rows or columns in relational databases will not degrade the quality of data due to the essential properties of relational data[1]. This extension of the scheme can further increase the precision in tamper localization in the case that the database relation consists of a large number of attributes (and tuples).

In such an extension, all attributes are securely divided into a number of groups, just as all tuples are securely divided into a number of groups. The only difference is that the attribute grouping is based on attribute name hash (more precisely, hash of a secret key concatenated with attribute name and relation name), while the tuple grouping is based on primary key hash. For each block of data that corresponds to a particular group of tuples and a

---

[1] The essential properties that are widely recognized for relational data include: (i) Entries in columns are single-valued; (ii) Columns values are of the same type of data; (iii) Each row has a unique primary key; (iv) Each column has a unique attribute name; (v) The sequence of columns is insignificant; and (vi) The sequence of rows is insignificant.

particular group of attributes, a watermark is calculated by hashing all data values in this block organized in a fixed order of tuples and attributes (e.g., ascending order of primary key hash and attribute name hash) and encoded into the block by manipulating both the order of tuples and the order of attributes. As a result, any tampering with the watermarked data can be localized at the block level. This solution is distortion-free and can be easily extended to watermarking multi-dimensional data cubes.

Recently, Guo et al. [8] proposed another fragile watermarking scheme that can further improve the precision in tamper localization, assuming that the database relation to be watermarked has numerical attributes and that the errors introduced in two least significant bits of each value can be tolerated. In this solution, the tuples are first divided into groups, as in Li, Guo, and Jajodia's scheme. Within each group, a (keyed) tuple hash is computed for each tuple (with attributes organized in a fixed order), and a (keyed) attribute hash for each attribute (with tuples organized in a fixed order). When these hash values are computed, the two least significant bits of all attribute values are ignored. Each tuple hash is embedded into the corresponding tuple and each attribute hash into the corresponding attribute. For any value $r_i.A_j$ in the embedding process, the least significant bit of $r_i.A_j$ is set to the i-th bit of attribute A_j's hash, and the next least significant bit of $r_i.A_j$ is set to the j-th bit of tuple r_i's hash. In this way, the embedded hash values actually form a watermark grid, which helps to detect, localize, and characterize database attacks.

In watermark detection, as in watermark embedding, all tuples are divided into groups and all tuple/attribute hash values are computed for each group. Then, each tuple/attribute hash is compared to the related information extracted from the data. Different database attacks will show different mismatch patterns in watermark detection with high probabilities. If a value is modified in a group, then the corresponding tuple hash and attribute hash will not match the related extracted information. In such a case, the precision of tamper localization is down to the element level. If a tuple is deleted, all attribute hash values in this group will not match the related extracted information. If a tuple is inserted into a group, then all attribute hash values in this group plus the corresponding tuple hash will not match the related extracted information. If an attribute is deleted, all tuple hashes in all groups will not match the related extracted information. Finally, if an attribute is inserted, all tuple hashes in all groups and the corresponding attribute hash in each group will not match the related extracted information. The false hit and false miss rates in detection can be made extremely low if there are enough tuples and attributes in each group.

5 Watermark Information

5.1 From One-Bit Watermark to Multiple Bit Watermark

Back to Agrawal and Kiernan's scheme, the watermark information that is embedded is one-bit only given a predetermined embedding key. This can be seen clearly by extending it to embedding a multiple bits watermark $W = (w_0, \ldots, w_{\ell-1})$, as proposed by Li, Swarup, and Jajodia [15]. To embed W, the same procedure as in Agrawal and Kiernan's scheme is used to: (i) select some tuples; (ii) for each selected tuple r, select one numerical attribute; (iii) for each selected attribute, select one of ξ least significant bits; and (iv) compute a mark bit x for each selected bit. Now the difference is that the mark bit x is not used directly to replace the selected least significant bit; instead, w_i XOR x is used to replace the selected bit, where w_i is a watermark bit selected from W for $i = \mathcal{S}_5 \mod \ell$ (note that the first four random sequence numbers $\mathcal{S}_1 \sim \mathcal{S}_4$ generated for each tuple have already been used in Agrawal and Kiernan's scheme). Similar to Agrawal and Kiernan's scheme, each watermark bit is embedded multiple times and is detected with a majority vote (i.e., the percentage of correctly detected bits should be greater than threshold τ). The whole watermark W is correctly detected if every bit in W is correctly detected. Agrawal and Kiernan's scheme is a special case of Li, Swarup, and Jajodia's scheme where W is 1-bit zero.

Assume ω_i bits are extracted from the data for each watermark bit w_i in watermark detection. When Li, Swarup, and Jajodia's multi-bit watermarking scheme is applied to unmarked data, the false hit rate is $\prod_{i=0}^{\ell-1} B(\lceil \tau\omega_i \rceil; \omega_i, 0.5)$ $\leq \frac{1}{2^\ell}$ (i.e., the probability of detecting a particular binary string of length ℓ from unmarked data), where $\tau \geq 0.5$ is the threshold in the majority vote. This false hit rate is extremely low if the watermark string is long enough, regardless of the value of τ. When the scheme is applied to watermarked data, the false hit rate is $\prod_{i=0}^{\ell-1} 2B(\lceil \tau\omega_i \rceil; \omega_i, 0.5)$ (i.e., the probability of any binary string of length ℓ can be detected from watermarked data). This false hit rate can be made low by increasing the threshold τ. The false miss rate can be analyzed under a typical modification attack in which an attacker randomly flips every least significant bit with a probability $p < 0.5$. Under this attack, the false miss rate is $1 - \prod_{i=0}^{\ell-1}(1 - B(\omega_i - \lfloor \tau\omega_i \rfloor - 1; \omega_i, p))$.

Another multi-bit watermark scheme was proposed by Sion, Atallah, and Prabhakar [22]. The scheme is designed primarily for watermarking a set of real numbers $\{x_1, \ldots x_n\}$ by manipulating its distributions. The first step of watermark insertion is to sort the values according to a cryptographically keyed hash of the set of most significant bits of the normalized values. Then, a maximum number of non-intersecting subsets of values are formed, where each subset consists of a certain number of adjacent items after sorting. Embedding a watermark bit into a subset is achieved by making minor changes to some of the data values in this subset such that the number of values that are "outliers" in the distribution is less than a smaller threshold (for watermark bit zero) or greater than a larger threshold (for watermark bit one). Note that some of the groups may not be watermarkable given user-specified change tolerance. Also note that some redundant bits must be embedded such that the original multi-bit watermark can be recovered in watermark detection even if some of the encoded bits are destroyed in data attacks. Compared with Li, Swarup, and Jajodia's multi-bit watermarking scheme, this scheme is robust against linear transformation and does not depend on the existence of a primary key. On the other hand, it incurs more watermarking overhead as it requires ordering, grouping, and distribution-manipulating.

5.2 From Multiple Bit Watermark to Fingerprint

Li, Swarup, and Jajodia's multi-bit watermarking scheme can be easily extended to fingerprinting relational databases [17]. Fingerprinting is a different class of information hiding techniques that insert digital marks into data with the purpose of identifying the users who have been provided data, as oppose to watermarking's purpose of identifying the sources of data. In fingerprinting, the owner of the data embeds a user-specific mark into a data copy provided to a user; he can subsequently detect the fingerprint in pirated data and use it to identify the traitor who distributed the data.

Li, Swarup, and Jajodia's fingerprinting scheme is the same as their multi-bit watermarking scheme except that the multi-bit watermark information $W = (w_0, \ldots, w_{\ell-1})$ is used to encode each user's identification information, instead of the owner's. The watermark information is called fingerprint, as it is used to distinguish among different users for traitor tracing.

Since different fingerprints are embedded into different data copies, it is impossible to determine what the correct fingerprint is before fingerprint detection. This is different from watermark detection, where the correct watermark is fixed and known. To solve this problem, two counters – one for bit value zero, and one for bit value one – are maintained for each fingerprint bit, recording the number of times that the fingerprint bit is recovered from the data as to be either zero or one. At the end of fingerprint detection, the fingerprint bit is set to be zero or one if the corresponding counter exceeds τ (in percentage) of the sum of the two counters for this bit; otherwise, the fingerprint detection terminates with no traitor detected. If a binary string is recovered at the end of fingerprint detection, it can be used to identify a traitor (e.g., via the tracing algorithm proposed in [3]).

Since fingerprinting aims to identify a traitor, it can be subject to attacks that cause an innocent principal (or no principal) to be identified as a traitor. As a result, the false hit rate in fingerprinting can be further classified as

- Misdiagnosis false hit: the probability of detecting a valid fingerprint from data that has not been fingerprinted.
- Misattribution false hit: the probability of detecting an incorrect but valid fingerprint from fingerprinted data.

When fingerprint detection is applied to unmarked data, it may return some binary string $(f_0, \ldots f_{\ell-1})$ as a potential fingerprint. Let f_i be extracted ω_i times from data. Then, f_i is detected to be zero or one with the same probability $B(\lfloor \tau \omega_i \rfloor; \omega_i, 0.5)$. The fingerprint scheme detects a binary string as a potential fingerprint with probability $\prod_{i=0}^{\ell-1} 2B(\lfloor \tau \omega_i \rfloor; \omega_i, 0.5)$, where the factor 2 means that each bit could be either zero or one. Let N be the total number of valid fingerprints. The probability that the binary string is a valid fingerprint is $\frac{N}{2^\ell}$. The overall misdiagnosis false hit is $\frac{N}{2^\ell} \prod_{i=0}^{\ell-1} 2B(\lfloor \tau \omega_i \rfloor; \omega_i, 0.5) = N \cdot \prod_{i=0}^{\ell-1} B(\lfloor \tau \omega_i \rfloor; \omega_i, 0.5)$. The misdiagnosis false hit has upper bound $\frac{N}{2^\ell}$, which is tight in the case that all ω_i are odd and $\tau = 0.5$. The upper bound is independent of the size of the database relation being checked.

The misattribution false hit and false miss rates can be analyzed under a typical modification attack in which an attacker randomly flips every least significant bit with a probability $p < 0.5$ in fingerprinted data. For the detection algorithm to extract a binary bit for fingerprint bit f_i, either at most $\omega_i - \lfloor \tau \omega_i \rfloor - 1$ of its embedded bits are toggled, or more than $\lfloor \tau \omega_i \rfloor$ of its embedded bits are toggled. If the detection algorithm extracts a binary string, the probability that the binary string is a valid but "innocent" fingerprint is $\frac{N-1}{2^\ell}$. Therefore, the false misattribution false hit is $\frac{N-1}{2^\ell} \Pi_{i=0}^{\ell-1} (1 - B(\omega_i - \lfloor \tau \omega_i \rfloor - 1; \omega_i, p) + B(\lfloor \tau \omega_i \rfloor; \omega_i, p)) \le \frac{N-1}{2^\ell}$. The misattribution false hit rate has an upper bound $\frac{N-1}{2^\ell}$ since $B(\lfloor \tau \omega_i \rfloor; \omega_i, p) \le B(\omega_i - \lfloor \tau \omega_i \rfloor - 1; \omega_i, p)$ when $\tau \ge 0.5$. The upper bound is tight in the case that all ω_i are odd and $\tau = 0.5$. It is straightforward to get the false miss rate

$$1 - \Pi_{i=0}^{\ell-1}(1 - B(\omega_i - \lfloor \tau \omega_i \rfloor - 1; \omega_i, p)) -$$
$$\frac{N-1}{2^\ell} \Pi_{i=0}^{\ell-1}(1 - B(\omega_i - \lfloor \tau \omega_i \rfloor - 1; \omega_i, p) + B(\lfloor \tau \omega_i \rfloor; \omega_i, p)).$$

where $1 - \Pi_{i=0}^{\ell-1}(1 - B(\omega_i - \lfloor \tau \omega_i \rfloor - 1; \omega_i, p))$ is the probability that the entire fingerprint is detected incorrectly.

Fingerprinting schemes are susceptible to collusion attacks. A collusion attack is launched by a coalition who has access to different fingerprinted copies of the same data. Members of a coalition can identify the differences in their fingerprinted copies, change the identified values to damage the corresponding fingerprint bits, and create a useful data copy that does not implicate any member of the coalition. Note that the collusion attack is specific to fingerprinting and there is no collusion attack in watermarking setting.

To thwart collusion attacks, the fingerprint codes need to be carefully designed so that information that a coalition cannot detect can be used to trace at least one of the traitors. Such fingerprinting codes have been rigorously studied in the literature of cryptography. A well-known fingerprinting code, called BoSh code (Boneh and Shaw [3]), is designed to be c-secure with ϵ-error, as it enables the capture of a member of a coalition of at most c members with probability at least $1 - \epsilon$, where c and ϵ are two design parameters (increasing c or reducing ϵ will result in longer BoSh codes).

BoSh codes can be adapted such that for each user, the owner of a database can generate a c-secure and ϵ-error BoSh code using a secret key and the user's identification information [17]. If this BoSh code is directly used as a fingerprint, the misdiagnosis false hit rate will be 100 percent, as the tracing algorithm proposed in [3] returns exactly one "traitor" no matter what the input is (the assumed input in [3] is pirated data under collusion attacks). The solution to reduce the misdiagnosis false hit is to partition each fingerprint $\mathcal{F}$ of ℓ bits into two parts. The first part, $\mathcal{F}_1$ of ℓ_1 bits, is used as a multi-bit watermark, while the second part, $\mathcal{F}_2$ of ℓ_2 bits, is the adapted BoSh code generated from a secret key and a user's identification information. The entire fingerprint $\mathcal{F} = \mathcal{F}_1|\mathcal{F}_2$ of length $\ell = \ell_1 + \ell_2$ is embedded into a data copy as in a multi-bit watermarking scheme. For fingerprint detection, a binary string $\mathcal{F}$ is extracted from a suspicious data copy also as in a multi-bit watermarking scheme. From the extracted fingerprint template $\mathcal{F}$, its watermark part $\mathcal{F}_1$ is first checked against the codeword used in fingerprint insertion. If there is a single bit mismatch, the detection procedure returns none suspected. If the watermark part passes the first phase examination, the fingerprint part $\mathcal{F}_2$ will become the input of the tracing algorithm proposed in [3] for identifying a traitor.

If fingerprint detection is applied to a pirated data copy in the presence of a collusion attack only, the watermark part can be detected correctly. This is because the collusion attack can only change the values if the coalition has data copies that differ in those values. Then, the fingerprint part is fed into the tracing algorithm proposed by Boneh and Shaw [3]. The tracing algorithm will return exactly one buyer with a probability that this returned buyer is indeed a traitor in the coalition being greater than $1 - \epsilon$, as proved in [3]. In such a case, the false miss rate is zero, and misattribution false hit is no larger than ϵ.

Now, consider the misdiagnosis false hit when fingerprint detection is applied to unmarked data. Note that the watermark part is the same for all users and it is examined first in the detection process. The probability of detecting a binary string for the watermark part is $\Pi_{i=0}^{\ell_1-1} 2B(\lfloor \tau\omega_i \rfloor; \omega_i, 0.5)$. Now there is only one valid watermark codeword. Thus, the probability that the detected binary string matches the watermark codeword is $\frac{1}{2^{\ell_1}}$. Since whenever watermark detection succeeds, fingerprint detection returns exactly one valid buyer's identity, the misdiagnosis false hit is $\frac{1}{2^{\ell_1}} \Pi_{i=0}^{\ell_1-1} 2B(\lfloor \tau\omega_i \rfloor; \omega_i, 0.5)$ $= \Pi_{i=0}^{\ell_1-1} B(\lfloor \tau\omega_i \rfloor; \omega_i, 0.5) \leq \frac{1}{2^{\ell_1}}$, which has an upper bound $\frac{1}{2^{\ell_1}}$. The upper bound is tight in the case that all ω_i are odd and $\tau = 0.5$. The misdiagnosis false hit rate can be reduced exponentially by increasing ℓ_1; it can also be decreased by increasing τ.

It should be noted that length of a collusion resistant fingerprint is quite long even for small c and moderate ϵ. (All collusion resistant fingerprints are intrinsically long and there is no significant improvement in this regard to BoSh codes so far.) For example, for $c = 2$ (where at most two buyers can formulate a coalition), $\epsilon = 0.01$ and $N = 1000$, the length of the collusion resistant codeword is $51,695$; when $c = 2$ increases to $c = 3$ and 4, the length increases to $317,185$ and $1,098,622$, respectively. Such long fingerprints are only suitable for very large databases such as terabyte scientific databases, surveillance databases, and anti-terror databases [17]. Nonetheless, the database fingerprinting scheme mitigates the damage of collusion attacks by embedding multiple copies of each fingerprint bit and recovering it with a majority vote. As a result, the probability of detecting a traitor in collusion attacks does not drop dramatically even as the coalition size goes beyond c. A high detection rate can be obtained by either increasing c or decreasing ϵ as shown experimentally in [17].

5.3 From One Watermark to Multiple Watermarks

A major concern in database watermarking is that a pirate may simply add additional watermarks to watermarked data so as to confuse watermark detection (i.e., additive attack). Defending against this type of additive attacks demands an in-depth analysis of multiple watermarks.

When a group of people jointly create a database, the participants may embed their own watermarks separately into the database, and thus can verify their ownership independently. Such an application also requires basic research on multiple watermarks.

We consider to extend Agrawal and Kiernan's watermarking scheme to allow for multiple watermarks. Assume that n watermarks $\mathcal{W}_1, \ldots \mathcal{W}_n$ are embedded into database relation R sequentially with different secret keys $\mathcal{K}_1, \ldots, \mathcal{K}_n$ but with the same parameters γ, ν and ξ. Interference exists among multiple watermarks, as an embedded bit of one watermark could be flipped back and forth by some later embedded watermarks. The interference among multiple watermarks can be quantified as follows. Let $p_c = \frac{1}{\gamma \nu \xi}$ be the probability that a least significant bit is used in embedding a single watermark. For any mark bit of watermark $\mathcal{W}_{n_1}$, the probability that this mark bit is modified by other watermarks is $p_{n_1, n} = \frac{1}{2}[1 - (1 - p_c)^{n-n_1}] < 0.5$. For any least significant bit of the original data, the probability that this bit is modified by all watermarks is $p_{0,n} = \frac{1}{2}[1 - (1 - p_c)^n] < 0.5$.

If watermark detection is applied to unmarked data using each of n different valid secret keys $\mathcal{K}_1, \ldots, \mathcal{K}_n$, then the probability that at least one valid watermark is detected, or the false hit rate, is $1 - (1 - B(\lfloor \tau \omega \rfloor; \omega, 0.5))^n$, assuming that ω bits are detected for each watermark.

The false miss rate can be analyzed under a typical modification attack in which an attacker randomly toggles each least significant bit with a probability $p < 0.5$. Under this attack, the probability that the n_1-th watermark cannot be detected from the modified data, or the false miss rate, is $B(\omega - \lfloor \tau \omega \rfloor - 1; \omega, p_{n_1,n}(1 - p) + (1 - p_{n_1,n})p)$. The reason is that after modification, each mark bit of the n_1-th watermark could be modified either due to watermark interference or by data modification. The probability of it being modified due to watermark interference is $p_{n_1,n}$, and the probability of it being modified by a data modification attack is p. Therefore, the probability of it being modified in any way is $p_{n_1,n}(1-p) + (1 - p_{n_1,n})p$. The false miss rate in this case is the probability of at least $\omega - \lfloor \tau\omega \rfloor$ embedded bits out of ω bits of the n_1-th watermark being modified.

It can be verified that as $n \to \infty$, the false hit rate approaches 100% and the false miss rate approaches 50%. The more watermarks embedded into a data copy, the larger the false detection rates in watermark detection, and the more errors introduced to the underlying data in watermark insertion.

The watermarking errors should be carefully evaluated so as to preserve data quality. The errors can be controlled at two different levels. At item level, the errors introduced to individual values are bounded because no alteration is allowed beyond ξ least significant bits. At aggregation level, the errors introduced to descriptive statistics of attribute values can be quantified. In particular, one can study the watermarking error introduced to the mean of an integer-valued attribute with values $x_1, \ldots x_\eta$. After embedding n watermarks, value x_i becomes $x_i + e_i(n)$, where $e_i(n)$ is a random variable. For value x_i, if its least significant bit j is modified in watermark insertion, the modification will cause change $+2^j$ or -2^j to x_i with the same probability $1/2$. Knowing that the least significant bit j will be modified in watermark insertion with a probability $p_{0,n}$ (due to watermark interference), one can derive that the mean of $e_i(n)$ is zero and the variance of $e_i(n)$ is $\frac{p_{0,n}(2^{2\xi}-1)}{3}$. Let $\mu = \frac{\sum_{i=1}^{\eta} x_i}{\eta}$ be the mean of original attribute values and let $\mu_e(n) = \frac{\sum_{i=1}^{\eta} e_i(n)}{\eta}$ be the error in computing μ after watermarking. The expected error in computing μ after watermarking is $E[\mu_e(n)] = 0$ and the variance of the error is $V[\mu_e(n)] = \frac{p_{0,n}(2^{2\xi}-1)}{3\eta}$. It can be verified that the variance of watermarking error is monotonic increasing with n to approach its upper limit $\frac{2^{2\xi}-1}{6\eta}$.

An application of multiple watermarks is to defend against additive attacks. In an additive attack, a pirate inserts additional watermarks to watermarked data so as to confuse ownership proof. A pirate can insert watermarks to claim ownership of the data or claim that the data were provided to a buyer legitimately. An additive attack can be thwarted by raising the watermarking error to a predetermined threshold such that any additive attack would introduce more errors than the limit [16]. In the case of additive attack, the ownership dispute can be resolved by comparing whose watermarks can be detected more. To gain advantage in an ownership dispute, a pirate is forced to embed a large enough number of watermarks. Consequently, the pirated data is less useful or less competitive compared to the originally-watermarked data and it is not necessary for the owner to claim ownership over such data.

Multiple watermarks can also be used for proving joint ownership in a scenario where a database relation is jointly created by n participants. Each participant can embed a watermark with his own key so that he can prove his ownership independently. The question is whether the underlying data can be watermarked. Given a certain robustness requirement and error constraint, a maximum number of watermarks can be determined based on our analysis on false detection rates and watermarking errors.

6 Verifiability

One common feature of most robust watermarking techniques is that they are secret key-based, where ownership is proven through the knowledge of a secret key that is used for both watermark insertion and detection. The secret key-based approach is not suitable for proving ownership to the public (e.g., in a court). To prove ownership of suspicious data, the owner has to reveal his secret key to the public for watermark detection. After being used one time, the key is no longer secret. With access to the key, a pirate can invalidate watermark detection by either removing watermarks from protected data or adding a false watermark to non-watermarked data.

Li and Deng [12] proposed a unique database watermarking scheme that can be used for publicly verifiable ownership protection. Given a database relation to be published or distributed, the owner of the data uses a public watermark key to generate a public watermark, which is a relation with binary attributes. Anyone can use the watermark key and the watermark to check whether a suspicious copy of the data is watermarked, and, if so, prove the ownership of the data by checking a watermark certificate officially signed by a trusted certificate authority, DB-CA. The watermark certificate contains the owner's ID, the watermark key, the hashes of both the watermark and DB relation, the first time the relation was certified, the validity period of the current certificate, and the DB-CA's signature. The watermark certificate may be revoked and re-certified in the case of identity change, ownership change, DB-CA compromise, or data update. Therefore, the revocation status also needs to be checked in proving the ownership.

Li and Deng's scheme watermarks a database relation R whose schema is $R(P, A_0, \ldots, A_{\nu-1})$, where P is a primary key attribute. There is no constraint on the types of attributes used for watermarking; the attributes can be integer numeric, real numeric, character, Boolean, or any other types. For each attribute of a tuple, *the most significant bit* (MSB) of its standard binary representation may be used in the generation of a watermark. It is assumed that any change to an MSB would introduce intolerable error to the underlying data value.

In this scheme, the watermark key $\mathcal{K}$ is public and may take any value (numerical, binary, or categorical) selected by the owner. There is no constraint on the formation of the key. To reduce unnecessary confusion, the watermark key should be unique to the owner with respect to the watermarked relation. The watermark key is used to decide the composition of a public *watermark* W. The watermark W is a database relation whose scheme is $W(P, W_0, \ldots,$

Algorithm 5 Generating public watermark W for DB relation R

1: **for** each tuple r in R **do**
2:     construct a tuple t in W with the same primary key $t.P = r.P$
3:     **for** i=0; i < ϑ; i= i+1 **do**
4:         $j = S_i$ mod (the number of attributes in r) // S is seeded with $\mathcal{K}$ and $r.P$.
5:         $t.W_i$ = MSB of the j-th attribute in r
6:         delete the j-th attribute from r
7:     **end for**
8: **end for**
9: return W

$W_{\vartheta-1}$), where $W_0, \ldots, W_{\vartheta-1}$ are binary attributes. Compared to DB relation R, the watermark (relation) W has the same number η of tuples and the same primary key attribute P. The number ϑ of binary attributes in W, which is called the watermark generation parameter, determines the number ω of bits in W, where $\omega = \eta \cdot \vartheta$ and $\vartheta \leq \nu$.

The process of generating watermark W is shown in Algorithm 5. The MSBs of selected values are used for generating the watermark. The whole process does not introduce any distortions to the original data. The use of MSBs is for thwarting potential attacks that modify the data. Since the watermark key K, the watermark W, and the watermark generation algorithm are publicly known, anyone can locate those MSBs in R that are used for generating W. However, an attacker cannot modify those MSBs without introducing intolerable errors to the data.

In the construction of watermark W, each tuple in relation R contributes ϑ MSBs from different attributes that are pseudo-randomly selected based on the watermark key and the primary key of the tuple. It is impossible for an attacker to remove all of the watermark bits by deleting some but not all of the tuples and/or attributes from the watermarked data. The larger the watermark generation parameter ϑ, the more robust the scheme is against such deletion attacks.

In watermark detection, as in watermark generation, the MSB bits of ϑ values from each tuple are located based on the watermark key and the primary key. Based on the primary key values (which are assumed to not change or else can be recovered), the detected MSBs are compared to the corresponding bits in the public watermark W. The ownership is claimed if the percentage of the matches is more than a threshold $\tau \geq 0.5$, where τ is called the watermark detection parameter. The watermark detection parameter is used to balance between false hit and false miss.

It can be assumed that each MSB in W has the same probability of $1/2$ to be 1 or 0. If this is not the case, one can randomize the MSBs in W by XOR'ing them with pseudo-random mask bits. The mask bits can be computed from the watermark key together with the primary key for each tuple. With this assumption, the false hit rate (i.e., the probability of claiming ownership over non-watermarked data) is $B(\lfloor \tau \eta \vartheta \rfloor; \eta \vartheta, 0.5)$. The false hit is monotonic decreasing with both watermark insertion parameter ϑ and detection parameter τ. On the one hand, the larger the insertion parameter ϑ, the more MSBs are included in the watermark and the smaller the false hit. On the other hand, the false hit can be decreased by increasing the detection parameter τ, which is the least fraction of watermark bits required for ownership assertion.

Since both the watermark key and the watermark are public in our scheme, an attacker can pinpoint the MSBs of the watermarked values. A simple attack would be to flip some of those MSBs so that the watermark detection will detect no match. In the presence of this attack, the false miss rate is 1 if no less than $\vartheta \eta - \lfloor \tau \vartheta \eta \rfloor$ watermarked MSBs are flipped, the false miss rate is 0 otherwise. To achieve the best robustness, one may choose $\vartheta = \nu$ and $\tau \approx 0.5$. (However, this would increase the false hit rate.) In this extreme case, approximately 50% of the data values would have to be intolerably modified so as to defeat the watermark detection.

While watermark detection can be performed by anyone who has access to the public watermark key, the ownership is proven by further checking the corresponding watermark certificate. A watermark certificate C of relation R is a tuple $\langle ID, \mathcal{K}, HASH(W), HASH(R), T, \text{DB-CA}, Sig \rangle$, where ID is the identity of the owner of R, $\mathcal{K}$ is the owner's watermark key, W is the public watermark, T is the validity information, DB-CA is the trusted authority who signs the certificate by generating a signature Sig. The validity information is a triple $T = \langle T_{origin}, T_{start}, T_{end} \rangle$ indicating the original time T_{origin} when the DB relation is first certified, the starting time T_{start}, and the ending time T_{end} of this certificate in the current binding. When the DB relation is certified for the first time, T_{origin} should be the same as T_{start}. Compared with the identity certificate or attribute certificate, the watermark certificate not only has a validity period defined by T_{start} and T_{end}, but also contains the original time T_{origin}.

The original time T_{origin} can be used to thwart additive attacks. We assume that the owner of the data will not make the data available to potential attackers unless the data is watermarked and a valid watermark certificate is obtained. Even if an attacker manages to obtain a valid watermark certificate with T'_{origin} for pirated data, one always has $T_{origin} < T'_{origin}$ by which the legitimate ownership can be proven in the case of an ownership dispute. The attacker's valid certificate should be officially revoked after dispute resolution.

In certain cases such as identity change, ownership change, validity period change, DB-CA compromise, and database update, an existing certificate needs to be renewed, updated, or revoked. In these cases, the original time T_{origin} must be kept unchanged in the renewed or updated certificates. To ensure that a watermark certificate is valid in proving the ownership, the revocation information of watermark certificates must be checked in an effective and efficient manner (e.g., using certificate revocation status [18]).

7 Data Structure

7.1 Virtual Primary Key

The structural information of the underlying data is taken into account in the design of the various watermarking schemes. The schemes discussed above are primarily designed for watermarking relational databases with primary keys. The primary keys are used to seed a pseudo-random sequence generator or hash function so as to generate non-correlated pseudo-random numbers for different tuples in a database relation. In watermark insertion and detection, the non-correlated pseudo-random numbers are used to select tuples and to locate and determine watermark values. These techniques cannot be directly applied to database relations without primary keys. Also, these techniques are vulnerable to simple attacks that alter or delete the primary key attributes.

The previous watermarking techniques can be extended in two different ways to address the primary key issues [14]. The first extension is to examine each watermarkable attribute in each tuple independently in watermark insertion and detection. For each attribute $r.A_i$ in each tuple r, the bits of $r.A_i$ are partitioned into two parts: (i) $mb(r.A_i)$: the ξ least significant bits of $r.A_i$; and (ii) $vpk(r.A_i)$: the remaining most significant bits. The most significant bit part $vpk(r.A_i)$ is used as a virtual primary key to determine whether, where, and how to embed a watermark bit to $r.A_i$ in a similar way as in the previous watermarking schemes.

However, $vpk(r.A_i)$ is not a true primary key and may not be unique for each value $r.A_i$. With duplicate virtual primary keys, some watermark bits may be embedded fewer times than others, and some watermark bits may not be embedded at all. Watermark detection may easily fail in the presence of attacks if some of the watermark bits are embedded too few times due to duplicate virtual primary keys.

The duplicate problem can be mitigated by selecting one attribute with the fewest duplicates to provide the virtual primary keys for all tuples. More generally, the virtual primary key can be constructed by combining most significant bits from several attributes so as to minimize duplicates. To thwart attribute deletion attacks, different attributes may be selected for different tuples for constructing virtual primary keys. For example, one may choose to construct a virtual primary key for tuple r by concatenating k ($k \leq \nu$) hash values in $\{HMAC(\mathcal{K}, vpk(r.A_i)) : i = 0, \ldots, \nu - 1\}$ that are closest to zero (hash values are interpreted as natural numbers when compared to zero).

7.2 Data Cube

Data cube is a common data model that supports exploration of a large amount of data in multiple dimensions. Conceptually, a cube consists of a base cuboid, surrounded by a collection of aggregation cuboids that represent the aggregation of the base cuboid along one or more dimensions. In many applications, valuable data cubes are outsourced to specialized parties or provided for direct and interactive uses.

Guo et al. [9] proposed a robust watermarking scheme to protect the owner's rights in data cube applications. The basic assumption is that all watermarkable values in a data cube are numeric, and that small changes in a small portion of these values are acceptable. For each cell in a data cube, the owner of the data seeds a cryptographically secure pseudo-random sequence generator $\mathcal{S}$ with a secret key $\mathcal{K}$ in concatenation with the cell's feature attributes. If $\mathcal{S}_1 \bmod \gamma = 0$, then the cell is selected to embed a watermark bit; otherwise it is ignored. Given η watermarkable cells, roughly η/γ cells are selected. For each selected cell, a bit position among ξ least significant bits is selected to embed a mark bit in the same way as in Agrawal and Kiernan's scheme.

The most prevalent data cube operations are aggregation queries. To eliminate errors introduced by watermark to aggregation queries, a mini-cube is constructed for each cell that is modified in watermark insertion. Suppose that the value $d(X_i, Y_j, Z_k)$ of cell at position (X_i, Y_j, Z_k) in a 3-dimensional data cube is decremented by one in watermark insertion. Based on the position of $d(X_i, Y_j, Z_k)$, three other cell values $d(X_{xc}, Y_j, Z_k)$, $d(X_i, Y_{yc}, Z_k)$, and $d(X_i, Y_j, Z_{zc})$ are selected. The values of these cells are incremented by one so as to balance the deviation in any 1-dimensional aggregation (i.e., aggregation along one feature dimension) that involves cell (X_i, Y_j, Z_k). Similarly, three more cell values $d(X_{xc}, Y_j, Z_{zc})$, $d(X_i, Y_{yc}, Z_{zc})$, and $d(X_{xc}, Y_{yc}, Z_k)$ are decremented by one, and one last cell value $d(X_{xc}, Y_{yc}, Z_{zc})$ is incremented by one. These seven cells, which are called the balance cells, form a mini-cube together with the watermarked cell (X_i, Y_j, Z_k). With a mini-cube constructed, any data cube aggregation that involves at least two cells in the mini-cube remains unchanged after watermark insertion.

The mini-cube should be constructed such that: (i) the balance cells should not be selected from any cell that is used in watermark insertion so as to avoid interfering with the watermark insertion and detection; (ii) most aggregation queries would involve at least two cells in the mini-cube; and (iii) the modification to the balance cells should be minimal. Guo et al. [9] have shown that this can be done effectively and efficiently in real world applications even for very large data cubes.

7.3 Streaming Data

A Robust Watermarking Scheme

Sion, Atallah, and Prabhakar [23] proposed a robust watermarking scheme for streaming data. The scheme embeds a multi-bit watermark wm to an infinite sequence of numerical data items $x_1, x_2, \ldots$, which are normalized in the interval $(-0.5, 0.5)$. The basic idea is to use some extreme values and their neighboring values as watermark bit-carriers. An extreme value is a local maximum or local minimum value satisfying the criteria that at least one of its δ-neighboring values can be found in any uniform random sampling of degree χ (i.e., randomly selecting one value out of every χ values) of the sequence, where the δ-neighboring values are defined to be a subset of stream items forming a complete "chunk", being immediately adjacent to the extreme value, and having a Euclid distance to the extreme value smaller than δ. The intuition of using extreme values as watermark bit-carriers is that the extreme values are likely to be largely preserved in value-preserving attacks or transforms as they reflect the fluctuating behavior of the data stream.

Each δ-neighboring value is partitioned into two parts: most significant part and least significant part, where the most significant part is used to determine whether, where, and how to embed a watermark bit, and the least significant part may be used to embed a watermark bit. It is assumed that all δ-neighboring values of an extreme value share the same most significant part. It is also assumed that it is tolerable to modify the least significant part but not the most significant part in both watermark insertion and value-preserving attacks.

The watermark insertion can be interpreted using a cryptographically secure pseudo-random sequence generator $\mathcal{S}$ as follows. For each extreme value, seed $\mathcal{S}$ with the significant part of the extreme value in concatenation with a secret key. If $\mathcal{S}_1 \mod \gamma = 0$, this extreme value is selected; otherwise it is ignored (roughly $1/\gamma$ of extreme values are selected). For each selected extreme value, watermark bit $wm[i]$ is selected, where $i = \mathcal{S}_2 \mod$ the length of the watermark. Then, bit position j is selected, where $j = \mathcal{S}_3 \mod$ the length of least significant part of the extreme value. Finally, for each δ-neighboring value including the extreme value, the bit position j is set to $wm[i]$ and the adjacent bits are set to zero (to prevent "overflow" in computing average of some δ-neighboring values). Since the entire set of δ-neighboring values are modified, any random sampling of degree χ will include some watermarked values. Also, the average of any combination of some δ-neighboring values would preserve the embedded bit. In watermark detection, a majority vote is used for recovering each watermark bit $wm[i]$, as in Agrawal and Kiernan's scheme. The analysis on false detection rates can be done similarly as for Li, Swarup, and Jajodia's multi-bit watermarking scheme.

It has been shown that this scheme can be further improved to be resilient to various transform attacks including sampling, averaging, random alteration, and some combined transforms [23].

A Fragile Watermarking Scheme

Guo, Li, and Jajodia [7] proposed a fragile watermarking scheme for detecting malicious modifications to streaming data. The scheme partitions a numerical data stream into groups based on synchronization points. A data element x_i is defined to be a synchronization point if its keyed hash $HMAC(\mathcal{K}, x_i)$ mod $m = 0$, where $\mathcal{K}$ is a secret key, and m is a secret parameter. When a keyed hash is computed on any data item x_i in this scheme, the last bit of x_i is ignored since it will be replaced with a watermark bit.

In watermark insertion, a group of data items are collected from the data stream until a synchronization point is met and the number of elements in the group is greater than L, where L is the lower bound of the group size. A group hash value is computed by hashing the concatenation of all individual hash values of data items in the group. The watermark embedder needs two buffers: $buff_0$ for the current group, and $buff_1$ for the next group. A watermark is computed based on the current group hash and the group hash of the next group. The length of the watermark is the same as the number of data items in the group. The watermark is embedded by replacing the least significant bits of all data items with the watermark bits, assuming that such change does not degrade the value of data.

The watermark detection is also performed on two buffers using the same $\mathcal{K}$, m, and L. As in watermark insertion, a watermark is computed from the group hash value of the current group and the next group. If the computed group hash matches the extracted watermark, the current group of data is authentic. Otherwise, one needs to investigate the integrity of the previous group before ascertaining the final verification result of the current group. Since the embedded watermarks are chained, watermark detection can detect and localize malicious modifications even if some whole groups are deleted from the stream. The parameters L and m can be used to analyze the tradeoffs between false detection rates and localization precision (in terms of the average size of the group) in tamper detection [7]. The greater the L or m, the smaller the false detection rates, and the lower the localization precision.

7.4 A Note on Watermarking XML Data

Agrawal and Kiernan's scheme has been extended by Ng and Lau to watermark XML data [20]. In this scheme, the owner of the XML data is responsible for selecting the XML elements that are suitable to be locators, where a locator is defined to have a unique value that can serve as a primary key in the watermarking process, as in Agrawal and Kiernan's scheme. The difference between this scheme and Agrawal and Kiernan's scheme is that if a textual value of an element is selected to embed a mark bit, one of its words is chosen and replaced by a synonym function based on a well-known synonym database WordNet. This scheme is further extended and deployed on a XML compression system.

Gross-Amblard considered relational or XML data that are only partially accessible through a set of parametric queries in his query-preserving watermarking scheme [6]. The scheme modifies some numerical values in watermark insertion in a way that the distortions introduced to the results of those parametric queries are small and that the watermark can be detected from the results of those queries.

Finally, Zhou, Pang, and Tan [25] proposed creating queries to identify the data elements in XML data that can be used for embedding watermarks. The identifying queries are resilient against data reorganization and redundancy removal through query rewriting. If an identified element is a leaf node, watermark insertion is performed by modifying its value; otherwise, it is performed by adding to or deleting its child nodes. The usability of XML data is measured by query templates. The results of certain basic queries on the data remain useful after watermarking or attacks.

8 Open Issues

The current research on database watermarking has been primarily focused on how to embed and detect a watermark so that the embedded watermark is robust or fragile against various database attacks. However, the study on the impact of watermarking to database usability is relatively limited and preliminary, especially in application contexts. This type of study is important since one of the greatest concerns in database applications is the usability of the data, which should not be affected by the watermarking process.

One future research direction is to model common database queries and minimize the watermarking impact on those queries. It is possible that different watermarking schemes should be designed to accommodate different types of queries. Another future research direction is to model various database attacks that exist in real-world settings. Special attention should be directed toward the impact of those attacks on watermark design and database usability. Finally, it is meaningful to collect typical real-world data sets, to standardize database usability measurements and database attack models, and to benchmark/ evaluate/ compare various watermarking schemes for typical database applications.

References

1. R. Agrawal and J. Kiernan. Watermarking relational databases. In *Proceedings of VLDB*, pages 155–166, 2002.
2. E. Bertino, B. C. Ooi, Y. Yang, and R. Deng. Privacy and ownership preserving of outsourced medical data. In *Proceedings of IEEE International Conference on Data Engineering*, pages 521–532, 2005.
3. D. Boneh and J. Shaw. Collusion secure fingerprinting for digital data. *IEEE Transactions on Information Theory*, 44(5):1897–1905, 1998.
4. I.J. Cox, M.L. Miller, and J.A. Bloom. *Digital Watermarking: Principles and Practice*. Morgan Kaufmann, 2001.
5. B. Gray and J. Gorelick. Database piracy plague. *The Washington Times*, March 1, 2004. http://www.washingtontimes.com.
6. D. Gross-Amblard. Query-preserving watermarking of relational databases and xml documents. In *Proceedings of ACM Symposium on Principles of Database Systems (PODS)*, pages 191–201, 2003.

7. H. Guo, Y. Li, and S. Jajodia. Chaining watermarks for detecting malicious modifications to streaming data. *Inf. Sci.*, 177(1):281–298, 2007.

8. H. Guo, Y. Li, A. Liu, and S. Jajodia. A fragile watermarking scheme for detecting malicious modifications of database relations. *Inf. Sci.*, 176(10):1350–1378, 2006.

9. J. Guo, Y. Li, R. H. Deng, and K. Chen. Rights protection for data cubes. In *ISC*, pages 359–372, 2006.

10. N.F. Johnson, Z. Duric, and S. Jajodia. *Information Hiding: Steganography and Watermarking–Attacks and Countermeasures*. Kluwer Publishers, 2000.

11. S. Katzenbeisser and F.A. Petitcolas, editors. *Information Hiding Techniques for Steganography and Digital Watermarking*. Artech House, 2000.

12. Y. Li and R. H. Deng. Publicly verifiable ownership protection for relational databases. In *ASIACCS*, pages 78–89, 2006.

13. Y. Li, H. Guo, and S. Jajodia. Tamper detection and localization for categorical data using fragile watermarks. In *Digital Rights Management Workshop*, pages 73–82, 2004.

14. Y. Li, V. Swarup, and S. Jajodia. Constructing a virtual primary key for fingerprinting relational data. In *Digital Rights Management Workshop*, pages 133–141, 2003.

15. Y. Li, V. Swarup, and S. Jajodia. A robust watermarking scheme for relational data. In *Proceedings of the 13th Workshop on Information Technology and Systems (WITS)*, pages 195–200, December 2003.

16. Y. Li, V. Swarup, and S. Jajodia. Defending against additive attacks with maximal errors in watermarking relational databases. In *Proc. the 18th Annual IFIP WG 11.3 Working Conference on Data and Applications Security*, pages 81–94, 2004.

17. Y. Li, V. Swarup, and S. Jajodia. Fingerprinting relational databases: Schemes and specialties. *IEEE Transactions on Dependable and Secure Computing*, 2:34–45, 2005.

18. S. Micali. Efficient certificate revocation. In *Technical Report: TM-542b*. Massachusetts Institute of Technology. Cambridge, MA, USA, 1996.

19. W. J. Myrvold and F. Ruskey. Ranking and unranking permutations in linear time. *Inf. Process. Lett.*, 79(6):281–284, 2001.

20. W. Ng and H. L. Lau. Effective approaches for watermarking xml data. In *DASFAA*, pages 68–80, 2005.

21. R. Sion. Proving ownership over categorical data. In *Proceedings of IEEE International Conference on Data Engineering*, pages 584–596, 2004.

22. R. Sion, M. Atallah, and S. Prabhakar. Rights protection for relational data. In *Proceedings of ACM SIGMOD International Conference on Management of Data*, pages 98–108, 2003.

23. R. Sion, M. Atallah, and S. Prabhakar. Resilient rights protection for sensor streams. In *Proceedings of the Very Large Databases Conference*, pages 732–743, 2004.

24. L. Vaas. Putting a stop to database piracy. *eWEEK, enterprise news and reviews*, September 24, 2003. http://www.eweek.com/print_article/0,3048,a=107965,00.asp.

25. X. Zhou, Pang H. H., and K. L. Tan. Query-based watermarking for xml data. In *ASIACCS*, pages 253–264, 2007.

15

Trustworthy Records Retention

Ragib Hasan[1], Marianne Winslett[1], Soumyadeb Mitra[1],Windsor Hsu[2], Radu Sion[3]

[1] Department of Computer Science, University of Illinois at Urbana-Champaign, (rhasan,winslett,mitra1)@cs.uiuc.edu
[2] Data Domain, Inc. windsor.hsu@datadomain.com
[3] Network Security and Applied Cryptography Lab, Stony Brook University sion@cs.stonybrook.edu

Summary. Trustworthy retention of electronic records has become a necessity to ensure compliance with laws and regulations in business and the public sector. Among other features, these directives foster accountability by requiring organizations to secure the entire life cycle of their records, so that records are created, kept accessible for an appropriate period of time, and deleted, without tampering or interference from organizational insiders or outsiders. In this chapter, we discuss existing techniques for trustworthy records retention and explore the open problems in the area.

1 Introduction

Modern enterprises create, process, and store large quantities of records. The internal operations of an enterprise rely heavily on these records when making business decisions. Further, public confidence in an enterprise depends on its ability to maintain the confidentiality, integrity, and authenticity of its records throughout their life cycle. In response to a number of incidents of corporate fraud involving inappropriate modification and/or disclosure of financial and personal records, governments have issued laws and regulations that mandate organizations to provide trustworthy storage of their records for a guaranteed retention period, and to completely dispose of the records after their retention period has passed.

Unfortunately, most traditional security techniques are of little help in ensuring trustworthy retention of records, because traditional techniques focus on outsiders as the source of threats to the system. With organizational fraud, the threat comes from inside the organization, often from highly-placed employees who can coerce system administrators into aiding their coverup attempts. Trustworthy records retention requires new types of storage servers and database management systems, along with new techniques for indexing, record placement, data migration, and deletion.

This chapter explains the problem of trustworthy retention of records and outlines proposed solutions and open problems. Section 2 defines the trustworthy record retention problem and discusses the laws and regulations that mandate trustworthy record retention. Section 3 discusses the threats to trustworthy record retention. Section 4 presents the current storage and deployment models for trustworthy storage, and Section 5 discusses ways in which current records servers could be made more resilient against physical attack. Sections 6, 7, and 8 discuss techniques used for trustworthy record indexing, migration, and deletion, respectively. Finally, we conclude with a general discussion of open problems and issues in Section 9.

2 Problem Definition

Information subject to compliance regulations includes both structured records, such as relational database entries; and semi-structured or unstructured records, such as email, spreadsheets, reports, memos, and instant messages. We use the terms *records* and *documents* interchangeably when referring to semi-structured or unstructured collections of information.

Definition 1. *The goal of **trustworthy record retention** is to provide long-term retention and eventual disposal of organizational records in such a manner that no user can delete, hide, or tamper with any record during its retention period, nor recreate a record's content once it has been deleted.*

Trustworthy records retention has become mandatory with the passing of regulatory legislation all around the world. In the United States alone, there are more than 10,000 regulations at the state and federal level that mandate the secure management of such records. In this section, we briefly discuss these laws and regulations.

In the United States, the Sarbanes-Oxley Act of 2002 requires public companies to provide disclosure and accountability of their financial reporting, subject to independent audits [30]. The Health Insurance Portability and Accountability Act (HIPAA) requires trustworthy storage of medical records [3]. The Securities and Exchange Commission (SEC) rule 17a-4 requires traders, brokers, and financial companies to maintain their business records, transactions, and communications for a number of years [38]. The Gramm-Leach-Bliley Act of 1999 mandates that financial institutions must have a policy to protect information from any foreseeable threats in integrity and data security [29]. There are also state laws mandating the accountability of financial institutions when breach of financial records occurs [48].

Other well-known US legislation that mandates trustworthy records retention includes the Federal Information Security Management Act [31], which regulates information systems used by the Federal government and affiliated parties, requiring yearly audits, risk assessments, certification, and continuous monitoring of such systems. The Department of Defense Records Management Program under directive 5015.2 regulates automated record management systems used by the Department of Defense [24]. Food and Drug Administration 21 CFR Part 11 [27] places controls over records of trials of potential medicines. The Family Educational Rights and Privacy Act [25] requires long-term trustworthy storage of student records from elementary school through the university level. The Occupational Safety and Health Administration requires that records on employee exposure to dangerous substances be kept for 30 years [37].

The European Parliament has issued several directives regarding the security and mandatory retention of electronic records. For example, Directive 2006/24/EC of the European Parliament regulates the retention of data generated or processed in connection with the provision of publicly available electronic communications services or public communications networks [33]. The Markets in Financial Instruments Directive (MiFID) regulates financial markets across Europe, and introduces strict requirements on electronic record-keeping [10]. In addition, there are country-specific laws that mandate secure records retention for businesses. For example, in the United Kingdom, the Companies (Audit, Investigations and Community Enterprise) Act of 2004 requires companies to adopt strict security measures to ensure the accuracy and integrity of financial records [28].

In Japan, the Financial Instruments and Exchange Law, nicknamed J-SOX, was promulgated in 2006 to regulate financial reporting [4]. It requires companies to automate their financial report audit process, and is applicable to Japanese companies as well as their foreign subsidiaries.

Many other countries have similar regulations in place. For example, in Australia, the Corporate Law Economic Reform Program Act of 2004 regulates auditing and corporate financial reporting [39]. In Canada, Bill 198 of 2002 (An Act to Implement Budget Measures and Other Initiatives of the Government, nicknamed C-SOX) regulates financial reporting [26]. In addition, the Ontario Securities Commission rule Multilateral Instrument 52-111 mandates management responsibility for reporting on internal control over financial reporting [40].

While each of the regulations mentioned above is designed for a particular application area and has its own unique features, a number of assurance criteria are common to many of the directives:

- **Guaranteed retention**. Organizations must store records in a manner that prevents deletion of the records or tampering with their contents, even by insiders, for a regulation-mandated lifespan.
- **Long-term retention**. The mandated retention periods are measured in years or even decades. For example, national intelligence information, educational records, and certain health records must be retained for over 20 years. Many mandated retention periods exceed the expected lifetime of today's storage devices.

- **Efficient access to data.** Authorized requests for access to records must be serviced in a timely manner.
- **Data confidentiality.** Only authorized parties can access confidential records.
- **Data integrity.** Records can only enter the system through authorized means. Further, there must be procedures in place for correcting errors in the data, once detected.
- **Guaranteed deletion.** Some laws require enterprises to properly dispose of records after a certain point in time (e.g., [24, 3]). In other situations, deletion may not be required by regulation, but still may be highly desirable from the organization's point of view, as the records may represent a liability. Once records are deleted, ideally it should be impossible to reconstruct any information about their contents, either directly or through metadata-based inference. We use the term *trustworthy deletion* to describe this combination of features.
- **Litigation holds.** Electronic information may be used in litigation [18]. If a *litigation hold* is placed on a record, it must remain accessible until the hold is lifted, even if it reaches the end of its mandated lifespan.
- **Insider adversaries.** Much recent high-profile corporate malfeasance has been at the behest of chief executive officers and chief financial officers who have the power to order the destruction or alteration of incriminating records. Thus many compliance regulations target powerful insiders as the primary adversaries. In effect, these adversaries have superuser powers coupled with full access to the storage system hardware.
- **Auditing.** The organization is subject to periodic audits of its records retention practices.
- **High penalties for non-compliance.** Non-compliance with the regulations can bring stiff financial and criminal penalties [32].

  For example, a chief financial officer can receive a prison sentence for publishing an incorrect financial report, even if the false information was included without his or her knowledge.

Compliance regulations do not specify *how* these assurances are to be provided, i.e., what technology should be used to attain compliance. Thus we expect that the legal interpretation of whether an organization is in compliance will evolve over time, with more stringent measures being required once the technology is available to support them. This assumption drives much of the current research on trustworthy records retention, which focuses on cost-effective means of providing a higher degree of assurance than is available from current compliance products.

3 Usage Scenario and Threat Model

A records retention system faces all the attacks that any computer system is vulnerable to (e.g., physical destruction, denial-of-service attacks), plus additional dangers that are unique to the compliance arena. In this section, we describe those latter dangers. For information on other kinds of threats and their countermeasures, we refer the reader to the other chapters in this volume and to any textbook on computer security.

The main focus in trustworthy records retention is on preventing malicious insiders from tampering with or destroying records. Further, the traditional notion of an insider attack is refined to assume a very powerful insider who is capable of gaining physical, root-level access to the storage media. While outside adversaries may also pose threats, measures that are effective against superuser insiders will also stymie external attackers.

A second key factor in the threat model for trustworthy records retention is that the visible alteration or destruction of records is tantamount to an admission of guilt, in the context of litigation. Thus a successful adversary must perform their misdeeds undetectably.

The target usage scenario for trustworthy records retention is as follows. First, a legitimate user Alice creates and stores a record R that is subject to compliance regulations. Later, a user Mallory starts to regret R's existence and will do everything he can to prevent a subsequent user Bob from accessing R or inferring its existence. For example, Bob may be a regulatory authority looking for evidence of malfeasance, while Mallory may be the superuser CEO or Alice herself. The primary goal of trustworthy records retention is to ensure that Bob can still find and read R until the end of R's mandated lifespan, no matter what Mallory does. For some applications, undetectable post hoc insertion of records is also considered a threat and must be addressed.

Once R reaches the end of its mandated lifespan and is deleted, then Mallory may wish to determine whether R ever existed or infer information about the contents of R, based on any traces of information about R that may remain in the system. A second goal of trustworthy records retention is to ensure that Mallory cannot make these inferences.

To illustrate some of the implications of the threat model, consider the following hypothetical scenarios:

Trustworthy retention. Mallory can employ his superuser powers to attempt to modify or delete R, or to hide R by modifying indexes so that they no longer lead to R. Mallory can also swap out the disks in the storage server, replacing them with disks that do not contain any trace of R. We must make sure that Bob can detect Mallory's attacks and, where feasible, we must prevent them.

Trustworthy access and migration. Suppose that Alice's organization needs to migrate its compliance records to a new compliance storage server. Mallory is effectively in charge of the migration, and he wants to omit incriminating record R during the transfer. For trustworthy record retention, Bob must be able to detect whether any such modifications or omissions occurred during migration.

Trustworthy deletion. When its mandatory retention period is over and any litigation holds on R have been lifted, Alice's organization removes

R. Mallory subsequently gains access to the storage server and looks for magnetic traces of *R*. He also looks in the current copies of indexes and other metadata and supporting data structures, to try to glean information about *R*. For many applications, trustworthy record retention needs to prevent Mallory from gaining any information about *R*.

4 Storage Architectures

As explained in detail in other chapters of this book, conventional file/storage system access control mechanisms and data outsourcing techniques are intended to ensure that records and their metadata are only modified by legitimate applications. Under the outsourcing threat model, insiders are trusted but the storage server is not. The correctness of outsourced query answers can be guaranteed by the data owner by attaching appropriate signatures to the data that can be verified by the querier. These signature-based approaches only detect whether a record has been tampered with; they do not prevent tampering. The techniques for outsourcing and traditional access control are powerless against an adversary with superuser powers who can obtain any secret key and control the behavior of applications. Data owner Alice could alter the contents of her record *R* and re-sign it after it has already been committed to the storage server, or superuser Mallory could obtain access to Alice's private key and alter and re-sign *R* himself. In many applications, a key requirement for trustworthy retention of records is to *prevent* deletion and modification of the records. To thwart these attacks, we need a new kind of storage architecture [14]:

- Based on the computer security principle of minimizing the trusted computing base, **the component for enforcing the storage security properties should be as small as possible**, both to reduce the probability that something could go wrong or be compromised, and to increase our ability to verify the correctness of the component. This means that we cannot rely on having a trusted database management system running on the storage server, or even a trusted indexing package.
- The **cost of any effective attack against the component must be high, and its results must be conspicuous**. For example, perhaps a simple auditing routine is guaranteed to be able to detect the aftereffects of the attack; or else many or all records insertions will fail after the attack. A number of design principles follow from this requirement; for example, the component should have a *simple and well-defined interface*, to robustly restrict traffic into the component to legitimate requests only. Further, the component must *mediate all requests*; in other words, the overwrite protection cannot be circumvented by, for example, directly accessing the rewritable disk.
- The resulting system must provide **end-to-end security guarantees**, not just guarantees for individual components.

- The **price per byte of storage must be modest**, as data volumes are very high. The conflict between security, cost-effectiveness, and efficiency makes the design of compliance storage extremely challenging.

To respond to regulations for trustworthy document retention, the storage industry has developed a variety of *compliance storage* products that aim to address the requirements outlined in the previous section. Vendors in this marketplace include IBM [16], HP [13], EMC [7], Hitachi Data Systems [12], Zantaz [49], StorageTek [44], Network Appliance [23], and Quantum Inc. [34]. Often their products are referred to simply as WORM (write once, read many) devices, though of course any product that supports deletion of expired records is not a true WORM device. In this section, we briefly discuss a set of representative systems and their security properties.

Tape-based products. Due to the favorable cost-per-MB ratio of tape-based storage in the past, tape was a natural choice for massive data storage in commercial enterprise deployments where regulatory compliance is of concern. Thus storage vendors offered tape-based compliance storage first. The Quantum DLTSage predictive, preventative and diagnostic tools for tape storage environments [34] are a representative instance. The WORM assurances of the tape systems are provided under the assumption that only Quantum tape readers are deployed: "DLTSage WORM provides features to assure compliance, placing an electronic key on each cartridge to ensure WORM integrity. This unique identifier cannot be altered, providing a tamper-proof archive cartridge that meets stringent compliance requirements to ensure integrity protection and full accessibility with reliable duplication" [34]. Such systems, however, make impractical assumptions. Given the nature of magnetic tape, an attacker can easily dismantle the plastic tape enclosure and access the underlying data on a different customized reader, thus compromising its integrity. Relying on the physical integrity of a "plastic yellow label," as in one product, to safeguard essential enterprise information is likely to be unacceptable in high-stakes commercial scenarios.

Optical-disk products. Optical disk media (CDs) have been around experimentally since 1969 and commercially available since 1983. Given the prohibitive costs of high-powered lasers in small form factors, in the early days, most CD devices were only capable of reading disk information. As the technology matured, write-once (and later read-write) media appeared. Optical WORM-disk solutions rely on irreversible physical write effects to ensure the inability to alter existing content. However, with ever increasing amounts of information being produced and requiring constant low-latency accessibility in commercial scenarios, it is challenging to deploy a scalable optical-only WORM solution. Moreover, optical WORM disks are plagued with other practical issues such as the inability to fine-tune WORM and secure deletion granularity (problems partially shared also by tape-based solutions). Moreover, due to bulk production requirements, optical disks are vulnerable to simple data replication attacks, with the end result that they do not provide any strong security features. Optical WORM disks also perform relatively poorly in price-performance measurements, because current technology is somewhat undersized for the volumes of data associated with compliance regulations. Sony's Professional Disk for Data optical disk system, for example, holds only 23 GB per disk side [43]. Nevertheless, because it is faster than tape and cheaper than hard disks, optical WORM storage technology is often deployed as a secondary, high-latency storage medium to be used as second-tier storage in the framework of a hard disk-based solution. In such an environment, care needs to be taken in establishing points of trust and data integrity when data leaves the secured hard disk store for the optical media. As we will discuss below, such integrity assurances can be maintained with the help of additional secure hardware hosted inside the main store.

Hard disk products. Magnetic disk recording currently offers better overall cost and performance than optical or tape recording. Moreover, while immutability is often specified as a requirement for records, what is required in practice is that they be "term-immutable", i.e., immutable for a specified retention period. Thus almost all recently-introduced WORM storage devices are built atop conventional rewritable magnetic disks, with write-once semantics enforced through software ("soft-WORM").

EMC Centera. The EMC Centera Compliance Edition [7] is a content addressed storage (CAS) product that also offers regulatory compliance capabilities. Each data record "has two components: the content and its associated content descriptor file (CDF) that is directly linked to the stored object (business record, e-mail, etc.). A digital fingerprint derived from the content itself is the content's locator (content address). The CDF contains metadata record attributes (e.g., creation date, time, format) and the object's content address. The CDF is used for access to and management of the record. Within this CDF, the application will assign a retention period for each individual business record. Centera will permit deletion of a pointer to a record upon expiration of the retention period. Once the last pointer to a record has been so deleted, the object will be eliminated" [7], and, in the Plus version, also "shredded" from the media. Given its software-only nature, these mechanisms are vulnerable to simple software-based attacks and physical attacks. Data integrity can be easily compromised by a determined insider who replaces a disk by one with slightly altered content, as described in the next section.

Hitachi Message Archive for Compliance. Hitachi Data Systems provides the Data Retention Utility [12], a software-based "virtual WORM" mechanism for mainstream Hitachi storage systems. The system allows customers to "lock down archived data, making it non-erasable and non-rewritable for prescribed periods, facilitating compliance with governmental or industry regulations". This approach has the same vulnerabilities as do the EMC products.

IBM LockVault compliance software. IBM offers multiple soft-WORM products. The LockVault compliance software is a layer that operates on top of IBM System Storage N series [15] to provide "disk-based regulatory compliance solutions for unstructured data". This approach has the same vulnerabilities as do the EMC products.

IBM System Storage Archive Manager. The IBM Tivoli Storage Manager [17] is part of the IBM TotalStorage Software [16] and "makes the deletion of data before its scheduled expiration extremely difficult. *Short of physical destruction to storage media or server, or deliberate corruption of data or deletion of the Archive Manager database,* Archive Manager will not allow data [...] to be deleted before its scheduled expiration date." From a security point of view, it is not desirable for the regulatory compliance mechanism to depend on the correct behavior of the main system. After all, the compliance mechanism's main role is to guarantee exactly such faultless behavior. The main adversary of concern in regulatory settings is *exactly* one with incentives for data corruption and physical attacks.

Network Appliance Snaplock Compliance/Enterprise Software. The NetApp SnapLock software suite [23] is designed to work on top of NetApp NearStore and FAS storage systems. It provides soft-WORM assurances, "preventing critical files from being altered or deleted until a specified retention date". Unlike several other vendors, NetApp SnapLock supports open industry standard protocols such as NFS and CIFS.

Sun StorageTek Compliance Archiving Software. Sun also offers soft-WORM assurances through its StorageTek Compliance Archiving Software [44]. The software runs on top of the Sun StorageTek 5320 NAS Appliance [45] to "provide compliance-enabling features for authenticity, integrity, ready access, and security".

Strong WORM. Today's compliance storage products do not really satisfy the criteria for trustworthy record retention. They are fundamentally vulnerable to faulty behavior or malicious adversaries with incentives to alter stored data, as they rely on enforcement primitives—such as software and/or simple hardware device-hosted on/off switches—ill-suited to their target adversarial setting. For sound designs, we believe the following properties are required:

- To prevent physical attacks such as disk replacement, strong tamper-resistant and reactive hardware is required to ensure data integrity. As discussed later, a determined adversary can circumvent today's physical protection.
- The requirement for efficient access to compliance records, coupled with the large volume of such records, indicates that the records will need to be searched using indexes. These indexes cannot be kept on traditional storage, as a superuser could hide a record by removing its index entries. Even with indexes designed to be kept on optical media [1, 6, 19, 35], an adversary can compromise the search results—even for an approach as simple as binary search. The design of trustworthy indexes is an open research area.

- Current products address the trustworthiness issues that arise during the backup process. However, they do not ensure that a record is trustworthy throughout its entire life cycle, from creation, through migration to newer storage servers, to eventual deletion.
- Current compliance storage products aim to address the problem of document retention; no product supports structured data, e.g., provides a trustworthy relational database management system.

We discuss these open problems and potential solutions in the sections that follow.

5 Resistance to Physical Attack

Our insider adversary Mallory has physical access to the storage media. To limit the damage that he can do, one potential approach is to house the storage in a tamperproof or tamper-evident box. However, such a box would trap heat, making it necessary to run the storage server at lower speeds and reducing its cost-effectiveness. Thus this solution is unlikely to be popular with customers or vendors. Further, disks do fail and require replacement, which is hard to reconcile with the notion of tamper-evidence.

As one example of vulnerability to physical attack, consider recent US patent 6879454 for an IBM disk-based WORM system whose drives selectively and permanently disable their write mode by using programmable read only memory (PROM) circuitry: "One method of use employs selectively blowing a PROM fuse in the arm electronics of the hard disk drive to prevent further writing to a corresponding disk surface in the hard disk drive. A second method of use employs selectively blowing a PROM fuse in processor-accessible memory, to prevent further writing to a section of logical block addresses (LBAs) corresponding to a respective set of data sectors in the hard disk drive".

Unfortunately, this method does not provide strong WORM guarantees. Using off-the-shelf resources, an insider can open the storage medium enclosures to gain physical access to the underlying data and to any flash-based checksum storage. She can then surreptitiously replace a device by copying an illicitly modified version of the stored data onto a identical replacement unit. Maintaining integrity-authenticating checksums at device or software level does not prevent this attack, due to the lack of tamper-resistant storage for keying material. The adversary can access integrity checksum keys and construct a new matching checksum for the modified data on the replacement device, thus remaining undetected. This attack will still be effective if we add tamper-resistant storage for keying material [11], because a superuser is likely to have access to keys while they are in active use: achieving reasonable data throughputs will require integrity keys to be available in main memory for the main (untrusted) run-time data processing components.

A potentially more effective approach is to leverage components that are both tamper-resistant and active, such as general-purpose secure coprocessors (SCPUs). By adding a trusted SCPU inside the storage server, we can guarantee the trustworthiness of records from that server, even if the records subsequently pass through untrusted and possibly hostile environments inside or outside the server. The SCPU can run certified code; its close proximity to the data storage, coupled with its tamper-resistance guarantees, offers the possibility of higher security assurances at minimal extra cost.

However, SCPUs are not a panacea. The heat dissipation limits caused by tamper-resistant enclosures reduce the maximum allowable spatial gate density in an SCPU. As a result, SCPUs are significantly constrained in both computation ability and memory capacity, being up to one order of magnitude slower than ordinary CPUs. Thus to be competitive in the marketplace, the SCPU cannot run all of the storage server code—additional ordinary untrusted CPUs must shoulder much of the computational burden. Even then, a straightforward implementation (such as having the SCPU sign each new record as it arrives) will be too inefficient, leaving the untrusted CPUs underutilized and defeating the intended cost advantage of having fast untrusted main CPUs and expensive slower secured CPUs. A good implementation must access the secure hardware sparsely, asynchronously from the main data flow to and from disk, so that document insertions, deletions, and reads proceed at the throughput rate of the storage server's ordinary CPUs.

Researchers have proposed such an architecture for compliance storage and data migration, based on commodity x86 architecture [41]. With a single SCPU, their approach can support over 2500 record insertions and deletions per second, using a deferred-signature scheme described below. To minimize the trusted computing base, their record-level WORM layer identifies records by monotonically increasing serial numbers and does not support name spaces, trustworthy indexing or content-based addressing; all of these can be layered on top of the record-level WORM support.

To achieve such high throughput rates, the SCPU is involved in document insertions and deletions but not in reads, thus minimizing the overhead if the workload is dominated by read queries. Clients who perform reads get an SCPU-certified guarantee that (i) the block was not tampered with, if the read is successful; and if the read fails, either (ii) the block was deleted according to its retention policy, or (iii) it never existed on this storage server.

To authenticate the contents of the records on the storage server, one option is to keep a Merkle tree whose entries are signed by the SCPU. However, the resulting $O(\log n)$ cost to insert or delete a record, where n is the number of documents, will reduce the throughput of the system, even if the SCPU updates the Merkle tree in parallel with the activities of the other CPUs. To address this problem, one can instead label data blocks with monotonically increasing consecutive serial numbers and then introduce a concept of sliding "windows" that are authenticated at $O(1)$ cost by only signing the window boundaries [41].

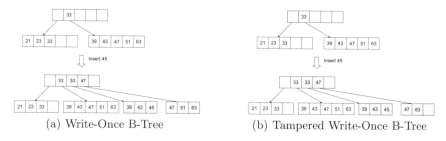

(a) Write-Once B-Tree   (b) Tampered Write-Once B-Tree

Fig. 1. An example of a write-once B-tree insert operation. (a) Inserting 45 requires a node split. Two new leaf nodes (shaded) are created and pointers to the new nodes are placed at the parent node. The parent node now has two pointers associated with 33. During querying, the latest pointer associated with a value is traversed. (b) Write-once B-trees are not trustworthy. The adversary can omit entries (e.g., value 51) during the copy operation.

Another trick to increase throughput during periods of high load is to temporarily replace expensive SCPU signature operations (e.g., 1024-bit signatures) with less expensive *short-term secure* variants (e.g., 512-bit signatures) [41]. The system can strengthen these weaker constructs when the load slackens, but within their security lifetime (e.g., before enough time has passed for an adversary to break the 512-bit signature scheme). This adaptivity helps the system amortize signature costs over time so that it gracefully handles high-load document insertion bursts.

6 Trustworthy Indexing

Indexing ensures that a target record can be quickly extracted from terabytes of data. In our discussion, we will assume that each record is assigned an integer identifier as it arrives at the storage server, and that identifiers are given out in increasing order. Any indexing approach for trustworthy records retention must have the following properties:

- The index itself must be trustworthy. As explained below, in practice this means that the search path to an index entry must be immutable for the lifetime of the record that it indexes.
- To keep the trusted computing base small, the indexing code should reside outside the storage server.
- To ensure that a record R is entered and retained in the appropriate indexes *before* Mallory regrets its existence, the insertion and indexing of R must be performed atomically.
- All traces of R must be removed from the index when R is deleted.

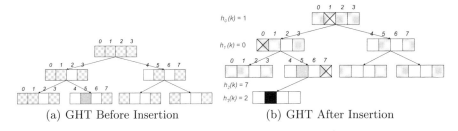

(a) GHT Before Insertion   (b) GHT After Insertion

Fig. 2. Inserting element k into a generalized hash tree. (a) The GHT before k is inserted. The shaded nodes are occupied and the white nodes are empty. (b) $h_0(k) = 1$, but node position 1 in the root node is already occupied. So k must be hashed again using h_1, with the goal of inserting k in the node that is the child of position 1 in the root node. $h_1(k) = 0$, but the 0th position in the appropriate subtree of the root is occupied, so k is hashed again using h_2. This again results in a collision. Finally, a new leaf is added and k is inserted at position $h_3(k) = 2$.

The first step in ensuring trustworthy indexing is to store the index on WORM. The problem of creating an index on write-once media has been studied before. For example, in *write-once B-trees* [6] (Figure 1(a)), a node is split into two new nodes when it overflows. Two pointers are added to the end of its parent node, superseding the earlier pointer to the old node. If the parent node overflows, it is split as well and only the most recent pointers are copied. When the root node splits, a new root is created. Unfortunately, the use of WORM alone is insufficient to make this or any other index trustworthy. For example, in a write-once B-tree, an adversary can effectively modify any record he wishes by creating a new version of the appropriate nodes, as shown in Figure 1(b). Although every alteration of the nodes is preserved in WORM storage, it is too expensive to examine each version of the tree on each lookup to guard against tampering.

Traditional hash-based structures are also not secure against tampering. For example, in dynamic hashing and its extensions (e.g., [5, 8, 2]), when the number of records in a hash table exceeds a high water mark, a new hash table with a larger size is allocated and all the records are rehashed and moved into the new table. In this way, dynamic data growth can be supported with good performance. The ability to relocate records, however, provides an opportunity for an adversary to alter the records during the copying step. A trie that stores records in its leaf nodes and moves records to new leaf nodes as the trie grows will also be untrustworthy. All these approaches are vulnerable because the search path to a particular record is not term-immutable.

To date, researchers have proposed trustworthy versions of hashing and inverted indexes, both of which guarantee term-immutable search paths. For example, a *generalized hash tree* (GHT) supports exact-match lookups of records based on attribute values [50]. One can use such an index, for example, to find all email sent from a particular address.

A GHT is a balanced tree-based data structure that does not require periodic rebalancing. In a GHT, predefined hashes of the record key determine all its possible lookup or insertion locations. The locations where a record can be inserted or looked up are therefore immutable. To insert or look up a record in a GHT, the record key is hashed to obtain a position within the root node (see Figure 2). If the corresponding node position at the root node is empty, the record is inserted there. If there is a collision, the key is rehashed (using a different hash function) and an attempt is made to insert the key in the appropriate subtree of the root node. This process is repeated until an empty node position is found. If a record cannot be inserted in any existing node of the tree, a new leaf node is added.

Full-text search (keyword search) is the most convenient way to query unstructured records such as email bodies and reports. Search engines typically use inverted indexes for this purpose [9]. As shown in Figure 3(a), an inverted index comprises a dictionary of terms (i.e., words that appear in documents) plus a *posting list* for each term, containing the identifiers of all records containing that term (with additional metadata such as term frequency within the record, term type, and term position within the record). Queries are answered by scanning the posting lists of the terms in the query. The records referenced in the posting lists are assigned scores for the query, based on similarity measures (e.g., cosine, Okapi, pivoted, Dirichlet [47, 36]). The scores are used to rank the records, producing an ordered list of results. Multi-keyword conjunctive queries can be answered by intersecting the posting lists of the query terms. To make the intersection fast, an additional index such as a B+ tree is usually kept for each posting list, and a zigzag join is used to perform the intersection [46].

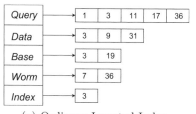
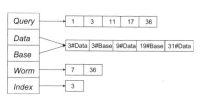

    (a) Ordinary Inverted Index   (b) Inverted Index After Merging

Fig. 3. Inverted indexes. With each keyword, a *posting list* of IDs of documents containing that keyword is stored. Each posting list is stored as a separate file on WORM. After merging, the keyword (or its hash) must also be stored in the posting list.

For a trustworthy version of inverted indexes, each posting list can be stored in a separate append-only file on WORM storage [20]. In a traditional inverted index, updates are processed in batches that involve sorting all the entries and regenerating the posting lists in their entirety; of course this is not trustworthy. To be trustworthy, we can append the terms of newly arriving records to the appropriate posting lists at the time the records arrive. Without additional optimizations, however, this approach is too slow to support real-time insertion of typical business documents: each new posting list entry requires a file append operation, which in turn requires a random I/O. The performance can be improved vastly by merging the posting lists for different terms until the tails of all posting lists fit into the storage server's cache (see Figure 3(b)). For example, with a cache of 256 MB (which is less than one would find in today's storage servers), one can index 500 new 500-keyword documents per second. Compared to a traditional unmerged implementation of an inverted index, query workload performance drops by less than 10%, which is quite good. Intuitively, merging posting lists has little effect on query performance because only a small set of terms is widely used in queries. As long as these "popular" terms are not merged together, performance is little affected by merging.

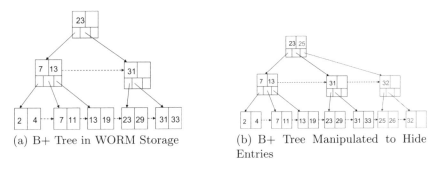

(a) B+ Tree in WORM Storage

(b) B+ Tree Manipulated to Hide Entries

Fig. 4. Why B+ trees are untrustworthy. (a) B+ tree in WORM storage. New elements are added at the leaf level. When a leaf node fills up, a new leaf is created and an entry is added to the parent that points to the new leaf. (b) The adversary can add entry 25 to the root and point it to a spurious subtree. This effectively hides entry 31 from subsequent queries.

For trustworthy conjunctive keyword search, the auxiliary B+ trees used in zigzag joins must also be trustworthy. One can create a B+ tree for an increasing sequence of document IDs without any node splits or merges, by building the tree from the bottom up, as shown in Figure 4 for the special case of a 2-3 tree. Unfortunately, such an index structure is also not trustworthy, even when kept on WORM storage, because the path to each entry is not immutable. For instance, Figure 4(b) shows that the adversary can hide entry 31 by creating a separate subtree that does not contain 31, and adding an entry 25 at the root to lead to the new subtree. Other techniques like binary search can also be compromised by the adversary, by appending smaller numbers at the tail of the sequence. For example, binary search on the leaves of the tree in Figure 4 would miss 31 because of the malicious entry 30 at the end.

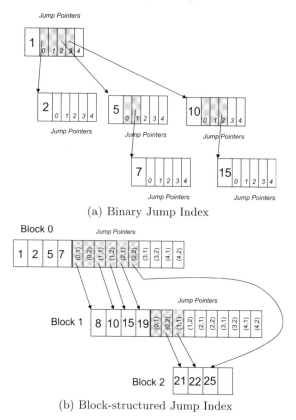

(a) Binary Jump Index

(b) Block-structured Jump Index

Fig. 5. (a) Simple jump index. Shaded pointers that are not filled in are null. Only the first five pointers in each node are shown. (b) Block-structured jump index. Only pointers with $i \leq 4$ are shown.

To address this problem, researchers have proposed *jump indexes* [20]. Jump indexes can be used to index monotonic sequences, such as document IDs in a posting list, as a replacement for the non-trustworthy B+ trees. Experiments show that overall, jump index lookup performance is within a factor of 1.4 of the performance of an equivalent B+ tree.

A jump index exploits the fact that to reach a particular number $k \leq N$, we can jump from 0 to k in powers of 2. For example, let $b_1, \ldots, b_p$ be the binary representation of k. We can reach k in p steps by starting at zero, then jumping forward by $b_1 \times 2^{p-1}$ integers, then jumping forward by $b_2 \times 2^{p-2}$ integers; and so on, until finally a $b_p \times 2^0$ jump brings us to the number k. In a jump index, of course, not all possible numbers (record IDs) will be stored in the index. Instead, as shown in Figure 5(a), a jump index node contains explicit jump pointers that correspond to the sequence of jumps to take forward. More precisely, the ith jump pointer stored with jump index entry (node) l will point to the smallest jump index entry (node) l' such that $l + 2^i \leq l' \leq l + 2^{i+1}$. As a result, lookups can be done in $O(\log_2 N)$ time, where $N = 2^p$. The jump index can be kept in WORM storage by storing each node of the index as a separate file, and appending new jump pointers to the end of the file.

As with B+ trees, one can tune the fanout of jump tree nodes for better space and time efficiency. Figure 5(b) shows a block-structured jump index, in which p posting entries are stored together in blocks of size L. Pointers are associated with blocks, rather than with every entry. Finally, jump pointers are calculated using powers of B rather than powers of two, where $p \geq B$. More specifically, $(B - 1) \log_B(N)$ pointers are stored with every block. Each pointer is uniquely identified by a pair (i, j), where $0 \leq i < \log_B(N)$ and $1 \leq j < B$. The pointers are set up as follows: let l_1 be the largest document ID stored in block b. The (i, j) pointer in b points to the block containing the smallest document ID s such that

$$l_1 + jB^i \leq s < l_1 + (j + 1)B^i.$$

In the trustworthy indexing approaches described above, an adversary can insert malicious entries into the index. For example, Mallory can insert a document ID into the posting list for a term that does not appear in the document, or can append an inappropriate jump pointer to a jump index node. Malicious entries fall into two categories: those that cause subsequent legitimate insertions to fail, and those that will only be noticed when a lookup operation finds a dangling pointer or returns a record that does not match the query. Both events will draw immediate unwanted attention to the attack, and neither prevents all matching records from being returned in the answer to a query. Thus these attacks are conspicuous and ineffective at hiding information.

If Mallory gains physical access to storage, he may tamper with the index contents. If we have trusted hardware that can periodically sign portions of the index (such as the secure coprocessor discussed in the previous section), then any discrepancy between the signature and the current index contents can be detected. Under such circumstances, the indexing system should support partial recovery and fault isolation [42], as it would be very expensive to regenerate the entire index from the data.

7 Trustworthy Migration

Storage systems technology evolves rapidly. It is impractical to store records on a single server for decades, as the server will become obsolete and too expensive to maintain. Organizations themselves may also evolve, via mergers, spin-offs, and reorganizations that require records to be copied or moved. When records must be moved, the migration process needs to be trustworthy; that is, it should be possible to verify that the migration was completed appropriately, even if a superuser adversary performed the migration.

To date, researchers have developed two schemes for trustworthy migration of records between compliance storage servers; both of these schemes rely on secure coprocessors (SCPUs). In the scheme proposed in [41], the SCPU of the original storage server (SCPU$_1$) should be provided assurances that the migration target environment (SCPU$_2$) is trustworthy and endorsed by the relevant regulatory authority (RA).

To achieve this, the migration process is initiated by (i) the system operator retrieving a migration certificate (MC) from the RA. The MC is in effect a signature on a message containing the timestamped identities of SCPU$_1$ and SCPU$_2$. Upon migration, (ii) the MC is presented to SCPU$_1$ (and possibly SCPU$_2$), who authenticates the signature of the RA. If this succeeds, SCPU$_1$ is ready to (iii) mutually authenticate and perform a key exchange with SCPU$_2$, using their internally stored key pairs and certificates. SCPU$_2$ will need backwards-compatible authentication capabilities, as the default authentication mechanisms of SCPU$_2$ may be unknown to SCPU$_1$. This backwards compatibility is relatively easy to achieve as long as the participating certificate authorities (i.e., SCPU manufacturer or delegates thereof) still exist and have not been compromised yet. A cross-certification chain can be set up between the old and the new certification authority root certificates. Once (iii) succeeds, SCPU$_1$ will be ready and willing to transfer a description of the state of the compliance records and index contents on a secure channel provided by an agreed-upon symmetric key (e.g., using a Diffie-Hellman variant). After the state information has been migrated, the actual records and index contents can be transferred by the main CPUs , without SCPU involvement.

The scheme proposed in [22] supports the migration of files through multiple servers while maintaining integrity guarantees. In this scheme, file and directories can be rearranged or omitted during the migration, based on corporate policies. The approach relies on the existence of a trusted third party, such as a storage system vendor, who records the public keys associated with the sequence of storage servers purchased by an organization.

The migration process is divided into three phases:

- In phase 1, the party in charge of migration prepares a plan for the migrations. The log of this plan includes the policies governing the migration and, in compact form, a representation of the list of files and directories to be migrated, the planned file and directory omissions, and the planned directory restructurings.
- In phase 2, the current storage server generates certificates that attest to the current state of the directory tree and file contents, and adds them to the log. The scheme assumes that the server will generate the certificates correctly, either because it is part of the trusted computing base or because it contains trusted hardware that is capable of perusing directories and creating certificates. In either case, these certificates can be generated reasonably quickly.

- Finally, in phase 3, the party in charge of migration moves the files to be migrated, and also copies the signed log to the new server.

After migration, anyone can look up the public keys used by an organization's series of storage servers, and then use validation routines to check whether the migration took place appropriately. For example, a trusted third-party auditor can certify the migration immediately after its completion, at approximately the same rate of speed as it took to generate the certificates in phase 2. At any point after the migration, a user can also quickly check whether a particular file was migrated appropriately.

A long-lived record may be migrated several times during its lifetime. If we migrate all previous logs during each of the component migrations, then the entire migration chain can be validated at any subsequent point. The disadvantage of this approach—and a potential concern in even a single-hop migration—is that a significant amount of information about deleted and/or omitted files may be present in the log. For example, if a file has been omitted during a previous migration, enough information must be present in the log for a verifier to be sure that the omission was appropriate. To address this problem, more complex schemes can be used to reduce the amount of migrated information about deleted files, to the point where a deleted file can appear in the log as just an opaque ID and expiration date.

Migration policies can be very complex. For example consider the policy *Delete all files containing the word* **Martha**. This deletion should preserve confidentiality: a person reading files and logs on the destination server should not learn anything other than the fact that the deleted file contained *Martha*. One can handle this problem in an elegant manner if the storage server contains a small amount of trusted hardware that can run downloaded query code and sign the results, to testify that only a certain set of files contained the word *Martha* [22]. Then this certificate can be included in the log file and migrated to the new server along with the appropriate subset of files. Anyone can verify that exactly the set of files listed in the query certificate was omitted during the migration.

8 Trustworthy Deletion

Since the primary purpose of WORM devices is to prevent data deletion, it is not surprising that cost-effective and trustworthy deletion of records is difficult. WORM devices use physical security measures, such as repeatedly overwriting the data blocks with certain patterns, to erase records from the media. However, simple erasure is not enough for trustworthy deletion, as an erased record can be recreated by reverse-engineering an index. Overall, no index entry deletion scheme developed so far meets all the requirements for trustworthy deletion.

For the deletion of document d to be *strongly secure*, the presence or absence of any word w in any reconstruction of d should not convey any information about its presence in the original document. More formally, let S be a reconstruction of the set of words in d, generated by the adversary by scanning directories, indexes, and migration logs. We say that d's deletion is strongly secure iff

$$\forall w.P(w \in d | w \in S) = P(w \in d)$$
$$\forall w.P(w \in d | w \notin S) = P(w \in d),$$

where $P(w \in d)$ denotes the probability of the word w belonging to document d, while $P(w \in d | w \in S)$ denotes the probability of w being in D given that w is in S.

Unfortunately, the trustworthy indexing schemes discussed earlier do not support strongly secure deletion. Generalized hash trees offer *weakly secure* deletion, in which Mallory cannot *prove* that a deleted record contained a specific set of terms [21]. (We can also define *probabilistically secure* deletion, in which the probability of the record having a specific reconstruction is bounded above.) Trustworthy inverted indexes and jump indexes are even more problematic with respect to deletion.

To see why deletion is difficult, consider an email from Alice to Bob with the text *Please sell 10,000 shares today.* An inverted index will contain entries for the terms in the email, and may also note the position of the words in the record. If the record containing the email is later deleted, it may be possible to exactly recreate the email by looking at its index entries. Therefore, the index entries must also be removed to ensure non-reproducibility of deleted records. WORM devices do not support erasure of short byte sequences, and they are unlikely to do so in the future.

Even if the WORM device does allow the corresponding index entries to be erased, structural properties of the index may allow an adversary to infer that they existed. For example, if the order of keyword insertion is significant in determining the current structure of the index (as is true for trustworthy inverted indexes and jump indexes), then the positions of the erased entries in the index may allow one to infer that a particular erased document contained certain keywords [21]. For example, one might be able to infer that Alice sent an email about shares to Bob on a certain day, without knowing the exact order of words in the email.

To address this problem, one might imagine dividing expiration times into epochs, and keeping a separate set of indexes for records expiring in each epoch. Then one could delete the entire epoch of indexes once the epoch is over. Unfortunately, litigation holds may require a document to be retained even after its mandatory retention period is over, making it impractical to delete large batches of records and index entries based simply on their expiration date. In general, there is a tradeoff between the ease and efficiency of the deletion approach and the trustworthiness guarantees of the approach to implementing litigation holds.

Another option is to rebuild the index in a trustworthy manner when records are deleted. However, the record arrival rate of today will be the

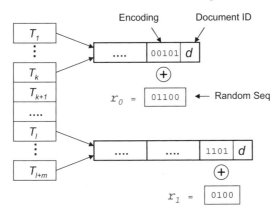

Fig. 6. Supporting deletions from a trustworthy inverted index. The term encoding E_i stored in each posting element has been XORed with a random sequence. The random sequence is stored in a separate file that is discarded when the record expires. Each posting list entry must also mention which random sequence to use to decrypt the encrypted term encoding (not shown).

required record deletion rate in the future. Thus this option is too expensive to be practical.

If document identifiers are encrypted with a per-document secret key before being stored in the index, one can still perform a join on the encrypted document identifiers to recover the document contents. Encrypting the document identifiers with a single key for each epoch is also problematic; Section 5 of [50] offers some solutions for the case of generalized hash trees.

An alternative for trustworthy inverted indexes is to merge posting lists together as usual, then encrypt the term encoding associated with each posting element and store it in the merged posting list entries (see Figure 6). One possible encryption technique is to replace the keyword encoding E in the posting element with its XOR with a random secret, which can be stored with the record and deleted upon its expiration. While the key is present (the record has not expired), the encoding E can be extracted from the posting element. Once the secret has been deleted, the keyword encoding E cannot be retrieved from the stored XOR value. The adversary will not be able to determine which of the q merged keywords corresponds to the posting element, after the secret is discarded.

We can generalize this scheme to handle multiple keywords per record, in such a manner that an adversary cannot determine which of the merged-together keywords a specific posting element corresponds to. The scheme does not achieve strongly secure deletion, though it is immune to a variety of possible attacks. Moreover, the scheme allows compression of posting list entries and has a modest space overhead. It does not require the records to be disposed of in epochs, and hence it can support litigation holds. However, the record anonymity provided by keyword merging critically depends on the set of keywords that are merged together, and this issue needs further investigation.

9 Open Problems

In this section, we briefly summarize the biggest open issues and challenges in trustworthy records retention.

- **Corrections**. Current models for records retention do not support corrections to record content. However, corrections are often necessary in practice (for example, when medical information is placed in the wrong record for a patient with a common name), and are mandated by law in some domains. An elegant, cost-effective approach is needed for supporting corrections and providing trustworthy provenance information and audit trails.
- **Deletions**. As discussed above, no entirely satisfactory scheme exists for trustworthy deletion of records. Traces of record metadata may remain in indexes or migration logs, potentially allowing an adversary to infer the contents of a deleted record.
- **Structured information**. This chapter has focused on the trustworthy retention of unstructured or semistructured data. Database records need a similar level of protection, but no work to date has addressed this problem.
- **Exploiting trusted hardware**. In addition to the trusted hardware based WORM layer, we believe it is important to explore how to deploy such hardware to achieve increased security and efficiency in the upper (e.g., indexing) layers. The challenge is to exploit a very small, cheap piece of trusted hardware along with off-the-shelf regular storage system components, in an architecture that provides good performance.

In addition to these major problems, many smaller questions remain open. For example, there are no trustworthy approaches to multidimensional indexing.

Acknowledgements

Authors Ragib Hasan, Soumyadeb Mitra, and Marianne Winslett were supported by NSF awards IIS-0331707, CNS-0331690, and CNS-0524695. Author Radu Sion was supported in part by the Stony Brook Office of the Vice President for Research and by the NSF award CNS-0627554.

References

1. Bruno Becker, Stephan Gschwind, Thomas Ohler, Bernhard Seeger, and Peter Widmayer. An asymptotically optimal multiversion b-tree. *The VLDB Journal*, 5(4):264–275, 1996.
2. Andrei Z. Broder and Anna R. Karlin. Multilevel Adaptive Hashing. In *1st ACM-SIAM Symposium on Discrete Algorithms*, 1990.
3. Centers for Medicare & Medicaid Services. The Health Insurance Portability and Accountability Act of 1996 (HIPAA). Online at http://www.cms.hhs.gov/hipaa/, 1996.
4. Protiviti Consulting. Frequently Asked Questions About J-SOX. Online at http://www.protiviti.jp/downloads/JSOXOverviewfinal_E.pdf, 2006.
5. Martin Dietzfelbinger, Anna Karlin, Kurt Mehlhorn, Friedhelm Meyer Auf Der Heide, Hans Rohnert, and Robert E. Tarjan. Dynamic Perfect Hashing: Upper and Lower Bounds. *SIAM Journal on Computing*, 23(4):738–761, 1994.
6. Malcolm C Easton. Key-sequence data sets on indelible storage. *IBM Journal of Research and Development*, 30(3):230–241, 1986.
7. EMC Corp. EMC Centera Content Addressed Storage System. Online at http://www.emc.com/products/systems/centera_ce.jsp, 2006.
8. R. J. Enbody and H. C. Du. Dynamic Hashing Schemes. *ACM Computing Surveys*, 20(2), June 1988.
9. Christos Faloutsos. Access methods for text. *ACM Computing Surveys*, 17(1):49–74, 1985.
10. Financial Security Authority. Markets in Financial Instruments Directive. Online at http://www.fsa.gov.uk/, 2006.
11. Trusted Computing Group. Trusted Platform Module (TPM) Specifications. Online at https://www.trustedcomputinggroup.org/specs/TPM, 2006.
12. Hitachi Data Systems. Content Archive Platform. Online at http://www.hds.com/products/storage-systems/content-archive-platform/, 2006.
13. HP. HP Storage Archiving Solutions. Online at http://h18006.www1.hp.com/storage/archiving/index.html, 2006.
14. Lan Huang, Windsor W. Hsu, and Fengzhou Zheng. CIS: Content Immutable Storage for Trustworthy Record Keeping. In *Proceedings of the Conference on Mass Storage Systems and Technologies (MSST)*, 2006.
15. IBM Corp. IBM Storage N Series. Online at http://www-03.ibm.com/systems/storage/nas/index.html, 2006.
16. IBM Corp. IBM TotalStorage DR550. Online at http://www-1.ibm.com/servers/storage/disk/dr, 2006.
17. IBM Corp. IBM Tivoli Storage Manager. Online at www.ibm.com/software/tivoli/products/storage-mgr/, 2007.
18. Judicial Conference of the United States. Federal Rules of Civil Procedure. Online at http://judiciary.house.gov/media/pdfs/printers/108th/civil2004.pdf, 2004.
19. T. Krijnen and L. G. L. T. Meertens. Making B-Trees Work for B.IW219/83. The Mathematical Centre, 1983.
20. Soumyadeb Mitra, Windsor W. Hsu, and Marianne Winslett. Trustworthy keyword search for regulatory-compliant record retention. In *International Conference on Very Large Data Bases*, pages 1001–1012, September 2006.

21. Soumyadeb Mitra and Marianne Winslett. Secure deletion from inverted indexes on compliance storage. In *StorageSS: ACM Workshop on Storage Security and Survivability*, pages 67–72, 2006.
22. Soumyadeb Mitra, Marianne Winslett, Windsor W. Hsu, and Xiaonan Ma. Trustworthy Migration and Retrieval of Regulatory Compliant Records. In *Proceedings of the Conference on Mass Storage Systems and Technologies (MSST)*, 2007.
23. Network Appliance, Inc. SnapLock^{TM} Compliance and SnapLock Enterprise Software. Online at http://www.netapp.com/products/filer/snaplock.html, 2006.
24. The U.S. Department of Defense. Directive 5015.2: DOD Records Management Program. Online at http://www.dtic.mil/whs/directives/corres/pdf/50152std_061902/p50152s.pdf, 2002.
25. The US Department of Education. 20 U.S.C. 1232g; 34 CFR Part 99: The Family Educational Rights and Privacy Act (FERPA). Online at http://www.ed.gov/policy/gen/guid/fpco/ferpa, 1974.
26. Janet Ecker (Minister of Finance). Bill 198 2002. An Act to Implement Budget Measures and Other Initiatives of the Government. Legislative Assembly of Ontario, 2002.
27. The U.S. Department of Health, Human Services Food, and Drug Administration. 21 CFR Part 11: Electronic Records and Signature Regulations. Online at http://www.fda.gov/ora/compliance_ref/part11/FRs/background/pt11finr.pdf, 1997.
28. Acts of the UK Parliament. Companies (Audit, Investigations and Community Enterprise) Act 2004. Online at http://www.opsi.gov.uk/ACTS/acts2004/20040027.htm, 2004.
29. Congress of the United States. Gramm-Leach-Bliley Financial Services Modernization Act. Public Law No. 106-102, 113 Stat. 1338, 1999.
30. Congress of the United States. Sarbanes-Oxley Act. Online at http://thomas.loc.gov, 2002.
31. Congress of the United States. The E-Government Act. U.S. Public Law 107-347, 2002.
32. Julie Owens. Best practices for emerging compliance challenges: Electronic messaging and communications. Online at http://www.facetime.com/pdf/reymann.pdf, 2004.
33. European Parliament. Legislative documents. Online at http://ec.europa.eu/justice_home/fsj/privacy/law/index_en.htm, 2006.
34. Quantum Inc. DLTSage WORM. Online at http://www.quantum.com/Products/TapeDrives/Index.aspx, 2006.
35. Peter Rathmann. Dynamic data structures on optical disks. In *Proceedings of the First International Conference on Data Engineering*, pages 175–180, Washington, DC, USA, 1984. IEEE Computer Society.
36. Stephen E. Robertson, Steve Walker, Micheline Hancock-Beaulieu, Aarron Gull, and Marianna Lau. Okapi at TREC. In *Text REtrieval Conference*, pages 21–30, 1992.
37. Occupational Safety and Health Administration. Regulation (Standards - 29 CFR), Access to employee exposure and medical records, Section 1910.1020(d)(1)(ii). Online at http://www.osha.gov/, 1993.

38. Securities and Exchange Commission. Guidance to Broker-Dealers on the Use of Electronic Storage Media under the National Commerce Act of 2000 with Respect to Rule 17a-4(f). Online at `http://www.sec.gov/rules/interp/34-44238.htm`, 2001.

39. Australian Securities and Exchange Commission. Clerp 9 corporate reporting and disclosure laws. Online at `http://www.asic.gov.au`, 2004.

40. Ontario Securities and Exchange Commission. Multilateral Instrument 52-111 - Reporting on Internal Control over Financial Reporting. Online at `http://www.osc.gov.on.ca`, 2005.

41. Radu Sion and Simona Boboila. Strong WORM, Network Security and Applied Cryptography Lab Technical Report 02-2007, Online at `http://crypto.cs.stonybrook.edu`, 2007.

42. Richard T. Snodgrass, Shilong (Stanley) Yao, and Christian S. Collberg. Tamper detection in audit logs. In *VLDB*, pages 504–515, 2004.

43. Sony Corp. Professional Disc for Data. Online at `www.sony.net/prodata`, 2006.

44. Sun Microsystems. Storagetek Volsafe secure media technology. Online at `http://www.storagetek.com/products/product_page2441.html`, 2006.

45. Sun Microsystems. Sun StorageTek 5320 NAS Appliance. Online at `http://www.sun.com/storagetek/nas/5320/`, 2006.

46. Jeffrey D. Ullman, Hector Garcia-Molina, and Jennifer Widom. *Database Systems: The Complete Book*. Prentice Hall, 2001.

47. Ian H. Witten, Alistair Moffat, and Timothy C. Bell. *Managing Gigabytes: Compressing and Indexing Documents and Images, Second Edition*. Morgan Kaufmann, 1999.

48. William Yurcik and Ragib Hasan. Toward one strong national breach disclosure law - justification and requirements. In *Workshop on the Economics of Securing the Information Infrastructure*, Alexandria, VA, USA, October 2006.

49. Zantaz. Zantaz Digital Safe. Online at `http://www.zantaz.com/digital-safe-product-family/`, 2006.

50. Qingbo Zhu and Windsor W. Hsu. Fossilized index: The linchpin of trustworthy non-alterable electronic records. In *Proceedings of the ACM SIGMOD International Conference on Management of Data*, pages 395–406. ACM, June 2005.

16

Damage Quarantine and Recovery in Data Processing Systems

Peng Liu[1], Sushil Jajodia[2], and Meng Yu[3]

[1] Pennsylvania State University, University Park, PA 16802, USA
   pliu@ist.psu.edu
[2] George Mason University, Fairfax, VA 22030, USA
   jajodia@gmu.edu
[3] Western Illinois University, Macomb, IL 61455, USA
   m-yu2@wiu.edu

Summary. In this article, we address transparent Damage Quarantine and Recovery (DQR), a very important problem faced today by a large number of mission, life, and/or business-critical applications and information systems that must manage risk, business continuity, and assurance in the presence of severe cyber attacks. Today, these critical applications still have a "good" chance to suffer from a big "hit" from attacks. Due to data sharing, interdependencies, and interoperability, the hit could greatly "amplify" its damage by causing catastrophic cascading effects, which may "force" an application to halt for hours or even days before the application is recovered. In this paper, we first do a thorough discussion on the limitations of traditional fault tolerance and failure recovery techniques in solving the DQR problem. Then we present a systematic review on how the DQR problem is being solved. Finally, we point out some remaining research issues in fully solving the DQR problem.

1 Introduction

In this article, we address transparent Damage Quarantine and Recovery (DQR), an important problem faced today by a large number of mission/life/ business-critical applications. These applications are the cornerstones of a variety of crucial information systems that must manage risk, business continuity, and data assurance in the presence of severe cyber attacks. Today, many of the nation's critical infrastructures (e.g., financial services, telecommunication infrastructure, transportation control) rely on these information systems to function.

There are at least two main reasons on why mission/life/business-critical applications have an urgent need for transparent damage quarantine and recovery. Firstly, despite that significant progress has been made in protecting applications and systems, mission/life/business-critical applications still have a "good" chance to suffer from a big "hit" from attacks. Due to data sharing, interdependencies, and interoperability between business processes and applications, the hit could greatly "amplify" its *damage* by causing catastrophic cascading effects, which may "force" an application to shut down itself for hours or even days before the application is recovered from the hit. (Note that high speed Internet, e-commerce, and global economy have greatly increased the speed and scale of damage spreading.) The cascading damage and loss of business continuity (i.e., DoS) may yield too much risk. Because not all intrusions can be prevented, DQR is an indispensable part of the corresponding security solution, and a quality DQR scheme may generate significant impact on risk management, business continuity, and assurance.

Secondly, due to several fundamental differences between failure recovery and attack recovery, the DQR problem cannot be solved by failure recovery technologies which are very mature in handling random failures. (a) Failure recovery in general assumes the semantics of *fail-stop*, while attack recovery in general cannot assume the semantics of attack-stop, since to achieve the adversary's goal, most attacks (except for DoS) do not allow themselves to simply crash the system; they prefer hidden damage and alive zombies, spyware, bots, etc. Assuming fail-stop, *quarantine* is not really a problem for failure recovery; however, intrusion/damage quarantine is a challenging research topic in attack recovery and it can make a big difference. (b) Failure recovery assumes that all operations (e.g., transactions) have equal rights to be recovered, while attack recovery can never assume "equal rights" because neither malicious operations nor corrupted operations should be recovered.

Towards understanding and solving the DQR problem, the rest of the article is organized as follows. In Section 2, we present a comprehensive yet tangible description of the DQR problem. In Section 3, we do in-depth discussions on the limitations of traditional fault tolerance and failure recovery techniques in solving the DQR problem. In Section 4, we present a systematic review on how the DQR problem is being solved. In Section 5, we propose a set of remaining research issues in fully solving the DQR problem and conclude the paper.

2 Overview of the DQR Problem

We are concerned with the DQR needs of mission/life/business-critical information systems. Since those information systems have been designed, implemented, deployed, and upgraded over several decades, they run both *conventional* applications, which typically use proprietary user interfaces and application-level client-server protocols [1], and *modern* applications, which are typically web-bounded running standard Web Services protocols.

Nevertheless, both conventional and modern mission/life/business-critical applications share some common characteristics: they are typically part of a large-scale, semantically rich, networked, interoperable information system;

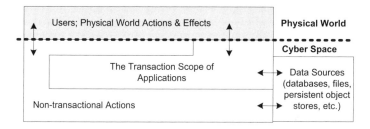

Fig. 1. Transaction Level Scope of Applications

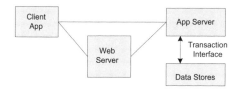

Fig. 2. The Transaction Model in Concern

they are typically stateful and data-intensive; they are typically 24*7 applications requiring superb business continuity (i.e., availability); and they typically require guaranteed recoverability (and data integrity).

Although the DQR problem may be addressed at several abstraction levels (e.g., disk level, OS level, DBMS level, transaction level, application level), solving the DQR problem at the transaction level is particularly appealing due to the following reasons. The *transaction* abstraction has revolutionized the way *reliability*, including *recoverability*, is engineered for applications. Through a simple API interface provided by an easy-to-use transaction (processing) package which is today an integral part of mainstream application development environments such as J2EE and .NET, programmers can make applications *transactional* in a rather automatic, effort-free fashion. And the benefits of making applications transactional are significant: "failure atomicity simplifies the maintenance of invariants on data" [2]; a guaranteed level of data consistency can be achieved without worrying about say race conditions; durability makes it much easier for programmers to get the luxury of recoverability.

As a result, the transaction mechanism is embraced by not only database systems [3], but also a large variety of computer systems and applications [4], including operating systems (e.g., VINO provides kernel transaction support [5]), file systems (e.g., Camelot provides transactional access to user-developed data structures stored in files [2]; and [6] argues that transactional file systems can be fast), distributed systems (e.g., QuickSilver uses transactions as a unified failure recovery mechanism [7]), persistent object stores (e.g., Augus supports transactions on abstract objects [8]), CORBA, and Web Services.

To leverage the strength, recovery facilities, and popularity of the transaction mechanism, and more important to make the proposed DQR solutions transparent to existing applications, it is a good idea to develop DQR theories and mechanisms at the transaction level. Since real world mission/life/business-critical applications typically deploy the transaction mechanism, transaction-level DQR solutions will have wide applicability.

2.1 Scope of Transaction Level DQR

In the rest of this paper, we will focus on transaction level DQR problems, models, and solutions. In particular, the transaction-level *scope* of an application and its *environment* are shown in Figure 1. In an information system, the transaction processing components of an application do not form an "isolated" system. Instead, these components will interact with their environment, which includes the Physical World, the various non-transactional actions, and the various types of data sources. Through these *interactions*, inputs are taken, physical world effects can be caused, and non-transactional attacking actions can "poison" the application's transaction scope. Although we are aware that the cyberspace damage and cascading effects can certainly cause damage in the physical world, this paper will focus on the *cyberspace* DQR solutions which will help minimize the damage caused in the physical world.

Based on how the transaction abstraction is implemented, different real world applications may deploy different transaction models. In this paper, we will focus on the transaction model shown in Figure 2. This model is widely used by conventional client-server applications and the well-known three-tier web applications. Applications running Transactional Web Services [1] and cross-site "business transactions" (a.k.a. workflows) require more advanced transaction models, which are out of the scope of this paper. As we will mention shortly in Section 5, these advanced transaction models would introduce additional challenges in solving the DQR problem.

2.2 The Threat Model and Intrusion Detection Assumption

Working at the transaction level does *not* mean that malicious transactions are the only threat we can handle. Instead, as shown in Figure 1, we allow threats to come from either inside or outside of the transaction-level scope of applications. Nevertheless, to exploit the application's transaction mechanism to achieve a malicious goal, both inside and outside threats need to either directly *corrupt* certain data objects or get certain malicious transactions launched. Outside non-transactional attack actions (e.g., Witty worm) may bypass the transaction interface and corrupt some data objects via low-level (e.g., file or disk) operations. In addition, non-transactional buffer overflow attacks may break in certain running program of the application; then the attacker can manipulate the program to launch certain malicious transactions.

Inside the transaction scope, *insider attack* [9] is probably the most serious threat. Since insiders (i.e., disgruntled employees of a bank) are typically not savvy in hacking, issuing malicious transactions (using a different user account) is typically the way they attack. Based on the study by [10], most (application level) attacks are from insiders. Besides insider attack, (a) *identity theft* may literally "transform" an outsider into an insider. (b) *SQL injection* attacks, though currently most used to steal sensitive information, has full capability to maliciously update data objects. (c) Five out of the top six web application vulnerabilities identified by OWASP [11] may enable the attacker to launched a malicious transaction. They are *unvalidated input, broken access control, broken authentication and session management, cross site scripting* (which helps the attacker to steal user name and passwords), and *injection flaws*. (d) Finally, *erroneous* transactions caused by user/operator mistakes instead of attacks are yet another major threat to data integrity.

The intrusion detection assumption: We assume that a set of *external* intrusion detection sensors will do their job and tell us which operations (or transactions) were malicious or which data objects were originally corrupted by the attack. These sensors may be a network-level (e.g., [12]), host-level (e.g., [13]), database-level (e.g., [14]) or transaction-level (e.g., [15, 16]) intrusion detection sensor. These sensors may enforce misuse detection (e.g., [17]), anomaly detection (e.g., [18, 19]), or specification-based (e.g., [20, 21]) detection mechanisms. We assume these sensors are usually associated with false positives, false negatives, and detection latency. Finally, sensors that detect data corruption (e.g., [22, 23, 24]) may also be used.

Remark   Although some intrusion detection sensors could raise a good number of false positives or false negatives, the alarms raised by many intrusion/error detection sensors can actually be *verified* before any DQR operation is performed. (In this way, the negative impact of false positives and false negatives on the correctness/quality of DQR may be avoided.) For example, (a) most user/operator mistakes can be easily verified by the operation audit trails. (b) Many data corruption detectors have 100% accuracy. (c) When a strong correlation is found between one alert X and some other alerts, alert X may be verified as a true intrusion.

2.3 The DQR Problem/Solution Space

In our view, the DQR problem is a 6-dimensional problem:

- (1) The *damage propagation* dimension explains why cascading effects can be caused and why quarantine is needed. Although some specific types of damage (e.g., when an individual credit card account is corrupted) could be self-contained, a variety types of damage are actually very infectious due to data sharing, interdependencies, and interoperability between business processes and applications. For example, in a travel assistant Web Service, if a set of air tickets are reserved due to malicious transactions, some other travelers may have to change their travel plans in terms of which airlines to go, which nights to stay in hotel, etc.. Furthermore, the changed travel plans can cause cascading effects to yet another group of travelers; and the propagation may go on and on.

- (2) The *recovery* dimension covers three semantics for recovery: the *coldstart* semantics mean that the system is "halted" while damage is being assessed and repaired. (Damage assessment is to identify the set of corrupted data objects. Damage repairing is to restore the value of each corrupted data object to the latest before-infection version.) To address the DoS threat, recovery mechanisms with *warmstart* or *hotstart* semantics are needed. Warmstart semantics allow continuous, but degraded, running of the application while damage is being recovered. Hotstart semantics make recovery transparent to the users.
- (3) The *quarantine* dimension covers a spectrum of quarantine strategies: (a) coldstart recovery without quarantine, (b) warmstart recovery with conservative, reactive quarantine, (c) warmstart recovery with proactive or predictive quarantine, (b) hotstart recovery with optimistic quarantine, to name a few.
- (4) The *application* dimension covers the various transaction models deployed by conventional and modern applications. The uniqueness of each model may introduce new challenges for solving the DQR problem.
- (5) The *correctness* dimension tells whether a DQR scheme is *correct* in terms of consistency, recoverability, and quarantinability.
- (6) The *quality* dimension allows people to measure and compare the *quality levels* achieved by a set of correct yet different DQR schemes.

2.4 What Transaction Level DQR Solutions Cannot Do

First, although transaction-level DQR solutions will help minimize the damage caused by cyberspace attacks in the physical world, they cannot repair physical damage, which is a different field of study. Second, transaction-level DQR solutions are not designed to patch software which is another critical intrusion recovery problem. Nevertheless, transaction-level DQR solutions and software patching are complementary to each other. Transaction-level DQR solutions can help quarantine and repair the damage done by unpatched software broken-in by the adversary.

3 Traditional Failure Recovery Techniques and Their Limitations

DQR theories and mechanisms draw on work from several areas of systems research such as survivable computing, fault-tolerant computing, and transaction processing. Among all the relevant areas, the closest one should be Failure Recovery, which is part of Fault Tolerance [25]. In the literature, failure recovery has not only been extensively studied in data processing systems [3, 26, 4], but also been thoroughly studied in other types of computing systems. In [27] and [28], operating systems failure recovery is investigated. In

[7], recovery management in distributed system is investigated. In [29], roll-back recovery techniques for long-run applications are thoroughly discussed. In [30, 31, 32, 33], checkpoint-based rollback recovery is discussed. In [34], reliability modeling and evaluation criteria are thoroughly discussed. More recently, (a) David Patterson et al. have proposed the concept of ROC (Recovery -Oriented Computing) [35] in which recovery is used as a general technique for dealing with failure in complex systems. For example, in [36] a model of "recursive recovery" is proposed in which a complex software system is decomposed into a multi-layer modular self-recovering implementation. (b) The Nooks approach [37] makes device driver failures transparent to operating systems.

Unfortunately, due to the fundamental differences mentioned in Section 1 between failure recovery and attack recovery, existing failure recovery techniques cannot effectively deal with malicious attacks. For example, (a) rolling back the application's state to a previous corruption-free *checkpoint* will lose *all* the good work done after the checkpoint. (b) Maintaining frequent checkpoints [38, 39, 40] may not work since no checkpoint taken between the time of attack and the time of recovery can be used. (c) Standy replica systems will not only replicate good work, but also replicate infection!

With DQR in *data processing systems* as the theme of this paper, this section will focus on failure recovery technologies for data processing systems and their limitations in solving the DQR problem. In the following, we classify failure recovery technologies for data processing systems into three categories: transactional undo/redo, replication-based recovery, and storage media backup-restore, and discuss them in three subsections, respectively.

3.1 Transactional Undo/Redo

The crux of transactional undo/redo techniques is correcting the application states that are corrupted due to failures. For data-processing systems or data-oriented applications in which doing read and write operations on various data objects (managed by a set of databases) represents the main activities, failure recovery is rooted in the *transaction concept* [41] which has been around for a long time. This concept encapsulates the *ACID* (Atomicity, Consistency, Isolation, and Durability) properties [3, 41]. Data-oriented applications are not limited to the database area [42, 43, 44, 7, 45, 46]. The basic recovery procedure is almost the same for all applications: when a failure happens, a set of *undo* operations will be performed to rollback the application's *state* to the most recent *checkpoint*, which is maintained through logging, then a set of *redo* operations will be performed to restore the state to exactly the failing point. Nevertheless, the concrete recovery algorithms depend heavily upon how changes are logged. WAL (Write Ahead Logging) is today the standard approach widely accepted by the database industry. Some of the commercial systems and prototypes based on WAL are ARIES [26], IBM's AS/400 [47],

IBM's DB2 [48], Microsoft's SQL Server [49], and Oracle's Oracle Database [50].

Besides the basic idea of WAL, a set of important enhancements such as (a) using log sequence number (LSN) to correlate the state of a page with respect to logged updates of that page and (b) fuzzy checkpoints are proposed by ARIES [26], the de facto (industry) standard for transaction recovery models.

Finally, in addition to such standard recovery techniques as WAL, the database industry has developed various proprietary recovery tools. For example, DB2 Log Analysis Tool [51] allows you to monitor data changes; DB2 Recovery Expert [52] analyzes and provides diagnostics of altered database assets, and can roll data changes backward or forward; Oracle Recovery Manager [53] manages the database backup and restore process; and Oracle Data Guard creates, maintains, manages and monitors one or more standby databases.

Limitations in Solving the DQR Problem: Although existing transaction recovery methods are matured in handling failures, they are not designed to deal with malicious attacks. In particular, first, the durability property ensures that traditional recovery mechanisms never undo committed transactions. However, the fact that a transaction commits does not guarantee that its effects are desirable. Specifically, a committed transaction may reflect inappropriate and/or malicious activity.

Second, although attack recovery is related to the notion of *cascading abort* [3], cascading aborts only capture the *read-from* relation between active transactions, and in standard recovery approaches cascading aborts are avoided by requiring transactions to read only committed data [54].

Third, there are two common approaches to handling the problem of undoing committed transactions: rollback and compensation. (3a) The rollback approach is simply to roll back all activity – desirable as well as undesirable – to a checkpoint believed to be free of damage. The rollback approach is effective, but expensive, in that all of the desirable work between the time of the checkpoint and the time of recovery is lost. Although there are algorithms for efficiently establishing snapshots on-the-fly [38, 39, 40], maintaining frequent checkpoints may not work since no checkpoint taken between the time of attack and the time of recovery can be used. (3b) The compensation approach [55, 56] seeks to undo either committed transactions or committed steps in long-duration or nested transactions [54] without necessarily restoring the data state to appear as if the malicious transactions or steps had never been executed. There are two kinds of compensation: action-oriented and effect-oriented [54, 57, 58, 59]. Action-oriented compensation for a transaction or step T_i compensates only the actions of T_i. Effect-oriented compensation for a transaction or step T_i compensates not only the actions of T_i, but also the actions that are affected by T_i. Although various types of compensation are possible, all of them require semantic knowledge of the application, and none of them is adopted by mainstream commercial systems.

Fourth, classic *redo* operations cannot repair damage because they do not reexecute affected transactions.

3.2 Replication-based Recovery

The crux of the replication based recovery is using redundancy to mask/tolerate failures. Replication-based recovery does not undo erroneous operations. In data-oriented applications, the replication idea is embodied through the widely adopted practice of data replication [60, 3] and *standby* databases [53]. In such replicated systems, each request (or transaction) will be processed by all the *replicas* in which each data object is replicated. When a failure happens to the primary database, the responses (or outputs) generated by a standby (or replicated) database can be returned to the client as if the failure had never happened. (In distributed computing, the replication idea is embodied through such techniques as RAPS (reliable array-structured partitioned service), the state-machine approach [61], and virtual synchrony [62].)

Limitations in Solving the DQR Problem: Both data replication and standy databases will not only replicate good work, but also replicate infection!

3.3 Storage Media Backup-Restore

The idea of storage media backup-restore is proven very practical and valuable. It is fully embraced by the IT industry: Computer Associates large enterprise backup solutions [63], Symantec LiveState recovery products [64], the Sonasoft Solution [65], just to name a few. This idea is complementary to the recovery idea and the replication idea, but in many cases it cannot achieve fine-grained data consistency, while the two other ideas can.

Limitations in Solving the DQR Problem: Among the data objects included in a *backup*, storage media backup-restore techniques cannot distinguish clean data objects from dirty, corrupted ones.

4 Solving the DQR Problem

In this section, we present a systematic review on how the DQR problem is being solved in the literature. Although self repairable file systems are proposed [66, 67], most DQR mechanisms proposed in the literature are transaction-level solutions. So here we concentrate on transaction-level DQR solutions.

4.1 The Model

In our model, a *transaction* is a set of *read* and *write* operations that either *commits* or *aborts*. For clarity, we assume there are no *blind* writes, although the theory can certainly be extended to handle blind writes. At the transaction level, an application (e.g., the application types shown in Figure 2) is a transaction execution *history*. Since recovery of uncommitted transactions is addressed by standard mechanisms [3], we can safely ignore aborted transactions and only consider the committed *projection* $C(H)$ of every history H. We define $<_H$ to be the usual partial order on $C(H)$, namely, $T_i <_H T_j$ if $<_H$ orders operations of T_i before conflicting operations of T_j (Note that in H the operations of different transactions are often interleaved). Two operations *conflict* if they are on the same data object and one is write.

In principle, the *correctness* of a DQR scheme (or solution) can be "checked" either by the operations performed by the scheme or by the resulted effects. Here, we use the resulted history of a DQR scheme to study its correctness. In our model, the DQR histories resulted from a DQR scheme may contain the following information:

- A DQR history may contain two types of *malicious* transactions, four types of *legitimate* transactions, and one type of *cleaning* transactions: Type 1 malicious transactions are issued by attackers or malicious code; more broadly, transactions executed by mistake can be viewed as a Type 2 malicious transaction A legitimate transaction may be either a *regular* transaction or a *reexecuted* transaction; and both regular and reexecuted transactions may be *affected* or *damaged* if they read any corrupted data object. Finally, cleaning transactions only contain backward or forward overwrite operations, depending upon how the recovery is performed.
- A classic history consists of only operations, while a DQR history is an interleaved sequence of operations and data store states. The *data store* contains all the data objects that a transaction may access. The *state* of the data store at time t is determined by the latest committed values of every data object in the store.
- A data store state (e.g., a database state) contains three types of *corrupted* data objects and two types of *clean* data objects. Type 1 corrupted data objects are originally generated by the writes of malicious transactions. Type 2 are originally generated by affected transactions. Type 3 are originally generated by non-transactional attacking actions outside of the application's transaction scope. Note that a corrupted data object may be read or updated several times before it is *repaired* (a.k.a. *cleaned*). Type 1 clean data objects are never corrupted. Type 2 clean data objects are once corrupted, but they are repaired.

Damage Propagation

Based on the threat model, we know where malicious transactions come from. To see how affected transactions are generated and how the damage spreads, we should do dependency (or causality) analysis.

Definition 4.1 (dependency graph)   As stated in [68], transaction T_j is *dependent upon* T_i in a history if there exists a data object o such that T_j

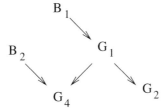

Fig. 3. Dependency Graph for History H_1

reads o after T_i has updated o; T_i does not abort before T_j reads o; and every transaction (if any) that updates o between the time T_i updates o and T_j reads o is aborted before T_j reads x. In a history, T_1 *affects* T_2 if the ordered pair (T_1, T_2) is in the transitive closure of the *dependent upon* relation. Finally, we define the *dependency graph* for a (any) set of transactions S in a history as $DG(S) = (V, E)$ in which V is the union of S and the set of transactions that are affected by S. There is an edge, $T_i \to T_j$, in E if $T_i \in V$, $T_j \in (V - S)$, and T_j is dependent upon T_i.   □

Example   Consider the following history over $(B_1, B_2, G_1, G_2, G_3, G_4)$:

$$H_1 : r_{B_1}[x]w_{B_1}[x]c_{B_1}r_{G_1}[x]w_{G_1}[x]r_{G_3}[z]w_{G_3}[z]c_{G_3}r_{G_1}[y]w_{G_1}[y]c_{G_1}$$
$$r_{G_2}[y]w_{G_2}[y]r_{B_2}[z]w_{B_2}[z]c_{B_2}r_{G_2}[v]w_{G_2}[v]c_{G_2}r_{G_4}[z]w_{G_4}[z]r_{G_4}[y]w_{G_4}[y]c_{G_4}$$

In H_1, B_1 and B_2 are malicious transactions while the other three are legitimate transactions; $r_T[x]$ ($w_T[x]$) is a read (write) operation by transaction T on data object x; c_T is the commit operation of T. Let $\mathbf{B} = \{B_1, B_2\}$, $DG(\mathbf{B})$ is shown in Figure 3.

Lemma 4.1   In a DQR history, a legitimate transaction is affected if and only if it is in dependency graph DG(all malicious transactions plus all the legitimate transactions that read the original version of any Type 3 corrupted data object). Being conservative, we assume all updates done by affected transactions may *spread* the damage.   □

Do We Have to Sacrifice Durability?

A main concern people may have on DQR solutions is whether they will compromise *Durability*, a fundamental property of transaction processing and transactional failure recovery mechanisms. In other words, do we have to sacrifice Durability in doing DQR? Fortunately, the answer is NO. To keep durability, DQR schemes never really need to undo a malicious or affected transaction; instead, they can execute cleaning transactions to *semantically* revoke the effect of a committed transaction. By semantically revoking the effect of a committed transaction, we can achieve the following: (a) The effect of a committed transaction will always be kept durable; we never revoke or reverse any physical effect of a committed transaction on the persistent storage. (b) A cleaning transaction will change the data store state in exactly the *same* way as a regular transaction performing a set of updates. Because executing regular transactions will never compromise Durability, executing cleaning transactions (to do damage recovery) will never compromise Durability.

The Spectrum of DQR Schemes

The concept of DQR histories allows us to see the differences between the ones on the "spectrum" of DQR schemes. (a) On one end of the spectrum, a *static* DQR scheme will stop processing new transactions until every corrupted data object is *repaired* or cleaned. (A corrupted data object is *repaired* if its value is restored to the latest clean version before corruption.) So since the *time of detection*, which is also the time when the recovery starts, the corresponding DQR history will proceed with only cleaning transactions until the repair is completed. In addition, affected transactions should be reexecuted; otherwise, DoS is caused. (b) On the other end, an optimistic, *dynamic* DQR scheme may do dependency analysis (a.k.a. damage assessment), execute cleaning transactions, execute to-be-reexecuted transactions, and execute new transactions *concurrently*. (c) Semi-dynamic DQR schemes may certainly stay on the spectrum between the two ends. For example, in [69, 70], there is a dedicated *scan* phase during which dependency analysis is performed, but *no* new transactions can be executed.

Section organization   In the rest of this section, without losing generality, we will focus on the two "ends" of the spectrum of DQR schemes, that is, we will review static DQR solutions and dynamic DQR solutions in Section 4.2 and Section 4.3, respectively.

4.2 Static DQR Solutions

Static DQR solutions "halt" the database (service) before the repair is completed. Since no new transactions can be executed during static DQR, the damage will not spread unless there are incorrect repair operations. Hence, damage quarantine is not an issue in static DQR. As a result, static DQR has two aspects: *damage assessment*, which identifies every corrupted data object, and *damage repair*, which restores the value of each corrupted data object to its pre-corruption version.

In terms of how damage assessment and repair can be done, existing static DQR methods are either *data-oriented* [71] or *transaction-oriented* [68]. Transaction-oriented methods assess and repair the damage by identifying and backing out affected transactions. In particular, they work as follows.

- *Damage Assessment*   Build the dependency graph defined in Definition 4.1 for the set of malicious transactions detected. Based on Lemma 4.1, the dependency graph consists of all and only the affected transactions that have "contributed" to damage propagation. Assuming that read operations are logged together with write operations, it is not difficult to build the dependency graph. It is shown in [68] that the log can be scanned forward only once (i.e., one-pass) from the entry where the first malicious transaction starts to locate every affected transaction.

- *Repair*   When the damage assessment part is done, scan backward from the end of the log to semantically revoke (or undo) the effects of all the malicious transactions and the transactions included in the dependency graph. Note that here the undoes should be performed in the reverse commit order.

In contrast, data-oriented methods use the read and write operations of transactions to trace the damage spreading from one data object to another, and compose a specific piece of code to repair each damaged data object. In particular, data-oriented methods work as follows.

- *Damage Assessment*   Construct a specific damage propagation graph in which each node is a (corrupted) data object while each directed edge from node x to y is a transaction T such that T reads x and writes y. The damage propagation graph can be built by one-pass scanning of the log.
- *Repair*   Once the damage propagation graph is constructed, for each data object x contained in the graph, search through the log to find the latest pre-corruption version of x. Then repair x by overwriting the value of x with the searched version.

Comparison   Data-oriented methods are more flexible and better at handling blind writes, however, composing cleaning code for each data object can be time consuming and prone to errors. Transaction-oriented methods use a cleaning transaction, which can be easily composed, to repair multiple data objects at the same time, thus they are more robust and efficient.

Maintaining Read Information

Both data-oriented methods and transaction-oriented methods rely on the read-from relationships between transactions. (Transaction T_1 *reads from* T_2 if there is a data object x such that T_1 reads x after T_2 updates x, and no other transaction updates x between these two operations.) However, the read-from information is not maintained by commercial DBMSes, since such information is not necessary for failure recovery. As a result, the transaction log maintained by a commercial DBMS actually does not contain sufficient information for the aforementioned DQR mechanisms to succeed. Therefore, maintaining the read-from information is an important task in engineering practical DQR systems.

In the literature, several representative techniques are proposed to maintain the read-from information. In [72], read operations are extracted from SQL statement texts. In particular, [72] assumes that each transaction belongs to a transaction *type*, and the *profile* (or source code) for each transaction type is known. For each transaction type ty_i, [72] extracts a *read set template* from

ty_i's profile. The template specifies the kind of objects that transactions of type ty_i could read. Later on when a transaction T_i is executed, the template for $type(T_i)$ will be *materialized* to produce the read set of T_i using the input arguments of T_i (Note that these input arguments are embedded in T_i's SQL statements). This method is transparent to the DBMS kernel, however, in some scenarios it can only obtain approximate read sets.

In [73], the DBMS is extended to provide support for read triggers. In contrast, commercial DBMSes only support insert/update triggers. This method can obtain the exact read sets and it has reasonable run-time overhead, but it requires a major extension to the kernel.

In [70], a more aggressive approach is taken to maintain the read-from information. In this approach, Recovery Manager, the "core" of commercial transaction management systems, is modified to log reads. In particular, when the system commits a transaction, all the read information about the transaction will be consolidated into a single log record; then this special reads-keeping log record will be forced onto the disk together with other writes-keeping log records. This approach has minimal run-time overhead, but it requires the largest amount of changes to the DBMS kernel.

Static Repair via History Rewriting

From the correctness point of view, both data-oriented methods and transaction-oriented methods would result in a history that is *conflict equivalent* to the *serial* history composed of only the legitimate, unaffected transactions. ($C(H_1)$ is conflict equivalent to $C(H_2)$ if they contain the same set of operations and they order every pair of conflicting operations in the same way.) Nevertheless, the history rewriting framework proposed in [74] shows that if we relax the correctness requirement from conflict equivalence to *view equivalence*, we may even save the work of affected transactions.

In particular, by exploiting two new semantic relationships between transactions, denoted *can-follow* and *can-precede*, respectively, the history rewriting framework can rewrite every "infected" history, which always starts with a malicious transaction, to a ready-to-repair history in which every legitimate, unaffected transaction precedes all the malicious transactions. Such a rewritten history typically looks like the following. Here, G_i is a legitimate, unaffected transaction and AG_i is an affected transaction. In addition, F_i is called a *fix*. A fix for a transaction like B_1 is a set of variables read by the transaction given values as in the original position of the transaction before the history is rewritten.

$$G_{i1}...AG_{j1}...G_{in}...AG_{jm}\ B_1^{F_1}\ AG_{k1}^{F_{k1}}...B_l^{F_l}...AG_{kp}^{F_{kp}}$$

The study in [74] shows that (a) each rewritten history and the original history will result in the same final database state, and (b) the work of all the legitimate transactions preceding $B_1^{F_1}$ in the rewritten history can be saved by executing a specific compensating transaction for each of the transactions

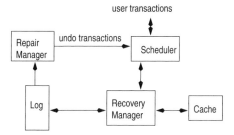

Fig. 4. Architecture of an On-the-fly Repair System

in the *suffix* of the rewritten history. The suffix starts with $B_1^{F_1}$. Note that the last transaction in the rewritten history should be the first one to compensate, and $B_1^{F_1}$ should be the last one. Since every legitimate, unaffected transaction will precede $B_1^{F_1}$, the work of all unaffected transactions will be kept. Moreover, since affected transactions may precede $B_1^{F_1}$, the work of many affected transactions may be saved as well.

4.3 Dynamic DQR Solutions

In static DQR, new transactions are blocked during the repair process. This prevents static DQR mechanisms from being deployed by 24*7 database applications. As 24*7 database applications are becoming more and more common, dynamic DQR solutions that can do non-stop, zero down-time attack recovery are in demand.

Dynamic DQR Solutions with Reactive Quarantine

To have zero down-time, neither damage assessment nor repair can block the execution of new transactions. This means that dependency analysis, execution of new transactions, execution of cleaning transactions, and reexecution of affected transactions need to be done in parallel. To meet this challenge, people may wonder if the traditional transaction management architecture needs to be rebuilt. Fortunately, Figure 4 shows that the traditional transaction management architecture [3] is adequate to accommodate on-the-fly repair. The *Repair Manager* is applied to the growing logs of on-the-fly histories to mark any bad as well as affected transactions. For every bad or affected transaction, the Repair Manager builds a cleaning transaction and submits it to the *Scheduler*. The cleaning transaction is only composed of write operations. The *Scheduler* schedules the operations submitted either by user transactions or by cleaning transactions to generate a correct on-the-fly history. Affected transactions that are semantically revoked (or undone) can be resubmitted to the Scheduler either by users or by the Repair Manager. Finally, the *Recovery Manager* executes the operations submitted by the Scheduler and logs them.

On-the-fly attack recovery faces several unique challenges. First, since new transactions may first read corrupted data objects then update clean data objects, the damage may continuously spread, and the attack recovery process may never *terminate*. Accordingly, we face two critical questions. (a) Will the attack recovery process terminate? (b) If the attack recovery process terminates, can we detect the termination? Second, we need to do repair *forwardly* since the assessment process may never stop. The assessment process may never stop since the damage may continuously spread. Third, cleaned data objects could be re-damaged during attack recovery.

To tackle challenge 2, we must ensure that a later on cleaning transaction will not accidentally damage an object cleaned by a previous cleaning transaction. For this purpose, the system should "remember" the data objects that are already repaired and not yet re-damaged. To tackle challenge 3, we must not mistake a cleaned object as damaged, and we must not mistake a re-damaged object as already cleaned. To tackle challenge 1, the study in [68] shows that when the damage spreading speed is quicker than the repair speed, the repair may never terminate. Otherwise, the repair process will terminate, and under the following three conditions we can ensure that the repair terminates: (1) every malicious transaction is cleaned; (2) every identified damaged object is cleaned; (3) further damage assessment scans will not identify any new damage (if no new attack comes).

From a state-transition angle, the job of attack recovery is to get a *state* of the database, which is determined by the values of the data objects, where (a) no effects of the malicious transactions are there and (b) the work of good transactions should be retained as much as possible. In particular, transactions transform the database from one state to another. Good transactions transform a good database state to another good state, but malicious transactions can transform a good state to a damaged one. Moreover, both malicious and affected (good) transactions can make an already damaged state even worse. We say a database state S_1 is *better* than another one S_2 if S_1 has fewer corrupted objects. The goal of on-the-fly attack recovery is to get the state better and better, although during the repair process new attacks and damage spreading could (temporarily) make the state even worse. (A state-oriented object-by-object attack recovery scheme is proposed in [71].)

Finally, it should be noticed that from the transaction scheduling viewpoint, on-the-fly repair introduces new scheduling constraints. For example, (a) when a read operation $r_T[x]$ is scheduled, x must be clean. (b) Conflicting cleaning transactions should be scheduled in the same order in which they are submitted by the Repair Manager. The order is critical to the correctness of repair. (c) When a cleaning operation $w_U[x]$ is scheduled, x must be dirty.

Dynamic DQR Solutions with Proactive Quarantine

From the viewpoint of on-the-fly non-stop recovery, fault/damage quarantine can be viewed as part of recovery. The goal of damage quarantine is to prevent

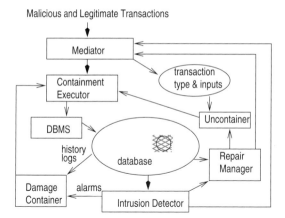

Fig. 5. Proactive Damage Quarantine

the damage from spreading out during recovery. One problem of the solution shown in Figure 4 is that its damage quarantine may not be effective, since it *contains* the damage by disallowing transactions to read the set of data objects that are identified (by the Damage Assessor) as corrupted. This reactive *one-phase* damage containment approach has a serious drawback, that is, it cannot prevent the damage caused on the objects that are corrupted but not yet located from spreading. Assessing the damage caused by a malicious transaction B can take a substantial amount of time, especially when there are a lot of transactions executed during the detection latency of B. During the *assessment latency*, the damage caused during the detection latency can spread to many other objects before being contained.

The approach shown in Figure 5 integrates a novel multi-phase damage containment technique to tackle this problem. In particular, the damage containment process has one containing phase, which instantly contains the damage that *might* have been caused (or spread) by the intrusion as soon as the intrusion is detected, and one or more later on uncontaining phases to uncontain the objects that are mistakenly contained during the containing phase, and the objects that are cleaned. In this approach, the *Damage Container* will enforce the containing phase (as soon as a malicious transaction is reported) by sending some containing instructions to the *Containment Executor*. The *Uncontainer*, with the help from the Damage Assessor, will enforce the uncontaining phases by sending some uncontaining instructions to the Containment Executor. The Containment Executor controls the access of the user transactions to the database according to these instructions.

When a malicious transaction B is detected, the containing phase must ensure that the damage caused directly or indirectly by B will be contained. In addition, the containing phase must be quick enough because otherwise either a lot of damage can leak out during the phase, or substantial availability can be lost. Time stamps can be exploited to achieve this goal. The containing phase can be done by just adding an access control rule to the Containment Executor, which denies access to the set of objects updated during the period of time from the time B commits to the time the containing phase starts. This period of time is called the *containing-time-window*. When the containing phase starts, every active transaction should be aborted because they could spread damage. New transactions can be executed only after the containing phase ends.

It is clear that the containing phase *overcontains* the damage in most cases. Many objects updated within the containing time window can be undamaged. And we must uncontain them as soon as possible to reduce the corresponding availability loss. Accurate uncontainment can be done based on the reports from the Damage Assessor, which could be too slow due to the assessment latency. [75] shows that transaction *types* can be exploited to do much *quicker* uncontainment. In particular, assuming that (a) each transaction T_i belongs to a transaction type $type(T_i)$ and (b) the *profile* for $type(T_i)$ is known, the *read set template* and *write set template* can be extracted from $type(T_i)$'s profile. The templates specify the kind of objects that transactions of $type(T_i)$ can read or write. As a result, the *approximate* read-from dependency among a history of transactions can be quickly captured by identifying the read-from dependency among the types of these transactions. Moreover, the type-based approach can be made more accurate by *materializing* the templates of transactions using their inputs before analyzing the read-from dependency among the types.

Other damage quarantine methods   (a) In [76], a color scheme for marking and containing damage is used to develop a mechanism by which databases under attack could still be safely used. This scheme assumes that each data record has an (accurate) initial damage mark or color (note that such marks may be generated by the damage assessment process), then specific color-based access controls are enforced to make sure that the damage will not spread from corrupted data objects to clean ones.

(b) *Attack Isolation*   The idea is to isolate likely suspicious transactions before a definite determination of intrusion is reported. In particular, when a suspicious session B is discovered, isolating B and the associated transactions transparently into a separate environment that still appears to B to be the actual system allows B's activities to be kept under surveillance without risking further harm to the system. An isolation strategy that has been used in such instances is known as *fishbowling*. Fishbowling involves setting up a separate look-alike host or file system and transparently redirecting the suspicious entity's requests to it. This approach allows the incident to be further studied to determine the real source, nature, and goal of the activity, but it has some limitations, particularly when considered at the application level. First, the substitute host or file system is essentially sacrificed during the suspected attack to monitor B, consuming significant resources that may be scarce. Second, since B is cut off from the real system, if B proves innocent, denial of service could still be a problem. While some types of service B receives from the substitute, fishbowl system may be adequate, in other cases the lack of interaction with the real system's resources may prevent B from continuing to produce valid results. On the other hand, if the semantics of the application are such that B can continue producing valid work, this work will be lost when the incident concludes even if B is deemed innocent and reconnected to the real system. The fishbowling mechanism makes no provision for re-merging updates from the substitute, fishbowl system back into the real system.

In [77, 78], these limitations are overcome by taking advantage of action semantics and the dependency relationships between transactions. In this method, as in the case of fishbowling, when B comes under suspicion, B is allowed to continue working while the security officer attempts to determine whether there is anything to worry about. At the same time, the system is isolated from any further damage B might have in mind. However, this method provides the isolation without consuming duplicate resources to construct an entirely separate environment, allows options for partial interaction across the boundary, and provides data-consistency-preserving algorithms for smoothly merging B's work back into the real system should B prove innocent. Among the partial interaction options, the *one-way isolation* concept is particularly interesting. One-way isolation allows being-isolated transactions to read the newest updates done by (trusted) transactions running on the main database, but forbids trusted transactions from reading any updates done by being-isolated transactions.

4.4 Quality Evaluation

Correctness does not always imply high quality. Two correct DQR schemes may yield very different quality levels in the DQR services they provide. In failure recovery, the MTTF-MTTR model (Mean Time To Failure - Mean Time To Recovery model) provides a neat yet precise way to gain concrete understanding of the quality of a recovery service which is measured by MTTF/(MTTF+MTTR), and this quality model has played a crucial role in advancing the theories and technologies of failure recovery. Unfortunately, due to the reasons mentioned in Section 1, the MTTF-MTTR model is no longer sufficient for defining the quality of DQR services.

In principle, the *quality* of DQR services can be evaluated by a vector composed of three criteria regarding *data integrity* and two criteria regarding *availability*:

- *C1: Dirtiness* depends on the percentage of corrupted data objects in each data store state.
- *C2: Data Freshness* When a clean yet older version of a corrupted data object o is made accessible during recovery, freshness depends on whether a fresher version of o is used by new transactions. Note that one clean

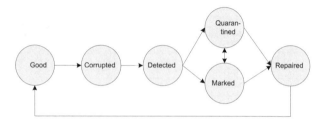

Fig. 6. DQR System State Transition

version can be much fresher than another clean version of the same data object.

- *C3: Data Consistency*   Violation of serializability can compromise data consistency no matter the history is multi-versioned or not.
- *C4: Rewarding Availability*   The more clean or cleaned data objects are made accessible to new transactions, the more *rewarding* availability (or business continuity) is achieved. The more rewarding availability, the less denial-of-service will be caused.
- *C5: Hurting Availability*   The more corrupted data objects are made accessible to new transactions, the more *hurting* availability is yielded. Because hurting availability will hurt data integrity and spread the damage, hurting availability is worse than letting the corrupted objects be quarantined.

An important finding gained in reliability evaluation research (e.g., [34, 79]) is that state transition models may play a big role in quality evaluation. A state transition model specific for DQR systems can be the model shown in Figure 6, where in terms of any portion of the application (e.g., a set of data objects), the system has 6 basic states: they are self explanatory except that the 'M' state means that the portion is Marked as damaged. Ignoring the 'Q' state, we could measure Dirtiness by (MTTC+MTTM+MTTR)/(MTTC+ MTTD+MTTM+MTTR); and Rewarding Availability by (MTTC+MTTR)/ (MTTC+MTTD+MTTM+MTTR). In [80], this idea is well justified in the context of intrusion tolerant database systems through Continuous Time Markov Chain based state transition model analysis and prototype experiments based validation.

5 Remaining Research Issues and Concluding Remarks

Although DQR is not a new concept, existing attack (or intrusion) recovery research activities (see Section 4) are still quite limited in satisfying the DQR needs of real world applications, for the following reasons: (1) A theoretic understanding of the correctness and quality of DQR schemes is still missing in the literature. Since classic failure recovery theories cannot handle quarantine or on-the-fly recovery, new DQR theories are necessary to understand the strength and weakness of existing DQR schemes, inspire the development of novel DQR schemes, and make DQR a rigor field of study, for example. (2) There is still a big gap in engineering practical DQR capabilities for real world applications. For one example, Web Services (WS) and service-oriented architectures have significantly changed the way applications are developed, but no WS aware techniques have yet been developed to do transparent DQR for WS-based applications. For another example, existing transaction-level DQR mechanisms either require major changes in system design or suffer from significant DoS or performance overhead.

Therefore, to fully solve the DQR problem, a holistic approach should be taken to make an integrated set of innovative contributions on four fundamental aspects of DQR: theories, mechanisms, applications, and systems.

- New DQR theories should be developed to (a) address quarantine and *transparency*, (b) define *quality* of DQR services, and (c) integrate *recoverability* and *quarantinability*.
- New DQR schemes should be developed to advance the state-of-the-art DQR techniques from the paradigm of read-write-dependency analysis to the new paradigm of mark-based causality tracing, which will significantly improve transparency and efficiency.
- Non-blocking repair schemes should be developed to advance the state-of-the-art DQR techniques, from the paradigm of "clean-then-reexecute" recovery to the new paradigm of "cleaning-free" recovery, which avoids the overhead introduced by cleaning transactions.
- New DQR schemes should be developed to advance the state-of-the-art from the paradigm of "lock-competing reexecution" to the new paradigm of "non-blocking repair".
- New DQR schemes should be developed to advance the state-of-the-art from the paradigm of "pre-programmed DQR" to "adaptive or self-reconfigurable DQR".
- DQR theories and mechanisms should handle both conventional applications (which require ACID properties) and modern applications which adopt a weaker consistency model to make distributed "business transaction" processing (on top of Web Services) practical, scalable, and efficient.
- From the perspective of system building, complete open-source DQR tools and systems should be prototyped and evaluated using the appropriate benchmarks.

Acknowledgement

Peng Liu was supported in part by NSF CCR-TC-0233324 and NSF/DHS 0335241.

References

1. Birman, K.P.: Reliable Distributed Systems: Technologies, Web Services, and Applications. Springer (2005)
2. Spector, A.Z., Daniels, D., Duchamp, D.: Distributed Transactions for Reliable Systems. In: ACM SOSP. (1985)
3. Bernstein, P.A., Hadzilacos, V., Goodman, N.: Concurrency Control and Recovery in Database Systems. Addison-Wesley, Reading, MA (1987)
4. Gray, J., ed.: The Benchmark Handbook for Database and Transaction Processing Systems. 2 edn. Morgan Kaufmann Publishers, Inc. (1993)
5. Seltzer, M.I., Endo, Y., Small, C., Smith, K.A.: Dealing With Disaster: Surviving Misbehaved Kernel Extensions. In: OSDI. (1996)
6. Liskov, B., Rodrigues, R.: Transactional File Systems Can Be Fast. In: 11th ACM SIGOPS European Workshop. (2004)
7. Haskin, R., Malachi, Y., Sawdon, W., Chan, G.: Recovery management in Quick-Silver. ACM Transactions on Computer Systems **6**(1) (1988)
8. Liskov, B., Curtis, D., Johnson, P., Scheifler, R.: Implementation of Argus . In: ACM SOSP. (1987) 111–122
9. Schneier, B.: Attack trends 2004 and 2005. ACM Queue **3**(5) (June 2005)
10. Carter, D.L., Katz, A.J.: Computer Crime: An Emerging Challenge for Law Enforcement. FBI Law Enforcement Bulletin **1**(8) (December 1996)
11. OWASP: Owasp top ten most critical web application security vulnerabilities. http://www.owasp.org/documentation/topten.html (January, 27 2004)
12. Paxson, V.: Bro: a system for detecting network intruders in real-time. Computer Networks (1999) 2435–2463
13. Forrest, S., Hofmeyr, S.A., Somayaji, A., Longstaff, T.A.: A Sense of Self for Unix Processes. In: Proceedings of 1996 IEEE Symposium on Computer Security and Privacy. (1996)
14. Chung, C.Y., Gertz, M., Levitt, K.: Demids: A misuse detection system for database systems. In: 14th IFIP WG11.3 Working Conference on Database and Application Security. (2000)
15. Stolfo, S., Fan, D., Lee, W.: Credit card fraud detection using meta-learning: Issues and initial results. In: AAAI Workshop on AI Approaches to Fraud Detection and Risk Management. (1997)
16. Bertino, E., Kamra, A., Terzi, E., Vakali, A.: Intrusion Detection in RBAC-administered Databases. In: Proceedings of the 21st Annual Computer Security Applications Conference. (2005)
17. Ilgun, K.: Ustat: A real-time intrusion detection system for unix. In: the IEEE Symposium on Security and Privacy, Oakland, CA (May 1993)
18. Javitz, H.S., Valdes, A.: The sri ides statistical anomaly detector. In: Proceedings IEEE Computer Society Symposium on Security and Privacy, Oakland, CA (May 1991)
19. Lee, W., Xiang, D.: Information-theoretic measures for anomaly detection. In: 2001 IEEE Symposium on Security and Privacy, Oakland, CA (May 2001)
20. Ko, C., Ruschitzka, M., Levitt, K.: Execution monitoring of security-critical programs in distributed systems: a Specification-based approach. In: Proceedings of the 1997 IEEE Symposium on Security and Privacy. (1997)
21. Sekar, R., Gupta, A., Frullo, J., Shanbhag, T., Tiwari, A., Yang, H., Zhou, S.: Implementation of Argus Specification-based anomaly detection: a new approach for detecting network intrusions. In: ACM CCS. (2002)

22. McDermott, J., Goldschlag, D.: Towards a model of storage jamming. In: the IEEE Computer Security Foundations Workshop, Kenmare, Ireland (June 1996) 176–185

23. Barbara, D., Goel, R., Jajodia, S.: "Using Checksums to Detect Data Corruption". In: Int'l Conf. on Extending Data Base Technology. (Mar 2000)

24. Maheshwari, U., Vingralek, R., Shapiro, W.: How to build a trusted database system on untrusted storage. In: 4th Symposium on Operating System Design and Implementation, San Diego, CA (October 2000)

25. Lee, P., Anderson, T.: Fault Tolerance: Principles and Practice. 2nd edn. Springer-Verlag (1990)

26. Mohan, C., Haderle, D., Lindsay, B., Pirahesh, H., Schwarz, P.: Aries: A transaction recovery method supporting fine-granularity locking. ACM Trans. on Database Systems 17(1) (1992) 94–162

27. Borg, A., Blau, W., Graetsch, W., Herrmann, F., Oberle, W.: Fault Tolerance Under UNIX. ACM Transactions on Computer Systems 7(1) (1989) 1–24

28. Muller, G., Banatre, M., Peyrouze, N., Rochat, R.: Lessons from FTM: An Experiment in the Design & Implementation of a Low-Cost Fault-Tolerant System. IEEE Transactions on Reliability 45(2) (1996) 332–340

29. Elnozahy, E.N.M., Alvisi, L., Wang, Y.M., Johnson, D.B.: A survey of rollback-recovery protocols in message-passing systems. ACM Computing Surveys 34(3) (September 2002) 375–408

30. Lin, J.L., Dunham, M.H.: A survey of distributed database checkpointing. Distributed and Parallel Databases 5(3) (1997) 289–319

31. Lin, J.L., Dunham, M.H.: A low-cost checkpointing technique for distributed databases. Distributed and Parallel Databases 10(3) (2001) 241–268

32. Jefferson, D.R.: Virtual time. ACM Transaction on Programming Languages and Systems 7(3) (July 1985) 404–425

33. Lin, Y., Lazowska, E.D.: A study of time warp rollback machanisms. ACM Transactions on Modeling and Computer Simulations 1(1) (January 1991) 51–72

34. Siewiorek, D.P., Swarz, R.S.: Reliable Computer Systems: Design and Evaluation. 3rd edn. A K Peters (1998)

35. Patterson, D., Brown, A., Broadwell, P., Candea, G., Chen, M., Cutler, J., Enriquez, P., Fox, A., Kycyman, E., Merzbacher, M., Oppenheimer, D., Sastry, N., Tetzlaff, W., Traupman, J., Treuhaft, N.: Recovery-oriented computing (roc): Motivation, definition, techniques, and case studies. Technical report, UC Berkeley Computer Science (2002) CSD-02-1175.

36. Candea, G., Fox, A.: Recursive restartability: Turning the reboot sledgehammer into a scalpel. In: Proceedings of the Eighth IEEE HOTOS. (2001)

37. Swift, M.M., Bershad, B.N., Levy, H.M.: Improving the Reliability of Commodity Operating Systems. In: ACM SOSP. (2003)

38. Ammann, P., Jajodia, S., Mavuluri, P.: On the fly reading of entire databases. IEEE Trans. on Knowledge and Data Engineering 7(5) (October 1995) 834–838

39. Mohan, C., Pirahesh, H., Lorie, R.: Efficient and flexible methods for transient versioning of records to avoid locking by read-only trans. In: ACM SIGMOD International Conference on Management of Data, San Diego, CA (June 1992) 124–133

40. Pu, C.: On-the-fly, incremental, consistent reading of entire databases. Algorithmica 1(3) (October 1986) 271–287

41. Gray, J., Reuter, A.: Transaction Processing: Concepts and Techniques. Morgan Kaufmann Publishers, Inc. (1993)
42. Dasgupta, P., Leblanc, R., Appelbe, W.: The Clouds distributed operating system. In: Proceedings 8th International Conference on Distributed Computing Systems, San Jose, Calif. (2002)
43. Dixon, G.N., Barrington, G.D., Shrivastava, S., Wheater, S.M.: The treatment of persistent objects in Arjuna. Comput. J. **32**(4) (1989)
44. Gheith, A., Schwan, K.: CHAOS: Support for real-time atomic transactions. In: Proc. 19th International Symposium on Fault-Tolerant Computing, Chicago (1989)
45. Liskov, B., Scheifler, R.: Guardians and actions: Linguistic support for robust, distributed programs. ACM Transactions on Program. Lang. Syst. **5**(3) (1983)
46. Nett, E., Kaiser, J., Kroger, R.: Providing recoverability in a transaction oriented distributed operating system. In: Proc. 6th International Symposium on Fault-Tolerant Computing, Cambridge (May 1986)
47. Clark, B.E., Corrtgan, M.J.: Application System/400 performance characteristics. IBM Syst. J. **28**(3) (1989)
48. Crus, R.: Data recovery in IBM Database 2. IBM Syst. J. **23**(2) (1984)
49. Sql server. http://www.microsoft.com/sql/default.mspx
50. Oracle database. http://www.oracle.com/database/index.html
51. Db2 log analysis tool for z/os. http://www-306.ibm.com/software/data/db2imstools/db2tools/db2lat.html
52. Db2 recovery expert for multiplatforms. http://www-306.ibm.com/software/data/db2imstools/db2tools/db2re/
53. Oracle data protection and disaster recovery solutions. http://www.oracle.com/technology/deploy/availability/htdocs/OracleDR Solutions.html
54. Korth, H., Levy, E., Silberschatz, A.: A formal approach to recovery by compensating trans. In: the International Conference on Very Large Databases, Brisbane, Australia (1990) 95–106
55. Garcia-Molina, H.: Using semantic knowledge for transaction processing in a distributed database. ACM Trans. on Database Systems **8**(2) (June 1983) 186–213
56. Garcia-Molina, H., Salem, K.: Sagas. In: ACM-SIGMOD International Conference on Management of Data, San Francisco, CA (1987) 249–259
57. Lomet, D.: MLR: A recovery method for multi-level systems. In: ACM-SIGMOD International Conference on Management of Data, San Diego, CA (June 1992) 185–194
58. Weikum, G., Hasse, C., Broessler, P., Muth, P.: Multi-level recovery. In: the Ninth ACM SIGACT-SIGMOD-SIGART Symposium of Principles of Database Systems, Nashville, Tenn (April 1990) 109–123
59. Weikum, G., Schek, H.J.: Concepts and applications of multilevel trans. and open nested trans. In Elmagarmid, A.K., ed.: Database Transaction Models for Advanced Applications. Morgan Kaufmann Publishers, Inc. (1992)
60. Gray, J., Helland, P., O'Neil, P., Shasha, S.: The dangers of replication and a solution. In: ACM SIGMOD. (1996)
61. Schneider, F.B.: Implementing fault-tolerant services using the state machine approach: a tutorial. ACM Computing Surveys **22**(4) (December 1990) 299–319
62. Berman, K., Cooper, R.: The ISIS Project: Real Experience with a Fault Tolerant Programming System. Operating Systems Review (1991) 103–107

63. CA data availability solutions.
    http://www3.ca.com/solutions/SubSolution.aspx?ID=312
64. Symantec livestate recovery products provide fast, reliable and cost-effective system and data recovery. http://www.symantec.com/press/2004/n041005.html
65. Sonasoft disaster recovery solutions.
    http://www.sonasoft.com/solutions/disaster.asp
66. Zhu, N., Chiueh, T.C.: Design, implementation, and evaluation of repairable file service. In: Proceedings of the IEEE Dependable Systems and Networks. (2003)
67. Goel, A., Po, K., Farhadi, K., Li, Z., Lara, E.D.: The Taser Intrusion Recovery System. In: ACM SOSP. (2005)
68. Ammann, P., Jajodia, S., Liu, P.: Recovery from malicious trans. IEEE Trans. on Knowledge and Data Engineering 15(5) (2002) 1167–1185
69. Yu, M., Liu, P., Zang, W.: "Self Healing Workflow Systems under Attacks". In: 24th IEEE Int'l Conf. on Distributed Computing Systems. (2004)
70. Lomet, D., Vagena, Z., Barga, R.: Recovery from Bad User Transactions. In: ACM SIGMOD. (2006)
71. Panda, B., Giordano, J.: Reconstructing the database after electronic attacks. In: the 12th IFIP 11.3 Working Conference on Database Security, Greece, Italy (July 1998)
72. Liu, P., Jing, J., Luenam, P., Wang, Y., Li, L., Ingsriswang, S.: "The Design and Implementation of a Self-Healing Database System". J. of Intelligent Information Systems (JIIS) 23(3) (2004) 247–269
73. Pilania, D., Chiueh, T.: Design, Implementation, and Evaluation of an Intrusion Resilient Database System. In: Proc. International Conference on Data Engineering. (2005)
74. Liu, P., Ammann, P., Jajodia, S.: Rewriting histories: Recovery from malicious trans. Distributed and Parallel Databases 8(1) (2000) 7–40
75. Liu, P., Jajodia, S.: Multi-phase damage confinement in database systems for intrusion tolerance. In: 14th IEEE Computer Security Foundations Workshop, Nova Scotia, Canada (June 2001)
76. Ammann, P., Jajodia, S., McCollum, C., Blaustein, B.: Surviving information warfare attacks on databases. In: the IEEE Symposium on Security and Privacy, Oakland, CA (May 1997) 164–174
77. Liu, P., Jajodia, S., McCollum, C.: Intrusion confinement by isolation in information systems. J. of Computer Security 8(4) (2000) 243–279
78. Liu, P., Wang, H., Li, L.: Real-time Data Attack Isolation for Commercial Database Applications. Elsevier Journal of Network and Computer Applications 29(4) (2006) 294–320
79. Trivedi, K.S.: "Probability and statistics with reliability, queuing and computer science applications". John Wiley and Sons (2002)
80. Wang, H., Liu, P.: Modeling and Evaluating the Survivability of an Intrusion Tolerant Database System. In: Proc. ESORICS (European Symposium on Research in Computer Security). (2006)

17

Hippocratic Databases: Current Capabilities and Future Trends

Tyrone Grandison[1], Christopher Johnson[2*], and Jerry Kiernan[1]

[1] IBM Almaden Research Center, 650 Harry Road, San Jose, CA 95120
{tyroneg,jkiernan}@us.ibm.com
[2] chrisjohnson@alum.berkeley.edu

Summary. Hippocratic databases (HDBs) are a class of database systems that accept responsibility for the privacy and security of information they manage without impeding legitimate use and disclosure. HDBs ensure that only authorized individuals have access to sensitive information and that any disclosure of this information is for proper purposes. They empower individuals to consent to specific uses and disclosures of their information and to verify the enterprise's compliance with its privacy policies. HDBs also employ technical safeguards to ensure the security of the information they manage. Further, they use advanced information sharing and analytics to enable enterprises to gain maximum value from information without compromising security or individual privacy. In this chapter, we outline the founding principles of a Hippocratic database, describe several technologies that advance these principles, evaluate the state of the art in HDB-enabling technologies, and suggest opportunities for future research.

1 Introduction

The Hippocratic database vision was developed at IBM's Almaden Research Center in response to significant privacy threats posed by the increasing availability of personal information in the modern technological environment. This vision was intended to provide guidance for the development of future information systems. Thus, HDB technology is not a fixed group of technologies, but rather an evolving set of capabilities that enable the responsible management of sensitive information. HDBs are inspired by the privacy provision of the Hippocratic Oath, which states that:

> ...about whatever I may see or hear in treatment, or even without treatment, in the life of human beings - things that should not ever be blurted outside - I will remain silent, holding such things to be unutterable [1].

---

* This work was done while the author was at IBM.

Hippocratic databases should be architected to regulate use and disclosure of personal information in strict accordance with privacy and security laws, enterprise policies, and individual choices. They should be designed to safeguard this information and protect individual privacy without impeding legitimate and beneficial uses of information. HDBs are founded upon a set of ten data protection principles and require a diverse set of technologies to realize these principles. In the following sections, we outline these founding principles, describe several technologies that advance these principles, evaluate the state of the art in HDB-enabling technologies, and suggest opportunities for future research.

2 Founding Principles of a Hippocratic Database

The founding principles of a Hippocratic database are based on concepts of information privacy drawn from international data protection laws and guidelines [2].

1. **Purpose Specification.** The purposes for which personal information has been collected shall be associated with that information in the database.
2. **Consent.** The purposes associated with personal information shall have the consent of the individual who is the subject of the information.
3. **Limited Collection.** The personal information collected shall be limited to the minimum necessary for accomplishing the specified purposes.
4. **Limited Use.** The database shall run only those queries and operations that are consistent with the purposes for which the information has been collected.
5. **Limited Disclosure.** Personal information stored in the database shall not be communicated outside of the database for purposes other than those to which the individual consented.
6. **Limited Retention.** Personal information shall be retained only as long as necessary to fulfill the purposes for which it was collected.
7. **Accuracy.** All personal information in the database shall be accurate and current.
8. **Safety.** Personal information shall be protected by security safeguards against theft and other misappropriation.
9. **Openness.** An individual shall be able to access all information about him or her stored in the database.
10. **Compliance.** An individual shall be able to verify compliance with the above principles, and the database capable of responding to these challenges.

3 Hippocratic Database Technologies

In the sections that follow, we describe a number of technologies that advance the principles of a Hippocratic database. These technologies are at various stages of development, but demonstrate the potential for future information systems to comply with the HDB vision.

3.1 Active Enforcement

One enabling technology of a Hippocratic database is an active enforcement system that limits access to and disclosure of personal information in accordance with fine-grained privacy policies, applicable laws, and individual opt-in and opt-out choices [3]. HDB active enforcement stores enterprise privacy policies and individual choices in database tables. It intercepts user queries at the database level and transforms these queries to comply with privacy policies and choices, ensuring that only authorized individuals have access to permitted information for proper purposes. Therefore, active enforcement satisfies the HDB principles of purpose specification, consent, limited use, and limited disclosure. Because it operates at the database level, HDB active enforcement enables enterprises to comply with detailed policies without modifying their applications or otherwise negatively impacting existing systems. In the current implementation (Figure 1), HDB active enforcement is executed in three stages: (1) policy creation, (2) preference negotiation, and (3) application data retrieval [4].

In the **policy creation stage**, an enterprise that safeguards personal information specifies its privacy policies. These policies govern access and disclosure of information in accordance with user authorization privileges, the purpose of the query, and the intended recipient of the query results, if different from the user issuing the query. The policies may also provide individuals with an opportunity to opt-in or opt-out of certain disclosures of their information. For example, an individual may opt to share his medical records with universities for research purposes, but opt not to disclose these records to drug companies for marketing purposes. The enterprise expresses these policies in a privacy language through a policy specification interface. The active enforcement component then parses the policies and installs them in the database as metadata. Subsequently, the enterprise may update or replace its policies through this one-step process without recoding any of its applications. The database stores all policy versions to allow accurate compliance verification.

In the **preference negotiation stage**, the active enforcement component notifies the individual of the enterprise's privacy policies. The individual formulates his or her own privacy preferences and expresses them in a preference language though a dedicated plug-in on the client side [5]. Prior to disclosing any personal information, the system matches these preferences with the enterprise's policies and informs the individual of any conflicts. The parties may either resolve these conflicts or terminate the process. If they proceed,

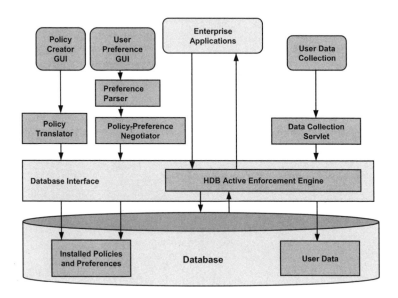

Fig. 1. HDB Active Enforcement Architecture

the system may then provide the individual with opt-in or opt-out choices concerning use and disclosure of their information. These choices are recorded in the database and enforced at the time of query processing. Successful preference negotiation confirms the terms of agreement between the parties.

In the **application data retrieval stage**, the active enforcement component intercepts and transforms an incoming query to comply with applicable privacy policies. The database runs the transformed query and retrieves only policy-compliant information. In this way, the system transparently enforces cell-level disclosure controls based upon the requestor's authorization, the purpose of access, the intended recipient, and individual opt-in and opt-out choices. Purpose and recipient information can either be inferred from the application or directly specified by the requestor issuing the query. This ensures that applications retrieve all information that a requestor is entitled to access for a particular purpose and intended recipient,

The current implementation of HDB active enforcement operates in an agnostic middleware layer above a relational database using any SQL compliant interface. Figure 2 shows the HDB Active Enforcement implementation as a Java Database Connectivity (JDBC) driver, which is a wrapper over a native JDBC driver (e.g., DB2's native JDBC driver). The JDBC application, shown at the top of the figure, connects to the HDB driver instead of the native driver and thereafter submits queries and commands as it would have done using the native driver. Using JDBC, queries are submitted with the execute-Query method, which accepts the query string as its argument. The submitted query is parsed and analyzed by the HDB driver for the purposes of policy enforcement. The query is converted into an internal representation called Query Graph Model (QGM), which is a convenient structure for semantic analysis and query transformation. Given the tables and columns referenced in a query, and contextual information, such as the business purpose for the query, the relevant policy metadata is extracted from the database and integrated into the model for the query. The original query is then transformed to integrate policy restrictions. The resulting model is converted back into an SQL string which is submitted to the database for execution. The submitted query implements policy restrictions as additional query predicates.

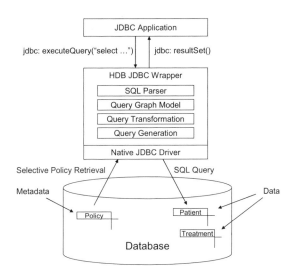

Fig. 2. HDB Active Enforcement JDBC Driver

Figure 3 is an example used to illustrate HDB query transformation for policy enforcement. An application submits a query for the purpose of medical research over the Patient and Treatment tables and selects diagnosis for patients in California. The query is parsed and a QGM representation is built for the query. Boxes represent operators such as select and tables. The example has a single select operator, which is a join of the two tables. HDB policy enforcement searches for policy metadata on these tables for the purpose of medical research and modifies the query by introducing additional restrictions between tables and query operators ranging over them. These newly introduced operators appear in the figure as boxes labeled AE. Further transformations and simplifications may be applied to the query before translating the query graph into a SQL query string. However, such transformations are not shown in the figure. Finally, a new SQL query is generated by HDB Active Enforcement component and submitted to the database using the native JDBC driver interfaces. In the figure, the generated query shows that patients can opt-in or out of having their information used for research purposes. A sub-query is used to verify the choices of individual patients in order to comply with the policy.

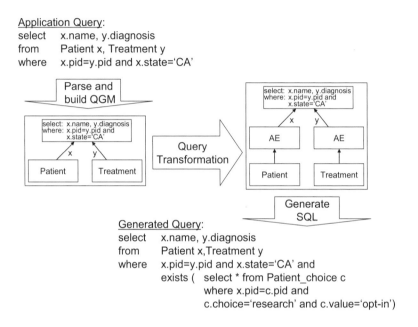

Fig. 3. Query Transformation for Policy Enforcement

HDB active enforcement can also be implemented within the database system to eliminate potential concerns about circumventing the enforcement component [6]. With the organization shown in Figure 2, policies are enforced provided that applications use JDBC to access the database and load the HDB JDBC driver rather than, say, a native JDBC driver. If database interfaces other than JDBC are used or the HDB driver is not loaded, policy enforcement is bypassed altogether. Nevertheless, there are application environments in which users only have database access through, say, a web portal supported by a restricted set of applications all using HDB to access the database. In such application environments, the configuration presented in Figure 2 can be used to protect sensitive data for large classes of users. In other environments, where all interfaces to the database must be policy-enabled to safeguard the sensitive data, policy enforcement must be pushed down into the database layer so that it takes place regardless of the external interface used to access the database. Within the database engine, SQL parsing and QGM transformation are the initial steps of query processing as described in Figure 2. Policy enforcement would be performed at this point in query processing, directly on the QGM representation of the database system. Thereafter, further database query processing occurs on the modified QGM graph implementing policy enforcement. Nevertheless, integrating enforcement within the database layer implies access to and knowledge of specific database product implementations and eliminates the database agnostic benefit of the middleware approach.

In addition, others have developed a system for enforcing fine-grained access control policies over XML data [7]. XML extends the flat tabular structure of relational tables with hierarchical structures used to model complex objects. XML represents complex objects as trees in which element nodes are root, intermediate or leaf nodes of the tree and other node types, such as text strings or attributes, are leaf nodes. Policy enforcement rules can target any part of the XML tree; not only the leaves. XML privacy/security policies are specified as individual positive or negative rules that grant or deny access to information represented as XML. A rule describes the users governed by the rule, the documents over which authority is granted or denied, the portion of the document governed by the rule (the portion is rooted at a sub-tree of the document), whether access is for the full sub-tree or only for root nodes of the sub-tree and the type of operation allowed or denied (access or update).

While these policy semantics are different than those defined for active enforcement for relational databases, a similar policy language for XML could be created to conform to HDB policy semantics. For example, HDB has only positive authorizations and access is denied in absence of any authorization; therefore, negative authorizations would not be used in the specification.

3.2 Compliance Auditing

A second enabling technology of a Hippocratic database is compliance auditing, which tracks past disclosures of information to support investigations of suspicious disclosures [8]. This HDB auditing component allows enterprises to ascertain the identities of those who have accessed a particular item of information in the database, the date and time of each query, the purpose of access, the final recipient, and the exact information disclosed. This capability greatly enhances the accountability of database systems and deters wrongful access and disclosure. By allowing enterprises to verify compliance with privacy policies and respond to individual challenges, this auditing component supports the HDB compliance principle.

HDB compliance auditing is a significant innovation over conventional auditing systems that log the results of every query. Enterprises often turn off these result logging systems because they consume considerable storage and computational resources [9]. HDB addresses this problem by logging only the queries and database updates. It records the query string and relevant contextual information (identity, time, purpose, and recipient) in a query log. It then records all updates, inserts, and deletions over source tables by insertions into backlog tables, which can be populated using database triggers or existing replication features. The query log and backlog tables are sufficient to track past disclosures by reconstructing any previous database state. Because HDB auditing does not incur additional cost for read queries, it requires much lower storage overhead than result logging systems.

HDB allows enterprises to formulate declarative "audit expressions," using a flexible query-like audit language, to specify the information they would like to audit. At the time of audit, HDB performs a static analysis of logged queries to generate a subset of candidate queries for further analysis. Candidate queries are identified as suspicious if they share an "indispensable tuple" with the audit expression. The system combines and transforms these queries into a single SQL audit query, which it runs against the backlog tables to determine the queries that accessed the data specified by the audit expression. For each suspicious query, the audit results reveal the requestor's identity, time, purpose, recipient, and actual information disclosed (Figure 4). This powerful and efficient auditing capability allows enterprises to investigate and account for past disclosures of information and verify compliance with policies, even if the information is updated over time.

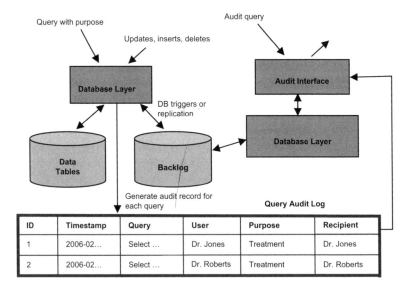

Fig. 4. Generic HDB Compliance Auditing Architecture

Audit Scenario. Suppose patient Adam complains to his primary care provider that his diabetes condition has been disclosed without his consent. A hospital auditor then initiates an audit by formulating an *audit expression* that declaratively specifies the information to be tracked, i.e. Adam's diagnosis. An audit expression is syntactically identical to an SQL query except that the SELECT clause is replaced by an audit clause of the form "**audit** *audit-list* **from** *audited-tables* **where** *conditions*" where *audit-list* is a list of column names, *audited-tables* are the tables containing the data which is the source of the audit and *conditions* identify the subset of the data that is the target of the audit. The auditor specifies the following audit expression to determine whether Adam's diagnosis information was improperly accessed.

> **audit** y.diagnosis
> **from** Patient x, Treatment y
> **where** x.pid=y.pcid **and** x.name = 'Adam'

After receiving the audit expression, the HDB auditing system performs a static analysis of the query log to isolate a set of *candidate queries*, which consists of all queries that accessed all columns specified in the audit-list. The system then combines the candidate queries with the audit expression to determine the *suspicious queries* that may have accessed Adam's information. A suspicious query is defined as a logged query that shares an *indispensable tuple* with the audit expression. A tuple t in T is *indispensable* in the computation of a SELECT-PROJECT-JOIN query Q over a database D if the result of the execution of Q over D is not identical to the result obtained from executing Q over D after deleting t from T.

The audit system then combines the suspicious queries into a single audit query and runs this query against the backlog tables to determine the exact information accessed by the query at the time it was issued. Finally, the results of the audit reveal those queries that accessed Adam's diagnosis information, including the identity of each query issuer, the date and time of the query, the purpose of the query (if available), and the state of the database at the time of the query.

Figure 5 illustrates audit query generation for the example audit given above. The figure shows the audit expression on the right and the logged query number 11 on the left. Query number 11 is a sample query that ran at time T15. After identifying query 11 as a candidate query, the audit component builds a QGM graph for this query and also builds a query model for the audit expression. The tables referenced by the query are substituted by their backlog tables. A temporal predicate is added over each backlog table to recover the snapshots of the source table at time T15, the time that query 11 ran. The audit expression is added over the logged query, thus creating a conjunction of its predicates with those of the logged query to determine if they share an indispensable tuple. If so, the resulting audit query produces an output tuple identifying query 11 as suspicious.

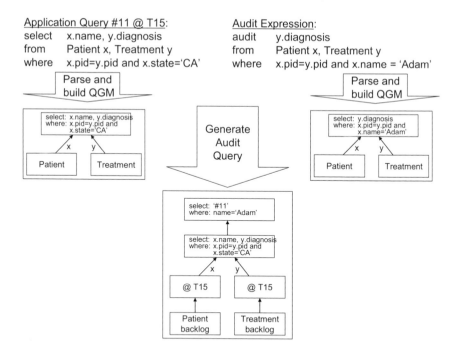

Fig. 5. Audit Query Generation

In addition to the flexibility and efficiency benefits, HDB auditing has an additional advantage over existing auditing approaches in that it captures information revealed by a query that may not be reflected in the query results. For example, the query "Select 'yes' if employee 'Adam' has a diagnosis = diabetes" would output only the word "yes" in the result, but actually reveal information about Adam's diagnosis to the user. The same is true for queries that aggregate values from the records accessed. In contrast, an HDB audit would reveal all information *accessed* by the query.

Additional research has explored auditing batches of SQL queries to determine whether the queries are suspicious with regard to unauthorized views of the data [10]. Beyond the notions of suspiciousness discussed above, this work also considers database instance independent notions of *syntactic suspiciousness* wherein the suspiciousness of the batch of queries is determined without the underlying database.

Auditing Disclosure by Relevance Ranking. Query ranking is an extension of HDB auditing that assists in tracking the origin of information after it has been leaked or misappropriated from a database. This auditing system ranks queries that accessed the data in accordance with the relevance of each query as the source of the improper disclosure [11]. The system uses a copy of the sensitive data that is the target of leakage, referred to as table S, to compute a ranking of queries in the query log over the database suspected of being the source of leakage. We refer to the output of each query in the query log as query table Qi. The ranking system ranks each Qi with respect to its similarity to S.

To perform the ranking, we use one of three measures of proximity between the sensitive table and the query table. The first, based on information retrieval's document frequency similarity measure, computes proximity by considering partial tuple matches between two tables, while factoring in the likelihood of the match. Partial tuples are formed by matching a tuple in Qi with a tuple in S and forming a partial tuple based upon matching attribute pairs. Document frequency is computed as the number of query tables having the partial tuple. The ranking method favors Qi's having partial tuples with low document frequency. This method has high sensitivity to even single partial tuple matches occurring in few query results.

The second, based on record linkage and expectation maximization, measures proximity by aggregating scores of individual tuple matches. This method was originally devised to match individuals appearing in different census records in the absence of surrogate keys uniquely identifying these individuals in each list such as social security number. The method is adaptive and estimates the number of record pairs that are true matches and non-matches based upon attributes that are common to both lists and the likelihood of a random match. It is applied to our information leakage problem by matching each query table Qi with S. This method has lower sensitivity than the previous one to unique combinations of matching attributes appearing in few Qi's.

The third is based on the minimum description length principle and measures proximity by computing the minimum length (maximum probability) derivation of the sensitive table from the query result. In contrast with the previous two methods, this method also examines the similarity of tuples within S when measuring the similarity of tuples in Qi with tuples in S. This method is therefore better at differentiating Qi's having multiple matches with near duplicates in S with Qi's having multiple matches with distinct information in S.

The following scenario describes a practical application of query ranking. Suppose that a major credit card company sells copies of its customer database to its business affiliates under a very strict confidentiality agreement. The affiliates are allowed to analyze the database for their own business intelligence purposes, but may not disclose any of the customer information to a third party. Several months later, a copy of this database is released into the public domain. The credit card company would like to determine the source of the disclosure so that it may terminate its business relationship with this affiliate. Using the HDB query ranking system, the company could evaluate the proximity of the leaked database to the queries that accessed the database by using the appropriate proximity measure algorithm, and rank the relative likelihood that each query resulted in the leaked data. The query that accessed the state of the database that is most similar to the leaked database should be examined first by the auditor. While this technique helps prioritize the leads, establishing the source of disclosure with certainty still requires forensic investigation. We assume that individual business affiliates are loaned separate copies of the database generated from queries that were run at different times. Since the company can identify the queries that disclosed information to specific third parties, this ranking method may help isolate the source of disclosure. Thus, query ranking enables the company to track the release of its data without perturbing the released data.

Auditing Curation. Another important feature of a Hippocratic database is the ability to audit modifications of information and policies. Suppose that NetCare Hospital is the subject of a malpractice investigation, in which plaintiff Betsy alleges that her husband Charles's death was due to an improper drug prescription and dosage. She claims that the doctor ignored her husband's reported allergy to the drug and that administration of this drug was inappropriate given the results of his most recent blood tests. His physician, Dr. Roberts, contends that there is no record of the patient's allergy to this drug and that the prescribed dosage was appropriate given the results of the patient's blood work. In the course of its internal investigation, NetCare would like to determine whether any potentially inculpating information in the patient's medical record was deleted or modified.

To address this problem, we proposed an auditing system called *curation auditing*, which tracks the history of modifications to sensitive information and the policies that govern such information, using logs of database updates [12]. By allowing entities to investigate the source of improprieties, such as improper data or policy modifications, curation auditing helps to address the HDB compliance principle more completely. The audit system maintains logs of all database operations in addition to the backlog structure used for auditing database access. The audit expression language discussed above with regard to compliance auditing is extended to declaratively specify the curation information to be audited. Because curation auditing tracks general updates, this language includes the *before* and *after* values of update operations. The following is an informal example of an audit expression that NetCare would issue to determine whether patient Charles's allergy information was updated or deleted subsequent to his death six months ago.

> Who updated or deleted patient Charles allergy to penicillin within the past six months?
>
> **During** current date - 6 months to current date
> **Audit-curation** Patient-Allergies s
> **Where** s.patient-name="Charles" and before s.allergy="penicillin"

The *during* clause of the audit expression specifies a time period for the audit, the *audit-curation* clause stipulates that the patient-allergies table is to be audited, and the where clause examines updates (or deletes) of the allergy information in patient Charles's medical record. The before and after images of updated tuples can be accessed using special *before* and *after* keywords. The audit returns the identities of logged commands having performed modifications that qualify the audit expression. The command log records all queries and commands submitted to the database along with annotations such as the identity of the user submitting the query, the time the query was submitted, and the purpose of the query (if available). Upon receiving the audit expression above, the system reveals that Dr. Roberts deleted Charles's allergy information in September, shortly after the patient's death. The hospital can then initiate similar audits to determine whether any information was modified regarding the patient's test results and to determine whether Dr. Roberts improperly deleted or modified information in any other patient records.

Currently, only the high-level design of HDB curation auditing has been articulated. Deeper technical and implementation issues are topics for further research.

3.3 Sovereign Information Integration

Another enabling technology of a Hippocratic database, called Sovereign Information Integration (SII), allows secure information sharing among multiple autonomous databases without using a trusted third party [13].

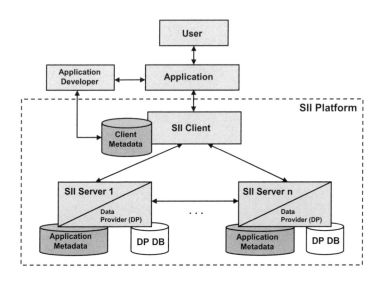

Fig. 6. Sovereign Information Integration Architecture

SII enables two or more enterprises to run queries across their databases that do not reveal any information among the databases apart from the results of the query. This technology is designed to foster beneficial uses of information without violating any of the HDB principles. Figure 6 shows the architecture of an arbitrary SII application. The SII data provider enables sovereign information sharing for its data. The SII server maintains the metadata needed to retrieve information from the data providers' databases. The SII client provides the necessary functionality to map the application schema to the data providers' schemas, construct and invoke query requests against multiple data providers, and receive query responses. The application is a thin layer on top of the SII client, which invokes the required SII operations. For example, suppose that a commercial airline and a government agency would like to compare a passenger manifest and a suspicious traveler database to identify any common names, without revealing any names that are not in common. SII processes such secure information sharing operations by applying a set of commutative encryption functions to data in different orders and at different locations. Only encrypted information is exchanged between participants and both data providers must participate in order to encrypt values and identify the values that are in common to both providers. SII compares the multiply-encrypted values and provides the query results without compromising the security or privacy of either data set. This technology is also useful in the clinical genomics arena, allowing enterprises to conduct secure join operations among sovereign databases to discover and investigate correlations between genetic sequences and phenotypic data.

Unlike other data integration approaches, such as centralized data warehouses and mediator-based data federations, which reveal all data among the databases, SII only reveals query results. SII is a software solution that can be integrated seamlessly into existing data environments without the need for any perturbation or anonymization of the original data. It enables multiple parties to conduct a range of useful operations over autonomous databases. SII has been implemented on a web services infrastructure to process sovereign join operations [14]. Recent research has also explored game theoretic approaches to assure that a dishonest SII participant cannot gain more information that an honest participant by providing false input data [15].

3.4 Encryption

An essential feature of a Hippocratic database is safety, which involves securing sensitive data against theft or misappropriation. Encryption prevents unauthorized users from circumventing database security by directly accessing the database files without using the database software. However, most encryption techniques significantly degrade system performance because they do not preserve the order of encrypted values and therefore, do not allow the use of indexes to compute range queries. To address this problem, an order preserving encryption scheme (OPES) was proposed for numeric data that processes range queries and MIN, MAX, and COUNT queries on the server without decrypting the data [16]. The OPES algorithm uses as input the source (or plaintext) distribution of a column's values and a target distribution for ciphertext column values and then transforms plaintext values, preserving their order, into ciphertext. The resulting ciphertext column values conform to the target distribution. With the two input distributions used for encryption, OPES decryption maps a target value to its plaintext value.

Revealing the order of plaintext values may not always be acceptable. Furthermore, column-level order preserving encryption as well as standard encryption reveals duplicate values which may not provide enough security for all application environments. Iyer, et al. address the problem of efficiency and duplicates by introducing a completely new storage model called the Partition Plaintext Ciphertext (PPC) model [17]. PPC pushes encryption to the lower levels of the database system, maintaining in-memory pages as plaintext in the buffer pool and writing encrypted pages to the disk. The upper levels of the database system software therefore remain unaffected and continue to operate on plaintext data. This protects data at rest by preventing users from circumventing database security. PPC reduces computation and storage costs by partitioning data into plaintext and ciphertext mini-pages. All sensitive values are stored as ciphertext on the mini-page. Only one encryption operation is needed when a page is written to disk and one decryption is required when ciphertext page is brought into memory. This PPC storage model uses standard and efficient cryptographic algorithms to encrypt personal information.

4 Future Work

Improved Policy Specification. For HDB controls to be completely effective, policies must accurately capture the data usage practices of enterprises and the preference and choices of individuals concerning the use and disclosure of their personal information. The policy language must be fine grained to allow enterprises to collect, use, and disclose the minimum necessary information to accomplish their intended purposes. It must also be simple enough that technically unsophisticated individuals can understand the consequences of their decisions to provide personal information.

Policy languages such as P3P [18] are machine interpretable and enable automated policy enforcement. Thus, they offer significant improvement over the complex and ambiguous legal language of written policies. While these machine interpretable languages allow enterprises to define policies that offer some individual choices regarding the usage of personal information, they currently do not allow the data subject to individually tailor her own rules regarding usage of her private information. Rather, the individual subscribes (or not) to a policy and make choices within the boundaries of the stated policy.

Further, the automated negotiation of an enterprise's policy with the preferences, choices and requirements of an individual remains an important challenge. Such automated mediation would relieve the individual from having to review each enterprise's policy and allow enterprises to gain the maximum usage of personal information while fully complying with and individual preferences. Also, given the current investment in information systems and their data disclosure mechanisms, HDB should allow refinement of policies based on actual information usage, such that the policy is a representation of a company's intent and practice. Future policy languages and systems must reconcile these requirements with the need for efficient computation, which is a difficult technical challenge [19].

Enforcement After Extraction. HDB active enforcement is currently adept at limiting disclosure of information contained within the database, but does not exert any control or safeguards over information that is legitimately extracted and transferred outside of the database. Enterprises that transfer private information to other entities must rely on those entities to enforce the appropriate disclosure policies. Their only means of assurance is to impose disclosure obligations on the transferee by written contract. Future HDBs should address this issue by extending active enforcement to distributed data environments having no central point of control and providing guarantees on the external systems with regards to policy compliance. When individuals disclose personal information to an enterprise under specific policies and conditions, they should know that these policies and conditions will be enforced after legitimate transfers of the information to other entities. Thus, HDBs should be able to attach policy annotations to each item of information that is transferred from the database to ensure that the transferee complies with the original disclosure policies. They should also be capable of applying source disclosure policies to any information received from another entity and resolving any policy conflicts. Compliance with attached policies should be reviewable by audit.

Filter and Deny Semantics. The HDB active enforcement solution described above uses query predicates to *filter* results in compliance with the applicable policy rules. The system transforms the query so that the database only returns information that is compliant with the database user's authorization, the enterprise's privacy policy, and any individual choices. Prohibited values that are sought by the query are returned as null values. However, in some circumstances, this type of filtering may not be desirable because it may mislead the user into thinking that the prohibited values do not actually exist.

For example, suppose that a military officer would like to know whether there are any friendly forces within a particular building before authorizing a missile strike. There are friendly intelligence operatives in the building, but the existence and locations of these operatives exceeds the security clearance of the officer. In this case, filtering the prohibited results would not be desirable because it would wrongly suggest to the officer that there are no friendly forces in the building. Rather, it would be preferable to *deny* the officer's query by suggesting that he is not authorized to view the results. This would prevent the officer from accessing prohibited information without returning inaccurate or incomplete results.

In other situations, filtering is more appropriate than denial. Suppose that a military officer would like to determine the safest path into a particular town, so he would like to know the current locations of all friendly and enemy forces within a ten mile radius of the town. Within this radius are covert friendly operatives that exceed the officer's clearance level. In this situation, the system should not broadly *deny* the officer's query, rather it should *filter* the results to remove the locations of the covert operatives, but return the locations of all other forces. Here, filtering is preferable because it would not mislead the officer into taking inappropriate action due to incomplete query results. To handle these types of situations, database access controls should support both filter and deny semantics depending on the context of the query. Rosenthal and Winslett originally highlighted this problem [20]. Ager, et al. proposed an initial solution to integrate filter and deny semantics involving policy scoping rules [21]. Miklau and Suciu have proposed a database instance independent approach to prevent disclosure on the basis of the query and the policies, regardless of the information that exists in the database [22]. However, Miklau and Suciu determined that discerning whether a particular query violates a policy rule for all possible database instances is an intractable problem [22].

Future HDB systems should seamlessly support both filter and deny semantics in an efficient manner.

Limited Retention. Another key principle of a Hippocratic database is that personal information should be kept for only as long as necessary to accomplish its intended purpose. Enterprises should comply with their own privacy policies, applicable legal regulations, and individual consents regarding the purposes for which they may use information and the duration for which they may keep information. Ananthanarayanan, et al. have explored how to automatically enforce policies related to handling personal information, and resolve conflicts among different policy obligations applicable to the same information [23]. However, in certain instances, an individual may want his or her information removed from a database after the enterprise has accomplished the purpose for which the information was collected. At the same time, there may be regulatory mandates that state that particular classes of documents must be retained for specific periods of time. Both (seemingly conflicting) requirements must be met by future systems. Obviously, there remains a significant research challenge in designing database systems that can entirely remove information, even beyond the point of recovery, without affecting their ability to recover non-expired information [2].

Limited Collection. The limited collection principle of a Hippocratic database is also not completely addressed by currently available technologies. This principle states that the information collected shall be limited to the minimum necessary to accomplish the specified purposes. In practice, knowing the minimal set of data elements needed for a particular purpose is difficult because systems do not distinguish between *minimum necessary to complete a task* and *necessary to complete a task*. Future HDB systems should be able to provide insight on this *minimum necessary* data set by analyzing the information that was collected for given purposes, but not used.

Intrusion Detection. Hippocratic databases in the future should also be able to detect illegitimate access by comparing a query access pattern to the usual and expected access pattern for that particular user and purpose. This capability advances the HDB safety principle by preventing inappropriate access through legitimate channels. Bertino, et al. have proposed an approach to intrusion detection in databases with role-based access control [24]. Their intrusion detection system uses a Nave Bayes Classifier to mine database logs formulate user profiles for particular roles within the organization. It then evaluates each query against the expected behavior for that particular role to identify intruders. However, the performance and false positive/negative ratio for similarly styled approaches must still be addressed. Additionally, constructing various optimization techniques and enforcement models for real-time database intrusion detection with minimal system impact is a higher level goal that the research community should target.

Data Integrity. HDB systems should provide guarantees on the soundness of the data that it contains. Individuals should have access to view and verify the accuracy of their information. Data cleansing [25] can be used to identify and correct erroneous data. Maintaining the provenance [26] of information can also provide an indication of the reliability of the information.

Openness. Hippocratic databases should support the principle of openness, which states that individuals should be able to access all information stored about them in the database. This allows individuals to know the extent of the information about them maintained by the data collector. It also ensures that the individual will be able to review this information, correct any inaccuracies, and request the deletion of certain information. There are two significant problems to supporting openness. First, before providing access to the individual's private information, the database must be able to verify the identity of the user [2]. Potential solutions include biometric identifiers, smart cards, speech recognition, or authentication mechanisms for anonymous entities [27]. Second, individuals should be able to anonymously determine whether a particular database contains any information about them [2].

5 Conclusion

Since the initial articulation of the Hippocratic Database vision in 2002, significant strides have been taken in developing technologies that adhere to the founding principles. Active enforcement technology supports the principles of purpose specification, consent, limited use and limited disclosure for relational database and XML-based systems. Compliance auditing, query ranking, and curation auditing technologies support the compliance principle. Sovereign Information Integration enables limited use and limited disclosure in distributed environments with no trusted third parties, while order-preserving encryption and the Partition Plaintext Ciphertext storage model promote the safety principle. Nevertheless, there are many interesting HDB technologies that require further research, such as improved policy specification, enforcement after data retrieval, support for filter and deny semantics, limited retention, limited collection, intrusion detection, data integrity, and openness. The growth of electronic medical and financial records accompanied by many highly publicized privacy breaches in recent years underscore the importance of continuing research in HDB technology.

References

1. H. Von Staden, translator, "In a Pure and Holy Way: Personal and Professional Conduct in the Hippocratic Oath," *Journal of the History of Medicine and Applied Sciences* 51, 406–408, 1966.
2. R. Agrawal, J. Kiernan, R. Srikant, Y. Xu., "Hippocratic Databases," *Proceedings of the 28th International Conference on Very Large Databases*, Hong Kong, China, August 2002.
3. K. LeFevre, R. Agrawal, R. Ercegovac, R. Ramakrishnan, Y. Xu, D. DeWitt, "Limiting Disclosure in Hippocratic Databases," *In Proceedings of the 30th International Conference on Very Large Databases*, Toronto, Canada, August 2004.
4. IBM Hippocratic Database Active Enforcement User Guide, http://www.almaden.ibm.com/software/projects/iis/hdb/Publications/papers/ HDBEnforcementUserGuide.pdf.
5. R. Agrawal, J. Kiernan, R. Srikant, Y. Xu, "An XPath-based Preference Language for P3P," *In Proceedings of the 12th International World Wide Web Conference*, Budapest, Hungary, May 2003.
6. R. Agrawal, P. Bird, T. Grandison, J. Kieman, S. Logan, W. Rjaibi, "Extending Relational Database Systems to Automatically Enforce Privacy Policies," *In Proceedings of the 21st Int'l Conf. on Data Engineering (ICDE 2005)*, Tokyo, Japan, April 2005.
7. E. Bertino, S. Castano, E. Ferrari, "On Specifying Security Policies for Web Documents with an XML-based Language," *In ACM Symposium on Access Control Models and Technologies*, Chantilly, Virginia, United States, May, 2001.
8. R. Agrawal, R. Bayardo, C. Faloutsos, J. Kiernan, R. Rantzau, R. Srikant, "Auditing Compliance with a Hippocratic Database," *In Proceedings of the 30th*

International Conference on Very Large Databases, Toronto, Canada, August 2004.

9. President's Information Technology Advisory Committee, Revolutionizing Health Care through Information Technology, Report to the President of the United States, June 2004.

10. R.. Motwani, S. Nabar, D, Thomas, "Auditing SQL Queries," Third International Workshop on Privacy Data Management, in conjunction with the 23rd International Conference on Data Engineering (ICDE 2007), April, 2007, Istanbul, Turkey.

11. R. Agrawal, A. Evfimievski, J. Kiernan, R. Velu, "Auditing Disclosure by Relevance Ranking," to appear in *Proceedings of the 26th ACM SIGMOD Intl Conference on Management of Data*, Beijing, China, June 2007.

12. T. Ager, C. Johnson, J. Kiernan, "Policy-Based Management and Sharing of Sensitive Information among Government Agencies," *Proceedings of the 25th IEEE Military Communications Conference (MILCOM)*, Washington DC, USA, October 2006.

13. R. Agrawal, A. Evfimievski, R. Srikant. "Information Sharing across Private Databases," *Proceedings of the ACM SIGMOD Conference on Management of Data*, San Diego, California. June 2003.

14. R. Agrawal, D. Asonov, M. Kantarcioglu, Y. Li, "Sovereign Joins," *Proceedings of the 22nd International Conference on Data Engineering*, Atlanta, Georgia, USA, April 2006.

15. R. Agrawal, E. Terzi, "On Honesty in Sovereign Information Sharing," *Proceedings of the 10th International Conference on Extending Database Technology*, Munich, Germany, March 2006.

16. R. Agrawal, J. Kiernan, R. Srikant, and Y. Xu, "Order-Preserving Encryption for Numeric Data," *Proceedings of the ACM SIGMOD Conference on Management of Data*, Paris, France, June 2004.

17. B. Iyer, S. Mehrotra, E. Mykletun, G. Tsudik, Y. Wu, "A Framework for Efficient Storage Security in RDBMS," *In Proceedings of the 9th International Conference on Extending DataBase Technology (EDBT 2004)*, Heraklion, Crete, Greece, March 2004.

18. L. Cranor, M. Langheinrich, M. Manchiori, M. Presler-Marshall, J. Reagle, Platform for Privacy Preferences 1.0 (P3P1.0) Specification, W3C Recommendation, 2002.

19. R. Agrawal, C. Johnson, "Securing Electronic Health Records without Impeding the Flow of Information," *International Journal of Medical Informatics*, Vol. 76, Nos. 5-6, May-June 2007.

20. A. Rosenthal, M. Winslett, "Security of Shared Data in Large Systems: State of the Art and Research Directions". *Proc. of the 30th Int'l Conf. on Very Large Databases*, Toronto, Canada, August 2004.

21. T. Ager, C. Johnson, J. Kiernan, "Policy-Based Management and Sharing of Sensitive Information among Government Agencies," *Proceedings of the 25th IEEE Military Communications Conference (MILCOM)*, Washington DC, USA, October 2006.

22. G. Miklau and D. Suciu, "A Formal Analysis of Information Disclosure in Data Exchange," *Proceedings. of the ACM SIGMOD International Conference on Management of Data*, Paris, France, June 2004.

23. R. Ananthanarayanan, M. Mohania, A. Gupta, "Management of Conflicting Obligations in Self-Protecting, Policy-Based Systems," *Second IEEE International Conference on Autonomic Computing*, Seattle, Washington, USA, June 2005.

24. E. Bertino, A. Kamra, E. Terzi, A. Vakali, "Intrusion Detection in RBAC-administered Databases," *Proceedings of the 21st Annual IEEE Computer Security Applications Conference*, Tucson, Arizona, USA, December 2005.

25. H Galhardas, D Florescu, D Shasha, E Simon, "An Extensible Framework for Data Cleaning.", *Proceedings of the Inter. Conference on Data Engineering*, San Diego, March, 2000.

26. J. Widom. "Trio: A System for Integrated Management of Data, Accuracy, and Lineage," *Proceedings of the Second Biennial Conference on Innovative Data Systems Research (CIDR '05)*, Pacific Grove, California, January 2005.

27. President's Information Technology Advisory Committee, "Revolutionizing Health Care Through Information Technology". Report to the President of the United States, June 2004.

18

Privacy-Preserving Data Mining: A Survey

Charu C. Aggarwal and Philip S. Yu

IBM T. J. Watson Research Center
19 Skyline Drive
Hawthorne, NY 10532
{charu,psyu}@us.ibm.com

Summary. In recent years, privacy-preserving data mining has been studied extensively, because of the wide proliferation of sensitive information on the internet. A number of algorithmic techniques have been designed for privacy-preserving data mining. In this paper, we provide a review of the state-of-the-art methods for privacy. We discuss methods for randomization, k-anonymization, and distributed privacy-preserving data mining. We also discuss cases in which the output of data mining applications needs to be sanitized for privacy-preservation purposes. We discuss the computational and theoretical limits associated with privacy-preservation over high dimensional data sets.

1 Introduction

In recent years, data mining has been viewed as a threat to privacy because of the widespread proliferation of electronic data maintained by corporations. This has lead to increased concerns about the privacy of the underlying data. In recent years, a number of techniques have been proposed for modifying or transforming the data in such a way so as to preserve privacy. A survey on some of the techniques used for privacy-preserving data mining may be found in [105]. In this chapter, we will study an overview of the state-of-the-art in privacy-preserving data mining.

Most methods for privacy computations use some form of transformation on the data in order to perform the privacy preservation. Typically, such methods reduce the granularity of representation in order to reduce the privacy. This reduction in granularity results in some loss of effectiveness of data management or mining algorithms. This is the natural trade-off between information loss and privacy. Some examples of such techniques are as follows:

- *The randomization method:* The randomization method is a technique for privacy-preserving data mining in which noise is added to the data in order to mask the attribute values of records [2, 5]. The noise added is sufficiently large so that individual record values cannot be recovered. Therefore, techniques are designed to derive aggregate distributions from the perturbed records. Subsequently, data mining techniques can be developed in order to work with these aggregate distributions. We will describe the randomization technique in greater detail in a later section.

- *The k-anonymity model and l-diversity:* The k-anonymity model was developed because of the possibility of indirect identification of records from public databases. This is because combinations of record attributes can be used to exactly identify individual records. In the k-anonymity method, we reduce the granularity of data representation with the use of techniques such as generalization and suppression. This granularity is reduced sufficiently that any given record maps onto at least k other records in the data. The l-diversity model was designed to handle some weaknesses in the k-anonymity model since protecting identities to the level of k-individuals is not the same as protecting the corresponding sensitive values, especially when there is homogeneity of sensitive values within a group. To do so, the concept of intra-group diversity of sensitive values is promoted within the anonymization scheme [77].

- *Distributed privacy preservation:* In many cases, individual entities may wish to derive *aggregate results* from data sets which are partitioned across these entities. Such partitioning may be horizontal (when the records are distributed across multiple entities) or vertical (when the attributes are distributed across multiple entities). While the individual entities may not desire to share their entire data sets, they may consent to limited information sharing with the use of a variety of protocols. The overall effect of such methods is to maintain privacy for each individual entity, while deriving aggregate results over the entire data.

- *Downgrading Application Effectiveness:* In many cases, even though the data may not be available, the output of applications such as association rule mining, classification or query processing may result in violations of privacy. This has lead to research in downgrading the effectiveness of applications by either data or application modifications. Some examples of such techniques include association rule hiding [106], classifier downgrading [83], and query auditing [1].

In this paper, we will provide a broad overview of the different techniques for privacy-preserving data mining. We will provide a review of the major algorithms available for each method, and the variations on the different techniques. We will also discuss a number of combinations of different concepts such as k-anonymous mining over vertically- or horizontally-partitioned data. We will also discuss a number of unique challenges associated with privacy-preserving data mining in the high dimensional case.

This paper is organized as follows. In section 2, we will introduce the randomization method for privacy preserving data mining. In section 3, we will discuss the k-anonymization method along with its different variations. In section 4, we will discuss issues in distributed privacy-preserving data mining. In section 5, we will discuss a number of techniques for privacy which arise in the context of sensitive output of a variety of data mining and data management applications. In section 6, we will discuss some unique challenges associated with privacy in the high dimensional case. Section 7 contains the conclusions and discussions.

2 The Randomization Method

In this section, we will discuss the randomization method for privacy-preserving data mining. The randomization method has been traditionally used in the context of distorting data by probability distribution for methods such as surveys which have an evasive answer bias because of privacy concerns [69, 111]. This technique has also been extended to the problem of privacy-preserving data mining [2].

The method of randomization can be described as follows. Consider a set of data records denoted by $X = \{x_1 \ldots x_N\}$. For record $x_i \in X$, we add a noise component which is drawn from the probability distribution $f_Y(y)$. These noise components are drawn independently, and are denoted $y_1 \ldots y_N$. Thus, the new set of distorted records are denoted by $x_1 + y_1 \ldots x_N + y_N$. We denote this new set of records by $z_1 \ldots z_N$. In general, it is assumed that the variance of the added noise is large enough, so that the original record values cannot be easily guessed from the distorted data. Thus, the original records cannot be recovered, but the distribution of the original records can be recovered.

Thus, if X be the random variable denoting the data distribution for the original record, Y be the random variable describing the noise distribution, and Z be the random variable denoting the final record, we have:

$$Z = X + Y$$
$$X = Z - Y$$

Now, we note that N instantiations of the probability distribution Z are known, whereas the distribution Y is known publicly. For a large enough number of values of N, the distribution Z can be approximated closely by using a variety of methods such as kernel density estimation. By subtracting Y from the approximated distribution of Z, it is possible to approximate the original probability distribution X. In practice, one can combine the process of approximation of Z with subtraction of the distribution Y from Z by using a variety of iterative methods such as those discussed in [2, 5]. Such iterative methods typically have a higher accuracy than the sequential solution of first approximating Z and then subtracting Y from it. In particular, the EM method proposed in [5] shows a number of optimal properties in approximating the distribution of X.

We note that at the end of the process, we only have a *distribution* containing the behavior of X. Individual records are not available. Furthermore, the distributions are available only along individual dimensions. Therefore, new data mining algorithms need to be designed to work with the uni-variate distributions rather than the individual records. This can sometimes be a challenge, since many data mining algorithms are inherently dependent on statistics which can only be extracted from either the individual records or the multi-variate probability distributions associated with the records. While the approach can certainly be extended to multi-variate distributions, density estimation becomes inherently more challenging [100] with increasing dimensionalities. For even modest dimensionalities such as 7 to 10, the process of density estimation becomes increasingly inaccurate, and falls prey to the curse of dimensionality.

One key advantage of the randomization method is that it is relatively simple, and does not require knowledge of the distribution of other records in the data. This is not true of other methods such as k-anonymity which require the knowledge of other records in the data. Therefore, the randomization method can be implemented at *data collection time*, and does not require the use of a trusted server containing all the original records in order to perform the anonymization process. While this is a strength of the randomization method, it also leads to some weaknesses, since it treats all records equally irrespective of their local density. Therefore, outlier records are more susceptible to adversarial attacks as compared to records in more dense regions in the data [10]. In order to guard against this, one may need to be needlessly more aggressive in adding noise to all the records in the data. This reduces the utility of the data for mining purposes.

The randomization method has been extended to a variety of data mining problems. In [2], it was discussed how to use the approach for classification. A number of other techniques [124, 126] have also been proposed which seem to work well over a variety of different classifiers. Techniques have also been proposed for privacy-preserving methods of improving the effectiveness of classifiers. For example, the work in [47] proposes methods for privacy-preserving boosting of classifiers. Methods for privacy-preserving mining of association rules have been proposed in [44, 95]. The problem of association rules is especially challenging because of the discrete nature of the attributes corresponding to presence or absence of items. In order to deal with this issue, the randomization technique needs to be modified slightly. Instead of adding quantitative noise, random items are dropped or included with a certain probability. The perturbed transactions are then used for aggregate association rule mining. This technique has shown to be extremely effective in [44]. The randomization approach has also been extended to other applications such as OLAP [3], and SVD based collaborative filtering [91].

2.1 Privacy Quantification

The quantity used to measure privacy should indicate how closely the original value of an attribute can be estimated. The work in [2] uses a measure that defines privacy as follows: If the original value can be estimated with $c\%$ confidence to lie in the interval $[\alpha_1, \alpha_2]$, then the interval width $(\alpha_2 - \alpha_1)$ defines the amount of privacy at $c\%$ confidence level. For example, if the perturbing additive is uniformly distributed in an interval of width 2α, then α is the amount of privacy at confidence level 50% and 2α is the amount of privacy at confidence level 100%. However, this simple method of determining privacy can be subtly incomplete in some situations. This can be best explained by the following example.

Example 1. Consider an attribute X with the density function $f_X(x)$ given by:

$$f_X(x) = \begin{array}{ll} 0.5 & 0 \le x \le 1 \\ 0.5 & 4 \le x \le 5 \\ 0 & \text{otherwise} \end{array}$$

Assume that the perturbing additive Y is distributed uniformly between $[-1, 1]$. Then according to the measure proposed in [2], the amount of privacy is 2 at confidence level 100%.

However, after performing the perturbation and subsequent reconstruction, the density function $f_X(x)$ will be approximately revealed. Let us assume for a moment that a large amount of data is available, so that the distribution function is revealed to a high degree of accuracy. Since the (distribution of the) perturbing additive is publically known, the two pieces of information can be combined to determine that if $Z \in [-1, 2]$, then $X \in [0, 1]$; whereas if $Z \in [3, 6]$ then $X \in [4, 5]$.

Thus, in each case, the value of X can be localized to an interval of length 1. This means that the actual amount of privacy offered by the perturbing additive Y is *at most* 1 at confidence level 100%. We use the qualifier 'at most' since X can often be localized to an interval of length less than one. For example, if the value of Z happens to be -0.5, then the value of X can be localized to an even smaller interval of $[0, 0.5]$. □

This example illustrates that the method suggested in [2] does not take into account the distribution of original data. In other words, the (aggregate) reconstruction of the attribute value also provides a certain level of knowledge which can be used to guess a data value to a higher level of accuracy. To accurately quantify privacy, we need a method which takes such side-information into account.

A key privacy measure [5] is based on the *differential entropy* of a random variable. The differential entropy $h(A)$ of a random variable A is defined as follows:

$$h(A) = -\int_{\Omega_A} f_A(a) \log_2 f_A(a) \, da \tag{1}$$

where Ω_A is the domain of A. It is well-known that $h(A)$ is a measure of uncertainty inherent in the value of A [99]. It can be easily seen that for a random variable U distributed uniformly between 0 and a, $h(U) = \log_2(a)$. For $a = 1$, $h(U) = 0$.

In [5], it was proposed that $2^{h(A)}$ is a measure of privacy inherent in the random variable A. This value is denoted by $\Pi(A)$. Thus, a random variable U distributed uniformly between 0 and a has privacy $\Pi(U) = 2^{log_2(a)} = a$. For a general random variable A, $\Pi(A)$ denote the length of the interval, over which a uniformly distributed random variable has the same uncertainty as A.

Given a random variable B, the *conditional* differential entropy of A is defined as follows:

$$h(A|B) = -\int_{\Omega_{A,B}} f_{A,B}(a, b) \log_2 f_{A|B=b}(a) \, da \, db \tag{2}$$

Thus, the average conditional privacy of A given B is $\Pi(A|B) = 2^{h(A|B)}$. This motivates the following metric $\mathcal{P}(A|B)$ for the conditional privacy loss of A, given B:

$$\mathcal{P}(A|B) = 1 - \Pi(A|B)/\Pi(A) = 1 - 2^{h(A|B)}/2^{h(A)} = 1 - 2^{-I(A;B)}. \tag{3}$$

where $I(A; B) = h(A) - h(A|B) = h(B) - h(B|A)$. $I(A; B)$ is also known as the *mutual information* between the random variables A and B. Clearly, $\mathcal{P}(A|B)$ is the fraction of privacy of A which is lost by revealing B.

As an illustration, let us reconsider Example 1 given above. In this case, the differential entropy of X is given by:

$$h(X) = -\int_{\Omega_X} f_X(x) \log_2 f_X(x) \, dx = 1 \tag{4}$$

Thus the privacy of X, $\Pi(X) = 2^1 = 2$. In other words, X has as much privacy as a random variable distributed uniformly in an interval of length 2. The density function of the perturbed value Z is given by $f_Z(z) = \int_{-\infty}^{\infty} f_X(\nu) f_Y(z - \nu) \, d\nu$.

Using $f_Z(z)$, we can compute the differential entropy $h(Z)$ of Z. It turns out that $h(Z) = 9/4$. Therefore, we have:

$$I(X; Z) = h(Z) - h(Z|X) = 9/4 - h(Y) = 9/4 - 1 = 5/4 \tag{5}$$

Here, the second equality $h(Z|X) = h(Y)$ follows from the fact that X and Y are independent and $Z = X + Y$. Thus, the fraction of privacy loss in this case is $\mathcal{P}(X|Z) = 1 - 2^{-5/4} = 0.5796$. Therefore, after revealing Z, X has privacy $\Pi(X|Z) = \Pi(X) \times (1 - \mathcal{P}(X|Z)) = 2 \times (1.0 - 0.5796) = 0.8408$. This value is less than 1, since X can be localized to an interval of length less than one for many values of Z.

2.2 Adversarial Attacks on Randomization

In the earlier section on privacy quantification, we illustrated an example in which the reconstructed distribution on the data can be used in order to reduce the privacy of the underlying data record. In general, a systematic approach can be used to do this in multi-dimensional data sets with the use of spectral filtering or PCA based techniques [50, 62]. The broad idea in techniques such as PCA [50] is that the correlation structure in the original data can be estimated fairly accurately (in larger data sets) even after noise addition. Once the broad correlation structure in the data has been determined, one can then try to remove the noise in the data in such a way that it fits the aggregate correlation structure of the data. It has been shown that such techniques can reduce the privacy of the perturbation process significantly since the noise removal results in values which are fairly close to their original values [50, 62]. Some other discussions on limiting breaches of privacy in the randomization method may be found in [43].

A second kind of adversarial attack is with the use of public information. Consider a record $X = (x_1 \ldots x_d)$, which is perturbed to $Z = (z_1 \ldots z_d)$. Then, since the distribution of the perturbations is known, we can try to use a maximum likelihood fit of the *potential perturbation* of Z to a public record. Consider the publicly public record $W = (w_1 \ldots w_d)$. Then, the *potential perturbation* of Z with respect to W is given by $(Z - W) = (z_1 - w_1 \ldots z_d - w_d)$. Each of these values $(z_i - w_i)$ should fit the distribution $f_Y(y)$. The corresponding log-likelihood fit is given by $-\sum_{i=1}^{d} \log(f_y(z_i - w_i))$. The higher the log-likelihood fit, the greater the probability that the record W corresponds to X. If it is known that the public data set always includes X, then the maximum likelihood fit can provide a high degree of certainty in identifying the correct record, especially in cases where d is large. We will discuss this issue in greater detail in a later section.

2.3 Randomization Methods for Data Streams

The randomization approach is particularly well suited to privacy-preserving data mining of streams, since the noise added to a given record is independent of the rest of the data. However, streams provide a particularly vulnerable target for adversarial attacks with the use of PCA based techniques [50] because of the large volume of the data available for analysis. In [73], an interesting technique for randomization has been proposed which uses the auto-correlations in different time series while deciding the noise to be added to any particular value. It has been shown in [73] that such an approach is more robust since the noise correlates with the stream behavior, and it is more difficult to create effective adversarial attacks with the use of correlation analysis techniques.

2.4 Multiplicative Perturbations

The most common method of randomization is that of additive perturbations. However, multiplicative perturbations can also be used to good effect for privacy-preserving data mining. Many of these techniques derive their roots in the work of [57] which shows how to use multi-dimensional projections in order to reduce the dimensionality of the data. This technique preserves the inter-record distances approximately, and therefore the transformed records can be used in conjunction with a variety of data mining applications. In particular, the approach is discussed in detail in [87, 88], in which it is shown how to use the method for privacy-preserving clustering. The technique can also be applied to the problem of classification as discussed in [25]. Multiplicative perturbations can also be used for distributed privacy-preserving data mining. Details can be found in [75]. A number of techniques for multiplicative perturbation in the context of masking census data may be found in [66]. A variation on this theme may be implemented with the use of distance preserving Fourier transforms, which work effectively for a variety of cases [82].

As in the case of additive perturbations, multiplicative perturbations are not entirely safe from adversarial attacks. In general, if the attacker has no prior knowledge of the data, then it is relatively difficult to attack the privacy of the transformation. However, with some prior knowledge, two kinds of attacks are possible [76]:

- **Known Input-Output Attack:** In this case, the attacker knows some linearly independent collection of records, and their corresponding perturbed version. In such cases, linear algebra techniques can be used to reverse-engineer the nature of the privacy preserving transformation.
- **Known Sample Attack:** In this case, the attacker has a collection of independent data samples from the same distribution from which the original data was drawn. In such cases, principal component analysis techniques can be used in order to reconstruct the behavior of the original data.

2.5 Data Swapping

We note that noise addition or multiplication is not the only technique which can be used to perturb the data. A related method is that of data swapping, in which the values across different records are swapped in order to perform the privacy-preservation [45]. One advantage of this technique is that the lower order marginal totals of the data are completely preserved and are not perturbed at all. Therefore certain kinds of aggregate computations can be exactly performed without violating the privacy of the data. We note that this technique does not follow the general principle in randomization which allows the value of a record to be perturbed independent;y of the other records. Therefore, this technique can be used in combination with other frameworks such as k-anonymity, as long as the swapping process is designed to preserve the definitions of privacy for that model.

3 The *k*-Anonymity Framework

The randomization method is a simple technique which can be easily implemented at *data collection time*, because the noise added to a given record is independent of the behavior of other data records. This is also a weakness because outlier records can often be difficult to mask. Clearly, in cases in which the privacy-preservation does not need to be performed at data-collection time, it is desirable to have a technique in which the level of inaccuracy depends upon the behavior of the locality of that given record. Another key weakness of the randomization framework is that it does not consider the possibility that publicly available records can be used to identify the identity of the owners of that record. In [10], it has been shown that the use of publicly available records can lead to the privacy getting heavily compromised in high-dimensional cases. This is especially true of outlier records which can be easily distinguished from other records in their locality.

In many applications, the data records are made available by simply removing key identifiers such as the name and social-security numbers from personal records. However, other kinds of attributes (known as pseudo-identifiers) can be used in order to accurately identify the records. Foe example, attributes such as age, zip-code and sex are available in public records such as census rolls. When these attributes are also available in a given data set, they can be used to infer the identity of the corresponding individual. A combination of these attributes can be very powerful, since they can be used to narrow down the possibilities to a small number of individuals.

In *k*-anonymity techniques [98], we reduce the granularity of representation of these pseudo-identifiers with the use of techniques such as *generalization* and *suppression*. In the method of *generalization*, the attribute values are generalized to a range in order to reduce the granularity of representation. For example, the date of birth could be generalized to a range such as year of birth, so as to reduce the risk of identification. In the method of *suppression*, the value of the attribute is removed completely. It is clear that such methods reduce the risk of identification with the use of public records, while reducing the accuracy of applications on the transformed data.

In order to reduce the risk of identification, the *k*-anonymity approach requires that every tuple in the table be indistinguishability related to no fewer than *k* respondents. This can be formalized as follows:

Definition 1. *Each release of the data must be such that every combination of values of quasi-identifiers can be indistinguishably matched to at least k respondents.*

The first algorithm for *k*-anonymity was proposed in [98]. The approach uses *domain generalization hierarchies* of the quasi-identifiers in order to build *k*-anonymous tables. The concept of *k*-minimal generalization has been proposed in [98] in order to limit the level of generalization for maintaining as much data precision as possible for a given level of anonymity. Subsequently, the topic of

k-anonymity has been widely researched. A good overview and survey of the corresponding algorithms may be found in [28].

We note that the problem of optimal anonymization is inherently a difficult one. In [80], it has been shown that the problem of optimal k-anonymization is NP-hard. Nevertheless, the problem can be solved quite effectively by the use of a number of heuristic methods. A method proposed by Bayardo and Agrawal [16] is the k-*Optimize* algorithm which can often obtain effective solutions.

The approach assumes an ordering among the quasi-identifier attributes. The values of the attributes are discretized into intervals (quantitative attributes) or grouped into different sets of values (categorical attributes). Each such grouping is an *item*. For a given attribute, the corresponding items are also ordered. An index is created using these attribute-interval pairs (or items) and a set enumeration tree is constructed on these attribute-interval pairs. This set enumeration tree is a systematic enumeration of all possible generalizations with the use of these groupings. The root of the node is the null node, and every successive level of the tree is constructed by appending one item which is lexicographically larger than all the items at that node of the tree. We note that the number of possible nodes in the tree increases exponentially with the data dimensionality. Therefore, it is not possible to build the entire tree even for modest values of n. However, the k-Optimize algorithm can use a number of pruning strategies to good effect. In particular, a node of the tree can be pruned when it is determined that no descendent of it could be optimal. This can be done by computing a bound on the quality of all descendents of that node, and comparing it to the quality of the current best solution obtained during the traversal process. A branch and bound technique can be used to successively improve the quality of the solution during the traversal process. Eventually, it is possible to terminate the algorithm at a maximum computational time, and use the current solution at that point, which is often quite good, but may not be optimal.

In [70], the *Incognito* method has been proposed for computing a k-minimal generalization with the use of bottom-up aggregation along domain generalization hierarchies. The Incognito method uses a bottom-up breadth-first search of the domain generalization hierarchy, in which it generates all the possible minimal k-anonymous tables for a given private table. First, it checks k-anonymity for each single attribute, and removes all those generalizations which do not satisfy k-anonymity. Then, it computes generalizations in pairs, again pruning those pairs which do not satisfy the k-anonymity constraints. In general, the Incognito algorithm computes $(i + 1)$-dimensional generalization *candidates* from the i-dimensional generalizations, and removes all those those generalizations which do not satisfy the k-anonymity constraint. This approach is continued until, no further candidates can be constructed, or all possible dimensions have been exhausted. We note that the methods in [71, 70] use a more general model for k-anonymity than that in [98]. This is because the method in [98] assumes that the value generalization hierarchy is a tree, whereas that in [71, 70] assumes that it is a graph.

Two interesting methods for top-down specialization and bottom-up generalization for k-anonymity have been proposed in [46, 107]. In [46], a top-down heuristic is designed, which starts with a general solution, and then specializes some attributes of the current solution so as to increase the information, but reduce the anonymity. The reduction in anonymity is always controlled, so that k-anonymity is never violated. At the same time each step of the specialization is controlled by a goodness metric which takes into account both the gain in information and the loss in anonymity. A complementary method to top down specialization is that of *bottom up generalization*, for which an interesting method is proposed in [107].

We note that generalization and suppression are not the only transformation techniques for implementing k-anonymity. For example in [35] it is discussed how to use micro-aggregation in which clusters of records are constructed. For each cluster, its representative value is the average value along each dimension in the cluster. A similar method for achieving anonymity via clustering is proposed in [13]. The work in [13] also provides constant factor approximation algorithms to design the clustering. In [8], a related method has been independently proposed for condensation based privacy-preserving data mining. This technique generates pseudo-data from clustered groups of k-records. The process of pseudo-data generation uses principal component analysis of the behavior of the records within a group. It has been shown in [8], that the approach can be effectively used for the problem of classification. We note that the use of pseudo-data provides an additional layer of protection, since it is difficult to perform adversarial attacks on synthetic data. At the same time, the aggregate behavior of the data is preserved, and this can be useful for a variety of data mining problems.

Since the problem of k-anonymization is essentially a search over a space of possible multi-dimensional solutions, standard heuristic search techniques such as genetic algorithms or simulated annealing can be effectively used. Such a technique has been proposed in [112] in which a simulated annealing algorithm is used in order to generate k-anonymous representations of the data. Another technique proposed in [55] uses genetic algorithms in order to construct k-anonymous representations of the data. Both of these techniques require high computational times, and provide no guarantees on the quality of the solutions found.

The only known techniques which provide guarantees on the quality of the solution are *approximation algorithms* [11, 12, 80], in which the solution found is guaranteed to be within a certain factor of the cost of the optimal solution. An approximation algorithm for k-anonymity was proposed in [80], and it provides an $O(k \cdot \log k)$ optimal solution. A number of techniques have also been proposed in [11, 12], which provide $O(k)$-approximations to the optimal cost k-anonymous solutions.

In many cases, associations between pseudo-identifiers and sensitive attributes can be protected by using multiple views, such that the pseudo-
identifiers and sensitive attributes occur in different views of the table. Thus,
only a small subset of the selected views may be made available. It may be
possible to achieve k-anonymity because of the lossy nature of the join across
the two views. In the event that the join is not lossy enough, it may result in
a violation of k-anonymity. In [121], the problem of violation of k-anonymity
using multiple views has been studied. It has been shown that the problem
is NP-hard in general. It has been shown in [121] that a polynomial time
algorithm is possible if functional dependencies exist between the different
views.

An interesting analysis of the safety of k-anonymization methods has been
discussed in [68]. It tries to model the effectiveness of a k-anonymous representation, given that the attacker has some prior knowledge about the data such
as a sample of the original data. Clearly, the more similar the sample data is
to the true data, the greater the risk. The technique in [68] uses this fact to
construct a model in which it calculates the expected number of items identified. This kind of technique can be useful in situations where it is desirable
to determine whether or not anonymization should be used as the technique
of choice for a particular situation.

3.1 Personalized Privacy Preservation

Not all individuals or entities are equally concerned about their privacy. For
example, a corporation may have very different constraints on the privacy of
its records as compared to an individual. This leads to the natural problem
that we may wish to treat the records in a given data set very differently
for anonymization purposes. From a technical point of view, this means that
the value of k for anonymization is not fixed but may vary with the record.
A condensation-based approach [9] has been proposed for privacy-preserving
data mining in the presence of variable constraints on the privacy of the data
records. This technique constructs groups of non-homogeneous size from the
data, such that it is guaranteed that each record lies in a group whose size is
at least equal to its anonymity level. Subsequently, pseudo-data is generated
from each group so as to create a synthetic data set with the same aggregate
distribution as the original data.

Another interesting model of personalized anonymity is discussed in [114]
in which a person can specify the level of privacy for his or her *sensitive
values*. This technique assumes that an individual can specify a node of the
domain generalization hierarchy in order to decide the level of anonymity that
he can work with. This approach has the advantage that it allows for direct
protection of the sensitive values of individuals than a vanilla k-anonymity
method which is susceptible to different kinds of attacks.

3.2 Utility Based Privacy Preservation

The process of privacy-preservation leads to loss of information for data mining purposes. This loss of information can also be considered a loss of *utility* for data mining purposes. Since some negative results [7] on the curse of dimensionality suggest that a lot of attributes may need to be suppressed in order to preserve anonymity, it is extremely important to do this carefully in order to preserve utility. We note that many anonymization methods [16, 46, 77, 108] use cost measures in order to measure the information loss from the anonymization process. examples of such utility measures include generalization height [16], size of anonymized group [77], discernability measures of attribute values [16], and privacy information loss ratio[108]. In addition, a number of metrics such as the classification metric [55] explicitly try to perform the privacy-preservation in such a way so as to tailor the results with use for specific applications such as classification.

The problem of utility-based privacy-preserving data mining was first studied formally in [65]. The broad idea in [65] is to ameliorate the curse of dimensionality by separately publishing marginal tables containing attributes which have utility, but are also problematic for privacy-preservation purposes. The generalizations performed on the marginal tables and the original tables in fact do not need to be the same. It has been shown that this broad approach can preserve considerable utility of the data set without violating privacy.

A method for utility-based data mining using local recoding was proposed in [116]. The approach is based on the fact that different attributes have different utility from an application point of view. Most anonymization methods are *global*, in which a particular tuple value is mapped to the same generalized value globally. In local recoding, the data space is partitioned into a number of regions, and the mapping of the tuple to the generalizes value is local to that region. Clearly, this kind of approach has greater flexibility, since it can tailor the generalization process to a particular region of the data set. In [116], it has been shown that this method can perform quite effectively because of its local recoding strategy.

Another indirect approach to utility based anonymization is to make the privacy-preservation algorithms more aware of the workload [72]. Typically, data recipients may request only a subset of the data in many cases, and the union of these different requested parts of the data set is referred to as the workload. Clearly, a workload in which some records are used more frequently than others tends to suggest a different anonymization than one which is based on the entire data set. In [72], an effective and efficient algorithm has been proposed for workload aware anonymization.

3.3 Sequential Releases

Privacy-preserving data mining poses unique problems for dynamic applications such as data streams because in such cases, the data is released sequentially. In other cases, different views of the table may be released sequentially.

Once a data block is released, it is no longer possible to go back and increase the level of generalization. On the other hand, new releases may sharpen an attacker's view of the data and may make the overall data set more susceptible to attack. For example, when different views of the data are released sequentially, then one may use a join on the two releases [109] in order to sharpen the ability to distinguish particular records in the data. A technique discussed in [109] relies on lossy joins in order to cripple an attack based on global quasi-identifiers. The intuition behind this approach is that if the join is lossy enough, it will reduce the confidence of the attacker in relating the release from previous views to the current release. Thus, the inability to link successive releases is key in preventing further discovery of the identity of records.

3.4 The *l*-diversity Method

The *k*-anonymity is an attractive technique because of the simplicity of the definition and the numerous algorithms available to perform the anonymization. Nevertheless the technique is susceptible to many kinds of attacks especially when background knowledge is available to the attacker. Some kinds of such attacks are as follows:

- **Homogeneity Attack:** In this attack, all the values for a sensitive attribute within a group of *k* records are the same. Therefore, even though the data is *k*-anonymized, the value of the sensitive attribute for that group of *k* records can be predicted exactly.
- **Background Knowledge Attack:** In this attack, the adversary can use an association between one or more quasi-identifier attributes with the sensitive attribute in order to narrow down possible values of the sensitive field further. An example given in [77] is one in which background knowledge of low incidence of heart attacks among Japanese could be used to narrow down information for the sensitive field of what disease a patient might have.

Clearly, while *k*-anonymity is effective in preventing *identification* of a record, it may not always be effective in preventing inference of the sensitive values of the attributes of that record. Therefore, the technique of *l*-diversity was proposed which not only maintains the minimum group size of *k*, but also focuses on maintaining the diversity of the sensitive attributes. Therefore, the *l*-diversity model [77] for privacy is defined as follows:

Definition 2. *Let a q^*-block be a set of tuples such that its non-sensitive values generalize to q^*. A q^*-block is l-diverse if it contains l "well represented" values for the sensitive attribute S. A table is l-diverse, if every q^*-block in it is l-diverse.*

A number of different instantiations for the *l*-diversity definition are discussed in [77]. We note that when there are multiple sensitive attributes, then the

l-diversity problem because especially challenging. Methods have been proposed in [77] for constructing l-diverse tables from the data set, though the technique remains susceptible to the curse of dimensionality [7]. Other methods for creating l-diverse tables are discussed in [115], in which a simple and efficient method for constructing the l-diverse representation is proposed.

4 Distributed Privacy-Preserving Data Mining

The key goal in most distributed methods for privacy-preserving data mining is to allow computation of useful aggregate statistics over the entire data set without compromising the privacy of the individual data sets within the different participants. Thus, the participants may wish to collaborate in obtaining aggregate results, but may not fully trust each other in terms of the distribution of their own data sets. For this purpose, the data sets may either be *horizontally partitioned* or be *vertically partitioned*. In horizontally partitioned data sets, the individual records are spread out across multiple entities, each of which have the same set of attributes. In vertical partitioning, the individual entities may have different attributes (or views) of the same set of records. Both kinds of partitioning pose different challenges to the problem of distributed privacy-preserving data mining.

The problem of distributed privacy-preserving data mining overlaps closely with a field in cryptography for determining secure multi-party computations. A broad overview of the intersection between the fields of cryptography and privacy-preserving data mining may be found in [90]. The broad approach to cryptographic methods tends to compute functions over inputs provided by multiple recipients without actually sharing the inputs with one another. For example, in a 2-party setting, Alice and Bob may have two inputs x and y respectively, and may wish to both compute the function $f(x, y)$ without revealing x or y to each other. This problem can also be generalized across k parties by designing the k argument function $h(x_1 \ldots x_k)$. Many data mining algorithms may be viewed in the context of repetitive computations of many such primitive functions such as the scalar dot product, secure sum etc. In order to compute the function $f(x, y)$ or $h(x_1 \ldots, x_k)$, a *protocol* will have to designed for exchanging information in such a way that the function is computed without compromising privacy. We note that the robustness of the protocol depends upon the level of trust one is willing to place on the two participants Alice and Bob. This is because the protocol may be subjected to various kinds of adversarial behavior:

- **Semi-honest Adversaries:** In this case, the participants Alice and Bob are curious and attempt to learn from the information received by them during the protocol, but do not deviate from the protocol themselves. In many situations, this may be considered a realistic model of adversarial behavior.

- **Malicious Adversaries:** In this case, Alice and Bob may vary from the protocol, and may send sophisticated inputs to one another to learn from the information received from each other.

A key building-block for many kinds of secure function evaluations is the 1 out of 2 oblivious-transfer protocol. This protocol was proposed in [42, 93] and involves two parties: a *sender*, and a *receiver*. The sender's input is a pair (x_0, x_1), and the receiver's input is a bit value $\sigma \in \{0, 1\}$. At the end of the process, the receiver learns x_σ only, and the sender learns nothing. A number of simple solutions can be designed for this task. In one solution [42, 49], the receiver generates two random public keys, K_0 and K_1, but the receiver knows only the decryption key for K_σ. The receiver sends these keys to the sender, who encrypts x_0 with K_0, x_1 with K_1, and sends the encrypted data back to the receiver. At this point, the receiver can only decrypt x_σ, since this is the only input for which they have the decryption key. We note that this is a semi-honest solution, since the intermediate steps require an assumption of trust. For example, it is assumed that when the receiver sends two keys to the sender, they indeed know the decryption key to only one of them. In order to deal with the case of malicious adversaries, one must ensure that the sender chooses the public keys according to the protocol. An efficient method for doing so is described in [85]. In [85], generalizations of the 1 out of 2 oblivious transfer protocol to the 1 out N case and k out of N case are described.

Since the oblivious transfer protocol is used as a building block for secure multi-party computation, it may be repeated many times over a given function evaluation. Therefore, the computational effectiveness of the approach is important. Efficient methods for both semi-honest and malicious adversaries are discussed in [85]. More complex problems in this domain include the computation of probabilistic functions over a number of multi-party inputs [118]. Such powerful techniques can be used in order to abstract out the primitives from a number of computationally intensive data mining problems. Many of the above techniques have been described for the 2-party case, though generic solutions also exist for the multiparty case. Some important solutions for the multiparty case may be found in [22].

The oblivious transfer protocol can be used in order to compute several data mining primitives related to vector distances in multi-dimensional space. A classic problem which is often used as a primitive for many other problems is that of computing the scalar dot-product in a distributed environment [54]. A fairly general set of methods in this direction are described in [36]. Many of these techniques work by sending changed or encrypted versions of the inputs to one another in order to compute the function with the different alternative versions followed by an oblivious transfer protocol to retrieve the correct value of the final output. A systematic framework is described in [36] to transform normal data mining problems to secure multi-party computation problems. The problems discussed in [36] include those of clustering, classification, association rule mining, data summarization, and generalization. A second set of methods for distributed privacy-preserving data mining is discussed in [29] in which the secure multi-party computation of a number of important data mining primitives is discussed. These methods include the secure sum, the secure set union, the secure size of set intersection and the scalar product. These techniques can be used as data mining primitives for secure multi-party computation over a variety of horizontally and vertically partitioned data sets. Next, we will discuss algorithms for secure multi-party computation over horizontally partitioned data sets.

4.1 Distributed Algorithms over Horizontally Partitioned Data Sets

In horizontally partitioned data sets, different sites contain different sets of records with the same (or highly overlapping) set of attributes which are used for mining purposes. Many of these techniques use specialized versions of the general methods discussed in [29, 36] for various problems. The work in [74] discusses the construction of a popular decision tree induction method called ID3 with the use of approximations of the best splitting attributes. Subsequently, a variety of classifiers have been generalized to the problem of horizontally-partitioned privacy preserving mining including the Naive Bayes Classifier [61], and the SVM Classifier with nonlinear kernels [122]. An extreme solution for the horizontally partitioned case is discussed in [120], in which privacy-preserving classification is performed in a *fully* distributed setting, where each customer has private access to only their own record. A host of other data mining applications have been generalized to the problem of horizontally partitioned data sets. These include the applications of association rule mining [60], clustering [53, 58, 59] and collaborative filtering [92]. Methods for cooperative statistical analysis using secure multi-party computation methods are discussed in [37, 38].

A related problem is that of information retrieval and document indexing in a network of content providers. This problem arises in the context of multiple providers which may need to cooperate with one another in sharing their content, but may essentially be business competitors. In [15], it has been discussed how an adversary may use the output of search engines and content providers in order to reconstruct the documents. Therefore, the level of trust required grows with the number of content providers. A solution to this problem [15] constructs a centralized privacy-preserving index in conjunction with a distributed access control mechanism. The privacy-preserving index maintains strong privacy guarantees even in the face of colluding adversaries, and even if the entire index is made public.

4.2 Distributed Algorithms over Vertically Partitioned Data

For the vertically partitioned case, many primitive operations such as computing the scalar product or the secure set size intersection can be useful in computing the results of data mining algorithms. For example, the methods in [54] discuss how to use to scalar dot product computation for frequent itemset counting. The process of counting can also be achieved by using the secure size of set intersection as described in [29]. Another method for association rule mining discussed in [101] uses the secure scalar product over the vertical bit representation of itemset inclusion in transactions, in order to compute the frequency of the corresponding itemsets. This key step is applied repeatedly within the framework of a roll up procedure of itemset counting. It has been shown in [101] that this approach is quite effective in practice.

The approach of vertically partitioned mining has been extended to a variety of data mining applications such as decision trees [104], SVM Classification [123], Naive Bayes Classifier [103], and k-means clustering [102]. A number of theoretical results on the ability to learn different kinds of functions in vertically partitioned databases with the use of cryptographic approaches are discussed in [39].

4.3 Distributed Algorithms for k-Anonymity

In many cases, it is important to maintain k-anonymity across different distributed parties. In [56], a k-anonymous protocol for data which is vertically partitioned across two parties is described. The broad idea is for the two parties to agree on the quasi-identifier to generalize to the same value before release. A similar approach is discussed in [110], in which the two parties agree on how the generalization is to be performed before release.

In [125], an approach has been discussed for the case of horizontally partitioned data. The work in [125] discusses an extreme case in which each site is a customer which owns exactly one tuple from the data. It is assumed that the data record has both sensitive attributes and quasi-identifier attributes. The solution uses encryption on the sensitive attributes. The sensitive values can be decrypted only if therefore are at least k records with the same values on the quasi-identifiers. Thus, k-anonymity is maintained.

The issue of k-anonymity is also important in the context of hiding identification in the context of distributed location based services [17, 48]. In this case, k-anonymity of the user-identity is maintained even when the location information is released. Such location information is often released when a user may send a message at any point from a given location.

A similar issue arises in the context of communication protocols in which the anonymity of senders (or receivers) may need to be protected. A message is said to be *sender k-anonymous*, if it is guaranteed that an attacker can at most narrow down the identity of the sender to k individuals. Similarly, a message is said to be *receiver k-anonymous*, if it is guaranteed that an attacker can at most narrow down the identity of the receiver to k individuals. A number of such techniques have been discussed in [52, 116, 119].

5 Privacy-Preservation of Application Results

In many cases, the output of applications can be used by an adversary in order to make significant inferences about the behavior of the underlying data. In this section, we will discuss a number of miscellaneous methods for privacy-preserving data mining which tend to preserve the privacy of the end results of applications such as association rule mining and query processing. This problem is related to that of disclosure control [1] in statistical databases, though advances in data mining methods provide increasingly sophisticated methods for adversaries to make inferences about the behavior of the underlying data. In cases, where the commercial data needs to be shared, the association rules may represent sensitive information for target-marketing purposes, which needs to be protected from inference.

In this section, we will discuss the issue of disclosure control for a number of applications such as association rule mining, classification, and query processing. The key goal here is to prevent adversaries from making inferences from the end results of data mining and management applications. A broad discussion of the security and privacy implications of data mining are presented in [30]. We will discuss each of the applications below:

5.1 Association Rule Hiding

Recent years have seen tremendous advances in the ability to perform association rule mining effectively. Such rules often encode important target marketing information about a business. Some of the earliest work on the challenges of association rule mining for database security may be found in [14]. Two broad approaches are used for association rule hiding:

- **Distortion:** In distortion [89], the entry for a given transaction is modified to a different value. Since, we are typically dealing with binary transactional data sets, the entry value is flipped.
- **Blocking:** In blocking [96], the entry is not modified, but is left incomplete. Thus, unknown entry values are used to prevent discovery of association rules.

We note that both the distortion and blocking processes have a number of side effects on the non-sensitive rules in the data. Some of the non-sensitive rules may be lost along with sensitive rules, and new *ghost rules* may be created because of the distortion or blocking process. Such side effects are undesirable since they reduce the utility of the data for mining purposes.

A formal proof of the NP-hardness of the distortion method for hiding association rule mining may be found in [14]. In [14], techniques are proposed for changing some of the 1-values to 0-values so that the support of the corresponding sensitive rules is appropriately lowered. The utility of the approach was defined by the number of non-sensitive rules whose support was also lowered by using such an approach. This approach was extended in [31] in which both support and confidence of the appropriate rules could be lowered. In this case, 0-values in the transactional database could also change to 1-values. In many cases, this resulted in spurious association rules (or ghost rules) which was an undesirable side effect of the process. A complete description of the various methods for data distortion for association rule hiding may be found in [106]. Another interesting piece of work which balances privacy and disclosure concerns of sanitized rules may be found in [89].

The broad idea of blocking was proposed in [20]. The attractiveness of the blocking approach is that it maintains the truthfulness of the underlying data, since it replaces a value with an unknown (often represented by '?') rather than a false value. Some interesting algorithms for using blocking for association rule hiding are presented in [97]. The work has been further extended in [96] with a discussion of the effectiveness of reconstructing the hidden rules. Another interesting set of techniques for association rule hiding with limited side effects is discussed in [113]. The objective of this method is to reduce the loss of non-sensitive rules, or the creation of ghost rules during the rule hiding process.

In [6], it has been discussed how blocking techniques for hiding association rules can be used to prevent discovery of sensitive entries in the data set by an adversary. In this case, certain entries in the data are classified as sensitive, and only rules which disclose such entries are hidden. An efficient depth-first association mining algorithm is proposed for this task [6]. It has been shown that the methods can effectively reduce the disclosure of sensitive entries with the use of such a hiding process.

5.2 Downgrading Classifier Effectiveness

An important privacy-sensitive application is that of classification, in which the results of a classification application may be sensitive information for the owner of a data set. Therefore the issue is to modify the data in such a way that the accuracy of the classification process is reduced, while retaining the utility of the data for other kinds of applications. A number of techniques have been discussed in [21, 83] in reducing the classifier effectiveness in context of classification rule and decision tree applications. The notion of *parsimonious downgrading* is proposed [21] in the context of blocking out inference channels for classification purposes while mining the effect to the overall utility. A system called Rational Downgrader [83] was designed with the use of these principles.

The methods for association rule hiding can also be generalized to rule based classifiers. This is because rule based classifiers often use association rule mining methods as subroutines, so that the rules with the class labels in their consequent are used for classification purposes. For a classifier downgrading approach, such rules are sensitive rules, whereas all other rules (with non-class attributes in the consequent) are non-sensitive rules. An example of a method for rule based classifier downgradation is discussed in [86] in which it has been shown how to effectively hide classification rules for a data set.

5.3 Query Auditing and Inference Control

Many sensitive databases are not available for public access, but may have a public interface through which *aggregate querying* is allowed. This leads to the natural danger that a smart adversary may pose a sequence of queries through which he or she may infer sensitive facts about the data. The nature of this inference may correspond to *full disclosure*, in which an adversary may determine the exact values of the data attributes. A second notion is that of *partial disclosure* in which the adversary may be able to narrow down the values to a range, but may not be able to guess the exact value. Most work on query auditing generally concentrates on the full disclosure setting.

Two broad approaches are designed in order to reduce the likelihood of sensitive data discovery:

- **Query Auditing:** In query auditing, we deny one or more queries from a sequence of queries. The queries to be denied are chosen such that the sensitivity of the underlying data is preserved. Some examples of query auditing methods include [34, 64, 84, 94].
- **Query Inference Control:** In this case, we perturb the underlying data or the query result itself. The perturbation is engineered in such a way, so as to preserve the privacy of the underlying data. Examples of methods which use perturbation of the underlying data include [3, 23, 81]. Examples of methods which perturb the query result include [19, 33, 39, 40, 41].

An overview of classical methods for query auditing may be found in [1]. The query auditing problem has an *online* version, in which we do not know the sequence of queries in advance, and an *offline* version, in which we do know this sequence in advance. Clearly, the offline version is open to better optimization from an auditing point of view.

The problem of query auditing was first studied in [34, 94]. This approach works for the online version of the query auditing problem. In these works, the sum query is studied, and privacy is protected by using restrictions on sizes and pairwise overlaps of the allowable queries. Let us assume that the query size is restricted to be at most k, and the number of common elements in pairwise query sets is at most m. Then, if q be the number of elements that the attacker already knows from background knowledge, it was shown that [34, 94] that the maximum number of queries allowed is $(2 \cdot k - (q + 1))/m$. We note that if N be the total number of data elements, the above expression is always bounded above by $2 \cdot N$. If for some constant c, we choose $k = N/c$ and $m = 1$, the approach can only support a constant number of queries, after which all queries would have to be denied by the auditor. Clearly, this is undesirable from an application point of view. Therefore, a considerable amount of research has been devoted to increasing the number of queries which can be answered by the auditor without compromising privacy.

In [63], the problem of sum auditing on sub-cubes of the data cube are studied, where a query expression is constructed using a string of 0, 1, and *. The elements to be summed up are determined by using matches to the query string pattern. In [67], the problem of auditing a database of boolean values is studied for the case of sum and max queries. In [18], and approach for query auditing is discussed which is actually a combination of the approach of denying some queries and modifying queries in order to achieve privacy.

In [64], the authors show that denials to queries depending upon the answer to the current query can leak information. The authors introduce the notion of simulatable auditing for auditing sum and max queries. In [84], the authors devise methods for auditing max queries and bags of max and min queries under the partial and full disclosure settings. The authors also examine the notion of *utility* in the context of auditing, and obtain results for sum queries in the full disclosure setting.

A number of techniques have also been proposed for the offline version of the auditing problem. In [26], a number of variations of the offline auditing problem have been studied. In the offline auditing problem, we are given a sequence of queries which have been truthfully answered, and we need to determine if privacy has been breached. In [26], effective algorithms were proposed for the sum, max, and max and min versions of the problems. On the other hand, the sum and max version of the problem was shown to be NP-hard. In [4], an offline auditing framework was proposed for determining whether a database adheres to its disclosure properties. The key idea is to create an audit expression which specifies sensitive table entries.

A number of techniques have also been proposed for sanitizing or randomizing the data for query auditing purposes. These are fairly general models of privacy, since they preserve the privacy of the data even when the entire database is available. The standard methods for perturbation [2, 5] or k-anonymity [98] can always be used, and it is always guaranteed that an adversary may not derive anything more from the queries than they can from the base data. Thus, since a k-anonymity model guarantees a certain level of privacy even when the entire database is made available, it will continue to do so under any sequence of queries. In [23], a number of interesting methods are discussed for measuring the effectiveness of sanitization schemes in terms of balancing privacy and utility.

Instead of sanitizing the base data, it is possible to use summary constructs on the data, and respond to queries using only the information encoded in the summary constructs. Such an approach preserves privacy, as long as the summary constructs do not reveal sensitive information about the underlying records. A histogram based approach to data sanitization has been discussed in [23, 24]. In this technique the data is recursively partitioned into multi-dimensional cells. The final output is the exact description of the cuts along with the population of each cell. Clearly, this kind of description can be used for approximate query answering with the use of standard histogram query processing methods. In [51], a method has been proposed for privacy-preserving indexing of multi-dimensional data by using bucketizing of the underlying attribute values in conjunction with encryption of identification keys. We note that a choice of larger bucket sizes provides greater privacy but less accuracy. Similarly, optimizing the bucket sizes for accuracy can lead to reductions in privacy. This tradeoff has been studied in [51], and it has been shown that reasonable query precision can be maintained at the expense of partial disclosure.

In the class of methods which use summarization structures for inference control, an interesting method was proposed by Mishra and Sandler in [81], which uses pseudo-random sketches for privacy-preservation. In this technique sketches are constructed from the data, and the sketch representations are used to respond to user queries. In [81], it has been shown that the scheme preserves privacy effectively, while continuing to be useful from a utility point of view.

Finally, an important class of query inference control methods changes the results of queries in order to preserve privacy. A classical method for aggregate queries such as the sum or relative frequency is that of random sampling [32]. In this technique, a random sample of the data is used to compute such aggregate functions. The random sampling approach makes it impossible for the questioner to precisely control the formation of query sets. The advantage of using a random sample is that the results of large queries are quite robust (in terms of *relative error*), but the privacy of individual records are preserved because of high *absolute error*.

Another method for query inference control is by adding noise to the results of queries. Clearly, the noise should be sufficient that an adversary cannot use small changes in the query arguments in order to infer facts about the base data. In [41], an interesting technique has been presented in which the result of a query is perturbed by an amount which depends upon the underlying sensitivity of the query function. This sensitivity of the query function is defined approximately by the change in the response to the query by changing one argument to the function. An important theoretical result [19, 33, 39, 40] shows that a surprisingly small amount of noise needs to be added to the result of a query, provided that the number of queries is sublinear in the number of database rows. With increasing sizes of databases today, this result provides fairly strong guarantees on privacy. Such queries together with their slightly noisy responses are referred to as the SuLQ primitive.

6 Limitations of Privacy: The Curse of Dimensionality

Many privacy-preserving data-mining methods are inherently limited by the curse of dimensionality in the presence of public information. For example, the technique in [7] analyzes the k-anonymity method in the presence of increasing dimensionality. The curse of dimensionality becomes especially important when adversaries may have considerable background information, as a result of which the boundary between pseudo-identifiers and sensitive attributes may become blurred. This is generally true, since adversaries may be familiar with the subject of interest and may have greater information about them than what is publicly available. This is also the motivation for techniques such as l-diversity [77] in which background knowledge can be used to make further privacy attacks. The work in [7] concludes that in order to maintain privacy, a large number of the attributes may need to be suppressed. Thus, the data loses its utility for the purpose of data mining algorithms. The broad intuition behind the result in [7] is that when attributes are generalized into wide ranges, the combination of a large number of generalized attributes is so sparsely populated, that even two anonymity becomes increasingly unlikely. While the method of l-diversity has not been formally analyzed, some observations made in [77] seem to suggest that the method becomes increasingly infeasible to implement effectively with increasing dimensionality.

The method of randomization has also been analyzed in [10]. This paper makes a first analysis of the ability to re-identify data records with the use of maximum likelihood estimates. Consider a d-dimensional record $X = (x_1 \ldots x_d)$, which is perturbed to $Z = (z_1 \ldots z_d)$. For a given public record $W = (w_1 \ldots w_d)$, we would like to find the probability that it could have been perturbed to Z using the perturbing distribution $f_Y(y)$. If this were true, then the set of values given by $(Z - W) = (z_1 - w_1 \ldots z_d - w_d)$ should be all drawn from the distribution $f_Y(y)$. The corresponding log-likelihood fit is given by $-\sum_{i=1}^{d} \log(f_y(z_i - w_i))$. The higher the log-likelihood fit, the greater the probability that the record W corresponds to X. In order to achieve greater anonymity, we would like the perturbations to be large enough, so that some of the spurious records in the data have greater log-likelihood fit to Z than the true record X. It has been shown in [10], that this probability reduces rapidly with increasing dimensionality for different kinds of perturbing distributions. Thus, the randomization technique also seems to be susceptible to the curse of high dimensionality.

We note that the problem of high dimensionality seems to be a fundamental one for privacy preservation, and it is unlikely that more effective methods can be found in order to preserve privacy when background information about a large number of features is available to even a subset of selected individuals. Indirect examples of such violations occur with the use of trail identifications [78, 79], where information from multiple sources can be compiled to create a high dimensional feature representation which violates privacy.

7 Summary

In this paper, we presented a survey of the broad areas of privacy-preserving data mining and the underlying algorithms. We discussed a variety of data modification techniques such as randomization and k-anonymity based techniques. We discussed methods for distributed privacy-preserving mining, and the methods for handling horizontally and vertically partitioned data. We discussed the issue of downgrading the effectiveness of data mining and data management applications such as association rule mining, classification, and query processing. Finally, we discussed some fundamental limitations of the problem of privacy-preservation in the presence of increased amounts of public information and background knowledge.

References

1. Adam N., Wortmann J. C.: Security-Control Methods for Statistical Databases: A Comparison Study. *ACM Computing Surveys*, 21(4), 1989.
2. Agrawal R., Srikant R. Privacy-Preserving Data Mining. *Proceedings of the ACM SIGMOD Conference*, 2000.
3. Agrawal R., Srikant R., Thomas D. Privacy-Preserving OLAP. *Proceedings of the ACM SIGMOD Conference*, 2005.
4. Agrawal R., Bayardo R., Faloutsos C., Kiernan J., Rantzau R., Srikant R.: Auditing Compliance via a hippocratic database. *VLDB Conference*, 2004.
5. Agrawal D. Aggarwal C. C. On the Design and Quantification of Privacy-Preserving Data Mining Algorithms. *ACM PODS Conference*, 2002.
6. Aggarwal C., Pei J., Zhang B. A Framework for Privacy Preservation against Adversarial Data Mining. *ACM KDD Conference*, 2006.
7. Aggarwal C. C. On k-anonymity and the curse of dimensionality. *VLDB Conference*, 2005.
8. Aggarwal C. C., Yu P. S.: A Condensation approach to privacy preserving data mining. *EDBT Conference*, 2004.
9. Aggarwal C. C., Yu P. S.: On Variable Constraints in Privacy-Preserving Data Mining. *SIAM Conference*, 2005.
10. Aggarwal C. C.: On Randomization, Public Information and the Curse of Dimensionality. *ICDE Conference*, 2007.
11. Aggarwal G., Feder T., Kenthapadi K., Motwani R., Panigrahy R., Thomas D., Zhu A.: Anonymizing Tables. *ICDT Conference*, 2005.
12. Aggarwal G., Feder T., Kenthapadi K., Motwani R., Panigrahy R., Thomas D., Zhu A.: Approximation Algorithms for k-anonymity. *Journal of Privacy Technology*, paper 20051120001, 2005.
13. Aggarwal G., Feder T., Kenthapadi K., Khuller S., Motwani R., Panigrahy R., Thomas D., Zhu A.: Achieving Anonymity via Clustering. *ACM PODS Conference*, 2006.
14. Atallah, M., Elmagarmid, A., Ibrahim, M., Bertino, E., Verykios, V.: Disclosure limitation of sensitive rules, *Workshop on Knowledge and Data Engineering Exchange*, 1999.

15. Bawa M., Bayardo R. J., Agrawal R.: Privacy-Preserving Indexing of Documents on the Network. *VLDB Conference*, 2003.
16. Bayardo R. J., Agrawal R.: Data Privacy through Optimal k-Anonymization. *Proceedings of the ICDE Conference*, pp. 217–228, 2005.
17. Bettini C., Wang X. S., Jajodia S.: Protecting Privacy against Location Based Personal Identification. *Proc. of Secure Data Management Workshop*, Trondheim, Norway, 2005.
18. Biskup J., Bonatti P.: Controlled Query Evaluation for Known Policies by Combining Lying and Refusal. *Annals of Mathematics and Artificial Intelligence*, 40(1-2), 2004.
19. Blum A., Dwork C., McSherry F., Nissim K.: Practical Privacy: The SuLQ Framework. *ACM PODS Conference*, 2005.
20. Chang L., Moskowitz I.: An integrated framwork for database inference and privacy protection. *Data and Applications Security*. Kluwer, 2000.
21. Chang L., Moskowitz I.: Parsimonious downgrading and decision trees applied to the inference problem. *New Security Paradigms Workshop*, 1998.
22. Chaum D., Crepeau C., Damgard I.: Multiparty unconditionally secure protocols. *ACM STOC Conference*, 1988.
23. Chawla S., Dwork C., McSherry F., Smith A., Wee H.: Towards Privacy in Public Databases, *TCC*, 2005.
24. Chawla S., Dwork C., McSherry F., Talwar K.: On the Utility of Privacy-Preserving Histograms, *UAI*, 2005.
25. Chen K., Liu L.: Privacy-preserving data classification with rotation perturbation. *ICDM Conference*, 2005.
26. Chin F.: Security Problems on Inference Control for SUM, MAX, and MIN Queries. *J. of the ACM*, 33(3), 1986.
27. Chin F., Ozsoyoglu G.: Auditing for Secure Statistical Databases. *Proceedings of the ACM'81 Conference*, 1981.
28. Ciriani V., De Capitiani di Vimercati S., Foresti S., Samarati P.: *k*-Anonimity. *Security in Decentralized Data Management*, ed. Jajodia S., Yu T., Springer, 2006.
29. Clifton C., Kantarcioglou M., Lin X., Zhu M.: Tools for privacy-preserving distributed data mining. *ACM SIGKDD Explorations*, 4(2), 2002.
30. Clifton C., Marks D.: Security and Privacy Implications of Data Mining., *Workshop on Data Mining and Knowledge Discovery*, 1996.
31. Dasseni E., Verykios V., Elmagarmid A., Bertino E.: Hiding Association Rules using Confidence and Support, *4th Information Hiding Workshop*, 2001.
32. Denning D.: Secure Statostical Databases with Random Sample Queries. *ACM TODS Journal*, 5(3), 1980.
33. Dinur I., Nissim K.: Revealing Information while preserving privacy. *ACM PODS Conference*, 2003.
34. Dobkin D., Jones A., Lipton R.: Secure Databases: Protection against User Influence. *ACM Transactions on Databases Systems*, 4(1), 1979.
35. Domingo-Ferrer J,, Mateo-Sanz J.: Practical data-oriented micro-aggregation for statistical disclosure control. *IEEE TKDE*, 14(1), 2002.
36. Du W., Atallah M.: Secure Multi-party Computation: A Review and Open Problems. *CERIAS Tech. Report* 2001-51, Purdue University, 2001.
37. Du W., Han Y. S., Chen S.: Privacy-Preserving Multivariate Statistical Analysis: Linear Regression and Classification, Proc. SIAM Conf. Data Mining, 2004.

38. Du W., Atallah M.: Privacy-Preserving Cooperative Statistical Analysis, 17th Annual Computer Security Applications Conference, 2001.
39. Dwork C., Nissim K.: Privacy-Preserving Data Mining on Vertically Partitioned Databases, *CRYPTO*, 2004.
40. Dwork C., Kenthapadi K., McSherry F., Mironov I., Naor M.: Our Data, Ourselves: Privacy via Distributed Noise Generation. *EUROCRYPT*, 2006.
41. Dwork C., McSherry F., Nissim K., Smith A.: Calibrating Noise to Sensitivity in Private Data Analysis, *TCC*, 2006.
42. Even S., Goldreich O., Lempel A.: A Randomized Protocol for Signing Contracts. *Communications of the ACM*, vol 28, 1985.
43. Evfimievski A., Gehrke J., Srikant R. Limiting Privacy Breaches in Privacy Preserving Data Mining. *ACM PODS Conference*, 2003.
44. Evfimievski A., Srikant R., Agrawal R., Gehrke J.: Privacy-Preserving Mining of Association Rules. *ACM KDD Conference*, 2002.
45. Fienberg S., McIntyre J.: Data Swapping: Variations on a Theme by Dalenius and Reiss. *Technical Report, National Institute of Statistical Sciences*, 2003.
46. Fung B., Wang K., Yu P.: Top-Down Specialization for Information and Privacy Preservation. *ICDE Conference*, 2005.
47. Gambs S., Kegl B., Aimeur E.: Privacy-Preserving Boosting. *Knowledge Discovery and Data Mining Journal*, to appear.
48. Gedik B., Liu L.: A customizable k-anonymity model for protecting location privacy, *ICDCS Conference*, 2005.
49. Goldreich O.: Secure Multi-Party Computation, Unpublished Manuscript, 2002.
50. Huang Z., Du W., Chen B.: Deriving Private Information from Randomized Data. pp. 37–48, *ACM SIGMOD Conference*, 2005.
51. Hore B., Mehrotra S., Tsudik B.: A Privacy-Preserving Index for Range Queries. *VLDB Conference*, 2004.
52. Hughes D, Shmatikov V.: Information Hiding, Anonymity, and Privacy: A modular Approach. *Journal of Computer Security*, 12(1), 3–36, 2004.
53. Inan A., Saygin Y., Savas E., Hintoglu A., Levi A.: Privacy-Preserving Clustering on Horizontally Partitioned Data. *Data Engineering Workshops*, 2006.
54. Ioannidis I., Grama A., Atallah M.: A secure protocol for computing dot products in clustered and distributed environments, *International Conference on Parallel Processing*, 2002.
55. Iyengar V. S.: Transforming Data to Satisfy Privacy Constraints. *KDD Conference*, 2002.
56. Jiang W., Clifton C.: Privacy-preserving distributed k-Anonymity. *Proceedings of the IFIP 11.3 Working Conference on Data and Applications Security*, 2005.
57. Johnson W., Lindenstrauss J.: Extensions of Lipshitz Mapping into Hilbert Space, *Contemporary Math.* vol. 26, pp. 189-206, 1984.
58. Jagannathan G., Wright R.: Privacy-Preserving Distributed k-means clustering over arbitrarily partitioned data. *ACM KDD Conference*, 2005.
59. Jagannathan G., Pillaipakkamnatt K., Wright R.: A New Privacy-Preserving Distributed k-Clustering Algorithm. *SIAM Conference on Data Mining*, 2006.
60. Kantarcioglu M., Clifton C.: Privacy-Preserving Distributed Mining of Association Rules on Horizontally Partitioned Data. *IEEE TKDE Journal*, 16(9), 2004.

61. Kantarcioglu M., Vaidya J.: Privacy-Preserving Naive Bayes Classifier for Horizontally Partitioned Data. *IEEE Workshop on Privacy-Preserving Data Mining*, 2003.
62. Kargupta H., Datta S., Wang Q., Sivakumar K.: On the Privacy Preserving Properties of Random Data Perturbation Techniques. *ICDM Conference*, pp. 99-106, 2003.
63. Karn J., Ullman J.: A model of statistical databases and their security. *ACM Transactions on Database Systems*, 2(1):1–10, 1977.
64. Kenthapadi K.,Mishra N., Nissim K.: Simulatable Auditing, *ACM PODS Conference*, 2005.
65. Kifer D., Gehrke J.: Injecting utility into anonymized datasets. *SIGMOD Conference*, pp. 217-228, 2006.
66. Kim J., Winkler W.: Multiplicative Noise for Masking Continuous Data, *Technical Report Statistics 2003-01, Statistical Research Division, US Bureau of the Census*, Washington D.C., Apr. 2003.
67. Kleinberg J., Papadimitriou C., Raghavan P.: Auditing Boolean Attributes. *Journal of Computer and System Sciences*, 6, 2003.
68. Lakshmanan L., Ng R., Ramesh G. To Do or Not To Do: The Dilemma of Disclosing Anonymized Data. *ACM SIGMOD Conference*, 2005.
69. Liew C. K., Choi U. J., Liew C. J. A data distortion by probability distribution. *ACM TODS*, 10(3):395-411, 1985.
70. LeFevre K., DeWitt D., Ramakrishnan R.: Incognito: Full Domain K-Anonymity. *ACM SIGMOD Conference*, 2005.
71. LeFevre K., DeWitt D., Ramakrishnan R.: Mondrian Multidimensional K-Anonymity. *ICDE Conference*, 25, 2006.
72. LeFevre K., DeWitt D., Ramakrishnan R.: Workload Aware Anonymization. *KDD Conference*, 2006.
73. Li F., Sun J., Papadimitriou S. Mihaila G., Stanoi I.: Hiding in the Crowd: Privacy Preservation on Evolving Streams through Correlation Tracking. *ICDE Conference*, 2007.
74. Lindell Y., Pinkas B.: Privacy-Preserving Data Mining. *CRYPTO*, 2000.
75. Liu K., Kargupta H., Ryan J.: Random Projection Based Multiplicative Data Perturbation for Privacy Preserving Distributed Data Mining. *IEEE Transactions on Knowledge and Data Engineering*, 18(1), 2006.
76. Liu K., Giannella C. Kargupta H.: An Attacker's View of Distance Preserving Maps for Privacy-Preserving Data Mining. *PKDD Conference*, 2006.
77. Machanavajjhala A., Gehrke J., Kifer D., and Venkitasubramaniam M.: l-Diversity: Privacy Beyond k-Anonymity. *ICDE*, 2006.
78. Malin B, Sweeney L. Re-identification of DNA through an automated linkage process. *American Medical Informatics Association*, 423–427, 2001.
79. Malin B. Why methods for genomic data privacy fail and what we can do to fix it, *AAAS Annual Meeting*, Seattle, WA, 2004.
80. Meyerson A., Williams R. On the complexity of optimal k-anonymity. *ACM PODS Conference*, 2004.
81. Mishra N., Sandler M.: Privacy vis Pseudorandom Sketches. *ACM PODS Conference*, 2006.
82. Mukherjee S., Chen Z., Gangopadhyay S.: A privacy-preserving technique for Euclidean distance-based mining algorithms using Fourier based transforms, *VLDB Journal*, 2006.

83. Moskowitz I., Chang L.: A decision theoretic system for information downgrading. *Joint Conference on Information Sciences*, 2000.

84. Nabar S., Marthi B., Kenthapadi K., Mishra N., Motwani R.: Towards Robustness in Query Auditing. *VLDB Conference*, 2006.

85. Naor M., Pinkas B.: Efficient Oblivious Transfer Protocols, *SODA Conference*, 2001.

86. Natwichai J., Li X., Orlowska M.: A Reconstruction-based Algorithm for Classification Rules Hiding. *Australasian Database Conference*, 2006.

87. Oliveira S. R. M., Zaane O.: Privacy Preserving Clustering by Data Transformation, *Proc. 18th Brazilian Symp. Databases*, pp. 304-318, Oct. 2003.

88. Oliveira S. R. M., Zaiane O.: Data Perturbation by Rotation for Privacy-Preserving Clustering, *Technical Report TR04-17*, Department of Computing Science, University of Alberta, Edmonton, AB, Canada, August 2004.

89. Oliveira S. R. M., Zaiane O., Saygin Y.: Secure Association-Rule Sharing. *PAKDD Conference*, 2004.

90. Pinkas B.: Cryptographic Techniques for Privacy-Preserving Data Mining. *ACM SIGKDD Explorations*, 4(2), 2002.

91. Polat H., Du W.: SVD-based collaborative filtering with privacy. *ACM SAC Symposium*, 2005.

92. Polat H., Du W.: Privacy-Preserving Top-N Recommendations on Horizontally Partitioned Data. *Web Intelligence*, 2005.

93. Rabin M. O.: How to exchange secrets by oblivious transfer, *Technical Report* TR-81, Aiken Corporation Laboratory, 1981.

94. Reiss S.: Security in Databases: A combinatorial Study, *Journal of ACM*, 26(1), 1979.

95. Rizvi S., Haritsa J.: Maintaining Data Privacy in Association Rule Mining. *VLDB Conference*, 2002.

96. Saygin Y., Verykios V., Clifton C.: Using Unknowns to prevent discovery of Association Rules, *ACM SIGMOD Record*, 30(4), 2001.

97. Saygin Y., Verykios V., Elmagarmid A.: Privacy-Preserving Association Rule Mining, *12th International Workshop on Research Issues in Data Engineering*, 2002.

98. Samarati P.: Protecting Respondents' Identities in Microdata Release. *IEEE Trans. Knowl. Data Eng.* 13(6): 1010-1027 (2001).

99. Shannon C. E.: The Mathematical Theory of Communication, University of Illinois Press, 1949.

100. Silverman B. W.: Density Estimation for Statistics and Data Analysis. *Chapman and Hall*, 1986.

101. Vaidya J., Clifton C.: Privacy-Preserving Association Rule Mining in Vertically Partitioned Databases. *ACM KDD Conference*, 2002.

102. Vaidya J., Clifton C.: Privacy-Preserving k-means clustering over vertically partitioned Data. *ACM KDD Conference*, 2003.

103. Vaidya J., Clifton C.: Privacy-Preserving Naive Bayes Classifier over vertically partitioned data. *SIAM Conference*, 2004.

104. Vaidya J., Clifton C.: Privacy-Preserving Decision Trees over vertically partitioned data. *Lecture Notes in Computer Science*, Vol 3654, 2005.

105. Verykios V. S., Bertino E., Fovino I. N., Provenza L. P., Saygin Y., Theodoridis Y.: State-of-the-art in privacy preserving data mining. *ACM SIGMOD Record*, v.33 n.1, 2004.

106. Verykios V. S., Elmagarmid A., Bertino E., Saygin Y.,, Dasseni E.: Association Rule Hiding. *IEEE Transactions on Knowledge and Data Engineering*, 16(4), 2004.
107. Wang K., Yu P., Chakraborty S.: Bottom-Up Generalization: A Data Mining Solution to Privacy Protection. *ICDM Conference*, 2004.
108. Wang K., Fung B. C. M., Yu P. Template based Privacy -Preservation in classification problems. *ICDM Conference*, 2005.
109. Wang K., Fung B. C. M.: Anonymization for Sequential Releases. *ACM KDD Conference*, 2006.
110. Wang K., Fung B. C. M., Dong G.: Integarting Private Databases for Data Analysis. *Lecture Notes in Computer Science*, 3495, 2005.
111. Warner S. L. Randomized Response: A survey technique for eliminating evasive answer bias. *Journal of American Statistical Association*, 60(309):63–69, March 1965.
112. Winkler W.: Using simulated annealing for k-anonymity. *Technical Report 7, US Census Bureau.*
113. Wu Y.-H., Chiang C.-M., Chen A. L. P.: Hiding Sensitive Association Rules with Limited Side Effects. *IEEE Transactions on Knowledge and Data Engineering*, 19(1), 2007.
114. Xiao X., Tao Y.. Personalized Privacy Preservation. *ACM SIGMOD Conference*, 2006.
115. Xiao X., Tao Y. Anatomy: Simple and Effective Privacy Preservation. *VLDB Conference*, pp. 139-150, 2006.
116. Xu J., Wang W., Pei J., Wang X., Shi B., Fu A. W. C.: Utility Based Anonymization using Local Recoding. *ACM KDD Conference*, 2006.
117. Xu S., Yung M.: k-anonymous secret handshakes with reusable credentials. *ACM Conference on Computer and Communications Security*, 2004.
118. Yao A. C.: How to Generate and Exchange Secrets. *FOCS Conferemce*, 1986.
119. Yao G., Feng D.: A new k-anonymous message transmission protocol. *International Workshop on Information Security Applications*, 2004.
120. Yang Z., Zhong S., Wright R.: Privacy-Preserving Classification of Customer Data without Loss of Accuracy. *SDM Conference*, 2006.
121. Yao C., Wang S., Jajodia S.: Checking for k-Anonymity Violation by views. *ACM Conference on Computer and Communication Security*, 2004.
122. Yu H., Jiang X., Vaidya J.: Privacy-Preserving SVM using nonlinear Kernels on Horizontally Partitioned Data. *SAC Conference*, 2006.
123. Yu H., Vaidya J., Jiang X.: Privacy-Preserving SVM Classification on Vertically Partitioned Data. *PAKDD Conference*, 2006.
124. Zhang P., Tong Y., Tang S., Yang D.: Privacy-Preserving Naive Bayes Classifier. *Lecture Notes in Computer Science*, Vol 3584, 2005.
125. Zhong S., Yang Z., Wright R.: Privacy-enhancing k-anonymization of customer data, In Proceedings of the ACM SIGMOD-SIGACT-SIGART Principles of Database Systems, Baltimore, MD. 2005.
126. Zhu Y., Liu L. Optimal Randomization for Privacy- Preserving Data Mining. *ACM KDD Conference*, 2004.

19

Privacy in Database Publishing: A Bayesian Perspective

Alin Deutsch*

Department of Computer Science and Engineering
University of California San Diego
9500 Gilman Dr., La Jolla, CA, 92093-0404, USA
deutsch@cs.ucsd.edu

Summary. We present a unifying perspective of privacy guarantees in view-based and generalization-based publishing. This perspective uses a generic Bayesian privacy model which generalizes both types of publishing scenarios and allows us to relate seemingly disparate privacy guarantees found in the literature.

1 Introduction

Database publishing systems export parts of a proprietary database for consumption by client applications. The design of a publishing system is subject to two conflicting requirements. On one hand, the data owner needs to publish appropriate parts of the proprietary data to support various interactions with her clients. On the other hand she must protect certain sensitive data from being disclosed to clients.

In this chapter, we discuss data *privacy* which pertains to defense against attackers who access the data legally. These attackers are regular clients who inspect the published data and potentially combine it with external knowledge to infer information about the secret data. Note that privacy is orthogonal to data *security*, whose goal is defense against unauthorized access to the database using access control mechanisms.

We focus on two classes of publishing systems. In *view-based* publishing, the owner specifies the data to be released by means of views defined in some standard query language. In *generalization-based* publishing, the released data is specified using a formalism of incomparable expressive power, namely anonymization using generalization functions. Examples of anonymization via generalization include replacing a person's actual age by an age range, removing the least significant digits of the zip code, etc.

* Funded by an Alfred P. Sloan fellowship and by NSF CAREER award IIS-0347968.

The two corresponding lines of privacy research have evolved independently, yielding different formalisms for stating privacy guarantees. In this chapter, we show that privacy guarantees in view-based and generalization-based publishing are related, being both particular cases of guarantees in a general privacy model. We call this model the Generic Bayesian Privacy (**GBP**) model as it offers guarantees based on the revision of the attacker's belief about the secret between the state before and after seeing the published data.

We start by developing in Section 2 a generic model for attacks attempting to glean knowledge about the sensitive part of the database starting from the published part thereof, also exploiting external knowledge. In Section 3, we show how privacy guarantees developed for view-based publishing systems can be cast as particular cases in the **GBP** model. Then in Section 4 we connect generalization-based publishing to the **GBP** model. Exploiting the uniform formalization using the **GBP** model, Section 5 compares various privacy guarantees from both view-based and generalization-based publishing. Finally, Section 6 shows how the **GBP** model can be applied to formulate and check meaningful privacy guarantees for publishing in open-world information integration systems.

2 GBP: A Generic Bayesian Privacy Model

The published data. The data owner publishes part of the database D, possibly after some processing such as filtering, aggregation, anonymization, etc. For the purpose of our discussion, this processing can be modeled as a function $\mathcal{V}$, whose result $\mathcal{V}(D)$ is being released.

The secret. The owner wishes to keep sensitive data secret. Since sensitivity depends on the application and is best judged by the data owner, she must be provided with the possibility to declare which data is to be kept secret. The secret may be a subset of the database, possibly altered by processing, which we shall model as another function $\mathcal{S}$, whose result $\mathcal{S}(D)$ is the secret.

We note that in the generic model, $\mathcal{V}$ and $\mathcal{S}$ are arbitrary functions from databases to databases. However, in the running example of this section, we shall express such functions by queries. We shall see in Section 4 examples of functions expressed differently, as anonymization functions.

Example 1. Consider a database whose only relation contains tuples associating the patient with the ailment he suffered from and the doctor who treated him:

$$PDA(patient, doctor, ailment).$$

The secret $\mathcal{S}$ is the association between patients and their ailment, specifiable by the owner for instance using query $\mathcal{S}(p, a) :\!- PDA(p, d, a)$.

2.1 Attacks

In this model we only consider attackers who access the data legally by inspecting the published data $\mathcal{V}(D)$, using it together with external knowledge to infer information about the secret $\mathcal{S}(D)$. The defense against unauthorized access to the database is beyond the scope of this model.

Possible databases. Ideally, the attacker would like to reverse-engineer D starting from the observed published data $\mathcal{V}(D)$. This would immediately lead to the full disclosure of the secret: the attacker could compute the secret by directly running $\mathcal{S}$ over D. Of course, $\mathcal{V}$ is likely to be a lossy data transformation, thus precluding the unequivocal identification of its arguments from its output. In general there may be (potentially infinitely) many databases which have the same image as D under $\mathcal{V}$. The attacker cannot distinguish among them solely by observing the published data $\mathcal{V}(D)$, regardless of the computational resources at his disposal. Therefore, in the absence of external knowledge about D, all databases with the same image are possible from the attacker's point of view (we will shortly introduce the attacker's external knowledge into the model). We therefore refer to the set $[D]_\mathcal{V}$ of databases as the *possible* databases given $\mathcal{V}(D)$:

$$[D]_\mathcal{V} := \{D' \mid \mathcal{V}(D') = \mathcal{V}(D)\}.$$

Example 2. Continuing Example 1, assume that the owner publishes a view listing all the patients $V_p(p) :- PDA(p,d,a)$ and one listing all ailments treated by the hospital: $V_a(a) :- PDA(p,d,a)$. Assume that on the actual database D, $V_p(D)$ yields {John, Jane} and $V_a(D)$ yields {flu, pneumonia}. Then some of the possible databases corresponding to the observed views are $D_1 = \{$ (John, doc$_1$, flu), (Jane, doc$_2$, pneumonia) $\}$, $D_2 = \{$ (John, doc$_3$, flu), (John, doc$_3$, pneumonia), (Jane, doc$_4$, flu) $\}$, etc., where doc$_i$ are unknown doctor names.

Clearly the set of possible databases may be very large. For example, consider the case when the published data is a projection of a table. By observing the published table (and using no external knowledge about the data), an attacker must assume any possible completion for the missing columns. This is the case in Example 2 if the attacker does not know the set of all possible doctors.

It is therefore not a priori given that the attacker is even able to enumerate all possible databases. In the following, we assume the worst-case scenario for the owner, namely that the attacker comes up with some finite representation of the set of possible databases which he uses for reasoning about the secret. Note that the more advantage we assume for the attacker, the stronger any privacy guarantees based on these assumptions.

Possible secrets. Since the owner cares about guarding only the secret (rather than the non-sensitive parts of the database), the privacy model focuses on possible secrets. From a reasonable attacker's point of view, a secret

s is *possible* only if it is witnessed by some possible database i.e. if there exists $D' \in [D]_\mathcal{V}$ such that $s = \mathcal{S}(D')$. Without worrying yet whether the attacker can even compute all possible secrets, note that they provide an upper bound on the set of candidates for the secret which an attacker needs to consider. Let us denote the set of possible secrets with $\mathcal{S}([D]_\mathcal{V})$:

$$\mathcal{S}([D]_\mathcal{V}) := \{\mathcal{S}(D') \mid D' \in [D]_\mathcal{V}\}.$$

In particular, the actual secret $S(D)$ is a possible secret: $\mathcal{S}(D) \in \mathcal{S}([D]_\mathcal{V})$.

Example 3. Continuing Example 2, the possible secrets are obtained by running the $\mathcal{S}$ over each possible database. We obtain $s_1 = \mathcal{S}(D_1) = \{(\text{John, flu}), (\text{Jane, pneumonia})\}$, $s_2 = \mathcal{S}(D_2) = \{ (\text{John, flu}), (\text{John, pneumonia}), (\text{Jane, flu}) \}$, etc.

The optimal attack: compute possible secrets and use external knowledge. In the absence of external knowledge, possible secrets are indistinguishable with respect to the published data $\mathcal{V}(D)$ and even with unlimited computational resources the best an attacker can hope for is to reverse-engineer $\mathcal{S}([D]_\mathcal{V})$. Towards a conservative privacy guarantee, let's assume that the attacker is successful at this task, handling the case of infinitely many possible secrets by coming up with a finite representation thereof.[2] If there is only one possible secret, then the actual secret is exposed and the attacker's task accomplished. In the (likely) case of several possible secrets, a sophisticated attacker improves his chances of singling out the actual secret by whittling down $\mathcal{S}([D]_\mathcal{V})$ using external knowledge. If several possible secrets remain even now, the attacker is forced to guess the actual secret among them. However, the guess does not have to be uneducated: while the attacker's external knowledge may be insufficient to further rule out any possible secrets, it could still influence the attacker's beliefs about the relative likelihood of the possible secrets. This would enable the attacker to pick the secret he believes likeliest. Finally, if the attacker deemed several possible secrets equally likely but likelier than all others, he would be forced to guess at random among them.

Modeling attacker's belief. The attacker's external knowledge can pertain to the possible databases or exclusively to the possible secrets. Note that any attacker who forms an opinion on how to rank possible databases can infer the ranking of the corresponding secrets and is therefore at least as knowledgeable (and dangerous) as an attacker who does not understand or care about the underlying database, focusing solely on the secret.

To defend against the more dangerous class of attackers, we model the attacker's *a priori* belief (i.e. before observing $\mathcal{V}(D)$) as a probability distribution δ on all databases. This induces a belief (probability distribution) $\mathbf{P}_\delta$ on all secrets as follows: given candidate secret s, the probability $\mathbf{P}_\delta[s]$ that s is the actual secret is the sum of probabilities of all databases witnessing s:

---

[2] We know such representations exist: (an admittedly crude) one is given by the definition of $\mathcal{V}$ together with $\mathcal{V}(D)$.

$$\mathbf{P}_\delta[s] := \sum_{s=\mathcal{S}(D')} \delta(D'). \tag{1}$$

δ also induces the probability $\mathbf{P}_\delta[\mathcal{V}(D)]$ that the published data is $\mathcal{V}(D)$:

$$\mathbf{P}_\delta[\mathcal{V}(D)] := \sum_{D' \in [D]_\mathcal{V}} \delta(D').$$

The actual release of the published data causes a revision of the attacker's belief about the probability of s being the actual secret. We call this the *a posteriori* probability, and it is the conditional probability $\mathbf{P}_\delta[s|\mathcal{V}(D)]$:

$$\mathbf{P}_\delta[s|\mathcal{V}(D)] = \frac{\mathbf{P}_\delta[s \wedge \mathcal{V}(D)]}{\mathbf{P}_\delta[\mathcal{V}(D)]} = \frac{\sum_{D' \in [D]_\mathcal{V}, \mathcal{S}(D')=s} \delta(D')}{\sum_{D' \in [D]_\mathcal{V}} \delta(D')}. \tag{2}$$

Classes of attackers. For all privacy guarantees we consider next, we conservatively assume that the attacker is able to reverse-engineer the possible databases and secrets from the published data. Attackers are therefore distinguished from each other exclusively by their belief about the likelihood of databases, as induced by the external knowledge they possess. Consequently, in the following we characterize an attacker by the probability distribution δ he associates on all databases. A class of attackers we wish to defend against is then described by a family $\mathcal{P}$ of probability distributions.

2.2 Privacy Guarantees

Privacy guarantees rule out privacy breaches. We list below several alternative guarantees that generalize guarantees considered in the literature. Each one is determined by the definition of what constitutes a "breach".

Extent-Dependent Guarantees. We start with a class of guarantees which depend on the extent of actual database D. Each of them take as argument a publishing function $\mathcal{V}$ and hold if and only if publishing $\mathcal{V}(D)$ does not breach privacy.

No complete database exposure ($\mathbf{NDE}^D$). The worst case of breach consists in complete exposure of the actual database D. That is, the breach is defined as the case when the only possible database is D: $[D]_\mathcal{V} = \{D\}$. In this case, an attacker who successfully reverse-engineers the possible databases retrieves the actual database and can then compute *any* secret function $\mathcal{S}$ on it. The guarantee of no database exposure, denoted $\mathrm{NDE}^D(\mathcal{V})$, requires at least two possible databases:

$$\mathrm{NDE}^D(\mathcal{V}) := |[D]_\mathcal{V}| \geq 2.$$

Example 4. Assume that in the setting of Example 1, the hospital publishes a view revealing which doctors every patient sees: $V_{PD}(p, d) :\!- PDA(p, d, a)$. An additional view is published as well, listing which ailments every doctor is treating: $V_{DA} := PDA(p, d, a)$. If for some database D the view extents are $V_{PD}(D) = \{$ (John, Dr. MacDonald) $\}$ and $V_{DA}(D) = \{$ (Dr. MacDonald, pneumonia) $\}$, then D is exposed since $[D]_{V_{PD}, V_{DA}}$ is the PDA table with the single tuple $\{$ (John, Dr. MacDonald, pneumonia) $\}$. If on the other hand the attacker observes $V_{PD}(D) = \{$ (John, Dr. MacDonald), (Jane, Dr. MacDonald) $\}$ and $V_{DA}(D) = \{$ (Dr. MacDonald, flu), (Dr. MacDonald, pneumonia) $\}$, then D is not exposed since there are several possible databases. One in which John has flu and Jane pneumonia, on in which John has both diseases and Jane has flu, etc.

No complete secret exposure ($\mathbf{NSE}_{\mathcal{S}}^{D}$). Even if the actual database is not exposed, it may be that all possible databases have the same image under $\mathcal{S}$, thus completely exposing the secret. To guard against this case, we define the breach as having a single possible secret: $\mathcal{S}([D]_{\mathcal{V}}) = \{\mathcal{S}(D)\}$. Non-exposure of the secret requires at least two possible secrets:

$$\mathrm{NSE}_{\mathcal{S}}^{D}(\mathcal{V}) := |\mathcal{S}([D]_{\mathcal{V}})| \geq 2.$$

Example 5. For the schema of Example 1, assume that the hospital publishes the view V_P from Example 1 and view V_{DA} from Example 4. If the attacker observes $V_P(D) = \{$ (John), (Jane) $\}$ and $V_{DA}(D) = \{$ (Dr. MacDonald, pneumonia), (Dr. Zhivago, pneumonia) $\}$, then D is not exposed since there are several possible databases: one in which John sees Dr. MacDonald and Jane Dr. Zhivago, one in which they swap doctors, one in which John sees both doctors and Jane only one of them, etc. And yet, the secret is exposed, since both doctors treat the same disease so no matter whom they see, both John and Jane must suffer from pneumonia.

No belief revision ($\mathbf{NBR}_{\mathcal{P}, \mathcal{S}}^{D}$). The non-exposure guarantees fulfill only the very basic owner expectations. They do not suffice to put her mind at ease since attackers can "learn" something about some candidate secret, thus improving their odds of guessing the actual secret.

For a given attacker described by probability distribution δ, we define "learning something about candidate secret s" in the strongest, information-theoretic sense, as revision of attacker's belief about the secret. The *belief revision* is the change between the δ-induced a priori and a posteriori beliefs that s is the secret. Formally, a belief revision occurs precisely when $\mathbf{P}_{\delta}[s|\mathcal{V}(D)] \neq \mathbf{P}_{\delta}[s]$. The guarantee that no attacker from a class $\mathcal{P}$ revises his belief amounts to

$$\mathrm{NBR}_{\mathcal{P}, \mathcal{S}}^{D}(\mathcal{V}) := \forall s \; \forall (\delta \in \mathcal{P}) \; \mathbf{P}_{\delta}[s|\mathcal{V}(D)] = \mathbf{P}_{\delta}[s].$$

This guarantee is preferred by the owner because it makes no assumptions on the attacker's computational resources. When the guarantee holds, the owner can rest assured that nothing can be learned about the secret. The following example however shows that such a guarantee is often unreasonably strong and is violated by most publishing functions, which is why we need to set our sights on more relaxed guarantees.

Example 6. Consider the database from Example 1. Suppose that the owner exports the projection of the PDA relation on its doctor attribute: $V(d) :- PDA(p, d, a)$. Since neither patients nor ailments are exported, this publishing is seemingly safe. However, an attacker can still learn from it some (small amount of) information about the secret. Indeed, if the published list of doctors is empty, then the actual database relation must be empty as well, so no patient can suffer from any ailment. An attacker whose belief assigns non-zero probability to a possible secret containing at least one ailing patient will therefore revise this belief a posteriori. If however there is even one doctor in the published list, then there is a non-zero probability of a certain patient suffering from some disease. An attacker who is a priori certain that there are no ailing patients must revise his belief as well. Clearly, at least these two attackers have learned something about the secret upon observing the list of doctors, and the idealized guarantee $\text{NBR}_{\mathcal{P}, \mathcal{S}}^{D}$ is violated. At the same time, ruling out this publishing amounts to asking the owner to release no data whatsoever, even if she avoids the attributes involved in the secret.

No further belief revision ($\text{NFBR}_{\mathcal{P}, \mathcal{S}}^{D}$). Since the guarantees NDE and $\text{NSE}_{\mathcal{S}}$ are too weak, and the ideal guarantee $\text{NBR}_{\mathcal{P}, \mathcal{S}}$ is too strong, we consider a more pragmatic guarantee: it assumes that the owner is willing to live with the current level in attacker's belief as induced by the already published data $\mathcal{V}(D)$, but wants to make sure that publishing any further data will not lead to further belief revision. Formally, denoting with $\mathcal{N}$ the new publishing function which the owner contemplates, a breach occurs when $\mathbf{P}_{\delta}[s|\mathcal{V}(D)] \neq \mathbf{P}_{\delta}[s|\mathcal{V}(D) \wedge \mathcal{N}(D)]$. Here, $\mathbf{P}_{\delta}[s|\mathcal{V}(D) \wedge \mathcal{N}(D)]$ is the belief of the attacker described by distribution δ that s is the secret, provided that both $\mathcal{V}(D)$ and $\mathcal{N}(D)$ are published:

$$\mathbf{P}_{\delta}[s|\mathcal{V}(D) \wedge \mathcal{N}(D)] = \frac{\mathbf{P}_{\delta}[s \wedge \mathcal{V}(D) \wedge \mathcal{N}(D)]}{\mathbf{P}_{\delta}[\mathcal{V}(D) \wedge \mathcal{N}(D)]} = \frac{\sum_{D' \in [D]_{\mathcal{V}} \cap [D]_{\mathcal{N}}, \mathcal{S}(D')=s} \delta(D')}{\sum_{D' \in [D]_{\mathcal{V}} \cap [D]_{\mathcal{N}}} \delta(D')}. (3)$$

The associated guarantee is the following:

$$\text{NFBR}_{\mathcal{P}, \mathcal{S}}^{D}(\mathcal{N}, \mathcal{V}) := \forall s \forall (\delta \in \mathcal{P}) \ \mathbf{P}_{\delta}[s|\mathcal{V}(D)] = \mathbf{P}_{\delta}[s|\mathcal{V}(D) \wedge \mathcal{N}(D)].$$

Example 7. Assume that on the schema from Example 1, the owner has already published $\mathcal{V} = (V_p, V_a)$ where V_p, V_a are the views from Example 2. The owner is currently contemplating the publishing of the two new views $\mathcal{N} = (V_{PD}, V_{DA})$ from Example 4. Suppose that $V_p(D) = \{(\text{John}),(\text{Jane}),(\text{Jack})\}$, and $V_a(D) = \{(\text{pneumonia}),(\text{flu}),(\text{cold})\}$. From this observation, any attacker can reverse-engineer the set of possible databases. This includes, among others, the database $D_1 = \{(\text{John,doc}_1,\text{pneumonia}), (\text{Jane,doc}_2,\text{flu}), (\text{Jack,doc}_3,\text{cold})\}$, yielding the secret $s_1 = \mathcal{S}(D_1) = \{(\text{John, pneumonia}), (\text{Jane,flu}), (\text{Jack,cold})\}$. Given an attacker described by some distribution δ, assume that his a priori belief that s_1 is the secret is non-zero

$\mathbf{P}_\delta[s_1|\mathcal{V}(D)] > 0$. Now assume that the attacker were to observe the extents of the new views, which are $V_{PD} = \{$ (John, Dr. MacDonald), (Jane,Dr. Zhivago), (Jack,Dr. Zhivago) $\}$ and $V_{DA} = \{$ (Dr. MacDonald, flu), (Dr. Zhivago, pneumonia), (Dr. Zhivago, cold) $\}$ The attacker must now revise to 0 his a posteriori belief that s_1 is the secret. Indeed, only Dr. Zhivago treats pneumonia, but John sees Dr. MacDonald, therefore John cannot have pneumonia: $\mathbf{P}_\delta[s_1|\mathcal{V}(D) \wedge \mathcal{N}(D)] = 0$.

An alternative intuition for the no-further-belief-revision guarantee is the following. After observing $\mathcal{V}(D)$, the attacker reverse-engineers the possible databases $[D]_\mathcal{V}$ and uses his background knowledge to assign a likelihood to each of them. After subsequently observing $\mathcal{N}(D)$, the attacker rules out all databases which are possible for $\mathcal{V}(D)$ but not for $\mathcal{N}(D)$, being left with only those in $[D]_\mathcal{V} \cap [D]_\mathcal{N}$. Ruling out even one database results in re-distributing its probability over the remaining ones, thus potentially modifying the attacker's a posteriori belief about the secret. For instance, in an extreme case, the possible databases in $[D]_\mathcal{V}$ may witness two secrets s_1 and s_2. If $[D]_\mathcal{V} \cap [D]_\mathcal{N}$ rules out all witnesses of s_2 (and maybe also some but not all witnesses of s_1), then by (3) the attacker's belief about the secret being s_2 drops to 0 and the belief of s_1 becomes 1, i.e. certainty.

This intuition is formalized by the following result.

Theorem 1 ([8]). *Let $\mathcal{P}$ contain all possible distributions, thus modeling all attackers. Then for every database D and secret $\mathcal{S}$ no attacker's belief is revised upon observing $\mathcal{N}(D)$ if and only if the possible databases do not change:*

$$\forall D \; \forall \mathcal{S} \; NFBR^D_{\mathcal{P},\mathcal{S}}(\mathcal{N}, \mathcal{V}) \Leftrightarrow [D]_\mathcal{V} = [D]_\mathcal{V} \cap [D]_\mathcal{N}$$

Note that despite being defined in probabilistic fashion, the no-further-belief-revision guarantee remarkably reduces by Theorem 1 to a purely model-theoretic problem involving reasoning solely about possible databases.

Bounded belief revision ($\mathbf{BBR}^D_{\mathcal{P},\mathcal{S}}$). It is often useful to consider relaxing privacy guarantees to allow desirable publishing functions. We next consider a natural relaxation of the $\mathrm{NBR}^D_{\mathcal{P},\mathcal{S}}$ guarantee of no belief revision, which offers the owner more control over the trade-off between privacy and utility of publishing functions. The idea is to allow revision, but only if bounded by an owner-defined threshold. In this case, a breach is formally defined as $|\mathbf{P}_\delta[s|\mathcal{V}(D)] - \mathbf{P}_\delta[s]| > \epsilon$, where $\epsilon \in [0, 1]$ is the threshold. This definition of breach induces a family of privacy guarantees, parameterized by the threshold:

$$\mathrm{BBR}^D_{\mathcal{P},\mathcal{S}}(\mathcal{V}, \epsilon) := \forall s \forall (\delta \in \mathcal{P}) \; |\mathbf{P}_\delta[s|\mathcal{V}(D)] - \mathbf{P}_\delta[s]| \leq \epsilon.$$

Bounded further belief revision ($\mathbf{BFBR}^D_{\mathcal{P},\mathcal{S}}$). The same idea of allowing bounded belief revision yields a natural relaxation of guarantee $\mathrm{NFBR}^D_{\mathcal{P},\mathcal{S}}$:

$$\mathrm{BFBR}^D_{\mathcal{P},\mathcal{S}}(\mathcal{N}, \mathcal{V}, \epsilon) := \forall s \forall (\delta \in \mathcal{P}) \; |\mathbf{P}_\delta[s|\mathcal{V}(D)] - \mathbf{P}_\delta[s|\mathcal{V}(D) \wedge \mathcal{N}(D)]| \leq \epsilon.$$

Extent-Independent Guarantees. The privacy guarantees we've considered so far depend on the extent of the actual database D. The owner is thus faced with the following dilemma. Checking the guarantee on a given extent D avoids being overly conservative and rejecting those publishing functions that preserve privacy on the actual database but breach it on some other database extent D'. On the other hand, this means re-checking the privacy guarantees upon each update to D. Alternatively, we consider strengthening the above guarantees to hold over all database extents. We obtain the following list of extent-independent privacy guarantees:

$$\mathrm{NDE}(\mathcal{V}) := \forall D \ \mathrm{NDE}^{D}(\mathcal{V})$$

$$\mathrm{NSE}_{\mathcal{S}}(\mathcal{V}) := \forall D \ \mathrm{NSE}_{\mathcal{S}}^{D}(\mathcal{V})$$

$$\mathrm{NBR}_{\mathcal{P},\mathcal{S}}(\mathcal{V}) := \forall D \ \mathrm{NBR}_{\mathcal{P},\mathcal{S}}^{D}(\mathcal{V})$$

$$\mathrm{NFBR}_{\mathcal{P},\mathcal{S}}(\mathcal{N},\mathcal{V}) := \forall D \ \mathrm{NFBR}_{\mathcal{P},\mathcal{S}}^{D}(\mathcal{N},\mathcal{V})$$

$$\mathrm{BBR}_{\mathcal{P},\mathcal{S}}(\mathcal{V},\epsilon) := \forall D \ \mathrm{BBR}_{\mathcal{P},\mathcal{S}}^{D}(\mathcal{V},\epsilon)$$

$$\mathrm{BFBR}_{\mathcal{P},\mathcal{S}}(\mathcal{N},\mathcal{V},\epsilon) := \forall D \ \mathrm{BFBR}_{\mathcal{P},\mathcal{S}}^{D}(\mathcal{N},\mathcal{V},\epsilon)$$

As before, it makes sense to carefully consider the trade-off between strength of the guarantee and utility of the publishing functions it allows. In many situations, the proprietary database is known to satisfy a set of integrity constraints $\mathcal{C}$. By imposing the unrestricted extent-independent guarantees above, the owner risks excluding a perfectly safe publishing function because it breaks the guarantees on some database that will never occur in practice since it violates the constraints. Clearly, the owner does not need the privacy guarantees to hold on all imaginable databases, but only on a subclass thereof: all databases D satisfying the constraints in $\mathcal{C}$ (denoted $D \models \mathcal{C}$). This natural relaxation yields guarantees that are extent-independent as long as the extents satisfy the constraints:

$$\mathrm{NDE}^{\mathcal{C}}(\mathcal{V}) := \forall (D \models \mathcal{C}) \ \mathrm{NDE}^{D}(\mathcal{V})$$

$$\mathrm{NSE}_{\mathcal{S}}^{\mathcal{C}}(\mathcal{V}) := \forall (D \models \mathcal{C}) \ \mathrm{NSE}_{\mathcal{S}}^{D}(\mathcal{V})$$

$$\mathrm{NBR}_{\mathcal{P},\mathcal{S}}^{\mathcal{C}}(\mathcal{V}) := \forall (D \models \mathcal{C}) \ \mathrm{NBR}_{\mathcal{P},\mathcal{S}}^{D}(\mathcal{V})$$

$$\mathrm{NFBR}_{\mathcal{P},\mathcal{S}}^{\mathcal{C}}(\mathcal{N},\mathcal{V}) := \forall (D \models \mathcal{C}) \ \mathrm{NFBR}_{\mathcal{P},\mathcal{S}}^{D}(\mathcal{N},\mathcal{V})$$

$$\mathrm{BBR}_{\mathcal{P},\mathcal{S}}^{\mathcal{C}}(\mathcal{V},\epsilon) := \forall (D \models \mathcal{C}) \ \mathrm{BBR}_{\mathcal{P},\mathcal{S}}^{D}(\mathcal{V},\epsilon)$$

$$\mathrm{BFBR}_{\mathcal{P},\mathcal{S}}^{\mathcal{C}}(\mathcal{N},\mathcal{V},\epsilon) := \forall (D \models \mathcal{C}) \ \mathrm{BFBR}_{\mathcal{P},\mathcal{S}}^{D}(\mathcal{N},\mathcal{V},\epsilon)$$

A Similar Privacy Model. [5, 6] propose a similar privacy model for relational databases, based on Bayesian belief revision. However the authors do not address the equivalent of the $\mathrm{NFBR}_{\mathcal{P},\mathcal{S}}$, $\mathrm{BBR}_{\mathcal{P},\mathcal{S}}$, and $\mathrm{BFBR}_{\mathcal{P},\mathcal{S}}$ guarantees, nor do they consider guarantees parameterized by classes of probability distributions, or integrity constraints.

3 View-Based Publishing

3.1 Independent-Tuple Attackers

The application of the privacy model from [5] to view-based publishing was pioneered in seminal work by Miklau and Suciu [19, 20].

In the setting of [19, 20], the publishing function $\mathcal{V}$ is given by a list of views. Both $\mathcal{V}$ and the secret $\mathcal{S}$ are specified by conjunctive queries with inequalities.

As in Section 2, an attacker is described by a probability distribution δ on the set of all databases. However, only attackers described by *independent-tuple* distributions are considered. These distributions treat the occurrences of any two tuples t_1, t_2 in a given database as independent events. Formally, given a domain **Dom**, denote the set of all tuples over **Dom** by *tuples(***Dom***)*. Any $D \subseteq tuples(\mathbf{Dom})$ is a database over domain **Dom**. δ is an independent-tuple distribution on the databases over **Dom** if it is induced by a distribution p on *tuples(***Dom***)*. That is, for any database D over **Dom** we have (by the independent-tuple assumption)

$$\delta(D) := \prod_{t \in D} p(t) \times \prod_{t \in tuples(\mathbf{Dom}) - D} (1 - p(t)).$$

The attacker's a priori and a posteriori beliefs about the secret $\mathcal{S}(R)$ are then induced by p via δ as in (1), respectively (2).

Perfect privacy. Given secret $\mathcal{S}(D)$, the views $\mathcal{V}$ are considered to preserve privacy against an attacker described by distribution δ if there is no change between the attacker's a posteriori belief (after seeing $\mathcal{V}(R)$) and his a priori belief (before seeing $\mathcal{V}(R)$) about secret $s = \mathcal{S}(D)$: $\mathbf{P}_\delta[s] = \mathbf{P}_\delta[s|\mathcal{V}(D)]$.

Given a domain **Dom**, denote with $\mathcal{P}_{\mathbf{Dom}}$ the set of all independent-tuple distributions on databases over **Dom** induced by distributions over *tuples(***Dom***)*.

Then $\mathcal{V}$ is said to maintain *perfect privacy* for secret $\mathcal{S}$, denoted $\mathbf{PerfP}_\mathcal{S}(\mathcal{V})$ if for every domain **Dom**, every database D over **Dom**, every secret value s and every distribution $\delta \in \mathcal{P}_{\mathbf{Dom}}$, upon observing $\mathcal{V}(D)$ the attacker does not revise his belief that s is the secret:

$$\mathbf{PerfP}_\mathcal{S}(\mathcal{V}) := \forall \mathbf{Dom}\ \forall(D \subseteq tuples(\mathbf{Dom}))\ \forall s\ \forall(\delta \in \mathcal{P}_{\mathbf{Dom}})$$
$$\mathbf{P}_\delta[s] = \mathbf{P}_\delta[s|\mathcal{V}(D)],$$

or, equivalently in the notation of the **GBP** model (Section 2.2),

$$\mathbf{PerfP}_\mathcal{S}(\mathcal{V}) := \forall \mathbf{Dom}\ \forall(D \subseteq tuples(\mathbf{Dom}))\ \mathrm{NBR}^D_{\mathcal{P}_{\mathbf{Dom}},\mathcal{S}}(\mathcal{V}). \tag{4}$$

Note that perfect privacy is an extent-independent guarantee. Therefore it need not be re-checked upon every update to the database.

[19] shows that perfect privacy is decidable in Π_2^p in the combined size of the queries defining $\mathcal{V}, \mathcal{S}$. The result follows from a key lemma showing that privacy holds for all domains if it holds for *some* domain of size polynomial in the number of variables and constants appearing in the view and secret queries. Essentially, to check the guarantee on such a domain **Dom**, one simply needs to enumerate the databases over **Dom**. There are only finitely many of them (though their number is exponential in the domain size). In a follow-up paper, Machanavajjhala et al. [15] provide an alternative decision procedure which reduces perfect privacy to checking a number of containments between queries constructed from the views and secret definitions. This allows them to leverage well-known results on the complexity of query containment to identify restrictions leading to a PTIME-checkability of the perfect privacy guarantee.

In addition to a decision procedure for perfect privacy, [19] introduce also a notion equivalent to the bounded belief revision guarantee $\text{BBR}_{\mathcal{P},\mathcal{S}}$ from Section 2.2 (again considering only independent-tuple distributions). Furthermore, Miklau and Suciu consider a limited flavor of the "no further belief revision" guarantee $\text{NFBR}_{\mathcal{P},\mathcal{S}}$, in which the already published views are defined by *boolean* queries.

As recognized in [19, 20], the fact that perfect privacy only defends against attackers described by independent-tuple distributions is a limitation because it ignores attackers whose background knowledge gives them correlations between tuples. For instance, the attacker's background knowledge that reviewers r_1 and r_2 have similar research expertise and taste can be modeled by a distribution in which the probability that r_1 bids for a paper is similar to the probability that r_2 does. In an additional example, the attacker may know that if a patient has a highly contagious disease, then her spouse likely has it, too. Such background information cannot be modeled by independent-tuple distributions.

However, limiting attackers to those characterized by independent-tuple distributions strikes a good balance in the trade-off between guarantee strength and feasibility of checking the guarantee. This conclusion is reinforced by a study (discussed next) of what happens if the limitation is removed.

3.2 More General Classes of Attackers

[8] explores an alternate way to balance the tension between the strength of the guarantee and the feasibility of checking it.

The study starts from the thesis that data owners cannot presume that attacker's beliefs are induced exclusively by the independent-tuple distributions of [19, 20]. However, strengthening the guarantees to consider more general classes of attackers carries the potential danger of rendering them too rigid, i.e. violated by too many desirable publishing scenarios. Therefore, [8] simultaneously considers a relaxation along a different dimension: data owners are assumed willing to accept the privacy breach caused by an already published set of views $\mathcal{V}$, but want to ensure that a new view $\mathcal{N}$ will cause no further breach. "Breach" is defined as a revision of belief from the a priori of having observed $\mathcal{V}(D)$ to the a posteriori of having also observed $\mathcal{N}(D)$.

In the terminology of Section 2.2, [8] introduces and studies precisely the various flavors of the NFBR$_{\mathcal{P},\mathcal{S}}$ guarantee: extent-dependent (NFBR$_{\mathcal{P},\mathcal{S}}^{D}$), and also extent-independent. Moreover, [8] argues that a privacy guarantee that holds for given D, $\mathcal{V}$, $\mathcal{S}$, and $\mathcal{N}$ may be violated if it is also known that D satisfies a set $\mathcal{C}$ of integrity constraints.

Example 8. Assume a hospital database consisting of four tables:

- PW associates patients with the ward they are in;
- WD associates doctors with the wards they are responsible for (several doctors may share responsibility for the same ward, and the same doctor may share responsibility for several wards);
- DA associates doctors with the ailments they treat;
- PA associates patients with the ailments they suffer from.

Assume that PW, WD, DA are published and PA is the secret. If the owner also discloses (or common sense leads the attacker to assume) the following integrity constraints, the attacker's belief can be affected.

- Patients can be treated only by doctors responsible for their ward.
- If a patient p suffers from an ailment a then some doctor treats p for a.

If these constraints do not hold, an attacker may consider a possible database associating a patient p with a doctor d who does not cover p's ward and hold a non-zero belief that p suffers from some ailment a treated only by d. However, under the constraints the secret patient-ailment association PA is a subset of $\Pi_{PA}(PW \bowtie WD \bowtie DA)$, to which (p, a) does not belong. This forces the attacker to revise to 0 his belief about any possible database witnessing (p, a).

[8] takes into account such semantic and integrity constraints when checking privacy.

Maybe the most interesting dimension of the study in [8] stems from proposing a natural way to classify attackers, yielding two groups.

First, we have the class of *all* attackers, described by set $\mathcal{P}_a$ of unrestricted distributions. Ideally, this is whom the owner wishes to defend against. $\mathcal{P}_a$ captures attackers who exploit correlations between tuples, and strictly includes attackers who don't (the ones described by the independent-tuple distributions of [19, 20]).

Second, [8] observes that the attacker is often unaware of (or uninterested in) the details of the possible database D witnessing a secret $\mathcal{S}(D)$, as D may also involve data that are tangential or irrelevant to the secret. For example, the attacker trying to link patients to their ailment does not care about the patient's insurance provider or the hospital's parking facilities, all of which could be also stored in the database.

[8] therefore considers attackers whose background knowledge enables them to form an opinion that discriminates among possible *secrets*, but who cannot (or do not care to) distinguish among the possible *databases* witnessing any given secret. In this survey we call such attackers *secret-focused*, and, given a secret $\mathcal{S}$, we denote with $\mathcal{P}_\mathcal{S}$ the set of distributions describing secret-focused attackers with respect to $\mathcal{S}$.

$\mathcal{P}_\mathcal{S}$ is defined as follows. Given a distribution $\delta_\mathcal{S}$ on possible secrets, we say that $\delta_\mathcal{S}$ induces a distribution δ on possible databases if δ satisfies both of the following conditions:

- for every s and every D such that $s = \mathcal{S}(D)$, we have $\sum_{s = \mathcal{S}(D')} \delta(D') = \delta_\mathcal{S}(s)$;
- all witnesses of the secret are equi-probable according to δ: $\forall D_1, D_2\ \mathcal{S}(D_1) = \mathcal{S}(D_2) \Rightarrow \delta(D_1) = \delta(D_2)$.

Observing that δ is uniquely determined by $\delta_\mathcal{S}$, we have that $\mathcal{P}_\mathcal{S}$ is the set of distributions on databases induced by all unrestricted distributions on secrets. Note that $\mathcal{P}_\mathcal{S}$ still allows for attackers with arbitrary capacity to discriminate among the secrets, as we start from arbitrary distributions on secrets.

[8] studies the setting in which the already published views $\mathcal{V}$, the secret $\mathcal{S}$, and the new view $\mathcal{N}$ are specified by unions of conjunctive queries with inequalities UCQ$^{\neq}$. The constraints in $\mathcal{C}$ are equivalent to containment statements between UCQ$^{\neq}$ queries. Such constraints extend classical embedded dependencies [1] with disjunction and inequalities, and can express such common integrity constraints as keys and foreign keys, functional, inclusion and join dependencies [1], cardinality constraints, and beyond.

For the extent-dependent guarantees, [8] shows that NFBR$^D_{\mathcal{P}_a,\mathcal{S}}(\mathcal{V},\mathcal{N})$ is Π^p_2-complete in the combined size of the queries and database, while NFBR$^D_{\mathcal{P}_\mathcal{S},\mathcal{S}}(\mathcal{V},\mathcal{N})$ is in PSPACE. These results hold even when the attacker knows that D satisfies a set $\mathcal{C}$ of constraints, as long as $\mathcal{C}$ is *weakly acyclic* [9, 10]. In addition, both extent-independent guarantees NFBR$_{\mathcal{P}_a,\mathcal{S}}(\mathcal{V},\mathcal{N})$ and NFBR$_{\mathcal{P}_\mathcal{S},\mathcal{S}}(\mathcal{V},\mathcal{N})$ are undecidable [8], even in the absence of constraints ($\mathcal{C} = \emptyset$).

These results should be viewed in light of the fact that in generalization-based publishing (discussed in Section 4), deciding whether an anonymization is optimal is NP-complete in the size of the database.

While the above results render the proposed privacy guarantees impractical in the current form, the study in [8] is a first step toward identifying restrictions leading to tractability on the views, secret and constraints. Moreover, the study proves that changing the class of attacker distributions yields a novel privacy guarantee, which is qualitatively different from the version in [19, 20], as witnessed by the different complexity and decidability bounds. Finally, the contrast between the various classes of attackers considered in [19, 20] and [8] shows the difficulty of striking the right balance between the strength of the guarantee and the feasibility of checking it.

4 Generalization-Based Publishing

The concept of anonymization by generalization [23, 24] was introduced to enable the publishing of data about individuals for the purpose of studies (e.g. computing statistics and data mining), while making it hard to pinpoint the exact individual associated with each data value. A canonical example pertains to a hospital that publishes seemingly anonymized data by releasing the age, gender and zip code of its patients together with the disease, in the hope that by leaving out the name and social security number attackers cannot infer who suffers from what disease.

Sweeney shows that this hope is unfounded [24], as over 85% of the US population is identified by the combination of age, gender and zip. This data is accessible to attackers either because they know the person, or simply from publicly available databases such as voter registration lists. In a notorious illustration of her point, Sweeney uncovered the medical history of a former governor of Massachusetts by combining the medical data with the registration list.

The attacks based on combining the anonymized data with external public databases are called *linking attacks*. Sweeney argues that in order to defend against linking attacks, the data owner must conservatively assume that the attacker has access to the public database, and that the information in this database uniquely identifies the individual. The upshot of this assumption is that the attacker has access to the identity of each individual, as if the owner had published it. Therefore, the best a defense against linking attacks can accomplish is to hide the *association* between the individual's identity and the sensitive data (such as her disease, salary, etc.).

In detail, work on anonymization by generalization considers a database containing a single relation $R(ID, QI, S)$, where

- the list of attributes ID comprises the person's identifier (e.g. (ssn) or (first name, middle name, last name)),
- the list of attributes QI gives the person's quasi-identifier (e.g. (age,gender,zip)) which can be used to look up the actual identifier in some public database of schema ID, QI, and
- S is the list of *sensitive* attributes (e.g. disease, salary, etc.).

Association between identity and sensitive attributes. We say that identity id is associated in R to sensitive attribute value s if there exists some tuple $r \in R$ with $r[ID] = id$ and $r[S] = s$.

Generalization function. To keep associations private, the owner anonymizes the QI attributes using a *generalization function* g. g hides the actual values of the QI attributes, replacing them with more general values. For instance, an age value is replaced by an age interval, a zip code changed by dropping some of its least significant digits. In the extreme, the generalization function can hide the attribute value completely by replacing it with the wild card "*". This is called attribute *suppression*.

Proprietary data

Name	Age	Gender	Zip	Ailment
John	20	M	92122	flu
Jane	22	F	92121	pneumonia
Jack	26	M	92093	cold
Jill	29	F	92094	bronchitis

Anonymized data

Age	Gender	Zip	Ailment
[20-25)	*	9212*	flu
[20-25)	*	9212*	pneumonia
[25-30)	*	9209*	cold
[25-30)	*	9209*	bronchitis

Fig. 1. Anonymization in Example 9

Anonymization. The generalization function g defines an anonymizing function $\mathcal{A}_g$ on R, which drops the ID attributes of each R-tuple, keeps the sensitive attributes unchanged, and substitutes the QI attributes with the result of g. If duplicates are created in this process, then they are all preserved. We have

$$\mathcal{A}_g(R) := \{\{t : QI, S| \ r \in R, t[QI] = g(r[QI]) \wedge t[S] = r[S]\}\},$$

where $t[X]$ denotes the projection of tuple t on attribute list X, and where $\{\{\}\}$ denote multi-set comprehensions (which preserve duplicates, as opposed to the set comprehensions denoted with $\{\}$).

Example 9. In Figure 1, the proprietary table R on the left has ID attribute *Name*, QI attributes *Age, Gender, Zip*, and S attribute *Ailment*. The table on the right is its anonymization $\mathcal{A}_g(R)$ where g replaces age with the 5-year interval it falls in, suppresses gender and hides the least significant digit of the zip code.

Given a tuple $r \in R$, the owner wishes to preserve the privacy of the association between the identifier $r[ID]$ and the sensitive attribute values $r[S]$. Since the sensitive attributes are published in clear, the attacker needs to guess only $r[ID]$. Intuitively, the anonymization $\mathcal{A}_g$ "hides the identity $r[ID]$ in a crowd" of possible identities, forcing the attacker to guess among them. The larger the crowd, the lower the chance of guessing right.

Equivalence under generalization. This crowd comprises the identities of all tuples whose projection on the quasi-identifiers generalizes under g to the same value. It is easy to see that the property of two tuples having the same image of their QI projection under g is an equivalence relation. Denoting with $[r]_g^R$ the equivalence class of r, we have

$$[r]_g^R := \{r' \in R \mid g(r'[QI]) = g(r[QI])\}.$$

In Example 9, the tuples of table R are partitioned by g into two equivalence classes, one comprising the tuples for John and Jane, the other the tuples for Jack and Jill.

Now consider a tuple $t \in \mathcal{A}_g(R)$ which is the image under $\mathcal{A}_g$ of some tuple $r \in R$. When the attacker observes the *occurrence* of sensitive attribute value s in t ($t[S] = s$), the identities which could be associated with $t[S]$ in the actual database R are those of the tuples in r's equivalence class: $\{c : ID \mid r \in [r]_g^R, c[ID] = r[ID]\}$. In Example 9, the attacker concludes that either Jack or Jill can have bronchitis.

Assumptions on the attacker's knowledge. As introduced in [23, 24], the defense against linking attacks relies on a few implicit assumptions, also adopted by follow-up work. We explicitly list them below:

A1 For every $r \in R$, the attacker *knows* that $r[ID]$ occurs in the database (e.g. because $r[ID]$ identifies an acquaintance or celebrity whose hospitalization the attacker is aware of).

A2 For every $r \in R$, the attacker knows the value of the quasi-identifier attributes $r[QI]$ (e.g. due to access to some external public database).

A3 The attacker has no additional external knowledge to discriminate among the possible identities, thus treating them as equi-probable.

Util The owner is willing to live with the privacy breach caused by publishing the projection of R on S *in the clear*, since this is a minimal utility requirement for statistical and data mining computations performed by consumers of the released data.

Note that assumptions **A1** and **A2** are conservative, and any guarantee holding under them also defends against less informed attackers. In contrast, assumption **A3** is optimistic and weakens any guarantee, as it ignores attackers who improve their guessing odds by exploiting background knowledge to discriminate among alternatives. We address below versions of anonymity which relax this assumption. Finally, regarding assumption **Util**, note that [23] and most of its follow-up work concerns itself with choosing generalizations of the quasi-identifier attributes so as to minimize information loss, with the understanding that the sensitive data is released in the clear.

Relationship to GBP Model. We show the connection between the **GBP** model and the privacy guarantees offered by an arbitrary anonymization of a table via generalization. This will enable a comparison to the privacy guarantees described in Section 3. Moreover, it will allow us to contrast various anonymization guarantees found in the literature using a uniform framework.

- In typical studies of generalization, the proprietary database D consists of a single relation R of schema (ID, QI, S).
- Assumptions **A1** and **A2** can be modeled by just as well assuming that the owner (or some other authority) has already published the projection of R on ID, QI:
$$V_{id}(R) := \Pi_{ID,QI}(R).$$

- In our modeling, we separate the owner's concerns on releasing the sensitive data (none according to assumption **Util**) and the quasi-identifier data (serious concerns, calling for generalization). To this end, we consider the projection of R on the sensitive attributes S as good as published, by a view

$$V_s(R) := \{\{t : S \mid r \in R, t[S] = r[S]\}\}.$$

Note that V_s is defined under multi-set semantics (it preserves duplicates), thus revealing the distribution of sensitive values in the underlying population for the benefit of statistical studies.

In addition, the owner contemplates a new data release: the table R anonymized using publishing function $\mathcal{A}_g$ which associates anonymized quasi-identifiers with clear sensitive values. [3]

Under assumption **Util**, the owner is not concerned about the attacker's belief revision caused by seeing the sensitive values. The only revision she wishes to bound is caused by considering $\mathcal{A}_g(R)$ *on top of* $V_s(R)$. To this end, we adopt the following convention: *a priori* every attacker has access to views $V_{id}(R)$ and $V_s(R)$. We denote with $\mathcal{V}$ the publishing function given by the pair of views V_{id}, V_s. A *posteriori* refers to having released $\mathcal{A}_g(R)$ on top of $\mathcal{V}(R)$.

- For each proprietary tuple $r \in R$, both the identity value $r[ID]$ and the sensitive value $r[S]$ are known a priori to the attacker via views V_{id}, respectively V_s. The attacker is uncertain only about whether the two are associated in R. To hide this association from the attacker, the owner declares as secret the boolean query that checks the existence of some tuple $r' \in R$ which witnesses the association:

$$\mathcal{S}_r := \exists (r' \in R) \; r'[ID] = r[ID] \wedge r'[S] = r[S].$$

  Note that the secret does not include the quasi-identifier attributes, as by assumption **A2**, these are known for every identifier anyway (via V_{id}).

- Under assumption **A3**, the owner guards only against a single type of attackers, namely those who for lack of additional external knowledge deem all possible databases equally likely. We model these attackers by the *uniform probability distribution u* on possible databases.

Denote the multiplicity of sensitive value s in table X with $\text{mult}(s, X)$. Then it is easy to verify that, under assumptions **A1**,**A2**, and **A3**, the probability that $id = r[ID]$ is associated to $s = r[S]$ in R (i.e. that secret $\mathcal{S}_r$ holds) is a priori (i.e. after seeing $\mathcal{V}(R)$) given by $\frac{\text{mult}(s, R)}{|R|}$. The a posteriori probability (after seeing $\mathcal{A}_g(R)$) equals $\frac{\text{mult}(s, [r]_g^R)}{|[r]_g^R|}$. It follows that g offers the following guarantee of bounded belief revision for secret $\mathcal{S}_r$:

$$\text{BFBR}_{\{u\}, \mathcal{S}_r}^R (\mathcal{V}, \mathcal{A}_g, |\frac{\text{mult}(r[S], [r]_g^R)}{|[r]_g^R|} - \frac{\text{mult}(r[S], R)}{|R|}|).$$

This immediately yields that the anonymization of R via g satisfies the following privacy guarantee:

---

[3] In practice, view $V_s(R)$ is released simultaneously with anonymized table $\mathcal{A}_g(R)$ (as its projection on S), not prior to it. Our modeling is merely a means to capture assumption **Util**.

$$\bigwedge_{r \in R} \mathrm{BFBR}^R_{\{u\}, \mathcal{S}_r}(\mathcal{V}, \mathcal{A}_g, |\frac{\mathrm{mult}(r[S], [r]^R_g)}{|[r]^R_g|} - \frac{\mathrm{mult}(r[S], R)}{|R|}|). \qquad (5)$$

Note that the frequency of a sensitive value s in the entire table R can diverge widely from the frequency of s in the equivalence class of some $r \in R$. In a worst-case scenario when s is predominant in R (its frequency in R is close to 1) but very infrequent in r's equivalence class, the belief revision for secret $\mathcal{S}_r$ is considerably close to 1, which is the maximum possible.

4.1 K-Anonymity

In this section, we expose the connection between the original work on k-anonymity and the attacker's Bayesian belief revision. Casting the terminology of [23, 24] in terms of the **GBP** model, we find that [23, 24] bounds the attacker's belief revision by requiring the generalization function g to induce only equivalence classes of cardinality at least k. In that case, g is called *k-anonymous*, which we shall denote $\mathrm{anon}^R_k(g)$:

$$\mathrm{anon}^R_k(g) := \forall (r \in R) \ |[r]^R_g| \geq k.$$

For instance, function g in Example 9 is 2-anonymous.

By the above discussion, k-anonymity immediately implies that for a given *occurrence* of sensitive attribute value s in some tuple t of the anonymized data, there are at least k distinct identities which could be associated with s in the actual database R. Under assumptions **A1**,**A2**, and **A3**, the attacker's odds of guessing that indeed $r[ID]$ is the correct identity are at most $1/k$.

Previous work has interpreted this fact as implying that the probability of correctly guessing that identity *id* is associated in R to sensitive data *value* s is at most $1/k$. As pointed out in [16] and detailed below, this conclusion is unjustified: it is caused by the confusion between the *value* of the sensitive attributes and their *occurrence*. Specifically, if sensitive value s occurs l times in r's equivalence class, then the probability that $r[ID]$ is associated with value s is the sum over all occurrences of s of the probability that $r[ID]$ is associated with that occurrence, yielding $\frac{l}{|[r]^R_g|}$. This quantity can be arbitrarily larger than $\frac{1}{k}$, reaching 1 in the extreme case when all tuples in r's equivalence class have the same sensitive value. This observation gives an alternative explanation why k-anonymity provides no meaningful privacy guarantees in general.

Before discussing in the following sections refinements of k-anonymity which address this problem, we first articulate an implicit assumption under which k-anonymity does bound by $\frac{1}{k}$ the probability of guessing secret $\mathcal{S}_r$.

A4 For every $r \in R$, sensitive value $r[S]$ occurs only once in $[r]^R_g$.

We are now ready to relate the definition of k-anonymity with the **GBP** model. Under additional assumption **A4**, if g yields a k-anonymization of R then the a priori probability of $\mathcal{S}_r$ is $\frac{1}{|R|}$ and the a posteriori probability is $\frac{1}{|[r]_g^R|} \leq \frac{1}{k}$:

$$(\mathrm{anon}_k^R(g) \wedge \mathbf{A4}) \Leftrightarrow \bigwedge_{r \in R} \mathrm{BFBR}_{\{u\}, \mathcal{S}_r}^R (\mathcal{V}, \mathcal{A}_g, \frac{1}{k} - \frac{1}{|R|}) \qquad (6)$$

$$\Rightarrow \bigwedge_{r \in R} \mathrm{BFBR}_{\{u\}, \mathcal{S}_r}^R (\mathcal{V}, \mathcal{A}_g, \frac{1}{k}). \qquad (7)$$

(7) states that under assumption **A4** the amount of belief revision for each secret $\mathcal{S}_r$ is bounded by a constant rather than the size of the database.

We discuss next a widely applicable guarantee that lifts restriction **A4**, relaxes restriction **A3**, and still bounds the amount of belief revision by an owner-defined constant.

4.2 L-Diversity

Machanavajjhala et al. [16] point out two key deficiencies of the k-anonymity guarantee: it does not withstand so-called *homogeneity* and *background* attacks.

In the general case when sensitive attribute values may occur more than once in R, vulnerability to homogeneity attacks arises whenever few sensitive values occur with high multiplicity in an equivalence class. In particular, when all tuples in r's equivalence class share the same sensitive value s, any attacker can infer with certainty that $r[ID]$ is associated with s. In this case, the attacker learns the maximum possible amount of information about the secret $\mathcal{S}_r$ since its a posteriori probability is 1.

In background attacks, the attacker exploits external background information to rule out a number of sensitive values as being definitely *not* associated to $r[ID]$. The remaining alternatives are considered equi-probable. This class of attackers is not covered by k-anonymity, which considers the single attacker who a priori deems all associations equi-probable.

[16] proposes the concept of *l-diversity* to remedy these deficiencies of k-anonymity. The intuition behind this concept is to defend against attackers who are able to rule out at most $l - 1$ sensitive values from the equivalence class of each $r \in R$, by ensuring that the frequency of each sensitive value in the remaining set of tuples is upper bounded by an owner-defined threshold. [16] introduces the notion of *recursive* (c, l)-*diversity* as a sufficient condition for l-diversity.

For every $r \in R$, let o be the number of distinct sensitive values occurring in r's equivalence class. Let their list be $s_1, \ldots, s_o$, and let m_i be the multiplicity of s_i in r's equivalence class. Assuming w.l.o.g. that $m_1 \geq m_2 \geq \ldots \geq m_o$, we say that the equivalence class of r satisfies recursive (c, l)-diversity if

$$m_1 \leq c(m_l + m_{l+1} + \ldots + m_o)$$

for some constant c. We say that g satisfies recursive (c, l)-diversity for R, denoted r-div$_{c,l}(g, R)$, if for every $r \in R$, r's equivalence class satisfies recursive (c, l)-diversity.

Example 10. The anonymized table in Fig. 1 satisfies recursive (1,2)-diversity.

Recursive (c, l)-diversity has two immediate implications.

First, it enables owners to drop assumption **A4**, thus extending applicability of the guarantee to tables with duplicate sensitive values. Indeed, it is easy to check that under assumptions **A1**, **A2** and **A3**, (c, l)-diversity imposes an upper bound of $\frac{c}{1+c}$ on the attacker's a posteriori and a priori belief, and hence on the belief revision that $\mathcal{S}_r$ holds. Recursive (c, l)-diversity thus provides defense even when assumption **A4** is violated.

Second, recursive (c, l)-diversity allows to relax assumption **A3** to accommodate defense against background attacks. [16] shows that this guarantee implies that regardless of which (at most) $l - 1$ sensitive values are pruned from r's equivalence class as being unassociated to $r[ID]$ (according to background information), the frequency of each remaining sensitive value in the pruned equivalence class is at most $\frac{c}{1+c}$. This is the upper bound on the a posteriori belief about secret $\mathcal{S}_r$.

[17] discusses additional refinements of (c, l)-diversity, relaxing the definition to allow for the disclosure of attributes for certain individuals with less stringent privacy concerns. The authors also show that l-diversity is a practical notion, not only because it defends against more realistic attacks than k-anonymity, but also because finding an optimal l-diverse generalization of a table can be done no less efficiently than finding an optimal k-anonymization. Machanavajjhala et al. show how to exploit the structural similarity of the two privacy notions to easily adapt to l-diversity the state-of-the-art techniques developed for k-anonymity, such as the Incognito algorithm [12].

In the remainder of this section, we connect l-diversity to the **GBP** model. **Relationship to the GBP Model.** The insight that when assumption **A4** does not hold K-anonymity provides no guarantees, is also reflected in the **GBP** model. Specifically, in the pathological case when all tuples in r's equivalence class share the same sensitive value, the posterior probability of $\mathcal{S}_r$ is given by

$$\mathbf{P}_u[\mathcal{S}_r | \mathcal{V}(R) \wedge \mathcal{A}_g(R)] = \frac{\text{mult}(r[S], [r]_g^R)}{|[r]_g^R|} = 1$$

so from (5) we obtain that the only guarantee possible for $\mathcal{S}_r$ is

$$\text{BFBR}_{\{u\}, \mathcal{S}_r}^R(\mathcal{V}, \mathcal{A}_g, 1 - \frac{\text{mult}(r[S], R)}{|R|}).$$

This is a trivial guarantee, satisfied by any anonymization, including those in which the secret $\mathcal{S}_r$ is completely exposed.

In contrast, it is easily verified that, even after dropping assumption **A4**, recursive (c, l)-diversity guarantees that

$$\frac{\text{mult}(r[S], R)}{|R|} \leq \frac{\text{mult}(r[S], [r]_g^R)}{|[r]_g^R|} \leq \frac{c}{1+c}$$

which implies that the further belief revision is bounded by $\frac{c}{1+c}$. Plugging this bound into (5), we obtain

$$\text{r-div}_{c,l}^R(g) \Rightarrow \bigwedge_{r \in R} \text{BFBR}_{\{u\}, \mathcal{S}_r}^R(\mathcal{V}, \mathcal{A}_g, \frac{c}{1+c}).$$

A remarkable fact about recursive (c, l)-diversity is that it represents the first anonymity flavor that looks beyond the uninformed attacker described by the uniform probability distribution. The class of attackers it considers can be described by the following family of probability distributions. We say that a probability distribution δ is *l-pruning* if it satisfies both conditions below:

- for every $r \in R$, there is a set V_r of sensitive values occurring in $[r]_g^R$, such that
  - $|V_r| < l$ and
  - for every database R', $\delta(R') = 0$ if and only if there are $r' \in R$ and $v \in V_{r'}$ such that R' contains the association of $r'[ID]$ with v;
- all databases with non-zero probability are equi-probable.

Intuitively, V_r is the set of alternatives which the attacker rules out as unassociated to $r[ID]$. Denoting with $\mathcal{LP}$ all l-pruning distributions given by R and g, we have

$$\text{r-div}_{c,l}^R(g) \Rightarrow \bigwedge_{r \in R} \text{BFBR}_{\mathcal{LP}, \mathcal{S}_r}^R(\mathcal{V}, \mathcal{A}_g, \frac{c}{1+c}).$$

Since $\mathcal{LP}$ is generated by all possible choices of V_r, the guarantee defends against all attackers able to rule out at most $l-1$ alternatives, no matter which these alternatives are, as dictated by the various attackers' backgrounds.

We conclude this section with a few remarks.

4.3 Additional Remarks on Anonymization Techniques

Complexity of Finding Optimal Anonymizations. Clearly one extreme way to ensure k-anonymity is to generalize tuples into a single equivalence class. This would of course minimize the utility of the released data. [18] studies the problem of finding the k-anonymization which incurs the least amount of data loss due to generalization (for various metric for data loss), showing that the problem of optimal k-anonymization is NP-complete. Several follow-up papers propose practical k-anonymization algorithms based on approximations and heuristics [12, 3, 7, 4]. While Machanavajjhala et al. do not provide a lower bound for finding optimal l-diverse anonymizations, they conjecture NP-hardness as well, and show how to adapt the Incognito Algorithm [12].

Sensitive Data Generalization. There are slight exceptions from assumption **Util**: an example occurs in [22]. In this work, sensitive data is not published in the clear, but generalized itself using a function f. The generalization function f exploits a hierarchy among concepts in the sensitive domain, treating ancestor concepts as more general than descendant concepts. For instance, instead of displaying "pneumonia", the owner may release a more general concept such as "respiratory tract problems" which in turn is generalized by "antibiotic-curable ailment". Evidently the objective in [22] is to minimize the information loss resulting from generalization of both quasi-identifiers and sensitive attributes. We can capture this scenario as well in the **GBP** model, by simply adjusting assumption **Util** to state that the owner is willing to live with the attacker's belief after seeing the generalized sensitive values described by view $V_s(R) := f(\Pi_S(R))$.

T-Closeness. One paper that explicitly states and exploits assumption **Util** is [14]. It considers the probability distribution p on the secrets $\{S_r\}_{r \in R}$ after seeing the entire anonymized table $\mathcal{A}_g(R)$, and the probability distribution q of the sensitive values in R, i.e. in $V_s(R)$. The authors introduce the privacy guarantee of *t-closeness*, which holds if the *distribution distance* between p and q is smaller than a parameter threshold t. The authors show shortcomings of standard metrics for comparing distributions and propose their own. They also show that the search for a t-close anonymization that maximizes utility (under a standard measure) can be performed by adapting efficient algorithms developed for k-anonymity. However, t-closeness does not subsume k-anonymity and the authors suggest combining the two before releasing an anonymized table.

An Alternative Bayesian Modeling. [17] compares the notion of l-diversity to a model called *Bayesian Optimal Privacy (BOP)* model. Just like the **GBP** model, the BOP model is based on belief revision. However, the authors conclude a mismatch between l-diversity and the BOP model. As demonstrated in this section, the reason is not due to any fundamental mismatch between Bayesian privacy models and l-diversity. Rather, it stems from the particular modeling choice in [17] which ignores assumption **Util**: [17] considers that a priori the attacker sees $V_{id}(R)$ but not $V_s(R)$. The difficulty with this modeling (identified in [17] as well) is that to estimate the attacker's a priori belief revision about S_r, we require knowledge of the attacker's probability distribution on the domain of all sensitive values, which is an unrealistic expectation. The modeling we describe in this section surmounts this obstacle, as under assumption **Util**, it needn't care about this distribution; it only considers belief revision starting from the attacker's adjusted belief *after seeing* $V_s(R)$. We can estimate this belief (as in (5)), regardless of the belief before seeing $V_s(R)$.

work	attacker classes considered
[8]	all $\mathcal{P}_a$; secret-focused $\mathcal{P}_\mathcal{S}$
[19, 20]	independent-tuple $\mathcal{P}_{it}$
[16, 17]	l-pruning $\mathcal{LP}$
[23, 24]	uniform distribution $\mathcal{P}_u = \{u\}$

$$\mathcal{P}_u \subset \mathcal{LP} \subset \begin{matrix} \mathcal{P}_\mathcal{S} \\ \mathcal{P}_{it} \end{matrix} \subset \mathcal{P}_a$$

Fig. 2. Classes of attackers considered by privacy guarantees in various works

k-Anonymous Views. An intriguing idea introduced by Jajodia et al in [25] is to apply the notion of k-anonymity to view-based publishing. The setting is similar to generalization-based publishing: we have a single table R with identity attributes ID and sensitive attributes S. The owner publishes data from R via views expressed as conjunctive queries. It is assumed that releasing all identifiers $\Pi_{ID}(R)$ and all sensitive attributes $\Pi_S(R)$ is acceptable to the owner, but releasing the *association* between them is not.

A view V is said to satisfy k-anonymity if for every identifier $id \in \Pi_{ID}(R)$, there are k distinct possible databases $\{R_1, \ldots, R_k\} \subseteq [R]_V$, each associating id with a distinct sensitive value $s_1, \ldots, s_k$.

This guarantee can be connected to the **GBP** model as follows. Say that an attacker is *uniform secret-focused* if he is described by a distribution on databases which is generated by a uniform distribution on secrets. Given secret $\mathcal{S}$, there is only one such uniform secret-focused distribution, $\delta_\mathcal{S}$. Then view V's k-anonymity implies

$$\bigwedge_{r \in R} \mathrm{BFBR}^R_{\{\delta_{\mathcal{S}_r}\}, \mathcal{S}_r}(\mathcal{V}, V, \frac{1}{k}).$$

where $\mathcal{V}$ are the views (considered a priori known to the attacker) $\Pi_{ID}(R)$ and $\Pi_S(R)$, and $\mathcal{S}_r$ is the secret association for tuple r, as defined in Section 4.1.

5 View-Based Versus Generalization-Based Publishing

The formalization of various privacy guarantees in terms of the **GBP** model allows us to qualitatively compare view-based and generalization-based privacy guarantees.

Abstracting from the different expressive powers of the publishing functions $\mathcal{V}$ and $\mathcal{N}$ (views versus generalizations), the fundamental difference between these guarantees remains the class of probability distributions used to model attackers.

The guarantee in [8] is the most conservative one, considering all types of attackers (with the drawback of high complexity for deciding the extent-dependent guarantees, and undecidability in the extent-independent case).

Miklau and Suciu's guarantee of perfect privacy considers a subclass of attackers described by independent-tuple distributions, with the benefit of featuring better decision complexity. Recursive (c, l)-diversity requires l-pruning distributions, which are a subclass of the distributions of [8]. L-pruning distributions are also particular cases of independent-tuple distributions. Finally, the uniform distribution u implicitly used to model attackers in k-anonymity is a particular case of l-pruning distributions (for $l = 1$). Figure 2 summarizes the relationship between the various classes of attackers.

Note that the classes $\mathcal{P}_a, \mathcal{P}_\mathcal{S}, \mathcal{P}_{it}$ were introduced for view-based privacy, while $\mathcal{LP}$ and $\mathcal{P}_u$ for generalization-based privacy. There is no reason why the various classes of attackers should not be considered uniformly, across both publishing paradigms.

6 Privacy in Open-World Integration

So far we have only considered publishing settings in which $\mathcal{V}$ is a function. However, this modeling leaves out an important publishing paradigm, namely open-world integration [11, 13].

In open-world integration, a collection L of data sources (also known as local databases) is registered into an integrated database G (also known as the global database). Each data source is registered by stating the inclusion of a publishable data subset into G. The publishable subset is typically specified by a query against the local database, and the global dataset containing it is specified by a query against the global database. This allows for instance a Toyota car dealer to register the classified deals in her database as a subset of the Toyota deals from the global database of a portal covering many dealerships. If the portal offers several brands, specifying its Toyota deals requires a selection query.

Such inclusion statements do not uniquely determine the global database, since whenever a global database G satisfies them, so does any other database strictly containing the tuples in G. Consequently, the relation $\mathcal{V}$ between local (proprietary) and global (public) database is not functional: $\mathcal{V}$ associates any extent of local databases L to an infinite family of global databases. Towards a well-defined semantics of answering application queries Q against the global schema, the notion of *certain answers* was introduced [11, 13]. Given a set L of local databases, the certain answer of Q against the global schema is the set of all tuples appearing in the answer of Q on all global databases G related to L: $cert_Q(L) = \cap_{(L,G) \in \mathcal{V}} Q(G)$.

Clients (and therefore attackers) can interact with the integration system only by posing queries against the global schema and receiving their certain answer. In such a setting, it still makes sense to allow the owner of an individual local database to specify the sensitive data using a query $\mathcal{S}$ against the local database. Privacy of the secret can still be defined in terms of no (or bounded) belief revision, which depends on the possible local databases, analogous to the **GBP** model.

However, the possible local databases now represent precisely those which are indistinguishable from the actual local database by an arbitrary interaction with the integration system. That is, they cannot be distinguished by posing arbitrary-length sequences of arbitrary queries against the global schema and observing their certain answer.

The problem is that the space of possible interactions between attacker and integration system is infinite, so this definition does not immediately lead to an algorithm for identifying the set of possible local databases, which in turn hinders the development of an algorithm for checking privacy guarantees.

[21] solves the problem in a setting where $\mathcal{V}$ is given by containment statements between a union of conjunctive queries with inequalities $(\text{UCQ}^{\neq})$ against the local data and a $\text{UCQ}^{\neq}$ query against the global data (such statements are also known as GLAV [11, 13] or source-target constraints [10]). The secret $\mathcal{S}$ is also given by a $\text{UCQ}^{\neq}$ query against the local database. [21] shows that, instead of considering the infinitely many possible interactions of an attacker with the integration system, it suffices to focus on a single, canonically built interaction. This canonical interaction is optimal in the sense that it poses a finite set of queries against the integration system, such that no further queries an attacker could conceive give additional information. More precisely, the certain answers of the canonical queries suffice to reverse-engineer precisely the set of possible local databases. This in turn enables formulating and checking all extent-dependent **GBP** privacy guarantees (Section 2).

7 Conclusions

In this chapter, we reduced various instantiations of the view-based and generalization-based publishing to the **GBP** model, also showing how to apply it to publishing in open-world integration. This reduction offers a unifying perspective on various seemingly disparate privacy guarantees developed independently for the various publishing paradigms.

We have applied the **GBP** model to settings in which the publishing transformation is deterministically defined as either a function or a relation. This assumption leaves out the mature line of research on preserving privacy by randomizing the data (see for instance [2] and references within).

References

1. Serge Abiteboul, Richard Hull, and Victor Vianu. *Foundations of Databases*. Addison-Wesley, 1995.
2. Charu C. Aggarwal. On randomization, public information and the curse of dimensionality. In *International Conference on Data Engineering (ICDE)*, pages 136–145, 2007.

3. G. Aggarwal, T. Feder, K. Kenthapadi, R. Motwani, R. Panigrahy, D. Thomas, and A. Zhu. Anonymizing tables. In *International Conference on Database Theory (ICDT)*, pages 246–258, 2005.
4. C. C. Aggrawal. On k-anonymity and the curse of dimensionality. In *International Conference on Very Large Data Bases (VLDB)*, pages 901–909, 2005.
5. Francois Bancilhon and Nicolas Spyratos. Protection of information in relational data bases. In *International Conference on Very Large Data Bases (VLDB)*, pages 494–500, 1977.
6. Francois Bancilhon and Nicolas Spyratos. Algebraic versus probabilistic independence in data bases. In *ACM Symposium on Principles of Database Systems (PODS)*, pages 149–153, 1985.
7. R. Bayardo and R. Agrawal. Data privacy through optimal k-anonymization. In *International Conference on Data Engineering (ICDE)*, pages 217–228, 2005.
8. Alin Deutsch and Yannis Papakonstantinou. Privacy in database publishing. In *International Conference on Database Theory (ICDT)*, pages 230–245, 2005.
9. Alin Deutsch and Val Tannen. Reformulation of XML queries and constraints. In *International Conference on Database Theory (ICDT)*, 2003.
10. R. Fagin, P. Kolaitis, R. Miller, and L. Popa. Data exchange: Semantics and query answering. In *International Conference on Database Theory (ICDT)*, 2003.
11. Alon Halevy. Answering queries using views: A survey. *VLDB Journal*, 10(4):270–294, 2001.
12. K. Lefevre, D. J. DeWitt, and R. Ramakrishnan. Incognito: Efficient full-domain k-anonymity. In *ACM Conference on Management of Data (SIGMOD)*, pages 49–60, 2005.
13. Maurizio Lenzerini. Data integration: A theoretical perspective. In *ACM Symposium on Principles of Database Systems (PODS)*, 2002.
14. Ninghui Li, Tiancheng Li, and Suresh Venkatasubramanian. t-closeness: Privacy beyond k-anonymity and l-diversity. In *International Conference on Data Engineering (ICDE)*, 2007.
15. Ashwin Machanavajjhala and Johannes Gehrke. On the efficiency of checking perfect privacy. In *ACM Symposium on Principles of Database Systems (PODS)*, pages 163–172, 2006.
16. Ashwin Machanavajjhala, Johannes Gehrke, Daniel Kifer, and Muthuramakrishnan Venkatasubramaniam. l-diversity: Privacy beyond k-anonymity. In *International Conference on Data Engineering (ICDE)*, page 24, 2006.
17. Ashwin Machanavajjhala, Johannes Gehrke, Daniel Kifer, and Muthuramakrishnan Venkitasubramaniam. l-diversity: Privacy beyond k-anonymity. *To appear in IEEE Transactions on Knowledge and Data Engineering (TKDE)*.
18. A. Meyerson and R.Williams. On the complexity of optimal k-anonymity. In *ACM Symposium on Principles of Database Systems (PODS)*, pages 223–228, 2004.
19. Gerome Miklau and Dan Suciu. A formal analysis of information disclosure in data exchange. In *ACM Conference on Management of Data (SIGMOD)*, pages 575–586, 2004.
20. Gerome Miklau and Dan Suciu. A formal analysis of information disclosure in data exchange. *Journal of Computer and Systems Sciences*, 73(3):507–534, 2007.
21. Alan Nash and Alin Deutsch. Privacy in GLAV information integration. In *International Conference on Database Theory (ICDT)*, pages 89–103, 2007.

22. Pierangela Samarati. Protecting respondents' identities in microdata release. *IEEE Transactions on Knowledge and Data Engineering (TKDE)*, 13(6):1010–1027, 2001.

23. Pierangela Samarati and Latanya Sweeney. Generalizing data to provide anonymity when disclosing information. In *ACM Symposium on Principles of Database Systems (PODS)*, page 188, 1998.

24. Latanya Sweeney. k-anonymity: a model for protecting privacy. *International Journal on Uncertainty, Fuzziness, and Knowlege-Based Systems*, 10(5):557–570, 2002.

25. Chao Yao, Xiaoyang Sean Wang, and Sushil Jajodia. Checking for k-anonymity violation by views. In *International Conference on Very Large Data Bases (VLDB)*, pages 910–921, 2005.

20

Privacy Preserving Publication: Anonymization Frameworks and Principles

Yufei Tao

Department of Computer Science and Engineering
Chinese University of Hong Kong
Sha Tin, New Territories, Hong Kong
taoyf@cse.cuhk.edu.hk

Summary. Given a microdata table T, the objective of *privacy preserving publication* is to release a distorted version T' of T such that T' does not allow an adversary to confidently derive the sensitive data of any individual, and yet, T' can be used to analyze the statistical patterns significant in T. The existing methods of privacy preserving publication is essentially the integration of an *anonymization framework* and an *anonymization principle*. Specifically, a framework describes how anonymization is performed, whereas a principle measures whether a sufficient amount of anonymization has been applied. In this chapter, we will discuss the characteristics of two existing frameworks: generalization and anatomy, and of two most popular principles: k-anonymity and l-diversity.

1 Introduction

This chapter will discuss an important problem, known as *privacy preserving publication*, in the literature of data privacy protection. Formally, we have a trustable publisher that has a *microdata* table T, where each tuple describes the information of an individual. For our discussion, assume that T has d non-sensitive attributes A_1^q, A_2^q, ..., A_d^q and a sensitive attribute A^s. The objective is to publish an anonymized version T' of T such that T' does not allow an adversary to confidently derive the sensitive data of any individual, and yet, T' can be used to analyze the statistical patterns significant in T.

As a concrete application example, consider that the publisher is a hospital, and T is given in Table 1a. Here, T has three non-sensitive attributes $A_1^q = Age$, $A_2^q = Sex$, $A_3^q = Zipcode$, and a sensitive attribute $A^s = Disease$. The column *Name* specifies the owners of the tuples, e.g., Tuple 1 indicates that Andy, aged 5, lives in a neighborhood with Zipcode 12000, and he contracted *gastric-ulcer*. Obviously, *Name* should not be published along with T, since it explicitly reveals the identities of all individuals.

Let T' be the resulting table after removing *Name* from T. At first glance, it appears that we can simply release T', which, *by itself*, does not contain any

row #	Name	Age	Sex	Zipcode	Disease
1	Andy	5	M	12000	gastric ulcer
2	Bill	9	M	14000	dyspepsia
3	Ken	6	M	18000	pneumonia
4	Nash	8	M	19000	bronchitis
5	Joe	12	M	22000	pneumonia
6	Sam	19	M	24000	pneumonia
7	Linda	21	F	58000	flu
8	Jame	26	F	36000	Alzeimer
9	Sarah	28	F	37000	pneumonia
10	Mary	56	F	33000	flu

Name	Age	Sex	Zipcode
Andy	5	M	12000
Bill	9	M	14000
Ken	6	M	18000
Nash	8	M	19000
Mike	*7*	*M*	*17000*
Joe	12	M	22000
Sam	19	M	24000
Linda	21	F	58000
Jane	26	F	36000
Sarah	28	F	37000
Mary	56	F	33000

(a) Microdata   (b) A voter registration list

Table 1. Illustration of linking attacks for privacy inferencing

hint about *who* is the owner of each tuple. This naive approach fails, because an adversary may combine T' with certain additional information, to recover the owner of a tuple. For instance, imagine that a neighbor of Sarah knows the age 28 of Sarah, and that Sarah has been hospitalized before, and thus, must have a record in T'. Since this neighbor has all the non-sensitive values of Sarah, s/he easily finds out that the last-but-one tuple in T' belongs to Sarah. In this way, the neighbor has successfully "linked" Sarah to her sensitive value *pneumonia*.

The above process exemplifies a type of privacy inferences called *linking attacks*, where an adversary accurately infers the sensitive value of a victim, via the victim's non-sensitive values. Since the non-sensitive attributes may be utilized to pinpoint the tuple owned by a person, they are commonly referred to as the *quasi-identifier* (QI) attributes. Linking attacks were first identified as a real threat by Sweeney [15]. In particular, she shows that when the QI attributes are *date-of-birth, gender*, and *Zipcode*, 87% of the Americans have a unique combination of the values on those attributes. Furthermore, leveraging a dataset released by a real publisher (the publication was done in the same way as described earlier for Table 1a), Sweeney convinces the community about the seriousness of linking attacks, by correctly extracting the medical history of an ex-governor of Massachusetts.

In reality, the QI-values of an individual may be acquired by an adversary through several channels. Knowing the victim is an obvious channel, as in our earlier example where the adversary is the neighbor of Sarah. Alternatively, an adversary may also obtain the QI-values from an *external database*, which can be completely separate from T, and its accessibility to the public cannot be controlled by the publisher of T. For instance, a worker in the government may have access to the voter registration list in Table 1b, which includes all the QI-attributes in the microdata of Table 1a, together with peoples' names. Note that an external database, most likely, does not include exactly the same set of individuals as in the microdata. For instance, Mike in the list of Table 1b is absent from Table 1a. Nevertheless, by performing an equi-join between the two tables, an adversary easily recovers the identities of all the patients in the microdata.

Prevention of linking attacks is important, because they strongly discourage a publisher (e.g., a hospital, a census bureau, etc.) from sharing its data with researchers, who rely on such data to verify their hypotheses from laboratories. Several methods have been developed in the database community to counter such attacks, by computing an adequately anonymized version T' of the microdata T. Each method is essentially the integration of an *anonymization framework* and an *anonymization principle*. Specifically, a framework describes how anonymization is performed, whereas a principle measures whether a sufficient amount of anonymization has been applied. In the sequel, we will discuss the characteristics of two existing frameworks: generalization and anatomy, and those of two most popular principles: k-anonymity and l-diversity.

The rest of this chapter is organized as follows. Section 2 introduces the concept of k-anonymous generalization, and points out its vulnerabilities to linking attacks. Section 3 clarifies l-diversity and how it remedies the defects of k-anonymity, again assuming generalization is the underlying anonymization framework. Section 4 explains how l-diversity can be implemented with anatomy, and compares the two anonymization frameworks. Section 5 identifies several limitations of l-diversity. Finally, Section 6 provides a summary of the chapter.

2 k-anonymous Generalization

Given a microdata table T, the *generalization* [13, 15] anonymization framework replaces each QI-value with a less specific form, such that the QI-values of a tuple become indistinguishable from those of some other tuples. Table 2 demonstrates a generalized version of the microdata in Table 1a. For example, the age 5 of Tuple 1 in Table 1a has been *generalized* to an interval $[1, 10]$ in Table 2. Semantically, the interval indicates that the original age of Tuple 1 may be any value in the range of $[1, 10]$.

Notice that Tuples 1 and 2 have exactly the same generalized value on every QI attribute, and therefore, constitute a "QI-group". Formally, a *QI-group* is a group resulting from grouping the tuples in a relation by all the QI attributes. Clearly, Table 2 involves 4 QI-groups: $\{1, 2\}$ (indicated by tuple IDs), $\{3, 4\}$, $\{5, 6\}$, and $\{7, 8, 9, 10\}$. It is worth mentioning that the notion of "QI-group" is also known by several other names, such as "equivalent class" [9], "q-block" [11], and so on.

Assume that the publisher releases Table 2. Consider the linking attack launched by the neighbor of Sarah who, as mentioned in Section 1, possesses the QI values $\{28, F, 37000\}$ of Sarah. To guess which tuples may belong to

row #	Age	Sex	Zipcode	Disease
1	[1, 10]	M	[10001, 15000]	gastric ulcer
2	[1, 10]	M	[10001, 15000]	dyspepsia
3	[1, 10]	M	[15001, 20000]	pneumonia
4	[1, 10]	M	[15001, 20000]	bronchitis
5	[11, 20]	M	[20001, 25000]	pneumonia
6	[11, 20]	M	[20001, 25000]	pneumonia
7	[21, 60]	F	[30000, 60000]	flu
8	[21, 60]	F	[30000, 60000]	Alzeimer
9	[21, 60]	F	[30000, 60000]	pneumonia
10	[21, 60]	F	[30000, 60000]	flu

Table 2. A 2-anonymous version of Table 1a

Sarah, the neighbor examines the generalized QI-values in Table 2. Obviously, Tuple 1 cannot be owned by Sarah, since it *Age*-value [1, 10] does not cover 28. By this reasoning, Tuples 7-10 (in the last QI-group) are the only candidates for the tuple of Sarah. Unable to make additional inferences from here, the adversary settles on a fuzzy fact: Sarah may have got *flu*, *pneumonia*, or *Alzeimer's*.

Unlike Table 1a which allows the adversary to exactly derive the private value of Sarah, Table 2 offers stronger protection. Evidently, protection is made possible by the fact that generalization prevents the unique association of a tuple to its owner. Specifically, since Tuples 7-10 share the same QI formats, with a random guess, an adversary has only a 1/4 chance of correctly identifying Tuple 9 as the real tuple owned by Sarah.

Based on the above idea, Sweeney and Samarati [14] propose *k-anonymity* as an anonymization principle to measure the degree of generalization. Formally, a generalized table is *k-anonymous* if each QI-group contains at least *k*-tuples. Table 2 is 2-anonymous, since the smallest QI-group (involving the first two rows) has a size 2. In general, a higher *k* provides stronger protection because, in general, *k*-anonymity guarantees that an adversary has at most $1/k$ probability of finding out the actual tuple owned by the victim individual. As a tradeoff, however, increasing *k* also brings down the utility of the generalized table, since more information must be lost in generalization. This can be easily understood through an extreme example: $k = |T|$. In that case, all the tuples in the microdata T must be included in a single QI-group. As a result, each generalized value must be a (very!) long interval encompassing all the values in T on the corresponding QI-attribute. For instance, if *k* equals 10 and T is Table 1a, after generalization each *Age*-value becomes an interval that covers the range [5, 56]. Releasing such an excessively generalized table is hardly more useful than publishing only the *Disease*-column of T.

A large bulk of research has been devoted to developing algorithms [3, 6, 7, 8, 9, 13, 15, 17, 19] for computing a *k*-anonymous version of T, which minimizes the amount of information loss gauged by an appropriate metric. Although different metrics exist, all of them capture the loss amount as a monotone function of the lengths of the generalized intervals (i.e., the longer the interval, the higher the loss). We do not discuss the details of those algorithms, most of which can be found in a nice survey [4]. For the subsequent discussion, however, we need to make two notes.

- **NP-Hardness.** Finding the optimal k-anonymity generalization (with the smallest information loss) is NP-hard [2, 5, 12], even for simple information-loss metrics. This fact forces a practitioner to accept an approximate algorithm. However, the existing solutions [2, 5, 12] cannot ensure a small approximation ratio (which varies according to the information-loss norm). In particular, the best known ratio is $O(k)$, which implies that the output of an algorithm may considerably deviate from the optimal quality, when strong privacy protection is required (e.g., $k = 20$).

- **Curse of Dimensionality.** Second, it is known [1] that, when the number of QI attributes is large, k-anonymous generalization *inevitably* lose a huge amount of information, even for $k = 2$.

Machanavajjhala et al. [11] observe two crucial defects of k-anonymity in guarding against linking attacks. They actually define two types of attacks that leverage these defects to breach the privacy of individuals. Next, we will illustrate them using the 2-anonymous generalization in Table 2 of the microdata Table 1a.

- **Homogeneity Attack.** Assume that an adversary knows the QI-values {19, M, 24000} of Sam. After inspecting the published Table 2, s/he realizes that the tuple of Sam must fall in the third QI-group consisting of Tuples 5 and 6. Since both tuples carry the sensitive value *pneumonia*, the adversary becomes affirmative that Sam must have contracted that disease. In other words, the 2-anonymity in Table 2 provides no protection to the privacy of Sam at all. Note that this observation does not contradict our earlier conclusion that, k-anonymity ensures that an adversary has only $1/k$ probability to correctly identify the real tuple of a victim. In our case here, the adversary is equally uncertain about whether Tuple 5 or 6 belongs to Sam. However, *it does not matter*, since, either way, Sam must have got the same disease.

- **Background Attack.** Now let us consider, once again, the neighbor of Sarah. As explained before, from Table 2, the neighbor can only figure out that Sarah may have had *flu*, *Alzeimer's*, or *pneumonia*. This conjecture, however, may be further improved, if the neighbor utilizes her/his "background knowledge". For example, s/he may know that a flu-vaccine shot had been offered to all the residents in the neighborhood a month before Sarah was hospitalized. Hence, it is rather unlikely that the hospitalization was caused by *flu*. Furthermore, obviously, Sarah is too young to get infected with Alzeimer's disease. Thus, the adversary becomes (almost fully) confident that Sarah contracted pneumonia.

The above drawbacks lead to the development of another anonymization principle as discussed in the next section.

3 l-diverse Generalization

Both homogeneity and background attacks are caused by the fact that there is not sufficient *diversity* in the set of sensitive values present in a QI-group. For example, in Figure 2, there is only one *Disease*-value *pneumonia* in the QI-group containing tuples 5-6, which is the reasoning behind the homogeneity attack illustrated in the previous section. Although more diversity exists in the last QI-group involving tuples 7-10 (where there are 3 sensitive values *flu, Alzeimer, pneumonia*), the degree of diversity is still not enough for preventing the background attack launched by the adversary (the neighbor of Sarah mentioned in Section 2) that can exclude 2 diseases *flu* and *Alzeimer* from being the real disease of Sarah.

Evidently, in the worst case, no matter how diverse the sensitive values are in a QI-group, a highly-knowledgable adversary can still precisely derive the privacy of the victim individual o. Specifically, assume that the QI-group accommodating the record of o has x different sensitive values, whereas the adversary can correctly assert that o cannot be associated with $x - 1$ of them; in this case, the adversary uniquely identifies the true sensitive value of o. Fortunately, the realistic situation is much more optimistic, since it is rare for an adversary to be able to exclude too many sensitive values with respect to o. For instance, among the vast number of possible diseases, the neighbor of Sarah most likely can exclude only a very small percentage as the real disease of Sarah.

l-diversity [11] was exactly motivated by this observation. It requires that, after generalization, every QI-group should contain at least l "well-represented" sensitive values. Intuitively, this requirement does not allow an adversary to accurately recover the sensitive value of any individual o, provided that the adversary can exclude up to $l - 2$ values (i.e., leaving at least 2 possibilities for o). Thus, with a sufficiently large l, l-diversity can effectively prevent privacy breaches.

There are multiple ways to interpret the meaning of "well-represented". The simplest one is

Definition 1. *A QI-group fulfills* **distinctness l-diversity**, *if it contains at least l different sensitive values.*

Although this interpretation can be easily understood, it does not offer strong privacy guarantees from a probabilistic point of view. For example, imagine a QI-group with 1000 tuples, 900 of which carry the same sensitive value *HIV*, and the remaining 100 tuples have distinct values different from *HIV*. Clearly, the QI-group satisfies distinctness 101-diversity. Nevertheless, the privacy of *HIV* patients is poorly preserved. Specifically, consider an adversary who aims at inferring the disease of such a patient *o*, and has no background knowledge, i.e., s/he cannot exclude any disease before studying the published table. With a random guess, the adversary concludes that *o* had *HIV* with probability $900/1000 = 90\%$. Notice that this process of privacy inference essentially captures homogeneity attacks as a special case; hence, we refer to the process as a *probabilistic homogeneity attack*.

This phenomenon leads to an improved version of *l*-diversity:

Definition 2. *A table fulfills* **frequency *l*-diversity** *if, in each QI-group, at most $1/l$ of the tuples carry the sensitive value.*

By this reasoning, the last QI-group of Table 2 satisfies frequency 2-diversity, as the most frequent *Disease*-value *flu* is possessed by half of the tuples in the group. This definition has an important property: if, before consulting the published table, an adversary cannot preclude any sensitive value as belonging to the victim individual *o*, with a probabilistic homogeneity attack, s/he can correctly reconstruct the real disease of *o* with at most $1/l$ probability.

Frequency *l*-diversity does not provide adequate protection to background attacks. To understand this, consider a QI-group with 1000 tuples, 500 of which have the sensitive value *HIV*, 499 tuples have *pneumonia*, and the remaining tuple carries *flu*. This QI-group qualifies frequency 2-diversity, since the most frequent value *HIV* belongs to 50% of the tuples. Let *o* be an *HIV*-patient. Now, imagine an adversary who knows that this group contains the record of *o*, and that *o* does not have *pneumonia*. As a result, the record of *o* must be one of the 500 *HIV*-tuples, or the *flu*-tuple. At this point, the adversary cannot exclude any other disease; hence, taking a random guess, s/he conjectures that *o* contracted *HIV* with an exceedingly high probability $500/501 > 99.8\%$.

The cause of the above problem is as follows: after removing the 2nd frequent sensitive value (i.e., *pneumonia*) in a QI-group, the most frequent sensitive (*HIV*) value accounts for an excessively high proportion of the *remaining* tuples in the group. The implication is that, it is not enough to limit the frequency of the most popular sensitive value with respect to the QI-group size (as is the case in frequency *l*-diversity). Instead, we should limit the frequency according to the number of remaining tuples, after eliminating those having the 2nd frequent sensitive value. Remember that, we arrived at this conclusion by assuming that an adversary can preclude a single sensitive value as owned by the victim. Carrying the reasoning to the general scenario, if an adversary can exclude at most $l - 2$ values, we ought to constrain the frequency of the most sensitive value, with respect to the remaining tuples, after discarding the 2nd, 3rd, ..., $(l - 1)$-th most frequent sensitive values. This leads to the next version of *l*-diversity.

Definition 3 ([11]). *Given a QI-group, use n_1, n_2, ..., n_m to denote the number of tuples having the most, 2nd most, ..., the least frequent sensitive values in the group, respectively. The QI-group obeys* **recursive (c, l)-diversity**, *if the next inequality holds*[1]:

$$n_1 \leq c \cdot (n_l + n_{l+1} + ... + n_m), \qquad (1)$$

where c is a certain constant, and l is an integer at most m.

For instance, the last QI-group in Figure 2 satisfies recursive $(2, 3)$-diversity. Specifically, for that QI-group, $n_1 = 2$, and $n_2 = n_3 = 1$. Setting c to 2 and l to 3, Inequality 1 becomes $2 \leq 2 \cdot 1$.

It is not hard to observe an interesting connection between Definitions 2 and 3. A QI-group obeys (c, l)-diversity, if and only if, after eliminating the tuples with any l different sensitive values, the remaining set of tuples still obeys frequency $\frac{c}{c+1}$-diversity. This connection leads to a crucial property of Definition 3: if all the QI-groups in a generalized table satisfy recursive (c, l)-diversity, an adversary can correctly discover the sensitive value of an individual with probability at most $c/(c+1)$, provided that the adversary can preclude at most $l - 2$ values as belonging to the victim individual.

We have discussed three different versions of l-diversity. Machanavajjhala et al. formulate several other versions, as can be found in [11], which also explains the computation of generalized tables conforming to this principle. Currently, we are not aware of any published work on the hardness of finding the optimal l-diverse table that minimizes a certain information-loss metric. Nevertheless, it appears that the problem should be NP-hard for most metrics. In any case, l-diverse generalization also inherits the defect of k-anonymity that the amount of information loss will be inevitably large, when the number of QI-attributes is high. This defect can have rather negative influences on the utility of the published table, as discussed in the next section.

4 Anatomy

So far our discussion has employed generalization as the underlying anonymization framework. In this section, we proceed to introduce another framework: anatomy. As with generalization, anatomy can be combined with k-anonymity and l-diversity. The following analysis focuses on l-diversity, due to its obvious advantages over k-anonymity. In particular, we adopt frequency l-diversity (Definition 2), to avoid the complication of recursive (c, l)-diversity. Accordingly, we will assume that probabilistic homogeneity attacks are the objective of privacy protection. The discussion in this section, however, can be extended to k-anonymity and other versions of l-diversity in a straightforward manner.

---

[1] In the original proposition of [11], the "$\leq$" in Inequality 1 is "$<$". We adopt "$\leq$" here to simplify discussion, but the rationale extends naturally to "$<$" as well.

tuple ID	Age	Sex	Zipcode	Disease
1 (Bob)	23	M	11000	pneumonia
2	27	M	13000	dyspepsia
3	35	M	59000	dyspepsia
4	59	M	12000	pneumonia
5	61	F	54000	flu
6	65	F	25000	gastritis
7 (Alice)	65	F	25000	flu
8	70	F	30000	bronchitis

(a) The microdata

tuple ID	Age	Sex	Zipcode	Disease
1	[21, 60]	M	[10001, 60000]	pneumonia
2	[21, 60]	M	[10001, 60000]	dyspepsia
3	[21, 60]	M	[10001, 60000]	dyspepsia
4	[21, 60]	M	[10001, 60000]	pneumonia
5	[61, 70]	F	[10001, 60000]	flu
6	[61, 70]	F	[10001, 60000]	gastritis
7	[61, 70]	F	[10001, 60000]	flu
8	[61, 70]	F	[10001, 60000]	bronchitis

(b) A 2-diverse table

Table 3. Another generalization example

4.1 Motivation

Although generalization preserves privacy, it often loses considerable information in the microdata, which severely compromises the accuracy of data analysis. We illustrate this by using the microdata in Table 3a and the 2-diverse generalization in Table 3b. Assume that a researcher wants to derive from this table an estimate for the following query:

A: SELECT COUNT(*) FROM Unknown-Microdata
    WHERE $Disease = $ 'pneumonia' AND $Age <= 30$
    AND $Zipcode$ IN $[10001, 20000]$

To illustrate how to process the query, Figure 1 shows a 2D space, where the x-, y-dimensions are Age and $Zipcode$, respectively. Each point denotes a tuple in the microdata of Table 3a. For example, the x-, y-coordinates of point 1 equal the age and zipcode of tuple 1, respectively. Rectangle R_1 (or R_2) is obtained from the generalized values in the first (or second) QI-group in Table 3b. For instance, the x- (y-) projection of R_1 is the generalized age [20, 60] (zipcode [10001, 60000]) of tuples 1-4. Query A is represented as the shaded rectangle Q, whose projection on the x- (y-) dimension is decided by the range condition $Age \leq 30$ ($10001 \leq Zipcode \leq 20000$).

Since the researcher sees only R_1 and R_2 (but not the points), s/he answers query A in a way similar to selectivity estimation on a multidimensional

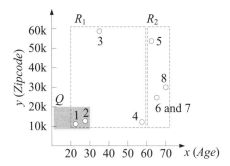

Fig. 1. The original and generalized data in the *Age-Zipcode* plane

histogram [16], as suggested in [9]. Clearly, as R_2 is disjoint with Q, no tuple in the second QI-group can satisfy the query. R_1, however, intersects Q, and hence, is examined as follows.

From the *Disease*-values in Table 3b, the researcher knows that 2 tuples in the first QI-group are associated with pneumonia. It remains to calculate the probability p that a tuple in the QI-group qualifies the range predicates of A, or equivalently, the tuple's point representation falls in Q (Figure 1). Once p is available, the query answer can be estimated as $2p$. Without additional knowledge, the researcher assumes uniform data distribution in R_1, and computes p as $Area(R_1 \cap R_Q)/Area(R_1) = 0.05$. This value leads to an approximate answer 0.1, which, however, is ten times smaller than actual query result 1 (see Table 3a).

The gross error is caused by the fact that the data distribution in R_1 significantly deviates from uniformity. Nevertheless, given only the generalized table, we cannot justify any other distribution assumption. This is an inherent problem of generalization: it prevents an analyst from correctly understanding the data distribution inside each QI-group.

4.2 Rationale of Anatomy

Anatomy overcomes the above defect of generalization, by releasing the exact QI-distribution without compromising the quality of privacy preservation. Specifically, anatomy releases a *quasi-identifier table* (QIT) and a *sensitive table* (ST), which separate QI-values from sensitive values. For example, Tables 4a and 4b demonstrate the QIT and ST obtained from the microdata Table 3a, respectively.

Construction of the anatomized tables can be (informally) understood as follows. First, we partition the tuples of the microdata into several QI-groups, based on a certain strategy. Here, following the grouping in Table 3b, let us place tuples 1-4 (or 5-8) of Table 3a into QI-group 1 (or 2).

Then, we create the QIT. Specifically, for each tuple in Table 3a, the QIT (Table 4a) includes all its *exact* QI-values, together with its group membership

row #	Age	Sex	Zipcode	Group-ID
1	23	M	11000	1
2	27	M	13000	1
3	35	M	59000	1
4	59	M	12000	1
5	61	F	54000	2
6	65	F	25000	2
7	65	F	25000	2
8	70	F	30000	2

(a) The quasi-identifier table (QIT)

Group-ID	Disease	Count
1	dyspepsia	2
1	pneumonia	2
2	bronchitis	1
2	flu	2
2	gastritis	1

(b) The sensitive table (ST)

Table 4. The anatomized tables

in a new column *Group-ID*. However, QIT does not store any *Disease* value. Finally, we produce the ST (Table 4b), which retains the *Disease* statistics of each QI-group. For instance, the first two records of the ST (to avoid confusion, we use 'record', instead of 'tuple', for the data of an ST) indicate that, two tuples of the first QI-group are associated with dyspepsia, and two with pneumonia. Similarly, the next three records imply that, the second QI-group has a tuple associated with bronchitis, two with flu, and one with gastritis.

Anatomy preserves privacy because the QIT does not indicate the sensitive value of any tuple, which must be randomly guessed from the ST. To explain this, consider again the adversary who has the age 23 and zipcode 11000 of Bob. Hence, from the QIT (Table 4a), the adversary knows that tuple 1 belongs to Bob, but does not obtain any information about his disease so far. Instead, s/he gets the id 1 of the QI-group containing tuple 1. Judging from the ST (Table 4b), the adversary realizes that, among the 4 tuples in QI-group 1, 50% of them are associated with dyspepsia (or pneumonia) in the microdata. Note that s/he does not gain any additional hints, regarding the exact diseases carried by these tuples. Hence, s/he arrives at the conclusion that Bob could have contracted dyspepsia (or pneumonia) with 50% probability. This is the same conjecture obtainable from the generalized Table 3b, as mentioned earlier.

By announcing the QI values directly, anatomy permits more effective analysis than generalization. Given query A in Section 4.1, we know, from the ST (Table 4b), that 2 tuples carry pneumonia in the microdata, and they are both in QI-group 1. Hence, we proceed to calculate the probability p that a tuple in the QI-group falls in Q (Figure 1). This calculation does not need any assumption about the data distribution in the *Age-Zipcode* plane, *because the distribution is precisely released*. Specifically, the QIT (Table 4a) shows that tuples 1 and 2 in QI-group 1 appear in Q, leading to the *exact $p = 50\%$*. Thus, we obtain an answer $2p = 1$, which is also the actual query result.

4.3 Formalization of Anatomy

As with generalization, Anatomy requires partitioning the microdata T.

Definition 4. *A **partition** consists of several subsets of T, such that each tuple in T belongs to exactly one subset. We refer to these subsets as **QI-groups**, and denote them as QI_1, QI_2, ..., QI_m. Namely, $\bigcup_{j=1}^{m} QI_j = T$ and, for any $1 \le j_1 \ne j_2 \le m$, $QI_{j_1} \cap QI_{j_2} = \emptyset$.*

We are interested only in l-diverse partitions that can lead to provably good privacy guarantees. Specifically, a partition with m QI-groups is *l-diverse*, if each QI-group QI_j ($1 \le j \le m$) satisfies the following condition. Let v be the most frequent A^s value in QI_j, and $c_j(v)$ the number of tuples $t \in QI_j$ with $t[d + 1] = v$; then

$$c_j(v)/|QI_j| \le 1/l \tag{2}$$

where $|QI_j|$ is the size (the number of tuples) of QI_j. Table 3a shows a partition with two QI-groups, where QI_1 contains tuples 1-4, and QI_2 includes tuples 5-8. In QI_1, dyspepsia and pneumonia are equally frequent, i.e., $c_1(\text{dyspepsia}) = c_1(\text{pneumonia}) = 2$. In QI_2, the most frequent A^s value is flu, i.e., $c_2(\text{flu}) = 2$. Since $|QI_1| = |QI_2| = 4$, according to Inequality 2, we know that QI_1 and QI_2 constitute a 2-diverse partition.

We are ready to formulate the QIT and ST tables published by anatomy.

Definition 5 ([18]). *Given an l-diverse partition with m QI-groups, anatomy produces a **quasi-identifier table** (QIT) and a **sensitive table** (ST) as follows. The QIT has schema*

$$(A_1^{qi}, A_2^{qi}, ..., A_d^{qi}, \textit{Group-ID}). \tag{3}$$

For each QI-group QI_j ($1 \le j \le m$) and each tuple $t \in QI_j$, QIT has a tuple of the form:

$$(t[1], t[2], ..., t[d], j). \tag{4}$$

The ST has schema

$$(\textit{Group-ID}, A^s, \textit{Count}). \tag{5}$$

For each QI-group QI_j ($1 \le j \le m$) and each distinct A^s value v in QI_j, the ST has a record of the form:

$$(j, v, c_j(v)) \tag{6}$$

where $c_j(v)$ is the number of tuples $t \in QI_j$ with $t[d+1] = v$. Apart from the tuples (or records) defined earlier, the QIT (or ST) does not contain any other data.

For instance, based on the 2-diverse partition suggested in Table 3b, anatomy produces the QIT and ST in Tables 4a and 4b respectively, as explained in Section 4.2.

When there is no ambiguity, we refer to a pair of QIT and ST collectively as the *anatomized tables*. In Section 4.6, we will show that anatomized tables capture the correlation in T more accurately than generalized tables. For this purpose, we also need to formalize generalization.

Definition 6. (Generalization) *Given a partition of T with m QI-groups, for any tuple $t \in T$, a generalized table of T contains a tuple of the form*

$$(QI_j[1], QI_j[2], ..., QI_j[d], t[d+1]) \tag{7}$$

where QI_j ($1 \le j \le m$) is the unique QI-group including t, and $QI_j[i]$ ($1 \le i \le d$) is an interval^2 covering $t[i]$. Furthermore, $QI_j[i]$ is identical for all tuples $t \in QI_j$. Apart from the tuples defined earlier, the table does not contain any other data.

For instance, let t be tuple 1 in the microdata Table 3a. We have $j = 1$, namely, t is contained in the first QI-group. In the generalized Table 3b, $QI_1[1] = [21, 60]$ (the generalized age of tuple 1), $QI_1[2] = $ M, and $QI_1[3] = [100001, 60000]$, which, together with $t[4] = $ pneumonia, form the first tuple.

We would like to point out that, although Definition 5 is based on an l-diverse partition, in general, anatomy produces a pair of QIT and ST from any partition (Definition 4) in exactly the same way. In particular, any k-anonymous or l-diverse table has an anatomized counterpart. We concentrate on l-diverse partitions to achieve strong privacy preservation. Several algorithms have been developed [18] to compute anatomized tables that minimize certain metrics of information loss. Interestingly, unlike optimal generalization that is NP-hard, optimal anatomy can be achieved in polynomial time.

4.4 Privacy Preservation

A pair of anatomized tables provide a convenient way for the data publisher to find out, for each tuple $t \in T$, all the A^s values that an adversary can associate t with, and the probability of each association. This is formally explained in the next lemma.

Lemma 1 ([18]). *If we perform a natural join $QIT \bowtie ST$, the join result is a table with $d+3$ attributes, containing records of the form*

---

^{2} If A_i^{qi} is categorical, following a common assumption in the literature, we consider that there is a total ordering on A_i^{qi}.

$$(t[1], t[2], ..., t[d], j, v, c_j(v)) \qquad (8)$$

where j is the ID of the QI-group including t (i.e., $t \in QI_j$), v an A^s value, and $c_j(v)$ the number of tuples in QI_j with A^s value v. Then, from an adversary's perspective,

$$Pr\{t[d+1] = v\} = c_j(v)/|QI_j| \qquad (9)$$

where $|QI_j|$ denotes the size of QI_j.

Corollary 1 ([18]). *Given a pair of QIT and ST, an adversary can correctly re-construct any tuple $t \in T$ with a probability at most $1/l$.*

Corollary 1 gives the privacy protection guarantee at the *tuple level*. It is also necessary to discuss the corresponding guarantee at the *individual level*, since in practice multiple individuals may have the same QI-values, thus complicating the privacy-attack process performed by an adversary.

To explain this, consider that an adversary has the age 65 and zipcode 25000 of Alice (the "owner" of tuple 7 in Table 3a), and wants to infer the medical record of Alice from the QIT and ST in Tables 4a and 4b, respectively. S/he consults the QIT, and sees that, in QI-group 2 (denoted as QI_2), both tuples 6 and 7 match the QI-values of Alice. Hence, s/he examines two scenarios.

First, assuming that tuple 6 belongs to Alice, the adversary uses Lemma 1 to derive the probability distribution for the tuple's disease value. According to Equation 9, tuple 6 has probability $c_2(\text{flu})/|QI_2| = 2/4 = 50\%$ to carry flu. Notice that, in the microdata, tuple 6 does not really belong to Alice. However, it does not matter — *the adversary may "happen to" use a wrong tuple to infer the correct sensitive value of Alice!* From tuple 6, the adversary actually has 50% probability to figure out that Alice contracted flu.

In the second scenario, the adversary assumes that tuple 7 belongs to Alice, through which (similar to tuple 6) s/he also has 50% probability to obtain the real disease of Alice. Finally, (without further knowledge) the adversary assumes that the two scenarios occur with the same likelihood $\frac{1}{2}$. Therefore, the overall breach probability should be calculated as $\frac{1}{2} \cdot 50\% + \frac{1}{2} \cdot 50\%$, where $\frac{1}{2}$ and 50% have the same semantics as in the above discussion.

In fact, Lemma 1 shows that tuple 7 (the real tuple of Alice) can be re-constructed with 50% likelihood. Namely, the breach probability at the individual level coincides with that at the tuple level. This happens because tuples 6 and 7 appear in the same QI-group. In general, as long as tuples with identical QI-values always end up in the same QI-group (as is true for "global-recoding" generalization [8]), the probabilities of the two levels are always equivalent. In this case, it suffices to discuss only the (simpler) tuple level; as a result, the individual level has not been addressed before (all the existing generalization schemes adopt global recoding).

Anatomy, however, allows high flexibility in forming QI-groups such that tuples with the same QI-values do not always belong to the same QI-group.

Therefore, we must provide a formal result regarding the individual-level breach probability.

Theorem 1 ([18]). *Given a pair of QIT and ST, an adversary can correctly infer the sensitive value of any individual with probability at most $1/l$.*

4.5 Comparison with Generalization

Intuitively, by releasing the QI-values directly, anatomy may allow a higher breach probability than generalization. Nevertheless, such probability is always bounded by $1/l$, as long as the background knowledge of an adversary is not stronger than the level allowed by the l-diversity model. Next, we will explain these observations in detail.

The derivation in Section 4.4 implicitly makes two assumptions:

• A1: the adversary has the QI-values of the target individual (i.e., Alice);
• A2: the adversary also knows that the individual is definitely involved in the microdata.

In fact, usually both assumptions are satisfied in practical privacy-attacking processes. For example, in her pioneering paper [15], Sweeney shows how to reveal the medical record of the governor of Massachusetts from the data released by the Group Insurance Commission, after obtaining the governor's QI-values from public sources. The revelation is possible because Sweeney knew in advance that the record of the governor must be present in the microdata. Otherwise, no inference could be drawn against the governor because the "privacy-leaking" record could as well just belong to a person who happens to share the same QI-values as the governor.

In general, if both Assumptions A1 and A2 are true, anatomy provides as much privacy control as generalization, that is, the privacy of a person is breached with a probability at most $1/l$. For instance, if an adversary is sure that Alice has been hospitalized before, from Alice's QI-values, s/he can assert that Alice must be described by one of tuples 5-8 in the generalized Table 3a. Then, s/he carries out the rest of her/his probabilistic conjecture (about the disease of Alice) in the same way as s/he would do after identifying Alice to be in Group 2 of the anatomized Table 4a.

Now, consider the case where A1 holds, but A2 does not. Accordingly, the overall breach probability of Alice has a Bayes form:

$$Pr_{A2}(\text{Alice}^{qi}) \cdot Pr_{breach}(\text{Alice}^{s}|A2) \qquad (10)$$

where $Pr_{A2}(\text{Alice}^{qi})$ is the chance for Alice to be involved in the microdata, and $Pr_{breach}(\text{Alice}^{s}|A2)$ the likelihood for the adversary to correctly guess the disease of Alice on condition that Alice appears in the microdata. As analyzed earlier, anatomy and generalization give the same $Pr_{breach}(\text{Alice}^{s}|A2)$, which is simply the preach probability when both A1 and A2 are valid.

Name	Age	Sex	Zipcode
Ada	61	F	54000
Alice	65	F	25000
Bella	65	F	25000
Emily	*67*	*F*	*33000*
Stephanie	70	F	30000
...	...	...	...

Table 5. The voter registration list (publicly accessible)

To compute $Pr_{A2}(\text{Alice}^{qi})$, an adversary typically needs to consult another external database [19], which relates QI-values to concrete personal identities for all the persons in the microdata, perhaps together with some other people. An example of such an external source is a voter registration list, partially demonstrated in Table 5, where the record of Emily is italicized to indicate that she is not involved in the microdata of Table 3a. In this scenario, generalization and anatomy make a difference. Specifically, judging from (the QI-values of tuples 5-8 in) the generalized Table 3a, the adversary sees that each person shown in Table 5 could be involved in the microdata with equal likelihood, and hence, calculates $Pr_{A2}(\text{Alice}^{qi})$ as 4/5. On the other hand, given the anatomized Table 4, the adversary concludes that $Pr_{A2}(\text{Alice}^{qi}) = 1$ (here s/he can figure out that Emily is definitely absent from the microdata). As a result, generalization provides a stronger overall privacy-preserving guarantee. Nevertheless, since anatomy ensures $Pr_{breach}(\text{Alice}^{s}|A2) \leq 1/l$, it also secures the same upper bound $1/l$ for Formula 10.

Although generalization has the above advantage over anatomy, *the advantage cannot be leveraged in computing the published data.* This is because the publisher cannot predict or control the external database to be utilized by an adversary, and therefore, must guard against an "accurate" external source that does not involve any person absent in the microdata. For instance, if Table 5 did not contain Emily, the voter list would produce $Pr_{A2}(\text{Alice}^{qi}) = 1$ in attacking the privacy of Alice from Table 3a (instead of 4/5 as discussed earlier). In other words, to ensure a maximum breach probability p using generalization, we must still set l to $\lceil 1/p \rceil$, i.e., same as in applying anatomy.

Finally, if neither assumption A1 nor A2 is satisfied, the breach probability of Alice becomes

$$\sum_{\forall x} Pr_{A1}(x) \cdot Pr_{A2}(x|A1) \cdot Pr_{breach}(\text{Alice}^{s}|A1, A2) \tag{11}$$

where x is a vector representing a possible set of QI-values of Alice, and $Pr_{A1}(x)$ equals the probability that x captures Alice's real QI-values, whereas Pr_{A2} and Pr_{breach} follow the same semantics as in Formula 10, but on condition that x is real. The comparison results between anatomy and generaliza-

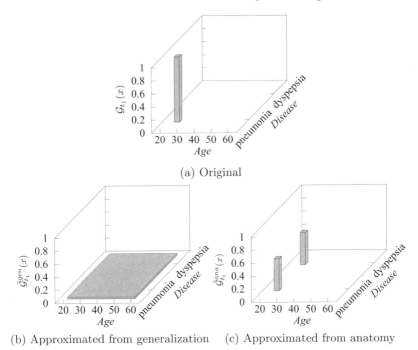

(a) Original

(b) Approximated from generalization   (c) Approximated from anatomy

Fig. 2. Original/re-constructed pdf of tuple 1 in Table 3a

tion are analogous to those discussed for the previous case where A1 is true and A2 is not.

4.6 Correlation Preservation

A good publication method should preserve both privacy and data correlation (between QI- and sensitive attributes). Using a concrete query, we have shown in Section 4.2 that anatomy allows more effective aggregate analysis than generalization. Next, we provide the underlying theoretical rationale.

Obviously, for any tuple $t \in T$, every publication method will lose certain information of t (if not, it is equivalent to disclosing t directly, contradicting the goal of privacy). On the other hand, the method should permit development of an approximate modeling of t (otherwise, the published table is useless for research). Hence, the quality of correlation preservation depends on how accurate the re-constructed modeling is.

Let us first examine the correlation between Age and $Disease$ in the microdata of Table 3a. The two attributes define a 2D space $DS_{A,D}$. Every tuple in the table can be mapped to a point in $DS_{A,D}$. For example, tuple 1, denoted as t_1, corresponds to point $(t_1[A], t_1[D])$, where $t_1[A]$ is the age 23 of t_1, and $t_1[D]$ its disease 'pneumonia'.

We can model t_1 using a probability density function (pdf) $\mathcal{G}_{t_1} : DS_{A,D} \rightarrow [0, 1]$. Specifically:

$$\mathcal{G}_{t_1}(x) = \begin{cases} 1 \text{ if } x = (t_1[A], t_1[D]) \\ 0 \text{ otherwise} \end{cases} \tag{12}$$

where x is a 2D random variable in $DS_{A,D}$. Figure 2a demonstrates the pdf.

Assume that a researcher wants to re-construct an approximate pdf $\tilde{\mathcal{G}}_{t_1}^{gen}$ of t_1 from the generalized Table 3b. From her/his perspective, $t_1[A]$ can be any value in the interval $[21, 60]$ with equality probability $1/40$, but $t_1[D]$ must be pneumonia. Hence,

$$\tilde{\mathcal{G}}_{t_1}^{gen}(x) = \begin{cases} 1/40 \text{ if } x[A] \in [21, 60] \text{ and} \\ \quad\quad x[D] =\text{pneumonia} \\ 0 \quad\quad \text{otherwise} \end{cases} \tag{13}$$

which is illustrated in Figure 2b.

Instead, suppose that the researcher re-constructs a pdf $\tilde{\mathcal{G}}_{t_1}^{ana}$ from the QIT and ST in Tables 4a and 4b. This time, s/he knows that $t_1[A]$ must be 23 (since age is published directly), but $t_1[D]$ can be pneumonia or dyspepsia with 50% probability (the ST shows that half of the tuples in QI-group 1 are associated with these two diseases, respectively). Therefore,

$$\tilde{\mathcal{G}}_{t_1}^{ana}(x) = \begin{cases} 1/2 \text{ if } x = (23, \text{ pneumonia}) \text{ or} \\ \quad\quad x = (23, \text{ dyspepsia}) \\ 0 \quad\quad \text{otherwise} \end{cases} \tag{14}$$

as shown in Figure 2c. Obviously, the pdf approximated from the anatomized tables is more accurate than that (Figure 2b) from the generalized table.

Towards a more rigorous comparison, given an approximate pdf $\tilde{\mathcal{G}}_{t_1}$ (Equation 13 or 14), a natural way of quantifying its approximation quality is to calculate its "L_2 distance" from the actual pdf $\mathcal{G}_{t_1}$ (Equation 12):

$$\sum_{x \in DS_{A,D}} \left(\tilde{\mathcal{G}}_{t_1}(x) - \mathcal{G}_{t_1}(x) \right)^2. \tag{15}$$

The distance of $\tilde{\mathcal{G}}_{t_1}^{ana}$ is 0.5, indeed significantly lower than the distance 22.5 of $\tilde{\mathcal{G}}_{t_1}^{gen}$. Although we focused on t_1, in the same way, it is easy to verify that the anatomized tables permit better re-construction of the pdfs of all tuples in Table 3a.

5 Summary

In this chapter, we studied two anonymization frameworks for privacy preserving data publication: generalization and anatomy. Generally speaking, anatomy publishes anonymized tables with higher utility (e.g., allowing more accurate aggregate analysis), by releasing the QI-values directly. However, there are applications where precise publication of QI-values is inappropriate. For instance, if the *presence* of an individual in the microdata is also considered sensitive, then anatomy should not be deployed since, as explained in Section 4.5, it may allow an adversary to assert that an individual definitely exists in the microdata (even though the adversary is not able to derive the individual's sensitive information confidently). In that case, generalization should be applied instead.

We also reviewed two most popular anonymization principles: k-anonymity and l-diversity. Due to its pioneering role in the literature, k-anonymity has several serious shortcomings, and does not provide good privacy guarantees. l-diversity offers much stronger protection, as mathematically elaborated in Section 3. Nevertheless, l-diversity also has some weaknesses, which have motivated the development of several other generalization principles. For example, a weakness of l-diversity is that it is not suitable for handling numeric sensitive attributes, as explained in [10], which alleviates the problem with an alternative principle called *t-closeness*. Another weakness of l-diversity is that it does not take into account the discrepancies of the privacy requirements from various data owners. A personalized approach [19] has been proposed to address this issue.

References

1. C. C. Aggarwal. On k-anonymity and the curse of dimensionality. In *Proc. of Very Large Data Bases (VLDB)*, pages 901–909, 2005.
2. G. Aggarwal, T. Feder, K. Kenthapadi, R. Motwani, R. Panigrahy, D. Thomas, and A. Zhu. Anonymizing tables. In *Proc. of International Conference on Database Theory (ICDT)*, pages 246–258, 2005.
3. R. Bayardo and R. Agrawal. Data privacy through optimal k-anonymization. In *Proc. of International Conference on Data Engineering (ICDE)*, pages 217–228, 2005.
4. V. Ciriani, D. C. di Vimercati, S. Foresti, and P. Samarati. *k-anonymity*. Springer, 2006.
5. Y. Du, T. Xia, Y. Tao, D. Zhang, and F. Zhu. On multidimensional k-anonymity with local recoding generalization. In *Proc. of International Conference on Data Engineering (ICDE)*, 2007.
6. B. C. M. Fung, K. Wang, and P. S. Yu. Top-down specialization for information and privacy preservation. In *Proc. of International Conference on Data Engineering (ICDE)*, pages 205–216, 2005.
7. V. Iyengar. Transforming data to satisfy privacy constraints. In *Proc. of ACM Knowledge Discovery and Data Mining (SIGKDD)*, pages 279–288, 2002.
8. K. LeFevre, D. J. DeWitt, and R. Ramakrishnan. Incognito: Efficient full-domain k-anonymity. In *Proc. of ACM Management of Data (SIGMOD)*, pages 49–60, 2005.

9. K. Lefevre, D. J. DeWitt, and R. Ramakrishnan. Mondrian multidimensional k-anonymity. In *Proc. of International Conference on Data Engineering (ICDE)*, 2006.

10. N. Li and T. Li. t-closeness: Privacy beyond k-anonymity and l-diversity. In *Proc. of International Conference on Data Engineering (ICDE)*, 2007.

11. A. Machanavajjhala, J. Gehrke, and D. Kifer. l-diversity: Privacy beyond k-anonymity. In *Proc. of International Conference on Data Engineering (ICDE)*, 2006.

12. A. Meyerson and R. Williams. On the complexity of optimal k-anonymity. In *Proc. of ACM Symposium on Principles of Database Systems (PODS)*, pages 223–228, 2004.

13. P. Samarati. Protecting respondents' identities in microdata release. *IEEE Transactions on Knowledge and Data Engineering (TKDE)*, 13(6):1010–1027, 2001.

14. P. Samarati and L. Sweeney. Generalizing data to provide anonymity when disclosing information. In *Proc. of ACM Symposium on Principles of Database Systems (PODS)*, page 188, 1998.

15. L. Sweeney. k-anonymity: a model for protecting privacy. *International Journal on Uncertainty, Fuzziness, and Knowlege-Based Systems*, 10(5):557–570, 2002.

16. N. Thaper, S. Guha, P. Indyk, and N. Koudas. Dynamic multidimensional histograms. In *Proc. of ACM Management of Data (SIGMOD)*, pages 428–439, 2002.

17. K. Wang, P. S. Yu, and S. Chakraborty. Bottom-up generalization: A data mining solution to privacy protection. In *Proc. of International Conference on Management of Data (ICDM)*, pages 249–256, 2004.

18. X. Xiao and Y. Tao. Anatomy: Simple and effective privacy preservation. In *Proc. of Very Large Data Bases (VLDB)*, pages 139–150, 2006.

19. X. Xiao and Y. Tao. Personalized privacy preservation. In *Proc. of ACM Management of Data (SIGMOD)*, pages 229–240, 2006.

21

Privacy Protection through Anonymity in Location-based Services[*]

Claudio Bettini[1], Sergio Mascetti[1], and X. Sean Wang[2]

[1] DICo, University of Milan, Italy
bettini@dico.unimi.it, mascetti@dico.unimi.it
[2] Department of Computer Science, University of Vermont, VT
xywang@emba.uvm.edu

Summary. The adoption of location-based services (LBS) brings new privacy threats to users. The user location information revealed in LBS requests may be used by attackers to associate sensitive information of the user with her identity. This contribution focuses on privacy protection through anonymity, i.e., keeping individual users indistinguishable in a large group of people that may have issued the same request. The contribution identifies different privacy threats to LBS users, discusses techniques for protecting user privacy under different threats, and gives a performance evaluation of the mentioned protection methods.

1 Introduction

Location-based services (LBS) have recently attracted much interest from both industry and research. Currently, the most popular commercial service is probably car navigation, but many other services are being offered and more are being experimented, as less expensive location aware devices are reaching the market. Consciously or unconsciously, many users are ready to give up one more piece of their private information in order to access the new services. Many other users, however, are concerned with releasing their exact location as part of the service request or with releasing the information of having used a particular service. To safeguard user privacy while rendering useful services is a critical issue on the growth path of the emerging LBS.

An obvious defense against privacy threats is to eliminate from the request any data that can directly reveal the issuer's identity, possibly using a pseudonym whenever this is required (e.g., for billing through a third party).

Unfortunately, simply dropping the issuer's personal identification data may not be sufficient to anonymize the request. For example, the location and time information in the request may be used, with the help of external

---

[*] The work was partially supported by the Italian MIUR InterLink project N.II04C0EC1D, and the US NSF grants IIS-0430402 & IIS-0430165.

knowledge, to restrict the possible user to a small group issuers. This problem is well-known for the release of data in databases tables [17]. In that case, the problem is to protect the association between the identity of an individual and a tuple containing her sensitive data; the attributes whose values could possibly be used to restrict the candidate identities for a given tuple are called *quasi-identifiers* [7, 5].

This contribution contains a classification of different privacy threats involved in LBS, and a discussion of different protection techniques based on user anonymity. More specifically, in Section 2, we first provide a general overview of the general LBS privacy problem, and a classification of different privacy threats. We then formalize the anonymity approach for privacy protection in Section 3, and detail a number of protection techniques for different threats in Section 4, also identifying some interesting research directions. In Section 5, we report an experimental evaluation of the presented techniques, and finally conclude with a brief summary and possible future works in Section 6.

2 Privacy threats with LBS

In general, there is a privacy threat when an attacker is able to associate the identity of a user to information that the user considers private. In the case of LBS, this *sensitive association* can be possibly derived from requests issued to service providers. More precisely, the identity and the private information of a single user can be derived from requests issued by a group of users. Figure 1 shows a graphical representation of this general view of privacy threats in LBS.

In order to infer the sensitive association, the attacker can exploit some *external knowledge* that is not transmitted with the requests. This information can be used, for example, to discover the identity of the issuer even if this information is not explicitly provided in the request or to derive private information associated with a particular location.

The assumption about the external knowledge that is available to the attacker strongly affects the defense techniques used to protect user's privacy. More generally, a privacy preserving technique can be provided once the *context assumption* is fixed. This assumption includes the external knowledge that is possibly available to the attacker and his reasoning abilities.

2.1 The reference scenario

Figure 2 shows our reference scenario that involves three entities:

- The **User** invokes or subscribes to location-based remote services that are going to be provided to her mobile device.

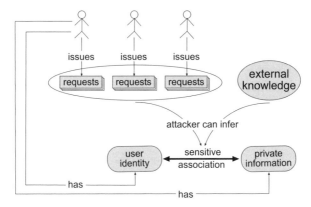

Fig. 1. General privacy threat in LBS

- The **Location-aware Trusted Server (LTS)** stores precise location data of all its users, using data directly provided by users' devices and/or acquired from the infrastructure. It also has the ability to efficiently perform spatio-temporal queries to determine, for example, which or how many users are in a certain region.
- The **Service Provider (SP)** fulfills user requests and communicates with the user through the LTS. Both pull and push communication service models are possible; We concentrate on the former but the framework we present can be easily extended to deal with the latter too.

In our model each request r is processed by the LTS into a request r' with the same logical components but appropriately generalized. Under the condition that user's privacy is guaranteed, this generalization should be as little as possible to ensure the best service quality for the user. Requests, once forwarded by the LTS, may be acquired by potential attackers in different ways: they may be stolen from SP storage, voluntarily published by the trusted parties, or may be acquired by eavesdropping on the communication lines. On the contrary, the communication between the user and the LTS is considered as trusted, and the data stored at the LTS is not considered accessible by the attacker.

Most of the approaches proposed in the literature [8, 9, 11, 16] to protect LBS privacy consider scenarios that can be easily mapped to the one depicted in Figure 2. Actually, scenarios where no location-aware intermediate entity is present have also been considered. For example, in [12] a direct communication between the user and the service provider is assumed, and the defense function is computed on the client system. Clearly in this model it is not possible to assume that the client has any awareness of the exact location of other clients; hence the generalization techniques proposed in this and in other papers would not be applicable. We believe that the current business models of mobile operators naturally support the existence and functionality of an entity like the LTS. Indeed, mobile users implicitly trust the operator infrastructure even if they know that very accurate information about their location and service requests is stored. Moreover, in most countries each operator has a very large number of customers, and hence a collection of data that may be more than sufficient to implement some of the defense techniques we are proposing.

Fig. 2. A general reference scenario

The format of a request is represented by the following triple:

$$\langle IdData, STData, SSData \rangle$$

- **IdData** contains the exact user identity in the original request; when the request is generalized it is either empty or it contains a pseudo-id.
- **STData** contains spatio-temporal information about the location of the user performing the requests, and the time the request was issued. For the sake of simplicity, we assume that this information is a point in 3-dimensional space (with time being the third dimension) for the original request, and a region in the same space for the generalized request.
- **SSData** contains parameters characterizing the required service and service provider.

2.2 Static case

Most of the approaches presented so far in the literature [9, 16, 11, 3] have proposed techniques to ensure a user's privacy in the case in which the attacker can acquire a single request issued by that user. More specifically, these approaches assume that:

- the attacker is not able to *link* a set of requests i.e., to understand that the requests have been issued by the same (anonymous) user;
- the attacker is not able to derive private information about the issuer of a request from the requests issued by other users.

In general, we can distinguish privacy threats according to two orthogonal dimensions: a) threats in *static* versus *dynamic* cases, b) threats involving requests from a single user (*single-issuer* case) versus threats involving requests from different users (*multiple-issuer* case).

Figure 3 shows a graphical representation of the privacy threat in the static, single-issuer case. In this case, in order to prevent the disclosure of the sensible association, it is sufficient to prevent the attacker from inferring either user's identity or user's sensitive information. The ongoing research in this field is tackling these two subproblems: prevent the attacker from inferring the user's identity and prevent the attacker from inferring the user's private information. Despite the solution of one of the two subproblems is sufficient to guarantee user's privacy, we argue that the solution of both subproblems could enhance better techniques for privacy protection. Indeed, the obfuscation of requests parameters usually involved in privacy protection techniques implies a degradation of the quality of service. A location based privacy preserving system that implements solutions for both the subproblems can combine them in order to to optimize quality of service while preserving privacy.

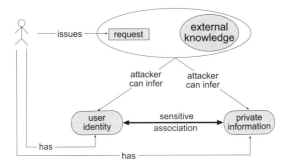

Fig. 3. The static, single-issuer case

Example 1 shows that, in the multiple-issuer case, an attacker can infer the sensitive association for a user even if the identity of that user is not revealed to the attacker.

Example 1. Suppose a user u issues a request generalized into r' by the LTS. Assume that, considering r', an attacker can only understand that the issuer of r' is one of the users in the set S of potential issuers. However, if all of the users in S issue requests from which the attacker can infer the same sensitive information inferred from r', then the attacker can associate that sensitive information to u.

In the area of privacy in databases, this kind of attack is known as *homogeneity attack* [14]. The problem in the area of LBS is depicted in Figure 4. Note that, differently from the general case (Figure 1), in the static, multiple-issuer case, a single request for each user is considered.

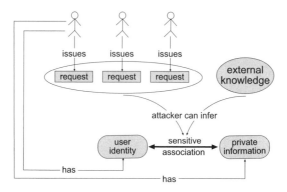

Fig. 4. The static, multiple-issuer case

2.3 The dynamic case

In contrast with the static case, in the dynamic case it is assumed that the attacker is able to recognize that a set of requests has been issued by the same user. Researchers [1, 10] have considered such a possibility. We call this *linking*. Several techniques exist to *link* different requests to the same user, with the most trivial ones being the observation of the same identity or pseudo-id in the requests. We call *request trace* a set of requests that the attacker can correctly associate to a single user.

Figure 5 shows a graphical representation of the dynamic case. The corresponding techniques to preserve privacy are facing two problems. First, preventing the attacker from linking the requests (called *linking problem*); Indeed, the longer is a trace, the higher the probability of the issuer to loose her privacy. Second, preventing the attacker from understanding the sensitive association from a request trace.

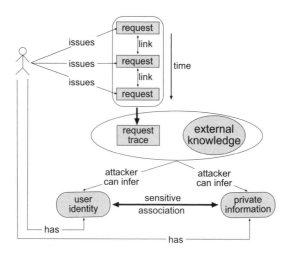

Fig. 5. The dynamic case

3 Privacy protection through anonymity

As we illustrated in Section 2, a privacy threat occurs when an attacker is able to obtain a user's sensitive association. When a LBS requires each request to contain explicit full identification of the user, the sensitive association can only be protected by avoiding the explicit and implicit release of the second component of the association: *private information*. However, most LBS either do not require full identification or they admit the use of pseudonyms for billing and/or personalization. In these cases, preserving the anonymity of the issuer is a successful technique to avoid releasing a sensitive association, while still providing precise service invocation parameters.

Note that the anonymity problem in LBS has at least two distinguishing aspects with respect to the analogous problem in the release of data from databases [17]. First, the fact that each request contains data about the location of the user at the time of request, introduces spatio-temporal data as a new kind of potential *quasi-identifier*, and it is well known that the effective management of this kind of data requires specific techniques. Second, anonymity in databases has been studied considering a one-time publication of a given set of records, while the problem in LBS is inherently dynamic: the position of users is continuously changing and this has to be taken into account each time a request has to be anonymized. Moreover, inferencing based on previously anonymized requests can be used by the attacker.

Anonymity as a LBS privacy protection technique has been only recently investigated. Several research contributions (among which [9, 16, 11, 3]) have proposed techniques that aim at enforcing the issuer of a request to be *anonymous*, in the sense that an attacker, that can acquire the requests, must not be able to associate each request to its issuer with likelihood greater than a threshold value. Unfortunately, a clear understanding of which techniques can be proved to be *safe* under which conditions is still missing, mostly because of the lack of an underlying formal model.

3.1 A formal model for anonymity in LBS

In this section we provide a formal model to define attack and defense techniques. The set R contains all the possible *original* requests issued by the users to the LTS and all the possible *generalized* requests that the LTS would forward to the SP. We also indicate with I the set of all users' identities and with $issuer(r)$ the identity of the user that issued the request r. A *generalization* function is used by the LTS to transform an original request into a generalized one to be forwarded to the SP.

Definition 1. *Given a set R of requests, we say that $g : R \rightarrow R$ is a* generalization function.

The purpose of a generalization function is to render requests *safe* from privacy threats. We claim that the safety of a generalization function can only be formally evaluated if it is clearly identified which part of a request can act as a so-called *quasi-identifier*. A quasi-identifier [17] is data that can be used by an attacker to identify the actual issuer of the request, through some external knowledge that we call *context* and that is assumed to be possibly reachable by the attacker. Clearly, what is a quasi-identifier in requests changes depending on the applicative context C.

A typical context assumed in almost all LBS privacy research, exemplified by [9, 8], is given in Example 2 below.

Example 2. Consider a location based yellow pages service and the following context C_{st}, in which the attacker can obtain at most the following knowledge:

1. the location of each user;
2. the fact that the *STData* field of the requests forwarded by the LTS always contains the location of the issuer of the original request.

Suppose that Alice issues a request asking for the closest shop where she can find some specialty items. Assume LTS wants to protect Alice's privacy by not revealing that the request issuer is Alice. The LTS now receives the request and deletes the information that could directly lead to Alice's identity (her name, for example). Moreover, the exact location of Alice is generalized into an area. Then, the resulting generalized request r' is forwarded to the SP.

If an attacker obtains r', he first uses the location knowledge (assumption 1) to restrict the set of possible issuers to the users whose location is in the region specified in r'. Suppose this set has only one person, who must be Alice due to assumption 2. In this case, the LTS has failed to provide privacy under this context. The LTS obviously has to enlarge the area a bit further to obtain r'' so the area of r'' covers the locations of three users: Alice, Bob and Carl. In this case, r'' provides 3-anonymity. Further enlarging the area in the requests generally provides k-anonymity with a greater k value.

Context C_{st} may seem too excessive because it assumes that an attacker knows the location of all users. However, if an attacker can possibly know the location of one user (not too outrageous an assumption), we are forced to assume the worst case, namely he knows the location of all users. This assumption may be relaxed by saying that the attacker can only know the locations of some users in some particular areas. But this is outside the scope of this paper.

Given a context C, the attacker aims to infer, from a generalized request, the identity of the user that issued it. We model a specific attack as the likelihood of associating a specific identity to a generalized request.

Definition 2. *An* attack *exploiting context C is a function* $Att_C : R \times I \to \mathbb{R}^+$.

A special case of Definition 2 is the one in which the attacker can identify, from the generalized request, a set of candidate issuers, each one having the same probability of being the real issuer. This is the situation described in Example 2, in which the three users Alice, Bob, and Carl are the candidate issuers identified from the generalized request r''. In this case, for each generalized request r', we call *anonymity set in context C*, denoted $Anon_C(r')$, the set of candidate issuers of r' obtained exploiting context C.

Once the anonymity set is specified, it is possible to derive the corresponding *uniform attack*:

Definition 3. *Given a context C and the complete function $Anon_C : R \to 2^I$, we say that $UAtt_C$ is the* uniform attack based on anonymity set $Anon_C$ *if, for each generalized request $r' \in R$ and for each $i \in I$:*

$$UAtt_C(r',i) = \begin{cases} 0 & \text{if } i \notin Anon_C(r') \\ \frac{1}{|Anon_C(r')|} & \text{otherwise} \end{cases}$$

The above definition formalizes the idea that each user in the candidate set $Anon_C(r')$ has the same probability to be the actual issuer. The question is when such an attack actually breaches the privacy of the issuer. We formally define this in Definition 4.

The idea of Definition 4 is that a generalized request is safe if the (normalization of the) attack associates it to the correct issuer with a likelihood smaller than a threshold value h. Formally,

Definition 4. *Let Att_C be an attack, h a value in $[0,1)$ and r' a generalized request. Moreover, let $\overline{Att}$ be the function*

$$\overline{Att}_C(r',i) = \begin{cases} \frac{1}{|I|} & \text{if } \forall i' \in I : Att_C(r',i') = 0 \\ \frac{Att_C(r',i)}{\sum_{i' \in I} Att_C(r',i')} & \text{otherwise} \end{cases}$$

We say that r' is a safe request against Att_C *with threshold h if, given $i = issuer(r')$, $\overline{Att}_C(r',i) \le h$.*

If a request is not safe, we say that it is unsafe.

For the uniform attack, the above safety definition is equivalent to asking if $UAtt_C(r',i) \le h$. Therefore, if $h = 1/3$, then the request r'' in Example 2 is safe for Alice, while request r' in the same example is not.

The task of the LTS is to avoid to forward to a SP a unsafe request. We call *defense function* a generalization function that generates only requests that are safe against a given attack.

Definition 5. *Let Att_C be an attack and h a value in $[0,1)$. A generalization function $g : R \to R$ is a* defense function against Att_C *with threshold h if for each original request $r \in R$ such that $g(r)$ is defined, $g(r)$ is a safe request against Att_C with threshold h.*

For the context C_{st} in Example 2, a generalization function is a defense function against $UAtt_{C_{st}}$ with threshold $1/3$ if the generalized request r' produced by the generalization function always has its area containing at least three users, including the actually issuer. A non-trivial question is to efficiently generalize a given request so that the generalized request is safe, while keeping the area in the request as small as possible. Interesting algorithms have appeared in the literature, e.g., [9, 8, 16].

Another interesting context consists of, in addition to the assumptions in Example 2, the assumption that the attacker knows the generalization function itself [11, 3]. We call it the "inversion assumption":

inver. The attacker knows the generalization algorithm.

The context with assumptions 1, 2 (in Example 2) and *inver* is denoted by C_{ist}.

The inversion assumption brings in an interesting twist on defense functions against C_{ist} in comparison to against C_{st}. Indeed, a typical defense against C_{st} for a request r is to start with the area in r and systematically expand this area until it includes $k - 1$ other users. This approach may not be safe against C_{ist} [11]. This is because the attacker can use the knowledge of the algorithm to rule out candidate issuers from the anonymity set whose location would have been generalized differently by the algorithm.

An intuitive defense against attack $UAtt_{C_{ist}}$ is to divide the users into regions without consulting the location of the given request r. Once each region contains at least k users, then pick up the region that contains r as its generalized area. It can be shown that the knowledge of this defense function is useless to an attacker. Kalnis et al. [11] and Bettini et al. [3] studied such defenses.

4 Techniques to enforce anonymity

In this section we present the main techniques proposed so far to enforce anonymity for LBS privacy preservation. We first address in detail techniques that consider the static single-issuer case, the only one extensively studied up to now, while we discuss open issues related to techniques for other cases in Subsection 4.3.

The presentation of the anonymization algorithms proposed for the static single-issuer case distinguishes C_I-safe from C_I-unsafe algorithms, depending on the fact that the knowledge of the specific generalization algorithm can be obtained by a potential attacker or not, respectively. More formally, we call C_I-safe the algorithms that achieve anonymity even in the case the current context includes the *inver* assumption, and C_I-unsafe those that consider a context without this assumption.

4.1 C_I-unsafe algorithms

The first generalization algorithm that appeared in the literature was named *IntervalCloaking* [9]. The idea of the algorithm is to iteratively divide the total region monitored by the LTS. At each iteration the current area q_{prev} is partitioned into quadrants of equal size. If less than k users are located in the quadrant q where the issuer of the request is located, then q_{prev} is returned. Otherwise, iteration continues considering q as the next area. In order to evaluate the time complexity of the algorithm it is necessary to make some assumptions about the data structures. In our implementation of the algorithm, we used a data structure consisting of a quadTree in which each leaf has a pointer to a user, and each internal node n stores the number of users "contained" in n i.e., the number of users stored in the subtree that has n as root. The generalization algorithm traverses the quadTree from the root to the first internal node that contains at least k users. Each iteration is constant time and the number of iterations is bounded by the height of the quadTree. In the worst case, the height of the tree is linear in the cardinality of the set I of users. However, if users are uniformly distributed (as in the case of the experimental results that we present in Section 5) the height of the tree is logarithmic in the number of users hence the algorithm has a worst-case time complexity of $O(\log(|I|))$.

Mokbel et al. [16] propose *Casper*, a framework for privacy protection that includes a generalization algorithm. In this paper we consider the "basic" data structure[3] used by Casper i.e., a balanced quadTree in which each node has a pointer to its parent, and users are stored in leaf nodes only. Moreover, the data structure consists of a table in which each user i is associated with the leaf node that contains i. The generalization algorithm starts from the leaf node that contains the issuer of the request, and iteratively traverses the tree towards the root until an area that contains at least k users is found. At each iteration, the algorithm considers the union of the area covered by the current node n and the horizontally (vertically, resp.) contiguous area covered by its sibling node. If only one of these two joined areas contains more than k users, that area is returned; if both of them contain more than k users, the one containing the minimum number is returned; otherwise, the algorithm proceeds with the next iteration. Similarly to *IntervalCloaking*, the worst case time complexity of *Casper* is linear in the height of the quadTree. However, in this case, this height is bounded by the logarithm of the number of leaf nodes if users are uniformly distributed, and it is at most linear in the same number, otherwise.

Conceptually, one of the simplest ways to generalize a request is to compute the k Nearest Neighbor query among the users and return the MBR of the result. We call *nnALG* this generalization algorithm. The problem of this approach is that in most cases the issuer of the request is located close to the center of the resulting area; hence, he can be easily discovered by the attacker [11]. To partially overcome this problem, Kalnis et al. [11] propose the *nnASR* generalization algorithm that picks a random user i in the set of

---

[3] For the purpose of this paper, there is no need to consider the "adaptive" data structure proposed in the paper.

the $k-1$ users that are the closest to the issuer, and returns the MBR of the set containing i, the issuer, and the $k-1$ users closest to i. In our implementation of the $nnASR$ algorithm we used a kd-Tree to store users' locations, making possible to compute k Nearest Neighbor queries in logarithmic expected time with respect to the number of users.

4.2 C_I-safe algorithms

To the best of our knowledge, the first C_I-safe generalization algorithm was proposed by Kalnis et al. [11], and it was called $hilbASR$. The idea of $hilbASR$ is to exploit the Hilbert space filling curve to define a total order among users' locations. A data structure is then used to store users in the order defined through the Hilbert space filling curve. Intuitively, the $hilbASR$ generalization algorithm partitions the data structure into blocks of k users: the first block from the user in position 0 to the user in position $k-1$ and so on (note that the last block can contain up to $2 \cdot k - 1$ users). The algorithm then returns the MBR computed considering the position of the users that are in the same block as the issuer. The worst case time complexity of $hilbASR$ is $O(log(|I|))$.

A different C_I-safe algorithm was proposed by Mascetti et al [15] and was called $dichotomicArea$. Starting from the total area monitored by the LTS, the $dichotomicArea$ algorithm (Algorithm 1) iteratively partitions the area into two adjacent rectangles of equal size. The partitioning is done along the horizontal and vertical axis, altenatively in each iteration. The input of the algorithm consists of the degree of anonymity k and the issuer i. The output is **null** if less than k users are located in the total area monitored by the LTS, otherwise the algorithm returns an area in which at least k users are located. The algorithm terminates when at least 1 and at most $k-1$ users are located in any of the two sub-areas. Algorithm $dichotomicArea$ is an instance of a class of algorithms presented in [3]; in that paper it is proved that any generalization algorithm that iteratively partitions the set of users, and that terminates when any block contains less then k users, is a C_I-safe algorithm. At each iteration, $dichotomicArea$ partitions the set of users according to their location with respect to the sub-areas. If no user is located in a sub-area, then the set of users is not partitioned and iteration continues. On the contrary, if one of the sub-areas contains more than one user but less than k, execution terminates. The data structure that we used in the implementation of the algorithm is similar to the one we used for the implementation of $IntervalCloaking$. The only difference is that each internal node has two children instead of four. Consequently, the time complexity of the algorithm is the same as the one for $IntervalCloaking$.

A second generalization algorithm belonging to the class presented in [3] is called $dichotomicPoints$. The idea is to use a different partitioning function, named $partitionPoints$. The users are totally ordered according to their locations considering first one axis, then the other, and if necessary even the

Algorithm 1 dichotomicArea

1: $orient := HOR$
2: $area :=$ the total area
3: **if** $(|usersIn(area)| < k)$ **then return null;**
4: **while true do**
5:   $subAreas := partitionArea(area, orient)$
6:   **if** $\exists a \in subAreas$ s.t. $0 < |usersIn(a)| < k$ **then**
7:     **return** $area$
8:   **else**
9:     $area := a_j \in subAreas$ s.t. $i \in usersIn(a_j)$
10:     **if** $orient = HOR$ **then** $orient := VER$
11:     **else** $orient := HOR$
12:   **end if**
13: **end while**

user identifier; Then, considering the user u in the middle[4], it partitions the users into two blocks: the ones before u, and the remaining ones. In order to choose the first axis used to order the users, *dichotomicPoints* computes, for each axis, the difference between the maximum and minimum value of users's locations projected on that axis and then choose the one having the higher difference[5].

Similarly to *dichotomicArea*, computation terminates when any of the two blocks of the partition contain less than k users; Then it returns the MBR of all the users' locations in those two blocks. This algorithm has some similarities with the *Anonymize* algorithm presented in [13] despite they have been independently designed. The data structure used in the implementation of *dichotomicPoints* consists of two arrays, $order_x$ and $order_y$, containing the users ordered according to the horizontal and vertical axis, respectively. At each iteration, the user locations that are not in the same block as the issuer are removed from the two arrays. So, at each iteration it is necessary to find the user location in the middle of the correct array, to count how many users will be in each block and to remove the users that are not in the same block as the issuer. The first two operations can be performed in constant time, while the last one requires a time linear in the size of the two arrays. Since the number of iterations is logarithmic in the number of users and each iteration requires time linear in the number of the users, the worst case time complexity of the algorithm is $O(|I| \cdot \log(|I|))$.

---

[4] When there is an even number r of users, user u is the one in position r/2 +1.
[5] A slightly different version of *dichotomicPoints* was presented in [15]; The only difference is the way the first axis used to order users is chosen.

4.3 Open problems

The techniques presented in Section 3 can guarantee anonymity in the static, single-issuer case. In this section we discuss three relevant open problems that are mostly related to the extension of these techniques to different cases.

Homogeneity attack.

Example 1 in Section 2 shows that, in the multiple-issuer case, a homogeneity attack is possible in LBS, and hence anonymity can be insufficient to guarantee user privacy. A technical solution proposed to contrast the homogeneity attack in the area of DB is called *l-diversity* [14]. Intuitively, a set of tuples in a DB table is *l*-diverse if the tuples contain at least *l* different values of private information.

A preliminary investigation on the extension of the *l*-diversity concept in the area of LBS has appeared [2]. Intuitively, the *l*-diversity property holds for a generalized request r' if the attacker can infer at least l different values of private information from the requests issued by the users in the anonymity set of r'. Further research is needed, for example, to formally characterize a) how the parameters k and l affect the probability distribution in the anonymity set, b) under which conditions close values in private information can really be considered different (e.g., location areas), and c) how the homogeneity attack changes in the dynamic case.

Personalization of the degree of anonymity.

In our discussion we never considered issues related to the personalization of defense parameters, as for example, the degree of anonymity k to be enforced by the LTS. Some approaches (e.g. [16]) actually explicitly allow different users to specify different values of k. A natural question is if the proposed techniques can be applied and can be considered safe even in this case. Once again, to answer this question it is essential to consider which knowledge an attacker may obtain. The degree of anonymity k desired by each user at the time of a request is not assumed to be known by the attacker in contexts C_{st} and C_{ist}, hence algorithms that are safe for these contexts remain safe even when the LTS admits different values of k.

However, it may be reasonable to consider contexts in which the attacker may obtain information about k. In the multiple-issuer case, the attacker may use, for example, data mining techniques. Example 3 shows that, in these contexts, C_I-safe algorithms need to be extended in order to provide an effective defense.

Example 3. User i_1 issues a request r asking the LTS a degree of anonymity $k = 2$. Using a C_I-safe algorithm, the LTS generalizes r to the request r' that has a spatio-temporal region containing only users i_1 and i_2. Since the generalization algorithm is C_I-safe, if r were issued by i_2 with $k = 2$, then it would be generalized to r'. However, if the attacker knows that i_2 always issues requests with $k \geq 3$, then he knows that if the issuer of r were i_2, the request would have been generalized to a request r'' different from r', because the spatio-temporal region of r'' should include at least 3 users. Hence the attacker would identify i_1 as the issuer of r'.

A straightforward solution to extend C_I-safe algorithms to these cases is the following: when a request r needs to be generalized with degree of anonymity k, the anonymity set is computed considering only the users that can possibly issue a request requiring that degree of anonymity. Clearly, the solution is viable only if a limited set of k values is available and a large number of users using each value exists. If this is not the case, more sophisticated strategies need to be devised to obtain C_I-safe generalization algorithms, and, to our knowledge, this is still an open research issue.

Anonymity in the dynamic case

The techniques presented in Section 3 to provide anonymity in the static, single-issuer case do not guarantee user's privacy in the dynamic, single-issuer case. Example 4 shows that the generalization of each request in a trace, using a C_I-safe algorithm, is not sufficient to guarantee user's anonymity.

Example 4. User i_1 issues a request r with $k = 3$. The LTS uses a C_I-safe algorithm to generalize r into a request r' whose spatio-temporal region includes only users i_1, i_2 and i_3. Afterwards, i_1 issues a new request r_1 with $k = 3$. The LTS generalizes it into a request r_1' whose spatio-temporal region includes only users i_1, i_4 and i_5. Suppose the attacker is able to link requests r' and r_1', i.e. he is able to understand that the two requests have been issued by the same user. The attacker can observe that neither i_2 nor i_3 can be the issuer of r_1', because they are not in the spatio-temporal region of r_1'; Consequently, they cannot be the issuers of r' either. Analogously, considering the spatio-temporal region in r', he can derive that i_4 and i_5 cannot be the issuers of the two request. Therefore, the attacker can identify i_1 as the issuer of r' and r_1'.

The problem of anonymity in the dynamic, single-issuer case has been investigated in [4]. The notion of k-anonymity along a trace of requests is called *historical k-anonymity*. Some preliminary definitions are necessary to formally define it. It is reasonable to assume that the LTS not only stores in its database the set of requests issued by each user, but also stores for each user the sequence of her location updates. This sequence is called *Personal History of Locations* (PHL). More formally, the PHL of user u is a sequence of 3D points $(\langle x_1, y_1, t_1 \rangle, \ldots, \langle x_m, y_m, t_m \rangle)$, where $\langle x_i, y_i \rangle$, for $i = 1, \ldots, m$, represents the position of u (in two-dimensional space) at the time instant t_i.

A PHL $(\langle x_1, y_1, t_1 \rangle, \ldots, \langle x_m, y_m, t_m \rangle)$ is defined to be *LT-consistent* with a set of requests $r_1, \ldots, r_n$ issued to a SP if for each request r_i there exists an element $\langle x_j, y_j, t_j \rangle$ in the PHL such that the area of r_i contains the location identified by the point x_j, y_j and the time interval of r_i contains the instant t_j.

Then, given the set $\bar{R}$ of all requests issued to a certain SP, a subset of requests $\bar{R}' = \{r_1, \ldots, r_m\}$ issued by the same user u is said to satisfy *Historical k-Anonymity* if there exist $k-1$ PHLs $P_1, \ldots, P_{k-1}$ for $k-1$ users different from u, such that each P_j, $j = 1, \ldots, k-1$, is LT-consistent with $\bar{R}'$.

The open problem in this case is how to generalize each request in order to obtain traces that are historical k-anonymous. One problem is that the LTS has to generalize each request when it is issued, without having the knowledge of the future users' locations nor the future requests that are to be issued. A separate problem is to avoid long traces; indeed, the longer is a trace, the more each request needs to be generalized in order to guarantee historical k-anonymity.

5 Experimental results

This section presents an extensive experimental evaluation of the algorithms in Section 4. Tests were performed using artificial data with uniform as well as non-uniform distribution of users in the considered area.[6] Users' locations were generated by the moving object generator developed by Brinkhoff [6] that was set to create $100,000$ user locations in the metropolitan area of San Francisco. The total area of the map is about $25,000$ km^2 while the total perimeter is about 630 km. The resulting average density of users for km^2 is 4.067. Two main parameters have been considered for each test: the value k, representing the degree of anonymity, and the total number p of users in the test. We are interested in three output values from the tests: a) the perimeter of the output region, b) the area of that region, and c) the computation time. We implemented the algorithms using Java, and performed our tests on a Linux machine with two 2,4Ghz Pentium Xeon processors and 4GB of shared RAM. All the output values presented in this section are obtained by running $1,000$ tests and taking the average or maximum value, as indicated in the specific experiment.

To compare the perimeter of the regions returned by the generalization algorithms with the one having the smallest perimeter, we implemented the *optimalUnsafe* algorithm. This algorithm computes the set of $k-1$ users such that the perimeter of the MBR including these users and the issuer is minimal. The idea of *optimalUnsafe* is to search the best perimeter of the MBRs for each set containing the issuer and other $k-1$ users. Hence, the complexity of the algorithm is exponential in p; However, we developed several optimization techniques that make the algorithm in most cases computable in time linear

---

[6] The experimental results summarized in the figures of this section are obtained on non-uniform distributions, if not explicitly said otherwise in the captions.

in the size of p, and exponential in the size of k. This makes it possible to compute the optimal perimeter, as a reference value for the evaluation of Γ_I-unsafe algorithms, for quite large values of p and practically relevant values of k.

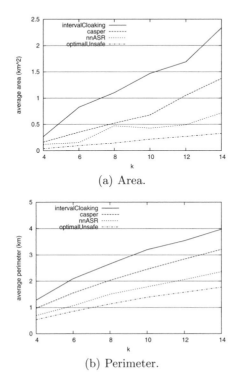

(a) Area.

(b) Perimeter.

Fig. 6. Area and perimeter as computed by C_I-unsafe algorithms with $p = 100,000$ and $k \leq 14$.

Figures 6(a) and 6(b) show the average area and perimeter, respectively, of four C_I-unsafe algorithms. Since the experimental results for the $nnALG$ and $nnASR$ algorithms are almost identical, in this section we report the results of the $nnASR$ algorithm only. The principle behind the $nnASR$ algorithm may induce the reader to think that the resulting region is minimal. Our empirical results show that that this is not the case. On average, $nnASR$ returns regions having a perimeter 30% larger than the one of the region returned by *optimalUnsafe*. We also computed the average number of times in which $nnASR$ returns the same result as *optimalUnsafe*. We noticed that this value rapidly decreases with the growing of k. For example, with $k = 4$ and $p = 100,000$, $nnASR$ returns the region with the minimal perimeter in about 13% of the cases, while the percentage drops below 1% for $k = 14$ and the same number of users. Unfortunately, the high computational complexity of *optimalUnsafe* makes it impossible to evaluate this algorithm for values of k larger than 14. For this reason, in the remaining of this section, this algorithm is ignored.

Figures 7(a) and 7(b) show the average area of the region returned by C_I-unsafe and C_I-safe algorithms, respectively, with values of k higher than in the previous test (up to $k = 180$). Similar results have been obtained considering the average perimeter. It can be noticed that *dichotomicPoints* returns smaller regions with respect to *hilbASR*, *dichotomicArea* and *intervalCloaking*. Figure 7(b) shows that the curve referring to *dichotomicPoints* does not grow regularly but has some "steps". This is due to the fact that the algorithm partitions the number of points until it finds a set containing less than k users. The number of iterations is given by: $\lceil \log(\frac{p}{k}) \rceil$. Therefore, there are executions of the algorithm with different values of k that iterate the same number of times, hence computing, at the last iteration, the same number of users. Consequently, these executions return regions with similar area. Predictably, the C_I-unsafe algorithms generally return smaller regions than the C_I-safe ones as, intuitively, the C_I-safe algorithms have more constraints on the output regions.

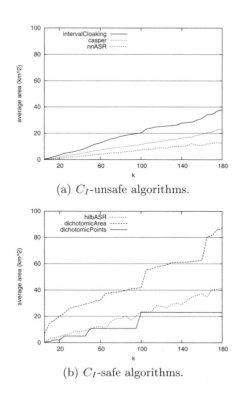

(a) C_I-unsafe algorithms.

(b) C_I-safe algorithms.

Fig. 7. Average area with $p = 100{,}000$ and $k \le 180$.

Figures 8(a) and 8(b) show the average area of the regions returned by the C_I-unsafe and C_I-safe algorithms when users' locations are uniformly distributed in the map. We can notice that the three algorithms of Figure 8(b) return regions with almost the same average area. Analogous results have been obtained considering the perimeter. Comparing Figure 7(b) and Figure 8(b), we can notice that the performance of $hilbASR$ does not significantly differ with the two distributions. On the other hand, $dichotomicArea$ has by far the worst performance in the non-uniform case. This is due to the fact that, with a non-uniform distribution, there are regions with few users that lead the $dichotomicArea$ algorithm to terminate the execution after few iterations. On the contrary, $dichotomicPoints$ has significantly better performance in the non-uniform distribution. This is due to the fact that the issuer of the request is randomly chosen among the users, and in the non-uniform distribution, users' density is much higher in some parts of the general area than in others; Hence, on average, we have many requests from densely populated regions.

Unlike in Figures 7(a) and 7(b), with the uniform data set, the C_I-unsafe algorithms generally perform similarly to the C_I-safe ones, with the exception of $intervalCloaking$. The poor performance of $intervalCloaking$, is mainly due to the fact that, by dividing at each step the area in 4 quadrants, it may happen to return areas that double those returned by the other algorithms. The similar performance of the other algorithms can be intuitively understood since, with uniform locations, i) it does not matter if we divide the region based on number of users or based on the area (that is the main difference between $dicothomicPoints$ and $dicothomicArea$), and ii) the termination condition of C_I-unsafe and C_I-safe algorithms is satisfied in a similar number of steps. Indeed, the termination condition of C_I-safe algorithms imposes that at least k users are included in each block of the partition, and this usually causes less iterations (and larger output regions); however with a uniform distribution this condition is likely to be satisfied whenever the one for C_I-unsafe algorithms is satisfied, leading to similar dimensions of the resulting areas.

Figure 9 shows the average computation time of the algorithms $dichotomicPoints$ for different values of p. The average computation time of Algorithms $nnASR$, $dichotomicArea$ and $hilbASR$ is less than 5 ms in each experiment and we did not observe significant changes in the computation time for values of p between $10,000$ and $200,000$. This is due to the fact that i) the time complexity of the algorithms depends logarithmically in the size of p and ii) the computation time of the algorithms is dominated by startup time. On the contrary, the computation time of $dichotomicPoints$ grows linearly with p. This result is consistent with the theoretical complexity analysis of the algorithm. We also evaluated the time complexity of the algorithms for a fixed p and different values of k and we observed that the execution time of the algorithms is almost not affected by the value of the parameter k.

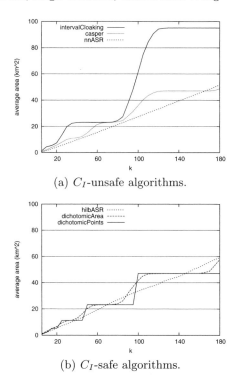

(a) C_I-unsafe algorithms.

(b) C_I-safe algorithms.

Fig. 8. Average area with $p = 100,000$, uniform distribution of users.

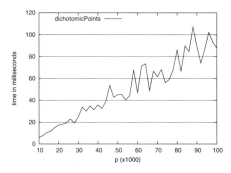

Fig. 9. Computation time of *dichotomicPoints* algorithm with $k = 80$.

6 Conclusion

In this contribution, we identified different privacy threats to users when location-based services are involved. We then discussed the use of anonymity for protection, and detailed different techniques for different threats. We also provided a performance evaluation of the different techniques.

In terms of future work, we pointed out a number of open problems in Section 4.3. More general future work should include studies of actual LBS users and their requests. In addition, usability studies of different protection techniques are also necessary and interesting.

References

1. Alastair R. Beresford and Frank Stajano. Mix zones: User privacy in location-aware services. In *PERCOMW '04: Proceedings of the Second IEEE Annual Conference on Pervasive Computing and Communications Workshops*, page 127, 2004.
2. Claudio Bettini, Sushil Jajodia, and Linda Pareschi. Anonymity and diversity in LBS: a preliminary investigation. In *Proc. of the 5th International Conference on Pervasive Computing and Communication (PerCom)*, 2007.
3. Claudio Bettini, Sergio Mascetti, X. Sean Wang, and Sushil Jajodia. Anonymity in location-based services: towards a general framework. In *Proc. of the 8th International Conference on Mobile Data Management (MDM)*. IEEE Computer Society, 2007.
4. Claudio Bettini, X. Sean Wang, and Sushil Jajodia. Protecting privacy against location-based personal identification. In *Proc. of the 2nd workshop on Secure Data Management (SDM)*, volume 3674 of *LNCS*, pages 185–199. Springer, 2005.
5. Claudio Bettini, X. Sean Wang, and Sushil Jajodia. The role of quasi-identifiers in k-anonymity revisited. Technical Report RT-11-06, DICo, University of Milan, 2006.
6. Thomas Brinkhoff. A framework for generating network-based moving objects. *GeoInformatica*, 6(2):153–180, 2002.
7. Tore Dalenius. Finding a needle in a haystack - or identifying anonymous census record. *Journal of Official Statistics*, 2(3):329–336, 1986.
8. Bugra Gedik and Ling Liu. Location privacy in mobile systems: A personalized anonymization model. In *Proc. of the 25th International Conference on Distributed Computing Systems (ICDCS)*, pages 620–629. IEEE Computer Society, 2005.
9. Marco Gruteser and Dirk Grunwald. Anonymous usage of location-based services through spatial and temporal cloaking. In *Proc. of the 1st International Conference on Mobile Systems, Applications and Services (MobiSys)*. The USENIX Association, 2003.
10. Baik Hoh and Marco Gruteser. Protecting location privacy through path confusion. In *Proc. of the 1st International Conference on Security and Privacy for Emerging Areas in Communications Networks (SecureComm)*, pages 194–205. IEEE Computer Society, 2005.
11. Panos Kalnis, Gabriel Ghinta, Kyriakos Mouratidis, and Dimitri Papadias. Preserving anonymity in location based services. Technical Report B6/06, National University of Singapore, 2006.
12. Hidetoshi Kido, Yutaka Yanagisawa, and Tetsuji Satoh. An anonymous communication technique using dummies for location-based services. In *Proc. of the International Conference on Pervasive Services (ICPS)*, pages 88–97. IEEE Computer Society, 2005.

13. Kristen Lefevre, David J. DeWitt, and Raghu Ramakrishnan. Mondrian multidimensional k-anonymity. In *Proc. of the 22nd International Conference on Data Engineering (ICDE)*. IEEE Computer Society, 2006.

14. Ashwin Machanavajjhala, Johannes Gehrke, Daniel Kifer, and Muthuramakrishnan Venkitasubramaniam. *l*-diversity: Privacy beyond *k*-anonymity. In *Proc. of the 22nd International Conference on Data Engineering (ICDE)*. IEEE Computer Society, 2006.

15. Sergio Mascetti and Claudio Bettini. A comparison of spatial generalization algorithms for LBS privacy preservation. In *Proc. of the 1st International Workshop on Privacy-Aware Location-based Mobile Services (PALMS)*, 2007.

16. Mohamed F. Mokbel, Chi-Yin Chow, and Walid G. Aref. The new casper: query processing for location services without compromising privacy. In *Proc. of the 32nd International Conference on Very Large Data Bases (VLDB)*, pages 763–774. VLDB Endowment, 2006.

17. P. Samarati. Protecting respondents' identities in microdata release. *IEEE Transactions on Knowledge and Data Engineering*, 13(6):1010–1027, 2001.

Privacy-enhanced Location-based Access Control

C.A. Ardagna, M. Cremonini, S. De Capitani di Vimercati, P. Samarati

Dipartimento di Tecnologie dell'Informazione
Università degli Studi di Milano
26013 Crema, Italy
{ardagna,cremonini,decapita,samarati}@dti.unimi.it

Summary. Advancements in location technologies reliability and precision are fostering the development of location-based services that make use of the location information of users. An increasingly important category of such services is represented by Location-based Access Control (LBAC) systems that integrate traditional access control mechanisms with access conditions based on the physical position of users and other attributes related to the users location. Since privacy is extremely important for users, protection of their location information is paramount to the success of such emerging location-based services.

In this chapter, we first present an overview of Location-based Access Control systems and then characterize the location privacy protection problem. We then discuss the main techniques that have been proposed to protect location information, focusing on the obfuscation-based techniques. We conclude the chapter by showing a privacy-aware LBAC architecture and describing how a location-based access control policy can be evaluated.

1 Introduction

The widespread diffusion of pervasive technologies, as well as of mobile devices relying on them, makes available a great amount of high-sensitive location information that can be used for a variety of purposes. Customer-oriented applications, social networks and monitoring services can be functionally enriched with data reporting where people are, how they are moving or whether they are close by specific locations. To this end, several commercial and enterprise-oriented location-based services are already available and have gained popularity. Location-based services are supported by modern location technologies that have reached good precision and reliability at costs that most people (e.g., the cost of mobile devices) and companies (e.g., the cost of integrating location technologies in existing telecommunication infrastructures) can economically sustain. Since these location-based services are very complex and may use the location information for different purposes, gathering and managing such information is a challenging aspect. Among the different issues that need to be addressed in the development of such services, *location privacy* is becoming increasingly important. Location privacy can be defined as the right of individuals to decide how, when, and for which purposes their location information could be released to other parties. The lack of location privacy protection could result in severe consequences that make users the target of fraudulent attacks such as [1]: *i) unsolicited advertising,* meaning that the location of the user could be exploited, without her consent, to provide advertisements of products and services available nearby the user position; *ii) physical attacks or harassment,* meaning that the location of the user could be used to carry physical assaults to individuals; *iii) users profiling,* meaning that the location of the user, which intrinsically carries personal information, could be used to infer other sensitive information such as state of health, personal habits, and professional duties; *iv) denial of services,* meaning that the location of the user could be used to deny accesses to services under some circumstances. In addition, location information can expose users to dangers such as stalking or physical harassment [2, 3].

Although location privacy is the subject of growing research efforts, there are no comprehensive solutions for location privacy protection in pervasive systems. The main branch of current research on location privacy focuses on users anonymity and on supporting online and mobile services that do not require the personal identification of a user for their provision [4, 5, 6]. When identification of users is required and, consequently, anonymity is not suitable, a viable solution to protect users privacy is to decrease the precision of personal information (including location) bound to identities [7, 8, 9]. For several online services personal information associated with identities does not need to be as accurate as possible to guarantee a certain service quality.

In this chapter, the issue of protecting location privacy is analyzed in the context of Location-based Access Control (LBAC) systems [10]. The remainder of this chapter is organized as follows. Section 2 presents basic concepts behind location-based access control systems. Section 3 provides a brief overview of different types of location privacy that must be preserved depending on the scenarios and on the requirements together with a description of the techniques that can be used to protect location privacy. Section 4 describes some obfuscation-based techniques aimed at privacy protection. Section 5 presents a privacy-aware LBAC architecture and discusses how the evaluation of location-based predicates can be performed. Finally, Section 6 gives our conclusions.

2 Location-based Access Control Systems

Novel access control mechanisms are based on the assumption that properties characterizing a requester, which are usually provided through *digital cre-*

dentials, are sufficient to decide which actions the requester is authorized to perform on resources [11]. However, requester's credentials are not the only information that should be considered in access control decisions. The rapid development in the field of wireless and mobile networking fostered a new generation of devices suitable for being used as sensors by location technologies, which are able to compute the relative position and movement of users in their environment. Therefore, the location of users, potentially available to access control modules, may also play an important role in determining access rights and allows the definition of a new class of location-based policies regulating access to and fruition of resources. When evaluating location-based access control policies, however, we need to consider that location-based information presents some peculiarities: location information is both *approximate* (all location system have a margin of error) and *time-variant* (the user position changes over time due to the on-going motion of requesters).

Location-based Access Control (LBAC) systems provide the infrastructure for managing and evaluating access control policies that include predicates and conditions based on the location information of users. LBAC systems should be designed to tolerate rapid context changes, because users are no longer forced to be at pre-defined fixed positions but they can freely access services through their mobile devices (e.g., mobile phones).

2.1 Location-based Conditions and Predicates

The first step towards the development of a LBAC system consists in the definition of location-based conditions. We identify three main classes of location-based conditions, which might be useful to include in access control policies and whose evaluation is possible with today's technology [10]:

- *position-based* conditions on the location of the user (e.g., to evaluate whether a user is in a certain building or city or in the proximity of other entities);
- *movement-based* conditions on the mobility of the users (e.g., velocity, acceleration, or direction where users are headed);
- *interaction-based* conditions relating multiple users or entities (e.g., the number of users within a given area).

The language presented in [10] supports such conditions and is based on the assumption that each user, who is unknown to the service responsible for location measurements, is univocally identified via a user identifier (UID). A unique identifier is also associated with physical and/or moving entities that may need to be located (e.g., a vehicle with an on-board GPRS card). A typical UID for location-based applications is the SIM number linking the user's identity to a mobile terminal. Moreover, the language is also based on the assumption that there is a set of map regions identified either via a geometric model (i.e., a range in a n-dimensional coordinate space) or a

Table 1. Examples of location-based predicates

Type	Predicate	Description
Position	inarea(*user*, *area*)	Evaluate whether *user* is located within *area*.
	disjoint(*user*, *area*)	Evaluate whether *user* is outside *area*.
	distance(*user*, *entity*, *min_dist*, *max_dist*)	Evaluate whether distance between *user* and *entity* is within interval [*min_dist*, *max_dist*].
Movement	velocity(*user*, *min_vel*, *max_vel*)	Evaluate whether *user*'s speed falls within range [*min_vel*, *max_vel*].
Interaction	density(*area*, *min_num*, *max_num*)	Evaluate whether the number of users currently in *area* falls within interval [*min_num*, *max_num*].
	local_density(*user*, *area*, *min_num*, *max_num*)	Evaluate the density within a 'relative' area surrounding *user*.

symbolic model (i.e., with reference to entities of the real world such as, for example, cells, streets, cities, zip code or buildings) [12].

Predicates are expressed as boolean queries of the form *predicate(parameters, value)*. Table 1 illustrates some examples of location predicates.

Example 1. Let `alice` be a user identifier, and `Milan` and `Director_Office` be two map regions. Three simple examples of location-based conditions are the following.

- `inarea(alice,Milan)`: request `alice` to be located in `Milan`.
- `velocity(alice,70,90)`: request `alice` to travel at a speed included in the interval [`70`,`90`].
- `density(Director_Office,0,1)`: request at most one person in the `Director_Office`.

2.2 Location-based Access Control Policies

Location-based access control policies can be considered as a means for enriching the expressive power of existing access control languages (e.g., [11, 13, 14, 15]) by introducing location-based predicates. We assume access control rules to be triples whose elements are generic boolean formula over the subject, object, and action domains. Formally, an access control rule is defined as follows.

Definition 1 (Access control rule). *An access control rule is a triple of the form ⟨subj_expr, obj_expr, action⟩, where:*

- subj_expr *is a boolean formula of terms referring to a set of subjects depending on whether they satisfy or not certain conditions that can evaluate the user's profile/information, location predicates, or the user's membership in groups, active roles, and so on;*

Table 2. Examples of access control rules regulating access to the Mobile Network Console and databases

	subject		action	object
	generic conditions	location-based conditions		
1	user.role=admin ∧ valid(user.username, user.password)	inarea(user.sim, Server_Room) ∧ density(Server_Room, 1, 1) ∧ velocity(user.sim, 0, 3)	execute	object.name=MNC
2	user.role=admin ∧ valid(user.username, user.password)	inarea(user.sim, Inf._System_Dept.) ∧ local_density(user.sim, Close_By, 1, 1) ∧ velocity(user.sim, 0, 3)	read	object.category= Log&Bill
3	user.role=CEO ∧ valid(user.username, user.password)	local_density(user.sim, Close_By, 1, 1) ∧ inarea(user.sim, Corp._Main_Office) ∧ velocity(user.sim, 0, 3)	read	object.category= customer
4	user.role=CEO ∧ valid(user.username, user.password)	local_density(user.sim, Close_By, 1, 1) ∧ disjoint(user.sim, Competitor_Location)	read	object.category= StatData
5	user.role=guest ∧ valid(user.username, user.password)	local_density(user.sim, Close_By, 1, 1) ∧ inarea(user.sim, Corporate_Location)	read	object.category= StatData

- obj_expr *is a boolean formula of terms referring to a set of objects depending on whether they satisfy or not certain conditions that can evaluate membership of the object in categories, values of properties on metadata, and so on;*
- action *is the action (or class of actions) to which the rule refers.*

Each profile is referenced with the identity of the corresponding user/object. Single properties within users and objects profiles are referenced with the traditional dot notation. For instance, alice.address indicates the address of user alice. Here, alice is the identity of the user (and therefore the identifier for the corresponding profile), and address is the name of the property. To refer to the user and the object involved in a request without introducing variables in the language, we use two keywords: **user** indicates the identifier of the person making the request; **object** indicates the identifier of the object to which access is requested.

Example 2. Consider a company responsible for the management of a mobile network that needs both strong authentication methods and expressive access control policies. Suppose that the Mobile Network Console (MNC) is the software that permits to reconfigure the mobile network. Managing a nation-wide mobile network is an extremely critical activity because reconfiguration privileges must be granted to strictly selected personnel only and must be performed according to high security standards (rule 1 in Table 2). In addition to reconfiguration privileges, also the access to mobile network's databases must be managed carefully and according to different security standards depending on the level of risk of the data to be accessed. In particular, access to logging and billing data is critical, because they include information about the position and movements of mobile operator's customers (rule 2 in Table 2). Access to customer-related information is usually less critical but still to be handled in a highly secured environment and to be granted only to selected personnel, according to the laws and regulations in force (rule 3 in Table 2). Finally, access to statistical data about the network's operation is at a lower criticality level, whereas they are still private information to be protected, for example, from disclosure to competitors (rules 4 and 5 in Table 2).

In the following, we discuss location privacy issues and present a location privacy solution suitable for location-based services along with a privacy-aware LBAC architecture.

3 Location Privacy

Although location information can be exploited for providing enhanced services, the high sensitivity of such an information increases concerns of users about their privacy. Location privacy can assume several meanings and pursue different objectives, depending on the services the users are interacting with. The following categories of location privacy have been identified.

- *Identity privacy.* The main goal is to protect users' identities that could be directly or indirectly inferred from location information [4, 5, 6, 16]. To this purpose, protection techniques aim at minimizing the disclosure of the data that can let an attacker infer a user identity, such as home and work addresses. This type of location privacy is suitable in application contexts that do not require the identification of the users as a fundamental information for service provisioning. For instance, many online services provide a person with the ability to establish a relationship with some other entities (e.g., anonymous chats) or with some applications (e.g., allergy warning) without her personal identity being disclosed to that entity. In this case, the best possible location measurement can be provided to the others entities but the actual user's identity must be preserved.
- *Position privacy.* The main goal is to protect the position information of individual users, by perturbing corresponding information and decreasing the accuracy of location information [7, 8, 9]. Position privacy is suitable for environments where users' identities are required for a successful service provisioning, and less accurate location information does not severely affect the service quality (e.g., access to services inside a production plant or friends finder services). A technique that most solutions exploit, either explicitly or implicitly, consists in reducing the accuracy by scaling a location to a coarser granularity (e.g., from meters to hundreds of meters, from a city block to the whole town).
- *Path privacy.* The main goal is to protect the privacy of information associated with users motion, such as the path followed while traveling or walking in a urban area [17, 18, 19]. There are several location-based services (e.g., personal navigation systems) that could be exploited to subvert path privacy or to illicitly track users. Path privacy is the most complex

class of location privacy problem and can refer to identity privacy and/or position privacy.

The above three privacy categories pose different requirements that are fulfilled by different techniques. The heterogeneity of location privacy problems results then in a lack of a general solution able to satisfy all the privacy requirements. In the following, different classes of techniques are discussed and analyzed.

3.1 Location Privacy Techniques

Location privacy techniques can be partitioned into three main classes that correspond to the different types of location privacy above-mentioned: *anonymity-based*, *policy-based*, and *obfuscation-based*. These classes are partially overlapped in scope and could be potentially suitable to cover requirements coming from one or more of the categories of location privacy. Anonymity-based and obfuscation-based techniques can be usually regarded as dual categories. While anonymity-based techniques have been primarily defined to protect identity privacy and are less suitable for protecting position privacy, obfuscation-based techniques are well suited for position protection and less appropriate for identity protection. Anonymity-based and obfuscation-based techniques are well-suited for protecting path privacy. Nevertheless, more studies and proposals have been focused on anonymity-based rather than on obfuscation-based techniques. Policy-based techniques are in general suitable for all the location privacy categories; however, they can be difficult to understand and manage for end users.

Anonymity-based techniques

This class of techniques focus both on identity privacy and path privacy protection [4, 5, 6, 20]. Beresford and Stajano [4, 21] propose a *mix zone* model and employs an anonymity service based on an infrastructure that delays and reorders messages from subscribers within pre-defined zones. The mix zone model is based on a trusted middleware positioned between location systems and third party applications, which is responsible for limiting the information collected by applications. An application selects a set of *application zones* representing application interests in specific geographic areas, such as hospital, supermarket, and so on. Users register interest in a specific set of applications and the middleware limits the location information that such applications can receive to the locations inside the application zones. Each user has one or more unregistered geographical regions, called *mix zones*, where users cannot be tracked, that is, when a user enters a mix zone her identity is mixed with all other users in the same mix zone. The mix zones model is then aimed at protecting long-term user movements still allowing the interaction with many location-based services. However, the effectiveness of such a solution is strongly dependent on the number of users joining the anonymity service and, in particular, on the number of users physically co-located in the same mix zone at the same time.

Bettini et. al. [5] propose a framework able to evaluate the risk of sensitive location-based information dissemination and introduce a technique aimed at supporting k-anonymity [8, 9]. The concept of k-anonymity captures a traditional requirement of statistical agencies stating that released data must be indistinguishably related to no less than a certain number (k) of users. Traditionally, k-anonymity is based on the definition of a *quasi-identifier* that is a set of attributes exploitable for linking data to identifiers. The k-anonymity requirement states that each release of data must guarantee that every combination of values of quasi-identifiers can be indistinctly linkable to at least k individuals. The proposal in [5] puts forward the idea that the geo-localized history of the requests submitted by a user can be considered as a quasi-identifier that can be used to discover sensitive information about that user. For instance, a user tracked during working days is likely to commute from her house to the workplace in a specific time frame in the morning and to come back in another specific time frame in the evening. This information could be used to identify the user. Consequently, the service provider gathering both user requests for services and personal history of locations (i.e., a sequence of user location updates) should never be able to link a subset of requests to a single user. To make this possible, there must exist k users having a personal history of locations consistent with the set of requests that have been issued. This solution is highly dependent on the availability of k indistinguishable histories of locations: the worst case happens when a given user has a unique history, which make her always identifiable.

Also other proposals [6, 20] rely on the concept of k-anonymity by requiring that a user should be indistinguishable from other $k - 1$ users in a given spatial area or temporal interval. Gruteser and Grunwald [6] propose a middleware architecture and an adaptive algorithm to adjust location information resolution, in spatial or temporal dimensions, to comply with specified anonymity requirements. To this purpose, the authors introduce the concepts of *spatial* and *temporal cloaking* used to transform the location of a user to a different location that satisfies the required level of anonymity. Spatial cloaking guarantees k-anonymity by applying an adaptive quad-tree algorithm that decreases the spatial resolution to an area that contains k indistinguishable users. Temporal cloaking, which is orthogonal to the spatial cloaking, provides spatial coordinates with higher accuracy but it reduces the accuracy in time. The key feature of the adaptive cloaking algorithm is that the required level of anonymity can be achieved for any location. Mokbel et al. [20] present a framework, named *Casper*, that changes traditional location-based servers and query processors to provide the users with anonymous services. Users can define their privacy preferences through two parameters: k, meaning that the user wants to be indistinguishable among other k entities; and A_{min} representing the minimal area that the user is willing to release. The core of the

Casper framework is composed by two components: a *location anonymizer,* which is responsible for perturbing the user location until user's privacy preferences are satisfied, and a *privacy-aware query processor,* which is responsible for the management of anonymous queries and cloaked spatial areas.

Anonymity-based techniques have also been exploited to guarantee *path privacy* protection [17, 18, 19]. In particular, path privacy involves the protection of users that are in motion and are continuously monitored during a time interval. This research field is particularly relevant for location tracking applications designed and developed for devices with limited capabilities (e.g., cellular phones), where data about users moving in a particular area are collected by external services. Gruteser et al. [17] propose a solution to path privacy protection by means of *path anonymization functions.* The authors argue that the association of a single or multiple pseudonyms, which change over time, with a user is not sufficient to provide path privacy protection. Privacy provided by pseudonyms can be actually subverted by applying an inference process that gathers path information, such as the place a user stays during the night. Therefore, since it is difficult to provide strong anonymity for path protection because it would require the existence of several users traveling along the same path at the same time, Gruteser et al. provide two techniques that guarantee a "weaker anonymity", meaning that users could potentially be linked to their identities but at price of huge computational efforts. The first technique relies on *path segmentation,* which partitions a user's path in a set of smaller paths changing, at the same time, the associated pseudonym. The second technique relies on *minutiae suppression* that suppresses those parts of a path that are more distinctive and could bring to an easy association between a path and an identity. The suitability of these techniques is highly dependent on the density of users in the area in which the adversary collects location samples. In areas with low density of users, an adversary has a good likelihood of tracking individuals, whereas in areas with many overlapping paths, linking segments to identities can be extremely difficult.

Other proposals consider path protection as a process whose outcome must be managed by a service provider and consequently privacy techniques have to preserve a given level of accuracy to permit a good quality of service provisioning. Gruteser and Liu [18] present a solution based on the definition of a *sensitivity map* composed by sensitive and insensitive zones. Sensitive zones are those area where the users prefer to hide their visits. The work defines three algorithms aimed at path privacy protection: *base, bounded-rate,* and k-area. Among the three, the k-area algorithm stands out, giving the best performance in terms of privacy, and minimizing the number of location updates suppression. In particular, the k-area algorithm is built on top of sensitivity maps that are composed of areas containing k sensitive zones. Location updates of a user entering a region with k sensitive areas are temporarily stored and not released. If a user leaving that region has visited at least one of the k sensitive areas, location updates are suppressed; they are released, otherwise. Finally, Ho and Gruteser [19] propose a path confusion algorithm. This algorithm introduces a level of uncertainty by creating cross paths between at least two users. In this case, the attacker observing different paths is not able to recognize which path has followed one specific user.

Policy-based techniques

Another class of location privacy techniques relies on the definition of *privacy policies*. Privacy policies define restrictions that regulate the release of the location of a user to third parties. Hauser and Kabatnik [22] address the location privacy problem in a privacy-aware architecture for a global location service, which allows users to define rules that will be evaluated to regulate access to location information. The IETF Geopriv working group addresses privacy and security issues related to the disclosure of location information over the Internet [23]. The main goal of the Geopriv working group is to define an environment (i.e., architecture, protocols, and policies) supporting both location information and policy data. Others works [24, 25] used the Platform for Privacy Preferences (P3P) [26] to encode users privacy preferences.

In summary, policy-based techniques allow a flexible definition of policies that fit the user needs of privacy by restricting the ability to manage locations and disclosing information. However, although policies-based solutions are suitable for privacy protection, users are often not willing to directly manage complex policies and, hence, may refuse participation in pervasive environments.

Obfuscation-based techniques

Obfuscation-based techniques are aimed at protecting location privacy by degrading the accuracy of the location information still maintaining an explicit association with the real user identity.

Duckham and Kulik [7] define a framework that provides a mechanism for balancing individual needs for high-quality information services and location privacy. The proposed solution is based on the concept of *imprecision*, which indicates the lack of specificity of location information. The authors suggest to degrade location information quality and to provide obfuscation features by adding n points with same probability of being the real user position. The algorithm assumes a graph-based representation of the environment. Also, the authors propose a validation and evaluation of their methods through a set of simulations [27]. The results show that obfuscation can provide at the same time a high service quality and a high privacy level.

Other proposals relies on a trusted middleware, which lies between location providers and location-based applications, responsible for enforcing users privacy preferences before releasing location information. Openwave [28], for example, includes a location gateway that obtains users location information from multiple sources and delivers them, possibly modified according to privacy requirements, to other parties. Users define their privacy preferences in terms of a minimum distance representing the maximum location accuracy they are willing to accept. Bellavista et al. [29] present a solution based on a middleware that balances the level of privacy requested by users and the need of service precision. Location information is perturbed depending on privacy/efficiency requirements negotiated by the parties and it is returned with lower precision and lower geographical granularity.

In summary, although obfuscation-based techniques are compatible with users specifying their privacy preferences in a common and intuitive manner (usually as a *minimum distance*), they do not provide a quantitative estimation of the provided privacy level, and they usually implement a single obfuscation technique, which provide an obfuscation effect by scaling up the extent of the location area.

4 Obfuscation Techniques for Location Privacy Protection

An interesting research direction is to use obfuscation-based techniques for location privacy protection in LBAC systems [30, 31, 32]. These recent proposals provide privacy by degrading the location accuracy of each measurement while offering a measurable accuracy to service providers and are based on two working assumptions that simplify the analysis with no loss of generality: *i)* the area returned by a location measurement is planar and circular, which is the actual shape resulting from many location technologies; *ii)* the distribution of measurement errors within a returned area is uniform. The first assumption derives from the fact that user location information is affected by an intrinsic measurement error introduced by sensing technologies, resulting in spatial areas rather than geographical points. This assumption represents a particular case of the general requirement of considering convex areas and a good approximation for actual shapes resulting from many location technologies (e.g., cellular phones location). A location measurement is then defined as follows.

Definition 2 (Location measurement). *A location measurement of a user u is a circular area $Area(r, x_c, y_c)$, centered on the geographical coordinates (x_c, y_c) and with radius r, which includes the real user's position (x_u, y_u) with probability $P((x_u, y_u) \in Area(r, x_c, y_c)) = 1$.*

Definition 2 comes from observing that sensing technologies based on cellular phones usually guarantee that the real user's position falls within the returned area.

The second assumption is introduced to discuss the effects of obfuscation techniques. Consider a random location within a location measurement

$Area(r, x_c, y_c)$, where a "random location" is a neighborhood of random point $(\hat{x}, \hat{y}) \in Area(r, x_c, y_c)$. The probability that the real user's position (x_u, y_u) belongs to a neighborhood of a random point $(\hat{x}, \hat{y})$ is uniformly distributed over the whole location measurement. Accordingly, the joint probability density function (pdf) of the real user's position can be defined as follows.

Definition 3 (Uniform joint pdf). *Given a location measurement $Area(r, x_c, y_c)$, the joint probability density function (joint pdf) $f_r(x, y)$ of real user's position (x_u, y_u) to be in the neighborhood of point (x, y) is:*

$$f_r(x, y) = \begin{cases} \frac{1}{\pi r^2} & if\ (x, y) \in Area(r, x_c, y_c) \\ 0 & otherwise. \end{cases}$$

Before analyzing the obfuscation techniques in details, we first describe how users can express their privacy preferences. Despite its importance for the effectiveness of a privacy solution, this issue has received little attention in previous works on location privacy. We then describe how the level of privacy can be quantitatively expressed as a functional term independently from any physical scale or specific technology.

4.1 User Preferences and Relevance Metric

Several works in location privacy field are based on the definition of users privacy preferences by means of a minimum distance [7, 28]. This choice is dictated by the fact that usually the users tend to adopt simple and intuitive way for expressing their privacy preference and tend to be averse to complex configurations. A user can define as her privacy preference a minimum distance, which results in a location area achieved by increasing the granularity of the actual location measurement. In particular, assuming location measurements as circular areas, the minimum distance privacy preference represents the minimum radius of the area that a user is willing to release to other parties. However, the definition of the minimum distance as user privacy preference exhibits some shortcomings: *i)* it is highly dependent on the adopted privacy solution; *ii)* it is suitable for only obfuscation techniques that increase the granularity of the measurement; *iii)* it is difficult to integrate in a full-fledged location-based application scenario [10, 33]; *iv)* it is not suitable for solutions using different obfuscation techniques.

To overcome these issues, others proposals [30, 31, 32] suggest a different way to manage users privacy preferences. In these works, users specify their privacy requirements through the definition of a *relative* degradation of the location accuracy with respect to the location measurement, which is modeled through an index $\lambda \in [0, \infty)$, where $\lambda = 0$ corresponds to no degradation, $\lambda \to \infty$ to maximum degradation, and intermediate values correspond to different degrees of degradation. For instance, $\lambda=0.5$ means 50% of degradation,

$\lambda=1$ means 100% of degradation and any value $\lambda >1$ corresponds to a degradation greater than 100%. Although both minimum distance d and index λ are easy to specify for users, λ is a more general solution because independent from a specific location measurement and obfuscation technique. However, the definition of λ is not sufficient, especially when we need to balance the users needs of privacy and the LBSs needs of location accuracy to maintain an acceptable quality of the online service.

To accommodate the peculiar characteristics of the above scenario, the concept of *relevance* is introduced as the adimensional metric of both the accuracy and the privacy of a location information, abstracting from any physical attribute of sensing technology. A relevance $\mathcal{R}$ is a value in $(0,1]$ associated with each location information, which depends on measurement errors and privacy preferences of users. In particular, $\mathcal{R}$ tends to 0 when the location information is considered unreliable for service provision; $\mathcal{R}=1$ when the location information is equal to the original location measurement; $\mathcal{R} \in (0,1)$ when the location information has various degrees of accurateness. The location privacy associated with an obfuscated location is evaluated by $(1\text{-}\mathcal{R})$.

Applying the concept of relevance to a LBAC scenario, an LBAC service has to manage the following different relevances:

- *Technological relevance* $(\mathcal{R}_{Tech})$ is the metric for the accuracy of the location measurement provided by a location service given a mobile technology and its technical quality.
- *Privacy relevance* $(\mathcal{R}_{Priv})$ is the metric for the accuracy of an obfuscated location and therefore the level of privacy provided to the users.
- *LBAC relevance* $(\mathcal{R}_{LBAC})$ is the metric for the lowest accuracy of the location information that an LBAC service is willing to accept. It is required by the business application for a location measurement or for a location-based predicate evaluation.
- *Evaluation relevance* $(\mathcal{R}_{Eval})$ is the metric for the accuracy of a LBAC predicate evaluation.

Among these relevances, $\mathcal{R}_{LBAC}$ and $\mathcal{R}_{Tech}$ are assumed to be known. $\mathcal{R}_{Priv}$ is derived from the privacy preferences expressed by users, while $\mathcal{R}_{Eval}$ is calculated by the system (see Sect. 5). In other words, $\mathcal{R}_{Priv}$ represents the relevance of the final obfuscated area that is calculated starting from the location measurement with relevance $\mathcal{R}_{Tech}$ and by degrading its accuracy according to the value of λ. Formally, $\mathcal{R}_{Priv}$ is calculated as:

$$\mathcal{R}_{Priv} = (\lambda + 1)^{-1}\mathcal{R}_{Tech} \tag{1}$$

If a privacy preference is expressed through a minimum distance r, it is straightforward to derive λ from r. The obfuscated area is then calculated by scaling up the radius of the location measurement until the user privacy preference λ is satisfied.

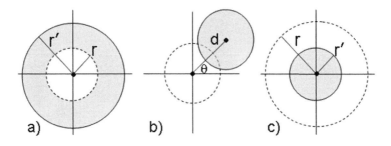

Fig. 1. Enlarging (a), shifting (b), and reducing (c)

4.2 Obfuscation Techniques

We present some obfuscation techniques that reduce the location accuracy of a location measurement until the privacy preferences are achieved. In particular, each technique takes λ as input and computes $\mathcal{R}_{Priv}$ and the obfuscated area.

Enlarging the Radius

Enlarging the radius of a location measurement represents the traditional solution adopted in the context of location privacy protection. Given a location measurement $Area(r, x_c, y_c)$, an obfuscated area $Area(r', x_c, y_c)$ is generated, where $r' > r$ (see Fig. 1(a)). The obfuscation effect directly derives from the fact that the joint pdf associated with the obfuscated area decreases, that is, $\forall r, r' \in \mathbb{R}^+ : r < r' \Rightarrow f_r(x, y) > f_{r'}(x, y)$. The relevance $\mathcal{R}_{Priv}$ of the location information after spatial obfuscation can be derived from $\mathcal{R}_{Tech}$ by considering the ratio of the two pdf as a scalar factor:

$$\mathcal{R}_{Priv} = \frac{f_{r'}(x, y)}{f_r(x, y)} \cdot \mathcal{R}_{Tech} = \frac{r^2}{r'^2} \cdot \mathcal{R}_{Tech}, \quad \text{with } r < r' \tag{2}$$

Given a privacy preference $\lambda \geq 0$, the radius of the obfuscated area r' is calculated from (1) and (2) as follows:

$$r' = r\sqrt{\lambda + 1}$$

This relation permits to generate the obfuscated area by enlarging radius r to radius r', which satisfies, according to our semantics, the user privacy preference λ. Note that, if the privacy preference of the user is provided by means of a minimum distance (i.e., radius r') relevance $\mathcal{R}_{Priv}$ of the obfuscated area is always calculated by equation (2).

Shifting the Center

Shifting the center of the area returned by a sensing technology is another way of obfuscating a location measurement. The obfuscated area is derived from the original area by calculating the distance d between the two centers and the shifting angle θ. Let $Area(r, x_c + \Delta x, y_c + \Delta y)$ be the obfuscated area. Note that, since LBAC applications cannot deal with false information to provide a service, obfuscated areas with no intersection with the original location measurement are considered not acceptable. The reason is that, since location measurements contain users positions with probability 1, all the areas disjoint with a location measurement have probability 0 of including the real user location, and then are indiscernible using the relevance metric. Therefore, these areas must be simply considered as false location information.

The privacy gain can be measured by considering the intersection of the original and obfuscated areas, denoted $Area_{Tech \cap Priv}$. Intuitively, the degree of privacy is inversely proportional to the intersection of the two areas and therefore it is directly proportional to the distance $d \in [0, 2r]$ between the two centers. In particular, if $d = 0$, there is no privacy gain and $P((x_u, y_u) \in Area(r, x_c + \Delta x, y_c + \Delta y)) = P((x_u, y_u) \in Area(r, x_c, y_c)) = 1$. If $d = 2r$, there is maximum privacy and $P((x_u, y_u) \in Area(r, x_c + \Delta x, y_c + \Delta y))$ tends to 0; and if $0 < d < 2r$, there is an increment of privacy and $0 < P((x_u, y_u) \in Area(r, x_c + \Delta x, y_c + \Delta y)) < 1$.

Angle θ (see Fig. 1(b)) is assumed to be randomly chosen, since all values of θ are equivalent with respect to the privacy preferences of users.

To measure the obfuscation effect and define the relation between relevances, two probabilities must be composed: $i)$ the probability that the real user's position belongs to the intersection $Area_{Tech \cap Priv}$, and $ii)$ the probability that a random point selected from the whole obfuscated area belongs to the intersection. Then, the relation between relevances $\mathcal{R}_{Tech}$ and $\mathcal{R}_{Priv}$ is represented by:

$$\mathcal{R}_{Priv} = P((x_u, y_u) \in Area_{Tech \cap Priv}) \cdot P((x, y) \in Area_{Tech \cap Priv}) \cdot \mathcal{R}_{Tech} =$$

$$\frac{Area_{Tech \cap Priv}}{Area(r, x_c, y_c)} \cdot \frac{Area_{Tech \cap Priv}}{Area(r, x_c + \Delta x, y_c + \Delta y)} \cdot \mathcal{R}_{Tech} = \frac{Area_{Tech \cap Priv}^2}{Area(r, x_c, y_c)^2} \cdot \mathcal{R}_{Tech} \quad (3)$$

Given the privacy preference expressed by $\lambda \geq 0$, the distance d between the centers of the original and obfuscated area is calculated from (1) and (3) as follows:

$$(\lambda + 1)^{-1} = \frac{Area_{Tech \cap Priv}^2}{Area(r, x_c, y_c)^2} \quad (4)$$

The distance d between the centers is the unknown variable to be derived to obtain the obfuscated area. It can be calculated by expanding the term $Area_{Tech \cap Priv}$ as a function of d and by solving the following system of equations, whose variables are d, σ and γ. σ and γ are the central angles of circular sectors identified by the two radii connecting the centers of the areas with the intersection points of original and obfuscated areas.[1]

$$\begin{cases} \left[\frac{\sigma}{2}r^2 - \frac{r^2}{2}\sin\sigma\right] + \left[\frac{\gamma}{2}R^2 - \frac{R^2}{2}\sin\gamma\right] = \sqrt{\delta}\pi r \cdot R \\ d = r\cos\frac{\sigma}{2} + R\cos\frac{\gamma}{2} \\ r\sin\frac{\sigma}{2} = R\sin\frac{\gamma}{2} \end{cases} \qquad (5)$$

Solutions of this system can be obtained numerically.

Reducing the Radius

The third obfuscation technique consists in reducing the radius of a location measurement from r to r', as showed in Fig. 1(c). The obfuscation effect is produced by a correspondent reduction of the probability to find the real user location within the returned area, whereas the joint pdf is fixed.

Let (x_u, y_u) be the real user position coordinates, By assumption, the probability that the real user position falls in the location measurement of radius r is $P((x_u, y_u) \in Area(r, x, y)) = 1$. When we obfuscate by reducing the radius, an area of radius $r' < r$ is returned, where $P((x_u, y_u) \in Area(r', x, y)) < P((x_u, y_u) \in Area(r, x, y))$, since a circular ring having pdf greater than zero has been excluded.

With regard to relevances $\mathcal{R}_{Tech}$ and $\mathcal{R}_{Priv}$, their relation can be defined as:

$$\mathcal{R}_{Priv} = \frac{P((x_u, y_u) \in Area(r', x, y))}{P((x_u, y_u) \in Area(r, x, y))} \cdot \mathcal{R}_{Tech} = \frac{r'^2}{r^2} \cdot \mathcal{R}_{Tech}, \quad \text{with } r' < r \qquad (6)$$

Given a privacy preference $\lambda \geq 0$, the radius of the obfuscated area r' is calculated from (1) and (6) as follows:

$$r' = \frac{r}{\sqrt{\lambda + 1}}$$

This relation permits to generate the obfuscated area by reducing radius r to radius r', which satisfies, according to our semantics, the user privacy preference λ.

5 Integrating Obfuscation Techniques with LBAC Systems

The definition of LBAC systems poses some architectural and functional issues that were never studied before in the context of traditional access control

---

[1] The system of equation (5) is presented in the most general form of two areas with different radii (i.e., r and R).

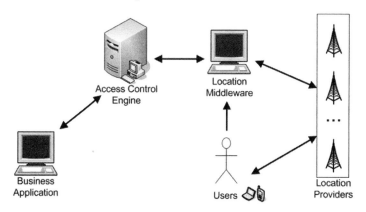

Fig. 2. A privacy-Aware LBAC Architecture

systems. A privacy-aware LBAC architecture must be developed integrating components logically tied with the applications that need location-based access control enforcement and components providing privacy-aware location services. One typical approach in the design of LBAC architectures is to provide a location middleware acting as a trusted gateway between the LBAC system and the location services. Such a component is in charge of managing all interactions with sensing technologies and enforce users privacy preferences. In [30, 31, 32] the authors present a privacy-aware LBAC architecture (see Fig. 2) whose logical components can be summarized as follows.

- *User.* It is the subject to be located through her mobile device during the interaction with the Business Application. The user first defines her privacy preferences at the Location Middleware and then interacts with the Access Control Engine to gain the access to the Business Application.
- *Business application.* It represents a service provider that offers resources protected by LBAC policies. It relies on the Access Control Engine for evaluating policies based on users location.
- *Access Control Engine (ACE).* It is the component responsible for the evaluation and enforcement of LBAC policies. It relies on functionalities provided by a specialized privacy-aware Location Middleware to collect information about the positions of the User involved in the access control decision process.
- *Location Middleware (LM).* It represents the core component of the architecture. It manages the low-level communications with the Location Provider and enforces both the privacy preferences of the User and the need of location accuracy requested by the Access Control Engine.
- *Location Provider (LP).* It is the component that manages sensing technologies to provide location measurement of the User to the Location Middleware.

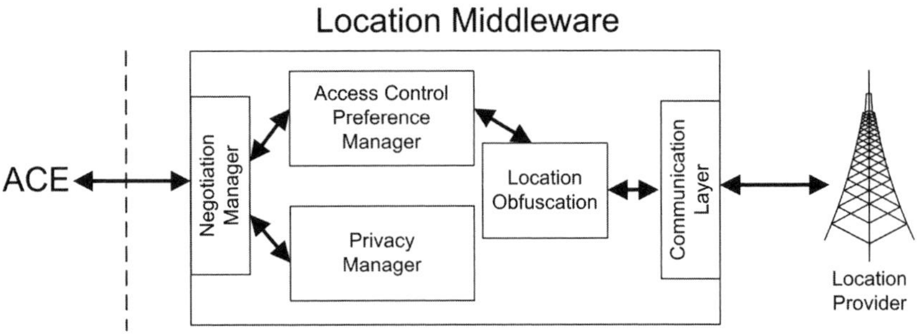

Location Middleware

Fig. 3. Location Middleware

The location middleware, whose logical schema is depicted in Fig. 3, includes the following components.

- *Communication Layer.* It manages the communication process with Location Providers by hiding low-level communication details to other components.
- *Negotiation Manager.* It acts as an interface with the Access Control Engine to provide negotiation functionalities regarding service quality and availability based on specific negotiation protocols [34].
- *Access Control Preference Manager.* It manages location service attributes and quality parameters by interacting with the Location Obfuscation component.
- *Location Obfuscation.* It applies obfuscation techniques to location measurements for protecting location privacy of users.
- *Privacy Manager.* It manages privacy preferences expressed by users and supports the privacy-aware location-based predicate evaluation.

A key aspect of such a privacy-aware LBAC architecture is the choice of the component in charge of evaluating LBAC predicates. Although LBAC policy evaluation and enforcement are logically provided by the ACE (i.e., the LBAC system), the LBAC predicates evaluation could take place in two different ways:

- *ACE Evaluation:* the ACE requests to the LM location information relevant to the access decision, without communicating the actual LBAC predicate to be evaluated. The returned response from the LM to the ACE is an obfuscated location measurement with associated a relevance value $\mathcal{R}_{Priv}$ that characterizes its accuracy. Given the relevance $\mathcal{R}_{LBAC}$, the ACE evaluates the LBAC predicate. Since $\mathcal{R}_{LBAC}$ represents the minimum accuracy level that the ACE is willing to accept for a certain service provisioning, $\mathcal{R}_{LBAC} \leq \mathcal{R}_{Eval}$ must hold or the evaluation of the location predicate is rejected.
- *LM Evaluation:* the ACE communicates to the LM the actual LBAC predicate and requests its evaluation based on location information managed by

the LM. The returned response from the LM to the ACE is assumed to be a boolean value with associated a relevance value $\mathcal{R}_{Eval}$ that characterizes the accuracy. $\mathcal{R}_{Eval}$ is derived from $\mathcal{R}_{Priv}$ by considering the obfuscated area generated by the LM and the LBAC predicate. The meaning of $\mathcal{R}_{Eval}$ is the reliability of the predicate evaluation, which depends on the accuracy $\mathcal{R}_{Priv}$ of the obfuscated location information. The LM calculates $\mathcal{R}_{Eval}$ as follows:

$$\mathcal{R}_{Eval} = \frac{Area_{Priv \cap LBAC}}{Area_{Priv}} \cdot \mathcal{R}_{Priv} \qquad (7)$$

where the scalar factor $\frac{Area_{Priv \cap LBAC}}{Area_{Priv}}$ depends on the degree of overlapping between the areas resulting by the application of the obfuscation techniques to the location measurement of the user and the area specified by the LBAC predicate (i.e., $Area_{Priv \cap LBAC}$). Again, $\mathcal{R}_{LBAC} \leq \mathcal{R}_{Eval}$ must hold.

Both solutions are viable, although well-suited for different sets of requirements. On the one side, the ACE Evaluation provides a clear separation between business-oriented components (i.e., ACE and Business Application) and location services (i.e., LM and LP). In addition, ACE Evaluation assures that the LM never deals with application-dependent predicates and the ACE never releases information about its access control policies. On the other side, LM Evaluation avoids releasing location information to the ACE. In this setting, location information is always managed by LM that becomes the only trusted component of the architecture with regard to location privacy.

6 Conclusions

Information regarding physical locations of users is rapidly becoming easily available for processing by online and mobile location-based services. Combined with novel application opportunities, however, threats to personal privacy are gaining special prominence, as witnessed by recent security incidents targeting privacy of individuals. This chapter has presented the main techniques aimed at protecting location privacy. The chapter has also described a privacy-aware LBAC architecture that integrates users privacy preferences, obfuscation techniques for location privacy protection, and privacy-enhanced location-based access control.

Acknowledgments

This work was partially supported by the European Union within the PRIME Project in the FP6/IST Programme under contract IST-2002-507591, by the Italian Ministry of Research Fund for Basic Research (FIRB) under project RBNE05FKZ2 and by the Italian MIUR under project MAPS.

References

1. Duckham, M., Kulik, L.: Location privacy and location-aware computing. In: Dynamic & Mobile GIS: Investigating Change in Space and Time. Taylor & Francis (2006) 34–51
2. Lee, J.W.: Location-tracing sparks privacy concerns. Korea Times. http://times.hankooki.com, 16 November 2004. Accessed 22 December 2006
3. Foxs News: Man Accused of Stalking Ex-Girlfriend With GPS. http://www.foxnews.com/story/0,2933,131487,00.html, 04 September 2004. Accessed 22 March 2007
4. Beresford, A.R., Stajano, F.: Location privacy in pervasive computing. IEEE Pervasive Computing **2**(1) (2003) 46–55
5. Bettini, C., Wang, X., Jajodia, S.: Protecting privacy against location-based personal identification. In: Proc. of the 2nd VLDB Workshop on Secure Data Management, LNCS 3674, Springer-Verlag (2005)
6. Gruteser, M., Grunwald, D.: Anonymous usage of location-based services through spatial and temporal cloaking. In: Proc. of the 1st International Conference on Mobile Systems, Applications, and Services. (May 2003)
7. Duckham, M., Kulik, L.: A formal model of obfuscation and negotiation for location privacy. In: Proc. of the 3rd International Conference PERVASIVE 2005, Munich, Germany (May 2005)
8. Ciriani, V., De Capitani di Vimercati, S., Foresti, S., Samarati, P.: K-Anonymity. In: Security in Decentralized Data Management. Springer (2007)
9. Samarati, P.: Protecting respondents' identities in microdata release. IEEE Transactions on Knowledge and Data Engineering **13**(6) (2001) 1010–1027
10. Ardagna, C., Cremonini, M., Damiani, E., De Capitani di Vimercati, S., Samarati, P.: Supporting location-based conditions in access control policies. In: Proc. of the ACM Symposium on Information, Computer and Communications Security (ASIACCS'06), Taipei, Taiwan (March 2006)
11. Bonatti, P., Samarati, P.: A unified framework for regulating access and information release on the web. Journal of Computer Security **10**(3) (2002) 241–272
12. Marsit, N., Hameurlain, A., Mammeri, Z., Morvan, F.: Query processing in mobile environments: a survey and open problems. In: Proc. of the 1st International Conference on Distributed Framework for Multimedia Applications (DFMA'05), Besancon, France (February 2005)
13. Jajodia, S., Samarati, P., Sapino, M., Subrahmanian, V.: Flexible support for multiple access control policies. ACM Transactions on Database Systems **26**(2) (June 2001) 214–260
14. OASIS: eXtensible Access Control Markup Language (XACML) Version 1.0. http://www.oasis-open.org/committees/xacml. (2003)
15. van der Horst, T., Sundelin, T., Seamons, K., Knutson, C.: Mobile trust negotiation: Authentication and authorization in dynamic mobile networks. In: Proc. of the 8th IFIP Conference on Communications and Multimedia Security, Lake Windermere, England (September 2004)
16. Gedik, B., Liu, L.: Location privacy in mobile systems: A personalized anonymization model. In: Proc. of the 25th International Conference on Distributed Computing Systems (IEEE ICDCS 2005), Columbus, Ohio (June 2005)
17. Gruteser, M., Bredin, J., Grunwald, D.: Path privacy in location-aware computing. In: Proc. of the Second International Conference on Mobile Systems,

Application and Services (MobiSys2004), Boston, Massachussetts, USA (June 2004)

18. Gruteser, M., Liu, X.: Protecting privacy in continuous location-tracking applications. IEEE Security & Privacy Magazine **2**(2) (March-April 2004) 28–34

19. Ho, B., Gruteser, M.: Protecting location privacy through path confusion. In: Proc. of IEEE/CreateNet International Conference on Security and Privacy for Emerging Areas in Communication Networks (SecureComm), Athens, Greece (September 2005)

20. Mokbel, M., Chow, C.Y., Aref, W.: The new casper: Query processing for location services without compromising privacy. In: Proceedings of the 32nd International Conference on Very Large Data Bases, Korea (September 2006) 763–774

21. Beresford, A.R., Stajano, F.: Mix zones: User privacy in location-aware services. In: Proc. of the 2nd IEEE Annual Conference on Pervasive Computing and Communications Workshops (PERCOMW04). (2004)

22. Hauser, C., Kabatnik, M.: Towards Privacy Support in a Global Location Service. In: Proc. of the IFIP Workshop on IP and ATM Traffic Management (WATM/EUNICE 2001), Paris, France (March 2001)

23. Geopriv: Geographic Location/Privacy.
http://www.ietf.org/html.charters/geopriv-charter.html. (September 2006)

24. Hong, D., Yuan, M., Shen, V.Y.: Dynamic privacy management: a plug-in service for the middleware in pervasive computing. In: Proc. of the 7th International Conference on Human Computer Interaction with Mobile Devices & Services (MobileHCI'05), Salzburg, Austria (2005)

25. Langheinrich, M.: A privacy awareness system for ubiquitous computing environments. In Borriello, G., Holmquist, L.E., eds.: Proc. of the 4th International Conference on Ubiquitous Computing (Ubicomp 2002). (September 2002) 237–245

26. W3C: Platform for privacy preferences (p3p) project.
http://www.w3.org/TR/P3P/. (April 2002)

27. Duckham, M., Kulik, L.: Simulation of obfuscation and negotiation for location privacy. In: Proc. of Conference On Spatial Information Theory (COSIT 2005). (September 2005) 31–48

28. Openwave: Openwave Location Manager. http://www.openwave.com/. (2006)

29. Bellavista, P., Corradi, A., Giannelli, C.: Efficiently managing location information with privacy requirements in wi-fi networks: a middleware approach. In: Proc. of the International Symposium on Wireless Communication Systems (ISWCS'05), Siena, Italy (September 2005)

30. Ardagna, C., Cremonini, M., Damiani, E., De Capitani di Vimercati, S., Samarati, P.: Managing privacy in LBAC systems. In: Proc. of the Second IEEE International Symposium on Pervasive Computing and Ad Hoc Communications (PCAC-07), Niagara Falls, Canada (May 2007)

31. Ardagna, C., Cremonini, M., Damiani, E., De Capitani di Vimercati, S., Samarati, P.: A middleware architecture for integrating privacy preferences and location accuracy. In: Proc. of the 22nd IFIP TC-11 International Information Security Conference (SEC 2007), Sandton, South Africa (May 2007)

32. Ardagna, C., Cremonini, M., Damiani, E., De Capitani di Vimercati, S., Samarati, S.: Location privacy protection through obfuscation-based techniques. In: Proc. of the 21st Annual IFIP WG 11.3 Working Conference on Data and Applications Security, Redondo Beach, CA, USA (July 2007)

33. Atluri, V., Shin, H.: Efficient enforcement of security policies based on tracking of mobile users. In: Proc. of the 20th Annual IFIP WG 11.3 Working Conference on Data and Applications Security, Sophia Antipolis, France (July-August 2006) 237–251
34. Ardagna, C., Cremonini, M., Damiani, E., De Capitani di Vimercati, S., Samarati, P.: Location-based metadata and negotiation protocols for LBAC in a one-to-many scenario. In: Proc. of the Workshop on Security and Privacy in Mobile and Wireless Networking (SecPri_MobiWi 2006), Coimbra, Portugal (May 2006)

Efficiently Enforcing the Security and Privacy Policies in a Mobile Environment

Vijayalakshmi Atluri[1] and Heechang Shin[2]

[1] Rutgers University, Newark, NJ `atluri@cimic.rutgers.edu`
[2] Rutgers University, Newark, NJ `hshin@cimic.rutgers.edu`

Summary. Effective delivery of *location-based services* (LBS) requires efficient processing of access requests to find the *past, present* and *future* location of the mobile customers (or moving objects) that match a certain profile. However, this gives rise to a number of security and privacy concerns because LBS may need to locate and track a mobile customer, and gain access to his/her profile. Location information has the potential to allow an adversary to physically locate a person, and user profile information may include sensitive attributes such as name, address, linguistic preference, age group, income level, marital status, education level, etc. As such, mobile customers have legitimate concerns about their personal safety, if such information should fall into the wrong hands. One way to take these concerns into account is by establishing security policies and enforcing them for every access. A comprehensive security policy can encode spatiotemporal restrictions on access to location and profile. To incorporate security, an appropriate access control mechanism must be in place to enforce the authorization specifications reflecting the above security and privacy policies. Serving an access request requires to search for the desired moving objects that satisfy the query, as well as identify and enforce the relevant security policies.

While this solves the security problem, it creates a performance problem. Often, enforcing security incurs overhead, and as a result may degrade the performance of a system. Thus, one way to alleviate this problem and to effectively serve access requests, is to efficiently organize the mobile objects, authorizations as well as mobile customers' profiles. The key insight is to realize that a lot of duplicate work is performed while searching for the relevant authorizations and mobile objects. In this book chapter, we present the different solutions proposed by researchers in a response to address the above issue. The solutions specifically propose unified index schemes for organizing moving object data, authorizations and profiles of users.

1 Introduction

In recent years, mobile phones and wireless PDAs have evolved into wireless terminals that are Global Positioning System (GPS) enabled. The market for location-aware mobile applications, often known as *location-based services*

(LBS), is very promising. LBS is to request usable, personalized information delivered at the point of need, which includes information about new or interesting products and services, promotions, and targeting of customers based on more advanced knowledge of customer profiles and preferences, automatic updates of travel reservations, etc. For example, a LBS provider can be designed to present users with targeted content such as clothing items on sale, based on prior knowledge of their profile, preferences and/or knowledge of their current location, such as proximity to a shopping mall [13]. Additionally, LBS can provide nearby points of interests based on the real-time location of the mobile customer, advising of current conditions such as traffic and weather, deliver personalized, location-aware, and context-sensitive advertising, again based on the mobile customer profiles and preferences.

Whether such LBS is delivered in a "push" or "pull" fashion, customization and personalization based on the location information, customer profiles and preferences, and vendor offerings are required. This is because, to be effective, targeted advertising should not overwhelm the mobile consumers and must push information only to a certain segment of mobile consumers based on their preferences and profiles, and based on certain marketing criteria. Obviously, these consumers should be targeted only if they are in the location where the advertisement is applicable at the time of the offer. As such, service providers require access to customers' preference profiles either through a proprietary database or use an arrangement with an LBS provider, who matches customer profiles to vendor offerings [2].

By definition, delivery of LBS requires knowledge of a mobile customer's location. Along with the location information, their preference profiles must also be maintained. Effective delivery requires efficient processing of access requests on this data to find the *past, present* and *future* status of the mobile customers (or moving objects) that match a certain profile.

However, this creates significant challenges. Since effective delivery of LBS may need to locate and track a mobile customer, and gain access to his/her profile, a number of security and privacy concerns are raised. Location information has the potential to allow an adversary to physically locate a person. As such, wireless subscribers carrying mobile devices have legitimate concerns about their personal safety, if such information should fall into the wrong hands.

Services such as targeted advertising may deliver the service based on the mobile customers' profile and preferences. It is important to note here that user profile information may include both sensitive and non-sensitive attributes such as name, address, linguistic preference, age group, income level, marital status, education level, etc. However, certain segment of mobile consumers are willing to trade-off privacy by sharing such sensitive data with selective merchants, either to benefit from personalization or to receive incentives offered by the merchants. For example, a security policy may specify that a customer is willing to reveal his age in order to enjoy a 20% discount coupon offered on sports clothing. But he is willing to do this only during the evening hours and while close to the store. As such, privacy of mobile users can be compromised if the sensitive profile information of the mobile users is revealed to unintended users. Therefore, it is important that the sensitive profile information is revealed to the respective merchants only on a need-to-know basis, when allowed. As a result, the security policies in such an environment are characterized by spatial and temporal attributes of the mobile customers (location and time), as well as their profile attributes.

In addition to the privacy concerns mentioned above, there are a number of applications that call for securing resources based on the criteria of mobile objects. These include context (location)-sensitive access control, and the ubiquitous computing environment, where access is permitted based on the location of the subjects/objects during a specific time.

In summary, in a mobile environment, there are a number of applications that require controlled access to the mobile user profiles, to their current location and movement trajectories, to mobile resources, stationary resources based on the user's spatiotemporal information. To incorporate security, an appropriate access control mechanism must be in place to enforce the authorization specifications reflecting the above security and privacy needs. One way to take these concerns into account is by establishing security policies and enforcing them for every access. A comprehensive security policy can encode spatio-temporal restrictions on access to location, profile, etc.

Traditionally, access policies are specified as a set of authorizations, where each authorization states if a given subject possesses privileges to access an object. Considering the basic authorization specification ⟨*subject, object, privilege*⟩, in a mobile environment, a moving object can be a subject, an object, or both. Access requests in such an environment can typically be on *past, present* and *future* status of the moving objects [15, 9]. Serving an access request requires to search for the desired moving objects that satisfy the query, as well as identify and enforce the relevant security policies.

While this solves the security problem, it creates a performance problem. Often, enforcing security incurs overhead, and as a result may degrade the performance of a system. However, the key insight is to realize that a lot of duplicate work is performed for both accesses. Thus, one way to alleviate this problem and to effectively serve access requests, is to efficiently organize the mobile objects, authorizations as well as mobile customers' profiles.

In this book chapter, we present the different solutions proposed by researchers in a response to address the above issue. The solutions specifically propose unified index schemes for organizing moving object data, authorizations and profiles of users.

2 System Architecture for a Mobile Application Environment

We assume the system in a location service environment comprises of the following components.

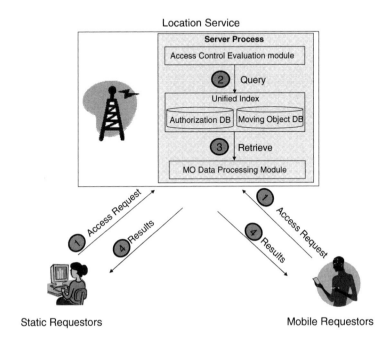

Fig. 1. System Architecture for Mobile Applications

Location Service (LS): We assume that there exists a location service that maintains the mobile customers' location and profile information, and LS is a trusted third party as in [16]. The current location of moving objects are stored and updated accordingly in order to provide most up-to-date location information to a requester. In this architecture, we assume that the moving object data is represented using the Moving Objects Spatio-Temporal (MOST) model [12] due to its simplicity and popularity in the literature. The continuous movement of mobile objects makes maintenance of location information extremely challenging. In the MOST, location information is treated as a dynamic attribute and is represented as a linear function of time [16]. This approach reduces the update frequency because the location information is updated only if the predicted location deviates from the actual location more than a certain threshold. Location information can be directly provided by users' mobile devices using wireless communication periodically, or acquired from the installed sensors. For example, the Active Badge [14] detects the location of each user in a building. Each individual carries a device called, badge, which is associated with the identifier of the user. A building is equipped with sensors detecting positions of badges. A person's location is determined by using an active badge which emits a signal every 15 seconds. A master station, which works as LS, collects the location information, and makes it available to users.

Requester: A requester is a subscriber to a service in order to gain access to the resources that LS offers. In a mobile environment, there are two types of resources that a requester can gain access to: static resources (e.g. repository room or printer) and mobile resources (location of vehicles). For example, consider a work environment where all the documents can only be accessed by employees only while they are physically located in the office. When a mobile requester submits an access request to the documents in the repository, LS checks the physical location of the requester, and only if the requester is within premises of the office, he is given access. ABng book library [1] is one such example to protect the books in the library. An Active Badge is used to authenticate the user and subsequently open the library door lock [1]. In this case, the requesters are obviously mobile.

We assume that the location information as well as the security policies are maintained by the LS. Under our framework, LS is also responsible for enforcing the specified security policies. Therefore, to efficiently enforce the access requests, LS maintains the proposed unified index, as shown in figure 1. The access requests are processed by the LS, which searches the index for the authorized data that adheres to the specified security policies. Specifically, when a user (mobile or stationary) sends an access request (1), access control evaluation module searches relevant authorizations that are applicable to the submitted access request. The query sent to the mobile object and authorization database essentially searches the unified index to identify the mobile objects that satisfy the query and the security policies of the user that are relevant to the query (2). The retrieved data from the unified index (3) is the identifiers of moving object data which satisfies the existing security policies as well as the user access request. If a user wants to access the location or trajectory information, moving object processing module associates the required information such as location or trajectory with the retrieved identifiers. Finally, the resultant mobile objects are sent to the requester (4).

The plausibility of considering LS as a trusted party is discussed in [16]: (1) enforcing spatiotemporal policies requires spatiotemporal processing which LS is normally capable of; (2) a LS is seen to be implemented as a globally distributed service which reduces the system susceptibility to the two major vulnerabilities: being a single point of failure, and being attractive to hacking attacks.

3 Authorization Model in a Mobile Environment

Specification of a security or privacy policy can be expressed as an authorization, $\alpha = \langle se, ge, p, \tau \rangle$ [3][4][5]. *se*, the subject expression specifies a set of auth-subjects such that they are associated with (1) a set of spatiotemporal and/or other traditional attributes, (2) a set of auth-subject identifiers, or (3) a combination of both. *se*, the object expression is used to specify a set of auth-objects such that they (1) are associated with a set of spatiotemporal and/or other types of attributes, (2) a set of auth-object identifiers, or (3) a combination of both. *p*, the privilege specifies the set of allowed actions by the auth-subjects specified by *se* on the auth-objects specified by *ge*. The supported privileges are not only traditional *read*, *write*, and *execute* privileges, but also include *view* that allows an auth-subject to access a mobile resource(s) within a spatiotemporal region, *locate* that allows auth-subjects to read the location information of mobile resources in the authorized spatiotemporal region, *track* that allows auth-subjects to read the trajectory information of mobile resources in the authorized spatiotemporal region, and *Compose* that allows auth-subjects to write information on the auth-objects. Finally, τ, the temporal expression is used to denote the basic temporal element in an expression. For example, τ can be a time point (e.g., Apr9:2007:17:12:39), a time interval (e.g., [Apr9:2007:17:12:39, Apr9:2007:19:12:39]), or a set of time intervals.

In a mobile environment, an authorization would be associated with spatiotemporal extents. In other words, for a given authorization α, $\alpha.se$ or $\alpha.ge$ would involve the spatiotemporal specifications for specifying auth-subjects or auth-objects respectively. There exist three different request scenarios based on the mobility of requesters and resources, and the corresponding authorizations in order to protect the resources.

- *Mobile Requesters upon Static Resources (MSR):* (e.g, an employee (mobile requester) tries to use the printer in the office (static resource).) In this scenario, the access control decision for the requester is dependent on the current location of the requester. To protect static resources from mobile requesters, a *Moving Auth-Subject upon Static Auth-Object Authorization* (α^{MS}) can be specified. Here, $\alpha.se$ is associated with the spatiotemporal extent. Examples of such security policies are as follows.
  Policy 1: Any employee can send a print job if she is currently located at the office during the office hours.
  Policy 2: A human resource employee is allowed to access performance records of employees only during office hours and while he is physically in his office.
- *Static Requesters upon Mobile Resources (SMR):* (e.g., a merchant (static requester) tries to send promotion deals to near-by mobile customers (mobile resources).) In this scenario, the location of mobile resources such as mobile customers plays an important role for evaluating the access control decision for the static requesters. Generally, mobile users have their

own privacy/security policies which are dependent on the locations and profiles. To protect mobile resources from static requesters, a *Static Auth-Subject upon Moving Auth-Object Authorization* (α^{SM}) can be specified. Here, $\alpha.se$ is associated with the spatiotemporal extent. An example of such a security policy is as follows.

Policy 3: In order to get a personalized promotion deal, a mobile customer is willing to reveal her age and salary information to a merchant, provided she is within 10 miles from the shopping mall during evening hours.

• *Mobile Requesters upon Mobile Resources (MMR):* (e.g., a boss (mobile requester) tries to access the locations of her employees (mobile resource).) In this scenario, locations of both entities (requesters and resources) are important. Mobile resources (employees) do not want their boss to know their current locations after the work hours, and these sensitive information must be available only for the work purposes. To protect mobile resources from mobile requesters, a *Moving Auth-Subject upon Moving Auth-Object Authorization* (α^{MM}) can be specified. Here, both of $\alpha.se$ and $\alpha.ge$ are associated with the spatiotemporal extents. An example of such a security policy is as follows.

Policy 4: A manager can access the location of his employee (John) information between "9am and 5pm" and while the manager is "in the office." Note that both the requester (manager in this case) and the resource (his employee) are mobile.

Observe that we do not include the case of "Static Requesters upon Static Resources" because this falls into the traditional static environment.

4 Unified Index for Authorizations and Profiles

The ASM-Trie model [16] considers static requesters (merchants) upon mobile resources (mobile users' profile and location information), and therefore can support example policies such as Policy 3 presented in section 3. The result of an access request by a merchant is a set of pseudonyms of the mobile customers that satisfy the authorizations and profiles, so that the merchant can "push" mass advertising to the mobile customers. In a pull scenario, non-expiring offers are stored at LS until the customer fetches them [16].

The basic idea in the proposed ASM-Trie model is to represent authorizations in the form of alphabetical strings. This is accomplished by first organizing that requesters (auth-subjects), resources (auth-objects), location and time interval as hierarchies. For example: (1) Because the model considers the mobile advertisement environment, auth-subjects are merchants. Therefore, the *Auth-Subject Hierarchy* comprises of all merchants, which may include hotels, retail businesses, etc., where the leaf nodes represent the individual merchants. (2) The *Auth-Object Hierarchy* is composed of two levels: the root node is $\{l+p\}$ and the leaves are $\{l\}$ and $\{p\}$ where l is the location information and p is the customer profile. (3) Similar to the auth-subject hierarchy, in the *Location Hierarchy* the root node represents all members, and the leaf node represents the members of the most specific representation. (4) Finally, the *Time Interval Hierarchy* in which an interval is represented by a node and all its component time intervals are represented as the children of it. One example would be the case where the root node represents the 24 hours in a day, and its children nodes could be "During Working Hours" and "After Working Hours." Observe that in case of the time interval hierarchy, children nodes are the exact decomposition of its parent node.

Each alphabetical string consists of five substrings that represent the ID, the object, the subject, the location, and the time. These substrings are drawn from preprocessed tables where the substrings are unique in each table. The path from the root to any node in a hierarchy is embedded in the substring of that node. For instance, the substring 'bcdbf' from the table 1 includes the letter 'b' for the USA, letter 'c' for Mid-Atlantic, letter 'd' for New Jersey and the two letters 'bf' for Essex County. Also, all the substrings are made equal length by adding a padding of letter 'a'. The ASM-trie allows search on the encoded strings. In the ASM-Trie, the path from the root to a leaf is an authorization rule.

Location	Code without padding	Code with padding
All USA	b	baaaa
New England	bb	bbaaa
Mid-Atlantic	bc	bcaaa
...	bc	bcaaa
New Jersey	bcd	bcdaa
New York	bce	bceaa
...		
Essex County	bcdbe	bcdbe
Hudson County	bcdbf	bcdbf

Table 1. A Sample from location encoding

Because authorizations are based on this hierarchy, evaluation of a user request may need to search different places in the hierarchy. Evaluation of user request is done by first creating a set of search keys. The search process extracts a letter from the search key and finds its order. This search operation is recursively performed until the end of the string is reached and an access control decision is returned if there exists a match.

For example, consider a query submitted by the Hilton for all customers in Essex County (which is the part of the state of NJ, USA) for a time interval 4:45 to 5:15 PM (which intersects with both time interval leaf nodes "During Working Hours" and "After Working Hours"). Assume that all customers who satisfy the query will be moving inside Essex County during the time interval. The evaluation proceeds as follows: In this case, for each customer and for each spatiotemporal window that the customer passes through, a set of search keys are created. Two spatiotemporal windows are possible: (Essex County, During Working Hours) and (Essex County, After Working Hours). Thus, the search key includes object $\{l\}$, the requester ID of Hilton, and a spatiotemporal window for each customer. The search operation is done in the order of the auth-object, the auth-subject, the location, and the time interval hierarchies since this same order is used in the authorization specification.

The approach using the ASM-Trie is not capable of providing unified index for authorizations and mobile objects. Moreover it considers the case where the auth-subjects are only static but cannot handle the cases when both subjects and objects are moving.

5 Unified Index for Authorizations and Moving Objects

The following two approaches have been proposed in the literature of unified index scheme for authorizations and moving objects.

- $^S TPR$-$Tree:$ Unified index for present and anticipated future locations of moving objects and authorizations.
- S^{PPF}-$Tree:$ Unified index for past, present, and anticipated future locations of moving objects and authorizations.

Both of unified index schemes consider the cases of mobile requesters upon static resources and static requesters upon mobile resources, but not mobile requesters upon mobile resources.

5.1 ^{S}TPR-Tree

^{S}TPR-tree is constructed by appropriately overlaying authorization on the TPR-tree [11], which in turn is a variant of the R-tree. Because the locations of moving objects are constantly updated, the main challenge for moving object database is to minimize the updating cost. For this purpose, in the TPR-tree, the moving object is represented as its initial location and its velocity vector; thus, a moving object is updated only if it deviates more than the specified tolerance level. This will reduce the necessity for frequent updating. Moreover, since the velocity of moving objects is also maintained, it can estimate their anticipated future locations.

Unlike the traditional *Minimum Bounding Rectangle* (MBR) in R-trees [8], a *Time-Parameterized bounding Rectangle* (TPR) is used to index velocity vectors as well as location information. However, given a moving object, it is unrealistic to assume that its velocity remains constant. The predicted future location of a object specified as a linear function of time becomes less and less accurate as time elapses [11]. To address this issue, the TPR-tree defines a *time horizon*, H, representing the time interval during which the velocities of the moving objects hold good. It assumes that the tree is constructed by bulkloading the moving objects at some point in time (say t_0) and reconstructs the tree after H. In essence, the tree is good during $[t_0, t_0 + H]$ interval and all predictions made within this interval are acceptable in terms of the degree of accuracy. The TPRs, organized as a hierarchical structure forms the TPR-tree. At the bottom-most level of the hierarchy, a set of moving objects could be grouped to form TPRs. Each TPR of the next higher level is the bounding TPR of the set of TPRs of all of its children. The root of the hierarchy is thus the bounding TPR covering all its lower level TPRs in a recursive manner.

The ^{S}TPR-Tree constructed by overlaying authorizations over the nodes of the TPR-tree. For a given authorization α, we denote the spatiotemporal extent of the authorization as $\alpha^\square$ if the type of the authorization is α^{MS} or α^{SM}. In case of α^{MM}, we denote the spatiotemporal extent associated with $\alpha.se$ as $\alpha^{\square s}$ and $\alpha.ge$ as $\alpha^{\square o}$ because we need to differentiate the spatiotemporal extents because it could be from *se* or *ge*. Also, we denote the spatiotemporal extent (TPR) of a node N as $N^\square$.

Overlaying is done by traversing the tree recursively starting from the root node to the leaf level and for each node N in the traversal path, $\alpha^\square$ is compared with $N^\square$. We encounter the following possible cases:

- **Case 1:** The spatiotemporal extent of α fully encloses that of the node N. In this case the tree traversal will be stopped and α is overlaid on N. This is because, if a subject is allowed to access objects within a certain spatiotemporal region, it is allowed to access objects in the *subregion* of that [4]. After overlaying an authorization on a node, it is not necessary to overlay the same authorization on any of its descendants.

- **Case 2:** The spatiotemporal extent of α overlaps with that of the node N. If N is a non-leaf node, for each of N's children a comparison between $\alpha^\square$ and $child^\square$ is done. The goal here is to check if there exists a child of N whose spatiotemporal extent is enclosed by that of α. On the other hand, if N is a leaf node, α is overlaid on N. This is because, when the spatiotemporal extent of the authorization $\alpha^\square$ does not enclose, but overlaps with that of the leaf node $N^\square$, we need to ensure that no relevant authorizations are discarded. Also, note that only part of the spatiotemporal extent of $N^\square$ is in the authorized region. The moving objects from the remaining unauthorized spatiotemporal region must be removed from the user's output, if the user request includes this region.

- **Case 3:** If neither of the above is true, $\alpha^\square$ is disjoint with that of $N^\square$. Then the overlaying process is stopped. This is because, if $\alpha.se$ does not have a privilege to the region covered by $N^\square$, then α is not applicable to that region. Also, since $N^\square$ includes spatiotemporal extent of all of its children nodes, $\alpha^\square$ is disjoint with the spatiotemporal extent of each child. Thus, there is no need to traverse further down the tree.

For all three different user request scenarios presented in section 3, the user access request evaluation is based on the overlaying procedure described above. In [4], only the situation of MSR is considered, and the SMR type of requests are supported in [5]. ^{s}TPR-tree only supports authorizations of type α^{SM} and α^{MS}, and they are not able to support MMR. The support of MMR is addressed in [7].

Static Requesters upon Mobile Resources (SMR): For a given user request SMR, the procedure traverses the subtree under the root node r until it reaches the leaf level. During this traversal, it compares the spatiotemporal extent of a user request with that of each node N in the traversal path. One would encounter three different cases:

- **enclosing:** If there exists any overlaid authorizations in N such that the set of auth-subjects evaluated by ge contains the requester of SMR, then all the moving objects that are located within the intersection area of $N^\square$ and $\alpha^\square$ are returned.
- **overlapping:** If there exists any overlaid authorization in N such that the set of auth-subjects evaluated by se contains the requester of SMR, only the objects overlapping with $SMR^\square$ are returned. However, one still needs to check authorizations overlaid on the descendants of N. This is because, those overlaid on the descendents of N may include another spatiotemporal region that $\alpha^\square$ does not cover. If N is a leaf node, all the moving objects that are overlapped with the intersection area of $N^\square$ and $\alpha^\square$ and $SMR^\square$ are returned.
- **disjoint:** The evaluation process is stopped because none of the moving objects that are stored at the subtree rooted at N are within $SMR^\square$.

Moving Requesters upon Static Resources (MSR): The evaluation starts by traversing the tree from the root node until it reaches the leaf level. During the traversal, it checks if the spatiotemporal extent of each node in the traversal path includes the current location of the requester of MSR. If so, all the auth-objects contained in the spatiotemporal region covered by ge such that the requester of MSR is in the set of subjects evaluated by se are collected. If the requested resources are among this auth-objects set, the traversal is stopped and a true is returned meaning that the requester is allowed to gain access to the requested resource. Otherwise, traversal is continued. In case N is a leaf node, for each authorization N in α^{MS}, the auth-objects of α^{MS} are included, if the intersection area of $N^\square$ and $\alpha^\square$ encloses the location of the requester.

Moving Requesters upon Moving Resources (MMR): Two traversals of the tree can process MMR. The first traversal is to evaluate if the requester is located in the authorized spatiotemporal region in order to access the moving resources. If this is true, another traversal can be performed to retrieve the moving resources that authorize the requester to access their resources.

The first operation can be performed using the steps used for MSR, and the second operation can be performed using the steps for SMR.

One main limitation of ^{S}TPR-tree is that it can only support the security/privacy policies based on the current and future locations of moving objects, but not on the past locations. As a result, it cannot support the security/privacy policies based on *track* privilege because the past status of moving objects is not being stored. The S^{PPF}-tree, presented next, eliminates this limitation using the concept of partial persistence.

5.2 S^{PPF}-Tree

The previously introduced ^{S}TPR-tree cannot support the security/privacy policies based on tracking of mobile users. It is important to note that tracking information could also be sensitive and therefore security policies are often specified to reflect this. To efficiently enforce these policies, the tree must support this functionality in the sense that all the location history of moving objects are preserved. S^{PPF}-tree, an extension of ^{S}TPR-tree, can maintain past, present and future positions of moving objects along with authorizations, by employing partial persistent storage. S^{PPF} is a variant of R^{PPF}-tree [10], which applies the concept of the partial persistence to the TPR-tree in order to preserve the past locations of moving objects, as well. Partial persistence is based on the following important concepts.

- **Evolution of Index Nodes and Data Entry:** In order to be transformed to a partially persistent structure, each index (leaf or non-leaf) node and data entry (moving objects) include two additional fields for maintaining the evolution of the index records: *insertion time* and *deletion time*. These are denoted as $N.insertionTime$ and $N.deletionTime$ for node N. If a new moving object is available and captured at time t_0, its insertion time is set to t_0 and deletion time is set to ∞. When the object is logically deleted from the index at time t_d, its deletion time is changed from ∞ to t_d. The same rule applies to index nodes. A node or a data entry is said to be *dead* if its deletion time is less than ∞, otherwise it is said to be *alive.*

- **Time Split:** When an update (insertion or deletion) occurs at a node N, it may result in structural changes if it becomes underfull or overfull. If this is the case, a *time-split* occurs to N. The time-split on a leaf node N at time t is performed by copying all alive entries in N at t to a new leaf node L and timestamp of both L and those copied entries are set to $[t, \infty)$. In addition, the deletion time of N is set to t and N is considered dead. Then, the new node L is investigated further in order to incorporate it into the tree. Essentially, three different cases may arise: (1) split: If L is overfull, split it into two nodes and then insert these two nodes into the tree. (2) merge: If L is underfull, accommodate by merging it with another node. (3) no change: If L is neither overfull nor underfull, insert it directly into the tree. After the structural change, the TPR of the parent node may need to be updated accordingly and the described process may be repeated up to the root node. If the root node is time-split at time t, a pointer to the new alive node together with timestamp $[t, \infty)$ is added to a special root array that is stored in the main memory [10].

Note that if the tree is constructed at t_0 and time split for the alive root element of the root array occurs at $\{t_1, t_2, \ldots, t_n\}$, each root element in the root array is associated with time interval $[t_0, t_1), [t_1, t_2), \ldots, [t_{n-1}, t_n)$, and $[t_n, \infty)$. The associated time interval for each root element represents the ephemeral structure of the tree during those time intervals. Thus, if we want to know the status of the tree at time t, we simply need to find a root element r from the root array R such that the time interval of r includes t.

Observe that there are two kinds of moving objects: one is currently moving objects so that their ending location is predicted but not decided (called alive moving objects), and another type is the objects that already stopped moving, or changes its velocity or anticipated future location above the predefined deviation level (called dead moving objects). During update (insertion or deletion) of moving objects in the tree, the leaf node where the update occurs are evaluated to see if there still exists a pre-specified range of alive moving objects. If the number is out of this specified range, alive objects in the node are copied into a new node (called time split). The original node is used for evaluating the past positions of moving objects; the newly created node is for the present and future positions of moving objects such as ^{S}TPR-tree. The similar process is applied to index nodes: in this case, the number of alive children nodes is checked if it is within the predefined range.

Because S^{PPF}-tree maintains past positions of moving objects as well, the overlaying process is more complicated than that of the ^{S}TPR-tree because authorizations are required to be maintained properly not only for present and future positions but also past positions: in case of ^{S}TPR-tree, the tree is re-constructed after some reasonable duration of time, and authorizations are batch-overlaid on the tree. Thus, there is no need to deal with maintenance of authorizations during the tree's life time. Since the S^{PPF}-tree handles all the history information as well, it is necessary to maintain the overlaid authorizations more carefully in order not to violate the overlaying strategy. An authorization log is introduced to handle this situation: whenever an authorization is applicable to the tree, the authorization log overlays the newly applicable authorization on the alive nodes, and relocate the authorizations from the alive nodes to the dead nodes if they are only applicable to the dead nodes. An authorization log is a data structure constructed by spreading all the authorizations on the time line. As time elapses, a new authorization becomes applicable to the tree when the valid time duration of the authorizations is overlapped with the tree's valid time duration, i.e. between current time and the time horizon. Then, the authorization log triggers an auth_begin

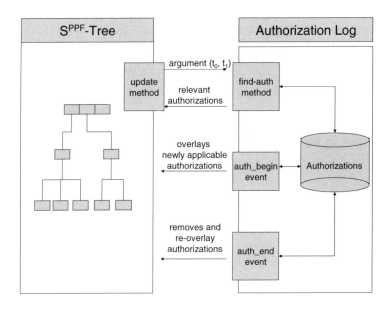

Fig. 2. Relationship of Authorization Log and S^{PPF}-Tree

event, which will overlay the authorization on the tree. On the other hand, certain overlaid authorizations become invalid when the valid time duration of the authorization is not applicable to the overlaid nodes. In this case, the authorization log triggers an auth_end event, which will remove the invalid authorizations from the overlaid nodes and re-overlay on the tree because the removed ones may satisfy the overlaying conditions of other nodes in the tree. Also, update must take care of the cases when the time-split occurs. Time-split creates a new node where some authorizations may be eligible to be overlaid on it. The authorization log supports a method, called find-auth, which computes all the authorizations overlapping with the valid interval of the newly created node. Then, the authorizations as a result of find-auth, will be overlaid on the new node if it meets the overlaying condition.

User request evaluation is similar to that of ^{S}TPR-tree except that it can now evaluate a user request that includes the tracking of moving objects as well due to the functionality of holding all the updates history. In this case, only the nodes of which initial creation time and the time when time-split occurs, if time-splitted (otherwise, this time can be considered as current time) are overlapped with the time interval of the user request are evaluated.

6 Unified Index for Authorizations, Moving Objects and Profiles

In this section, we present S^{STP}-tree [6] that supports efficient enforcement of security/privacy policies based on the user locations as well as profiles. Each node in the S^{STP}-tree comprises of the spatiotemporal attributes as well as a profile bounding vector, denoted as PV^B (explained later), in order to support the profile conditions. The role of profile bounding vector is to filter profile conditions that do not satisfy the designated profile query conditions.

One can assume that user profile as a set of attributes associated with a mobile customer that characterizes the user. These attributes may include (1) demographic information (e.g. country, race, age, gender, etc.), (2) contact information (e.g., name, address, zip code, telephone number, e-mail, etc.), (3) personal preferences (e.g., hobbies, favorite activities, favorite magazines, etc.), and (4) behavioral profile (e.g., level of activity, type of activity, etc.)[3]

Discretization is used to represent user profiles. All the possible discrete values for the profile attributes are represented simply use as many bits as the number of different discrete values. If the attribute is numerical data type, the continuous data space is partitioned into disjoint mutually-exclusive intervals, as shown for attribute age in figure 3.

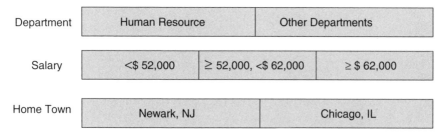

Fig. 3. Profile Attribute Discretization

For example, if $Salary < \$52,000$, we represent it with '100', and '001' if $Salary \geq \$62,000$. Table 2 shows the examples of user profile vectors. For example, profile representation of the user, Doe, is $\langle 10, 001, 10 \rangle$ because his department 'Human Resource', is represented as '10', salary, \$63,000, as 001, and home town, 'Newark, NJ' as '10'.

---

[3] The behavioral profile is created by observing activities and habits of a user continuously. For example, Sony TiVo box records frequently-watched television shows and generates a behavioral profile based on the past patterns. In order to do so, information such as what kind of activity has been done by a user at what intensity needs to be captured. In case of TiVo, type of activity can be 'watching drama' and level of activity can be '2 hours.'

Name	Department	Salary	Home Town	Profile Vector
Doe	Human Resource	$63,000	Newark, NJ	$\langle 10,001,10 \rangle$
James	Other Departments	$45,000	Chicago, IL	$\langle 01,100,01 \rangle$
Robert	Human Resource	$53,000	Chicago, IL	$\langle 01,010,01 \rangle$

Table 2. User Profile Information

All the different profile attribute representations are concatenated to form a profile vector, which is used to represent the profile of a mobile user. Because the same discretization is applied to all the mobile users, the length of profile vector is the same for all mobile users.

The idea of profile bounding vector, PV^B, is to represent a set of users' profiles by applying bitwise 'OR' operations of the profile vectors. For example, suppose that the set of profile attributes is department, salary, and home town. Consider three profile vectors, $pv_{\text{Doe}} = \langle 10,001,10 \rangle$, $pv_{\text{James}} = \langle 01,100,01 \rangle$, and $pv_{\text{Robert}} = \langle 01,010,01 \rangle$. Then, PV^B of two users, Doe and James is $\langle 11,101,11 \rangle$, and PV^B of all three users is $\langle 11,111,11 \rangle$.

Given a set of PV^Bs, hierarchical structure can be formed, also. Suppose we have three PV^Bs.

$$PV_1^B = \langle 11,011,10 \rangle$$
$$PV_2^B = \langle 10,010,10 \rangle$$
$$PV_3^B = \langle 01,001,10 \rangle$$

These PV^Bs can be organized in a hierarchical structure with PV_2^B and PV_3^B as the children of PV_1^B. Each PV^B bounds PV^Bs of all of its children. Therefore, the root of the hierarchy covers the set of PV^Bs of all of its descendants.

The S^{STP}-tree is constructed similar to that of ^sTPR-tree, but PV^B is also updated accordingly during the insertion of new objects. Each moving object is represented with its spatiotemporal and profile attributes. Thus, each node in the S^{STP}-tree includes a TPR and a PV^B for specifying the spatiotemporal and profile conditions, respectively. When a new moving object is inserted into S^{STP}-tree, the first operation is to find a leaf node that enlarges the TPR of the node smallest among all the other leaf nodes. After inserting the object into the target leaf node, the TPR and PV^B of the target leaf node are updated if necessary. If TPR or PV^B of the parent node does not enclose all of its children as a result of inserting a new object into the leaf node, the parent node is updated accordingly. The same operation is applied to its parent node until the root node is reached recursively.

Given an authorization α and a node N, the following different cases of spatiotemporal and PV^B relationships between α and N arise. The PV^B of an authorization and a node are denoted as $\alpha^{\rightarrow}$ and $N^{\rightarrow}$, respectively.

- *Spatiotemporal Relationship*
  - $\alpha^{\square} \supset_{st} N^{\square}$: Spatiotemporal extent of α encloses that of N.

- $\alpha^{\square} \cap_{st} N^{\square}$: Spatiotemporal extent of α overlaps with that of N.
- $\alpha^{\square} \otimes_{st} N^{\square}$: Spatiotemporal extent of α is disjoint with that of N
- *Profile Bounding Vector Relationship*
  - $\alpha^{\rightarrow} \supset_p N^{\rightarrow}$: $\alpha^{\rightarrow}$ encloses $N^{\rightarrow}$ if for each non-zero profile attribute vector [4] of $\alpha^{\rightarrow}$ and $N^{\rightarrow}$, bitwise 'OR' operation of $\alpha^{\rightarrow}$ and $N^{\rightarrow}$ results in $\alpha^{\rightarrow}$.
  - $\alpha^{\rightarrow} \cap_p N^{\rightarrow}$: $\alpha^{\rightarrow}$ overlaps with $N^{\rightarrow}$ if for each non-zero profile attribute of $\alpha^{\rightarrow}$ and $N^{\rightarrow}$, their bitwise 'AND' operation results in a non-zero profile attribute vector.
  - $\alpha^{\rightarrow} \otimes_p N^{\rightarrow}$: $\alpha^{\rightarrow}$ is disjoint with $N^{\rightarrow}$ if for each non-zero profile attribute of $\alpha^{\rightarrow}$ and $N^{\rightarrow}$, their bitwise 'XOR' operation results in all "1"s in the resultant vector.

The spatiotemporal relationships are handled similar to that in earlier sections. Profile bounding vector relationships between an authorization and a node are handled as follows. First, in case of enclosing relationship, observe that for every bit value of '0' of $\alpha^{\rightarrow}$, the corresponding bit value of $N^{\rightarrow}$ must be '0' because there must not exist any profile attribute value that only $N^{\rightarrow}$ includes but $\alpha^{\rightarrow}$ does not. Therefore, bitwise 'OR' operation would generate the same value with $\alpha^{\rightarrow}$. Also, in case of overlapping relationship, one need to see if there exists any common profile attribute value between α and $N^{\rightarrow}$. Therefore, if bitwise 'AND' operation results in a non-zero profile vector, we know that there exists common value set. Finally, in case of disjoint relationship, it is obvious that α and $N^{\rightarrow}$ should not share any profile attribute value that is common to each other. The bitwise 'XOR' operation is used for checking this condition, and the result of 'XOR' must include all '1's in the resultant $N^{\rightarrow}$.

$\alpha^{\rightarrow}$	$N^{\rightarrow}$	AND	OR	XOR	Relationship
110	011	010	111	101	$\alpha^{\rightarrow} \cap_p N^{\rightarrow}$
110	010	010	110	100	$\alpha^{\rightarrow} \cap_p N^{\rightarrow}$, $\alpha^{\rightarrow} \supset_p N^{\rightarrow}$
110	001	000	111	111	$\alpha^{\rightarrow} \otimes_p N^{\rightarrow}$

Table 3. Bitwise Operation Results

The authorizations overlaying procedure traverses the S^{STP}-tree from the root node to leaf level by recursively comparing both the spatiotemporal extents and PV^Bs of the overlaying authorization and each node in the traversal path. The following possible cases are encountered.

- **Case 1:** If $(\alpha^{\square}$ encloses $N^{\square}) \wedge (\alpha^{\rightarrow}$ encloses $N^{\rightarrow})$ is true, traversal is stopped and α is overlaid on N.

---

[4] A non-zero profile attribute vector refers to a binary vector that includes the value "1" in at least one bit

- **Case 2:** Else if ($\alpha^{\square}$ is disjoint with $N^{\square}$) $\vee$ ($\alpha^{\rightarrow}$ is disjoint with $N^{\rightarrow}$) is true, overlaying process is stopped.
- **Case 3:** Else if ($\alpha^{\square}$ overlaps $N^{\square}$) $\vee$ ($\alpha^{\rightarrow}$ overlaps $N^{\rightarrow}$) is true, the over-laying strategy is different depending on the level of N. If N is a non-leaf node, traversal to each of N's children node C is done, and the same comparison between α and C is performed. If N is a leaf node, α is overlaid on N.

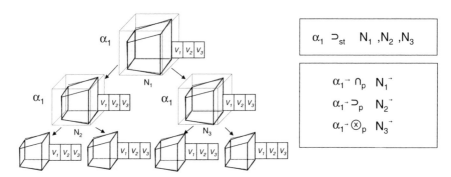

Fig. 4. Authorization Overlaying Process in S^{STP}-tree

Figure 4 presents the overlaying process in the S^{STP}-tree. It shows that a node N_1 is a root node of the tree, and N_2, N_3 are the children nodes of N_1. Consider an authorization α_1 to be overlaid on the S^{STP}-tree. α_1 cannot be overlaid on the node N_1 since $\alpha_1^{\rightarrow} \cap_p N_1^{\rightarrow}$, which belongs to the case 3 above. Therefore, we need to traverse down to N_1's children nodes N_2 and N_3. The first traversal path is to N_2, and α_1 can actually be overlaid on N_2 because $\alpha_1^{\square} \supset_{st} N_2^{\square}$ and $\alpha_1^{\rightarrow} \supset_p N_2^{\rightarrow}$, which is case 1 above. Another traversal path to N_3 is stopped because $\alpha_1^{\rightarrow} \otimes_p N_3^{\rightarrow}$, which belongs to the case 2 above.

The user access request evaluation process is very similar to that of ^{s}TPR-tree. A user request typically is of the form of requesting objects in the area of interest that satisfy a certain profile criteria. For example, a merchant is interested in sending promotion deals to mobile customers who are near a mall and whose salary is greater than \$52,000. However, such promotion deals should be reached to only to the customers who are willing to reveal their salary information to that merchant (specified in the authorization) to receive the promotion deal. In the following, how such a request can be processed is discussed while enforcing the specified authorizations.

We discuss the request type of SMR only because the application of PV^B to the request type of MSR is straightforward. Observe that SMR includes spatiotemporal extent condition as well as profile condition. The profile condition of SMR is represented as PV^B and denoted as $SMR^{\rightarrow}$. The evaluation process starts with the root node by comparing the spatiotemporal extents and the profile vectors of the user request and the corresponding counterparts of each node N involved in the top-down traversal recursively. The comparison between N and SMR during the traversal results in the following cases.

- If ($SMR^\square$ is disjoint with $N^\square$) $\vee$ ($U^\rightarrow$ is disjoint with $N^\rightarrow$): The disjoint relationship implies that all the moving objects stored at the subtree rooted at N are not within the spatiotemporal region or do not meet the profile condition for the user request SMR. Regardless of the existence of authorizations for the requester at N, the moving objects stored at the subtree rooted at N are not within the user's interests. Therefore, the traversal stops regardless of the existence of overlaid authorizations.

- Else if ($SMR^\square$ overlaps with $N^\square$) $\vee$ ($SMR^\rightarrow$ overlaps with $N^\rightarrow$)): If there is no authorization for the requester which is overlaid on N, the level of node decides the evaluation result. If N is a non-leaf node, access control decision cannot be made at the node N because there is a possibility that a relevant authorization may be overlaid on a descendent node of N. Thus, the evaluation process will be performed for all the children nodes of N. If N is a leaf node, we reject the access request because there exists no relevant authorization during the traversal.

  If there exist an authorization for the requester among the overlaid authorizations in N, the node level also decides the decision as well. If N is a non-leaf node, although all the moving objects stored at the subtree rooted at N are authorized, the user wants to retrieve a subset of moving objects whose locations are within $SMR^\square$ and whose profiles are enclosed by $SMR^\rightarrow$. Therefore, for the subtree rooted at N, we retrieve moving objects whose location overlaps with $SMR^\square$ and whose profile condition overlaps with $SMR^\rightarrow$. Thus, evaluation is delayed to each child node of N, and the same comparison will occur recursively. If N is a leaf node, because we overlay authorizations on a leaf-node in an enclosing case as well as overlapping case, not all of the moving objects in N are authorized. Thus, for all the authorizations overlaid on N, return the moving objects that are located within the intersection area between $\alpha^\square$ and $U^\square$ and whose profiles are overlapped with the bitwise AND operation of $\alpha^\rightarrow$ and $U^\rightarrow$.

- Else, implying the case of ($SMR^\square$ encloses $N^\square$) $\wedge$ ($SMR^\rightarrow$ encloses $N^\rightarrow$): If there exists at least one relevant authorization for the requester on N, the node level of N decides the access control decision. If N is a non-leaf node, because the spatiotemporal extents and profiles stored at the subtree rooted at N are authorized, all the moving objects stored at leaf nodes of the subtree rooted at N are allowed to be accessed by the requester. Therefore, there is no need to evaluate authorizations on the subtree rooted at N. In addition, spatiotemporal and profile vector comparisons would not be required because all the moving objects stored at the subtree rooted at N are within the user's interests. If N is a leaf node, some of the moving objects in N may not be authorized if the overlaid authorizations does not fully enclose the node. Thus, for all α issued for the requester, only the moving objects that are located within $\alpha^{\square}$ and whose profiles are overlapped with those of $\alpha^{\rightarrow}$ are returned.

If there exists no authorization overlaid on N, although all the moving objects stored at the subtree rooted at non-leaf node N meet the spatiotemporal and profile conditions of SMR, access control decision cannot be made because there is a possibility that a relevant authorization may be overlaid on a descendent node of N. Thus, the evaluation process is recursively performed in the children nodes of N. If N is a leaf node, we simply reject the access request because there exists no relevant authorization for the requester.

7 Open Issues

All the above proposed unified index trees except the ASM-Trie Model do not support negative authorizations. Providing such support is not trivial since they give rise to conflicts among the authorizations. Moreover, it may require changes to the fundamental assumptions used in the construction and access request evaluation. The overlaying strategy assumes only the positive authorizations. Thus, an authorization is overlaid as high level as possible in the tree because as long as there exists an authorization that allows the user to access the given region, there will not exist any conflicting negative authorization that will not allow the user to access some parts of the allowed region. Based on this assumption, authorization evaluation halts whenever a relevant authorization is located during the traversal from the root node towards the leaf level. However, if negative authorizations are supported, all the authorizations overlaid on traversal path need to be evaluated due to the possibility of conflicts among the authorizations: although an authorization that allows a user to access a region is overlaid in an index node, it is possible that another negative authorization that prohibits the user to access a part of the region may exist in the leaf node.

Also, formal analysis of the proposed approaches are necessary to be developed in order to show that unified index schemes actually perform better than separate index schemes. Development of cost models for proposed unified index schemes can actually determine how well the models perform compared to the optimal performance achievable by any other security enforcement method. If there is any room for improvement of performance, more refined model of unified index schemes can be developed so that the performance of the new model would be similar to that of the optimal solution.

References

1. Active Badge Next Generation Applications.
   http://www.cs.agh.edu.pl/ABng/applications.html

2. V. Atluri, Mobile Commerce, in The Handbook of Computer Networks, Volume III Distributed Networks, Network Planning, Control, Management and Applications, Part 3: Computer Network Popular Applications, John Wiley & Sons, to appear.

3. V. Atluri and S. Chun. An authorization model for geospatial data. IEEE Trans. Dependable Sec. Comput., 1(4):238-254, 2004.

4. V. Atluri and Q. Guo. Unified index for mobile object data and authorizations. In ESORICS, pages 80-97, 2005.

5. V. Atluri and H. Shin. Efficient Enforcement of Security Policies based on Tracking of Mobile Users. In DBSec, pages 237-251, 2006.

6. V. Atluri and H. Shin. Efficient Security Policy Enforcement in a Location Based Service Environment. In DBSec, 2007.

7. V. Atluri, H. Shin, and J. Vaidya. Efficient Security Policy Enforcement for the Mobile Environment. Journal of Computer Security. Submitted under review.

8. A. Guttman. R-trees: a dynamic index structure for spatial searching. Proceedings of the 1984 ACM SIGMOD international conference on Management of data, June 18-21, 1984, Boston, MA.

9. J. Moreira, C. Ribeiro, and T. Abdessalem. Query operations for moving objects database systems. In proceedings of the eighth ACM international symposium on Advances in geographic information systems, ACM Press, pages 108-114, 2000.

10. M. Pelanis, S. Saltenis, and C.S. Jensen. Indexing the past, present and anticipated future positions of moving objects. TIMECENTER Technical Report TR-78, 2004.

11. S. Saltenis, C.S. Jensen, S.T. Leutenegger, and M.A. Lopez. Indexing the positions of continuously moving objects. In SIGMOD Conference, pages 331-342, 2000.

12. A. P. Sistla, O. Wolfson, S. Chamberlain, and S. Dao. Modeling and Querying Moving Objects. In Proceedings of the Thirteenth international Conference on Data Engineering, pages 422-432, 1997.

13. V. Venkatesh, V. Ramesh, Anne P. Massey, Understanding usability in mobile commerce, Communications of the ACM, Volume 46, Issue 12, December 2003.

14. R. Want, A. Hopper, V. Falcao, and J. Gibbons. The active badge location system. ACM Trans. Inf. Syst. 10, 1, pages 91-102, 1992.

15. O. Wolfson, B. Xu, S. Chamberlain, and L. Jiang. Moving objects databases: Issues and solutions. In Rafanelli, M., Jarke, M., eds. 10th International Conference on Scientic and Statistical Database Management, Proceedings, Capri, Italy, July 1-3, 1998, IEEE Computer Society, pages 111-122, 1998.

16. M. Youssef, V. Atluri and N. R. Adam . Preserving Mobile Customer Privacy: An Access Control System for Moving Objects and Customer Profiles, In Proceedings of the 6th International Conference on Mobile Data Management (MDM) 2005.

Index

Printed in the United States of America.